# Modern Parallel Programming with C++ and Assembly Language

## X86 SIMD Development Using AVX, AVX2, and AVX-512

Daniel Kusswurm

Apress®

*Modern Parallel Programming with C++ and Assembly Language: X86 SIMD Development Using AVX, AVX2, and AVX-512*

Daniel Kusswurm
Geneva, IL, USA

ISBN-13 (pbk): 978-1-4842-7917-5                    ISBN-13 (electronic): 978-1-4842-7918-2
https://doi.org/10.1007/978-1-4842-7918-2

Managing Director, Apress Media LLC: Welmoed Spahr
Acquisitions Editor: Steve Anglin
Development Editor: James Markham
Coordinating Editor: Mark Powers

Cover designed by eStudioCalamar

Cover image by Viktor Forgacs on Unsplash (www.unsplash.com)

Distributed to the book trade worldwide by Apress Media, LLC, 1 New York Plaza, New York, NY 10004, U.S.A. Phone 1-800-SPRINGER, fax (201) 348-4505, e-mail orders-ny@springer-sbm.com, or visit www.springeronline.com. Apress Media, LLC is a California LLC and the sole member (owner) is Springer Science + Business Media Finance Inc (SSBM Finance Inc). SSBM Finance Inc is a **Delaware** corporation.

For information on translations, please e-mail booktranslations@springernature.com; for reprint, paperback, or audio rights, please e-mail bookpermissions@springernature.com.

Apress titles may be purchased in bulk for academic, corporate, or promotional use. eBook versions and licenses are also available for most titles. For more information, reference our Print and eBook Bulk Sales web page at http://www.apress.com/bulk-sales.

Any source code or other supplementary material referenced by the author in this book is available to readers on GitHub (https://github.com/Apress). For more detailed information, please visit http://www.apress.com/source-code.

Printed on acid-free paper

# Table of Contents

# About the Author

**Daniel Kusswurm** has over 35 years of professional experience as a software developer, computer scientist, and author. During his career, he has developed innovative software for medical devices, scientific instruments, and image processing applications. On many of these projects, he successfully employed C++ intrinsic functions, x86 assembly language, and SIMD programming techniques to significantly improve the performance of computationally intense algorithms or solve unique programming challenges. His educational background includes a BS in electrical engineering technology from Northern Illinois University along with an MS and PhD in computer science from DePaul University. Daniel Kusswurm is also the author of *Modern X86 Assembly Language Programming* (ISBN: 978-1484200650), *Modern X86 Assembly Language Programming, Second Edition* (ISBN: 978-1484240625), and *Modern Arm Assembly Language Programming* (ISBN: 978-1484262665), all published by Apress.

# About the Technical Reviewer

**Mike Kinsner** is a principal engineer at Intel developing languages and parallel programming models for a variety of computer architectures. He has recently been one of the architects of Data Parallel C++. He started his career at Altera working on high-level synthesis for field-programmable gate arrays and still contributes to spatial programming models and compilers. Mike is a representative within the Khronos Group standards organization, where he works on the SYCL and OpenCL open industry standards for parallel programming. Mike holds a PhD in computer engineering from McMaster University and recently coauthored the industry's first book on SYCL and Data Parallel C++.

# Acknowledgments

The production of a motion picture and the publication of a book are somewhat analogous. Movie trailers extol the performances of the lead actors. The front cover of a book trumpets the authors' names. Actors and authors ultimately receive public acclamation for their efforts. It is, however, impossible to produce a movie or publish a book without the dedication, expertise, and creativity of a professional behind-the-scenes team. This book is no exception.

I would like to thank the talented editorial team at Apress including Steve Anglin, Mark Powers, and Jim Markham for their efforts and contributions. I would also like to thank the entire production staff at Apress. Michael Kinsner warrants applause and a thank you for his comprehensive technical review and constructive comments. Ed Kusswurm merits kudos for reviewing each chapter and offering helpful suggestions. I accept full responsibility for any remaining imperfections.

Thanks to my professional colleagues for their support and encouragement. Finally, I would like to recognize parental nodes Armin (RIP) and Mary along with sibling nodes Mary, Tom, Ed, and John for their inspiration during the writing of this book.

# Introduction

SIMD (single instruction multiple data) is a parallel computing technology that simultaneously executes the same processor operation using multiple data items. For example, a SIMD-capable processor can carry out an arithmetic operation using several elements of a floating-point array concurrently. Programs often use SIMD operations to accelerate the performance of computationally intense algorithms in machine learning, image processing, audio/video encoding and decoding, data mining, and computer graphics.

Since the late 1990s, both AMD and Intel have incorporated various SIMD instruction set extensions into their respective x86 processors. The most recent x86 SIMD instruction set extensions are called AVX (Advanced Vector Extensions), AVX2, and AVX-512. These SIMD resources facilitate arithmetic and other data processing operations using multiple elements in a 128-, 256-, or 512-bit wide processor register (most standard x86 arithmetic operations are carried out using scalar values in an 8-, 16-, 32-, or 64-bit wide register).

Despite the incorporation of advanced SIMD capabilities in x86 modern processors, high-level language compilers are sometimes unable to fully exploit these resources. To optimally utilize the SIMD capabilities of a modern x86 processor, a software developer must occasionally write SIMD code that explicitly employs the AVX, AVX2, or AVX-512 instruction sets. A software developer can use either C++ SIMD intrinsic functions or assembly language programming to accomplish this. A C++ SIMD intrinsic function is code that looks like an ordinary C++ function but is handled differently by the compiler. More specifically, the compiler directly translates a C++ SIMD intrinsic function into one or more assembly language instructions without the overhead of a normal function (or subroutine) call.

Before continuing, a couple of caveats are warranted. First, the SIMD programming techniques described in this book are not appropriate for every "slow" algorithm or function. Both C++ SIMD intrinsic function use and assembly language code development should be regarded as specialized programming tools that can significantly accelerate the performance of an algorithm or function when judiciously employed. However, it is important to note that explicit SIMD coding usually requires extra effort during initial development and possibly when performing future maintenance. Second, it should be noted that SIMD parallelism is different than other types of parallel computing you may have encountered. For example, the task-level parallelism of an application that exploits multiple processor cores or threads to accelerate the performance of an algorithm is different than SIMD parallelism. Task-level parallelism and SIMD parallelism are not mutually exclusive; they are frequently utilized together. The focus of this book is x86 SIMD parallelism and software development, specifically the computational resources of AVX, AVX2, and AVX-512.

## Modern Parallel Programming with C++ and Assembly Language

*Modern Parallel Programming with C++ and Assembly Language* is an instructional text that explains x86 SIMD programming using both C++ intrinsic functions and assembly language. The content and organization of this book are designed to help you quickly understand and exploit the computational resources of AVX, AVX2, and AVX-512. This book also contains an abundance of source code that is structured to accelerate learning and comprehension of essential SIMD programming concepts and algorithms. After reading this book, you will be able to code performance-enhanced AVX, AVX2, and AVX-512 functions and algorithms using either C++ SIMD intrinsic functions or x86-64 assembly language.

# Target Audience

The target audience for *Modern Parallel Programming with C++ and Assembly Language* is software developers including

- Software developers who are creating new programs for x86 platforms and want to learn how to code performance-enhancing SIMD algorithms using AVX, AVX2, or AVX-512

- Software developers who need to learn how to write x86 SIMD functions to accelerate the performance of existing code using C++ SIMD intrinsic functions or x86-64 assembly language functions

- Software developers, computer science/engineering students, or hobbyists who want to learn about or need to gain a better understanding of x86 SIMD architectures and the AVX, AVX2, and AVX-512 instruction sets

Readers of this book should have some previous programming experience with modern C++ (i.e., ISO C++11 or later). Some familiarity with Microsoft's Visual Studio and/or the GNU toolchain will also be helpful.

# Content Overview

The primary objective of this book is to help you learn x86 SIMD programming using C++ SIMD intrinsic functions and x86-64 assembly language. The book's chapters and content are structured to achieve this goal. Here is a brief overview of what you can expect to learn.

Chapter 1 discusses SIMD fundamentals including data types, basic arithmetic, and common data manipulation operations. It also includes a brief historical overview of x86 SIMD technologies including AVX, AVX2, and AVX-512.

Chapters 2 and 3 explain AVX arithmetic and other essential operations using C++ SIMD intrinsic functions. These chapters cover both integer and floating-point operands. The source code examples presented in these (and subsequent) chapters are packaged as working programs, which means that you can run, modify, or otherwise experiment with the code to enhance your learning experience.

Chapters 4, 5, and 6 cover AVX2 using C++ SIMD intrinsic functions. In these chapters, you will learn how to code practical SIMD algorithms including image processing functions, matrix operations, and signal processing algorithms. You will also learn how to perform SIMD fused-multiply-add (FMA) arithmetic.

Chapters 7 and 8 describe AVX-512 integer and floating-point operations using C++ SIMD intrinsic functions. These chapters also highlight how to take advantage of AVX-512's wider operands to improve algorithm performance.

Chapter 9 covers supplemental x86 SIMD programming techniques. This chapter explains how to programmatically detect whether the target processor and its operating system support the AVX, AVX2, or AVX-512 instruction sets. It also describes how to utilize SIMD versions of common C++ library functions.

Chapter 10 explains x86-64 processor architecture including data types, register sets, memory addressing modes, and condition codes. The purpose of this chapter is to provide you with a solid foundation for the subsequent chapters on x86-64 SIMD assembly language programming.

Chapters 11 and 12 cover the basics of x86-64 assembly language programming. In these chapters, you will learn how to perform scalar integer and floating-point arithmetic. You will also learn about other essential assembly language programming topics including for-loops, compare operations, data conversions, and function calling conventions.

Chapter 13 and 14 explain AVX arithmetic and other operations using x86-64 assembly language. These chapters also illustrate how to code x86-64 assembly language functions that perform operations using arrays and matrices.

Chapters 15 and 16 demonstrate AVX2 and x86-64 assembly language programming. In these chapters, you will learn how to code x86-64 assembly language functions that perform image processing operations, matrix calculations, and signal processing algorithms using the AVX2 instruction set.

Chapters 17 and 18 focus on developing x86-64 assembly language code using the AVX-512 instruction set.

Chapter 19 discusses some usage guidelines and optimization techniques for both C++ SIMD intrinsic functions and assembly language code development.

Appendix A describes how to download and set up the source code. It also includes some basic instructions for using Visual Studio and the GNU toolchain. Appendix B contains a list of references and resources that you can consult for additional information about x86 SIMD programming and the AVX, AVX2, and AVX-512 instruction sets.

# Source Code

The source code published in this book is available on GitHub at https://github.com/Apress/modern-parallel-programming-cpp-assembly.

---

■ **Caution** The sole purpose of the source code is to elucidate programming topics that are directly related to the content of this book. Minimal attention is given to essential software engineering concerns such as robust error handling, security risks, numerical stability, rounding errors, or ill-conditioned functions. You are responsible for addressing these concerns should you decide to use any of the source code in your own programs.

---

The C++ SIMD source code examples (Chapters 2–9) can be built using either Visual Studio (version 2019 or later, any edition) on Windows or GNU C++ (version 8.3 or later) on Linux. The x86-64 assembly language source code examples (Chapters 11–18) require Visual Studio and Windows. If you are contemplating the use of x86-64 assembly language with Linux, you can still benefit from this book since most of the x86-AVX instruction explanations are OS independent (developing assembly language code that runs on both Windows and Linux is challenging due to differences between the various development tools and runtime calling conventions). To execute the source code, you must use a computer with a processor that supports AVX, AVX2, or AVX-512. You must also use a recent 64-bit operating system that supports these instruction sets. Compatible 64-bit operating systems include (but not limited to) Windows 10 (version 1903 or later), Windows 11, Debian (version 9 or later), and Ubuntu (version 18.04 LTS or later). Appendix A contains additional information about the source code and software development tools.

# Additional Resources

An extensive set of x86-related SIMD programming documentation is available from both AMD and Intel. Appendix B lists several important resources that both aspiring and experienced SIMD programmers will find useful. Of all the resources listed in Appendix B, two stand out.

The Intel Intrinsics Guide website (`https://software.intel.com/sites/landingpage/IntrinsicsGuide`) is an indispensable online reference for information regarding x86 C++ SIMD intrinsic functions and data types. This site documents the C++ SIMD intrinsic functions that are supported by the Intel C++ compiler. Most of these functions can also be used in programs that are developed using either Visual C++ or GNU C++. Another valuable programming resource is Volume 2 of the reference manual entitled *Intel 64 and IA-32 Architectures Software Developer's Manual, Combined Volumes: 1, 2A, 2B, 2C, 2D, 3A, 3B, 3C, 3D, and 4* (`www.intel.com/content/www/us/en/developer/articles/technical/intel-sdm.html`). Volume 2 contains comprehensive information for every AVX, AVX2, and AVX-512 processor instruction including detailed operational descriptions, lists of valid operands, affected status flags, and potential exceptions. You are strongly encouraged to consult this reference manual when developing your own x86 SIMD code to verify correct instruction usage.

# CHAPTER 1

■ ■ ■

# SIMD Fundamentals

Chapter 1 introduces x86 SIMD fundamentals and essential concepts. It begins with a section that defines SIMD. This section also introduces SIMD arithmetic using a concise source code example. The next section presents a brief historical overview of x86 SIMD instruction set extensions. The principal sections of Chapter 1 are next. These highlight x86 SIMD concepts and programming constructs including data types, arithmetic calculations, and data manipulation operations. These sections also describe important particulars related to AVX, AVX2, and AVX-512. It is important for you to understand the material presented in this chapter since it provides the necessary foundation to successfully comprehend the topics and source code discussed in subsequent chapters.

Before proceeding, a few words about terminology are warranted. In all ensuing discussions, I will use the official acronyms AVX, AVX2, and AVX-512 when explaining specific features or instructions of these x86 SIMD instruction set extensions. I will use the term x86-AVX as an umbrella expression for x86 SIMD instructions or computational resources that pertain to more than one of the aforementioned x86 SIMD extensions. The terms x86-32 and x86-64 are used to signify x86 32-bit and 64-bit processors and execution environments. This book focuses exclusively on the latter, but the former is occasionally mentioned for historical context or comparison purposes.

## What Is SIMD?

SIMD (single instruction multiple data) is a parallel computing technique whereby a CPU (or processing element incorporated within a CPU) performs a single operation using multiple data items concurrently. For example, a SIMD-capable CPU can carry out a single arithmetic operation using several elements of a floating-point array simultaneously. SIMD operations are frequently employed to accelerate the performance of computationally intense algorithms and functions in machine learning, image processing, audio/video encoding and decoding, data mining, and computer graphics.

The underlying concepts behind a SIMD arithmetic calculation are probably best illustrated by a simple source code example. Listing 1-1 shows the source code for three different calculating functions that perform the same arithmetic operation using single-precision floating-point arrays.

*Listing 1-1.* Example Ch01_01

```
//-----------------------------------------------
//              Ch01_01_fcpp.cpp
//-----------------------------------------------

#include <immintrin.h>
#include "Ch01_01.h"
```

© Daniel Kusswurm 2022
D. Kusswurm, *Modern Parallel Programming with C++ and Assembly Language*,
https://doi.org/10.1007/978-1-4842-7918-2_1

```
void CalcZ_Cpp(float* z, const float* x, const float* y, size_t n)
{
    for (size_t i = 0; i < n; i++)
        z[i] = x[i] + y[i];
}

void CalcZ_Iavx(float* z, const float* x, const float* y, size_t n)
{
    size_t i = 0;
    const size_t num_simd_elements = 8;

    for (; n - i >= num_simd_elements; i += num_simd_elements)
    {
        // Calculate z[i:i+7] = x[i:i+7] + y[i:i+7]
        __m256 x_vals = _mm256_loadu_ps(&x[i]);
        __m256 y_vals = _mm256_loadu_ps(&y[i]);
        __m256 z_vals = _mm256_add_ps(x_vals, y_vals);

        _mm256_storeu_ps(&z[i], z_vals);
    }

    // Calculate z[i] = x[i] + y[i] for any remaining elements
    for (; i < n; i += 1)
        z[i] = x[i] + y[i];
}
```

```
;----------------------------------------------------
;                  Ch01_01_fasm.asm
;----------------------------------------------------


;-----------------------------------------------------------------------------
; extern "C" void CalcZ_Aavx(float* z, const float* x, const float* x, size_t n);
;-----------------------------------------------------------------------------

NSE     equ 8                                   ;num_simd_elements


        .code
CalcZ_Aavx proc
        xor rax,rax                             ;i = 0;

Loop1:  mov r10,r9                              ;r10 = n
        sub r10,rax                             ;r10 = n - i
        cmp r10,NSE                             ;is n - i < NSE?
        jb Loop2                                ;jump if yes

; Calculate z[i:i+7] = x[i:i+7] + y[i:i+7]
        vmovups ymm0,ymmword ptr [rdx+rax*4]    ;ymm0 = x[i:i+7]
        vmovups ymm1,ymmword ptr [r8+rax*4]     ;ymm1 = y[i:i+7]
        vaddps ymm2,ymm0,ymm1                   ;z[i:i+7] = x[i:i+7] + y[i:i+7]
        vmovups ymmword ptr [rcx+rax*4],ymm2    ;save z[i:i+7]
```

```
        add rax,NSE                        ;i += NSE
        jmp Loop1                          ;repeat Loop1 until done

Loop2:  cmp rax,r9                         ;is i >= n?
        jae Done                           ;jump if yes

; Calculate z[i] = x[i] + y[i] for remaining elements
        vmovss xmm0,real4 ptr [rdx+rax*4]  ;xmm0 = x[i]
        vmovss xmm1,real4 ptr [r8+rax*4]   ;xmm1 = y[i]
        vaddss xmm2,xmm0,xmm1              ;z[i] = x[i] + y[i]
        vmovss real4 ptr [rcx+rax*4],xmm2  ;save z[i]

        inc rax                            ;i += 1
        jmp Loop2                          ;repeat Loop2 until done

Done:   vzeroupper                         ;clear upper bits of ymm regs
        ret                                ;return to caller
CalcZ_Aavx endp
        end
```

The function CalcZ_Cpp(), shown at the beginning of Listing 1-1, is a straightforward non-SIMD C++ function that calculates z[i] = x[i] + y[i]. However, a modern C++ compiler may generate SIMD code for this function as explained later in this section.

The next function in Listing 1-1, CalcZ_Iavx(), calculates the same result as CalcZ_Cpp() but employs C++ SIMD intrinsic functions to accelerate the computations. In CalcZ_Iavx(), the first for-loop uses the C++ SIMD intrinsic function _mm256_loadu_ps() to load eight consecutive elements from array x (i.e., elements x[i:i+7]) and temporarily saves these elements in an __m256 object named x_vals. An __m256 object is a generic container that holds eight values of type float. The ensuing _mm256_load_ps() call performs the same operation using array y. This is followed by a call to _mm256_add_ps() that calculates z[i:i+7] = x[i:i+7] + y[i:i+7]. What makes this code different from the code in the non-SIMD function CalcZ_Cpp() is that _mm256_add_ps() performs all eight array element additions concurrently. The final C++ intrinsic function in the first for-loop, _mm256_storeu_ps(), saves the resulting array element sums to z[i:i+7].

It is important to note that since the first for-loop in CalcZ_Iavx() processes eight array elements per iteration, it must terminate if there are fewer than eight elements remaining to process. The second for-loop handles any remaining (or residual) elements and only executes if n is not an integral multiple of eight. It is also important to mention that the C++ compiler treats C++ SIMD intrinsic function calls differently than normal C++ function calls. In the current example, the C++ compiler directly translates each __mm256 function into its corresponding AVX assembly language instruction. The overhead associated with a normal C++ function call is eliminated.

The final function in Listing 1-1 is named CalcZ_Aavx(). This is an x86-64 assembly language function that performs the same array calculation as CalcZ_Cpp() and CalcZ_Iavx(). What is noteworthy about this function is that the AVX instructions vmovps and vaddps contained in the code block are the same instructions that the C++ compiler emits for the C++ SIMD intrinsic functions _mm256_loadu_ps() and _mm256_add_ps(), respectively. The remaining code in CalcZ_Aavx() implements the two for-loops that are also implemented in function CalcZ_Cpp().

Do not worry if you are somewhat perplexed by the source code in Listing 1-1. The primary purpose of this book is to teach you how to develop and code SIMD algorithms like this using either C++ SIMD intrinsic functions or x86-64 assembly language. There are two takeaway points from this section. First, the CPU executes most SIMD arithmetic operations on the specified data elements concurrently. Second, similar design patterns are often employed when coding a SIMD algorithm regardless of whether C++ or assembly language is used.

One final note regarding the code in Listing 1-1. Recent versions of mainstream C++ compilers such as Visual C++ and GNU C++ are sometimes capable of automatically generating efficient x86 SIMD code for trivial arithmetic functions like CalcZ_Cpp(). However, these compilers still have difficulty generating efficient SIMD code for more complicated functions, especially ones that employ nested for-loops or nontrivial decision logic. In these cases, functions written using C++ SIMD intrinsic functions or x86-64 assembly language code can often outperform the SIMD code generated by a modern C++ compiler. However, employing C++ SIMD intrinsic functions does not improve performance in all cases. Many programmers will often code computationally intensive algorithms using standard C++ first, benchmark the code, and then recode bottleneck functions using C++ SIMD intrinsic functions or assembly language.

# Historical Overview of x86 SIMD

For aspiring x86 SIMD programmers, having a basic understanding about the history of x86 SIMD and its various extensions is extremely beneficial. This section presents a brief overview that focuses on noteworthy x86 SIMD instruction set extensions. It does not discuss x86 SIMD extensions incorporated in special-use processors (e.g., Intel Xeon Phi) or x86 SIMD extensions that were never widely used. If you are interested in a more comprehensive chronicle of x86 SIMD architectures and instruction set extensions, you can consult the references listed in Appendix B.

Intel introduced the first x86 SIMD instruction set extension, called MMX, in 1997. This extension added instructions that facilitated simple SIMD operations using 64-bit wide packed integer operands. The MMX extension did not add any new registers to the x86 platform; it simply repurposed the registers in the x87 floating-point unit for SIMD integer arithmetic and other operations. In 1998, AMD launched an x86 SIMD extension called 3DNow, which facilitated vector operations using single-precision floating-point values. It also added a few new integer SIMD instructions. Like MMX, 3DNow uses x87 FPU registers to hold instruction operands. Both MMX and 3DNow have been superseded by newer x86 SIMD technologies and should not be used to develop new code.

In 1999, Intel launched a new SIMD technology called Streaming SIMD extensions (SSE). SSE adds 128-bit wide registers to the x86 platform and instructions that perform packed single-precision (32-bit) floating-point arithmetic. SSE also includes a few packed integer instructions. In 2000, SSE2 was launched and extends the floating-point capabilities of SSE to cover packed double-precision (64 bit) values. SSE2 also significantly expands the packed integer capabilities of SSE. Unlike x86-32 processors, all x86-64-compatible processors from both AMD and Intel support the SSE2 instruction set extension. The SIMD extensions that followed SSE2 include SSE3 (2004), SSSE3 (2006), SSE4.1 (2008), and SSE4.2 (2008). These extensions incorporated additional SIMD instructions that perform operations using either packed integer or floating-point operands, but no new registers or data types.

In 2011, Intel introduced processors that supported a new x86 SIMD technology called Advanced Vector Extensions (AVX). AVX adds packed floating-point operations (both single precision and double precision) using 256-bit wide registers. AVX also supports a new three-operand assembly language instruction syntax, which helps reduce the number of register-to-register data transfers that a software function must perform. In 2013, Intel unveiled AVX2, which extends AVX to support packed-integer operations using 256-bit wide registers. AVX2 also adds enhanced data transfer capabilities with its broadcast, gather, and permute instructions. Processors that support AVX or AVX2 may also support fused-multiply-add (FMA) operations. FMA enables software algorithms to perform sum-of-product (e.g., dot product) calculations using a single floating-point rounding operation, which can improve both performance and accuracy.

Beginning in 2017, high-end desktop and server-oriented processors marketed by Intel included a new SIMD extension called AVX-512. This architectural enhancement supports packed integer and floating-point operations using 512-bit wide registers. AVX-512 also includes SIMD extensions that facilitate instruction-level conditional data merging, floating-point rounding control, and embedded broadcast operations.

In addition to the abovementioned SIMD extensions, numerous non-SIMD instructions have been added to the x86 platform during the past 25 years. This ongoing evolution of the x86 platform presents some challenges to software developers who want to exploit the latest instruction sets and computational resources. Fortunately, there are techniques that you can use to determine which x86 SIMD and non-SIMD instruction set extensions are available during program execution. You will learn about these methods in Chapter 9. To ensure software compatibility with future processors, a software developer should *never* assume that a particular x86 SIMD or non-SIMD instruction set extension is available based on processor manufacturer, brand name, model number, or underlying microarchitecture.

## SIMD Data Types

An x86 SIMD data type is a contiguous collection of bytes that is used by the processor to perform an arithmetic calculation or data manipulation operation using multiple values. An x86 SIMD data type can be regarded as a generic container object that holds multiple instances of the same fundamental data type (e.g., 8-, 16-, 32-, or 64-bit integers, single-precision or double-precision floating-point values, etc.). The bits of an x86 SIMD data type are numbered from right to left with *0* and *size – 1* denoting the least and most significant bits, respectively. X86 SIMD data types are stored in memory using little-endian byte ordering. In this ordering scheme, the least significant byte of an x86 SIMD data type is stored at the lowest memory address as illustrated in Figure 1-1. In this figure, the terms xmmword, ymmword, and zmmword are x86 assembly language expressions for 128-, 256-, and 512-bit wide SIMD data types and operands.

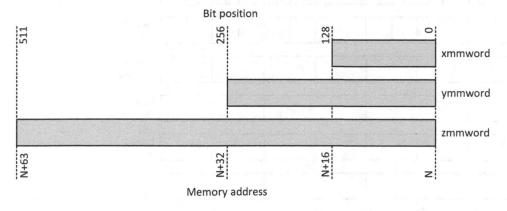

***Figure 1-1.*** *X86 SIMD data types*

A program can use x86 SIMD (also called packed) data types to perform simultaneous calculations using either integer or floating-point values. For example, a 256-bit wide packed operand can hold thirty-two 8-bit integers, sixteen 16-bit integers, eight 32-bit integers, or four 64-bit integers. It can also be used to hold eight single-precision or four double-precision floating-point values. Table 1-1 contains a complete list of x86 SIMD data types and the maximum number of elements for various integer and floating-point types.

**Table 1-1.** *SIMD Data Types and Maximum Number of Elements*

| Numerical Type | xmmword | ymmword | zmmword |
|---|---|---|---|
| 8-bit integer | 16 | 32 | 64 |
| 16-bit integer | 8 | 16 | 32 |
| 32-bit integer | 4 | 8 | 16 |
| 64-bit integer | 2 | 4 | 8 |
| Single-precision floating point | 4 | 8 | 16 |
| Double-precision floating-point | 2 | 4 | 8 |

The width of an x86 SIMD instruction operand varies depending on the x86 SIMD extension and the underlying fundamental data type. AVX supports packed integer operations using 128-bit wide operands. It also supports packed floating-point operations using either 128- or 256-bit wide operands. AVX2 also supports these same operand sizes and adds support for 256-bit wide packed integer operands. Figure 1-2 illustrates the AVX and AVX2 operand types in greater detail. In this figure, the terms byte, word, doubleword, and quadword signify 8-, 16-, 32-, and 64-bit wide integers; SPFP and DPFP denote single-precision and double-precision floating-point values, respectively.

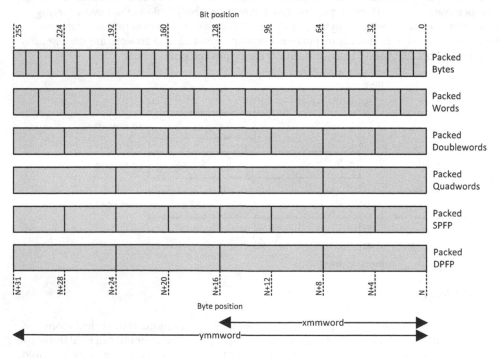

**Figure 1-2.** *AVX and AVX2 operands*

AVX-512 extends maximum width of an x86 SIMD operand from 256 to 512 bits. Many AVX-512 instructions can also be used with 128- and 256-bit wide SIMD operands. However, it should be noted at this point that unlike AVX and AVX2, AVX-512 is not a cohesive x86 SIMD instruction set extension. Rather, it is a collection of interrelated but distinct instruction set extensions. An AVX-512-compliant processor must minimally support 512-bit wide operands of packed floating-point (single-precision or double-precision) and packed integer (32- or 64-bit wide) elements. The AVX-512 instructions that exercise 128- and 256-bit wide operands are a distinct x86 SIMD extension as are the instructions that support packed 8- and 16-bit wide integers. You will learn more about this in the chapters that explain AVX-512 programming. AVX-512 also adds eight opmask registers that a function can use to perform masked moves or masked zeroing.

# SIMD Arithmetic

Source code example Ch01_01 introduced simple SIMD addition using single-precision floating-point elements. In this section, you will learn more about SIMD arithmetic operations that perform their calculations using either integer or floating-point elements.

## SIMD Integer Arithmetic

Figure 1-3 exemplifies integer addition using 128-bit wide SIMD operands. In this figure, integer addition is illustrated using eight 16-bit integers, four 32-bit integers, or two 64-bit integers. Like the floating-point example that you saw earlier, faster processing is possible when using SIMD arithmetic since the processor can perform the required calculations in parallel. For example, when 16-bit integer elements are used in a SIMD operand, the processor performs all eight 16-bit additions simultaneously.

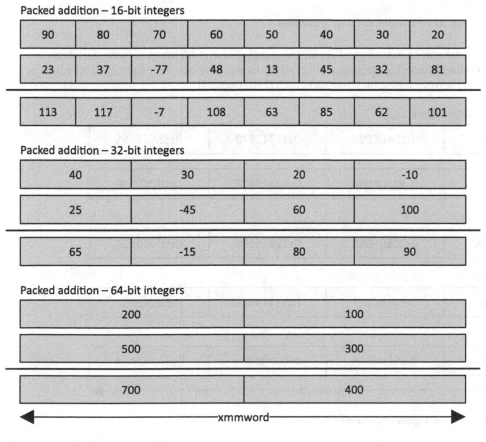

*Figure 1-3.* SIMD integer addition using various element sizes

Besides packed integer addition, x86-AVX includes instructions that perform other common arithmetic calculations with packed integers including subtraction, multiplication, shifts, and bitwise logical operations. Figure 1-4 illustrates various packed shift operations using 32-bit wide integer elements.

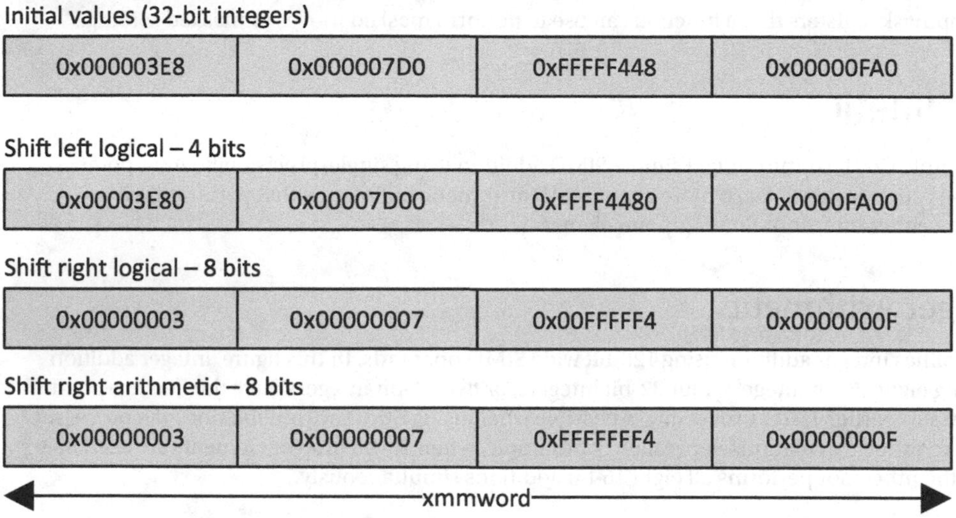

Initial values (32-bit integers)

| 0x000003E8 | 0x000007D0 | 0xFFFFF448 | 0x00000FA0 |
|---|---|---|---|

Shift left logical – 4 bits

| 0x00003E80 | 0x00007D00 | 0xFFFF4480 | 0x0000FA00 |
|---|---|---|---|

Shift right logical – 8 bits

| 0x00000003 | 0x00000007 | 0x00FFFFF4 | 0x0000000F |
|---|---|---|---|

Shift right arithmetic – 8 bits

| 0x00000003 | 0x00000007 | 0xFFFFFFF4 | 0x0000000F |
|---|---|---|---|

◄—————————————xmmword——————————————►

***Figure 1-4.*** *SIMD logical and arithmetic shift operations*

Figure 1-5 demonstrates bitwise logical operations using packed 32-bit integers. Note that when performing SIMD bitwise logical operations, distinct elements are irrelevant since the logical operation is carried out using the corresponding bit positions of each SIMD operand.

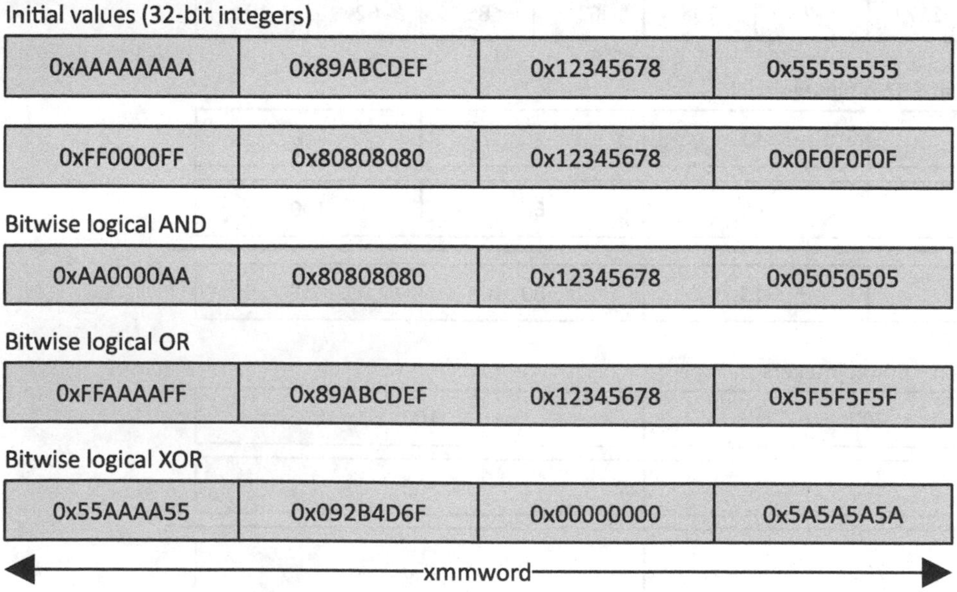

Initial values (32-bit integers)

| 0xAAAAAAAA | 0x89ABCDEF | 0x12345678 | 0x55555555 |
|---|---|---|---|

| 0xFF0000FF | 0x80808080 | 0x12345678 | 0x0F0F0F0F |
|---|---|---|---|

Bitwise logical AND

| 0xAA0000AA | 0x80808080 | 0x12345678 | 0x05050505 |
|---|---|---|---|

Bitwise logical OR

| 0xFFAAAAFF | 0x89ABCDEF | 0x12345678 | 0x5F5F5F5F |
|---|---|---|---|

Bitwise logical XOR

| 0x55AAAA55 | 0x092B4D6F | 0x00000000 | 0x5A5A5A5A |
|---|---|---|---|

◄—————————————xmmword——————————————►

***Figure 1-5.*** *SIMD bitwise logical operations*

# Wraparound vs. Saturated Arithmetic

One notable feature of x86-AVX is its support for saturated integer arithmetic. When performing saturated integer arithmetic, the processor automatically clips the elements of a SIMD operand to prevent an arithmetic overflow or underflow condition from occurring. This is different from normal (or wraparound) integer arithmetic where an overflow or underflow result is retained. Saturated arithmetic is extremely useful when working with pixel values since it eliminates the need to explicitly check each pixel value for an overflow or underflow. X86-AVX includes instructions that perform packed saturated addition and subtraction using 8- or 16-bit wide integer elements, both signed and unsigned.

Figure 1-6 shows an example of packed 16-bit signed integer addition using both wraparound and saturated arithmetic. An overflow condition occurs when the two 16-bit signed integers are summed using wraparound arithmetic. With saturated arithmetic, however, the result is clipped to the largest possible 16-bit signed integer value. Figure 1-7 illustrates a similar example using 8-bit unsigned integers. Besides addition, x86-AVX also supports saturated packed integer subtraction as shown in Figure 1-8. Table 1-2 summarizes the saturated addition and subtraction range limits for all supported integer sizes and sign types.

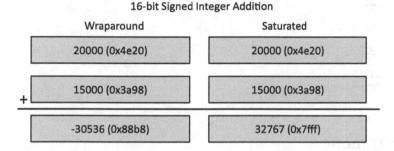

***Figure 1-6.*** *16-bit signed integer addition using wraparound and saturated arithmetic*

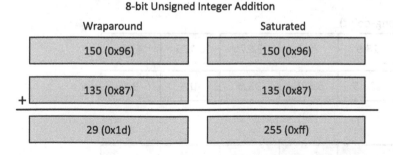

***Figure 1-7.*** *8-bit unsigned integer addition using wraparound and saturated arithmetic*

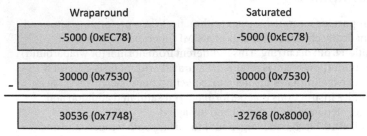

16-bit Signed Integer Subtraction

| Wraparound | Saturated |
|---|---|
| -5000 (0xEC78) | -5000 (0xEC78) |
| 30000 (0x7530) | 30000 (0x7530) |
| 30536 (0x7748) | -32768 (0x8000) |

*Figure 1-8.* *16-bit signed integer subtraction using wraparound and saturated arithmetic*

*Table 1-2.* *Range Limits for Saturated Arithmetic*

| Integer Type | Lower Limit | Upper Limit |
|---|---|---|
| 8-bit signed | -128 | 127 |
| 8-bit unsigned | 0 | 255 |
| 16-bit signed | -32768 | 32767 |
| 16-bit unsigned | 0 | 65535 |

# SIMD Floating-Point Arithmetic

X86-AVX supports arithmetic operations using packed SIMD operands containing single-precision or double-precision floating-point elements. This includes addition, subtraction, multiplication, division, and square roots. Figures 1-9 and 1-10 illustrate a few common SIMD floating-point arithmetic operations.

Initial values (single-precision floating-point)

| 12.0 | 17.5 | 37.25 | 18.9 | 20.2 | -23.75 | 0.125 | 47.5 |
|---|---|---|---|---|---|---|---|
| 88.0 | 17.5 | 28.0 | 100.5 | 5.625 | 33.0 | -0.5 | 0.1 |

Packed floating-point addition

| 100.0 | 35.0 | 65.25 | 119.4 | 25.825 | 9.25 | -0.375 | 47.6 |
|---|---|---|---|---|---|---|---|

Packed floating-point multiplication

| 1056.0 | 306.25 | 1043.0 | 1899.45 | 113.625 | -783.75 | -0.0625 | 4.75 |
|---|---|---|---|---|---|---|---|

◄───────────ymmword───────────►

*Figure 1-9.* *SIMD single-precision floating-point addition and multiplication*

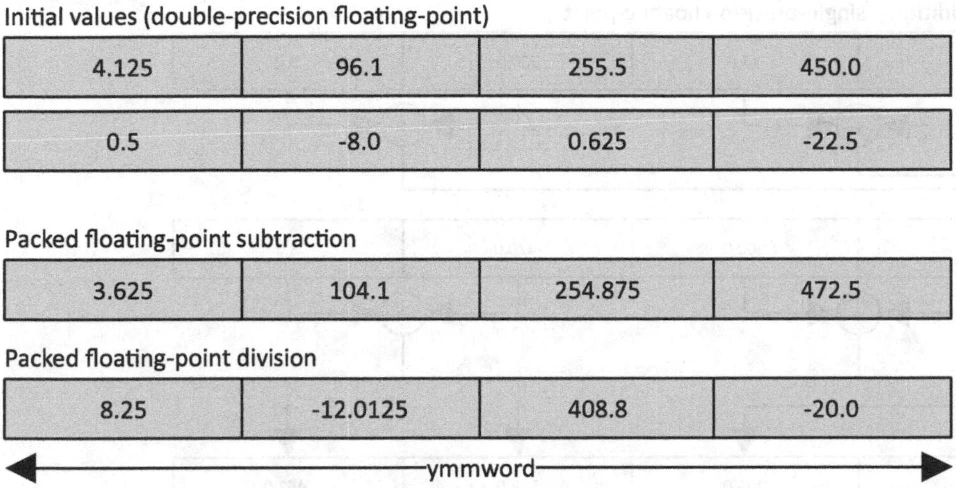

Initial values (double-precision floating-point)

| 4.125 | 96.1 | 255.5 | 450.0 |
|-------|------|-------|-------|

| 0.5 | -8.0 | 0.625 | -22.5 |
|-----|------|-------|-------|

Packed floating-point subtraction

| 3.625 | 104.1 | 254.875 | 472.5 |
|-------|-------|---------|-------|

Packed floating-point division

| 8.25 | -12.0125 | 408.8 | -20.0 |
|------|----------|-------|-------|

◄―――――――――――――――ymmword―――――――――――――――►

***Figure 1-10.*** *SIMD double-precision floating-point subtraction and division*

The SIMD arithmetic operations that you have seen thus far perform their calculations using corresponding elements of the two source operands. These types of operations are usually called vertical arithmetic. X86-AVX also includes arithmetic instructions that carry out operations using the adjacent elements of a SIMD operand. Adjacent element calculations are termed horizonal arithmetic. Horizontal arithmetic is frequently used to reduce the elements of a SIMD operand to a single scalar value. Figure 1-11 illustrates horizontal addition using packed single-precision floating-point elements and horizontal subtraction using packed double-precision floating-point elements. X86-AVX also supports integer horizontal addition and subtraction using packed 16- or 32-bit wide integers.

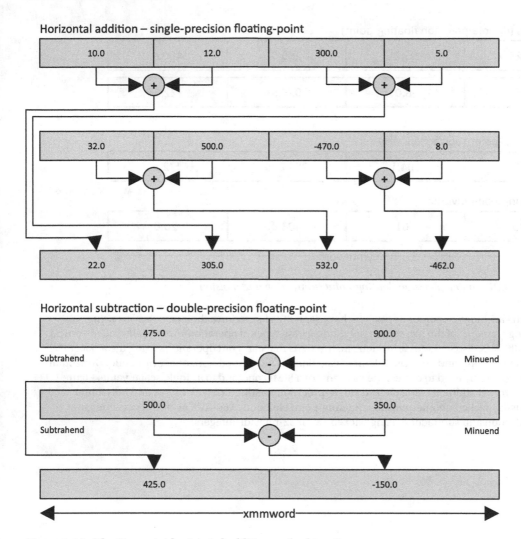

*Figure 1-11.* *Floating-point horizontal addition and subtraction*

# SIMD Data Manipulation Operations

Besides arithmetic calculations, many algorithms frequently employ SIMD data manipulation operations. X86-AVX SIMD data manipulation operations include element compares, shuffles, permutations, blends, conditional moves, broadcasts, size promotions/reductions, and type conversions. You will learn more about these operations in the programming chapters of this book. A few common SIMD data manipulation operations are, however, employed regularly to warrant a few preliminary comments in this chapter.

One indispensable SIMD data manipulation operation is a data compare. Like a SIMD arithmetic calculation, the operations performed during a SIMD compare are carried out simultaneously using all operand elements. However, the results generated by a SIMD compare are different than those produced by an ordinary scalar compare. When performing a scalar compare such as a > b, the processor conveys the result using status bits in a flags register (on x86-64 processors, this flags register is named RFLAGS). A SIMD compare is different in that it needs to report the results of multiple compare operations, which means a single set of status bits in a flags register is inadequate. To overcome this limitation, SIMD compares return a mask value that signifies the result of each SIMD element compare operation.

Figure 1-12 illustrates a couple of SIMD compare operations using packed 16-bit integers and packed single-precision floating-point elements. In this example, the result of each corresponding element compare is a mask of all ones if the compare predicate is true; otherwise, zero is returned. The use of all ones or all zeros for each element compare result facilitates subsequent operations using simple Boolean operations. You will learn how to do this in the programming chapters.

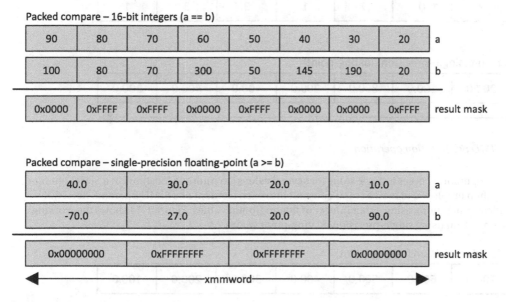

**Figure 1-12.** *SIMD compare operations*

Another common SIMD data manipulation operation is a permutation. SIMD permutations are employed to rearrange the elements of a SIMD operand. They are often applied prior to a specific calculation or to accelerate the performance of a SIMD arithmetic operation. A permutation generally requires two SIMD operands: a packed source operand of elements to permute and a packed operand of integer indices. Figure 1-13 illustrates an x86-AVX permutation using single-precision floating-point elements. In this example, the elements of the top-most SIMD operand are reordered using the element indices specified by the middle SIMD operand. Note that the same source operand element can be copied to multiple destination elements by simply specifying the appropriate index.

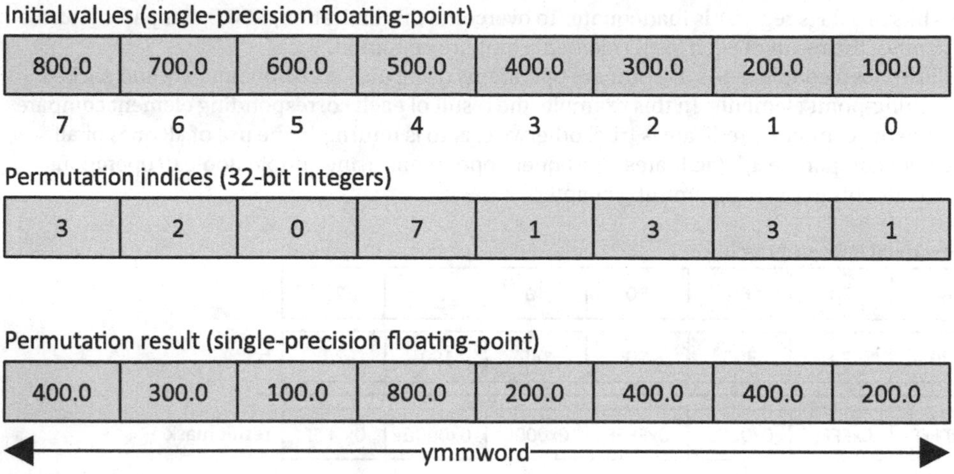

Initial values (single-precision floating-point)

| 800.0 | 700.0 | 600.0 | 500.0 | 400.0 | 300.0 | 200.0 | 100.0 |
|-------|-------|-------|-------|-------|-------|-------|-------|
| 7     | 6     | 5     | 4     | 3     | 2     | 1     | 0     |

Permutation indices (32-bit integers)

| 3 | 2 | 0 | 7 | 1 | 3 | 3 | 1 |
|---|---|---|---|---|---|---|---|

Permutation result (single-precision floating-point)

| 400.0 | 300.0 | 100.0 | 800.0 | 200.0 | 400.0 | 400.0 | 200.0 |
|-------|-------|-------|-------|-------|-------|-------|-------|

◄──────────────────ymmword──────────────────►

*Figure 1-13.* *SIMD permutation operation*

A broadcast operation copies a single value (or several values) to multiple locations in a SIMD operand. Broadcasts are often employed to load a scalar constant into each element of a SIMD operand. X86-AVX supports broadcast operations using either integer or floating-point values. Figure 1-14 shows the workings of a broadcast operation using single-precision floating-point values.

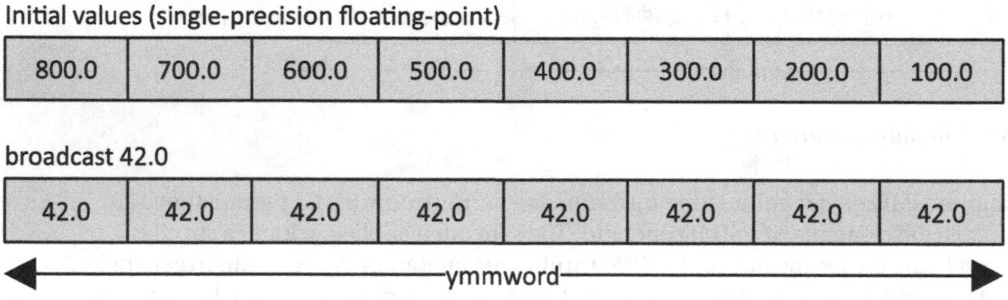

Initial values (single-precision floating-point)

| 800.0 | 700.0 | 600.0 | 500.0 | 400.0 | 300.0 | 200.0 | 100.0 |
|-------|-------|-------|-------|-------|-------|-------|-------|

broadcast 42.0

| 42.0 | 42.0 | 42.0 | 42.0 | 42.0 | 42.0 | 42.0 | 42.0 |
|------|------|------|------|------|------|------|------|

◄──────────────────ymmword──────────────────►

*Figure 1-14.* *Single-precision broadcast*

Figure 1-15 shows one more common manipulation operation. A masked move conditionally copies the elements from one SIMD operand to another SIMD operand based on the values in a control mask. In Figure 1-15, elements from Operand B are conditionally copied to Operand A if the most significant bit of the corresponding control mask is set to 1; otherwise, the element value in Operand A remains unaltered. Both AVX and AVX2 support masked moves using SIMD control masks. On processors that support AVX-512, functions use an opmask register to perform masked moves. They can also use an opmask register to perform a masked zeroing operation.

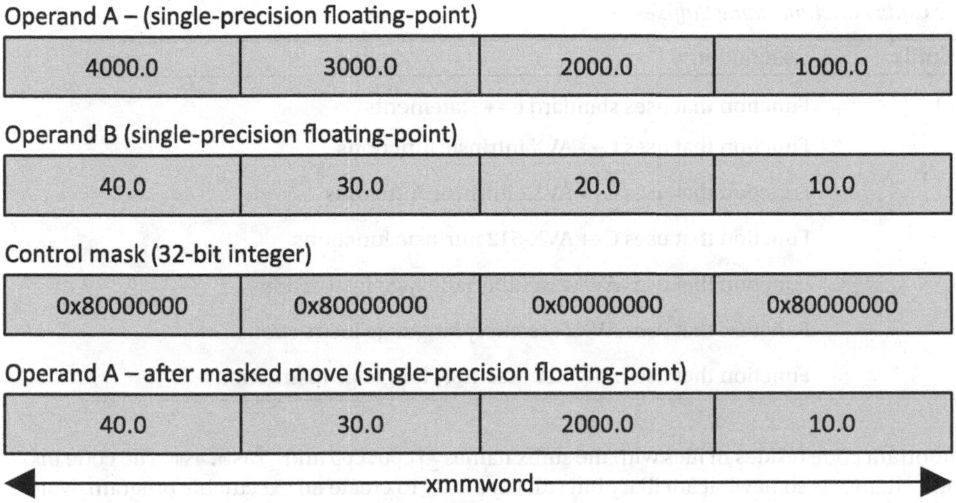

Operand A – (single-precision floating-point)

| 4000.0 | 3000.0 | 2000.0 | 1000.0 |
|--------|--------|--------|--------|

Operand B (single-precision floating-point)

| 40.0 | 30.0 | 20.0 | 10.0 |
|------|------|------|------|

Control mask (32-bit integer)

| 0x80000000 | 0x80000000 | 0x00000000 | 0x80000000 |
|------------|------------|------------|------------|

Operand A – after masked move (single-precision floating-point)

| 40.0 | 30.0 | 2000.0 | 10.0 |
|------|------|--------|------|

◄──────────────────────────xmmword──────────────────────────►

*Figure 1-15. Masked move operation*

# SIMD Programming

As mentioned in the Introduction, the primary objective of this book is to help you learn x86 SIMD programming using C++ SIMD intrinsic functions and x86-64 assembly language. The source code examples that you will see in the subsequent chapters are structured to help you achieve this goal.

Most of the source code examples published in this book follow the same design pattern. The first part of each example includes code that performs data initialization. The second part contains the SIMD code, which includes functions that use either C++ SIMD intrinsic functions or x86-AVX assembly language instructions. The final part of each example formats and displays the output. Some of the source code examples also include a rudimentary benchmarking function. Given the variety and scope of the source code in this book, I decided to create a (hopefully) straightforward naming convention for both file and function names. These are outlined Tables 1-3 and 1-4.

*Table 1-3. Source Code File Name Suffixes*

| File Name Suffix | Description |
|------------------|-------------|
| .h | Standard C++ header file |
| .cpp | Standard C++ source code file |
| _fcpp.cpp | C++ algorithm code (non-SIMD and SIMD) |
| _misc.cpp | Miscellaneous C++ functions |
| _bm.cpp | Benchmarking code |
| _fasm.asm | Assembly language algorithm code (SIMD) |

**Table 1-4.** *Source Code Function Name Suffixes*

| Function Name Suffix | Description |
| --- | --- |
| _Cpp (or no suffix) | Function that uses standard C++ statements |
| _Iavx | Function that uses C++ AVX intrinsic functions |
| _Iavx2 | Function that uses C++ AVX2 intrinsic functions |
| _Iavx512 | Function that uses C++ AVX-512 intrinsic functions |
| _Aavx | Function that uses AVX assembly language instructions |
| _Aavx2 | Function that uses AVX2 assembly language instructions |
| _Avx512 | Function that uses AVX-512 assembly language instructions |

The most important code resides in files with the suffix names `_fcpp.cpp` and `_fasm.asm`. The code in files with other suffix names is somewhat ancillary but still necessary to create an executable program. Note that function names incorporating the substrings avx, avx2, and avx512 will only work on processors that support the AVX, AVX2, and AVX-512 instruction set extensions, respectively. You can use one of the free utilities listed in Appendix B to verify the processing capabilities of your computer.

Finally, it should be noted that the C++ SIMD intrinsic functions used in the source code examples were originally developed by Intel for their compilers. Most of these functions are also supported by other x86-64 C++ compilers including Visual Studio C++ and GNU C++. Appendix A contains additional information about the source code including download and build instructions for both Visual Studio and the GNU toolchain. Depending on your personal preference, you may want to download and install the source code first before proceeding to the next chapter.

# Summary

Here are the key learning points for Chapter 1:

- SIMD is a parallel computing technique that carries out concurrent calculations using multiple data items.

- AVX supports 128- and 256-bit wide packed floating-point operands. It also supports packed 128-bit wide integer operands.

- AVX2 extends AVX to support 256-bit wide integer operands. It also adds additional broadcast and permutation instructions.

- AVX-512 minimally supports 512-bit wide packed operands of single-precision or double-precision floating-point values. It also supports 512-bit wide operands of packed 32- and 64-bit wide integers.

- The terms xmmword, ymmword, and zmmword are x86 assembly language expressions for 128-, 256-, and 512-bit wide SIMD data types and operands.

- The terms byte, word, doubleword, and quadword are x86 assembly language designations for 8-, 16-, 32-, and 64-bit integers.

- X86-AVX supports both wraparound and saturated arithmetic for packed 8- and 16-bit integers, both signed and unsigned.

# CHAPTER 2

■ ■ ■

# AVX C++ Programming: Part 1

The previous chapter explained SIMD fundamentals including packed types, arithmetic calculations, and data manipulation operations. It also highlighted a few details regarding the history of x86-AVX and its computational capabilities. The focus of this chapter is AVX integer arithmetic using 128-bit wide operands. The first section contains several concise source code examples that illustrate how to use C++ SIMD intrinsic functions to perform packed integer arithmetic. This followed by a section that highlights common programming operations with packed integers including bitwise logical operations and shifts. The third and final section includes source code examples that demonstrate elementary image processing tasks using C++ SIMD intrinsic functions. As you will soon see, SIMD techniques are ideal for many types of image processing algorithms.

## Integer Arithmetic

In this section, you will learn the basics of x86-AVX packed integer arithmetic using 128-bit wide SIMD operands. It begins with a simple program that demonstrates packed integer addition using both wraparound and saturated arithmetic. This is followed by a similar program that focuses on packed integer subtraction. The final source code example of this section details packed integer multiplication.

---

■ **Note**    Most of the source code examples is this book are shown using a single listing. This is done to minimize the number of listing references in the main text. The actual source code is partitioned into separate files using the naming conventions described in Chapter 1.

---

### Integer Addition

The first source code example is named Ch02_01. This example explains how to perform packed integer addition using C++ SIMD intrinsic functions. It also illustrates proper use of commonly used C++ SIMD data types. Listing 2-1 shows the source code for example Ch02_01.

***Listing 2-1.*** Example Ch02_01

```cpp
//----------------------------------------------------
//                  XmmVal.h
//----------------------------------------------------

#pragma once
#include <string>
#include <cstdint>
#include <sstream>
#include <iomanip>

struct alignas(16) XmmVal
{
public:
    union
    {
        int8_t m_I8[16];
        int16_t m_I16[8];
        int32_t m_I32[4];
        int64_t m_I64[2];
        uint8_t m_U8[16];
        uint16_t m_U16[8];
        uint32_t m_U32[4];
        uint64_t m_U64[2];
        float m_F32[4];
        double m_F64[2];
    };

    // rest of file XmmVal.h ...

//----------------------------------------------------
//                  Ch02_01.h
//----------------------------------------------------

#pragma once
#include "XmmVal.h"

// Ch02_01_fcpp.cpp
extern void AddI16_Iavx(XmmVal* c1, XmmVal* c2, const XmmVal* a, const XmmVal* b);
extern void AddU16_Iavx(XmmVal* c1, XmmVal* c2, const XmmVal* a, const XmmVal* b);

//----------------------------------------------------
//                  Ch02_01.cpp
//----------------------------------------------------

#include <iostream>
#include "Ch02_01.h"

static void AddI16(void);
static void AddU16(void);
```

```cpp
int main()
{
    AddI16();
    AddU16();
    return 0;
}

static void AddI16(void)
{
    const char nl = '\n';
    XmmVal a, b, c1, c2;

    a.m_I16[0] = 10;          b.m_I16[0] = 100;
    a.m_I16[1] = 200;         b.m_I16[1] = -200;
    a.m_I16[2] = 30;          b.m_I16[2] = 32760;
    a.m_I16[3] = -32766;      b.m_I16[3] = -400;
    a.m_I16[4] = 50;          b.m_I16[4] = 500;
    a.m_I16[5] = 60;          b.m_I16[5] = -600;
    a.m_I16[6] = 32000;       b.m_I16[6] = 1200;
    a.m_I16[7] = -32000;      b.m_I16[7] = -950;

    AddI16_Iavx(&c1, &c2, &a, &b);

    std::cout << "\nResults for AddI16_Iavx - Wraparound Addition\n";
    std::cout << "a:  " << a.ToStringI16() << nl;
    std::cout << "b:  " << b.ToStringI16() << nl;
    std::cout << "c1: " << c1.ToStringI16() << nl;
    std::cout << "\nResults for AddI16_Iavx - Saturated Addition\n";
    std::cout << "a:  " << a.ToStringI16() << nl;
    std::cout << "b:  " << b.ToStringI16() << nl;
    std::cout << "c2: " << c2.ToStringI16() << nl;
}

static void AddU16(void)
{
    const char nl = '\n';
    XmmVal a, b, c1, c2;

    a.m_U16[0] = 10;          b.m_U16[0] = 100;
    a.m_U16[1] = 200;         b.m_U16[1] = 200;
    a.m_U16[2] = 300;         b.m_U16[2] = 65530;
    a.m_U16[3] = 32766;       b.m_U16[3] = 40000;
    a.m_U16[4] = 50;          b.m_U16[4] = 500;
    a.m_U16[5] = 20000;       b.m_U16[5] = 25000;
    a.m_U16[6] = 32000;       b.m_U16[6] = 1200;
    a.m_U16[7] = 32000;       b.m_U16[7] = 50000;

    AddU16_Iavx(&c1, &c2, &a, &b);

    std::cout << "\nResults for AddU16_Iavx - Wraparound Addition\n";
    std::cout << "a:  " << a.ToStringU16() << nl;
```

19

```
    std::cout << "b:  " << b.ToStringU16() << nl;
    std::cout << "c1: " << c1.ToStringU16() << nl;
    std::cout << "\nResults for AddU16_Iavx - Saturated Addition\n";
    std::cout << "a:  " << a.ToStringU16() << nl;
    std::cout << "b:  " << b.ToStringU16() << nl;
    std::cout << "c2: " << c2.ToStringU16() << nl;
}

//-------------------------------------------------
//                 Ch02_01_fcpp.cpp
//-------------------------------------------------

#include <immintrin.h>
#include "Ch02_01.h"

void AddI16_Iavx(XmmVal* c1, XmmVal* c2, const XmmVal* a, const XmmVal* b)
{
    __m128i a_vals = _mm_load_si128 ((__m128i*)a);
    __m128i b_vals = _mm_load_si128 ((__m128i*)b);

    __m128i c1_vals = _mm_add_epi16(a_vals, b_vals);
    __m128i c2_vals = _mm_adds_epi16 (a_vals, b_vals);

    _mm_store_si128 ((__m128i*)c1, c1_vals);
    _mm_store_si128 ((__m128i*)c2, c2_vals);
}

void AddU16_Iavx(XmmVal* c1, XmmVal* c2, const XmmVal* a, const XmmVal* b)
{
    __m128i a_vals = _mm_load_si128 ((__m128i*)a);
    __m128i b_vals = _mm_load_si128 ((__m128i*)b);

    __m128i c1_vals = _mm_add_epi16 (a_vals, b_vals);
    __m128i c2_vals = _mm_adds_epu16 (a_vals, b_vals);

    _mm_store_si128 ((__m128i*)c1, c1_vals);
    _mm_store_si128 ((__m128i*)c2, c2_vals);
}
```

Listing 2-1 begins with the declaration of a C++ structure named XmmVal, which is declared in the header file XmmVal.h. This structure contains a publicly accessible anonymous union whose members correspond to the packed data types that can be used with a 128-bit wide x86-AVX operand. Note that XmmVal is declared using the alignas(16) specifier. This specifier instructs the C++ compiler to align each instance of an XmmVal on a 16-byte boundary. When an x86 processor executes an x86-AVX instruction that references an operand in memory, maximum performance is achieved when the operand is aligned on its natural boundary (e.g., 16-, 32-, or 64-byte boundaries for 128-, 256-, or 512-bit wide data types, respectively). Some x86-AVX instructions *require* their operands to be properly aligned, and these instructions will raise an exception if they attempt to access a misaligned operand in memory. You will learn more about this later. The structure XmmVal also contains several member functions that format the contents of an XmmVal variable for streaming to std::cout. The source code for these member functions is not shown in Listing 2-1 but is included in the software download package. Structure XmmVal is used in this example and in later source code examples to demonstrate x86-AVX SIMD operations.

The next file in Listing 2-1, Ch02_01.h, incorporates the requisite C++ function declarations for this source code example. Note that the function declarations in this header file use the previously defined XmmVal structure. Also note that file Ch02_01.h begins with a short comment block that includes its name to make it identifiable in the listing.

The file Ch02_01.cpp is next. This file contains the function main() and two other static functions named AddI16() and AddU16(). Function AddI16() begins its execution by initializing two XmmVal variables with packed 16-bit signed integer data. This is followed by a call to the function AddI16_Iavx(), which performs packed 16-bit signed integer addition. The remaining code in AddI16() displays the results calculated by AddI16_Iavx(). The function AddU16() is almost identical to AddI16() except that it uses unsigned instead of signed integers.

The final file in Listing 2-1 is Ch02_01_fcpp.cpp. This file contains two SIMD calculating functions named AddI16_Iavx() and AddU16_Iavx(). Near the top of this file is an #include statement for the header file immintrin.h. This file contains the declarations for the C++ SIMD intrinsic functions that are used in Ch02_01_fcpp.cpp. Function AddI16_Iavx() begins its execution with a call to _mm_load_si128 (). This C++ SIMD intrinsic function loads the contents of argument a into a_vals. Note that a_vals is declared as an __m128i, which a 128-bit wide C++ SIMD intrinsic type of 8-, 16-, 32-, or 64-bit integers. The _mm_load_si128 () function requires its source operand to be properly aligned on a 16-byte boundary. This requirement is satisfied by the alignas(16) specifier that was used in the declaration of XmmVal. Another call to _mm_load_si128 () is then employed to initialize b_vals.

Following SIMD variable initialization, AddI16_Iavx() employs the C++ SIMD intrinsic function _mm_add_epi16 (), which performs packed 16-bit integer addition using operands a_vals and b_vals. The result of this addition is saved in an __m128i variable named c1_vals. The ensuing call to _mm_adds_epi16 () also performs packed 16-bit integer addition but carries out its calculations using saturated instead of wraparound arithmetic. The final two code statements of AddI16_Iavx() employ the C++ SIMD intrinsic function _mm_store_si128 (). This function saves a 128-bit wide packed integer value to the specified target buffer, which must be aligned on 16-byte boundary.

Function AddU16_Iavx() performs its calculations using packed 16-bit unsigned integers. This function is identical to AddI16_Iavx() except for the use of _mm_adds_epu16 (), which performs 16-bit unsigned integer addition using saturated arithmetic. Here are the results for source code example Ch02_01:

```
Results for AddI16_Iavx - Wraparound Addition
a:       10     200       30  -32766  |     50       60    32000   -32000
b:      100    -200    32760    -400  |    500     -600     1200     -950
c1:     110       0   -32746   32370  |    550     -540   -32336    32586

Results for AddI16_Iavx - Saturated Addition
a:       10     200       30  -32766  |     50       60    32000   -32000
b:      100    -200    32760    -400  |    500     -600     1200     -950
c2:     110       0    32767  -32768  |    550     -540    32767   -32768

Results for AddU16_Iavx - Wraparound Addition
a:       10     200      300   32766  |     50    20000    32000    32000
b:      100     200    65530   40000  |    500    25000     1200    50000
c1:     110     400      294    7230  |    550    45000    33200    16464

Results for AddU16_Iavx - Saturated Addition
a:       10     200      300   32766  |     50    20000    32000    32000
b:      100     200    65530   40000  |    500    25000     1200    50000
c2:     110     400    65535   65535  |    550    45000    33200    65535
```

Other C++ SIMD intrinsic functions are available for packed integer addition. You can use the C++ intrinsic function _mm_add_epi8(), _mm_add_epi32(), or _mm_add_epi64() to perform packed addition using 8-, 32-, or 64-bit wide signed or unsigned integers. You can also use the function _mm_adds_epi8() or _mm_adds_epu8() to carry out packed saturated addition using 8-bit signed or unsigned integers. Note that distinct C++ SIMD intrinsic functions are used for wraparound and saturated integer addition since these operations can generate different results as explained in Chapter 1.

## Integer Subtraction

The next source code example, named Ch02_02, illustrates packed SIMD subtraction using 32- and 64-bit signed integers. Listing 2-2 shows the source code for example Ch02_02.

*Listing 2-2.* Example Ch02_02

```
//--------------------------------------------------
//                  Ch02_02.h
//--------------------------------------------------

#pragma once
#include "XmmVal.h"

// Ch02_02_fcpp.cpp
extern void SubI32_Iavx(XmmVal* c, const XmmVal* a, const XmmVal* b);
extern void SubI64_Iavx(XmmVal* c, const XmmVal* a, const XmmVal* b);

//--------------------------------------------------
//                  Ch02_02.cpp
//--------------------------------------------------

#include <iostream>
#include "Ch02_02.h"

static void SubI32(void);
static void SubI64(void);

int main()
{
    SubI32();
    SubI64();
    return 0;
}

static void SubI32(void)
{
    XmmVal a, b, c;
    const char nl = '\n';

    a.m_I32[0] = 1000000;        b.m_I32[0] = 100;
    a.m_I32[1] = 200;            b.m_I32[1] = -200;
    a.m_I32[2] = -30;            b.m_I32[2] = 30000;
```

```
        a.m_I32[3] = 40000000;    b.m_I32[3] = 5000;

        SubI32_Iavx(&c, &a, &b);

        std::cout << "\nResults for SubI32_Iavx\n";
        std::cout << "a:   " << a.ToStringI32() << nl;
        std::cout << "b:   " << b.ToStringI32() << nl;
        std::cout << "c:   " << c.ToStringI32() << nl;
}

static void SubI64(void)
{
        XmmVal a, b, c;
        const char nl = '\n';

        a.m_I64[0] = 100000000000; b.m_I64[0] = 99;
        a.m_I64[1] = 200;          b.m_I64[1] = 300000000000;

        SubI64_Iavx(&c, &a, &b);

        std::cout << "\nResults for SubI64_Iavx\n";
        std::cout << "a:   " << a.ToStringI64() << nl;
        std::cout << "b:   " << b.ToStringI64() << nl;
        std::cout << "c:   " << c.ToStringI64() << nl;
}

//--------------------------------------------------
//                 Ch02_02_fcpp.cpp
//--------------------------------------------------

#include <immintrin.h>
#include "Ch02_02.h"

extern void SubI32_Iavx(XmmVal* c, const XmmVal* a, const XmmVal* b)
{
        __m128i a_vals = _mm_load_si128 ((__m128i*)a);
        __m128i b_vals = _mm_load_si128 ((__m128i*)b);
        __m128i c_vals = _mm_sub_epi32 (a_vals, b_vals);

        _mm_store_si128 ((__m128i*)c, c_vals);
}

extern void SubI64_Iavx(XmmVal* c, const XmmVal* a, const XmmVal* b)
{
        __m128i a_vals = _mm_load_si128 ((__m128i*)a);
        __m128i b_vals = _mm_load_si128 ((__m128i*)b);
        __m128i c_vals = _mm_sub_epi64 (a_vals, b_vals);

        _mm_store_si128 ((__m128i*)c, c_vals);
}
```

The organization of the source code in example Ch02_02 parallels the previous example. In the file Ch02_02.cpp, the function SubI32() initializes XmmVal variables a and b using 32-bit signed integers. It then calls SubI32_Iavx(), which performs the packed subtraction. Function SubI64() is akin to SubI32() but uses 64-bit signed integers.

Function SubI32_Iavx() begins its execution with two _mm_load_si128 () calls that initialize XmmVal variables a and b. It then uses the C++ SIMD intrinsic function _mm_sub_epi32 () to perform packed 32-bit integer subtraction. The results are then saved using _mm_store_si128 (). Function SubI64_Iavx() is almost identical to SubI32_Iavx() except that it employs _mm_sub_epi64 () to carry out packed 64-bit integer subtraction. Here are the results for source code example Ch02_02:

```
Results for SubI32_Iavx
a:        1000000            200   |       -30       40000000
b:            100           -200   |     30000           5000
c:         999900            400   |    -30030       39995000

Results for SubI64_Iavx
a:               100000000000   |                        200
b:                         99   |               300000000000
c:                99999999901   |              -299999999800
```

You can use the C++ SIMD intrinsic function _mm_sub_epi8() or _mm_sub_epi16() to perform packed subtraction using 8- or 16-bit wide signed or unsigned integers, respectively. To perform saturated packed subtraction, you can use the C++ SIMD intrinsic function _mm_subs_epi8(), _mm_subs_epi16(), _mm_subs_epu8(), or _mm_subs_epu16().

# Integer Multiplication

There are also C++ SIMD intrinsic functions that perform packed integer multiplication. These functions are used somewhat differently than the packed integer addition and subtraction functions you saw in the previous two examples. Listing 2-3 shows the source code for example Ch02_03. This example demonstrates packed multiplication using 16- and 32-bit signed integers.

**Listing 2-3.** Example Ch02_03

```
//--------------------------------------------------
//              Ch02_03.h
//--------------------------------------------------

#pragma once
#include "XmmVal.h"

// Ch02_03_fcpp.cpp
extern void MulI16_Iavx(XmmVal c[2], const XmmVal* a, const XmmVal* b);
extern void MulI32a_Iavx(XmmVal* c, const XmmVal* a, const XmmVal* b);
extern void MulI32b_Iavx(XmmVal c[2], const XmmVal* a, const XmmVal* b);


//--------------------------------------------------
//              Ch02_03.cpp
//--------------------------------------------------
```

```cpp
#include <iostream>
#include <iomanip>
#include <string>
#include "Ch02_03.h"

static void MulI16(void);
static void MulI32a(void);
static void MulI32b(void);

int main()
{
    const char nl = '\n';
    std::string sep(75, '-');

    MulI16();
    std::cout << nl << sep << nl;
    MulI32a();
    std::cout << nl << sep << nl;
    MulI32b();
    return 0;
}

static void MulI16(void)
{
    const char nl = '\n';
    XmmVal a, b, c[2];

    a.m_I16[0] = 10;        b.m_I16[0] = -5;
    a.m_I16[1] = 3000;      b.m_I16[1] = 100;
    a.m_I16[2] = -2000;     b.m_I16[2] = -9000;
    a.m_I16[3] = 42;        b.m_I16[3] = 1000;
    a.m_I16[4] = -5000;     b.m_I16[4] = 25000;
    a.m_I16[5] = 8;         b.m_I16[5] = 16384;
    a.m_I16[6] = 10000;     b.m_I16[6] = 3500;
    a.m_I16[7] = -60;       b.m_I16[7] = 6000;

    MulI16_Iavx(c, &a, &b);

    std::cout << "\nResults for MulI16_Iavx\n";
    for (size_t i = 0; i < 8; i++)
    {
        std::cout << "a[" << i << "]: " << std::setw(8) << a.m_I16[i] << "   ";
        std::cout << "b[" << i << "]: " << std::setw(8) << b.m_I16[i] << "   ";

        if (i < 4)
        {
            std::cout << "c[0][" << i << "]: ";
            std::cout << std::setw(12) << c[0].m_I32[i] << nl;
        }
```

```cpp
        else
        {
            std::cout << "c[1][" << i - 4 << "]: ";
            std::cout << std::setw(12) << c[1].m_I32[i - 4] << nl;
        }
    }
}

static void MulI32a(void)
{
    const char nl = '\n';
    XmmVal a, b, c;

    a.m_I32[0] = 10;        b.m_I32[0] = -500;
    a.m_I32[1] = 3000;      b.m_I32[1] = 100;
    a.m_I32[2] = -2000;     b.m_I32[2] = -12000;
    a.m_I32[3] = 4200;      b.m_I32[3] = 1000;

    MulI32a_Iavx(&c, &a, &b);

    std::cout << "\nResults for MulI32a_Iavx\n";
    for (size_t i = 0; i < 4; i++)
    {
        std::cout << "a[" << i << "]: " << std::setw(10) << a.m_I32[i] << "  ";
        std::cout << "b[" << i << "]: " << std::setw(10) << b.m_I32[i] << "  ";
        std::cout << "c[" << i << "]: " << std::setw(10) << c.m_I32[i] << nl;
    }
}

static void MulI32b(void)
{
    const char nl = '\n';
    XmmVal a, b, c[2];

    a.m_I32[0] = 10;        b.m_I32[0] = -500;
    a.m_I32[1] = 3000;      b.m_I32[1] = 100;
    a.m_I32[2] = -40000;    b.m_I32[2] = -120000;
    a.m_I32[3] = 4200;      b.m_I32[3] = 1000;

    MulI32b_Iavx(c, &a, &b);

    std::cout << "\nResults for MulI32b_Iavx\n";
    for (size_t i = 0; i < 4; i++)
    {
        std::cout << "a[" << i << "]: " << std::setw(10) << a.m_I32[i] << "  ";
        std::cout << "b[" << i << "]: " << std::setw(10) << b.m_I32[i] << "  ";

        if (i < 2)
        {
            std::cout << "c[0][" << i << "]: ";
            std::cout << std::setw(14) << c[0].m_I64[i] << nl;
        }
```

```
        else
        {
            std::cout << "c[1][" << i - 2 << "]: ";
            std::cout << std::setw(14) << c[1].m_I64[i - 2] << nl;
        }
    }
}

//-------------------------------------------------
//                Ch02_03_fcpp.cpp
//-------------------------------------------------

#include <immintrin.h>
#include "Ch02_03.h"

void MulI16_Iavx(XmmVal c[2], const XmmVal* a, const XmmVal* b)
{
    __m128i a_vals = _mm_load_si128 ((__m128i*)a);
    __m128i b_vals = _mm_load_si128 ((__m128i*)b);

    __m128i temp_lo = _mm_mullo_epi16 (a_vals, b_vals);
    __m128i temp_hi = _mm_mulhi_epi16 (a_vals, b_vals);

    __m128i result_lo = _mm_unpacklo_epi16 (temp_lo, temp_hi);
    __m128i result_hi = _mm_unpackhi_epi16 (temp_lo, temp_hi);

    _mm_store_si128 ((__m128i*)&c[0], result_lo);
    _mm_store_si128 ((__m128i*)&c[1], result_hi);
}

void MulI32a_Iavx(XmmVal* c, const XmmVal* a, const XmmVal* b)
{
    __m128i a_vals = _mm_load_si128 ((__m128i*)a);
    __m128i b_vals = _mm_load_si128 ((__m128i*)b);
    __m128i c_vals = _mm_mullo_epi32 (a_vals, b_vals);

    _mm_store_si128 ((__m128i*)c, c_vals);
}

void MulI32b_Iavx(XmmVal c[2], const XmmVal* a, const XmmVal* b)
{
    __m128i a_vals = _mm_load_si128 ((__m128i*)a);
    __m128i b_vals = _mm_load_si128 ((__m128i*)b);

    __m128i temp1 = _mm_mul_epi32 (a_vals, b_vals);      // q2 | q0
    __m128i temp2 = _mm_srli_si128 (a_vals, 4);
    __m128i temp3 = _mm_srli_si128 (b_vals, 4);
    __m128i temp4 = _mm_mul_epi32 (temp2, temp3);        // q3 | q1
```

```
    *(&c[0].m_I64[0]) = _mm_extract_epi64 (temp1, 0);    // q0
    *(&c[0].m_I64[1]) = _mm_extract_epi64 (temp4, 0);    // q1
    *(&c[1].m_I64[0]) = _mm_extract_epi64 (temp1, 1);    // q2
    *(&c[1].m_I64[1]) = _mm_extract_epi64 (temp4, 1);    // q3
}
```

In file ChO2_03.cpp, the C++ function MulI16() contains code that initializes XmmVal variables a and b using 16-bit signed integers. It then calls MulI16_Iavx(), which performs the packed integer multiplication. The results are then streamed to std::cout. The other two static functions in ChO2_03.cpp, MulI32a() and Mul32b(), perform similar initialization tasks for 32-bit packed integer multiplication and then call MulI32a_Iavx() and MulI32b_Iavx(), respectively.

Recall that when performing integer multiplication, the product of two *n-bit* wide integers is always *2n* bits. When performing packed integer multiplication, additional processing is sometimes necessary to form the final products as you will soon see. Function MulI16_Iavx() starts with two _mm_load_si128 () calls that initialize XmmVal variables a and b. It then employs the C++ SIMD intrinsic function _mm_mullo_epi16 () to perform packed 16-bit integer multiplication. This function returns an __m128i value that contains only the low-order 16 bits of each 32-bit product. Function MulI16_Iavx() then uses the C++ SIMD intrinsic function _mm_mulhi_epi16 () to calculate the high-order 16 bits of each 32-bit product. The next function call, _mm_unpacklo_epi16 (), interleaves the four low-order 16-bit integer elements of source operands temp_lo and temp_hi to form 32-bit integer products. The subsequent call to _mm_unpackhi_epi16 () performs a similar operation using the four high-order 16-bit integer elements of the same source operands. Figure 2-1 illustrates the product calculation that MulI16_Iavx() employs.

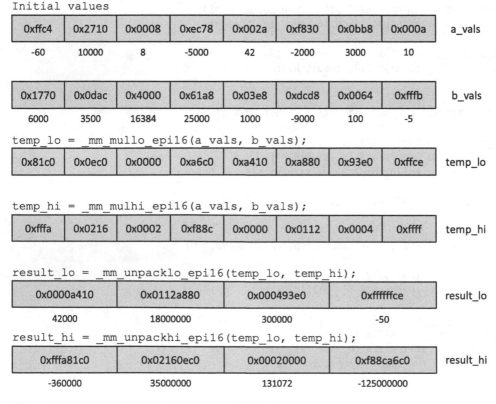

*Figure 2-1.* *Packed 16-bit signed integer multiplication*

Function MulI32a_Iavx() highlights one method of performing packed 32-bit signed integer multiplication. This function uses the C++ SIMD intrinsic function _mm_mullo_epi32 () to calculate the low-order 32 bits of each product. The packed 32-bit integer products are then saved using _mm_store_si128 (). This technique is suitable when calculating multiplicative products that will not exceed the value limits of a 32-bit signed integer.

Function Mul32b_Iavx() demonstrates another technique for calculating products using packed 32-bit signed integers. Following the initialization of a_vals and b_vals, Mul32b_Iavx() uses the C++ SIMD intrinsic function _mm_mul_epi32 () to calculate a.m_I32[0] * b.m_I32[0] and a.m_I32[2] * b.m_I32[2]. Note that _mm_mul_epi32 () computes complete 64-bit products. The subsequent _mm_srli_si128 () and _mm_srli_si128 () calls right shift a_vals and b_vals by 4 bytes (zeros are shifted in). The reason for these shifts is that _mm_mul_epi32 () carries out its calculations using only the even numbered elements of its two operands. The right shift operations facilitate calculation of the products a.m_I32[1] * b.m_I32[1] and a.m_I32[3] * b.m_I32[3] by the ensuing call to _mm_mul_epi32 () as shown in Figure 2-2. The final 64-bit products are then extracted from temp1 and temp4 using a series of calls to _mm_extract_epi64 (). The constant that is specified in each _mm_extract_epi64 () call designates which 64-bit integer to extract from the 128-bit wide source operand.

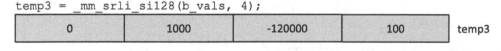

Initial values

| 4200 | -40000 | 3000 | 10 | a_vals |
|---|---|---|---|---|

| 1000 | -120000 | 100 | -500 | b_vals |
|---|---|---|---|---|

temp1 = _mm_mul_epi32(a_vals, b_vals);

| 4800000000 | -5000 | temp1 |
|---|---|---|

temp2 = _mm_srli_si128(a_vals, 4);

| 0 | 4200 | -40000 | 3000 | temp2 |
|---|---|---|---|---|

temp3 = _mm_srli_si128(b_vals, 4);

| 0 | 1000 | -120000 | 100 | temp3 |
|---|---|---|---|---|

temp4 = _mm_mul_epi32(temp2, temp3);

| 4200000 | 300000 | temp4 |
|---|---|---|

**Figure 2-2.** *Packed 32-bit signed integer multiplication*

Here are the results for source code example Ch02_03:

```
Results for MulI16_Iavx
a[0]:        10  b[0]:        -5  c[0][0]:          -50
a[1]:      3000  b[1]:       100  c[0][1]:       300000
a[2]:     -2000  b[2]:     -9000  c[0][2]:     18000000
a[3]:        42  b[3]:      1000  c[0][3]:        42000
a[4]:     -5000  b[4]:     25000  c[1][0]:   -125000000
```

```
a[5]:         8  b[5]:    16384  c[1][1]:         131072
a[6]:     10000  b[6]:     3500  c[1][2]:       35000000
a[7]:       -60  b[7]:     6000  c[1][3]:        -360000


-------------------------------------------------------------------


Results for MulI32a_Iavx
a[0]:        10  b[0]:     -500  c[0]:            -5000
a[1]:      3000  b[1]:      100  c[1]:           300000
a[2]:     -2000  b[2]:   -12000  c[2]:         24000000
a[3]:      4200  b[3]:     1000  c[3]:          4200000


-------------------------------------------------------------------


Results for MulI32b_Iavx
a[0]:        10  b[0]:     -500  c[0][0]:          -5000
a[1]:      3000  b[1]:      100  c[0][1]:         300000
a[2]:    -40000  b[2]:  -120000  c[1][0]:     4800000000
a[3]:      4200  b[3]:     1000  c[1][1]:        4200000
```

# Integer Bitwise Logical and Shift Operations

Besides standard arithmetic operations, x86-AVX also supports other common operations using 128-bit wide packed integer operands. In this section, you will learn how to carry out bitwise logical and shift operations.

## Bitwise Logical Operations

Listing 2-4 shows the source code for example Ch02_04. This example demonstrates how to perform bitwise logical (e.g., AND, OR, and exclusive OR) operations using packed integer operands.

*Listing 2-4.* Example Ch02_04

```
//--------------------------------------------------
//              Ch02_04.h
//--------------------------------------------------

#pragma once
#include "XmmVal.h"

// Ch02_04_fcpp.cpp
extern void AndU16_Iavx(XmmVal* c, const XmmVal* a, const XmmVal* b);
extern void OrU16_Iavx(XmmVal* c, const XmmVal* a, const XmmVal* b);
extern void XorU16_Iavx(XmmVal* c, const XmmVal* a, const XmmVal* b);


//--------------------------------------------------
//              Ch02_04.cpp
//--------------------------------------------------
```

```cpp
#include <iostream>
#include "Ch02_04.h"

static void BitwiseLogical(void);

int main()
{
    BitwiseLogical();
    return 0;
}

static void BitwiseLogical(void)
{
    XmmVal a, b, c;
    const char nl = '\n';

    a.m_U16[0] = 0x1234;        b.m_U16[0] = 0xFF00;
    a.m_U16[1] = 0xABDC;        b.m_U16[1] = 0x00FF;
    a.m_U16[2] = 0xAA55;        b.m_U16[2] = 0xAAAA;
    a.m_U16[3] = 0x1111;        b.m_U16[3] = 0x5555;
    a.m_U16[4] = 0xFFFF;        b.m_U16[4] = 0x8000;
    a.m_U16[5] = 0x7F7F;        b.m_U16[5] = 0x7FFF;
    a.m_U16[6] = 0x9876;        b.m_U16[6] = 0xF0F0;
    a.m_U16[7] = 0x7F00;        b.m_U16[7] = 0x0880;

    AndU16_Iavx(&c, &a, &b);
    std::cout << "\nResults for AndU16_Iavx\n";
    std::cout << "a: " << a.ToStringX16() << nl;
    std::cout << "b: " << b.ToStringX16() << nl;
    std::cout << "c: " << c.ToStringX16() << nl;

    OrU16_Iavx(&c, &a, &b);
    std::cout << "\nResults for OrU16_Iavx\n";
    std::cout << "a: " << a.ToStringX16() << nl;
    std::cout << "b: " << b.ToStringX16() << nl;
    std::cout << "c: " << c.ToStringX16() << nl;

    XorU16_Iavx(&c, &a, &b);
    std::cout << "\nResults for XorU16_Iavx\n";
    std::cout << "a: " << a.ToStringX16() << nl;
    std::cout << "b: " << b.ToStringX16() << nl;
    std::cout << "c: " << c.ToStringX16() << nl;
}

//-------------------------------------------------
//                Ch02_04_fcpp.cpp
//-------------------------------------------------

#include <immintrin.h>
#include "Ch02_04.h"
```

```
void AndU16_Iavx(XmmVal* c, const XmmVal* a, const XmmVal* b)
{
    __m128i a_vals = _mm_load_si128 ((__m128i*)a);
    __m128i b_vals = _mm_load_si128 ((__m128i*)b);
    __m128i c_vals = _mm_and_si128(a_vals, b_vals);

    _mm_store_si128 ((__m128i*)c, c_vals);
}

void OrU16_Iavx(XmmVal* c, const XmmVal* a, const XmmVal* b)
{
    __m128i a_vals = _mm_load_si128 ((__m128i*)a);
    __m128i b_vals = _mm_load_si128 ((__m128i*)b);
    __m128i c_vals = _mm_or_si128 (a_vals, b_vals);

    _mm_store_si128 ((__m128i*)c, c_vals);
}

void XorU16_Iavx(XmmVal* c, const XmmVal* a, const XmmVal* b)
{
    __m128i a_vals = _mm_load_si128 ((__m128i*)a);
    __m128i b_vals = _mm_load_si128 ((__m128i*)b);
    __m128i c_vals = _mm_xor_si128 (a_vals, b_vals);

    _mm_store_si128 ((__m128i*)c, c_vals);
}
```

In Listing 2-4, the function BitwiseLogical() initializes XmmVal variables a and b as test values. It then invokes the calculating functions AndU16_Iavx(), OrU16_Iavx(), and XorU16_Iavx(). These functions call the corresponding C++ SIMD intrinsic functions _mm_and_si128 (), _mm_or_si128 (), and _mm_xor_si128 (). Unlike packed integer arithmetic operations, there are no distinct integer elements in a packed bitwise logical operation. The processor simply carries out the specified Boolean operation using the corresponding bit positions of each SIMD operand. Here are the results for source code example Ch02_04:

```
Results for AndU16_Iavx
a:    1234    ABDC    AA55    1111    |    FFFF    7F7F    9876    7F00
b:    FF00    00FF    AAAA    5555    |    8000    7FFF    F0F0    0880
c:    1200    00DC    AA00    1111    |    8000    7F7F    9070    0800

Results for OrU16_Iavx
a:    1234    ABDC    AA55    1111    |    FFFF    7F7F    9876    7F00
b:    FF00    00FF    AAAA    5555    |    8000    7FFF    F0F0    0880
c:    FF34    ABFF    AAFF    5555    |    FFFF    7FFF    F8F6    7F80

Results for XorU16_Iavx
a:    1234    ABDC    AA55    1111    |    FFFF    7F7F    9876    7F00
b:    FF00    00FF    AAAA    5555    |    8000    7FFF    F0F0    0880
c:    ED34    AB23    00FF    4444    |    7FFF    0080    6886    7780
```

# Shift Operations

Listing 2-5 shows the source code for example Ch02_05. This example illustrates use of several C++ SIMD intrinsic functions that perform logical and arithmetic shift operations.

*Listing 2-5.* Example Ch02_05

```
//--------------------------------------------------
//                  Ch02_05.h
//--------------------------------------------------

#pragma once
#include "XmmVal.h"

// Ch02_05_fcpp.cpp
extern void SllU16_Iavx(XmmVal* c, const XmmVal* a, int count);
extern void SrlU16_Iavx(XmmVal* c, const XmmVal* a, int count);
extern void SraU16_Iavx(XmmVal* c, const XmmVal* a, int count);

//--------------------------------------------------
//                  Ch02_05.cpp
//--------------------------------------------------

#include <iostream>
#include "Ch02_05.h"

static void ShiftU16(void);

int main()
{
    ShiftU16();
    return 0;
}

static void ShiftU16(void)
{
    XmmVal a, c;
    const int count_l = 8;
    const int count_r = 4;
    const char nl = '\n';

    a.m_U16[0] = 0x1234;
    a.m_U16[1] = 0xFFB0;
    a.m_U16[2] = 0x00CC;
    a.m_U16[3] = 0x8080;
    a.m_U16[4] = 0x00FF;
    a.m_U16[5] = 0xAAAA;
    a.m_U16[6] = 0x0F0F;
    a.m_U16[7] = 0x0101;
```

```
    SllU16_Iavx(&c, &a, count_l);
    std::cout << "\nResults for SllU16_Aavx - count = " << count_l << nl;
    std::cout << "a: " << a.ToStringX16() << nl;
    std::cout << "c: " << c.ToStringX16() << nl;

    SrlU16_Iavx(&c, &a, count_r);
    std::cout << "\nResults for SrlU16_Aavx - count = " << count_r << nl;
    std::cout << "a: " << a.ToStringX16() << nl;
    std::cout << "c: " << c.ToStringX16() << nl;

    SraU16_Iavx(&c, &a, count_r);
    std::cout << "\nResults for SraU16_Aavx - count = " << count_r << nl;
    std::cout << "a: " << a.ToStringX16() << nl;
    std::cout << "c: " << c.ToStringX16() << nl;
}

//-------------------------------------------------
//                 Ch02_05_fcpp.cpp
//-------------------------------------------------

#include <immintrin.h>
#include "Ch02_05.h"

void SllU16_Iavx(XmmVal* c, const XmmVal* a, int count)
{
    __m128i a_vals = _mm_load_si128 ((__m128i*)a);
    __m128i b_vals = _mm_slli_epi16 (a_vals, count);

    _mm_store_si128 ((__m128i*)c, b_vals);
}

void SrlU16_Iavx(XmmVal* c, const XmmVal* a, int count)
{
    __m128i a_vals = _mm_load_si128 ((__m128i*)a);
    __m128i b_vals = _mm_srli_epi16 (a_vals, count);

    _mm_store_si128 ((__m128i*)c, b_vals);
}

void SraU16_Iavx(XmmVal* c, const XmmVal* a, int count)
{
    __m128i a_vals = _mm_load_si128 ((__m128i*)a);
    __m128i b_vals = _mm_srai_epi16 (a_vals, count);

    _mm_store_si128 ((__m128i*)c, b_vals);
}
```

Source code example Ch02_05 begins its execution with the initialization of XmmVal variable a using 16-bit wide integer elements. It then executes several calculating functions that perform various shift operations. The function SllU16_Iavx() uses the C++ SIMD intrinsic function _mm_slli_epi16 () to left shift each 16-bit integer element by count bits. Similarly, function SrlU16_Iavx() employs the C++ SIMD intrinsic function _mm_srli_epi16 () to logically right shift each 16-bit integer element by count bits. Note that both _mm_slli_epi16 () and _mm_srli_epi16 () shift in zeros for each element from the left or right, respectively. The final calculation is carried out by SraU16_Iavx(), which uses the C++ SIMD intrinsic function _mm_srai_epi16 () to perform an arithmetic right shift of each 16-bit integer element. Recall that an integer arithmetic right shift fills empty bit positions using the value of the sign bit. Here are the results for source code example Ch02_05:

```
Results for SllU16_Aavx - count = 8
a:    1234    FFB0    00CC    8080    |    00FF    AAAA    0F0F    0101
c:    3400    B000    CC00    8000    |    FF00    AA00    0F00    0100

Results for SrlU16_Aavx - count = 4
a:    1234    FFB0    00CC    8080    |    00FF    AAAA    0F0F    0101
c:    0123    0FFB    000C    0808    |    000F    0AAA    00F0    0010

Results for SraU16_Aavx - count = 4
a:    1234    FFB0    00CC    8080    |    00FF    AAAA    0F0F    0101
c:    0123    FFFB    000C    F808    |    000F    FAAA    00F0    0010
```

# C++ SIMD Intrinsic Function Naming Conventions

If you haven't done so already, now might be a good time to take a quick look at the Intel Intrinsics Guide website (https://software.intel.com/sites/landingpage/IntrinsicsGuide/). This site includes comprehensive information that describes the operation of all C++ SIMD instruction functions. When exploring the Intel Intrinsics Guide website, it is easy to get overwhelmed by the number of available C++ SIMD (and non-SIMD) intrinsic functions. Fortunately, most of the C++ SIMD intrinsic functions and data types follow a straightforward naming convention. Functions are named using a <prefix>_<intrinop>_<suffix> pattern. The <intrinop> component is a short descriptive text string that describes the operation (e.g., add, sub, and, xor, etc.). Table 2-1 shows the text strings that are used for the <prefix> and <suffix> components of a function name. Most AVX-512 C++ SIMD intrinsic function names also include the text string _mask_ or _maskz_ to signify that they require an integer mask operand.

***Table 2-1.*** *C++ SIMD Intrinsic Function Name Prefixes and Suffixes*

| String | Type | Description |
|---|---|---|
| _mm | Prefix | X86-AVX function that uses 128-bit wide operands |
| _mm256 | Prefix | X86-AVX function that uses 256-bit wide operands |
| _mm512 | Prefix | X86-AVX function that uses 512-bit wide operands |
| _epi8 | Suffix | Packed 8-bit signed integers |
| _epi16 | Suffix | Packed 16-bit signed integers |
| _epi32 | Suffix | Packed 32-bit signed integers |
| _epi64 | Suffix | Packed 64-bit signed integers |
| _epu8 | Suffix | Packed 8-bit unsigned integers |
| _epu16 | Suffix | Packed 16-bit unsigned integers |
| _epu32 | Suffix | Packed 32-bit unsigned integers |
| _epu64 | Suffix | Packed 64-bit signed integers |
| _ss | Suffix | Scalar single-precision floating-point |
| _sd | Suffix | Scalar double-precision floating-point |
| _ps | Suffix | Packed single-precision floating-point |
| _pd | Suffix | Packed double-precision floating-point |

It should be noted that many of the C++ SIMD intrinsic functions that carry out their operations using 128-bit wide SIMD operands will also execute on processors that support SSE, SSE2, SSE3, SSSE3, SSE4.1, or SSE4.2. For more information, you can consult the previously mentioned Intel Intrinsics Guide website.

Table 2-2 lists the principal C++ SIMD intrinsic data types.

***Table 2-2.*** *C++ SIMD Intrinsic Data Types*

| Type | Description |
|---|---|
| __m128 | 128-bit wide packed single-precision floating-point |
| __m128d | 128-bit wide packed double-precision floating-point |
| __m128i | 128-bit wide packed integers |
| __m256 | 256-bit wide packed single-precision floating-point |
| __m256d | 256-bit wide packed double-precision floating-point |
| __m256i | 256-bit wide packed integers |
| __m512 | 512-bit wide packed single-precision floating-point |
| __m512d | 512-bit wide packed single-precision floating-point |
| __m512i | 512-bit wide packed integers |

It is important to keep in mind that none of the C++ SIMD intrinsic functions and data types are defined in any of the ISO C++ standards. Minor discrepancies exist between mainstream compilers such as Visual C++ and GNU C++. Also, these compilers employ different techniques to implement the various SIMD functions and data types. If you are developing code that needs to work on multiple platforms, you should avoid directly referencing any of the internal members of the data types shown in Table 2-2. You can employ the portable SIMD data types used in this book (e.g., XmmVal) or define your own portable SIMD data type.

# Image Processing Algorithms

The source code examples presented thus far were designed to familiarize you with basic C++ SIMD intrinsic functions and common packed integer operations. To fully exploit the performance benefits of x86-AVX, you must develop complete SIMD functions. The source code examples in this section explain how to code a few simple image processing functions.

In the first example, you will learn how to utilize x86-AVX and C++ SIMD intrinsic functions to find the minimum and maximum value in an array of 8-bit unsigned integers. This example has real-world utility since digital images are often arranged in memory using arrays or matrices of 8-bit unsigned integers. Also, many image processing algorithms (e.g., contrast enhancement) often need to ascertain the minimum (darkest) and maximum (brightest) pixel values in an image. The second source code example illustrates how to calculate the mean value of an array of 8-bit unsigned integers using SIMD arithmetic. This is another example of a realistic algorithm that is directly relevant to the province of image processing. Finally, you will learn some straightforward techniques for benchmarking the performance of a SIMD function.

## Pixel Minimum and Maximum

Source code example Ch02_06 demonstrates how to find the minimum and maximum values in an array of 8-bit unsigned integers. This example also illuminates the use of dynamically allocated arrays that are properly aligned for use in x86-AVX calculating functions and some performance benchmarking techniques. Listing 2-6 shows the source code for example Ch02_06.

***Listing 2-6.*** Example Ch02_06

```
//--------------------------------------------------
//                 Ch02_06.h
//--------------------------------------------------

#pragma once
#include <cstddef>
#include <cstdint>

// Ch02_06_fcpp.cpp
extern bool CalcMinMaxU8_Cpp(uint8_t* x_min, uint8_t* x_max, const uint8_t* x, size_t n);
extern bool CalcMinMaxU8_Iavx(uint8_t* x_min, uint8_t* x_max, const uint8_t* x, size_t n);

// Ch02_06_misc.cpp
extern void InitArray(uint8_t* x, size_t n, unsigned int rng_seed);

// Ch02_06_BM.cpp
extern void CalcMinMaxU8_bm();
```

```cpp
// c_NumElements must be > 0 and even multiple of 16
const size_t c_NumElements = 10000000;
const unsigned int c_RngSeedVal = 23;

//-------------------------------------------------
//                 Ch02_06_misc.cpp
//-------------------------------------------------

#include "Ch02_06.h"
#include "MT.h"

void InitArray(uint8_t* x, size_t n, unsigned int rng_seed)
{
    int rng_min_val = 5;
    int rng_max_val = 250;
    MT::FillArray(x, n, rng_min_val, rng_max_val, rng_seed);

    // Use known values for min & max (for test purposes)
    x[(n / 4) * 3 + 1] = 2;
    x[n / 4 + 11] = 3;
    x[n / 2] = 252;
    x[n / 2 + 13] = 253;
    x[n / 8 + 5] = 4;
    x[n / 8 + 7] = 254;
}

//-------------------------------------------------
//                 Ch02_06.cpp
//-------------------------------------------------

#include <iostream>
#include "Ch02_06.h"
#include "AlignedMem.h"

static void CalcMinMaxU8();

int main()
{
    CalcMinMaxU8();
    CalcMinMaxU8_bm();
}

static void CalcMinMaxU8()
{
    size_t n = c_NumElements;
    AlignedArray<uint8_t> x_aa(n, 16);
    uint8_t* x = x_aa.Data();

    InitArray(x, n, c_RngSeedVal);
```

```cpp
    uint8_t x_min1 = 0, x_max1 = 0;
    uint8_t x_min2 = 0, x_max2 = 0;

    bool rc1 = CalcMinMaxU8_Cpp(&x_min1, &x_max1, x, n);
    bool rc2 = CalcMinMaxU8_Iavx(&x_min2, &x_max2, x, n);

    std::cout << "\nResults for CalcMinMaxU8_Cpp\n";
    std::cout << "rc1: " << rc1 << "   x_min1: " << (int)x_min1;
    std::cout << "   x_max1: " << (int)x_max1 << '\n';
    std::cout << "\nResults for CalcMinMaxU8_Iavx\n";
    std::cout << "rc2: " << rc2 << "   x_min2: " << (int)x_min2;
    std::cout << "   x_max2: " << (int)x_max2 << '\n';
}

//------------------------------------------------
//                  Ch02_06_fcpp.cpp
//------------------------------------------------

#include <immintrin.h>
#include "Ch02_06.h"
#include "AlignedMem.h"

bool CalcMinMaxU8_Cpp(uint8_t* x_min, uint8_t* x_max, const uint8_t* x, size_t n)
{
    if (n == 0 || ((n % 16) != 0))
        return false;

    if (!AlignedMem::IsAligned(x, 16))
        return false;

    uint8_t min_val = 0xff;
    uint8_t max_val = 0;

    for (size_t i = 0; i < n; i++)
    {
        uint8_t x_val = x[i];

        if (x_val < min_val)
            min_val = x_val;
        else if (x_val > max_val)
            max_val = x_val;
    }

    *x_min = min_val;
    *x_max = max_val;
    return true;
}
```

```cpp
bool CalcMinMaxU8_Iavx(uint8_t* x_min, uint8_t* x_max, const uint8_t* x, size_t n)
{
    if (n == 0 || ((n % 16) != 0))
        return false;

    if (!AlignedMem::IsAligned(x, 16))
        return false;

    __m128i min_vals = _mm_set1_epi8 ((char)0xff);
    __m128i max_vals = _mm_setzero_si128 ();

    const size_t num_simd_elements = 16;

    for (size_t i = 0; i < n; i += num_simd_elements)
    {
        __m128i x_vals = _mm_load_si128 ((__m128i*)&x[i]);

        min_vals = _mm_min_epu8 (x_vals, min_vals);
        max_vals = _mm_max_epu8 (x_vals, max_vals);
    }

    __m128i temp1, temp2, temp3, temp4;
    __m128i vals_r1, vals_r2, vals_r3, vals_r4;

    // Reduce min_vals to final min_val
    temp1 = _mm_srli_si128 (min_vals, 8);
    vals_r1 = _mm_min_epu8 (min_vals, temp1);
    temp2 = _mm_srli_si128 (vals_r1, 4);
    vals_r2 = _mm_min_epu8 (vals_r1, temp2);
    temp3 = _mm_srli_si128 (vals_r2, 2);
    vals_r3 = _mm_min_epu8 (vals_r2, temp3);
    temp4 = _mm_srli_si128 (vals_r3, 1);
    vals_r4 = _mm_min_epu8 (vals_r3, temp4);

    *x_min = (uint8_t)_mm_extract_epi8 (vals_r4, 0);

    // Reduce max_vals to final max_val
    temp1 = _mm_srli_si128 (max_vals, 8);
    vals_r1 = _mm_max_epu8 (max_vals, temp1);
    temp2 = _mm_srli_si128 (vals_r1, 4);
    vals_r2 = _mm_max_epu8 (vals_r1, temp2);
    temp3 = _mm_srli_si128 (vals_r2, 2);
    vals_r3 = _mm_max_epu8 (vals_r2, temp3);
    temp4 = _mm_srli_si128 (vals_r3, 1);
    vals_r4 = _mm_max_epu8 (vals_r3, temp4);

    *x_max = (uint8_t)_mm_extract_epi8 (vals_r4, 0);
    return true;
}
```

```
//----------------------------------------------------
//                  Ch02_06_bm.cpp
//----------------------------------------------------

#include <iostream>
#include "Ch02_06.h"
#include "AlignedMem.h"
#include "BmThreadTimer.h"

void CalcMinMaxU8_bm(void)
{
    std::cout << "\nRunning benchmark function CalcMinMaxU8_bm - please wait\n";

    size_t n = c_NumElements;
    AlignedArray<uint8_t> x_aa(n, 16);
    uint8_t* x = x_aa.Data();

    InitArray(x, n, c_RngSeedVal);

    uint8_t x_min0 = 0, x_max0 = 0;
    uint8_t x_min1 = 0, x_max1 = 0;

    const size_t num_it = 500;
    const size_t num_alg = 2;
    BmThreadTimer bmtt(num_it, num_alg);

    for (size_t i = 0; i < num_it; i++)
    {
        bmtt.Start(i, 0);
        CalcMinMaxU8_Cpp(&x_min0, &x_max0, x, n);
        bmtt.Stop(i, 0);

        bmtt.Start(i, 1);
        CalcMinMaxU8_Iavx(&x_min1, &x_max1, x, n);
        bmtt.Stop(i, 1);
    }

    std::string fn = bmtt.BuildCsvFilenameString("Ch02_06_CalcMinMaxU8_bm");
    bmtt.SaveElapsedTimes(fn, BmThreadTimer::EtUnit::MicroSec, 2);
    std::cout << "Benchmark times save to file " << fn << '\n';
}
```

The first file in Listing 2-6 is Ch02_06.h. This file contains the requisite function declarations and a few miscellaneous constants. Note that the function declarations use the fixed-width integer type uint8_t, which is defined in the header file <cstdint>. Some programmers (including me) prefer to use the fixed-width integer types in SIMD calculating functions since it eschews the size ambiguities of the standard C++ integer types char, short, int, long, and long long.

The next file in Listing 2-6, Ch02_06_misc.cpp, contains a simple function named InitArray(). This function fills an array of 8-bit unsigned integers using random values. The actual filling of the array is performed by a template function named MT::FillArray(), which is defined in the header file MT.h. The driver function for this example is named CalcMinMaxU8() and is defined in Ch02_06.cpp. Near the top of CalcMinMaxU8() is the statement AlignedArray<uint8_t> x_aa(n, 16). This statement dynamically allocates an n element array of uint8_t integers that is aligned on a 16-byte boundary. The source code for both MT.h and AlignedMem.h (which contains the template class AlignedMem<T>) is not shown in Listing 2-6 but is included in the software download package.

The principal calculating functions for example Ch02_06 are defined in the file Ch02_06_fcpp.cpp. The first function in this module, CalcMinMaxU8_Cpp(), finds the minimum and maximum value in an array of uint8_t integers. This function is coded using typical C++ statements sans any C++ SIMD intrinsic functions and will be used later for comparison and benchmarking purposes. Note that prior to the start of the for-loop, two error checks are performed. The first error check ensures that n is not equal to zero and an integral multiple of 16. Requiring n to be an integral multiple of 16 is not as restrictive as it might appear since the number of pixels in a digital camera image is often an integral multiple of 64 due to the processing requirements of the JPEG algorithms. Later examples will include additional code that can process arrays of any size. The second error check ensures that the source pixel buffer x is properly aligned on a 16-byte boundary.

The SIMD counterpart function to CalcMinMaxU8_Cpp() is named CalcMinMaxU8_Iavx(). This function starts its execution by validating n for size and x for proper alignment. The next statement uses the C++ SIMD intrinsic function _mm_set1_epi8 () to set each 8-bit element in min_vals to 0xFF. This is also known as a broadcast operation. Unlike the non-SIMD min-max function, the for-loop in CalcMinMaxU8_Iavx() maintains 16 intermediate pixel minimums as it sweeps through pixel buffer x and the variable min_val holds these values. The next statement uses _mm_setzero_si128 () to initialize each 8-bit element in max_vals to 0x00. This variable holds intermediate pixel maximums during execution of the for-loop.

Immediately before the start of the for-loop, the constant variable num_simd_elements is set to 16 and represents the number of pixels processed during each iteration of the for-loop. This is the reason for requiring n to be an integral multiple of 16. The for-loop itself begins with a call to _mm_load_si128 () that loads 16 8-bit unsigned integer elements from pixel buffer x into x_vals. The next statement uses the C++ SIMD function _mm_min_epu8 () to update the intermediate minimum values maintained in min_vals. This function compares the two 128-bit wide operands of 8-bit unsigned integers and returns an __m128i value that contains the minimum value of each element compare as shown in Figure 2-3. The C++ SIMD intrinsic function _mm_max_epu8 () performs the corresponding 8-bit unsigned integer packed maximum compare and is also shown in Figure 2-3.

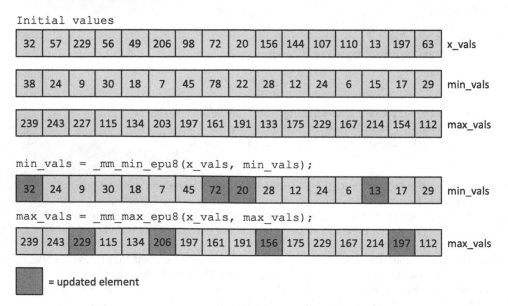

Figure 2-3. Pixel minimum and maximum compares using _mm_min_epu8 () and _mm_max_epu8 ()

Following execution of the for-loop, packed variables min_vals and max_vals contain the final 16 minimum and maximum values, respectively. The true pixel minimum and maximum value is one of the elements in these variables. To find the true minimum and maximum values, both min_vals and max_vals must be reduced to a single scalar value. For min_vals, this is accomplished using a series of _mm_srli_si128 () and _mm_min_epu8 () calls as shown in Figure 2-4. The code that reduces max_vals to a scalar value is almost identical except that it uses the C++ SIMD intrinsic function _mm_max_epu8 () instead. Following each reduction operation, CalcMinMaxU8_Iavx() employs _mm_extract_epi8 () to extract the final 8-bit unsigned integer value.

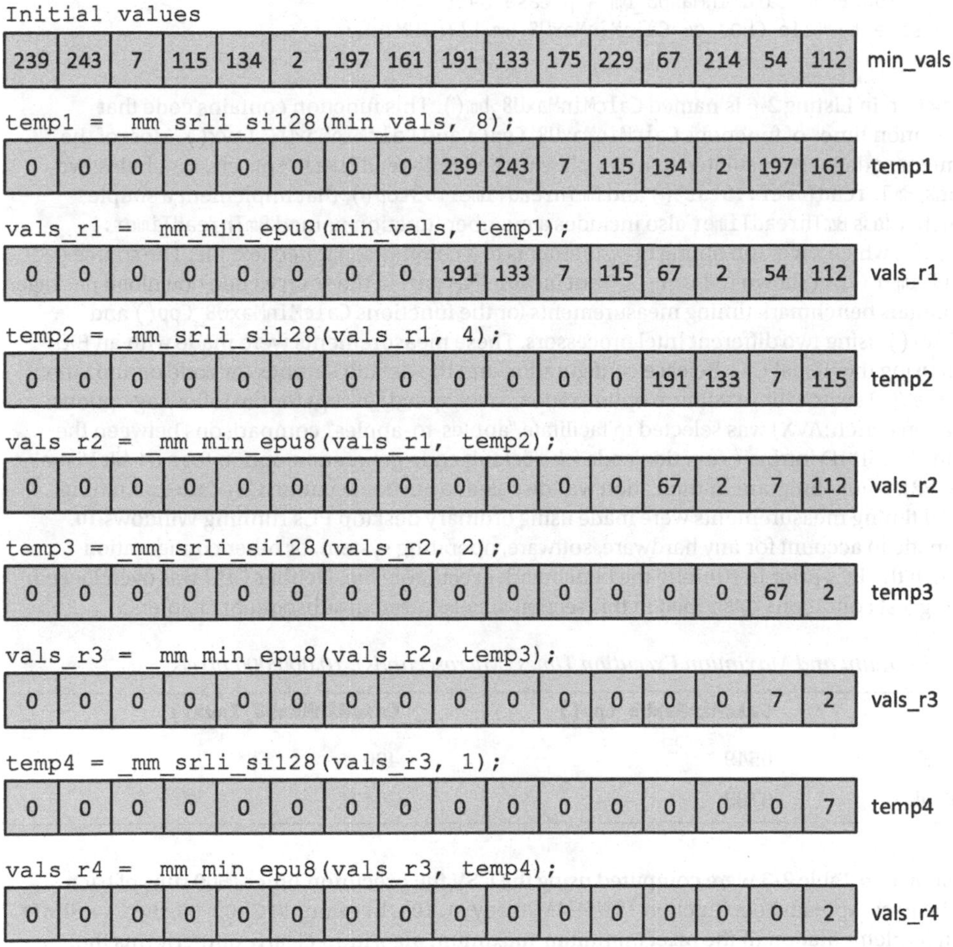

```
Initial values
```

| 239 | 243 | 7 | 115 | 134 | 2 | 197 | 161 | 191 | 133 | 175 | 229 | 67 | 214 | 54 | 112 | min_vals |

```
temp1 = _mm_srli_si128(min_vals, 8);
```

| 0 | 0 | 0 | 0 | 0 | 0 | 0 | 0 | 239 | 243 | 7 | 115 | 134 | 2 | 197 | 161 | temp1 |

```
vals_r1 = _mm_min_epu8(min_vals, temp1);
```

| 0 | 0 | 0 | 0 | 0 | 0 | 0 | 0 | 191 | 133 | 7 | 115 | 67 | 2 | 54 | 112 | vals_r1 |

```
temp2 = _mm_srli_si128(vals_r1, 4);
```

| 0 | 0 | 0 | 0 | 0 | 0 | 0 | 0 | 0 | 0 | 0 | 0 | 191 | 133 | 7 | 115 | temp2 |

```
vals_r2 = _mm_min_epu8(vals_r1, temp2);
```

| 0 | 0 | 0 | 0 | 0 | 0 | 0 | 0 | 0 | 0 | 0 | 0 | 67 | 2 | 7 | 112 | vals_r2 |

```
temp3 = _mm_srli_si128(vals_r2, 2);
```

| 0 | 0 | 0 | 0 | 0 | 0 | 0 | 0 | 0 | 0 | 0 | 0 | 0 | 0 | 67 | 2 | temp3 |

```
vals_r3 = _mm_min_epu8(vals_r2, temp3);
```

| 0 | 0 | 0 | 0 | 0 | 0 | 0 | 0 | 0 | 0 | 0 | 0 | 0 | 0 | 7 | 2 | vals_r3 |

```
temp4 = _mm_srli_si128(vals_r3, 1);
```

| 0 | 0 | 0 | 0 | 0 | 0 | 0 | 0 | 0 | 0 | 0 | 0 | 0 | 0 | 0 | 7 | temp4 |

```
vals_r4 = _mm_min_epu8(vals_r3, temp4);
```

| 0 | 0 | 0 | 0 | 0 | 0 | 0 | 0 | 0 | 0 | 0 | 0 | 0 | 0 | 0 | 2 | vals_r4 |

*Figure 2-4.* Reduction of min_vals using _mm_srli_i128() and _mm_min_epu8 ()

Here are the results for source code example Ch02_06:

```
Results for CalcMinMaxU8_Cpp
rc1: 1  x_min1: 2  x_max1: 254

Results for CalcMinMaxU8_Iavx
rc2: 1  x_min2: 2  x_max2: 254

Running benchmark function CalcMinMaxU8_bm - please wait
Benchmark times save to file Ch02_06_CalcMinMaxU8_bm_LITHIUM.csv
```

The final function in Listing 2-6 is named CalcMinMaxU8_bm(). This function contains code that measures the execution times of functions CalcMinMaxU8_Cpp() and CalcMinMaxU8_Iavx(). Most of the timing measurement code is encapsulated in a C++ class named BmThreadTimer. This class includes two member functions, BmThreadTimer::Start() and BmThreadTimer::Stop(), that implement a simple software stopwatch. Class BmThreadTimer also includes a member function named BmThreadTimer::SaveElapsedTimes(), which saves the timing measurements to a comma-separated text file. The source code for class BmThreadTimer is not shown in Listing 2-6 but included as part of the source code download package.

Table 2-3 contains benchmark timing measurements for the functions CalcMinMaxU8_Cpp() and CalcMinMaxU8_Iavx() using two different Intel processors. These measurements were made with an EXE file that was built using the Visual C++ Release configuration and the default settings for code optimization (which includes the /O2 switch for maximum optimization, favor speed) except for the following options: AVX code generation (/arch:AVX) was selected to facilitate "apples-to-apples" comparisons between the standard C++ and C++ SIMD intrinsic function code (the default code generation option for a 64-bit Visual C++ EXE file is SSE2); whole program optimization was disabled to ensure accurate C++ function timing measurements. All timing measurements were made using ordinary desktop PCs running Windows 10. No attempt was made to account for any hardware, software, operating system, or other configuration differences between the PCs prior to running the benchmark executable file. Neither CPU was overclocked. The benchmarking test conditions described in this section are also used in subsequent chapters.

*Table 2-3.* *Pixel Minimum and Maximum Execution Times (Microseconds), 10,000,000 pixels*

| CPU | CalcMinMaxU8_Cpp() | CalcMinMaxU8_Iavx() |
|-----|--------------------|--------------------|
| Intel Core i7-8700K | 6549 | 406 |
| Intel Core i5-11600K | 6783 | 304 |

The values shown in Table 2-3 were computed using the CSV file execution times (500 runs of each algorithm) and the Excel spreadsheet function TRIMMEAN(array,0.10). In example Ch02_06, the C++ SIMD intrinsic function implementation of the pixel minimum-maximum algorithm clearly outperforms the standard C++ version by a wide margin. It is not uncommon to achieve significant speed improvements when using C++ intrinsic functions, especially by algorithms that can fully exploit the SIMD parallelism of an x86 processor. You will see additional examples of accelerated algorithmic performance throughout the remainder of this book.

The benchmark timing measurements cited in this book provide reasonable approximations of function execution times. They are intended to provide some insights regarding the performance of a function coded using standard C++ statements vs. a function coded using C++ SIMD intrinsic functions. Like automobile fuel economy and mobile device battery runtime estimates, software performance benchmarking is not an exact science and subject to a variety of uncontrollable factors. It is also important to keep mind that this book is an introductory primer about x86 SIMD programming and not benchmarking. The source code examples are structured to hasten the study of x86 SIMD programming techniques. In addition, the Visual C++ options described earlier were selected mostly for practical reasons and may not yield optimal performance in all cases. Both Visual C++ and GNU C++ include a plethora of code generation options that can affect performance. Benchmark timing measurements should always be construed in a context that is correlated with the software's purpose. The methods described in this section are generally worthwhile, but measurement results occasionally vary. Appendix A contains additional information about the software tools used to develop the source code examples in this book.

## Pixel Mean Intensity

The final source code example of this chapter, Ch02_07, demonstrates how to calculate the arithmetic mean of an array of 8-bit unsigned integers using packed integer arithmetic. Listing 2-7 shows the source code for example Ch02_07.

*Listing 2-7.* Example Ch02_07

```
//--------------------------------------------------
//                  Ch02_07.h
//--------------------------------------------------

#pragma once
#include <cstddef>
#include <cstdint>

// Ch02_07_fcpp.cpp
extern bool CalcMeanU8_Cpp(double* mean_x, uint64_t* sum_x, const uint8_t* x, size_t n);
extern bool CalcMeanU8_Iavx(double* mean_x, uint64_t* sum_x, const uint8_t* x, size_t n);

// Ch02_07_misc.cpp
extern void InitArray(uint8_t* x, size_t n, unsigned int seed);
extern bool CheckArgs(const uint8_t* x, size_t n);

// Ch02_07_bm.cpp
extern void CalcMeanU8_bm(void);

// Miscellaneous constants
const size_t c_NumElements = 10000000;
const size_t c_Alignment = 16;
const unsigned int c_RngSeedVal = 29;
extern "C" size_t g_NumElementsMax;


//--------------------------------------------------
//                  Ch02_07_misc.cpp
//--------------------------------------------------

#include "Ch02_07.h"
#include "MT.h"
#include "AlignedMem.h"
```

```
size_t g_NumElementsMax = 64 * 1024 * 1024;

bool CheckArgs(const uint8_t* x, size_t n)
{
    if (n == 0 || n > g_NumElementsMax)
        return false;

    if ((n % 64) != 0)
        return false;

    if (!AlignedMem::IsAligned(x, c_Alignment))
        return false;

    return true;
}

void InitArray(uint8_t* x, size_t n, unsigned int rng_seed)
{
    int rng_min_val = 0;
    int rng_max_val = 255;
    MT::FillArray(x, n, rng_min_val, rng_max_val, rng_seed);
}

//--------------------------------------------------
//                  Ch02_07.cpp
//--------------------------------------------------

#include <iostream>
#include <iomanip>
#include "Ch02_07.h"
#include "AlignedMem.h"

static void CalcMeanU8(void);

int main()
{
    CalcMeanU8();
    CalcMeanU8_bm();
}

static void CalcMeanU8(void)
{
    const char nl = '\n';
    const size_t n = c_NumElements;
    AlignedArray<uint8_t> x_aa(n, 16);
    uint8_t* x = x_aa.Data();

    InitArray(x, n, c_RngSeedVal);

    bool rc0, rc1;
    uint64_t sum_x0, sum_x1;
```

```
    double mean_x0, mean_x1;

    rc0 = CalcMeanU8_Cpp(&mean_x0, &sum_x0, x, n);
    rc1 = CalcMeanU8_Iavx(&mean_x1, &sum_x1, x, n);

    std::cout << std::fixed << std::setprecision(6);

    std::cout << "\nResults for CalcMeanU8_Cpp\n";
    std::cout << "rc0: " << rc0 << "  ";
    std::cout << "sum_x0: " << sum_x0 << "   ";
    std::cout << "mean_x0: " << mean_x0 << nl;

    std::cout << "\nResults for CalcMeanU8_Iavx\n";
    std::cout << "rc1: " << rc1 << "   ";
    std::cout << "sum_x1: " << sum_x1 << "   ";
    std::cout << "mean_x1: " << mean_x1 << nl;
}

//-------------------------------------------------
//                 Ch02_07_fcpp.cpp
//-------------------------------------------------

#include <immintrin.h>
#include "Ch02_07.h"

bool CalcMeanU8_Cpp(double* mean_x, uint64_t* sum_x, const uint8_t* x, size_t n)
{
    if (!CheckArgs(x, n))
        return false;

    uint64_t sum_x_temp = 0;

    for (size_t i = 0; i < n; i++)
        sum_x_temp += x[i];

    *sum_x = sum_x_temp;
    *mean_x = (double)sum_x_temp / n;
    return true;
}

bool CalcMeanU8_Iavx(double* mean_x, uint64_t* sum_x, const uint8_t* x, size_t n)
{
    if (!CheckArgs(x, n))
        return false;

    const size_t num_simd_elements = 16;

    __m128i packed_zero = _mm_setzero_si128 ();
    __m128i pixel_sums_u32 = _mm_setzero_si128 ();
```

```cpp
for (size_t i = 0; i < n; i += num_simd_elements * 4)
{
    __m128i pixel_vals_u8, pixel_vals_lo_u16, pixel_vals_hi_u16;

    __m128i pixel_sums_u16 = _mm_setzero_si128 ();

    // Process pixels x[i:i+15]
    pixel_vals_u8 = _mm_load_si128 ((__m128i*)&x[i]);
    pixel_vals_lo_u16 = _mm_unpacklo_epi8 (pixel_vals_u8, packed_zero);
    pixel_vals_hi_u16 = _mm_unpackhi_epi8 (pixel_vals_u8, packed_zero);
    pixel_sums_u16 = _mm_add_epi16 (pixel_sums_u16, pixel_vals_lo_u16);
    pixel_sums_u16 = _mm_add_epi16 (pixel_sums_u16, pixel_vals_hi_u16);

    // Process pixels x[i+16:i+31]
    pixel_vals_u8 = _mm_load_si128 ((__m128i*)&x[i + 16]);
    pixel_vals_lo_u16 = _mm_unpacklo_epi8 (pixel_vals_u8, packed_zero);
    pixel_vals_hi_u16 = _mm_unpackhi_epi8 (pixel_vals_u8, packed_zero);
    pixel_sums_u16 = _mm_add_epi16 (pixel_sums_u16, pixel_vals_lo_u16);
    pixel_sums_u16 = _mm_add_epi16 (pixel_sums_u16, pixel_vals_hi_u16);

    // Process pixels x[i+32:i+47]
    pixel_vals_u8 = _mm_load_si128 ((__m128i*)&x[i + 32]);
    pixel_vals_lo_u16 = _mm_unpacklo_epi8 (pixel_vals_u8, packed_zero);
    pixel_vals_hi_u16 = _mm_unpackhi_epi8 (pixel_vals_u8, packed_zero);
    pixel_sums_u16 = _mm_add_epi16 (pixel_sums_u16, pixel_vals_lo_u16);
    pixel_sums_u16 = _mm_add_epi16 (pixel_sums_u16, pixel_vals_hi_u16);

    // Process pixels x[i+48:i+63]
    pixel_vals_u8 = _mm_load_si128 ((__m128i*)&x[i + 48]);
    pixel_vals_lo_u16 = _mm_unpacklo_epi8 (pixel_vals_u8, packed_zero);
    pixel_vals_hi_u16 = _mm_unpackhi_epi8 (pixel_vals_u8, packed_zero);
    pixel_sums_u16 = _mm_add_epi16 (pixel_sums_u16, pixel_vals_lo_u16);
    pixel_sums_u16 = _mm_add_epi16 (pixel_sums_u16, pixel_vals_hi_u16);

    // Convert pixel_sums_u16 to u32, then update pixel_sums_u32
    __m128i pixel_sums_lo_u32 = _mm_unpacklo_epi16 (pixel_sums_u16, packed_zero);
    __m128i pixel_sums_hi_u32 = _mm_unpackhi_epi16 (pixel_sums_u16, packed_zero);
    pixel_sums_u32 = _mm_add_epi32(pixel_sums_u32, pixel_sums_lo_u32);
    pixel_sums_u32 = _mm_add_epi32(pixel_sums_u32, pixel_sums_hi_u32);
}

// Reduce pixel_sums_u32 to single sum value
uint64_t pixel_sum = _mm_extract_epi32 (pixel_sums_u32, 0);
pixel_sum += _mm_extract_epi32 (pixel_sums_u32, 1);
pixel_sum += _mm_extract_epi32 (pixel_sums_u32, 2);
pixel_sum += _mm_extract_epi32 (pixel_sums_u32, 3);

// Calculate mean
*sum_x = pixel_sum;
*mean_x = (double)pixel_sum / n;
return true;
}
```

The organization of the code in this example is similar to Ch02_06. File Ch02_07_misc.cpp contains two functions, CheckArgs() and InitArray(), which perform argument checking and array initialization, respectively. Note that the size of the source array must be an integral multiple of 64 and aligned on a 16-byte boundary. The function CheckArgs() also verifies that the number of array elements n is less than g_NumElementsMax. This size restriction enables the C++ SIMD code to perform intermediate calculations using packed 32-bit unsigned integers without any safeguards for arithmetic overflows.

Calculation of an array mean is straightforward; a function must sum the elements of the array and then divide this sum by the total number of elements. The function CalcMeanU8_Cpp() accomplishes this using a simple for-loop and scalar floating-point division.

The C++ SIMD counterpart function is named CalcMeanU8_Iavx(). Following argument validation using CheckArgs(), CalcMeanU8_Iavx() initializes variables packed_zero and pixel_sums_u32 to all zeros. The former variable is employed by the for-loop to perform unsigned integer size promotions, and the latter maintains four 32-bit unsigned integer intermediate sum values. The main for-loop is next. Note that each for-loop iteration processes 64 array elements since the index variable i is incremented by num_simd_elements * 4. The reason for doing this is that it reduces the number of 8-bit to 32-bit unsigned integer size promotions required to calculate the final pixel sum.

The first executable statement of the for-loop sets pixel_sums_u16 to zero. This variable holds eight 16-bit unsigned integer sums. The _mm_load_si128() call that follows loads 16 pixels into the variable pixel_vals_u8. The next two statements employ the C++ SIMD intrinsic functions _mm_unpacklo_epi8() and _mm_unpackhi_epi8() to size-promote the pixel values from 8 bits to 16 bits. Following this size promotion task, the for-loop executes two _mm_add_epi16() calls to update the intermediate packed sum value pixel_sums_u16 as shown in Figure 2-5. The for-loop repeats this pixel-load and size-promotion summing sequence three more times. The final code block in the for-loop promotes the 16-bit unsigned integer values in pixel_sums_u16 to 32 bits and adds these values to pixel_sums_u32. The for-loop uses the C++ SIMD intrinsic functions _mm_unpacklo_epi16() and _mm_unpackhi_epi16() to carry out the size promotions and _mm_add_epi32() to perform the packed 32-bit addition.

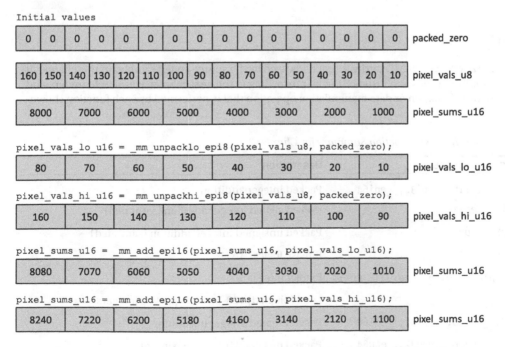

*Figure 2-5.* Pixel size-promotion and summing sequence used in CalcMeanU8_Iavx()

Following execution of the for-loop, four _mm_extract_epi32 () calls are employed to extract each 32-bit unsigned integer intermediate sum value from pixel_sums_u32. After summing these values, the final pixel mean is calculated using scalar floating-point division. Here are the results for source code example Ch02_07:

```
Results for CalcMeanU8_Cpp
rc0: 1  sum_x0: 1275046509  mean_x0: 127.504651

Results for CalcMeanU8_Iavx
rc1: 1  sum_x1: 1275046509  mean_x1: 127.504651

Running benchmark function CalcMeanU8_bm - please wait
Benchmark times save to file Ch02_07_CalcMeanU8_bm_LITHIUM.csv
```

Table 2-4 shows some benchmark timing measurements for source code example Ch02_07. While not as large as the previous example, using C++ SIMD intrinsic functions to calculate the arithmetic mean of a pixel array still yielded a considerable increase in performance compared to the standard C++ method.

*Table 2-4.* *Pixel Array Arithmetic Mean Execution Times (Microseconds), 10,000,000 pixels*

| CPU | CalcMeanU8_Cpp() | CalcMeanU8_Iavx() |
|---|---|---|
| Intel Core i7-8700K | 2234 | 462 |
| Intel Core i5-11600K | 1856 | 288 |

# Summary

Table 2-5 summarizes the C++ SIMD intrinsic functions used by the source code examples in this chapter. It also lists suffixes for the various size variants. Before proceeding to the next chapter, you should understand the SIMD arithmetic calculation or data manipulation operation that is performed by each function shown in Table 2-5.

*Table 2-5.* *C++ SIMD Intrinsic Function Summary for Chapter 2*

| C++ SIMD Function Names | Description |
|---|---|
| _mm_add_epi8, _epi16, _epi32, _epi64 | Packed integer addition |
| _mm_adds_epi8, _epi16 | Packed signed integer addition (saturated) |
| _mm_adds_epu8, _epu16 | Packed unsigned integer addition (saturated) |
| _mm_and_si128 | Bitwise logical AND |
| _mm_extract_epi8, _epi16, _epi32, _epi64 | Extract integer |
| _mm_load_si128 | Load (aligned) 128-bit wide packed integers |
| _mm_max_epi8, _epi16, _epi32, _epi64 | Packed signed integer maximum |
| _mm_max_epu8, _epu16, _epu32, _epu64 | Packed unsigned integer maximum |

*(continued)*

**Table 2-5.** (*continued*)

| C++ SIMD Function Names | Description |
|---|---|
| _mm_min_epi8, _epi16, _epi32, _epi64 | Packed signed integer minimum |
| _mm_min_epu8, _epu16, _epu32, _epu64 | Packed unsigned integer minimum |
| _mm_mul_epi32 | Packed 32-bit signed integer multiplication |
| _mm_mul_epu32 | Packed 32-bit unsigned integer multiplication |
| _mm_mulhi_epi16 | Packed 16-bit signed integer multiplication (high result) |
| _mm_mulhi_epu16 | Packed 16-bit unsigned integer multiplication (high result) |
| _mm_mullo_epi16, _epi32, _epi64 | Packed signed integer multiplication (low result) |
| _mm_or_si128 | Bitwise logical OR |
| _mm_set1_epi8, _epi16, _epi32, _epi64 | Broadcast integer constant to all elements |
| _mm_setzero_si128 | Set 128-bit wide SIMD operand to all zeros |
| _mm_slli_epi16, _epi32, _epi64 | Packed integer shift left logical |
| _mm_slli_si128 | 128-bit wide shift left logical |
| _mm_srai_epi16, _epi32, _epi64 | Packed integer shift right arithmetic |
| _mm_srli_epi16, _epi32, _epi64 | Packed integer shift right logical |
| _mm_srli_si128 | 128-bit wide shift right logical |
| _mm_store_si128 | Store (aligned) 128-bit wide packed integers |
| _mm_sub_epi8, _epi16, _epi32, _epi64 | Packed integer subtraction |
| _mm_subs_epi8, _epi16 | Packed signed integer subtraction (saturated) |
| _mm_subs_epu8, _epu16 | Packed unsigned integer subtraction (saturated) |
| _mm_unpackhi_epi8, _epi16, _epi32, _epi64 | Unpack and interleave high-order integers |
| _mm_unpacklo_epi8, _epi16, _epi32, _epi64 | Unpacked and interleave low-order integers |
| _mm_xor_si128 | Bitwise logical XOR |

# CHAPTER 3

■ ■ ■

# AVX C++ Programming: Part 2

The source code examples of the previous chapter elucidated the fundamentals of AVX using packed integer operands and C++ SIMD intrinsic functions. In this chapter, you will learn how to exploit the floating-point capabilities of AVX using C++ SIMD intrinsic functions. The chapter begins with a series of examples that demonstrate common arithmetic operations using packed floating-point operands. This is followed by a section that explains how to carry out SIMD calculations using floating-point arrays. The final section illustrates SIMD operations with floating-point matrices.

## Floating-Point Operations

In this section, you will study three source code examples that illustrate elementary SIMD floating-point operations using both single-precision and double-precision values. The first example explains basic packed floating-point arithmetic. The second source code example demonstrates packed floating-point compare operations. The final source code example of this section describes packed floating-point conversions.

### Floating-Point Arithmetic

Listing 3-1 shows the source code for example Ch03_01. This example highlights common floating-point arithmetic operations including addition, subtraction, multiplication, division, and square roots using 256-bit wide packed operands.

***Listing 3-1.*** Example Ch03_01

```
//-------------------------------------------------
//              YmmVal.h
//-------------------------------------------------

#pragma once
#include <string>
#include <cstdint>
#include <sstream>
#include <iomanip>
```

```cpp
struct alignas(32) YmmVal
{
public:
    union
    {
        int8_t m_I8[32];
        int16_t m_I16[16];
        int32_t m_I32[8];
        int64_t m_I64[4];
        uint8_t m_U8[32];
        uint16_t m_U16[16];
        uint32_t m_U32[8];
        uint64_t m_U64[4];
        float m_F32[8];
        double m_F64[4];
    };

        // Rest of file YmmVal.h ...
```

```cpp
//---------------------------------------------------
//                  Ch03_01.h
//---------------------------------------------------

#pragma once
#include "YmmVal.h"

// Ch03_01_fcpp.cpp
extern void PackedMathF32_Iavx(YmmVal c[8], const YmmVal* a, const YmmVal* b);
extern void PackedMathF64_Iavx(YmmVal c[8], const YmmVal* a, const YmmVal* b);
```

```cpp
//---------------------------------------------------
//                  Ch03_01.cpp
//---------------------------------------------------

#include <iostream>
#include <iomanip>
#include <string>
#define _USE_MATH_DEFINES
#include <math.h>
#include "Ch03_01.h"

static void PackedMathF32();
static void PackedMathF64();

static const char* c_OprStr[8] =
{
    "Add", "Sub", "Mul", "Div", "Min", "Max", "Sqrt a", "Abs b"
};
```

```
int main()
{
    const char nl = '\n';

    PackedMathF32();
    std::cout << nl << std::string(78, '-') << nl;
    PackedMathF64();
}

static void PackedMathF32(void)
{
    YmmVal a, b, c[8];
    const char nl = '\n';

    a.m_F32[0] = 36.0f;                 b.m_F32[0] = -(float)(1.0 / 9.0);
    a.m_F32[1] = (float)(1.0 / 32.0);   b.m_F32[1] = 64.0f;
    a.m_F32[2] = 2.0f;                  b.m_F32[2] = -0.0625f;
    a.m_F32[3] = 42.0f;                 b.m_F32[3] = 8.666667f;
    a.m_F32[4] = (float)M_PI;           b.m_F32[4] = -4.0f;
    a.m_F32[5] = 18.6f;                 b.m_F32[5] = -64.0f;
    a.m_F32[6] = 3.0f;                  b.m_F32[6] = -5.95f;
    a.m_F32[7] = 142.0f;                b.m_F32[7] = (float)M_SQRT2;

    PackedMathF32_Iavx(c, &a, &b);

    size_t w = 9;
    std::cout << ("\nResults for PackedMathF32_Iavx\n");

    for (unsigned int i = 0; i < 2; i++)
    {
        std::string s0 = (i == 0) ? "a lo:    " : "a hi:    ";
        std::string s1 = (i == 0) ? "b lo:    " : "b hi:    ";
        std::cout << s0 << a.ToStringF32(i) << nl;
        std::cout << s1 << b.ToStringF32(i) << nl;

        for (unsigned int j = 0; j < 8; j++)
        {
            std::cout << std::setw(w) << std::left << c_OprStr[j];
            std::cout << c[j].ToStringF32(i) << nl;
        }

        if (i == 0)
            std::cout << nl;
    }
}

static void PackedMathF64(void)
{
    YmmVal a, b, c[8];
    const char nl = '\n';
```

```
    a.m_F64[0] = 2.0;              b.m_F64[0] = M_PI;
    a.m_F64[1] = 4.0 ;            b.m_F64[1] = M_E;
    a.m_F64[2] = 7.5;              b.m_F64[2] = -9.125;
    a.m_F64[3] = 3.0;              b.m_F64[3] = -M_PI;

    PackedMathF64_Iavx(c, &a, &b);

    size_t w = 9;
    std::cout << ("\nResults for PackedMathF64_Iavx\n");

    for (unsigned int i = 0; i < 2; i++)
    {
        std::string s0 = (i == 0) ? "a lo:     " : "a hi:     ";
        std::string s1 = (i == 0) ? "b lo:     " : "b hi:     ";
        std::cout << s0 << a.ToStringF64(i) << nl;
        std::cout << s1 << b.ToStringF64(i) << nl;

        for (unsigned int j = 0; j < 8; j++)
        {
            std::cout << std::setw(w) << std::left << c_OprStr[j];
            std::cout << c[j].ToStringF64(i) << nl;
        }

        if (i == 0)
            std::cout << nl;
    }
}

//----------------------------------------------------
//               Ch03_01_fcpp.cpp
//----------------------------------------------------

#include <cstdint>
#include <immintrin.h>
#include "Ch03_01.h"

void PackedMathF32_Iavx(YmmVal c[8], const YmmVal* a, const YmmVal* b)
{
    __m256 a_vals = _mm256_load_ps((float*)a);
    __m256 b_vals = _mm256_load_ps((float*)b);
    const uint32_t abs_mask_val = 0x7FFFFFFF;
    __m256 abs_mask = _mm256_broadcast_ss((float*)&abs_mask_val);

    __m256 c_vals0 = _mm256_add_ps(a_vals, b_vals);
    __m256 c_vals1 = _mm256_sub_ps(a_vals, b_vals);
    __m256 c_vals2 = _mm256_mul_ps(a_vals, b_vals);
    __m256 c_vals3 = _mm256_div_ps(a_vals, b_vals);
    __m256 c_vals4 = _mm256_min_ps(a_vals, b_vals);
    __m256 c_vals5 = _mm256_max_ps(a_vals, b_vals);
    __m256 c_vals6 = _mm256_sqrt_ps(a_vals);
    __m256 c_vals7 = _mm256_and_ps(b_vals, abs_mask);
```

```
    _mm256_store_ps((float*)&c[0], c_vals0);
    _mm256_store_ps((float*)&c[1], c_vals1);
    _mm256_store_ps((float*)&c[2], c_vals2);
    _mm256_store_ps((float*)&c[3], c_vals3);
    _mm256_store_ps((float*)&c[4], c_vals4);
    _mm256_store_ps((float*)&c[5], c_vals5);
    _mm256_store_ps((float*)&c[6], c_vals6);
    _mm256_store_ps((float*)&c[7], c_vals7);
}

void PackedMathF64_Iavx(YmmVal c[8], const YmmVal* a, const YmmVal* b)
{
    __m256d a_vals = _mm256_load_pd((double*)a);
    __m256d b_vals = _mm256_load_pd((double*)b);
    const uint64_t abs_mask_val = 0x7FFFFFFFFFFFFFFF;
    __m256d abs_mask = _mm256_broadcast_sd((double*)&abs_mask_val);

    __m256d c_vals0 = _mm256_add_pd(a_vals, b_vals);
    __m256d c_vals1 = _mm256_sub_pd(a_vals, b_vals);
    __m256d c_vals2 = _mm256_mul_pd(a_vals, b_vals);
    __m256d c_vals3 = _mm256_div_pd(a_vals, b_vals);
    __m256d c_vals4 = _mm256_min_pd(a_vals, b_vals);
    __m256d c_vals5 = _mm256_max_pd(a_vals, b_vals);
    __m256d c_vals6 = _mm256_sqrt_pd(a_vals);
    __m256d c_vals7 = _mm256_and_pd(b_vals, abs_mask);

    _mm256_store_pd((double*)&c[0], c_vals0);
    _mm256_store_pd((double*)&c[1], c_vals1);
    _mm256_store_pd((double*)&c[2], c_vals2);
    _mm256_store_pd((double*)&c[3], c_vals3);
    _mm256_store_pd((double*)&c[4], c_vals4);
    _mm256_store_pd((double*)&c[5], c_vals5);
    _mm256_store_pd((double*)&c[6], c_vals6);
    _mm256_store_pd((double*)&c[7], c_vals7);
}
```

Listing 3-1 begins with the declaration of a C++ structure named YmmVal. Like the XmmVal structure that you saw in Chapter 2, this structure contains a publicly accessible anonymous union whose members correspond to the packed data types that can be used with a 256-bit wide x86-AVX operand. Note that YmmVal is declared using the alignas(32) specifier, which instructs the C++ compiler to align each YmmVal instance on a 32-byte boundary. Some of the C++ intrinsic functions used in this example require their memory operands to be aligned on a 32-byte boundary. This can improve performance as explained in Chapter 2. The structure YmmVal also defines several member functions that format and display the contents of an YmmVal variable. The source code for these member functions is not shown in Listing 3-1 but is included in the software download package.

Following the declaration of YmmVal is the header file Ch03_01.h. This file incorporates the C++ function declarations for this source code example. Note that the functions declared in Ch03_01.h require the previously declared YmmVal structure. The next file in Listing 3-1, Ch03_01.cpp, includes the functions PackedMathF32() and PackedMathF64(). These functions perform YmmVal variable initialization for the SIMD calculating functions. They also contain code that streams the results to std::cout. Note that the functions YmmVal::ToStringF32() and YmmVal::ToStringF64() require an integer argument value. This value specifies which element group to format as a string.

The final file in Listing 3-1 is named Ch03_01_fcpp.cpp. This file contains the SIMD calculating functions PackedMathF32_Iavx() and PackedMathF64_Iavx(). The first executable statement of PackedMathF32_Iavx() uses the C++ SIMD intrinsic function _mm256_load_ps() to load eight single-precision floating-point values into a_vals. Note that a_vals is declared as an __m256, which is a 256-bit wide C++ SIMD intrinsic data type that holds eight single-precision floating-point values. The ensuing statement also uses the C++ SIMD intrinsic function _mm256_load_ps() to initialize b_vals. Note that function _mm256_load_ps() requires the specified source operand to be aligned in a 32-byte boundary.

Following initialization of a_vals and b_vals, function PackedMathF32_Iavx() uses the C++ SIMD intrinsic function _mm256_broadcast_ss() to create a packed mask that will be used to calculate packed single-precision floating-point absolute values. This function broadcasts the constant 0x7FFFFFFF to each floating-point element in abs_mask. The absolute value of a single-precision floating-point value can be calculated by setting its sign (or most significant) bit to zero, and the mask value 0x7FFFFFFF facilitates absolute value calculations using a bitwise logical AND operation.

The next code block in PackedMathF32_Iavx() performs various packed floating-point arithmetic operations using a_vals and b_vals. The arithmetic operation performed by each C++ SIMD intrinsic function should be apparent based on the middle text of each function name. The function name suffix _ps signifies that a C++ SIMD intrinsic function carries out its calculation using packed single-precision floating-point values. Chapter 2 contains additional information about the naming conventions that are used for the C++ SIMD intrinsic functions.

The final function in Listing 3-1, PackedMathF64_Iavx(), is the packed double-precision floating-point counterpart of PackedMathF32_Iavx(). Note that this function uses the __m256d C++ SIMD intrinsic data type, which holds four double-precision floating-point values. The only other change between the functions PackedMathF32_Iavx() and PackedMathF64_Iavx() is that the latter uses the packed double-precision floating-point versions of the C++ SIMD intrinsic functions. These functions incorporate a _pd suffix in their names instead of a _ps suffix. Here is the output for source code example Ch03_01:

```
Results for PackedMathF32_Iavx
a lo:         36.000000        0.031250    |      2.000000     42.000000
b lo:         -0.111111       64.000000    |     -0.062500      8.666667
Add           35.888889       64.031250    |      1.937500     50.666668
Sub           36.111111      -63.968750    |      2.062500     33.333332
Mul           -4.000000        2.000000    |     -0.125000    364.000000
Div         -324.000000        0.000488    |    -32.000000      4.846154
Min           -0.111111        0.031250    |     -0.062500      8.666667
Max           36.000000       64.000000    |      2.000000     42.000000
Sqrt a         6.000000        0.176777    |      1.414214      6.480741
Abs b          0.111111       64.000000    |      0.062500      8.666667

a hi:          3.141593       18.600000    |      3.000000    142.000000
b hi:         -4.000000      -64.000000    |     -5.950000      1.414214
Add           -0.858407      -45.400002    |     -2.950000    143.414215
Sub            7.141593       82.599998    |      8.950000    140.585785
Mul          -12.566371    -1190.400024    |    -17.849998    200.818329
Div           -0.785398       -0.290625    |     -0.504202    100.409164
Min           -4.000000      -64.000000    |     -5.950000      1.414214
Max            3.141593       18.600000    |      3.000000    142.000000
Sqrt a         1.772454        4.312772    |      1.732051     11.916375
Abs b          4.000000       64.000000    |      5.950000      1.414214


------------------------------------------------------------------------
```

```
Results for PackedMathF64_Iavx
a lo:               2.000000000000  |        4.000000000000
b lo:               3.141592653590  |        2.718281828459
Add                 5.141592653590  |        6.718281828459
Sub                -1.141592653590  |        1.281718171541
Mul                 6.283185307180  |       10.873127313836
Div                 0.636619772368  |        1.471517764686
Min                 2.000000000000  |        2.718281828459
Max                 3.141592653590  |        4.000000000000
Sqrt a              1.414213562373  |        2.000000000000
Abs b               3.141592653590  |        2.718281828459

a hi:               7.500000000000  |        3.000000000000
b hi:              -9.125000000000  |       -3.141592653590
Add                -1.625000000000  |       -0.141592653590
Sub                16.625000000000  |        6.141592653590
Mul               -68.437500000000  |       -9.424777960769
Div                -0.821917808219  |       -0.954929658551
Min                -9.125000000000  |       -3.141592653590
Max                 7.500000000000  |        3.000000000000
Sqrt a              2.738612787526  |        1.732050807569
Abs b               9.125000000000  |        3.141592653590
```

# Floating-Point Compares

The next source code example, Ch03_02, demonstrates packed floating-point compares using packed single-precision and double-precision values. Listing 3-2 shows the source code for example Ch03_02.

*Listing 3-2.* Example Ch03_02

```cpp
//--------------------------------------------------
//                 Ch03_02.h
//--------------------------------------------------

#pragma once
#include "YmmVal.h"

// Ch03_02_fcpp.cpp
extern void PackedCompareF32_Iavx(YmmVal c[8], const YmmVal* a, const YmmVal* b);
extern void PackedCompareF64_Iavx(YmmVal c[8], const YmmVal* a, const YmmVal* b);


//--------------------------------------------------
//                 Ch03_02.cpp
//--------------------------------------------------

#include <iostream>
#include <iomanip>
#include <string>
#define _USE_MATH_DEFINES
```

```cpp
#include <math.h>
#include <limits>
#include "Ch03_02.h"

static void PackedCompareF32();
static void PackedCompareF64();

static const char* c_CmpStr[8] =
{
    "EQ", "NE", "LT", "LE", "GT", "GE", "ORDERED", "UNORDERED"
};

int main()
{
    const char nl = '\n';

    PackedCompareF32();
    std::cout << nl << std::string(80, '-') << nl;
    PackedCompareF64();
}

static void PackedCompareF32()
{
    YmmVal a, b, c[8];
    const char nl = '\n';
    constexpr float qnan_f32 = std::numeric_limits<float>::quiet_NaN();

    a.m_F32[0] = 2.0f;              b.m_F32[0] = 1.0f;
    a.m_F32[1] = 7.0f;              b.m_F32[1] = 12.0f;
    a.m_F32[2] = -6.0f;             b.m_F32[2] = -6.0f;
    a.m_F32[3] = 3.0f;              b.m_F32[3] = 8.0f;
    a.m_F32[4] = -16.0f;            b.m_F32[4] = -36.0f;
    a.m_F32[5] = 3.5f;              b.m_F32[5] = 3.5f;
    a.m_F32[6] = (float)M_PI;       b.m_F32[6] = -6.0f;
    a.m_F32[7] = (float)M_SQRT2;    b.m_F32[7] = qnan_f32;

    PackedCompareF32_Iavx(c, &a, &b);

    size_t w = 9;
    std::cout << ("\nResults for PackedCompareF32_Iavx\n");

    for (unsigned int i = 0; i < 2; i++)
    {
        std::string s0 = (i == 0) ? "a lo:     " : "a hi:     ";
        std::string s1 = (i == 0) ? "b lo:     " : "b hi:     ";
        std::cout << s0 << a.ToStringF32(i) << nl;
        std::cout << s1 << b.ToStringF32(i) << nl;
```

```cpp
        for (unsigned int j = 0; j < 8; j++)
        {
            std::cout << std::setw(w) << std::left << c_CmpStr[j];
            std::cout << c[j].ToStringX32(i) << nl;
        }

        if (i == 0)
            std::cout << nl;
    }
}

static void PackedCompareF64()
{
    YmmVal a, b, c[8];
    const char nl = '\n';
    constexpr double qnan_f64 = std::numeric_limits<double>::quiet_NaN();

    a.m_F64[0] = 2.0;        b.m_F64[0] = M_E;
    a.m_F64[1] = M_PI;       b.m_F64[1] = -M_1_PI;
    a.m_F64[2] = 12.0;       b.m_F64[2] = 42;
    a.m_F64[3] = qnan_f64;   b.m_F64[3] = M_SQRT2;

    PackedCompareF64_Iavx(c, &a, &b);

    size_t w = 9;
    std::cout << ("\nResults for PackedCompareF64_Iavx\n");

    for (unsigned int i = 0; i < 2; i++)
    {
        std::string s0 = (i == 0) ? "a lo:    " : "a hi:    ";
        std::string s1 = (i == 0) ? "b lo:    " : "b hi:    ";
        std::cout << s0 << a.ToStringF64(i) << nl;
        std::cout << s1 << b.ToStringF64(i) << nl;

        for (unsigned int j = 0; j < 8; j++)
        {
            std::cout << std::setw(w) << std::left << c_CmpStr[j];
            std::cout << c[j].ToStringX64(i) << nl;
        }

        if (i == 0)
            std::cout << nl;
    }
}

//-------------------------------------------------
//                  Ch03_02_fcpp.cpp
//-------------------------------------------------
```

```
#include <immintrin.h>
#include "Ch03_02.h"

void PackedCompareF32_Iavx(YmmVal c[8], const YmmVal* a, const YmmVal* b)
{
    __m256 a_vals = _mm256_load_ps((float*)a);
    __m256 b_vals = _mm256_load_ps((float*)b);

    __m256 c_vals0 = _mm256_cmp_ps(a_vals, b_vals, _CMP_EQ_OQ);
    __m256 c_vals1 = _mm256_cmp_ps(a_vals, b_vals, _CMP_NEQ_OQ);
    __m256 c_vals2 = _mm256_cmp_ps(a_vals, b_vals, _CMP_LT_OQ);
    __m256 c_vals3 = _mm256_cmp_ps(a_vals, b_vals, _CMP_LE_OQ);
    __m256 c_vals4 = _mm256_cmp_ps(a_vals, b_vals, _CMP_GT_OQ);
    __m256 c_vals5 = _mm256_cmp_ps(a_vals, b_vals, _CMP_GE_OQ);
    __m256 c_vals6 = _mm256_cmp_ps(a_vals, b_vals, _CMP_ORD_Q);
    __m256 c_vals7 = _mm256_cmp_ps(a_vals, b_vals, _CMP_UNORD_Q);

    _mm256_store_ps((float*)&c[0], c_vals0);
    _mm256_store_ps((float*)&c[1], c_vals1);
    _mm256_store_ps((float*)&c[2], c_vals2);
    _mm256_store_ps((float*)&c[3], c_vals3);
    _mm256_store_ps((float*)&c[4], c_vals4);
    _mm256_store_ps((float*)&c[5], c_vals5);
    _mm256_store_ps((float*)&c[6], c_vals6);
    _mm256_store_ps((float*)&c[7], c_vals7);
}

void PackedCompareF64_Iavx(YmmVal c[8], const YmmVal* a, const YmmVal* b)
{
    __m256d a_vals = _mm256_load_pd((double*)a);
    __m256d b_vals = _mm256_load_pd((double*)b);

    __m256d c_vals0 = _mm256_cmp_pd(a_vals, b_vals, _CMP_EQ_OQ);
    __m256d c_vals1 = _mm256_cmp_pd(a_vals, b_vals, _CMP_NEQ_OQ);
    __m256d c_vals2 = _mm256_cmp_pd(a_vals, b_vals, _CMP_LT_OQ);
    __m256d c_vals3 = _mm256_cmp_pd(a_vals, b_vals, _CMP_LE_OQ);
    __m256d c_vals4 = _mm256_cmp_pd(a_vals, b_vals, _CMP_GT_OQ);
    __m256d c_vals5 = _mm256_cmp_pd(a_vals, b_vals, _CMP_GE_OQ);
    __m256d c_vals6 = _mm256_cmp_pd(a_vals, b_vals, _CMP_ORD_Q);
    __m256d c_vals7 = _mm256_cmp_pd(a_vals, b_vals, _CMP_UNORD_Q);

    _mm256_store_pd((double*)&c[0], c_vals0);
    _mm256_store_pd((double*)&c[1], c_vals1);
    _mm256_store_pd((double*)&c[2], c_vals2);
    _mm256_store_pd((double*)&c[3], c_vals3);
    _mm256_store_pd((double*)&c[4], c_vals4);
    _mm256_store_pd((double*)&c[5], c_vals5);
    _mm256_store_pd((double*)&c[6], c_vals6);
    _mm256_store_pd((double*)&c[7], c_vals7);
}
```

Before examining the source code, a few words about floating-point compare operations are warranted. Unlike integer compares, a floating-point compare has four possible outcomes: less than, equal, greater than, or unordered. An unordered result occurs when one of the operands is a NaN (Not a Number) or an illegal value. An x86 processor will generate a NaN when the result of a floating-point operation is undefined (e.g., division by zero or square root of a negative number) per the IEEE-754 standard for floating-point arithmetic. It is the programmer's responsibility to prevent NaNs from occurring or to include additional error handling code. Appendix B contains several references that you can consult for more information about floating-point arithmetic and the IEEE-754 standard. You will also learn more about x86-AVX floating-point architecture in Chapter 10.

Listing 3-2 includes a function named PackedCompareF32(). This function initializes YmmVal variables a and b using single-precision floating-point values. Note that the value qnan_f32, which is a QNaN, is assigned to b.m_F32[7]. A QNaN (Quiet NaN) is a type of NaN that the processor propagates through most arithmetic operations without raising an exception. Following variable initialization is a call to the function PackedComareF32_Iavx(), which performs several packed floating-point compare operations. Subsequent to the execution of PackedCompareF32_Iavx(), results are streamed to std::cout. The function PackedCompareF64() is similar to PackedCompareF32() except that it uses double-precision instead of single-precision values.

The function PackedCompareF32_Iavx(),also shown in Listing 3-2, begins its execution with two _mm256_load_ps() calls that initialize a_vals and b_vals. The next code block performs packed single-precision floating-point compares using the C++ SIMD intrinsic function _mm256_cmp_ps(). This function performs eight concurrent floating-point compares using the corresponding elements of a_vals and b_vals. The type of compare is specified by the third argument to _mm256_cmp_ps(), and this constant value is often called a compare predicate. The result of each single-precision floating-point element compare is all ones if the compare predicate is true or all zeros if the compare predicate is false. The compare predicates used in this example include equal, not equal, less than, less than or equal, greater than, greater than or equal, ordered, and unordered. The letter O that is included in some of the compare predicate constants signifies an ordered compare (i.e., both compare values must not be NaNs). The letter Q instructs the processor not to raise an exception if one of the compare values is a QNaN. The programming reference manuals published by AMD and Intel contain additional information about other compare predicates. You can find a list of these manuals in Appendix B.

Function PackedCompareF64_Iavx() is the double-precision floating-point counterpart of PackedCompareF32_Iavx(). Like the previous example, PackedCompareF64_Iavx() uses double-precision C++ SIMD intrinsic functions for loads, compares, and stores. These functions are named using a _pd suffix. Here are the results for source code example Ch03_02:

```
Results for PackedCompareF32_Iavx
a lo:       2.000000        7.000000   |    -6.000000        3.000000
b lo:       1.000000       12.000000   |    -6.000000        8.000000
EQ          00000000        00000000   |     FFFFFFFF        00000000
NE          FFFFFFFF        FFFFFFFF    |     00000000        FFFFFFFF
LT          00000000        FFFFFFFF    |     00000000        FFFFFFFF
LE          00000000        FFFFFFFF    |     FFFFFFFF        FFFFFFFF
GT          FFFFFFFF        00000000    |     00000000        00000000
GE          FFFFFFFF        00000000    |     FFFFFFFF        00000000
ORDERED     FFFFFFFF        FFFFFFFF    |     FFFFFFFF        FFFFFFFF
UNORDERED   00000000        00000000    |     00000000        00000000

a hi:     -16.000000        3.500000   |     3.141593        1.414214
b hi:     -36.000000        3.500000   |    -6.000000             nan
EQ          00000000        FFFFFFFF    |     00000000        00000000
NE          FFFFFFFF        00000000    |     FFFFFFFF        00000000
```

```
LT         00000000        00000000    |    00000000        00000000
LE         00000000        FFFFFFFF    |    00000000        00000000
GT         FFFFFFFF        00000000    |    FFFFFFFF        00000000
GE         FFFFFFFF        FFFFFFFF    |    FFFFFFFF        00000000
ORDERED    FFFFFFFF        FFFFFFFF    |    FFFFFFFF        00000000
UNORDERED  00000000        00000000    |    00000000        FFFFFFFF

-------------------------------------------------------------------------

Results for PackedCompareF64_Iavx
a lo:                 2.000000000000    |              3.141592653590
b lo:                 2.718281828459    |             -0.318309886184
EQ          0000000000000000    |    0000000000000000
NE          FFFFFFFFFFFFFFFF    |    FFFFFFFFFFFFFFFF
LT          FFFFFFFFFFFFFFFF    |    0000000000000000
LE          FFFFFFFFFFFFFFFF    |    0000000000000000
GT          0000000000000000    |    FFFFFFFFFFFFFFFF
GE          0000000000000000    |    FFFFFFFFFFFFFFFF
ORDERED     FFFFFFFFFFFFFFFF    |    FFFFFFFFFFFFFFFF
UNORDERED   0000000000000000    |    0000000000000000

a hi:                12.000000000000    |                         nan
b hi:                42.000000000000    |              1.414213562373
EQ          0000000000000000    |    0000000000000000
NE          FFFFFFFFFFFFFFFF    |    0000000000000000
LT          FFFFFFFFFFFFFFFF    |    0000000000000000
LE          FFFFFFFFFFFFFFFF    |    0000000000000000
GT          0000000000000000    |    0000000000000000
GE          0000000000000000    |    0000000000000000
ORDERED     FFFFFFFFFFFFFFFF    |    0000000000000000
UNORDERED   0000000000000000    |    FFFFFFFFFFFFFFFF
```

# Floating-Point Conversions

A common operation in many C++ functions is to cast a single-precision or double-precision floating-point value to an integer or vice versa. It is also common for a function to promote a single-precision floating-point value to double precision or narrow a double-precision floating-point value to single precision. Source code example Ch03_03, shown in Listing 3-3, illustrates how to perform these types of conversions using C++ SIMD intrinsic functions.

*Listing 3-3.* Example Ch03_03

```
//-------------------------------------------------
//               Ch03_03.h
//-------------------------------------------------

#pragma once
#include "XmmVal.h"
```

```
enum class CvtOp : unsigned int
{
    I32_TO_F32, F32_TO_I32, I32_TO_F64, F64_TO_I32, F32_TO_F64, F64_TO_F32,
};

// Ch03_03_fcpp.cpp
extern void PackedConvertFP_Iavx(XmmVal* c, const XmmVal* a, CvtOp cvt_op);

//------------------------------------------------
//                  Ch03_03.cpp
//------------------------------------------------

#include <iostream>
#include <string>
#define _USE_MATH_DEFINES
#include <math.h>
#include "Ch03_03.h"

static void  PackedConvertF32(void);
static void  PackedConvertF64(void);

int main()
{
    std::string sep(80, '-');

    PackedConvertF32();
    std::cout << '\n' << sep << '\n';
    PackedConvertF64();
}

static void  PackedConvertF32(void)
{
    XmmVal a, c;

    a.m_I32[0] = 10;
    a.m_I32[1] = -500;
    a.m_I32[2] = 600;
    a.m_I32[3] = -1024;
    PackedConvertFP_Iavx(&c, &a, CvtOp::I32_TO_F32);
    std::cout << "\nResults for CvtOp::I32_TO_F32\n";
    std::cout << "a: " << a.ToStringI32() << '\n';
    std::cout << "c: " << c.ToStringF32() << '\n';

    a.m_F32[0] = 1.0f / 3.0f;
    a.m_F32[1] = 2.0f / 3.0f;
    a.m_F32[2] = -a.m_F32[0] * 2.0f;
    a.m_F32[3] = -a.m_F32[1] * 2.0f;
    PackedConvertFP_Iavx(&c, &a, CvtOp::F32_TO_I32);
    std::cout << "\nResults for CvtOp::F32_TO_I32\n";
    std::cout << "a: " << a.ToStringF32() << '\n';
    std::cout << "c: " << c.ToStringI32() << '\n';
```

```
    // F32_TO_F64 converts the two low-order F32 values of 'a'
    a.m_F32[0] = 1.0f / 7.0f;
    a.m_F32[1] = 2.0f / 9.0f;
    a.m_F32[2] = 0;
    a.m_F32[3] = 0;
    PackedConvertFP_Iavx(&c, &a, CvtOp::F32_TO_F64);
    std::cout << "\nResults for CvtOp::F32_TO_F64\n";
    std::cout << "a: " << a.ToStringF32() << '\n';
    std::cout << "c: " << c.ToStringF64() << '\n';
}

static void  PackedConvertF64(void)
{
    XmmVal a, c;

    // I32_TO_F64 converts the two low-order doubleword integers of 'a'
    a.m_I32[0] = 10;
    a.m_I32[1] = -20;
    a.m_I32[2] = 0;
    a.m_I32[3] = 0;
    PackedConvertFP_Iavx(&c, &a, CvtOp::I32_TO_F64);
    std::cout << "\nResults for CvtOp::I32_TO_F64\n";
    std::cout << "a: " << a.ToStringI32() << '\n';
    std::cout << "c: " << c.ToStringF64() << '\n';

    // F64_TO_I32 sets the two high-order doublewords of 'b' to zero
    a.m_F64[0] = M_PI;
    a.m_F64[1] = M_E;
    PackedConvertFP_Iavx(&c, &a, CvtOp::F64_TO_I32);
    std::cout << "\nResults for CvtOp::F64_TO_I32\n";
    std::cout << "a: " << a.ToStringF64() << '\n';
    std::cout << "c: " << c.ToStringI32() << '\n';

    // F64_TO_F32 sets the two high-order F32 values of 'b' to zero
    a.m_F64[0] = M_SQRT2;
    a.m_F64[1] = M_SQRT1_2;
    PackedConvertFP_Iavx(&c, &a, CvtOp::F64_TO_F32);
    std::cout << "\nResults for CvtOp::F64_TO_F32\n";
    std::cout << "a: " << a.ToStringF64() << '\n';
    std::cout << "c: " << c.ToStringF32() << '\n';
}

//--------------------------------------------------
//                  Ch03_03_fcpp.cpp
//--------------------------------------------------

#include <stdexcept>
#include <immintrin.h>
#include "Ch03_03.h"
```

```cpp
void PackedConvertFP_Iavx(XmmVal* c, const XmmVal* a, CvtOp cvt_op)
{
    __m128 temp_ps;
    __m128i temp_si;
    __m128d temp_pd;

    switch (cvt_op)
    {
        case CvtOp::I32_TO_F32:
            temp_si = _mm_load_si128((__m128i*)a);
            temp_ps = _mm_cvtepi32_ps(temp_si);
            _mm_store_ps((float*)c, temp_ps);
            break;

        case CvtOp::F32_TO_I32:
            temp_ps = _mm_load_ps((float*)a);
            temp_si = _mm_cvtps_epi32(temp_ps);
            _mm_store_si128((__m128i*)c, temp_si);
            break;

        case CvtOp::I32_TO_F64:
            temp_si = _mm_load_si128((__m128i*)a);
            temp_pd = _mm_cvtepi32_pd(temp_si);
            _mm_store_pd((double*)c, temp_pd);
            break;

        case CvtOp::F64_TO_I32:
            temp_pd = _mm_load_pd((double*)a);
            temp_si = _mm_cvtpd_epi32(temp_pd);
            _mm_store_si128((__m128i*)c, temp_si);
            break;

        case CvtOp::F32_TO_F64:
            temp_ps = _mm_load_ps((float*)a);
            temp_pd = _mm_cvtps_pd(temp_ps);
            _mm_store_pd((double*)c, temp_pd);
            break;

        case CvtOp::F64_TO_F32:
            temp_pd = _mm_load_pd((double*)a);
            temp_ps = _mm_cvtpd_ps(temp_pd);
            _mm_store_ps((float*)c, temp_ps);
            break;

        default:
            throw std::runtime_error("Invalid value for cvt_op");
    }
}
```

Listing 3-3 begins with an enumerated class named CvtOp, which defines symbolic names for the conversions demonstrated in this example. Next in Listing 3-3 is the file Ch03_03.cpp. This file contains two static functions. The first function, PackedConvertF32(), performs data initialization for single-precision floating-point conversions. The second function, PackedConvertF64(), does the same for double-precision floating-point conversions. Note that both functions initialize test objects of type XmmVal.

The final function in Listing 3-3 is named PackedConvertFP_Iavx(). This function uses the argument cvt_op and a simple switch construct to perform a conversion operation. Immediately following each case statement is a C++ SIMD intrinsic function call that loads source operand a into a temporary variable. Next is a C++ SIMD intrinsic function call that performs the actual packed conversion. This is followed by a store call that saves the result. The specific load, convert, and save functions used in each case statement code block vary depending on cvt_op. Note that when performing a conversion involving elements whose sizeof() sizes are different (i.e., I32 to F64, F64 to I32, F32 to F64, and F64 to F32), only the two low-order elements in the SIMD source operand are converted. This example uses 128-bit wide SIMD operands, but C++ SIMD intrinsic functions that carry out conversions using 256-bit wide SIMD operands are also available as are conversion functions for 64-bit integers. Here are the results for source code example Ch03_03:

```
Results for CvtOp::I32_TO_F32
a:             10            -500    |          600           -1024
c:      10.000000      -500.000000   |    600.000000    -1024.000000

Results for CvtOp::F32_TO_I32
a:       0.333333        0.666667    |    -0.666667       -1.333333
c:              0               1    |           -1              -1

Results for CvtOp::F32_TO_F64
a:       0.142857        0.222222    |    0.000000        0.000000
c:           0.142857149243          |        0.222222223878


------------------------------------------------------------------------

Results for CvtOp::I32_TO_F64
a:             10             -20    |           0               0
c:          10.000000000000           |      -20.000000000000

Results for CvtOp::F64_TO_I32
a:          3.141592653590           |       2.718281828459
c:              3               3    |           0               0

Results for CvtOp::F64_TO_F32
a:          1.414213562373           |       0.707106781187
c:        1.414214        0.707107    |    0.000000        0.000000
```

# Floating-Point Arrays

In C++, the elements of a one-dimensional array are stored in a contiguous block of memory that can be statically allocated at compile time or dynamically allocated during program execution. The elements of a C++ array are accessed using zero-based indexing, which means that valid indices for an array of size $N$

range from *0* to *N - 1*. In this section, you will learn how to carry out SIMD calculations using floating-point arrays. The first two source examples explain how to compute the sample mean and standard deviation of a floating-point array. The next two source examples illustrate square root and compare operations using the elements of a floating-point array.

## Mean and Standard Deviation

Listing 3-4 shows the source code for example Ch03_04. This example explains how to calculate the sample mean and standard deviation of an array of single-precision floating-point elements. It also illustrates execution of several SIMD data manipulation operations including element extractions and horizontal addition.

*Listing 3-4.* Example Ch03_04

```
//---------------------------------------------------
//                  Ch03_04.h
//---------------------------------------------------

#pragma once
#include <cstddef>

// Ch03_04_fcpp.cpp
extern bool CalcMeanF32_Cpp(float* mean, const float* x, size_t n);
extern bool CalcStDevF32_Cpp(float* st_dev, const float* x, size_t n, float mean);
extern bool CalcMeanF32_Iavx(float* mean, const float* x, size_t n);
extern bool CalcStDevF32_Iavx(float* st_dev, const float* x, size_t n, float mean);

// Ch03_04_misc.cpp
extern bool CheckArgs(const float* x, size_t n);
extern void InitArray(float* x, size_t n);

// Miscellaneous constants
const size_t c_NumElements = 91;
const unsigned int c_RngSeed = 13;
const float c_ArrayFillMin = 1.0f;
const float c_ArrayFillMax = 100.0f;
const size_t c_Alignment = 32;


//---------------------------------------------------
//                  Ch03_04_misc.cpp
//---------------------------------------------------

#include "Ch03_04.h"
#include "AlignedMem.h"
#include "MT.h"

bool CheckArgs(const float* x, size_t n)
{
    return ((n >= 2) && AlignedMem::IsAligned(x, c_Alignment));
}
```

```cpp
void InitArray(float* x, size_t n)
{
    MT::FillArrayFP(x, n, c_ArrayFillMin, c_ArrayFillMax, c_RngSeed);
}

//-------------------------------------------------
//                  Ch03_04.cpp
//-------------------------------------------------

#include <iostream>
#include <iomanip>
#include "Ch03_04.h"
#include "AlignedMem.h"

static void CalcMeanStDevF32(void);

int main()
{
    CalcMeanStDevF32();
    return 0;
}

static void CalcMeanStDevF32(void)
{
    size_t n = c_NumElements;
    AlignedArray<float> x_aa(n, c_Alignment);
    float* x = x_aa.Data();

    InitArray(x, n);

    float mean1, mean2, st_dev1, st_dev2;

    bool rc1 = CalcMeanF32_Cpp(&mean1, x, n);
    bool rc2 = CalcStDevF32_Cpp(&st_dev1, x, n, mean1);
    bool rc3 = CalcMeanF32_Iavx(&mean2, x, n);
    bool rc4 = CalcStDevF32_Iavx(&st_dev2, x, n, mean2);

    if (!rc1 || !rc2 || !rc3 || !rc4)
    {
        std::cout << "Invalid return code\n";
        return;
    }

    unsigned int w = 10;
    const char nl = '\n';
    std::cout << std::fixed << std::setprecision(6);
    std::cout << "Results for CalcMeanF32_Cpp and CalcStDevF32_Cpp" << nl;
    std::cout << "mean1:   " << std::setw(w) << mean1 << "   ";
    std::cout << "st_dev1: " << std::setw(w) << st_dev1 << nl << nl;
    std::cout << "Results for CalcMeanF32_Iavx and CalcStDevF32_Iavx" << nl;
```

```
    std::cout << "mean2:    " << std::setw(w) << mean2 << " ";
    std::cout << "st_dev2: " << std::setw(w) << st_dev2 << nl;
}

//------------------------------------------------
//              Ch03_04_fcpp.cpp
//------------------------------------------------

#include <cmath>
#include <immintrin.h>
#include "Ch03_04.h"

bool CalcMeanF32_Cpp(float* mean, const float* x, size_t n)
{
    if (!CheckArgs(x, n))
        return false;

    float sum = 0.0f;

    for (size_t i = 0; i < n; i++)
        sum += x[i];

    *mean = sum / n;
    return true;
}

bool CalcStDevF32_Cpp(float* st_dev, const float* x, size_t n, float mean)
{
    if (!CheckArgs(x, n))
        return false;

    float sum_squares = 0.0f;

    for (size_t i = 0; i < n; i++)
    {
        float temp = x[i] - mean;
        sum_squares += temp * temp;
    }

    *st_dev = sqrt(sum_squares / (n - 1));
    return true;
}

bool CalcMeanF32_Iavx(float* mean, const float* x, size_t n)
{
    if (!CheckArgs(x, n))
        return false;

    __m256 sums = _mm256_setzero_ps();
```

```
    size_t i = 0;
    const size_t num_simd_elements = 8;

    for (; n - i >= num_simd_elements; i += num_simd_elements)
    {
        __m256 x_vals = _mm256_load_ps(&x[i]);
        sums = _mm256_add_ps(x_vals, sums);
    }

    // Perform reduction, final sum in low-order element of temp4
    __m128 temp0 = _mm256_extractf128_ps(sums, 0);
    __m128 temp1 = _mm256_extractf128_ps(sums, 1);
    __m128 temp2 = _mm_add_ps(temp0, temp1);
    __m128 temp3 = _mm_hadd_ps(temp2, temp2);
    __m128 temp4 = _mm_hadd_ps(temp3, temp3);

    // Process remaining elements
    float sum;
    _mm_store_ss(&sum, temp4);

    for (; i < n; i++)
        sum += x[i];

    *mean = sum / n;
    return true;
}

bool CalcStDevF32_Iavx(float* st_dev, const float* x, size_t n, float mean)
{
    if (!CheckArgs(x, n))
        return false;

    __m256 packed_mean = _mm256_broadcast_ss(&mean);
    __m256 packed_sum_squares = _mm256_setzero_ps();

    size_t i = 0;
    const size_t num_simd_elements = 8;

    for (; n - i >= num_simd_elements; i += num_simd_elements)
    {
        __m256 x_vals = _mm256_load_ps(&x[i]);
        __m256 temp1 = _mm256_sub_ps(x_vals, packed_mean);
        __m256 temp2 = _mm256_mul_ps(temp1, temp1);

        packed_sum_squares = _mm256_add_ps(packed_sum_squares, temp2);
    }

    // Peform reduction, final sum_squares in low-order element of temp4
    __m128 temp0 = _mm256_extractf128_ps(packed_sum_squares, 0);
    __m128 temp1 = _mm256_extractf128_ps(packed_sum_squares, 1);
    __m128 temp2 = _mm_add_ps(temp0, temp1);
```

```
    __m128 temp3 = _mm_hadd_ps(temp2, temp2);
    __m128 temp4 = _mm_hadd_ps(temp3, temp3);

    // Process remaining elements
    float sum_squares;
    _mm_store_ss(&sum_squares, temp4);

    for (; i < n; i++)
    {
        float temp1 = x[i] - mean;
        sum_squares += temp1 * temp1;
    }

    *st_dev = sqrt(sum_squares / (n - 1));
    return true;
}
```

Here are the formulas that source code example Ch03_04 uses to calculate the sample mean and standard deviation:

$$\bar{x} = \frac{1}{n}\sum_i x_i$$

$$s = \sqrt{\frac{1}{n-1}\sum_i (x_i - \bar{x})^2}$$

Listing 3-4 starts with the header file Ch03_04.h. This file includes the requisite function declarations and some miscellaneous constants. The next file in Listing 3-4 is Ch03_04_misc.cpp. This file include two function definitions: CheckArgs() and InitArray(). The calculating functions use CheckArgs() to perform argument validation. Function CalcMeanStDevF32(), located in Ch03_04.cpp, uses InitArray() to initialize a test array with random values. Note that the test array is of type AlignedArray<float>. As explained in Chapter 2, the template class AlignedArray<T> allocates an array that is aligned on a specific boundary for use in x86-AVX calculating functions.

Following test array initialization, CalcMeanStDevF32() calls CalcMeanF32_Cpp() and CalcMeanF32_Iavx() to calculate the sample means. It then calculates the sample standard deviations using the calculating functions CalcStDevF32_Cpp() and CalcStDevF32_Iavx(). As explained in Chapter 1, this book uses the suffix _Cpp for functions that perform their calculations using standard C++ code. Functions that have an _Iavx in their names employ AVX C++ SIMD intrinsic functions to carry out their calculations. Two different mean and standard deviation calculating functions are used in this example for both edification (the non-SIMD functions are usually easier to understand) and benchmarking purposes. Other source code examples in this and subsequent chapters also follow this pattern.

The first function in Ch03_04_fcpp.cpp is CalcMeanF32_Cpp(). This function calculates the mean of an array of single-precision floating-point values. The code in CalcMeanF32_Cpp() uses a single for-loop to sum the elements in the array. It then employs scalar floating-point division to calculate the mean. Following CalcMeanF32_Cpp() in Listing 3-1 is the function CalcStDevF32_Cpp(). This function also uses a single for-loop and some straightforward C++ code to calculate the standard deviation.

Function CalcMeanF32_Iavx() begins its execution with a call to CheckArgs(), which validates argument n for size and array pointer x for proper alignment. It then uses the C++ SIMD intrinsic function _mm256_setzero_ps() to initialize sums to zero. This variable holds eight intermediate sum values. The first for-loop in CalcMeanF32_Iavx() updates sums during each iteration. CalcMeanF32_Iavx() uses _mm256_load_ps() to load eight elements from array x into x_vals. It then uses the function _mm256_add_ps() to update the intermediate values in sums.

Following execution of the first for-loop, the packed intermediate values in sums are reduced to a scalar value. This is accomplished using the C++ SIMD intrinsic functions _mm256_extractf128_ps(), _mm_add_ps, _mm_hadd_ps(), and _mm_store_ss() as shown in Figure 3-1. Note that the _mm_store_ss() function saves the current sum to a local variable so that it can be used in the second for-loop. Following the reduction operation, CalcMeanF32_Iavx() uses a second for-loop to calculate the final sum. This second for-loop executes only if the number of array elements n is not an integral multiple of num_simd_elements. (In this and subsequent chapters, I will call any elements leftover from a SIMD for-loop residual elements, residual values, or residual pixels.) The C++ statement that computes the mean follows the second for-loop.

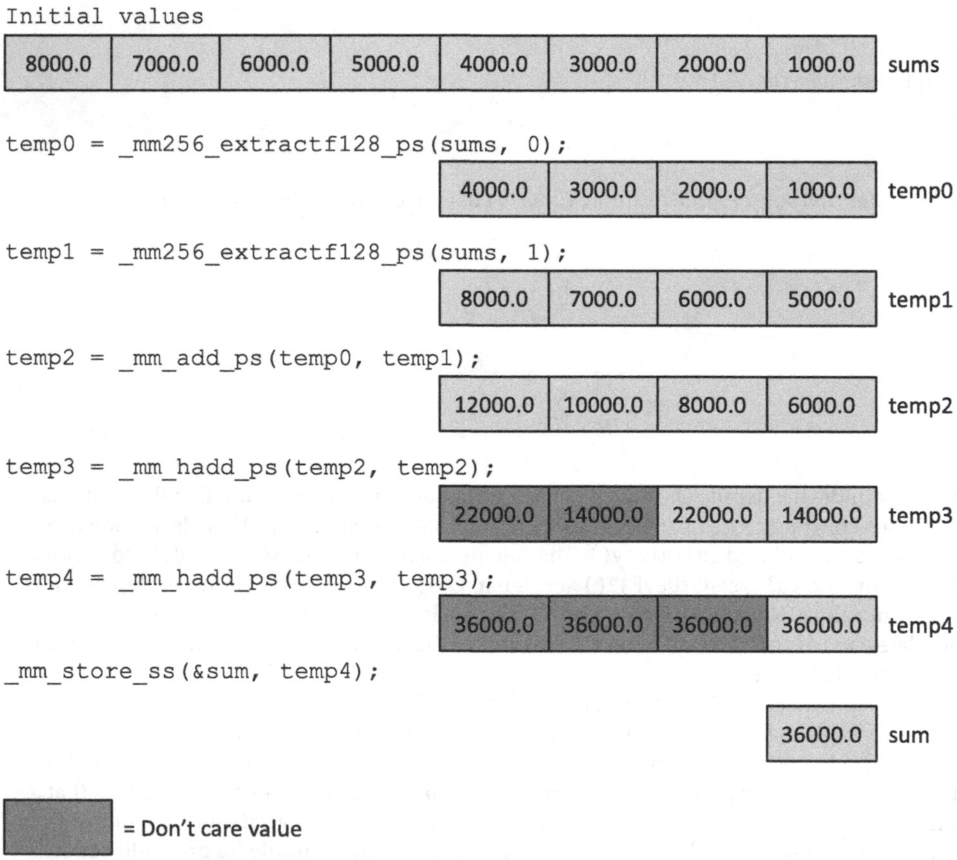

```
Initial values
```

| 8000.0 | 7000.0 | 6000.0 | 5000.0 | 4000.0 | 3000.0 | 2000.0 | 1000.0 | sums |

```
temp0 = _mm256_extractf128_ps(sums, 0);
```

| | | | | 4000.0 | 3000.0 | 2000.0 | 1000.0 | temp0 |

```
temp1 = _mm256_extractf128_ps(sums, 1);
```

| | | | | 8000.0 | 7000.0 | 6000.0 | 5000.0 | temp1 |

```
temp2 = _mm_add_ps(temp0, temp1);
```

| | | | | 12000.0 | 10000.0 | 8000.0 | 6000.0 | temp2 |

```
temp3 = _mm_hadd_ps(temp2, temp2);
```

| | | | | 22000.0 | 14000.0 | 22000.0 | 14000.0 | temp3 |

```
temp4 = _mm_hadd_ps(temp3, temp3);
```

| | | | | 36000.0 | 36000.0 | 36000.0 | 36000.0 | temp4 |

```
_mm_store_ss(&sum, temp4);
```

| | | | | | | | 36000.0 | sum |

▓ = Don't care value

*Figure 3-1. Reduction of eight single-precision floating-point values in a 256-bit wide SIMD operand*

The function CalcStdDevF32_Iavx() uses a similar design pattern to calculate the standard deviation. Following argument validation, CalcStDevF32() calls the C++ SIMD intrinsic functions _mm256_broadcast_ss() and _mm256_setzero_ps() to initialize packed_mean and packed_sum_squares, respectively. The first for-loop calculates packed_sum_squares. This for-loop uses _mm256_sub_ps() to calculate x[i:i+7] - packed_mean[i:i+7] and _mm256_mul_ps() to update packed_sum_squares[i:i+7]. Following completion of the first for-loop, packed_sum_squares is reduced to a scalar value using that same C++ SIMD intrinsic function sequence that is shown in Figure 3-1. The final block of code in CalcStDevF32_Iavx() processes any residual elements and calculates the final standard deviation. Here are the results for source code example Ch03_04:

```
Results for CalcMeanF32_Cpp and CalcStDevF32_Cpp
mean1:    49.602146  st_dev1:  27.758242

Results for CalcMeanF32_Iavx and CalcStDevF32_Iavx
mean2:    49.602154  st_dev2:  27.758245
```

You may have noticed that slight value discrepancies exist between the standard C++ and SIMD C++ implementations of the two calculating functions. Numerical discrepancies like this are not uncommon when using different sequences of code to implement the same algorithm due to the non-associativity of floating-point arithmetic. The possibility of value discrepancies like this is something that you should keep in mind if you are developing an application that includes both non-SIMD and SIMD versions of the same calculating function.

The next source code example, Ch03_05, is similar to the previous source code example except that it uses double-precision instead of single-precision floating-point SIMD arithmetic. Listing 3-5 shows the source code for example Ch03_05. Note that Listing 3-5 only shows the code for the calculating functions that are in Ch03_05_fcpp.cpp since the noncalculating code (test array initialization, error checking, etc.) closely resembles the code that you saw in Listing 3-4. The source code download package includes the complete code for this and all other source code examples published in this book.

***Listing 3-5.*** Example Ch03_05

```cpp
//--------------------------------------------------
//                 Ch03_05_fcpp.cpp
//--------------------------------------------------

#include <cmath>
#include <xmmintrin.h>
#include <immintrin.h>
#include "Ch03_05.h"
#include "AlignedMem.h"

bool CalcMeanF64_Cpp(double* mean, const double* x, size_t n)
{
    if (!CheckArgs(x, n))
        return false;

    double sum = 0.0;

    for (size_t i = 0; i < n; i++)
        sum += x[i];

    *mean = sum / n;
    return true;
}
```

```cpp
bool CalcStDevF64_Cpp(double* st_dev, const double* x, size_t n, double mean)
{
    if (!CheckArgs(x, n))
        return false;

    double sum_squares = 0.0;

    for (size_t i = 0; i < n; i++)
    {
        double temp = x[i] - mean;
        sum_squares += temp * temp;
    }

    *st_dev = sqrt(sum_squares / (n - 1));
    return true;
}

bool CalcMeanF64_Iavx(double* mean, const double* x, size_t n)
{
    if (!CheckArgs(x, n))
        return false;

    __m256d sums = _mm256_setzero_pd();

    size_t i = 0;
    const size_t num_simd_elements = 4;

    for (; n - i >= num_simd_elements; i += num_simd_elements)
    {
        __m256d x_vals = _mm256_load_pd(&x[i]);
        sums = _mm256_add_pd(x_vals, sums);
    }

    // Peform reduction, final sum in low-order element of temp3
    __m128d temp0 = _mm256_extractf128_pd(sums, 0);
    __m128d temp1 = _mm256_extractf128_pd(sums, 1);
    __m128d temp2 = _mm_add_pd(temp0, temp1);
    __m128d temp3 = _mm_hadd_pd(temp2, temp2);

    // Process remaining elements
    double sum;
    _mm_store_sd(&sum, temp3);

    for (; i < n; i++)
        sum += x[i];

    *mean = sum / n;
    return true;
}
```

```
bool CalcStDevF64_Iavx(double* st_dev, const double* x, size_t n, double mean)
{
    if (!CheckArgs(x, n))
        return false;

    __m256d packed_mean = _mm256_broadcast_sd(&mean);
    __m256d packed_sum_squares = _mm256_setzero_pd();

    size_t i = 0;
    const size_t num_simd_elements = 4;

    for (; n - i >= num_simd_elements; i += num_simd_elements)
    {
        __m256d x_vals = _mm256_load_pd(&x[i]);
        __m256d temp1 = _mm256_sub_pd(x_vals, packed_mean);
        __m256d temp2 = _mm256_mul_pd(temp1, temp1);

        packed_sum_squares = _mm256_add_pd(packed_sum_squares, temp2);
    }

    // Peform reduction, final sum_squares in low-order element of temp3
    __m128d temp0 = _mm256_extractf128_pd(packed_sum_squares, 0);
    __m128d temp1 = _mm256_extractf128_pd(packed_sum_squares, 1);
    __m128d temp2 = _mm_add_pd(temp0, temp1);
    __m128d temp3 = _mm_hadd_pd(temp2, temp2);

    // Process remaining elements
    double sum_squares;
    _mm_store_sd(&sum_squares, temp3);

    for (; i < n; i++)
    {
        double temp1 = x[i] - mean;
        sum_squares += temp1 * temp1;
    }

    *st_dev = sqrt(sum_squares / (n - 1));
    return true;
}
```

If you look closely at the function CalcMeanF64_Iavx() in Listing 3-5, you will notice only a few minor differences compared to the function CalcMeanF32_Iavx() that is shown in Listing 3-4. The function CalcMeanF64_Iavx() uses double-precision versions of the same C++ SIMD intrinsic functions that were used in example Ch03_04. The other critical change in CalcMeanF64_Iavx() is that num_simd_elements is initialized to four instead of eight, which means that the first for-loop processes four elements from array x during each iteration. The reduction of sums is also similar except that it requires only a single horizontal add operation.

The function CalcStDevF64_Iavx() also parallels its single-precision floating-point counterpart CalcStDevF32_Iavx(). One key takeaway point from this example is that with a little forethought, it is often relatively easy to develop a SIMD calculating algorithm that can be easily adapted for both single-precision and double-precision floating-point arithmetic. You will see other examples later in this chapter and in subsequent chapters. Here are the results for source code example Ch03_05:

```
Results for CalcMeanF64_Cpp and CalcStDevF64_Cpp
mean1:    49.60215657  st_dev1: 27.75824464

Results for CalcMeanF64_Iavx and CalcStDevF64_Iavx
mean2:    49.60215657  st_dev2: 27.75824464
```

## Distance Calculations

Listing 3-6 shows the source code for example Ch03_06. This example uses single-precision floating-point arithmetic to calculate Euclidean distances between two points on a 2D grid. It also explains how to use AVX compare operations to conditionally update the elements of an array.

*Listing 3-6.* Example Ch03_06

```
//--------------------------------------------------
//                  Ch03_06.h
//--------------------------------------------------

#pragma once
#include <cstddef>

struct PointArrays
{
    float* X1;
    float* Y1;
    float* X2;
    float* Y2;
    float* Dist1;
    float* Dist2;
    float* DistCmp1;
    float* DistCmp2;
    size_t NumPoints;
};

// Ch03_06_fcpp.cpp
extern bool CalcDistancesF32_Cpp(PointArrays& pa);
extern bool CalcDistancesF32_Iavx(PointArrays& pa);
extern void CompareDistancesF32_Cpp(PointArrays& pa, float cmp_val);
extern void CompareDistancesF32_Iavx(PointArrays& pa, float cmp_val);

// Ch03_06_misc.cpp
extern bool CheckArgs(PointArrays& pa);
extern void FillPointArraysF32(PointArrays& pa, float min_val, float max_val, unsigned int
rng_seed);
```

```cpp
// Miscellaneous constants
const size_t c_NumPoints = 21;
const unsigned int c_RngSeed = 39;
const float c_ArrayFillMin = 1.0f;
const float c_ArrayFillMax = 75.0f;
const float c_CmpVal = 50.0f;
const size_t c_Alignment = 32;


//-------------------------------------------------
//                  Ch03_06_misc.cpp
//-------------------------------------------------

#include <random>
#include "Ch03_06.h"
#include "AlignedMem.h"

bool CheckArgs(PointArrays& pa)
{
    if (!AlignedMem::IsAligned(pa.X1, c_Alignment))
        return false;
    if (!AlignedMem::IsAligned(pa.X2, c_Alignment))
        return false;
    if (!AlignedMem::IsAligned(pa.Y1, c_Alignment))
        return false;
    if (!AlignedMem::IsAligned(pa.Y2, c_Alignment))
        return false;
    if (!AlignedMem::IsAligned(pa.Dist1, c_Alignment))
        return false;
    if (!AlignedMem::IsAligned(pa.Dist2, c_Alignment))
        return false;
    if (!AlignedMem::IsAligned(pa.DistCmp1, c_Alignment))
        return false;
    if (!AlignedMem::IsAligned(pa.DistCmp2, c_Alignment))
        return false;

    return true;
}

void FillPointArraysF32(PointArrays& pa, float min_val, float max_val, unsigned int
rng_seed)
{
    std::mt19937 rng {rng_seed};
    std::uniform_real_distribution<float> dist {min_val, max_val};

    size_t num_points = pa.NumPoints;

    for (size_t i = 0; i < num_points; i++)
    {
        pa.X1[i] = dist(rng);
        pa.X2[i] = dist(rng);
```

```
        pa.Y1[i] = dist(rng);
        pa.Y2[i] = dist(rng);
    }
}

//--------------------------------------------------
//                  Ch03_06.cpp
//--------------------------------------------------

#include <iostream>
#include <iomanip>
#include <string>
#include "Ch03_06.h"
#include "AlignedMem.h"

static void CalcDistanceF32(void);

int main()
{
    CalcDistanceF32();
    return 0;
}

static void CalcDistanceF32(void)
{
    AlignedArray<float> x1(c_NumPoints, c_Alignment);
    AlignedArray<float> y1(c_NumPoints, c_Alignment);
    AlignedArray<float> x2(c_NumPoints, c_Alignment);
    AlignedArray<float> y2(c_NumPoints, c_Alignment);
    AlignedArray<float> dist1(c_NumPoints, c_Alignment);
    AlignedArray<float> dist2(c_NumPoints, c_Alignment);
    AlignedArray<float> dist_cmp1(c_NumPoints, c_Alignment);
    AlignedArray<float> dist_cmp2(c_NumPoints, c_Alignment);

    PointArrays pa;

    pa.X1 = x1.Data();
    pa.Y1 = y1.Data();
    pa.X2 = x2.Data();
    pa.Y2 = y2.Data();
    pa.Dist1 = dist1.Data();
    pa.Dist2 = dist2.Data();
    pa.DistCmp1 = dist_cmp1.Data();
    pa.DistCmp2 = dist_cmp2.Data();
    pa.NumPoints = c_NumPoints;

    FillPointArraysF32(pa, c_ArrayFillMin, c_ArrayFillMax, c_RngSeed);

    CalcDistancesF32_Cpp(pa);
    CompareDistancesF32_Cpp(pa, c_CmpVal);
    CalcDistancesF32_Iavx(pa);
    CompareDistancesF32_Iavx(pa, c_CmpVal);
```

```cpp
    const size_t w = 9;
    const char nl = '\n';
    std::cout << std::fixed << std::setprecision(3);
    std::cout << std::setw(w) << "X1" << " ";
    std::cout << std::setw(w) << "Y1" << " ";
    std::cout << std::setw(w) << "X2" << " ";
    std::cout << std::setw(w) << "Y2" << " |";
    std::cout << std::setw(w) << "Dist1" << " ";
    std::cout << std::setw(w) << "Dist2" << " |";
    std::cout << std::setw(w) << "DistCmp1" << " ";
    std::cout << std::setw(w) << "DistCmp2" << nl;
    std::cout << std::string(82, '-') << nl;

    for (size_t i = 0; i < c_NumPoints; i++)
    {
        std::cout << std::setw(w) << pa.X1[i] << " ";
        std::cout << std::setw(w) << pa.Y1[i] << " ";
        std::cout << std::setw(w) << pa.X2[i] << " ";
        std::cout << std::setw(w) << pa.Y2[i] << " |";
        std::cout << std::setw(w) << pa.Dist1[i] << " ";
        std::cout << std::setw(w) << pa.Dist2[i] << " |";
        std::cout << std::setw(w) << pa.DistCmp1[i] << " ";
        std::cout << std::setw(w) << pa.DistCmp2[i] << nl;
    }
}

//--------------------------------------------------
//                  Ch03_06_fcpp.cpp
//--------------------------------------------------

#include <cmath>
#include <immintrin.h>
#include "Ch03_06.h"
#include "AlignedMem.h"

bool CalcDistancesF32_Cpp(PointArrays& pa)
{
    if (!CheckArgs(pa))
        return false;

    size_t num_points = pa.NumPoints;

    for (size_t i = 0; i < num_points; i++)
    {
        float temp1 = pa.X1[i] - pa.X2[i];
        float temp2 = pa.Y1[i] - pa.Y2[i];
        pa.Dist1[i] = sqrt(temp1 * temp1 + temp2 * temp2);
    }

    return true;
}
```

```cpp
void CompareDistancesF32_Cpp(PointArrays& pa, float cmp_val)
{
    size_t num_points = pa.NumPoints;

    for (size_t i = 0; i < num_points; i++)
    {
        float temp1 = pa.Dist1[i];
        float temp2 = (temp1 >= cmp_val) ? temp1 * -2.0f : temp1;
        pa.DistCmp1[i] = temp2;
    }
}

bool CalcDistancesF32_Iavx(PointArrays& pa)
{
    if (!CheckArgs(pa))
        return false;

    size_t i = 0;
    size_t num_points = pa.NumPoints;
    const size_t num_simd_elements = 8;

    for (; num_points - i >= num_simd_elements; i += num_simd_elements)
    {
        __m256 x1_vals = _mm256_load_ps(&pa.X1[i]);
        __m256 y1_vals = _mm256_load_ps(&pa.Y1[i]);
        __m256 x2_vals = _mm256_load_ps(&pa.X2[i]);
        __m256 y2_vals = _mm256_load_ps(&pa.Y2[i]);

        __m256 temp_x = _mm256_sub_ps(x1_vals, x2_vals);
        __m256 temp_y = _mm256_sub_ps(y1_vals, y2_vals);
        __m256 temp_xx = _mm256_mul_ps(temp_x, temp_x);
        __m256 temp_yy = _mm256_mul_ps(temp_y, temp_y);
        __m256 temp_sum = _mm256_add_ps(temp_xx, temp_yy);
        __m256 temp_dist = _mm256_sqrt_ps(temp_sum);

        _mm256_store_ps(&pa.Dist2[i], temp_dist);
    }

    for (; i < num_points; i++)
    {
        float temp1 = pa.X1[i] - pa.X2[i];
        float temp2 = pa.Y1[i] - pa.Y2[i];
        pa.Dist2[i] = sqrt(temp1 * temp1 + temp2 * temp2);
    }

    return true;
}
```

```
void CompareDistancesF32_Iavx(PointArrays& pa, float cmp_val)
{
    size_t i = 0;
    size_t num_points = pa.NumPoints;
    const size_t num_simd_elements = 8;
    const float minus2 = -2.0f;

    __m256 cmp_vals = _mm256_broadcast_ss(&cmp_val);
    __m256 packed_minus2 = _mm256_broadcast_ss(&minus2);

    for (; num_points - i >= num_simd_elements; i += num_simd_elements)
    {
        __m256 dist2_vals = _mm256_load_ps(&pa.Dist2[i]);

        // Elements in cmp_mask contain 0xFFFFFFFF or 0x00000000
        __m256 cmp_mask = _mm256_cmp_ps(dist2_vals, cmp_vals, _CMP_GE_OQ);

        // Elements in temp1 contain -2.0 or 0.0
        __m256 temp1 = _mm256_and_ps(cmp_mask, packed_minus2);

        // Elements in temp2 contain -2.0 * dist2_vals or 0.0
        __m256 temp2 = _mm256_mul_ps(temp1, dist2_vals);

        // Elements in temp3 contain 0.0 or dist2_vals
        __m256 temp3 = _mm256_andnot_ps(cmp_mask, dist2_vals);

        // Elements in temp4 contain -2.0 * dist2_vals or dist2_vals
        __m256 temp4 = _mm256_or_ps(temp2, temp3);

        _mm256_store_ps(&pa.DistCmp2[i], temp4);
    }

    for (; i < num_points; i++)
    {
        float temp1 = pa.Dist2[i];
        float temp2 = (temp1 >= cmp_val) ? temp1 * -2.0f : temp1;
        pa.DistCmp2[i] = temp2;
    }
}
```

The distance between two points on a 2D grid can be calculated using the following formula:

$$dist = \sqrt{(x_1 - x_2)^2 + (y_1 - y_2)^2}$$

The first file in Listing 3-6, Ch03_06.h, begins with the definition of a structure named PointArrays. This structure contains pointers to the arrays that are used by the calculating functions. It also includes the requisite function declarations. The file Ch03_06_misc.cpp incorporates the functions CheckArgs() and FillPointArraysF32(). These functions carry out argument validation and test array initialization, respectively. The file Ch03_06.cpp contains the function CalcDistance(), which initializes the PointArrays object pa. This function also calls the SIMD calculating functions CalcDistancesF32_Cpp(), CompareDistancesF32_Cpp(), CalcDistancesF32_Iavx(), and CompareDistancesF32_Iavx().

The file Ch03_06.cpp begins with the definition of function CalcDistancesF32()_Cpp. This function performs its distance calculations using standard C++ code and the previously defined formula. Function CompareDistancesF32_Cpp() is next. Function CompareDistancesF32_Cpp() compares each distance value pa.Dist1[i] that was calculated in CalcDistancesF32_Cpp() to cmp_val. If pa.Dist1[i] >= cmp_val is true, pa.Dist1[i] is multiplied by -2.0 (-2.0 is just an arbitrary value for ternary operator demonstration purposes). Note that CompareDistancesF32_Cpp() uses a C++ ternary operator to perform the comparison and multiplication.

The function CalcDistancesF32_Iavx() is the SIMD counterpart of CalcDistancesF32_Cpp(). Following argument validation, CalcDistancesF32_Iavx() initializes the for-loop index variable i to zero and num_simd_elements to eight. The first for-loop in CalcDistancesF32_Iavx() performs distance calculations using C++ SIMD intrinsic functions. It begins with a series of _mm256_load_ps() calls that load array elements x1[i:i+7], y1[i:i+7], x2[i:i+7], and y2[i:i+7]. The ensuing code block performs the distance calculations using the C++ SIMD intrinsic functions _mm256_sub_ps(), _mm256_mul_ps(), _mm256_add_ps(), and _mm256_sqrt_ps(). The final statement in the first for-loop is a call to _mm256_store_ps(), which saves the calculated distance values to pa.Dist2[i:i+7]. The second for-loop in CalcDistancesF32_Iavx() uses scalar arithmetic to calculate distances when num_points is not an integral multiple of num_simd_elements.

The final function in Ch03_06_fcpp.cpp implements the same comparison and multiplication operations that were performed by CompareDistancesF32_Cpp() using C++ SIMD intrinsic functions. It begins with two _mm256_broadcast_ss() calls that initialize cmp_vals and packed_minus2. The first for-loop begins its execution with an _mm256_load_ps() call that loads elements pa.Dist2[i:i+7].

The next set of executable statements in CompareDistancesF32_Iavx() implement a SIMD ternary operator, as shown in Figure 3-2. In this figure, the function _m256_cmp_ps() performs a packed compare operation using operands dist2_vals and cmp_vals and the compare predicate _CMP_GE_OQ. Recall from the discussions earlier in this chapter that for each corresponding element pair in a SIMD operand, the result of packed compare is all ones (0xFFFFFFFF) if the compare predicate is true; otherwise, the result is all zeros (0x00000000). Depending on the result of the compare operation, _mm256_and_ps() sets each element in temp1 to either -2.0 or 0.0. The ensuing _mm256_mul_ps() call multiplies the values in temp1 by the original distance values, which yields -2.0 * distance or 0.0 for each single-precision floating-point element in temp2.

Initial values

| 50.0 | 50.0 | 50.0 | 50.0 | 50.0 | 50.0 | 50.0 | 50.0 | cmp_vals |

| -2.0 | -2.0 | -2.0 | -2.0 | -2.0 | -2.0 | -2.0 | -2.0 | packed_minus2 |

| 63.158 | 54.071 | 56.728 | 28.513 | 23.898 | 8.544 | 62.132 | 40.060 | dist2_vals |

cmp_mask = _mm256_cmp_ps(dist2_vals, cmp_vals, _CMP_GE_OQ);

| FFFFFFFFh | FFFFFFFFh | FFFFFFFFh | 00000000h | 00000000h | 00000000h | FFFFFFFFh | 00000000h | cmp_mask |

temp1 = _mm256_and_ps(cmp_mask, packed_minus2);

| -2.0 | -2.0 | -2.0 | 0.0 | 0.0 | 0.0 | -2.0 | 0.0 | temp1 |

temp2 = _mm256_mul_ps(temp1, dist2_vals);

| -126.315 | -108.141 | -113.457 | 0.0 | 0.0 | 0.0 | -124.264 | 0.0 | temp2 |

temp3 = _mm256_andnot_ps(cmp_mask, dist2_vals);

| 0.0 | 0.0 | 0.0 | 28.513 | 23.898 | 8.544 | 0.0 | 40.060 | temp3 |

temp4 = _mm256_or_ps(temp2, temp3);

| -126.315 | -108.141 | -113.457 | 28.513 | 23.898 | 8.544 | -124.264 | 40.060 | temp4 |

*Figure 3-2.* *SIMD ternary calculation performed by CompareDistancesF32_Iavx()*

The C++ SIMD intrinsic function call _mm256_andnot_ps() sets each element in temp3 to 0.0 or the original distance value. This function performs a bitwise logical AND using the SIMD operands ~cmp_mask and dist2_vals. The final SIMD ternary operation call, _mm256_or_ps(), results in each element of temp4 having its original distance value or that value multiplied by -2.0. The next C++ SIMD intrinsic function call of the first for-loop, _mm256_store_ps(), saves temp4 to pa.CmpDist2[i:i+7]. The second for-loop in CompareDistancesF32_Iavx() handles any residual elements using scalar arithmetic. Here are the results for source code example Ch03_06:

```
    X1      Y1      X2      Y2   |   Dist1    Dist2 |  DistCmp1  DistCmp2
----------------------------------------------------------------------
 41.470  60.045   1.419  60.938 |  40.060   40.060 |   40.060    40.060
 61.710  10.032  28.150  62.320 |  62.132   62.132 | -124.264  -124.264
 45.548  39.888  45.621  31.345 |   8.544    8.544 |    8.544     8.544
 35.329  35.887  17.867  52.203 |  23.898   23.898 |   23.898    23.898
 47.821  69.499  19.309  69.724 |  28.513   28.513 |   28.513    28.513
 61.347  70.889  40.176  18.259 |  56.728   56.728 | -113.457  -113.457
 69.049  31.697  35.764  74.309 |  54.071   54.071 | -108.141  -108.141
 62.110  71.023  25.831  19.325 |  63.158   63.158 | -126.315  -126.315
 47.475  19.668  26.502  28.675 |  22.826   22.826 |   22.826    22.826
 44.834  64.670  27.339  51.671 |  21.796   21.796 |   21.796    21.796
  4.585  64.255  22.440  68.924 |  18.455   18.455 |   18.455    18.455
 54.296  22.902   8.905  19.004 |  45.558   45.558 |   45.558    45.558
```

| | | | | | | | |
|--------|--------|--------|--------|--------|--------|----------|----------|
| 36.920 | 63.476 | 64.079 | 12.002 | 58.200 | 58.200 | -116.400 | -116.400 |
| 45.584 | 12.629 | 37.245 | 66.029 | 54.048 | 54.048 | -108.096 | -108.096 |
| 39.932 | 14.882 | 25.214 | 24.382 | 17.518 | 17.518 | 17.518 | 17.518 |
| 50.613 | 41.607 | 53.261 | 18.449 | 23.309 | 23.309 | 23.309 | 23.309 |
| 12.576 | 70.005 | 33.699 | 39.280 | 37.286 | 37.286 | 37.286 | 37.286 |
| 41.179 | 49.289 | 15.620 | 56.153 | 26.464 | 26.464 | 26.464 | 26.464 |
| 50.680 | 61.602 | 51.222 | 26.242 | 35.364 | 35.364 | 35.364 | 35.364 |
| 2.003 | 63.741 | 21.990 | 17.102 | 50.740 | 50.740 | -101.481 | -101.481 |
| 33.195 | 36.332 | 49.349 | 62.033 | 30.357 | 30.357 | 30.357 | 30.357 |

Source code example Ch03_07 is similar to example Ch03_06 but uses double-precision instead of single-precision floating-point arithmetic. Listing 3-7 shows the source code for the file Ch03_07_fcpp.cpp, which contains the code for the calculating functions CalcDistancesF64_Cpp(), CompareDistancesF64_Cpp(), CalcDistancesF64_Iavx(), and CompareDistancesF64_Iavx().

***Listing 3-7.*** Example Ch03_07

```
//-------------------------------------------------
//                 Ch03_07_fcpp.cpp
//-------------------------------------------------

#include <cmath>
#include <immintrin.h>
#include "Ch03_07.h"

bool CalcDistancesF64_Cpp(PointArrays& pa)
{
    if (!CheckArgs(pa))
        return false;

    size_t num_points = pa.NumPoints;

    for (size_t i = 0; i < num_points; i++)
    {
        double temp1 = pa.X1[i] - pa.X2[i];
        double temp2 = pa.Y1[i] - pa.Y2[i];
        pa.Dist1[i] = sqrt(temp1 * temp1 + temp2 * temp2);
    }

    return true;
}

void CompareDistancesF64_Cpp(PointArrays& pa, double cmp_val)
{
    size_t num_points = pa.NumPoints;

    for (size_t i = 0; i < num_points; i++)
    {
        double temp1 = pa.Dist1[i];
        double temp2 = (temp1 >= cmp_val) ? temp1 * -2.0 : temp1;
```

```
                pa.DistCmp1[i] = temp2;
        }
}

bool CalcDistancesF64_Iavx(PointArrays& pa)
{
    if (!CheckArgs(pa))
        return false;

    size_t i = 0;
    size_t num_points = pa.NumPoints;
    const size_t num_simd_elements = 4;

    for (; num_points - i >= num_simd_elements; i += num_simd_elements)
    {
        __m256d x1_vals = _mm256_load_pd(&pa.X1[i]);
        __m256d y1_vals = _mm256_load_pd(&pa.Y1[i]);
        __m256d x2_vals = _mm256_load_pd(&pa.X2[i]);
        __m256d y2_vals = _mm256_load_pd(&pa.Y2[i]);

        __m256d temp_x = _mm256_sub_pd(x1_vals, x2_vals);
        __m256d temp_y = _mm256_sub_pd(y1_vals, y2_vals);
        __m256d temp_xx = _mm256_mul_pd(temp_x, temp_x);
        __m256d temp_yy = _mm256_mul_pd(temp_y, temp_y);
        __m256d temp_sum = _mm256_add_pd(temp_xx, temp_yy);
        __m256d temp_dist = _mm256_sqrt_pd(temp_sum);

        _mm256_store_pd(&pa.Dist2[i], temp_dist);
    }

    for (; i < num_points; i++)
    {
        double temp1 = pa.X1[i] - pa.X2[i];
        double temp2 = pa.Y1[i] - pa.Y2[i];
        pa.Dist2[i] = sqrt(temp1 * temp1 + temp2 * temp2);
    }

    return true;
}

void CompareDistancesF64_Iavx(PointArrays& pa, double cmp_val)
{
    size_t i = 0;
    size_t num_points = pa.NumPoints;
    const size_t num_simd_elements = 4;
    const double minus2 = -2.0;

    __m256d cmp_vals = _mm256_broadcast_sd(&cmp_val);
    __m256d packed_minus2 = _mm256_broadcast_sd(&minus2);
```

```
    for (; num_points - i >= num_simd_elements; i += num_simd_elements)
    {
        __m256d dist2_vals = _mm256_load_pd(&pa.Dist2[i]);

        // Elements in cmp_mask contain 0xFFFFFFFFFFFFFFFF or 0x0000000000000000
        __m256d cmp_mask = _mm256_cmp_pd(dist2_vals, cmp_vals, _CMP_GE_OQ);

        // Elements in temp1 contain -2.0 or 0.0
        __m256d temp1 = _mm256_and_pd(cmp_mask, packed_minus2);

        // Elements in temp2 contain -2.0 * dist2_vals or 0.0
        __m256d temp2 = _mm256_mul_pd(temp1, dist2_vals);

        // Elements in temp3 contain 0.0 or dist2_vals
        __m256d temp3 = _mm256_andnot_pd(cmp_mask, dist2_vals);

        // Elements in temp4 contain -2.0 * dist2_vals or dist2_vals
        __m256d temp4 = _mm256_or_pd(temp2, temp3);

        _mm256_store_pd(&pa.DistCmp2[i], temp4);
    }

    for (; i < num_points; i++)
    {
        double temp1 = pa.Dist2[i];
        double temp2 = (temp1 >= cmp_val) ? temp1 * -2.0 : temp1;
        pa.DistCmp2[i] = temp2;
    }
}
```

The double-precision floating-point versions of the calculating functions shown in Listing 3-7 are straightforward ports of the single-precision versions shown in Listing 3-6. The double-precision functions use the C++ SIMD data type __m256d instead of __m256. They also employ the _pd versions of the C++ SIMD intrinsic functions. Also note that in both CalcDistancesF64_Iavx() and CompareDistancesF64_Iavx(), num_simd_elements is initialized to four instead of eight. The results for source code example Ch03_07 are the same as Ch03_06.

# Floating-Point Matrices

C++ also uses a contiguous block of memory to store the elements of a two-dimensional array or matrix. The elements of a C++ matrix in memory are organized using row-major ordering. Row-major ordering arranges the elements of a matrix first by row and then by column. For example, the elements of matrix int x[3][2] are stored in memory as follows: x[0][0], x[0][1], x[1][0], x[1][1], x[2][0], and x[2][1]. In order to access matrix element x[i][j], a function (or a compiler) must know the starting address of the matrix (i.e., the address of element x[0][0]), the row and column indices, the number of matrix columns, and the size in bytes of each element. Using this information, a function can use simple multiplication and addition to access a specific matrix element.

# Column Means

Listing 3-8 shows the source code for example Ch03_08. This example illustrates how to calculate the arithmetic mean of each column in a matrix of single-precision floating-point elements using C++ SIMD intrinsic functions.

*Listing 3-8.* Example Ch03_08

```
//-------------------------------------------------
//                 Ch03_08.h
//-------------------------------------------------

#pragma once
#include <vector>
#include "MatrixF32.h"

// Ch03_08_fcpp.cpp
extern std::vector<float> CalcColumnMeansF32_Cpp(const MatrixF32& x);
extern std::vector<float> CalcColumnMeansF32_Iavx(const MatrixF32& x);

// Miscellaneous constants
const unsigned int c_RngSeed = 41;
const float c_MatrixFillMin = 1.0f;
const float c_MatrixFillMax = 80.0f;


//-------------------------------------------------
//                 Ch03_08.cpp
//-------------------------------------------------

#include <iostream>
#include <iomanip>
#include "Ch03_08.h"
#include "MT.h"

static void CalcColumnMeansF32(void);

int main()
{
    CalcColumnMeansF32();
    return 0;
}

static void CalcColumnMeansF32(void)
{
    const char nl = '\n';
    const size_t nrows = 21;
    const size_t ncols = 15;
    MatrixF32 x(nrows, ncols);
    float* x_data = x.Data();
```

89

```cpp
    MT::FillMatrixFP(x_data, nrows, ncols, c_MatrixFillMin, c_MatrixFillMax, c_RngSeed);

    std::vector<float> col_means1 = CalcColumnMeansF32_Cpp(x);
    std::vector<float> col_means2 = CalcColumnMeansF32_Iavx(x);

    size_t w = 5;
    std::cout << std::fixed << std::setprecision(1);
    std::cout << "----- Test Matrix -----\n";

    for (size_t i = 0; i < nrows; i++)
    {
        for (size_t j = 0; j < ncols; j++)
            std::cout << std::setw(w) << x_data[i * ncols + j] << " ";
        std::cout << nl;
    }

    std::cout << "\n----- Column Means -----\n";

    for (size_t j = 0; j < ncols; j++)
        std::cout << std::setw(w) << col_means1[j] << " ";
    std::cout << nl;
    for (size_t j = 0; j < ncols; j++)
        std::cout << std::setw(w) << col_means2[j] << " ";
    std::cout << nl;

    if (!MT::CompareVectorsFP(col_means1, col_means2, 1.0e-6f))
        std::cout << "MT::CompareVectorsFP() failed\n";
}

//--------------------------------------------------
//                  Ch03_08_fcpp.cpp
//--------------------------------------------------

#include <immintrin.h>
#include "Ch03_08.h"

std::vector<float> CalcColumnMeansF32_Cpp(const MatrixF32& x)
{
    size_t nrows = x.GetNumRows();
    size_t ncols = x.GetNumCols();
    const float* x_data = x.Data();
    std::vector<float> col_means(ncols, 0.0f);

    for (size_t i = 0; i < nrows; i++)
    {
        for (size_t j = 0; j < ncols; j++)
            col_means[j] += x_data[i * ncols + j];
    }
```

```
    for (size_t j = 0; j < ncols; j++)
        col_means[j] /= (float)nrows;
    return col_means;
}


std::vector<float> CalcColumnMeansF32_Iavx(const MatrixF32& x)
{
    size_t nrows = x.GetNumRows();
    size_t ncols = x.GetNumCols();
    const float* x_data = x.Data();
    std::vector<float> col_means(ncols, 0.0f);
    float* cm = col_means.data();

    const size_t num_simd_elements = 8;
    const size_t num_simd_elements2 = 4;

    for (size_t i = 0; i < nrows; i++)
    {
        size_t j = 0;

        while (j < ncols)
        {
            if (j + num_simd_elements <= ncols)
            {
                __m256 x_vals = _mm256_loadu_ps(&x_data[i * ncols + j]);
                __m256 cm_vals = _mm256_loadu_ps(&cm[j]);

                cm_vals = _mm256_add_ps(cm_vals, x_vals);
                _mm256_storeu_ps(&cm[j], cm_vals);

                j += num_simd_elements;
            }
            else if (j + num_simd_elements2 <= ncols)
            {
                __m128 x_vals = _mm_loadu_ps(&x_data[i * ncols + j]);
                __m128 cm_vals = _mm_loadu_ps(&cm[j]);

                cm_vals = _mm_add_ps(cm_vals, x_vals);
                _mm_storeu_ps(&cm[j], cm_vals);

                j += num_simd_elements2;
            }
            else
            {
                for (; j < ncols; j++)
                    cm[j] += x_data[i * ncols + j];
            }
        }
    }
```

```
    for (size_t j = 0; j < ncols; j++)
        col_means[j] /= (float)nrows;
    return col_means;
}
```

Listing 3-8 begins with the header file Ch03_08.h. Note that the declaration statements for the calculating functions CalcColumnMeansF32_Cpp() and CalcColumnMeansF32_Iavx() require an argument of type MatrixF32. Class MatrixF32 is a simple wrapper class for a matrix of single-precision floating-point values. The internal buffer allocated by MatrixF32 is aligned on a 64-byte boundary, which means that it is properly aligned for use with AVX, AVX2, and AVX-512 C++ SIMD intrinsic functions. Class MatrixF32 is used in this example and several other source code examples in later chapters for matrix buffer management and benchmarking purposes. The source code for MatrixF32 is not shown in Listing 3-8 but included in the source code download package.

The function CalcColumnMeansF32() in Ch03_08.cpp begins its execution with the initialization of matrix x using random values. It then calls CalcColumnMeansF32_Cpp() and CalcColumnMeansF32_Iavx() to calculate the column means. Note that both of these functions return a std::vector<float> object that contains the calculated column means. The remaining code in CalcColumnMeansF32() streams results to std::cout and confirms that no value discrepancies exist between the two calculated column mean vectors.

The function CalcColumnMeansF32_Cpp() employs straightforward C++ code to calculate the column means of matrix x. Note that in the variable initialization code block, CalcColumnMeansF32_Cpp() uses several member functions of class MatrixF32 to obtain the number of rows and number of columns. It also acquires a pointer named x_data, which points to the first element (i.e., x[0][0]) in matrix x. Following variable initialization, a pair of nested for-loops sums the elements in each matrix column. The arithmetic that is used to calculate the offset of matrix element x[i][j] is humdrum C++ code; however, it is important to fully understand it since this type of calculation is used extensively in later chapters. The second for-loop in CalcColumnMeansF32_Cpp() calculates the final means.

The function CalcColumnMeansF32_Iavx() uses C++ SIMD intrinsic functions to calculate the column means. This function also uses a pair of nested for-loops to calculate the column sums but in a manner that is somewhat different than CalcColumnMeansF32_Cpp(). When traversing the elements of a matrix row, CalcColumnMeansF32_Iavx() must determine how many columns are available before the end of the row. If eight or more columns are available, the inner for-loop can use __m256 operands and intrinsic functions to add matrix elements x[i][j:j+7] to the eight intermediate sum values in cm. If four or more columns remain, the intermediate sums in cm are updated using __m128 operands and intrinsic functions using matrix elements x[i][j:j+3]. If fewer than four columns remain, ordinary scalar arithmetic is used. Processing matrices (or arrays) using groups of __m256 elements first followed by an __m128 group and then scalar elements maximizes the number of operations that are performed using SIMD arithmetic, which usually results in faster performance.

All of the source code examples prior to this one have used the C++ SIMD intrinsic functions _mm256_load_ps(), _mm256_store_ps(), _mm_load_ps(), and _mm_store_ps() to perform SIMD data load and store operations. These functions require the specified memory operand to be properly aligned. When accessing elements in a standard C++ matrix (or array), it is impossible to guarantee that any group of consecutive elements in memory will be aligned on a particular boundary. This is why the inner for-loop in CalcColumnMeansF32_Iavx() uses the C++ SIMD intrinsic functions _mm256_loadu_ps(), _mm256_storeu_ps(), _mm_loadu_ps(), and _mm_storeu_ps() for data load and store operations. These functions do not require their operand to be properly aligned in memory. The drawback of using these unaligned load and store functions is potentially slower performance since the processor may need to carry out more than one memory read or write operation.

Following completion of the summing operation, CalcColumnMeansF32_Iavx() employs a simple for-loop to calculate the final column means using scalar arithmetic. C++ SIMD intrinsic functions could also be used to calculate the column means, but straightforward scalar arithmetic is employed since this is a one-time operation. Here are the results for source code example Ch03_08:

```
----- Test Matrix -----
54.8  26.4 13.3  48.4   74.0  63.2  61.3  56.5 66.9  64.4  15.1  37.4  56.1 70.0  41.5
19.9   3.9 11.5  32.3   58.2  41.0  55.0  45.9 34.4  20.4  56.1   9.7  56.3 75.9  50.2
26.7   7.1 44.2  37.9   61.3  16.3  38.2  62.0 47.7  61.7  72.9  70.0   8.9 55.7  44.4
30.3   5.3 64.4   7.8   33.8  51.6  20.4  30.3 61.3  14.1  50.0  37.8  14.4 43.0  63.0
20.8  51.8  7.2  12.1   38.8  38.4  27.7  46.5 66.0  61.9  11.2  11.4  41.1 59.7  77.5
54.6  62.5 59.7  61.8   18.3  34.0  60.6  68.8 78.4  33.1  74.9  50.0   7.8 29.4  35.2
11.9  41.3  7.7  19.9   31.5  37.8  35.8  19.4 32.6  56.4  27.3   5.3  27.5 10.5  53.1
32.5  23.3 14.7  19.1   69.2   8.2  65.0  42.6 27.8  30.8  36.1  29.9  37.5 78.0  10.8
75.7  43.1 16.5  77.1   17.6  72.3  35.1  17.6 27.9  46.7  72.3  68.0  72.3 44.4  38.3
68.8  46.8 32.0  36.8   43.7  66.8  45.7  77.1 15.9  33.5  59.2  76.0  15.4 32.4  56.1
64.0  56.1 39.8  74.0   31.6  43.6   4.1  29.1 42.8  27.7  41.7   6.2  43.5 29.0  61.5
31.0  33.6 62.9  58.9   30.4  66.2  63.6  27.1 64.7  11.6   3.5  77.1  75.3 25.5  53.2
22.9  48.4 35.7   6.8    7.3  33.5  40.8  20.5 61.5   3.4  76.4   9.3  69.9 62.4  78.8
71.5  13.6 55.1  15.7   79.7  63.9  40.0  66.5 39.0  75.3  63.1  51.8  10.1 25.5   4.1
68.3  34.4 44.7  69.5   39.4  13.9   6.0  78.6 52.4  20.3  62.1  22.4  44.9 48.1  14.2
75.6  77.4 24.9  16.7   12.5  61.4  59.2  65.7 34.4  21.9  77.8  45.6  13.3 57.7  56.8
66.1  48.6 57.7  77.4   11.9  53.2  50.6  24.4 58.1  58.9  29.7  19.1  57.0  9.5  42.4
61.7  68.2 21.5  52.3   43.1  25.3  37.3  77.9 67.1  11.6  30.9  21.8  74.5 34.9  76.0
55.0  42.5  8.8   3.6   72.3  48.6  26.8  62.8 24.7  42.6  22.9  19.7   7.0 45.5  11.6
23.1  37.2 21.6  77.1   16.4  59.3  60.4  46.7 43.5  61.2  10.6  68.9  23.7 41.6  24.2
22.3  20.9 36.8  17.4   30.8  24.8   4.3  21.2 55.6  20.2  40.1  51.5  78.4 13.1  26.0

----- Column Means -----
45.6  37.7 32.4  39.2   39.1  44.0  39.9  47.0 47.8  37.0  44.5  37.6 39.8  42.5  43.8
45.6  37.7 32.4  39.2   39.1  44.0  39.9  47.0 47.8  37.0  44.5  37.6 39.8  42.5  43.8
```

Listing 3-9 shows the calculating functions for source code example Ch03_09. These functions calculate column means for a matrix that contains double-precision floating-point values.

*Listing 3-9.* Example Ch03_09

```cpp
//-------------------------------------------------
//                  Ch03_09_fcpp.cpp
//-------------------------------------------------

#include <immintrin.h>
#include "Ch03_09.h"

std::vector<double> CalcColumnMeansF64_Cpp(const MatrixF64& x)
{
    size_t nrows = x.GetNumRows();
    size_t ncols = x.GetNumCols();
    const double* x_data = x.Data();
    std::vector<double> col_means(ncols, 0.0);
```

```
    for (size_t i = 0; i < nrows; i++)
    {
        for (size_t j = 0; j < ncols; j++)
            col_means[j] += x_data[i * ncols + j];
    }

    for (size_t j = 0; j < ncols; j++)
        col_means[j] /= (double)nrows;
    return col_means;
}

std::vector<double> CalcColumnMeansF64_Iavx(const MatrixF64& x)
{
    size_t nrows = x.GetNumRows();
    size_t ncols = x.GetNumCols();
    const double* x_data = x.Data();
    std::vector<double> col_means(ncols, 0.0);
    double* cm = col_means.data();

    const size_t num_simd_elements = 4;
    const size_t num_simd_elements2 = 2;

    for (size_t i = 0; i < nrows; i++)
    {
        size_t j = 0;

        while (j < ncols)
        {
            if (j + num_simd_elements <= ncols)
            {
                __m256d x_vals = _mm256_loadu_pd(&x_data[i * ncols + j]);
                __m256d cm_vals = _mm256_loadu_pd(&cm[j]);

                cm_vals = _mm256_add_pd(cm_vals, x_vals);
                _mm256_storeu_pd(&cm[j], cm_vals);

                j += num_simd_elements;
            }
            else if (j + num_simd_elements2 <= ncols)
            {
                __m128d x_vals = _mm_loadu_pd(&x_data[i * ncols + j]);
                __m128d cm_vals = _mm_loadu_pd(&cm[j]);

                cm_vals = _mm_add_pd(cm_vals, x_vals);
                _mm_storeu_pd(&cm[j], cm_vals);

                j += num_simd_elements2;
            }
```

```
        else
        {
            cm[j] += x_data[i * ncols + j];
            j += 1;
        }
    }
}

for (size_t j = 0; j < ncols; j++)
    col_means[j] /= (float)nrows;
return col_means;
}
```

Like the previous two double-precision examples, only a few minor changes are required to transform the single-precision code of example Ch03_08 into the double-precision code that is used in this example. One of the changes is that source code example Ch03_09 employs the C++ class MatrixF64, which is the double-precision counterpart of class MatrixF32. The other noteworthy change is that the number row elements processed during each iteration of the inner loop in function CalcColumnMeansF64_Iavx() is cut in half. The results for source code example Ch03_09 are the same as Ch03_08.

# Summary

Table 3-1 summarizes the C++ SIMD intrinsic functions introduced in this chapter along with other commonly used type variants. Before proceeding to the next chapter, you should understand the SIMD arithmetic calculation or data manipulation operation that is performed by each function shown in Table 3-1.

***Table 3-1.*** *C++ SIMD Intrinsic Function Summary for Chapter 3*

| C++ SIMD Function Names | Description |
| --- | --- |
| _mm256_add_pd, _ps | Packed floating-point addition |
| _mm256_and_pd, _ps | Packed floating-point bitwise logical AND |
| _mm256_andnot_pd, _ps | Packed floating-point bitwise logical AND NOT |
| _mm256_broadcast_sd, _ss | Broadcast floating-point constant to all elements |
| _mm256_cmp_pd, _ps | Packed floating-point compare |
| _mm256_div_pd, _ps | Packed floating-point division |
| _mm256_extractf128_pd, _ps | 128-bit packed floating-point extract |
| _mm256_load_pd, _ps | Packed floating-point load (aligned) |
| _mm256_loadu_pd, _ps | Packed floating-point load (unaligned) |
| _mm256_max_pd, _ps | Packed floating-point maximum |
| _mm256_min_pd, _ps | Packed floating-point minimum |
| _mm256_mul_pd, _ps | Packed floating-point multiplication |

(*continued*)

***Table 3-1.*** (*continued*)

| C++ SIMD Function Names | Description |
|---|---|
| _mm256_or_pd, _ps | Packed floating-point bitwise logical OR |
| _mm256_setzero_pd, _ps | Set 256-bit wide SIMD operand to all zeros |
| _mm256_sqrt_pd, _ps | Packed floating-point square root |
| _mm256_store_pd, _ps | Packed floating-point store (aligned) |
| _mm256_storeu_pd, _ps | Packed floating-point store (unaligned) |
| _mm256_sub_pd, _ps | Packed floating-point subtraction |
| _mm_add_pd, _ps | Packed floating-point addition |
| _mm_cvtepi32_pd, _ps | Packed 32-bit integer to floating-point conversion |
| _mm_cvtpd_epi32 | Packed floating-point to integer conversion |
| _mm_cvtpd_ps | Packed double-precision to single-precision conversion |
| _mm_cvtps_epi32 | Packed single-precision floating-point to 32-bit integer |
| _mm_cvtps_pd | Packed single-precision to double-precision conversion |
| _mm_div_pd, _ps | Packed floating-point division |
| _mm_hadd_pd, _ps | Packed floating-point horizontal addition |
| _mm_hsub_pd, _ps | Packed floating-point horizontal subtraction |
| _mm_load_pd, _ps | Packed floating-point load (aligned) |
| _mm_loadu_pd, _ps | Packed floating-point load (unaligned) |
| _mm_mul_pd, _ps | Packed floating-point multiplication |
| _mm_sqrt_pd, _ps | Packed floating-point square root |
| _mm_store_pd, _ps | Packed floating-point store (aligned) |
| _mm_store_sd, _ss | Scalar floating-point store |
| _mm_storeu_pd, _ps | Packed floating-point store (unaligned) |
| _mm_sub_pd, _ps | Packed floating-point subtraction |

# CHAPTER 4

■ ■ ■

# AVX2 C++ Programming: Part 1

In Chapter 2, you learned how to use AVX C++ SIMD intrinsic functions to perform packed integer arithmetic and other data manipulation operations using 128-bit wide operands. In this chapter, you will learn how to exploit AVX2 to perform similar operations using 256-bit wide packed integer operands. Chapter 4 is partitioned into two sections. The first section highlights SIMD integer arithmetic, unpacking and packing, and size promotions. The second section includes source code examples that illustrate additional image processing techniques including pixel clipping, RGB to grayscale conversions, and thresholding.

The source code examples in this chapter and the next two require a processor and operating system that support AVX2. You can use one of the free utilities listed in Appendix B to ensure that your computer meets this requirement.

## Integer Arithmetic

In this section, you will learn how to carry out fundamental packed integer arithmetic and other data manipulation operations using 256-bit wide SIMD operands. The first source code example expounds packed integer addition and subtraction. This is followed by a source code example that illustrates integer unpacking and packing. The final source example explains packed integer size promotions.

### Addition and Subtraction

Listing 4-1 shows the source code for example Ch04_01. This example demonstrates packed integer addition and subtraction using 256-bit wide SIMD operands.

*Listing 4-1.* Example Ch04_01

```
//------------------------------------------------
//              Ch04_01.h
//------------------------------------------------

#pragma once
#include "YmmVal.h"

// Ch04_01_fcpp.cpp
extern void MathI16_Iavx2(YmmVal c[6], const YmmVal* a, const YmmVal* b);
extern void MathI32_Iavx2(YmmVal c[6], const YmmVal* a, const YmmVal* b);
```

© Daniel Kusswurm 2022
D. Kusswurm, *Modern Parallel Programming with C++ and Assembly Language*,
https://doi.org/10.1007/978-1-4842-7918-2_4

```cpp
//-------------------------------------------------
//                   Ch04_01.cpp
//-------------------------------------------------

#include <iostream>
#include <string>
#include "Ch04_01.h"

static void MathI16(void);
static void MathI32(void);
static const std::string c_ Line(75, '-');

int main()
{
    MathI16();
    MathI32();
    return 0;
}

static void MathI16(void)
{
    YmmVal a, b, c[6];
    const size_t w = 8;
    const char nl = '\n', sp = ' ';

    a.m_I16[0] = 10;        b.m_I16[0] = 1000;
    a.m_I16[1] = 20;        b.m_I16[1] = 2000;
    a.m_I16[2] = 3000;      b.m_I16[2] = 30;
    a.m_I16[3] = 4000;      b.m_I16[3] = 40;

    a.m_I16[4] = 30000;     b.m_I16[4] = 3000;      // add overflow
    a.m_I16[5] = 6000;      b.m_I16[5] = 32000;     // add overflow
    a.m_I16[6] = 2000;      b.m_I16[6] = -31000;    // sub overflow
    a.m_I16[7] = 4000;      b.m_I16[7] = -30000;    // sub overflow

    a.m_I16[8] = 4000;      b.m_I16[8] = -2500;
    a.m_I16[9] = 3600;      b.m_I16[9] = -1200;
    a.m_I16[10] = 6000;     b.m_I16[10] = 9000;
    a.m_I16[11] = -20000;   b.m_I16[11] = -20000;

    a.m_I16[12] = -25000;   b.m_I16[12] = -27000;   // add overflow
    a.m_I16[13] = 8000;     b.m_I16[13] = 28700;    // add overflow
    a.m_I16[14] = 3;        b.m_I16[14] = -32766;   // sub overflow
    a.m_I16[15] = -15000;   b.m_I16[15] = 24000;    // sub overflow

    MathI16_Iavx2(c, &a, &b);

    std::cout <<"\nResults for MathI16_Iavx2\n\n";
    std::cout << " i        a        b        add       adds";
    std::cout << "        sub       subs       min       max\n";
    std::cout << c_Line << nl;
```

```cpp
    for (size_t i = 0; i < 16; i++)
    {
        std::cout << std::setw(2)  << i << sp;
        std::cout << std::setw(w) << a.m_I16[i] << sp;
        std::cout << std::setw(w) << b.m_I16[i] << sp;
        std::cout << std::setw(w) << c[0].m_I16[i] << sp;
        std::cout << std::setw(w) << c[1].m_I16[i] << sp;
        std::cout << std::setw(w) << c[2].m_I16[i] << sp;
        std::cout << std::setw(w) << c[3].m_I16[i] << sp;
        std::cout << std::setw(w) << c[4].m_I16[i] << sp;
        std::cout << std::setw(w) << c[5].m_I16[i] << nl;
    }
}

static void MathI32(void)
{
    YmmVal a, b, c[6];
    const size_t w = 8;
    const char nl = '\n', sp = ' ';

    a.m_I32[0] = 64;        b.m_I32[0] = 4;
    a.m_I32[1] = 1024;      b.m_I32[1] = 5;
    a.m_I32[2] = -2048;     b.m_I32[2] = 2;
    a.m_I32[3] = 8192;      b.m_I32[3] = 5;
    a.m_I32[4] = -256;      b.m_I32[4] = 8;
    a.m_I32[5] = 12288;     b.m_I32[5] = 7;
    a.m_I32[6] = 16;        b.m_I32[6] = 3;
    a.m_I32[7] = -512;      b.m_I32[7] = 6;

    MathI32_Iavx2(c, &a, &b);

    std::cout << "\nResults for MathI32_Iavx2\n\n";
    std::cout << " i          a         b         add       sub";
    std::cout << "      mull      sll       sra       abs\n";
    std::cout << c_Line << nl;

    for (size_t i = 0; i < 8; i++)
    {
        std::cout << std::setw(2) << i << sp;
        std::cout << std::setw(w) << a.m_I32[i] << sp;
        std::cout << std::setw(w) << b.m_I32[i] << sp;
        std::cout << std::setw(w) << c[0].m_I32[i] << sp;
        std::cout << std::setw(w) << c[1].m_I32[i] << sp;
        std::cout << std::setw(w) << c[2].m_I32[i] << sp;
        std::cout << std::setw(w) << c[3].m_I32[i] << sp;
        std::cout << std::setw(w) << c[4].m_I32[i] << sp;
        std::cout << std::setw(w) << c[5].m_I32[i] << nl;
    }
}
```

```cpp
//-------------------------------------------------
//                  Ch04_01_fcpp.cpp
//-------------------------------------------------

#include <immintrin.h>
#include "Ch04_01.h"

void MathI16_Iavx2(YmmVal c[6], const YmmVal* a, const YmmVal* b)
{
    __m256i a_vals = _mm256_load_si256((__m256i*)a);
    __m256i b_vals = _mm256_load_si256((__m256i*)b);

    __m256i c_vals0 = _mm256_add_epi16(a_vals, b_vals);
    __m256i c_vals1 = _mm256_adds_epi16(a_vals, b_vals);
    __m256i c_vals2 = _mm256_sub_epi16(a_vals, b_vals);
    __m256i c_vals3 = _mm256_subs_epi16(a_vals, b_vals);
    __m256i c_vals4 = _mm256_min_epi16(a_vals, b_vals);
    __m256i c_vals5 = _mm256_max_epi16(a_vals, b_vals);

    _mm256_store_si256((__m256i*)&c[0], c_vals0);
    _mm256_store_si256((__m256i*)&c[1], c_vals1);
    _mm256_store_si256((__m256i*)&c[2], c_vals2);
    _mm256_store_si256((__m256i*)&c[3], c_vals3);
    _mm256_store_si256((__m256i*)&c[4], c_vals4);
    _mm256_store_si256((__m256i*)&c[5], c_vals5);
}

void MathI32_Iavx2(YmmVal c[6], const YmmVal* a, const YmmVal* b)
{
    __m256i a_vals = _mm256_load_si256((__m256i*)a);
    __m256i b_vals = _mm256_load_si256((__m256i*)b);

    __m256i c_vals0 = _mm256_add_epi32(a_vals, b_vals);
    __m256i c_vals1 = _mm256_sub_epi32(a_vals, b_vals);
    __m256i c_vals2 = _mm256_mullo_epi32(a_vals, b_vals);
    __m256i c_vals3 = _mm256_sllv_epi32(a_vals, b_vals);
    __m256i c_vals4 = _mm256_srav_epi32(a_vals, b_vals);
    __m256i c_vals5 = _mm256_abs_epi32(a_vals);

    _mm256_store_si256((__m256i*)&c[0], c_vals0);
    _mm256_store_si256((__m256i*)&c[1], c_vals1);
    _mm256_store_si256((__m256i*)&c[2], c_vals2);
    _mm256_store_si256((__m256i*)&c[3], c_vals3);
    _mm256_store_si256((__m256i*)&c[4], c_vals4);
    _mm256_store_si256((__m256i*)&c[5], c_vals5);
}
```

Listing 4-1 begins with the C++ header file `Ch04_01.h`. This file includes the requisite function declarations for this example. Note that the functions declared in `Ch04_01.h` make use of the `YmmVal` structure. As explained in Chapter 3, the `YmmVal` structure contains a simple C++ union whose members correspond to the packed data types of a 256-bit wide x86-AVX operand. The next file in Listing 4-1 is `Ch04_01.cpp`. This file contains two functions named `MathI16()` and `MathI32()`. These functions initialize test cases for the SIMD calculating functions `MathI16_Iavx2()` and `Math32_Iavx2()`. They also format and stream the results to `std::cout`.

The final file in Listing 4-1, `Ch04_02_fcpp.cpp`, starts with the definition of function `MathI16_Iavx2()`. This function begins its execution with an `_mm256_load_si256()` call that initializes a_vals. Note that a_vals is declared as an `__m256i`, which is a 256-bit wide C++ SIMD intrinsic data type of packed integers. Function `MathI16_Iavx2()` then uses another `_mm256_load_si256()` call to initialize b_vals. Note that function `_mm256_load_si256()` requires its source operand to be properly aligned on a 32-byte boundary.

The next code block in `MathI16_Iavx2()` contains C++ SIMD intrinsic function calls that carry out packed arithmetic calculations using 16-bit signed integer elements. The functions `_mm256_add_epi16()` and `_mm256_adds_epi16()` perform packed integer addition using wraparound and saturated arithmetic, respectively. The next two function calls, `_mm256_sub_epi16()` and `_mm256_subs_epi16()`, execute packed integer subtraction. The final two function calls, `_mm256_min_epi16()` and `_mm256_max_epi16()`, perform packed minimum and maximum compares. Following the arithmetic calculations, `MathI16_Iavx2()` employs a series of `_mm256_store_si256()` calls to save the results. Like the function `_mm256_load_si256()`, the function `_mm256_store_si256()` requires the specified destination operand to be aligned on 32-byte boundary.

Function `MathI32_Iavx2()` illustrates the use of C++ SIMD intrinsic functions that perform arithmetic operations using packed 32-bit signed integers. The C++ SIMD intrinsic functions `_mm256_add_epi32()`, `_mm256_sub_epi32()`, and `_mm_mullo_epi32()` are the 256-bit counterparts of the intrinsic functions that you saw in source code examples Ch02_01, Ch02_02, and Ch02_03. The C++ SIMD intrinsic function `_mm256_sllv_epi32()` left shifts each 32-bit element in a_vals using the bit counts that are specified by the corresponding element position in b_vals as shown in Figure 4-1. Also shown in Figure 4-1 is execution of the ensuing function call `_mm256_srav_epi32()`, which performs arithmetic right shifts of the elements in a_vals using the bit counts that are specified in b_vals. The final arithmetic calculation in `MathI32_Iavx2()` is a packed absolute value that is performed by the C++ SIMD intrinsic function `_mm256_abs_epi32()`.

Initial values

| 64 | 1024 | -2048 | 8192 | -256 | 12288 | 16 | -512 | a_vals |
|---|---|---|---|---|---|---|---|---|

| 4 | 5 | 2 | 5 | 8 | 7 | 3 | 6 | b_vals |
|---|---|---|---|---|---|---|---|---|

`c_vals3 = _mm256_sllv_epi32(a_vals, b_vals);`

| 1024 | 32768 | -8192 | 262144 | -65536 | 1572864 | 128 | -32768 | c_vals3 |
|---|---|---|---|---|---|---|---|---|

`c_vals4 = _mm256_srav_epi32(a_vals, b_vals);`

| 4 | 32 | -512 | 256 | -1 | 96 | 2 | -8 | c_vals4 |
|---|---|---|---|---|---|---|---|---|

***Figure 4-1.** Packed 32-bit integer shifts using `_mm256_sllv_epi32()` and `_mm256_srav_epi32()`*

Following its arithmetic calculations, MathI32_Iavx2() uses a sequence of _mm256_store_si256() calls to save the results. Here are the results for source code example Ch04_01:

Results for MathI16_Iavx2

| i | a | b | add | adds | sub | subs | min | max |
|---|---|---|---|---|---|---|---|---|
| 0 | 10 | 1000 | 1010 | 1010 | -990 | -990 | 10 | 1000 |
| 1 | 20 | 2000 | 2020 | 2020 | -1980 | -1980 | 20 | 2000 |
| 2 | 3000 | 30 | 3030 | 3030 | 2970 | 2970 | 30 | 3000 |
| 3 | 4000 | 40 | 4040 | 4040 | 3960 | 3960 | 40 | 4000 |
| 4 | 30000 | 3000 | -32536 | 32767 | 27000 | 27000 | 3000 | 30000 |
| 5 | 6000 | 32000 | -27536 | 32767 | -26000 | -26000 | 6000 | 32000 |
| 6 | 2000 | -31000 | -29000 | -29000 | -32536 | 32767 | -31000 | 2000 |
| 7 | 4000 | -30000 | -26000 | -26000 | -31536 | 32767 | -30000 | 4000 |
| 8 | 4000 | -2500 | 1500 | 1500 | 6500 | 6500 | -2500 | 4000 |
| 9 | 3600 | -1200 | 2400 | 2400 | 4800 | 4800 | -1200 | 3600 |
| 10 | 6000 | 9000 | 15000 | 15000 | -3000 | -3000 | 6000 | 9000 |
| 11 | -20000 | -20000 | 25536 | -32768 | 0 | 0 | -20000 | -20000 |
| 12 | -25000 | -27000 | 13536 | -32768 | 2000 | 2000 | -27000 | -25000 |
| 13 | 8000 | 28700 | -28836 | 32767 | -20700 | -20700 | 8000 | 28700 |
| 14 | 3 | -32766 | -32763 | -32763 | -32767 | 32767 | -32766 | 3 |
| 15 | -15000 | 24000 | 9000 | 9000 | 26536 | -32768 | -15000 | 24000 |

Results for MathI32_Iavx2

| i | a | b | add | sub | mull | sll | sra | abs |
|---|---|---|---|---|---|---|---|---|
| 0 | 64 | 4 | 68 | 60 | 256 | 1024 | 4 | 64 |
| 1 | 1024 | 5 | 1029 | 1019 | 5120 | 32768 | 32 | 1024 |
| 2 | -2048 | 2 | -2046 | -2050 | -4096 | -8192 | -512 | 2048 |
| 3 | 8192 | 5 | 8197 | 8187 | 40960 | 262144 | 256 | 8192 |
| 4 | -256 | 8 | -248 | -264 | -2048 | -65536 | -1 | 256 |
| 5 | 12288 | 7 | 12295 | 12281 | 86016 | 1572864 | 96 | 12288 |
| 6 | 16 | 3 | 19 | 13 | 48 | 128 | 2 | 16 |
| 7 | -512 | 6 | -506 | -518 | -3072 | -32768 | -8 | 512 |

Most of the C++ SIMD intrinsic functions demonstrated in example Ch04_01 have variant forms that can be used with different integer element sizes. These functions are listed in the summary section at the end of this chapter.

# Unpacking and Packing

The next source code example is named Ch04_02. This example illustrates unpacking and packing operations using 256-bit wide SIMD integer operands. Unpacking and packing operations are often employed to size-promote or size-reduce the elements of a SIMD integer operand.

*Listing 4-2.* Example Ch04_02

```
//--------------------------------------------------
//                 Ch04_02.h
//--------------------------------------------------

#pragma once
#include "YmmVal.h"

// Ch04_02_fcpp.cpp
extern void UnpackU32_U64_Iavx2(YmmVal c[2], const YmmVal* a, const YmmVal* b);
extern void PackI32_I16_Iavx2(YmmVal* c, const YmmVal* a, const YmmVal* b);

//--------------------------------------------------
//                 Ch04_02.cpp
//--------------------------------------------------

#include <iostream>
#include <string>
#include "Ch04_02.h"

static void UnpackU32_U64(void);
static void PackI32_I16(void);

static const std::string c_Line(82, '-');

int main()
{
    UnpackU32_U64();
    PackI32_I16();
    return 0;
}

static void UnpackU32_U64(void)
{
    YmmVal a, b, c[2];
    const char nl = '\n';

    a.m_U32[0] = 0x00000000;  b.m_U32[0] = 0x88888888;
    a.m_U32[1] = 0x11111111;  b.m_U32[1] = 0x99999999;
    a.m_U32[2] = 0x22222222;  b.m_U32[2] = 0xaaaaaaaa;
    a.m_U32[3] = 0x33333333;  b.m_U32[3] = 0xbbbbbbbb;

    a.m_U32[4] = 0x44444444;  b.m_U32[4] = 0xcccccccc;
    a.m_U32[5] = 0x55555555;  b.m_U32[5] = 0xdddddddd;
    a.m_U32[6] = 0x66666666;  b.m_U32[6] = 0xeeeeeeee;
    a.m_U32[7] = 0x77777777;  b.m_U32[7] = 0xffffffff;

    UnpackU32_U64_Iavx2(c, &a, &b);
```

```cpp
    std::cout << "\nResults for UnpackU32_U64_Iavx2\n" << c_Line << nl;

    std::cout << "a lo          " << a.ToStringX32(0) << nl;
    std::cout << "b lo          " << b.ToStringX32(0) << nl << nl;
    std::cout << "a hi          " << a.ToStringX32(1) << nl;
    std::cout << "b hi          " << b.ToStringX32(1) << nl << nl;

    std::cout << "c[0] lo qword" << c[0].ToStringX64(0) << nl;
    std::cout << "c[0] hi qword" << c[0].ToStringX64(1) << nl << nl;
    std::cout << "c[1] lo qword" << c[1].ToStringX64(0) << nl;
    std::cout << "c[1] hi qword" << c[1].ToStringX64(1) << nl << nl;
}

static void PackI32_I16(void)
{
    YmmVal a, b, c;
    const char nl = '\n';

    a.m_I32[0] = 10;          b.m_I32[0] = 32768;
    a.m_I32[1] = -200000;     b.m_I32[1] = 6500;
    a.m_I32[2] = 300000;      b.m_I32[2] = 42000;
    a.m_I32[3] = -4000;       b.m_I32[3] = -68000;

    a.m_I32[4] = 9000;        b.m_I32[4] = 25000;
    a.m_I32[5] = 80000;       b.m_I32[5] = 500000;
    a.m_I32[6] = 200;         b.m_I32[6] = -7000;
    a.m_I32[7] = -32769;      b.m_I32[7] = 12500;

    PackI32_I16_Iavx2(&c, &a, &b);

    std::cout << "\nResults for PackI32_I16_Iavx2\n" << c_Line << nl;

    std::cout << "a lo " << a.ToStringI32(0) << nl;
    std::cout << "a hi " << a.ToStringI32(1) << nl << nl;

    std::cout << "b lo " << b.ToStringI32(0) << nl;
    std::cout << "b hi " << b.ToStringI32(1) << nl << nl;
    std::cout << "c lo " << c.ToStringI16(0) << nl;
    std::cout << "c hi " << c.ToStringI16(1) << nl << nl;
}

//-------------------------------------------------
//                Ch04_02_fcpp.cpp
//-------------------------------------------------

#include <immintrin.h>
#include "Ch04_02.h"
```

```
void UnpackU32_U64_Iavx2(YmmVal c[2], const YmmVal* a, const YmmVal* b)
{
    __m256i a_vals = _mm256_load_si256((__m256i*)a);
    __m256i b_vals = _mm256_load_si256((__m256i*)b);

    __m256i c_vals0 = _mm256_unpacklo_epi32(a_vals, b_vals);
    __m256i c_vals1 = _mm256_unpackhi_epi32(a_vals, b_vals);

    _mm256_store_si256((__m256i*)&c[0], c_vals0);
    _mm256_store_si256((__m256i*)&c[1], c_vals1);
}

void PackI32_I16_Iavx2(YmmVal* c, const YmmVal* a, const YmmVal* b)
{
    __m256i a_vals = _mm256_load_si256((__m256i*)a);
    __m256i b_vals = _mm256_load_si256((__m256i*)b);

    __m256i c_vals = _mm256_packs_epi32(a_vals, b_vals);

    _mm256_store_si256((__m256i*)c, c_vals);
}
```

In Listing 4-2, the function UnpackU32_U64() begins its execution by initializing YmmVal variables a and b. It then calls the SIMD calculation function UnpackU32_U64_Iavx2(), which performs a SIMD unpacking operation using the 32-bit integer elements of a and b. The ensuing function PackI32_I16() initializes two YmmVal variables and then calls PackI32_I64_Iavx2() to carry out a 32- to 16-bit integer packing operation.

Also shown in Listing 4-2 is the function UnpackU32_U64_Iavx2(). This function begins its execution with two _mm256_load_si256() calls that initialize __m256i objects a_vals and b_vals. It then uses the C++ SIMD intrinsic functions _mm256_unpacklo_epi32() and _mm256_unpackhi_epi32() to interleave the 32-bit wide elements of a_vals and b_vals as shown in Figure 4-2. Note that in this figure, the C++ SIMD intrinsic functions _mm256_unpacklo_epi32() and _mm256_unpackhi_epi32() carry out independent interleave operations using the lower and upper 128 bits of the specified 256-bit wide operands. The lower or upper 128 bits of a 256-bit wide x86-AVX operand is called a lane.

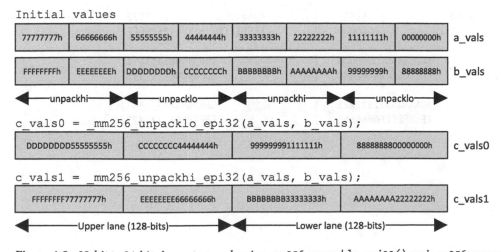

*Figure 4-2.* *32-bit to 64-bit element unpack using _mm256_unpacklo_epi32() and _mm256_unpackhi_epi32()*

105

The final function in Listing 4-2, PackI32_I16_Iavx(), illustrates the use of the C++ intrinsic function _mm256_packs_epi32(). Function _mm256_packs_epi32() packs the 32-bit signed integer elements of its two __m256i source operands into a single __m256i object of 16-bit signed integers using signed saturation. Recall from the discussions in Chapter 1 that saturated arithmetic is often used in image processing algorithms since it eliminates the need to explicitly check each pixel value for an overflow or underflow. Figure 4-3 illustrates this operation in greater detail. Note that _mm256_packs_epi32() also performs independent packing operations using the lower and upper lanes of the two source operands.

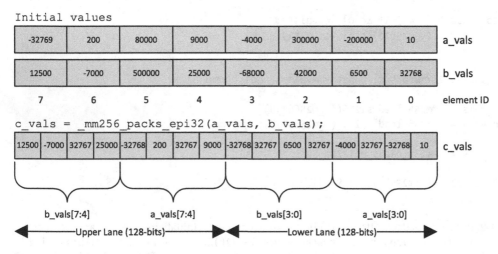

**Figure 4-3.** *32-bit to 16-bit element pack using_mm256_packs_epi32()*

Here are the results for source code example Ch04_02:

```
Results for UnpackU32_U64_Iavx2
-------------------------------------------------------------------------
a lo         00000000      11111111    |    22222222      33333333
b lo         88888888      99999999    |    AAAAAAAA      BBBBBBBB

a hi         44444444      55555555    |    66666666      77777777
b hi         CCCCCCCC      DDDDDDDD    |    EEEEEEEE      FFFFFFFF

c[0] lo qword        8888888800000000    |        9999999911111111
c[0] hi qword        CCCCCCCC44444444    |        DDDDDDDD55555555

c[1] lo qword        AAAAAAAA22222222    |        BBBBBBBB33333333
c[1] hi qword        EEEEEEEE66666666    |        FFFFFFFF77777777
```

```
Results for PackI32_I16_Iavx2
------------------------------------------------------------------------
a lo             10        -200000  |        300000         -4000
a hi           9000         80000   |           200        -32769

b lo          32768          6500   |         42000        -68000
b hi          25000        500000   |         -7000         12500

c lo     10 -32768 32767   -4000    | 32767   6500 32767   -32768
c hi   9000  32767   200  -32768    | 25000  32767 -7000    12500
========================================================================
```

## Size Promotions

In Chapter 2, you learned how to size-promote packed integers using the C++ SIMD intrinsic functions
_mm_unpacklo_epi8() and _mm_unpackhi_epi8() (see example Ch02_07). The source code example of this
section, shown in Listing 4-3, highlights several alternative AVX2 C++ SIMD intrinsic functions that also size-
promote packed integer operands.

*Listing 4-3.* Example Ch04_03

```
//-------------------------------------------------
//              Ch04_03.h
//-------------------------------------------------

#pragma once
#include "YmmVal.h"

// Ch04_03_fcpp.cpp
extern void ZeroExtU8_U16_Iavx2(YmmVal c[2], YmmVal* a);
extern void ZeroExtU8_U32_Iavx2(YmmVal c[4], YmmVal* a);
extern void SignExtI16_I32_Iavx2(YmmVal c[2], YmmVal* a);
extern void SignExtI16_I64_Iavx2(YmmVal c[4], YmmVal* a);

//-------------------------------------------------
//              Ch04_03.cpp
//-------------------------------------------------

#include <iostream>
#include <string>
#include <cstdint>
#include "Ch04_03.h"

static void ZeroExtU8_U16(void);
static void ZeroExtU8_U32(void);
static void SignExtI16_I32(void);
static void SignExtI16_I64(void);
```

```cpp
static const std::string c_Line(80, '-');

int main()
{
    ZeroExtU8_U16();
    ZeroExtU8_U32();
    SignExtI16_I32();
    SignExtI16_I64();
}

static void ZeroExtU8_U16(void)
{
    YmmVal a, c[2];
    const char nl = '\n';

    for (size_t i = 0; i < 32; i++)
        a.m_U8[i] = (uint8_t)(i * 8);

    ZeroExtU8_U16_Iavx2(c, &a);

    std::cout << "\nResults for ZeroExtU8_U16_Iavx2\n" << c_Line << nl;

    std::cout << "a (0:15):   " << a.ToStringU8(0) << nl;
    std::cout << "a (16:31):  " << a.ToStringU8(1) << nl;
    std::cout << nl;
    std::cout << "c (0:7):    " << c[0].ToStringU16(0) << nl;
    std::cout << "c (8:15):   " << c[0].ToStringU16(1) << nl;
    std::cout << "c (16:23):  " << c[1].ToStringU16(0) << nl;
    std::cout << "c (24:31):  " << c[1].ToStringU16(1) << nl;
}

static void ZeroExtU8_U32(void)
{
    YmmVal a, c[4];
    const char nl = '\n';

    for (size_t i = 0; i < 32; i++)
        a.m_U8[i] = (uint8_t)(255 - i * 8);

    ZeroExtU8_U32_Iavx2(c, &a);

    std::cout << "\nResults for ZeroExtU8_U32_Iavx2\n" << c_Line << nl;

    std::cout << "a (0:15):   " << a.ToStringU8(0) << nl;
    std::cout << "a (16:31):  " << a.ToStringU8(1) << nl;
    std::cout << nl;
    std::cout << "c (0:3):    " << c[0].ToStringU32(0) << nl;
    std::cout << "c (4:7):    " << c[0].ToStringU32(1) << nl;
    std::cout << "c (8:11):   " << c[1].ToStringU32(0) << nl;
    std::cout << "c (12:15):  " << c[1].ToStringU32(1) << nl;
    std::cout << "c (16:19):  " << c[2].ToStringU32(0) << nl;
```

```cpp
    std::cout << "c (20:23):   " << c[2].ToStringU32(1) << nl;
    std::cout << "c (24:27):   " << c[3].ToStringU32(0) << nl;
    std::cout << "c (28:31):   " << c[3].ToStringU32(1) << nl;
}

static void SignExtI16_I32(void)
{
    YmmVal a, c[2];
    const char nl = '\n';

    for (size_t i = 0; i < 16; i++)
        a.m_I16[i] = (int16_t)(-32768 + i * 4000);

    SignExtI16_I32_Iavx2(c, &a);

    std::cout << "\nResults for SignExtI16_I32_Iavx2\n" << c_Line << nl;

    std::cout << "a (0:7):     " << a.ToStringI16(0) << nl;
    std::cout << "a (8:15):    " << a.ToStringI16(1) << nl;
    std::cout << nl;
    std::cout << "c (0:3):     " << c[0].ToStringI32(0) << nl;
    std::cout << "c (4:7):     " << c[0].ToStringI32(1) << nl;
    std::cout << "c (8:11):    " << c[1].ToStringI32(0) << nl;
    std::cout << "c (12:15):   " << c[1].ToStringI32(1) << nl;
}

static void SignExtI16_I64(void)
{
    YmmVal a, c[4];
    const char nl = '\n';

    for (size_t i = 0; i < 16; i++)
        a.m_I16[i] = (int16_t)(32767 - i * 4000);

    SignExtI16_I64_Iavx2(c, &a);

    std::cout << "\nResults for SignExtI16_I64_Iavx2\n" << c_Line << nl;

    std::cout << "a (0:7):     " << a.ToStringI16(0) << nl;
    std::cout << "a (8:15):    " << a.ToStringI16(1) << nl;
    std::cout << nl;
    std::cout << "c (0:1):     " << c[0].ToStringI64(0) << nl;
    std::cout << "c (2:3):     " << c[0].ToStringI64(1) << nl;
    std::cout << "c (4:5):     " << c[1].ToStringI64(0) << nl;
    std::cout << "c (6:7):     " << c[1].ToStringI64(1) << nl;
    std::cout << "c (8:9):     " << c[2].ToStringI64(0) << nl;
    std::cout << "c (10:11):   " << c[2].ToStringI64(1) << nl;
    std::cout << "c (12:13):   " << c[3].ToStringI64(0) << nl;
    std::cout << "c (14:15):   " << c[3].ToStringI64(1) << nl;
}
```

```cpp
//----------------------------------------------------
//                  Ch04_03_fcpp.cpp
//----------------------------------------------------

#include <immintrin.h>
#include "Ch04_03.h"

void ZeroExtU8_U16_Iavx2(YmmVal c[2], YmmVal* a)
{
    __m128i a_vals_u8_lo = _mm_load_si128((__m128i*)&a->m_U8[0]);
    __m128i a_vals_u8_hi = _mm_load_si128((__m128i*)&a->m_U8[16]);

    __m256i c_vals_u16_lo = _mm256_cvtepu8_epi16(a_vals_u8_lo);
    __m256i c_vals_u16_hi = _mm256_cvtepu8_epi16(a_vals_u8_hi);

    _mm256_store_si256((__m256i*)&c[0], c_vals_u16_lo);
    _mm256_store_si256((__m256i*)&c[1], c_vals_u16_hi);
}

void ZeroExtU8_U32_Iavx2(YmmVal c[4], YmmVal* a)
{
    __m128i a_vals_u8_0 = _mm_loadl_epi64((__m128i*)&a->m_U8[0]);
    __m128i a_vals_u8_1 = _mm_loadl_epi64((__m128i*)&a->m_U8[8]);
    __m128i a_vals_u8_2 = _mm_loadl_epi64((__m128i*)&a->m_U8[16]);
    __m128i a_vals_u8_3 = _mm_loadl_epi64((__m128i*)&a->m_U8[24]);

    __m256i c_vals_u32_0 = _mm256_cvtepu8_epi32(a_vals_u8_0);
    __m256i c_vals_u32_1 = _mm256_cvtepu8_epi32(a_vals_u8_1);
    __m256i c_vals_u32_2 = _mm256_cvtepu8_epi32(a_vals_u8_2);
    __m256i c_vals_u32_3 = _mm256_cvtepu8_epi32(a_vals_u8_3);

    _mm256_store_si256((__m256i*)&c[0], c_vals_u32_0);
    _mm256_store_si256((__m256i*)&c[1], c_vals_u32_1);
    _mm256_store_si256((__m256i*)&c[2], c_vals_u32_2);
    _mm256_store_si256((__m256i*)&c[3], c_vals_u32_3);
}

void SignExtI16_I32_Iavx2(YmmVal c[2], YmmVal* a)
{
    __m128i a_vals_i16_lo = _mm_load_si128((__m128i*)&a->m_I16[0]);
    __m128i a_vals_i16_hi = _mm_load_si128((__m128i*)&a->m_I16[8]);

    __m256i c_vals_i32_lo = _mm256_cvtepi16_epi32(a_vals_i16_lo);
    __m256i c_vals_i32_hi = _mm256_cvtepi16_epi32(a_vals_i16_hi);

    _mm256_store_si256((__m256i*)&c[0], c_vals_i32_lo);
    _mm256_store_si256((__m256i*)&c[1], c_vals_i32_hi);
}
```

```
void SignExtI16_I64_Iavx2(YmmVal c[4], YmmVal* a)
{
    __m128i a_vals_i16_0 = _mm_loadl_epi64((__m128i*)&a->m_I16[0]);
    __m128i a_vals_i16_1 = _mm_loadl_epi64((__m128i*)&a->m_I16[4]);
    __m128i a_vals_i16_2 = _mm_loadl_epi64((__m128i*)&a->m_I16[8]);
    __m128i a_vals_i16_3 = _mm_loadl_epi64((__m128i*)&a->m_I16[12]);

    __m256i c_vals_i64_0 = _mm256_cvtepi16_epi64(a_vals_i16_0);
    __m256i c_vals_i64_1 = _mm256_cvtepi16_epi64(a_vals_i16_1);
    __m256i c_vals_i64_2 = _mm256_cvtepi16_epi64(a_vals_i16_2);
    __m256i c_vals_i64_3 = _mm256_cvtepi16_epi64(a_vals_i16_3);

    _mm256_store_si256((__m256i*)&c[0], c_vals_i64_0);
    _mm256_store_si256((__m256i*)&c[1], c_vals_i64_1);
    _mm256_store_si256((__m256i*)&c[2], c_vals_i64_2);
    _mm256_store_si256((__m256i*)&c[3], c_vals_i64_3);
}
```

The file Ch04_03.cpp that is located toward the top of Listing 4-3 includes four data setup functions named ZeroExtU8_U16(), ZeroExtU8_U32(), SignExtI16_I32(), and SignExtI16_I64(). These functions perform data initialization tasks for uint8_t to uint16_t, uint8_t to uint32_t, int16_t to int32_t, and int16_t to int64_t size promotions. They also format and stream the results from the C++ SIMD calculating functions to std::cout.

The file Ch04_03_fcpp.cpp starts with the definition of function ZeroExtU8_U16_Iavx2(), which size-promotes a 256-bit wide operand of packed 8-bit unsigned integers to packed 16-bit unsigned integers. This function begins its execution with an _mm_load_si128() call that loads the 16 low-order 8-bit integers from YmmVal argument a into a_vals_u8_lo. Function ZeroExtU8_U16_Iavx2() uses another _mm_load_si128() call to load the 16 high-order 8-bit integers from a into a_vals_u8_hi. It then employs the C++ SIMD intrinsic function _mm256_cvtepu8_epi16() to size-promote the 8-bit unsigned integers in a_vals_u8_lo and a_vals_u8_hi to 16 bits. These values are then saved in c_vals_u16_lo and c_vals_u16_hi, respectively. Note that both a_vals_u8_lo and a_vals_u8_hi are declared as type __m128i while c_vals_u16_lo and c_vals_u16_hi are declared as type __m256i.

The function that follows, ZeroExtU8_U32_Iavx2(), size-promotes a 256-bit wide operand of packed 8-bit unsigned integers to packed 32-bit unsigned integers. This function begins its execution with a series of four _mm_loadl_epi64() calls that load eight 8-bit elements from YmmVal a into variables a_vals_u8_0, a_vals_u8_1, a_vals_u8_2, and a_vals_u8_3. Note that these variables are declared as type __m128i but each _mm_loadl_epi64() call stores its result in the low-order 64 bits. The function _mm_loadl_epi64() also sets the high-order 64 bits of the destination operand to zero; these values are ignored in this example. The next code block employs a sequence of four _mm256_cvtepu8_epi32() calls to perform the packed 8-bit to 32-bit size promotions as shown in Figure 4-4.

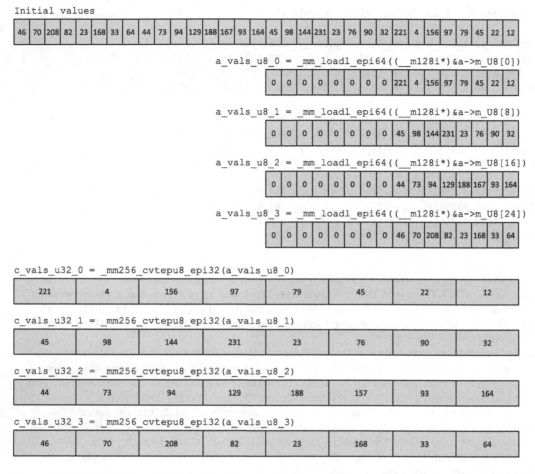

**Figure 4-4.** *Packed 8-bit to 32-bit unsigned integer size promotion using _mm256_cvtepu8_epi32()*

Also present in file ChO4_03_fcpp.cpp are the functions SignExtI16_I32_Iavx2() and SignExtI16_I64_Iavx2(). Function SignExtI16_I32_Iavx2() size-promotes a 256-bit wide operand of packed 16-bit signed integers to 32 bits using the C++ intrinsic function _mm256_cvtepi16_epi32(). The function SignExtI16_I64_Iavx2() size-promotes a 256-bit wide operand of packed 16-bit signed integers to 64 bits using a series of calls to the C++ SIMD intrinsic functions _mm_loadl_epi64() and _mm256_cvtepi16_epi16(). Here are the results for source code example Ch04_03:

```
Results for ZeroExtU8_U16_Iavx2
-----------------------------------------------------------------------
a (0:15):    0   8  16  24  32  40  48  56 |  64  72  80  88  96 104 112 120
a (16:31): 128 136 144 152 160 168 176 184 | 192 200 208 216 224 232 240 248

c (0:7):       0       8      16      24 |     32      40      48      56
c (8:15):     64      72      80      88 |     96     104     112     120
c (16:23):   128     136     144     152 |    160     168     176     184
c (24:31):   192     200     208     216 |    224     232     240     248
```

```
Results for ZeroExtU8_U32_Iavx2
-------------------------------------------------------------------------
a (0:15):   255 247 239 231 223 215 207 199 | 191 183 175 167 159 151 143 135
a (16:31):  127 119 111 103  95  87  79  71 |  63  55  47  39  31  23  15   7

c (0:3):                 255             247 |             239             231
c (4:7):                 223             215 |             207             199
c (8:11):                191             183 |             175             167
c (12:15):               159             151 |             143             135
c (16:19):               127             119 |             111             103
c (20:23):                95              87 |              79              71
c (24:27):                63              55 |              47              39
c (28:31):                31              23 |              15               7

Results for SignExtI16_I32_Iavx2
-------------------------------------------------------------------------
a (0:7):   -32768   -28768   -24768   -20768 | -16768  -12768   -8768   -4768
a (8:15):    -768     3232     7232    11232 |  15232   19232   23232   27232

c (0:3):            -32768           -28768 |          -24768          -20768
c (4:7):            -16768           -12768 |           -8768           -4768
c (8:11):             -768             3232 |            7232           11232
c (12:15):           15232            19232 |           23232           27232

Results for SignExtI16_I64_Iavx2
-------------------------------------------------------------------------
a (0:7):   32767    28767    24767    20767 |  16767   12767    8767    4767
a (8:15):    767    -3233    -7233   -11233 | -15233  -19233  -23233  -27233

c (0:1):                              32767 |                          28767
c (2:3):                              24767 |                          20767
c (4:5):                              16767 |                          12767
c (6:7):                               8767 |                           4767
c (8:9):                                767 |                          -3233
c (10:11):                            -7233 |                         -11233
c (12:13):                           -15233 |                         -19233
c (14:15):                           -23233 |                         -27233
```

The SIMD source code in example Ch04_03 illustrates a basic design pattern for size-promoting 8-, 16-, and 32-bit integers, both signed and unsigned integers. You will see other examples of integer size promotions later in this book.

# Image Processing

In Chapter 2, you learned how to carry out some elementary image processing operations using C++ SIMD intrinsic functions. The source code examples in this section demonstrate additional image processing techniques using 256-bit wide SIMD operands. The first example illustrates how to clip the intensity values of a grayscale image. The second example explains how to convert an RGB image to grayscale. This is followed by a source code example that performs image thresholding. The final example highlights unsigned 8-bit integer to floating-point pixel conversions.

As mentioned in Chapter 2, SIMD techniques are ideal for many types of image processing algorithms. Moreover, the C++ SIMD intrinsic functions used by the source code examples in this section are suitable for both image processing applications and a wide variety of algorithms that process large arrays or matrices of integer data.

## Pixel Clipping

Pixel clipping is an image processing technique that bounds the intensity value of each pixel in an image between two threshold limits. This method is often used to reduce the dynamic range of an image by eliminating its extremely dark and light pixels. Source code example Ch04_04, shown in Listing 4-4, illustrates how to use C++ SIMD intrinsic functions to clip the pixels of an 8-bit grayscale image.

*Listing 4-4.* Example Ch04_04

```
//--------------------------------------------------
//                Ch04_04.h
//--------------------------------------------------

#pragma once
#include <cstddef>
#include <cstdint>

// Data structure for pixel clipping algorithms
struct ClipData
{
    uint8_t* m_PbSrc;              // source buffer pointer
    uint8_t* m_PbDes;              // destination buffer pointer
    size_t m_NumPixels;            // number of pixels
    size_t m_NumClippedPixels;     // number of clipped pixels
    uint8_t m_ThreshLo;            // low threshold
    uint8_t m_ThreshHi;            // high threshold
};

// Ch04_04_fcpp.cpp
extern void ClipPixels_Cpp(ClipData* clip_data);
extern void ClipPixels_Iavx2(ClipData* clip_data);

// Ch04_04_misc.cpp
extern bool CheckArgs(const ClipData* clip_data);

// Ch04_04_bm.cpp
extern void ClipPixels_bm(void);

// Miscellaneous constants
const size_t c_Alignment = 32;
const int c_RngMinVal = 0;
const int c_RngMaxVal = 255;
const unsigned int c_RngSeed = 157;
const uint8_t c_ThreshLo = 10;
const uint8_t c_ThreshHi = 245;
```

```cpp
const size_t c_NumPixels = 8 * 1024 * 1024 + 31;
const size_t c_NumPixelsBM = 10000000;

//--------------------------------------------------
//                  Ch04_04_misc.cpp
//--------------------------------------------------

#include "Ch04_04.h"
#include "AlignedMem.h"

bool CheckArgs(const ClipData* clip_data)
{
    if (clip_data->m_NumPixels == 0)
        return false;
    if (!AlignedMem::IsAligned(clip_data->m_PbSrc, c_Alignment))
        return false;
    if (!AlignedMem::IsAligned(clip_data->m_PbDes, c_Alignment))
        return false;
    return true;
}

//--------------------------------------------------
//                  Ch04_04.cpp
//--------------------------------------------------

#include <iostream>
#include <cstring>
#include <limits>
#include <stdexcept>
#include "Ch04_04.h"
#include "AlignedMem.h"
#include "MT.h"

static void ClipPixels(void);

int main()
{
    try
    {
        ClipPixels();
        ClipPixels_bm();
    }

    catch (std::exception& ex)
    {
        std::cout << "Ch04_04 exception: " << ex.what() << '\n';
    }

}
```

```cpp
static void ClipPixels(void)
{
    const char nl = '\n';
    const uint8_t thresh_lo = c_ThreshLo;
    const uint8_t thresh_hi = c_ThreshHi;
    const size_t num_pixels = c_NumPixels;

    AlignedArray<uint8_t> pb_src(num_pixels, c_Alignment);
    AlignedArray<uint8_t> pb_des0(num_pixels, c_Alignment);
    AlignedArray<uint8_t> pb_des1(num_pixels, c_Alignment);

    MT::FillArray(pb_src.Data(), num_pixels, c_RngMinVal, c_RngMaxVal, c_RngSeed);

    ClipData cd0, cd1;

    cd0.m_PbSrc = pb_src.Data();
    cd0.m_PbDes = pb_des0.Data();
    cd0.m_NumPixels = num_pixels;
    cd0.m_NumClippedPixels = (std::numeric_limits<size_t>::max)();
    cd0.m_ThreshLo = thresh_lo;
    cd0.m_ThreshHi = thresh_hi;

    cd1.m_PbSrc = pb_src.Data();
    cd1.m_PbDes = pb_des1.Data();
    cd1.m_NumPixels = num_pixels;
    cd1.m_NumClippedPixels = (std::numeric_limits<size_t>::max)();
    cd1.m_ThreshLo = thresh_lo;
    cd1.m_ThreshHi = thresh_hi;

    ClipPixels_Cpp(&cd0);
    ClipPixels_Iavx2(&cd1);

    std::cout << "\nResults for ClipPixels_Cpp\n";
    std::cout << "  cd1.m_NumClippedPixels: " << cd0.m_NumClippedPixels << nl;
    std::cout << "\nResults for ClipPixels_Iavx2\n";
    std::cout << "  cd2.m_NumClippedPixels: " << cd1.m_NumClippedPixels << nl;

    bool ncp_check = cd0.m_NumClippedPixels == cd1.m_NumClippedPixels;
    bool mem_check = memcmp(pb_des0.Data(), pb_des1.Data(), num_pixels) == 0;

    if (ncp_check && mem_check)
        std::cout << "\nResult compare checks passed\n";
    else
        std::cout << "\nResult compare checks failed!\n";
}

//---------------------------------------------------
//                Ch04_04_fcpp.cpp
//---------------------------------------------------
```

```cpp
#include <immintrin.h>
#include "Ch04_04.h"
#include "AlignedMem.h"

void ClipPixels_Cpp(ClipData* clip_data)
{
    if (!CheckArgs(clip_data))
        throw std::runtime_error("ClipPixels_Cpp() - CheckArgs failed");

    uint8_t* pb_src = clip_data->m_PbSrc;
    uint8_t* pb_des = clip_data->m_PbDes;
    size_t num_pixels = clip_data->m_NumPixels;
    size_t num_clipped_pixels = 0;
    uint8_t thresh_lo = clip_data->m_ThreshLo;
    uint8_t thresh_hi = clip_data->m_ThreshHi;

    for (size_t i = 0; i < num_pixels; i++)
    {
        uint8_t pixel = pb_src[i];

        if (pixel < thresh_lo)
        {
            pb_des[i] = thresh_lo;
            num_clipped_pixels++;
        }
        else if (pixel > thresh_hi)
        {
            pb_des[i] = thresh_hi;
            num_clipped_pixels++;
        }
        else
            pb_des[i] = pb_src[i];
    }

    clip_data->m_NumClippedPixels = num_clipped_pixels;
}

void ClipPixels_Iavx2(ClipData* clip_data)
{
    if (!CheckArgs(clip_data))
        throw std::runtime_error("ClipPixels_Iavx2() - CheckArgs failed");

    uint8_t* pb_src = clip_data->m_PbSrc;
    uint8_t* pb_des = clip_data->m_PbDes;
    size_t num_pixels = clip_data->m_NumPixels;
    size_t num_clipped_pixels = 0;
    uint8_t thresh_lo = clip_data->m_ThreshLo;
    uint8_t thresh_hi = clip_data->m_ThreshHi;

    size_t i = 0;
    const size_t num_simd_elements = 32;
```

```
    // Create packed versions of thresh_lo and thresh_hi
    __m256i packed_thresh_lo = _mm256_set1_epi8(thresh_lo);
    __m256i packed_thresh_hi = _mm256_set1_epi8(thresh_hi);

    for (; num_pixels - i >= num_simd_elements; i += num_simd_elements)
    {
        __m256i pb_src_vals = _mm256_load_si256((__m256i*)&pb_src[i]);
        __m256i temp1 = _mm256_max_epu8(pb_src_vals, packed_thresh_lo);
        __m256i pb_des_vals = _mm256_min_epu8(temp1, packed_thresh_hi);

        _mm256_store_si256((__m256i*)&pb_des[i], pb_des_vals);

        __m256i temp2 = _mm256_cmpeq_epi8(pb_des_vals, pb_src_vals);
        unsigned int count_mask_eq = _mm256_movemask_epi8(temp2);
        num_clipped_pixels += _mm_popcnt_u32(~count_mask_eq);
    }

    for (; i < num_pixels; i++)
    {
        uint8_t pixel = pb_src[i];

        if (pixel < thresh_lo)
        {
            pb_des[i] = thresh_lo;
            num_clipped_pixels++;
        }
        else if (pixel > thresh_hi)
        {
            pb_des[i] = thresh_hi;
            num_clipped_pixels++;
        }
        else
            pb_des[i] = pb_src[i];
    }

    clip_data->m_NumClippedPixels = num_clipped_pixels;
}
```

Listing 4-4 begins with the declaration of a structure named ClipData. This structure contains the data that is used by the pixel clipping algorithms. The next item in Listing 4-4 is the function CheckArgs(), which performs argument checking. The file Ch04_04.cpp contains the function ClipPixels(). This function performs ClipData structure initialization. Note that structure member m_NumClippedPixels is set to std::numeric_limits<size_t>::max() to differentiate between an error condition and the case of zero clipped pixels. It also calls the SIMD calculating functions and displays the results.

The principal calculating functions of source code example Ch04_04 are in the file Ch04_04_fcpp.cpp. The first function in this file, ClipPixels_Cpp(), implements the pixel clipping algorithm using standard C++ statements. During execution of the for-loop, ClipPixels_Cpp() checks each pixel to see if its intensity value is below thresh_lo or above thresh_hi. If a pixel intensity value exceeds one of these limits, it is clipped. Note that ClipPixels_Cpp() updates num_clipped_pixels each time it clips a pixel. This count will be used to verify the results of both clipping functions.

The next function in Ch04_04_fcpp.cpp, ClipPixels_Iavx2(), implements the same algorithm as ClipPixels_Cpp() using C++ SIMD intrinsic functions. Following argument validation, the function ClipPixels_Iavx2() initializes num_simd_elements to 32. It then employs two calls to _mm256_set1_epi8() to initialize packed versions of thresh_lo and thresh_hi. The C++ SIMD intrinsic function _mm256_set1_epi8() broadcasts an 8-bit integer value to each element position of a 256-bit wide SIMD value.

The first for-loop in ClipPixels_Iavx2() starts each iteration with a call to _mm256_load_si256() that loads 32 pixels from the source pixel buffer into pb_src_vals. Then the next two calls, _mm256_max_epu8() and _mm256_min_epu8(), clip the just loaded pixel values to thresh_lo and thresh_hi. The ensuing call to _mm256_store_si256() saves the clipped result to the destination pixel buffer.

Following the pixel store operation, ClipPixels_Iavx2() uses the C++ SIMD intrinsic function _mm256_cmpeq_epi8() to compare the pixel values before and after clipping. This function sets each 8-bit element in temp2 to 0xFF if the corresponding elements in pb_src_vals and pb_des_vals are the same (i.e., the pixel was not clipped); otherwise, the element is set to 0x00. Then the next call, _mm256_movemask_epi8(), creates a 32-bit wide scalar integer mask named count_mask_eq using the most significant bit of each 8-bit element in temp2. Each "1" bit in temp2 signifies an unclipped pixel. Thus, the number of pixels clipped during each for-loop iteration corresponds to the number of "1" bits in ~count_mask_eq. These bits are counted using the C++ non-SIMD intrinsic function _mm_popcnt_u32().

If the number of pixels is not an integral multiple of 32, the second for-loop processes any residual pixels using standard C++ statements. Here are the results for source code example Ch04_04:

```
Results for ClipPixels_Cpp
  cd1.m_NumClippedPixels: 654950

Results for ClipPixels_Iavx2
  cd2.m_NumClippedPixels: 654950

Result compare checks passed

Running benchmark function ClipPixels_bm - please wait
Benchmark times save to file Ch04_04_ClipPixels_bm_OXYGEN4.csv
```

Table 4-1 shows some benchmark timing measurements for source code example Ch04_04.

*Table 4-1.* *Pixel Clipping Algorithm Execution Times (Microseconds), 10,000,000 Pixels*

| CPU | ClipPixels_Cpp() | ClipPixels_Iavx2() |
|---|---|---|
| Intel Core i7-8700K | 12109 | 810 |
| Intel Core i5-11600K | 9695 | 665 |

# RGB to Grayscale

Listing 4-5 shows the source code for example Ch04_05. This example explains how to use C++ SIMD intrinsic functions to convert an RGB color image to an 8-bit grayscale image. It also demonstrates the intermixing of both packed integer and packed floating-point operands in the same calculating function. And unlike the previous image processing examples, Ch04_05 uses a PNG image file instead of an array of randomly generated pixel values.

***Listing 4-5.*** Example Ch04_05

```
//--------------------------------------------------
//                Ch04_05.h
//--------------------------------------------------

#pragma once
#include <cstddef>
#include <cstdint>
#include "ImageMisc.h"

// Ch04_05.cpp
extern const float c_Coef[4];
extern const char* c_TestImageFileName;

// Ch04_05_fcpp.cpp
extern void ConvertRgbToGs_Cpp(uint8_t* pb_gs, const RGB32* pb_rgb, size_t num_pixels, const
float coef[4]);
extern void ConvertRgbToGs_Iavx2(uint8_t* pb_gs, const RGB32* pb_rgb, size_t num_pixels,
const float coef[4]);

// Ch04_05_misc.cpp
extern bool CheckArgs(const uint8_t* pb_gs, const RGB32* pb_rgb, size_t num_pixels, const
float coef[4]);

// Ch04_05_bm.cpp
extern void ConvertRgbToGs_bm(void);
extern bool CompareGsPixelBuffers(const uint8_t* pb_gs1, const uint8_t* pb_gs2, size_t num_
pixels);

// Miscellaneous constants
const size_t c_Alignment = 32;
const size_t c_NumPixelsMax = 256 * 1024 * 1024;

//--------------------------------------------------
//                Ch04_05_misc.cpp
//--------------------------------------------------

#include "Ch04_05.h"
#include "AlignedMem.h"

bool CheckArgs(const uint8_t* pb_gs, const RGB32* pb_rgb, size_t num_pixels, const float
coef[4])
{
    if (num_pixels > c_NumPixelsMax)
        return false;
    if (num_pixels % 8 != 0)
        return false;
    if (!AlignedMem::IsAligned(pb_gs, c_Alignment))
        return false;
    if (!AlignedMem::IsAligned(pb_rgb, c_Alignment))
        return false;
```

```cpp
        if (coef[0] < 0.0f || coef[1] < 0.0f || coef[2] < 0.0f)
            return false;
        return true;
}

bool CompareGsPixelBuffers(const uint8_t* pb_gs1, const uint8_t* pb_gs2, size_t num_pixels)
{
    for (size_t i = 0; i < num_pixels; i++)
    {
        if (abs((int)pb_gs1[i] - (int)pb_gs2[i]) > 1)
            return false;
    }
    return true;
}

//--------------------------------------------------
//                  Ch04_05.cpp
//--------------------------------------------------

#include <iostream>
#include <stdexcept>
#include "Ch04_05.h"
#include "ImageMatrix.h"

// Test image file
const char* c_TestImageFileName = "../../Data/ImageC.png";

// RGB to grayscale conversion coefficients, values must be >= 0
const float c_Coef[4] {0.2126f, 0.7152f, 0.0722f, 0.0f};

static void ConvertRgbToGs(void);

int main()
{
    try
    {
        ConvertRgbToGs();
        ConvertRgbToGs_bm();
    }

    catch (std::exception& ex)
    {
        std::cout << "Ch04_05 exception: " << ex.what() << '\n';
    }
}

static void ConvertRgbToGs(void)
{
    const char nl = '\n';
    const char* fn_gs0 = "Ch04_05_GsImage0.png";
    const char* fn_gs1 = "Ch04_05_GsImage1.png";
```

```cpp
    ImageMatrix im_rgb(c_TestImageFileName, PixelType::Rgb32);
    size_t im_h = im_rgb.GetHeight();
    size_t im_w = im_rgb.GetWidth();
    size_t num_pixels = im_h * im_w;

    ImageMatrix im_gs0(im_h, im_w, PixelType::Gray8);
    ImageMatrix im_gs1(im_h, im_w, PixelType::Gray8);
    RGB32* pb_rgb = im_rgb.GetPixelBuffer<RGB32>();
    uint8_t* pb_gs0 = im_gs0.GetPixelBuffer<uint8_t>();
    uint8_t* pb_gs1 = im_gs1.GetPixelBuffer<uint8_t>();

    std::cout << "Results for ConvertRgbToGs\n";
    std::cout << "  Converting RGB image " << c_TestImageFileName << nl;
    std::cout << "  im_h = " << im_h << " pixels\n";
    std::cout << "  im_w = " << im_w << " pixels\n";

    // Exercise conversion functions
    ConvertRgbToGs_Cpp(pb_gs0, pb_rgb, num_pixels, c_Coef);
    ConvertRgbToGs_Iavx2(pb_gs1, pb_rgb, num_pixels, c_Coef);

    // Save results
    std::cout << "Saving grayscale image #0 - " << fn_gs0 << nl;
    im_gs0.SaveImage(fn_gs0, ImageFileType::PNG);
    std::cout << "Saving grayscale image #1 - " << fn_gs1 << nl;
    im_gs1.SaveImage(fn_gs1, ImageFileType::PNG);

    if (CompareGsPixelBuffers(pb_gs0, pb_gs1, num_pixels))
        std::cout << "Grayscale pixel buffer compare OK\n";
    else
        std::cout << "Grayscale pixel buffer compare failed!\n";
}

//-------------------------------------------------
//              Ch04_05_fcpp.cpp
//-------------------------------------------------

#include <iostream>
#include <stdexcept>
#include <immintrin.h>
#include "Ch04_05.h"
#include "ImageMisc.h"

void ConvertRgbToGs_Cpp(uint8_t* pb_gs, const RGB32* pb_rgb, size_t num_pixels, const float
coef[4])
{
    if (!CheckArgs(pb_gs, pb_rgb, num_pixels, coef))
        throw std::runtime_error("ConvertRgbToGs_Cpp() - CheckArgs failed");

    for (size_t i = 0; i < num_pixels; i++)
    {
        uint8_t r = pb_rgb[i].m_R;
```

```
            uint8_t g = pb_rgb[i].m_G;
            uint8_t b = pb_rgb[i].m_B;
            float gs_temp = r * coef[0] + g * coef[1] + b * coef[2] + 0.5f;

            if (gs_temp > 255.0f)
                gs_temp = 255.0f;

            pb_gs[i] = (uint8_t)gs_temp;
        }
}

void ConvertRgbToGs_Iavx2(uint8_t* pb_gs, const RGB32* pb_rgb, size_t num_pixels, const
float coef[4])
{
    if (!CheckArgs(pb_gs, pb_rgb, num_pixels, coef))
        throw std::runtime_error("ConvertRgbToGs_Iavx2() - CheckArgs failed");

    __m256 packed_0p5_f32 = _mm256_set1_ps(0.5f);
    __m256 packed_255p0_f32 = _mm256_set1_ps(255.0f);
    __m256i packed_zero = _mm256_setzero_si256();
    __m256i u32_byte0_mask = _mm256_set1_epi32(0x000000ff);

    __m256 packed_coef_r = _mm256_set1_ps(coef[0]);
    __m256 packed_coef_g = _mm256_set1_ps(coef[1]);
    __m256 packed_coef_b = _mm256_set1_ps(coef[2]);

    const size_t num_simd_elements = 8;

    for (size_t i = 0; i < num_pixels; i += num_simd_elements)
    {
        // Load next block of eight RGB32 pixels
        __m256i pixel_vals = _mm256_load_si256((__m256i*)&pb_rgb[i]);

        // De-interleave color components and size promote to U32
        __m256i pixel_vals_r = pixel_vals;
        __m256i pixel_vals_g = _mm256_srli_epi32(pixel_vals, 8);
        __m256i pixel_vals_b = _mm256_srli_epi32(pixel_vals, 16);
        __m256i pixel_vals_r_u32 = _mm256_and_si256(pixel_vals_r, u32_byte0_mask);
        __m256i pixel_vals_g_u32 = _mm256_and_si256(pixel_vals_g, u32_byte0_mask);
        __m256i pixel_vals_b_u32 = _mm256_and_si256(pixel_vals_b, u32_byte0_mask);

        // Convert color components from U32 to F32
        __m256 pixel_vals_r_f32 = _mm256_cvtepi32_ps(pixel_vals_r_u32);
        __m256 pixel_vals_g_f32 = _mm256_cvtepi32_ps(pixel_vals_g_u32);
        __m256 pixel_vals_b_f32 = _mm256_cvtepi32_ps(pixel_vals_b_u32);

        // Multiply color components by conversion coefficients
        pixel_vals_r_f32 = _mm256_mul_ps(pixel_vals_r_f32, packed_coef_r);
        pixel_vals_g_f32 = _mm256_mul_ps(pixel_vals_g_f32, packed_coef_g);
        pixel_vals_b_f32 = _mm256_mul_ps(pixel_vals_b_f32, packed_coef_b);
```

```
        // Sum color components
        __m256 temp1_f32 = _mm256_add_ps(pixel_vals_r_f32, pixel_vals_g_f32);
        __m256 pixel_vals_gs_f32 = _mm256_add_ps(pixel_vals_b_f32, temp1_f32);

        // Clip grayscale pixel values
        pixel_vals_gs_f32 = _mm256_add_ps(pixel_vals_gs_f32, packed_0p5_f32);
        pixel_vals_gs_f32 = _mm256_min_ps(pixel_vals_gs_f32, packed_255p0_f32);

        // Convert grayscale values from F32 to U8
        __m256i pixel_vals_gs_u32 = _mm256_cvtps_epi32(pixel_vals_gs_f32);
        __m256i pixel_vals_gs_u16 = _mm256_packus_epi32(pixel_vals_gs_u32, packed_zero);
        __m256i temp2_u16 = _mm256_permute4x64_epi64(pixel_vals_gs_u16, 0b01011000);
        __m256i pixel_vals_gs_u8 = _mm256_packus_epi16(temp2_u16, packed_zero);

        // Save result to gs pixel buffer
        uint64_t gs_vals = _mm256_extract_epi64(pixel_vals_gs_u8, 0);
        *((uint64_t*)&pb_gs[i]) = gs_vals;
    }
}
```

A variety of algorithms exist to convert an RGB image into a grayscale image. One frequently used technique calculates grayscale pixel values using a weighted sum of the RGB color components. In this source code example, RGB pixel values are converted to grayscale values using the following equation:

$$GS(x,y) = R(x,y)W_r + G(x,y)W_g + B(x,y)W_b$$

In the conversion equation, each RGB color conversion coefficient is a floating-point number between 0.0 and 1.0. The sum of these coefficients normally equals 1.0. The exact values used for the coefficients are based on published standards that reflect a multitude of visual factors including properties of the target color space, display device characteristics, and perceived image quality. Appendix B lists some references that you can consult if you are interested in learning more about RGB to grayscale image conversions.

Listing 4-5 opens with the declaration of a structure named RGB32. This structure is declared in the header file ImageMisc.h and specifies the color component ordering scheme for each RGB pixel. Note that in this example, RGB32 structure member m_A is not used. Next is the header file Ch04_05.h. This file contains function declarations and a few miscellaneous constants. Following the header file Ch04_05.h in Listing 4-5 is the file Ch04_05_misc.cpp, which contains the argument validation function CheckArgs() and the pixel buffer compare function CompareGsPixelBuffers(). Next is the file Ch04_05.cpp. In this file, the function ConvertRgbToGs() contains the code that loads a PNG image file, executes the conversion functions, and saves the results. Note that image file loading and saving is handled by a C++ class named ImageMatrix. The source code for ImageMatrix is not shown in Listing 4-5 but included in the download source code package.

The final file in Listing 4-5, Ch04_05_fcpp.cpp, contains the RGB to grayscale conversion functions. The function ConvertRgbToGs_Cpp() uses standard C++ statements to convert an RGB image to grayscale using the aforementioned conversion equation, while the function ConvertRgbToGs_Iavx2() uses C++ SIMD intrinsic functions. Function ConvertRgbToGs_Iavx2() begins its execution with a pair of _mm256_set1_ps() calls that prepare packed versions of the floating-point constants 0.0 and 255.0. Initialization of the constants packed_zero and u32_byte0_mask is next. The former is used for unsigned integer size reductions, and the latter is a color component mask. The final three initialization statements use the C++ SIMD intrinsic function _mm256_set1_ps() to create packed versions of the color conversion coefficients.

Each iteration of the for-loop in ConvertRgbToGs_Iavx2() begins with an _mm256_load_si256() call that loads eight RGB32 pixel values into the variable pixel_vals. Then the next code block uses the C++ SIMD intrinsic functions _mm256_srli_epi32() and _mm256_and_si256() to de-interleave and size-promote the RGB color component values from 8 bits to 32 bits as shown in Figure 4-5. This is followed by a code block that uses the C++ SIMD intrinsic function _mm256_cvtepi32_ps() to convert the packed 32-bit integer values to packed single-precision floating-point.

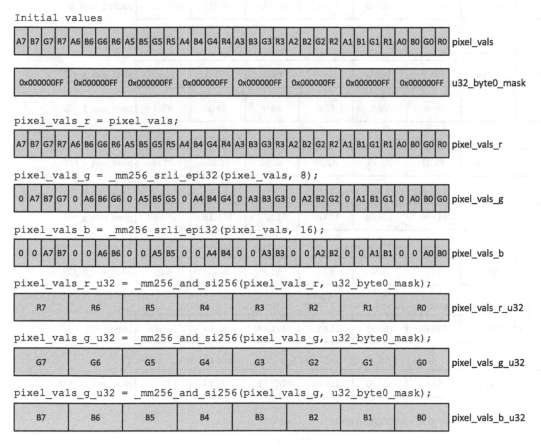

Figure 4-5. *RGB pixel de-interleaving and integer size promotions*

Following conversion of the color component pixel values to floating point, ConvertRgbToGs_Iavx2() uses the C++ SIMD intrinsic function _mm256_mul_ps() to multiply the red, green, and blue pixel values by the specified color conversion coefficients. The next two calls to _mm256_add_ps() sum the color component values, which yields floating-point grayscale pixel values. Figure 4-6 illustrates these steps in greater detail. After the summing operation, the function _mm256_add_ps(pixel_vals_gs_f32, packed_0p5_f32) adds 0.5 to each floating-point grayscale pixel value. This is the same technique that is often used in C++ to round a scalar floating-point value to an integer. The ensuing call to _mm256_min_ps(pixel_vals_gs_f32, packed_255p0_f32) prevents floating-point pixel values greater than 255.0 from occurring. Following these two operations, the floating-point grayscale pixel values are clipped to [0.0, 255.0].

Initial values

| 0.2126 | 0.2126 | 0.2126 | 0.2126 | 0.2126 | 0.2126 | 0.2126 | 0.2126 | packed_coef_r |
|---|---|---|---|---|---|---|---|---|
| 0.7152 | 0.7152 | 0.7152 | 0.7152 | 0.7152 | 0.7152 | 0.7152 | 0.7152 | packed_coef_g |
| 0.0722 | 0.0722 | 0.0722 | 0.0722 | 0.0722 | 0.0722 | 0.0722 | 0.0722 | packed_coef_b |
| 222.0 | 218.0 | 212.0 | 202.0 | 199.0 | 224.0 | 227.0 | 229.0 | pixel_vals_r_f32 |
| 162.0 | 158.0 | 156.0 | 165.0 | 155.0 | 159.0 | 161.0 | 164.0 | pixel_vals_g_f32 |
| 88.0 | 84.0 | 83.0 | 79.0 | 82.0 | 86.0 | 89.0 | 87.0 | pixel_vals_b_f32 |

`pixel_vals_r_f32 = _mm256_mul_ps(pixel_vals_r_f32, packed_coef_r);`

| 47.20 | 46.35 | 45.07 | 42.95 | 42.31 | 47.62 | 48.26 | 48.69 | pixel_vals_r_f32 |
|---|---|---|---|---|---|---|---|---|

`pixel_vals_g_g32 = _mm256_mul_ps(pixel_vals_g_f32, packed_coef_g);`

| 115.86 | 113.00 | 111.57 | 118.01 | 110.86 | 113.72 | 115.15 | 117.29 | pixel_vals_g_f32 |
|---|---|---|---|---|---|---|---|---|

`pixel_vals_b_f32 = _mm256_mul_ps(pixel_vals_b_f32, packed_coef_b);`

| 6.35 | 6.06 | 5.99 | 5.70 | 5.92 | 6.21 | 6.43 | 6.28 | pixel_vals_b_f32 |
|---|---|---|---|---|---|---|---|---|

`temp1_f32 = _mm256_add_ps(pixel_vals_r_f32, pixel_vals_g_f32);`

| 163.06 | 159.35 | 156.64 | 160.95 | 153.16 | 161.34 | 163.41 | 165.98 | temp1_f32 |
|---|---|---|---|---|---|---|---|---|

`pixel_vals_gs_f32 = _mm256_add_ps(pixel_vals_b_f32, temp1_f32);`

| 169.41 | 165.41 | 162.64 | 166.66 | 159.08 | 167.55 | 169.83 | 172.26 | pixel_vals_gs_f32 |
|---|---|---|---|---|---|---|---|---|

***Figure 4-6.*** *SIMD RGB to grayscale calculation*

The final set of statements in ConvertRgbToGs_Iavx2() converts the packed floating-point grayscale values in pixel_vals_gs_f32 to packed 8-bit unsigned integers. This process begins with a call to _mm256_cvtps_epi32(), which converts packed single-precision values to packed 32-bit integers. The following call to _mm256_packus_epi32() size-reduces the 32-bit unsigned integer values in pixel_vals_gs_u32 to 16 unsigned integers using unsigned saturation as illustrated in Figure 4-7. Note that _mm256_packus_epi32() performs independent packing operations using the lower and upper lanes of its operands. The next C++ SIMD intrinsic function, _mm256_permute4x64_epi64(), permutes the values in pixel_vals_gs_u16 to relocate the grayscale values into the low-order lane of temp2_u16. Note that function _mm256_permute4x64_epi64() performs its permutations using 64-bit wide integer elements. Each two-bit pair of the immediate constant 0b01011000 specifies which 64-bit wide element to copy from the source operand pixel_vals_gs_u16. In the current example, the four most significant bits of the immediate constant are don't care values.

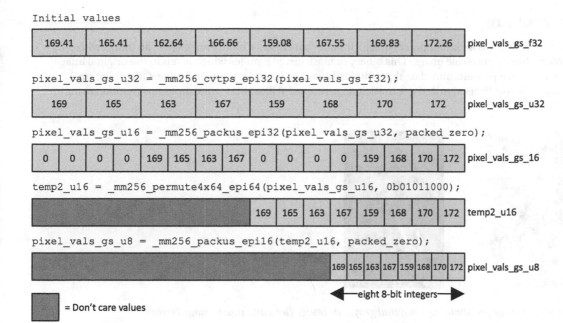

*Figure 4-7. Grayscale floating-point to 8-bit unsigned integer conversion*

Following the permutation, ConvertRgbToGs_Iavx2() uses the C++ intrinsic function _mm256_extract_epi64() to extract the eight grayscale pixel values from pixel_vals_gs_u8. Here are the results for source code example Ch04_05:

```
Results for ConvertRgbToGs
  Converting RGB image ../../Data/ImageC.png
  im_h = 960 pixels
  im_w = 640 pixels
Saving grayscale image #0 - Ch04_05_GsImage0.png
Saving grayscale image #1 - Ch04_05_GsImage1.png
Grayscale pixel buffer compare OK

Running benchmark function ConvertRgbToGs_bm - please wait
Benchmark times save to file Ch04_05_ConvertRgbToGs_bm_OXYGEN4.csv
```

Table 4-2 shows some benchmark timing measurements for source code example Ch04_05.

*Table 4-2. RGB to Grayscale Algorithm Execution Times (Microseconds) Using ImageC.png*

| CPU | ConvertRgbToGs_Cpp() | ConvertRgbToGs_Iavx2() |
|-----|----------------------|------------------------|
| Intel Core i7-8700K | 875 | 162 |
| Intel Core i5-11600K | 773 | 132 |

# Thresholding

Image thresholding is an image processing technique that creates a binary image (i.e., an image with only two colors) from a grayscale image. This binary or mask image signifies which pixels in the original image are greater than a predetermined or algorithmically derived intensity threshold value. Other relational operators can also be used to derive a mask image. Figure 4-8 illustrates a thresholding operation using an 8-bit grayscale image.

***Figure 4-8.*** *Image thresholding – original grayscale image (left) and mask image (right)*

Following a thresholding operation, the mask image is often used to perform additional calculations using the grayscale pixels of the original image. For example, one typical use of the mask image that is shown in Figure 4-8 is to compute the mean intensity of all above-threshold pixels in the original grayscale image. The application of a mask image simplifies calculating the mean since it facilitates the use of simple Boolean expressions to exclude unwanted pixels from the computations. Source code example Ch04_06 demonstrates how to calculate the mean intensity of image pixel greater than a predetermined threshold. Listing 4-6 shows the source code for example Ch04_06.

***Listing 4-6.*** Example Ch04_06

```
//-------------------------------------------------
//              Ch04_06.h
//-------------------------------------------------

#pragma once
#include <cstddef>
#include <cstdint>

struct ITD
{
    uint8_t* m_PbSrc;               // Source image pixel buffer
    uint8_t* m_PbMask;              // Mask mask pixel buffer
    size_t m_NumPixels;            // Number of source image pixels
    uint64_t m_NumMaskedPixels;    // Number of masked pixels
    uint64_t m_SumMaskedPixels;    // Sum of masked pixels
    double m_MeanMaskedPixels;     // Mean of masked pixels
    uint8_t m_Threshold;           // Image threshold value
};
```

```cpp
// Ch04_06_fcpp.cpp
extern void ThresholdImage_Cpp(ITD* itd);
extern void ThresholdImage_Iavx2(ITD* itd);
extern void CalcImageMean_Cpp(ITD* itd);
extern void CalcImageMean_Iavx2(ITD* itd);

// Ch04_06_misc.cpp
extern bool CheckArgs(size_t num_pixels, const uint8_t* pb_src, const uint8_t* pb_mask);

// Ch04_06_bm.cpp
extern void ProcessImage_bm(void);

// Miscellaneous constants
const size_t c_Alignment = 32;
const size_t c_NumSimdElements = 32;
const size_t c_NumPixelsMax = 16 * 1024 * 1024;
const uint8_t c_TestThreshold = 224;
extern const char* c_TestImageFileName;

//------------------------------------------------
//                 Ch04_06_misc.cpp
//------------------------------------------------

#include "Ch04_06.h"
#include "AlignedMem.h"

bool CheckArgs(size_t num_pixels, const uint8_t* pb_src, const uint8_t* pb_mask)
{
    if ((num_pixels == 0) || (num_pixels > c_NumPixelsMax))
        return false;
    if ((num_pixels % c_NumSimdElements) != 0)
        return false;
    if (!AlignedMem::IsAligned(pb_src, c_Alignment))
        return false;
    if (!AlignedMem::IsAligned(pb_mask, c_Alignment))
        return false;
    return true;
}

//------------------------------------------------
//                 Ch04_06.cpp
//------------------------------------------------

#include <iostream>
#include <iomanip>
#include <stdexcept>
#include "Ch04_06.h"
#include "ImageMatrix.h"
```

```cpp
const char* c_TestImageFileName = "../../Data/ImageA.png";

static void ProcessImage(void);

int main()
{
    try
    {
        ProcessImage();
        ProcessImage_bm();
    }

    catch (std::exception& ex)
    {
        std::cout << "Ch04_06 exception: " << ex.what() << '\n';
    }
}

static void ProcessImage(void)
{
    const char nl = '\n';
    const char* fn_mask0 = "Ch04_06_ProcessImage_Mask0.png";
    const char* fn_mask1 = "Ch04_06_ProcessImage_Mask1.png";

    ImageMatrix im_src(c_TestImageFileName, PixelType::Gray8);
    size_t im_h = im_src.GetHeight();
    size_t im_w = im_src.GetWidth();
    ImageMatrix im_mask0(im_h, im_w, PixelType::Gray8);
    ImageMatrix im_mask1(im_h, im_w, PixelType::Gray8);

    ITD itd0;
    itd0.m_PbSrc = im_src.GetPixelBuffer<uint8_t>();
    itd0.m_PbMask = im_mask0.GetPixelBuffer<uint8_t>();
    itd0.m_NumPixels = im_src.GetNumPixels();
    itd0.m_Threshold = c_TestThreshold;

    ITD itd1;
    itd1.m_PbSrc = im_src.GetPixelBuffer<uint8_t>();
    itd1.m_PbMask = im_mask1.GetPixelBuffer<uint8_t>();
    itd1.m_NumPixels = im_src.GetNumPixels();
    itd1.m_Threshold = c_TestThreshold;

    // Threshold image
    ThresholdImage_Cpp(&itd0);
    ThresholdImage_Iavx2(&itd1);
    im_mask0.SaveImage(fn_mask0, ImageFileType::PNG);
    im_mask1.SaveImage(fn_mask1, ImageFileType::PNG);

    // Calculate mean of masked pixels
    CalcImageMean_Cpp(&itd0);
    CalcImageMean_Iavx2(&itd1);
```

```cpp
    const unsigned int w = 12;
    std::cout << std::fixed << std::setprecision(4);
    std::cout << "\nResults for ProcessImage() using file ";
    std::cout  << c_TestImageFileName << nl << nl;
    std::cout << "                                         Cpp         Iavx2\n";
    std::cout << "---------------------------------------------------\n";
    std::cout << "SumPixelsMasked:   ";
    std::cout << std::setw(w) << itd0.m_SumMaskedPixels << "   ";
    std::cout << std::setw(w) << itd1.m_SumMaskedPixels << nl;
    std::cout << "NumPixelsMasked:   ";
    std::cout << std::setw(w) << itd0.m_NumMaskedPixels << "   ";
    std::cout << std::setw(w) << itd1.m_NumMaskedPixels << nl;
    std::cout << "MeanMaskedPixels:  ";
    std::cout << std::setw(w) << itd0.m_MeanMaskedPixels << "   ";
    std::cout << std::setw(w) << itd1.m_MeanMaskedPixels << nl;
}


//---------------------------------------------------
//                 Ch04_06_fcpp.cpp
//---------------------------------------------------

#include <stdexcept>
#include <immintrin.h>
#include "Ch04_06.h"

inline uint64_t Sum_u32x8(__m256i x)
{
    uint64_t sum = _mm256_extract_epi32(x, 0);
    sum += _mm256_extract_epi32(x, 1);
    sum += _mm256_extract_epi32(x, 2);
    sum += _mm256_extract_epi32(x, 3);
    sum += _mm256_extract_epi32(x, 4);
    sum += _mm256_extract_epi32(x, 5);
    sum += _mm256_extract_epi32(x, 6);
    sum += _mm256_extract_epi32(x, 7);
    return sum;
}

inline __m256i SumMasked_u8x32(__m256i a_u8x32, __m256i mask_u8x32)
{
    __m256i vals_u8x32 =_mm256_and_si256(a_u8x32, mask_u8x32);

    __m128i vals_u8x16_0 = _mm256_extracti128_si256(vals_u8x32, 0);
    __m128i vals_u8x16_1 = _mm256_extracti128_si256(vals_u8x32, 1);

    __m256i vals_u32x8_0 = _mm256_cvtepu8_epi32(vals_u8x16_0);
    __m128i temp0 =  _mm_srli_si128(vals_u8x16_0, 8);
    __m256i vals_u32x8_1 = _mm256_cvtepu8_epi32(temp0);
```

```
    __m256i vals_u32x8_2 = _mm256_cvtepu8_epi32(vals_u8x16_1);
    __m128i temp1 = _mm_srli_si128(vals_u8x16_1, 8);
    __m256i vals_u32x8_3 = _mm256_cvtepu8_epi32(temp1);

    __m256i temp1_u32x8 = _mm256_add_epi32(vals_u32x8_0, vals_u32x8_1);
    __m256i temp2_u32x8 = _mm256_add_epi32(vals_u32x8_2, vals_u32x8_3);
    __m256i sum_u32x8 = _mm256_add_epi32(temp1_u32x8, temp2_u32x8);
    return sum_u32x8;
}

void ThresholdImage_Cpp(ITD* itd)
{
    uint8_t* pb_src = itd->m_PbSrc;
    uint8_t* pb_mask = itd->m_PbMask;
    uint8_t threshold = itd->m_Threshold;
    size_t num_pixels = itd->m_NumPixels;

    if (!CheckArgs(num_pixels, pb_src, pb_mask))
        throw std::runtime_error("ThreshholdImage_Cpp() - CheckArgs failed");

    // Threshold the image
    for (size_t i = 0; i < num_pixels; i++)
        *pb_mask++ = (*pb_src++ > threshold) ? 0xff : 0x00;
}

void ThresholdImage_Iavx2(ITD* itd)
{
    uint8_t* pb_src = itd->m_PbSrc;
    uint8_t* pb_mask = itd->m_PbMask;
    size_t num_pixels = itd->m_NumPixels;
    uint8_t threshold = itd->m_Threshold;
    const size_t num_simd_elements = c_NumSimdElements;

    if (!CheckArgs(num_pixels, pb_src, pb_mask))
        throw std::runtime_error("ThreshholdImage_Iavx2() - CheckArgs() failed");

    __m256i pixel_sf = _mm256_set1_epi8((char)0x80);
    __m256i pixel_threshold = _mm256_set1_epi8(threshold);
    __m256i pixel_threshold2 = _mm256_sub_epi8(pixel_threshold, pixel_sf);

    for (size_t i = 0; i < num_pixels; i += num_simd_elements)
    {
        // Load next block of 32 pixels
        __m256i pixel_vals_u8x32 = _mm256_load_si256((__m256i*)&pb_src[i]);

        // Calculate and save mask pixels
        pixel_vals_u8x32 = _mm256_sub_epi8(pixel_vals_u8x32, pixel_sf);

        __m256i mask_vals_u8x32 = _mm256_cmpgt_epi8(pixel_vals_u8x32, pixel_threshold2);
        _mm256_store_si256((__m256i*)&pb_mask[i], mask_vals_u8x32);
    }
}
```

```
void CalcImageMean_Cpp(ITD* itd)
{
    uint8_t* pb_src = itd->m_PbSrc;
    uint8_t* pb_mask = itd->m_PbMask;
    size_t num_pixels = itd->m_NumPixels;
    uint64_t sum_masked_pixels = 0;
    uint64_t num_masked_pixels = 0;

    for (size_t i = 0; i < num_pixels; i++)
    {
        uint8_t mask_val = *pb_mask++;
        num_masked_pixels += mask_val & 1;
        sum_masked_pixels += (*pb_src++ & mask_val);
    }

    itd->m_NumMaskedPixels = num_masked_pixels;
    itd->m_SumMaskedPixels = sum_masked_pixels;

    if (num_masked_pixels > 0)
        itd->m_MeanMaskedPixels = (double)sum_masked_pixels / num_masked_pixels;
    else
        itd->m_MeanMaskedPixels = -1.0;
}

void CalcImageMean_Iavx2(ITD* itd)
{
    uint8_t* pb_src = itd->m_PbSrc;
    uint8_t* pb_mask = itd->m_PbMask;
    size_t num_pixels = itd->m_NumPixels;
    const size_t num_simd_elements = c_NumSimdElements;

    __m256i count_mask_u8x32 = _mm256_set1_epi8(0x01);
    __m256i num_masked_pixels_u32x8 = _mm256_setzero_si256();
    __m256i sum_masked_pixels_u32x8 = _mm256_setzero_si256();

    for (size_t i = 0; i < num_pixels; i += num_simd_elements)
    {
        // Load the next block of 32 image pixels and the corresponding mask pixels
        __m256i pixel_vals_u8x32 = _mm256_load_si256((__m256i*)&pb_src[i]);
        __m256i mask_vals_u8x32 = _mm256_load_si256((__m256i*)&pb_mask[i]);

        // Update num_masked_pixels
        __m256i temp0 = SumMasked_u8x32(mask_vals_u8x32, count_mask_u8x32);
        num_masked_pixels_u32x8 = _mm256_add_epi32(num_masked_pixels_u32x8, temp0);

        // Update sum_masked_pixels
        __m256i temp1 = SumMasked_u8x32(pixel_vals_u8x32, mask_vals_u8x32);
        sum_masked_pixels_u32x8 = _mm256_add_epi32(sum_masked_pixels_u32x8, temp1);
    }
```

```
// Calculate mean and save results
uint64_t num_masked_pixels = Sum_u32x8(num_masked_pixels_u32x8);
uint64_t sum_masked_pixels = Sum_u32x8(sum_masked_pixels_u32x8);
itd->m_NumMaskedPixels = num_masked_pixels;
itd->m_SumMaskedPixels = sum_masked_pixels;

if (num_masked_pixels > 0)
    itd->m_MeanMaskedPixels = (double)sum_masked_pixels / num_masked_pixels;
else
    itd->m_MeanMaskedPixels = -1;
}
```

The algorithm used in example Ch04_06 consists of two phases. The first phase constructs the mask image shown in Figure 4-8. The second phase computes the mean intensity of all pixels in the original grayscale image whose corresponding mask pixel is white (i.e., above the specified threshold).

Listing 4-6 begins with the definition of a structure named ITD, which contains the thresholding algorithm data. Note that this structure includes two distinct pixel count members: m_NumPixels and m_NumMaskedPixels. The former member is the total number of image pixels, while the latter member represents the number of grayscale image pixels greater than m_Threshold. The next file in Listing 4-6, Ch04_06_misc.cpp, contains the CheckArgs() function for this example. This is followed by the file Ch04_06. cpp. In this file, the function ProcessImage() includes code that initializes two instances of IDT. It also invokes the calculating functions and saves the results. Like the previous example, ProcessImage() uses the C++ class ImageMatrix to handle the minutiae of PNG image file loading and saving.

The final file in Listing 4-6 is Ch04_06_fcpp.cpp. Near the top of this file is the definition of an inline function named Sum_u32x8(). This function sums the eight 32-bit integer elements of SIMD argument x. Note that Sum_u32x8() uses the C++ SIMD intrinsic function _mm256_extract_epi32() to extract each 32-bit from argument x. Using extract operations here allows straightforward calculation of the return value, which is a scalar integer of type uint64_t. Following Sum_u32x8() is another inline function named SumMasked_u8x32(). This function size-promotes and partially sums the 32 8-bit integer values in argument a_u8x32 using only those pixels whose corresponding element in argument mask_u8x32 is set to 0xFF. Figure 4-9 illustrates this operation in greater detail. Function SumMasked_u8x32() returns an __m256i type of eight 32-bit integers, and these values are used by the SIMD calculating functions described later in this section.

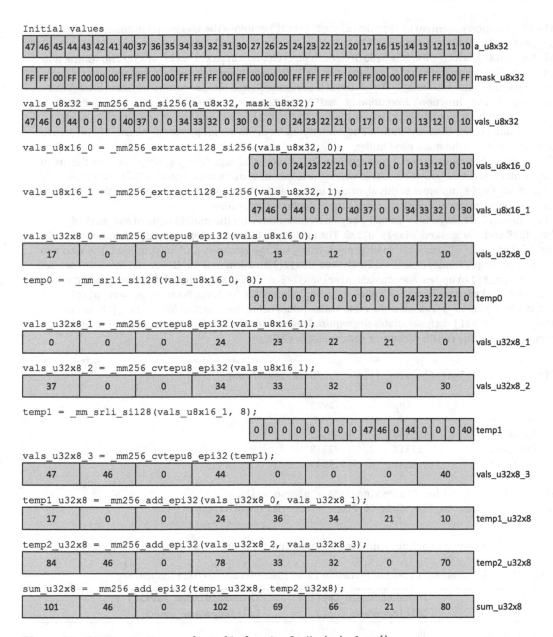

*Figure 4-9.* *SIMD operations performed in function SumMasked_u8x32()*

The next function in file Ch04_06_fcpp.cpp is named ThresholdImage_Cpp(). This function implements the image thresholding algorithm using standard C++ statements. The SIMD counterpart of ThresholdImage_Cpp() is named ThresholdImage_Iavx2(). Following argument validation, ThresholdImage_Iavx2() sets each 8-bit integer element of pixel_sf to 0x80. The variable pixel_sf is used to rescale the image's pixel values for reasons that will be explained shortly. Then the next two C++ SIMD intrinsic function calls, _mm256_set1_epi8() and _mm256_sub_epi8(), create a packed version of m_Threshold.

The first for-loop statement in `ThresholdImage_Iavx2()` employs the C++ SIMD intrinsic function `_mm256_load_si256()` to load a block of 32 pixels from the source pixel buffer. This is followed by a call to `_mm256_sub_epi8()`, which subtracts 0x80 from each pixel element in `pixel_vals_u8x32`. The subtraction operation rescales each pixel from [0, 255] to [-128, 127]. The reason for doing this is that the next C++ SIMD intrinsic function call, `_mm256_cmpgt_epi8()`, performs signed integer compares (there is no AVX2 `_mm256_cmpgt_epu8()` function). Execution of `_mm256_cmpgt_epi8()` yields the 256-bit wide value `mask_vals_u8x32`. Each 8-bit element of this mask is either 0x00 (pixel value less than or equal to threshold) or 0xFF (pixel value greater than threshold). The final statement of the for-loop, `_mm256_store_si256()`, saves the calculated mask to the mask pixel buffer.

The final two functions in file `CalcImageMean_Cpp()` and `CalcImageMean_Iavx2()` calculate the mean intensity of all pixels in the grayscale image whose corresponding mask image pixel is 0xFF. Function `CalcImageMean_Cpp()` implements this algorithm using standard C++ statements. Note that the for-loop in this function performs its calculations using simple Boolean expressions.

The function `CalcImageMean_Iavx2()` begins its execution with the initialization of `num_masked_pixels_u32x8` and `sum_masked_pixels_u32x8`. The for-loop in `CalcImageMean_Iavx2()` commences with two `_mm256_load_si256()` calls that load 32 pixels from both the grayscale and mask images. The next two statements use the previously described `SumMasked_u8x32()` function and the C++ SIMD intrinsic function `_mm256_add_epi32()` to update `num_masked_pixels_u32x8`. A similar sequence of function calls is then used to update `sum_masked_pixels_u32x8`. Following completion of the for-loop, both `num_masked_pixels_u32x8` and `sum_masked_pixels_u32x8` are reduced to scalar values using the function `Sum_u32x8()`. Function `CalcImageMean_Iavx2()` then calculates the required mean intensity value using scalar floating-point arithmetic. Here are the results for source code example Ch04_06:

```
Results for ProcessImage() using file ../../Data/ImageA.png

                        Cpp          Iavx2
-------------------------------------------------
SumPixelsMasked:      6555340        6555340
NumPixelsMasked:        27318          27318
MeanMaskedPixels:     239.9641       239.9641

Running benchmark function ProcessImage_Bm - please wait
Benchmark times save to file Ch04_06_ProcessImage_bm_OXYGEN4.csv
```

Table 4-3 shows some benchmark timing measurements for source code example Ch04_06.

*Table 4-3.* *Pixel Thresholding Algorithm Execution Times (Microseconds) Using* ImageA.png

| CPU | ThresholdImage_Cpp() + CalcImageMean_Cpp() | ThresholdImage_Iavx2() + CalcImageMean_Iavx2() |
|---|---|---|
| Intel Core i7-8700K | 2341 | 278 |
| Intel Core i5-11600K | 1654 | 204 |

You may have noticed the gap in the mask image of Figure 4-8. This is caused by the shadow that the left tusk casts over the right tusk. To address artifacts like this, real-word image processing often requires a pixel cleanup or border refinement step following a thresholding operation. Appendix B contains some helpful references that you can consult for additional information about thresholding and image processing algorithms.

# Pixel Conversions

To implement certain image processing algorithms, it is often necessary to convert the pixel values of a grayscale image from 8 bits [0, 255] to normalized floating point [0.0, 1.0]. The final source code example of this chapter, Ch04_07, demonstrates how to perform this type of conversion using a simple lookup table (LUT) and gather operations. Listing 4-7 shows the source code for example Ch04_07.

*Listing 4-7.* Example Ch04_07

```
//-------------------------------------------------
//                  Ch04_07.h
//-------------------------------------------------

#pragma once
#include <cstddef>
#include <cstdint>

// Ch04_07_fcpp.cpp
extern void ConvertU8ToF32_Cpp(float* pb_des, const uint8_t* pb_src, size_t num_pixels);
extern void ConvertU8ToF32_Iavx2(float* pb_des, const uint8_t* pb_src, size_t num_pixels);

// Ch04_07_misc.cpp
extern void BuildLUT_U8ToF32(void);
extern bool CheckArgs(const void* pb1, const void* pb2, size_t num_pixels);
extern size_t CompareArraysF32(const float* pb_src1, const float* pb_src2, size_t num_
pixels);

// Ch04_07_bm.cpp
extern void ConvertU8ToF32_bm(void);

// Miscellaneous constants
const size_t c_Alignment = 32;
const size_t c_NumPixels = 1024 * 1024 + 19;
const size_t c_NumPixelsBM = 10000000;
const size_t c_NumPixelsMax = 16 * 1024 * 1024;
const int c_FillMinVal = 0;
const int c_FillMaxVal = 255;
const unsigned int c_RngSeed = 71;
extern float g_LUT_U8ToF32[];

//-------------------------------------------------
//                  Ch04_07_misc.cpp
//-------------------------------------------------

#include <iostream>
#include "Ch04_07.h"
#include "AlignedMem.h"

float g_LUT_U8ToF32[256];
```

```cpp
void BuildLUT_U8ToF32(void)
{
    size_t n = sizeof(g_LUT_U8ToF32) / sizeof(float);

    for (size_t i = 0; i < n; i++)
        g_LUT_U8ToF32[i] = (float)i / 255.0f;
}

bool CheckArgs(const void* pb1, const void* pb2, size_t num_pixels)
{
    if (num_pixels == 0 || num_pixels > c_NumPixelsMax)
        return false;
    if (!AlignedMem::IsAligned(pb1, c_Alignment))
        return false;
    if (!AlignedMem::IsAligned(pb2, c_Alignment))
        return false;
    return true;
}

size_t CompareArraysF32(const float* pb_src1, const float* pb_src2, size_t num_pixels)
{
    size_t num_diff = 0;

    for (size_t i = 0; i < num_pixels; i++)
    {
        if (pb_src1[i] != pb_src2[i])
        {
            std::cout << i << ", " << pb_src1[i] << ", " << pb_src2[i] << '\n';
            num_diff++;
        }
    }

    return num_diff;
}

//--------------------------------------------------
//                  Ch04_07.cpp
//--------------------------------------------------

#include <iostream>
#include <iomanip>
#include <stdexcept>
#include "Ch04_07.h"
#include "AlignedMem.h"
#include "MT.h"

static void ConvertU8ToF32();

int main()
{
    try
```

```cpp
    {
        BuildLUT_U8ToF32();
        ConvertU8ToF32();
        ConvertU8ToF32_bm();
    }

    catch (std::exception& ex)
    {
        std::cout << "Ch04_07 exception: " << ex.what() << '\n';
    }
}

static void ConvertU8ToF32()
{
    const char nl = '\n';
    size_t num_pixels = c_NumPixels;
    AlignedArray<uint8_t> pb_src_aa(num_pixels, c_Alignment);
    AlignedArray<float> pb_des0_aa(num_pixels, c_Alignment);
    AlignedArray<float> pb_des1_aa(num_pixels, c_Alignment);
    uint8_t* pb_src = pb_src_aa.Data();
    float* pb_des0 = pb_des0_aa.Data();
    float* pb_des1 = pb_des1_aa.Data();

    MT::FillArray(pb_src, num_pixels, c_FillMinVal, c_FillMaxVal, c_RngSeed);
    ConvertU8ToF32_Cpp(pb_des0, pb_src, num_pixels);
    ConvertU8ToF32_Iavx2(pb_des1, pb_src, num_pixels);

    std::cout << "\nResults for ConvertU8ToF32\n";
    size_t num_diff = CompareArraysF32(pb_des0, pb_des1, num_pixels);
    std::cout << "  num_pixels: " << num_pixels << nl;
    std::cout << "  num_diff:   " << num_diff << nl;
}

//--------------------------------------------------
//                  Ch04_07_fcpp.cpp
//--------------------------------------------------

#include <stdexcept>
#include <immintrin.h>
#include "Ch04_07.h"

void ConvertU8ToF32_Cpp(float* pb_des, const uint8_t* pb_src, size_t num_pixels)
{
    if (!CheckArgs(pb_des, pb_src, num_pixels))
        throw std::runtime_error("ConvertU8ToF32_Cpp() CheckArgs failed");

    const float* lut = g_LUT_U8ToF32;
    for (size_t i = 0; i < num_pixels; i++)
        pb_des[i] = lut[pb_src[i]];
}
```

```
void ConvertU8ToF32_Iavx2(float* pb_des, const uint8_t* pb_src, size_t num_pixels)
{
    if (!CheckArgs(pb_des, pb_src, num_pixels))
        throw std::runtime_error("ConvertU8ToF32_Iavx2() CheckArgs failed");

    size_t i = 0;
    const size_t num_simd_elements = 32;
    const float* lut = g_LUT_U8ToF32;
    for (; num_pixels - i >= num_simd_elements; i += num_simd_elements)
    {
        // Load next block of 32 pixels
        __m256i pixel_vals_u8x32 = _mm256_load_si256((__m256i*)&pb_src[i]);
        __m128i pixel_vals_u8x16_0 = _mm256_extracti128_si256(pixel_vals_u8x32, 0);
        __m128i pixel_vals_u8x16_1 = _mm256_extracti128_si256(pixel_vals_u8x32, 1);

        // Convert pixels pb_src[0:15] from U8 to F32
        __m256i pixel_vals_u32x8_0 = _mm256_cvtepu8_epi32(pixel_vals_u8x16_0);
        __m256 pixel_vals_f32x8_0 = _mm256_i32gather_ps(lut, pixel_vals_u32x8_0, 4);
        __m128i temp0 = _mm_srli_si128(pixel_vals_u8x16_0, 8);
        __m256i pixel_vals_u32x8_1 = _mm256_cvtepu8_epi32(temp0);
        __m256 pixel_vals_f32x8_1 = _mm256_i32gather_ps(lut, pixel_vals_u32x8_1, 4);

        // Convert pixels pb_src[16:31] from U8 to F32
        __m256i pixel_vals_u32x8_2 = _mm256_cvtepu8_epi32(pixel_vals_u8x16_1);
        __m256 pixel_vals_f32x8_2 = _mm256_i32gather_ps(lut, pixel_vals_u32x8_2, 4);
        __m128i temp1 = _mm_srli_si128(pixel_vals_u8x16_1, 8);
        __m256i pixel_vals_u32x8_3 = _mm256_cvtepu8_epi32(temp1);
        __m256 pixel_vals_f32x8_3 = _mm256_i32gather_ps(lut, pixel_vals_u32x8_3, 4);

        // Save results
        _mm256_store_ps(&pb_des[i], pixel_vals_f32x8_0);
        _mm256_store_ps(&pb_des[i + 8], pixel_vals_f32x8_1);
        _mm256_store_ps(&pb_des[i + 16], pixel_vals_f32x8_2);
        _mm256_store_ps(&pb_des[i + 24], pixel_vals_f32x8_3);
    }

    // Process final block of pixels
    for (; i < num_pixels; i++)
        pb_des[i] = lut[pb_src[i]];
}
```

Listing 4-7 begins with the file Ch04_07.h, which includes the function declarations for this example. The next file, Ch04_07_misc.cpp, opens with the definition of a function named BuildLUT_U8ToF32(). This function builds a 256-element LUT of single-precision floating-point values ranging from 0.0 to 1.0. Each entry in the LUT will be used to match an 8-bit grayscale pixel value to its normalized single-precision floating-point counterpart (e.g., 0 = 0.0, 1 = 0.0039215, 2 = 0.0078431, ... 255 = 1.0). The remaining functions in Ch04_07_misc.cpp, CheckArgs() and CompareArraysF32(), are used by the calculating functions to validate arguments and compare results.

The next file in Listing 4-7 is named Ch04_07.cpp. This file includes the function main(). Note that main() calls BuildLUT_U8ToF32() to build the pixel conversion LUT. Also present in Ch04_07.cpp is the function ConvertU8ToF32(). This function initializes the test arrays, calls the conversion functions ConvertU8ToF32_Cpp() and ConvertU8ToF32_Iavx2(), and displays results.

The file Ch04_07_fcpp.cpp begins with the conversion function ConvertU8ToF32_Cpp(). This function converts an array of uint8_t values to normalized single-precision floating-point values. Following argument validation, function ConvertU8ToF32_Cpp() calls GetLUT_U8ToF32() to obtain a pointer to conversion LUT. The next block of code contains a simple two-statement for-loop that converts each pixel from uint8_t to single-precision floating-point.

The SIMD counterpart of ConvertU8ToF32_Cpp() is named ConvertU8ToF32_Iavx2(). This function employs SIMD techniques to carry out packed uint8_t to single-precision floating-point conversions. The first for-loop in ConvertU8ToF32_Iavx2() begins each iteration with a call to the C++ SIMD function _mm256_load_si256(), which loads 32 uint8_t values from pb_src into pixel_vals_u8x32. The ensuing two _mm256_extracti128_si256() calls extract pb_src[0:15] and pb_src[16:31] from pixel_vals_u8x32.

The next code block converts pixels pb_src[0:15] from uint8_t to single-precision floating-point. It begins with a call to the C++ SIMD intrinsic function _mm256_cvtepu8_epi32, which size-promotes the eight low-order pixel values in pixel_vals_u8x16_0 from 8-bit integers to 32-bit integers. These integer values are used as indices into the LUT by the ensuing call to _mm256_i32gather_ps(). The function _mm256_i32gather_ps() loads eight elements from an array and packs these elements into an __mm256 object. The specific elements loaded from the array are designated by the second argument of _mm256_i32gather_ps(), which contains array indices. Figure 4-10 illustrates this process in greater detail. The next three function calls, _mm_srli_si128(), _mm256_cvtepu8_epi32(), and _mm256_i32gather_ps(), convert the eight high-order pixel values in pixel_vals_u8x16_0.

Initial values

| 0.000000 | 0.003921 | 0.007843 | ... | | 0.992156 | 0.996078 | 1.000000 | lut |
|----------|----------|----------|-----|-----|----------|----------|----------|-----|
| 0 | 1 | 2 | | | 253 | 254 | 255 | |

| 12 | 2 | 188 | 253 | 0 | 135 | 255 | 87 | pixel_vals_u32x8_0 |
|----|---|-----|-----|---|-----|-----|----|--------------------|

pixel_vals_f32x8_0 = _mm256_i32gather_ps(lut, pixel_vals_u32x8_0, 4);

| 0.047058 | 0.007843 | 0.737254 | 0.992156 | 0.000000 | 0.529411 | 1.000000 | 0.341176 | pixel_vals_f32x8_0 |
|----------|----------|----------|----------|----------|----------|----------|----------|--------------------|

***Figure 4-10.*** *Packed 32-bit integer to packed single-precision floating-point using _mm256_i32gather_ps()*

The remaining code in the for-loop converts pixels pb_src[16:31] using the same technique. This is followed by a series of calls to _mm256_store_ps(), which saves the converted floating-point values. The second for-loop in ConvertU8ToF32_Iavx2() processes any residual pixels if num_pixels is not an integral multiple of 32. Here are the results for source code example Ch04_07:

```
Results for ConvertU8ToF32
  num_pixels: 1048595
  num_diff:    0

Running benchmark function ConvertU8ToF32_bm - please wait
Benchmark times save to file Ch04_07_ConvertU8ToF32_bm_OXYGEN4.csv
```

Table 4-4 shows some benchmark timing measurements for source code example Ch04_07.

*Table 4-4.* *Pixel Conversion Algorithm Execution Times (Microseconds) Using 10,000,000 Pixels*

| CPU | ConvertU8ToF32_Cpp() | ConvertU8ToF32_Iavx2() |
|---|---|---|
| Intel Core i7-8700K | 3397 | 2893 |
| Intel Core i5-11600K | 2788 | 2456 |

# Summary

Table 4-5 summarizes the C++ SIMD intrinsic functions introduced in this chapter along with other commonly used type variants. Before proceeding to the next chapter, you should understand the SIMD arithmetic calculation or data manipulation operation that is performed by each function shown in Table 4-5.

*Table 4-5.* *C++ SIMD Intrinsic Function Summary for Chapter 4*

| C++ SIMD Function Names | Description |
|---|---|
| _mm_loadl_epi64 | Load 64-bit integer into low-order element |
| _mm_popcnt_u32, _u64 | Count number of bits set to one |
| _mm256_abs_epi8, _epi16, _epi32 | Packed integer absolute value |
| _mm256_add_epi8, _epi16, _epi32, _epi64 | Packed integer addition |
| _mm256_adds_epi8, _epi16 | Packed signed integer addition (saturated) |
| _mm256_and_si256 | Bitwise logical AND |
| _mm256_cmpeq_epi8, _epi16, _epi32, _epi64 | Packed integer signed compare (equal) |
| _mm256_cmpgt_epi8, _epi16, _epi32, _epi64 | Packed integer signed compare (greater than) |
| _mm256_cvtepi16_epi32 | Packed integer sign-extend (16 bits to 32 bits) |
| _mm256_cvtepi32_ps | Packed signed integer to packed single precision |
| _mm256_cvtepu8_epi16, _epi32, _epi64 | Packed integer zero-extend |
| _mm256_cvtps_epi32 | Packed single precision to packed signed integer |
| _mm256_extract_epi32, _epi64 | Extract integer |
| _mm256_extracti128_si256 | Extract 128-bit wide packed integer data |
| _mm256_i32gather_psf | Gather single-precision elements using 32-bit indices |
| _mm256_load_si256 | Load (aligned) 256-bit wide packed integers |
| _mm256_max_epi8, _epi16, _epi32 | Packed integer signed maximum |
| _mm256_max_epu8, _epu16, _epu32 | Packed integer unsigned maximum |

*(continued)*

***Table 4-5.*** (*continued*)

| C++ SIMD Function Names | Description |
| --- | --- |
| _mm256_min_epi8, _epi16, _epi32 | Packed integer signed minimum |
| _mm256_min_epu8, _epu16, _epu32 | Packed integer unsigned minimum |
| _mm256_movemask_epi8 | Build mask using the most significant bit |
| _mm256_mullo_epi32 | Packed signed integer multiplication (low result) |
| _mm256_packs_epi16, _epi32 | Convert packed integers using signed saturation |
| _mm256_packus_epi16, _epi32 | Convert packed integers using unsigned saturation |
| _mm256_permute4x64_epi64 | Permute 64-bit integer |
| _mm256_set1_epi8, _epi16, _epi32, _epi64x | Broadcast integer value to all elements |
| _mm256_set1_pd, _ps | Broadcast floating-point value to all elements |
| _mm256_setzero_si256 | Set packed integers to all zeros |
| _mm256_sllv_epi32, _epi64 | Packed integer shift left logical |
| _mm256_srav_epi32 | Packed integer shift right arithmetic |
| _mm256_srli_epi32 | Packed integer shift right logical |
| _mm256_store_si256 | Store (aligned) 256-bit wide packed integers |
| _mm256_sub_epi8, _epi16, _epi32, _epi64 | Packed integer subtraction |
| _mm256_subs_epi8, _epi16 | Packed signed integer subtraction (saturated) |
| _mm256_subs_epu8, _epu16 | Packed unsigned integer subtraction (saturated) |
| _mm256_unpackhi_epi8, _epi16, _epi32, _epi64 | Unpack and interleave integers (upper bits of each lane) |
| _mm256_unpacklo_epi8, _epi16, _epi32, _epi64 | Unpack and interleave integers (lower bits of each lane) |

# CHAPTER 5

▦ ▦ ▦

# AVX2 C++ Programming: Part 2

In Chapter 3, you learned how to carry out elementary arithmetic using packed floating-point operands and AVX C++ SIMD intrinsic functions. You also learned how to code simple SIMD functions that performed computations using the elements of a floating-point array or matrix. In this chapter, you will study source code examples that perform floating-point calculations using AVX2 and C++ SIMD intrinsic functions. The first section highlights an array-based algorithm that demonstrates a least-squares calculation using double-precision SIMD arithmetic. The second section includes several examples that illustrate how to perform common matrix arithmetic using either packed single-precision or double-precision floating-point operands. As you will soon see, SIMD techniques are suitable for matrix arithmetic.

As a reminder, the source code examples in this chapter (and the next one) require a processor and operating system that support AVX2. You can use one of the free utilities listed in Appendix B to verify that your computer meets this requirement.

## Floating-Point Arrays

Source code examples Ch03_04 through Ch03_07 spotlighted SIMD calculations using single-precision and double-precision floating-point arrays. Later in this section, you will examine another SIMD processing algorithm that uses floating-point arrays. This one differs from the examples you saw in Chapter 3 in that it uses fused-multiply-add (FMA) arithmetic. Before looking at the source code for the next example, a few words about FMA operations are warranted.

When performing elementary floating-point arithmetic (e.g., addition, subtraction, multiplication, etc.), the processor executes a distinct rounding step as part of the computation. Rounding operations are defined as part of the IEEE-754 standard for floating-point arithmetic. X86-64 processors support several different floating-point rounding modes and you will learn more about these in Chapters 10 and 12. An FMA calculation combines multiplication and addition (or subtraction) into a single operation. More specifically, a fused-multiply-add (or fused-multiply-subtract) computation performs a multiplication followed by an addition (or subtraction) using only a single rounding operation instead of two.

Consider, for example, the expression $a = b * c + d$. Using standard floating-point arithmetic, the processor initially calculates the product $b * c$, and this calculation includes a rounding step. It then performs the floating-point addition, which also includes a rounding step. If the expression $a = b * c + d$ is evaluated using FMA arithmetic, the processor does not round the intermediate product $b * c$. Rounding is carried out only once using the calculated product-sum $b * c + d$. FMA operations are often used to improve the performance and accuracy of multiply-accumulate computations such as dot products, matrix-vector multiplications, and convolutions. On x86 processors, the FMA instruction set is a distinct extension just like AVX or AVX2. This means that you must never assume a processor supports FMA just because it also supports AVX or AVX2. You should always test for the presence of the FMA instruction set extension. You will learn how to do this in Chapter 9.

© Daniel Kusswurm 2022
D. Kusswurm, *Modern Parallel Programming with C++ and Assembly Language*,
https://doi.org/10.1007/978-1-4842-7918-2_5

## Least Squares

Simple linear regression is a statistical technique that models a linear relationship between two variables. One popular method of simple linear regression is called least-squares fitting. This method uses a set of sample data points to determine a best-fit curve between the two variables. When used with a simple linear regression mode, the curve is a straight line whose equation is $y = mx + b$. In this equation, $x$ denotes the independent variable, $y$ denotes the dependent (or measured) variable, $m$ is the line's slope, and $b$ is the line's y-axis intercept point. The slope and intercept point of a least-squares line are determined using a series of computations that minimize the sum of the squared deviations between the line and the sample data points. Following calculation of its slope and intercept, a least-squares line is often used to predict an unknown $y$ value using a known $x$ value. Appendix B contains some references that you can consult if you are interested in learning more about linear regression and least-squares fitting.

The following equations are used to calculate the slope and intercept point of a least-squares line:

$$m = \frac{n\sum_i x_i y_i - \sum_i x_i \sum_i y_i}{n\sum_i x_i^2 - \left(\sum_i x_i\right)^2}$$

$$b = \frac{\sum_i x_i^2 \sum_i y_i - \sum_i x_i \sum_i x_i y_i}{n\sum_i x_i^2 - \left(\sum_i x_i\right)^2}$$

At first glance, the slope and intercept equations may appear a little daunting. However, upon closer examination, a couple of simplifications become apparent. First, the slope and intercept denominators are the same, which means that this quantity only needs to be computed once. Second, it is only necessary to calculate four simple summation values (or sum variables) as shown in the following equations:

$$sum_x = \sum_i x_i$$

$$sum_y = \sum_i y_i$$

$$sum_{xy} = \sum_i x_i y_i$$

$$sum_{xx} = \sum_i x_i^2$$

Following calculation of the sum variables, the least-squares slope and intercept point are easily derived using simple scalar floating-point arithmetic. Source code example Ch05_01, shown in Listing 5-1, details the calculation of a least-squares regression line using packed double-precision floating-point arithmetic.

***Listing 5-1.*** Example Ch05_01

```
//--------------------------------------------------
//              Ch05_01.h
//--------------------------------------------------

#pragma once

// Ch05_01_fcpp.cpp
extern void CalcLeastSquares_Cpp(double* m, double* b, const double* x,
```

```
        const double* y, size_t n);
extern void CalcLeastSquares_Iavx2(double* m, double* b, const double* x,
    const double* y, size_t n);

// Ch05_01_misc.cpp
extern bool CheckArgs(const double* x, const double* y, size_t n);
extern void FillArrays(double* x, double* y, size_t n);

// Miscellaneous constants
const size_t c_Alignment = 32;
const double c_LsEpsilon = 1.0e-12;

//--------------------------------------------------
//                  Ch05_01_misc.cpp
//--------------------------------------------------

#include <cmath>
#include "Ch05_01.h"
#include "AlignedMem.h"
#include "MT.h"

bool CheckArgs(const double* x, const double* y, size_t n)
{
    if (n < 2)
        return false;
    if (!AlignedMem::IsAligned(x, c_Alignment))
        return false;
    if (!AlignedMem::IsAligned(y, c_Alignment))
        return false;

    return true;
}

void FillArrays(double* x, double* y, size_t n)
{
    const unsigned int rng_seed1 = 73;
    const unsigned int rng_seed2 = 83;
    const double fill_min_val = -25.0;
    const double fill_max_val = 25.0;

    MT::FillArrayFP(x, n, fill_min_val, fill_max_val, rng_seed1);
    MT::FillArrayFP(y, n, fill_min_val, fill_max_val, rng_seed2);

    for (size_t i = 0; i < n; i++)
        y[i] = y[i] * y[i];
}

//--------------------------------------------------
//                  Ch05_01.cpp
//--------------------------------------------------
```

```cpp
#include <iostream>
#include <iomanip>
#include "Ch05_01.h"
#include "AlignedMem.h"

static void CalcLS(void);

int main()
{
    try
    {
        CalcLS();
    }

    catch (std::exception& ex)
    {
        std::cout << "Ch05_01 exception: " << ex.what() << '\n';
    }

    return 0;
}

void CalcLS(void)
{
    const size_t n = 59;
    AlignedArray<double> x_aa(n, c_Alignment);
    AlignedArray<double> y_aa(n, c_Alignment);
    double* x = x_aa.Data();
    double* y = y_aa.Data();

    FillArrays(x, y, n);

    double m1, m2;
    double b1, b2;
    CalcLeastSquares_Cpp(&m1, &b1, x, y, n);
    CalcLeastSquares_Iavx2(&m2, &b2, x, y, n);

    size_t w = 12;
    const char nl = '\n';
    std::cout << std::fixed << std::setprecision(8);

    std::cout << "\nCalcLeastSquares_Cpp Results\n";
    std::cout << "  slope:     " << std::setw(w) << m1 << nl;
    std::cout << "  intercept: " << std::setw(w) << b1 << nl;
    std::cout << "\nCalcLeastSquares_Iavx2 Results\n";
    std::cout << "  slope:     " << std::setw(w) << m2 << nl;
    std::cout << "  intercept: " << std::setw(w) << b2 << nl;
}
```

```cpp
//-------------------------------------------------
//                Ch05_01_fcpp.cpp
//-------------------------------------------------

#include <cmath>
#include <stdexcept>
#include <immintrin.h>
#include "Ch05_01.h"

void CalcLeastSquares_Cpp(double* m, double* b, const double* x, const double* y, size_t n)
{
    *m = 0.0;
    *b = 0.0;

    if (!CheckArgs(x, y, n))
        throw std::runtime_error("CalcLeastSquares_cpp() CheckArgs failed");

    double sum_x = 0.0, sum_y = 0.0, sum_xx = 0.0, sum_xy = 0.0;

    for (size_t i = 0; i < n; i++)
    {
        sum_x += x[i];
        sum_y += y[i];
        sum_xx += x[i] * x[i];
        sum_xy += x[i] * y[i];
    }

    double denom = n * sum_xx - sum_x * sum_x;

    if (fabs(denom) >= c_LsEpsilon)
    {
        *m = (n * sum_xy - sum_x * sum_y) / denom;
        *b = (sum_xx * sum_y - sum_x * sum_xy) / denom;
    }
}

inline double SumF64x4(__m256d x)
{
    double sum;
    __m128d temp0 = _mm256_extractf128_pd(x, 0);
    __m128d temp1 = _mm256_extractf128_pd(x, 1);
    __m128d temp2 = _mm_add_pd(temp0, temp1);
    __m128d temp3 = _mm_hadd_pd(temp2, temp2);

    _mm_store_sd(&sum, temp3);
    return sum;
}
```

```
void CalcLeastSquares_Iavx2(double* m, double* b, const double* x, const double* y,
size_t n)
{
    *m = 0.0;
    *b = 0.0;

    if (!CheckArgs(x, y, n))
        throw std::runtime_error("CalcLeastSquares_Iavx2() CheckArgs failed");

    __m256d packed_sum_x = _mm256_setzero_pd();
    __m256d packed_sum_y = _mm256_setzero_pd();
    __m256d packed_sum_xx = _mm256_setzero_pd();
    __m256d packed_sum_xy = _mm256_setzero_pd();

    size_t i = 0;
    const size_t num_simd_elements = 4;

    for (; n - i >= num_simd_elements; i += num_simd_elements)
    {
        __m256d x_vals = _mm256_load_pd(&x[i]);
        __m256d y_vals = _mm256_load_pd(&y[i]);

        packed_sum_x = _mm256_add_pd(packed_sum_x, x_vals);
        packed_sum_y = _mm256_add_pd(packed_sum_y, y_vals);
        packed_sum_xx = _mm256_fmadd_pd(x_vals, x_vals, packed_sum_xx);
        packed_sum_xy = _mm256_fmadd_pd(x_vals, y_vals, packed_sum_xy);
    }

    // Reduce packed sum values to scalars
    double sum_x = SumF64x4(packed_sum_x);
    double sum_y = SumF64x4(packed_sum_y);
    double sum_xx = SumF64x4(packed_sum_xx);
    double sum_xy = SumF64x4(packed_sum_xy);

    // Process final values
    for (; i < n; i++)
    {
        sum_x += x[i];
        sum_y += y[i];
        sum_xx += x[i] * x[i];
        sum_xy += x[i] * y[i];
    }

    // Calculate slope and intercept
    double denom = n * sum_xx - sum_x * sum_x;

    if (fabs(denom) >= c_LsEpsilon)
    {
        *m = (n * sum_xy - sum_x * sum_y) / denom;
        *b = (sum_xx * sum_y - sum_x * sum_xy) / denom;
    }
}
```

The first file in Listing 5-1 is the header file Ch05_01.h, and this file contains the function declarations for this example. The next file in Listing 5-1 is Ch05_01_misc.cpp, which includes the function definitions for CheckArgs() and FillArrays(). The former function is used by the least-squares calculating functions to validate arguments. The latter function contains code that fills two double-precision floating-point test arrays with random values. The file Ch05_01.cpp contains the function CalcLS(). This function is responsible for test array allocation and initialization, calling the calculating functions, and streaming the results to std::cout.

The first function in Ch05_01_fcpp.cpp is named CalcLeastSquares_Cpp(). This function calculates a least-squares slope and intercept point using standard C++ statements and is included for comparison purposes. Note that the for-loop in CalcLeastSquares_Cpp() contains only four executable code statements. These statements correspond to the equations for the previously defined sum variables. Following execution of the for-loop, CalcLeastSquares_Cpp() verifies that fabs(denom) >= c_LsEpsilon is true before calculating the final slope and intercept point. If this expression is false, the variable denom is considered too close to zero to be valid.

Following CalcLeastSquares_Cpp() is a short inline helper function named SumF64x4(). This function sums the four double-precision elements of an __m256d data type.

The SIMD counterpart of CalcLeastSquares_Cpp() is named CalcLeastSquares_Iavx2(). Subsequent to argument validation, CalcLeastSquares_Iavx2() uses four consecutive calls to _mm256_setzero_pd() to initialize packed_sum_x, packed_sum_y, packed_sum_xx, and packed_sum_xy. The first for-loop in CalcLeastSquares_Iavx2() begins each iteration with two _mm256_load_pd() calls that load x[i:i+3] and y[i:i+3] into x_vals and y_vals, respectively. It then uses the C++ SIMD intrinsic function _mm256_add_pd() to update packed_sum_x and packed_sum_y.

Next is a call to _mm256_fmadd_pd(), which updates the variable packed_sum_xx. CalcLeastSquares_Iavx2() employs this C++ SIMD intrinsic function to calculate packed_sum_xx[0:3] += x_vals[i:i+3] * x_vals[i:i+3] using FMA arithmetic. Another call to _mm256_fmadd_pd() updates the variable packed_sum_xy and calculates packed_sum_xy[0:3] += x_vals[i:i+3] * y_vals[i:i+3]. Following the summation for-loop, the four packed variable sums are reduced to scalar values using SumF64x4(). The function CalcLeastSquares_Iavx2() then executes a second for-loop to process any residual elements. Calculation of the slope and mean is carried out using scalar floating-point arithmetic. Here are the results for source code example Ch05_01:

---

```
CalcLeastSquares_Cpp Results
  slope:        -1.00874909
  intercept:  196.22610714

CalcLeastSquares_Iavx2 Results
  slope:        -1.00874909
  intercept:  196.22610714
```

---

# Floating-Point Matrices

Many software applications make extensive use of matrices. For example, 3D computer graphics software typically employs matrices to perform common transformations such as translation, scaling, and rotation. When using homogeneous coordinates, each of these operations can be efficiently represented using a single 4 × 4 matrix. Multiple transformations also can be applied by merging a series of distinct transformation matrices into a single matrix using matrix multiplication. This combined matrix is typically applied to an array of object vertices. It is important for 3D computer graphics (or similar) software to carry out operations such as matrix-matrix or matrix-vector multiplication as quickly as possible since 3D models often contain thousands or millions of object vertices.

In this section, you will examine several source code examples that utilize C++ SIMD intrinsic functions to perform common matrix operations. The first section explains how to perform matrix-matrix multiplication. The second and third sections contain code that illustrates matrix-matrix and matrix-vector multiplication using 4 × 4 matrices and 4 × 1 vectors. The final section expounds matrix inversion.

## Matrix Multiplication

The product of two matrices is defined as follows. Let **A** be an $m \times p$ matrix where $m$ and $p$ denote the number of rows and columns, respectively. Let **B** be a $p \times n$ matrix. The matrix product **C** = **AB** is an $m \times n$ matrix where the value of each $c(i, j)$ in **C** is calculated using the following equation:

$$c_{ij} = \sum_{k=0}^{p-1} a_{ik} b_{kj} \quad i = 0,\ldots,m-1; \quad j = 0,\ldots,n-1$$

Note that the matrix multiplication equation uses zero-based subscripts since this simplifies translating the equation into C++ source code; most mathematical texts use one-based subscripts.

According to the definition of matrix multiplication, the number of columns in **A** must equal the number of rows in **B**. For example, if **A** is a 3 × 4 matrix and **B** is a 4 × 2 matrix, the product **AB** is a 3 × 2 matrix but the product **BA** is undefined. Note that each element $c(i, j)$ in **C** is simply the dot product (or inner product) of row $i$ in matrix **A** and column $j$ in matrix **B**. Dot product calculations are relatively easy to implement using FMA C++ SIMD intrinsic functions.

The archetypal method for calculating the product of two matrices using scalar arithmetic employs three nested for-loops to implement the previously defined matrix equation. The same technique can be utilized when employing SIMD techniques but with some minor modifications. The reason for this is that depending on the matrix sizes, a subset of the calculations may need to be carried out using partially filled SIMD data types. Figure 5-1 shows a block diagram of matrix **C** ($m \times n$), which is the product of matrix **A** ($m \times p$) and matrix **B** ($p \times n$). Note that the SIMD element groups in each row of **C**, except for the far right one, contain eight elements. If the number of columns in matrix **C** is not an integral multiple of eight, each row in matrix **C** will also contain a residual SIMD element group that contains between one and seven elements.

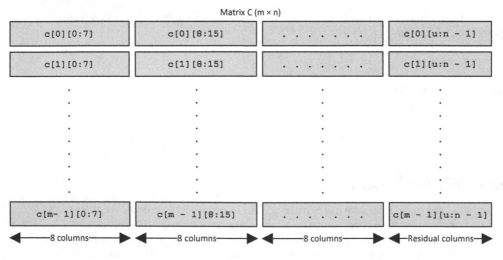

Matrix C (m × n)

| c[0][0:7] | c[0][8:15] | . . . . . . | c[0][u:n - 1] |
| c[1][0:7] | c[1][8:15] | . . . . . . | c[1][u:n - 1] |

| c[m- 1][0:7] | c[m - 1][8:15] | . . . . . . | c[m - 1][u:n - 1] |

◄——8 columns——► ◄——8 columns——► ◄——8 columns——► ◄—Residual columns—►

Notes:
Number of residual columns equals n % 8. if (n % 8) != 0 then u = n - (n % 8)

***Figure 5-1.*** *SIMD element groups for matrix* **C** *(m × n)*

Figure 5-2 underscores the handling of residual elements when using SIMD arithmetic to calculate a matrix product. In this figure, assume that matrix **A** is $5 \times 6$ and matrix **B** is $6 \times 10$. The first row of **C** = **AB**, where matrix **C** is $5 \times 10$, can be calculated using the equations shown in Figure 5-2. Note that the computations for matrix elements $c(0, 0)$ through $c(0, 7)$ can be carried out using an eight-element SIMD data type such as __m256. The two residual elements in the first row, $c(0, 8)$ and $c(0, 9)$, must be handled differently since there are fewer than eight elements. These elements can be calculated using masked load and store operations as you will soon see.

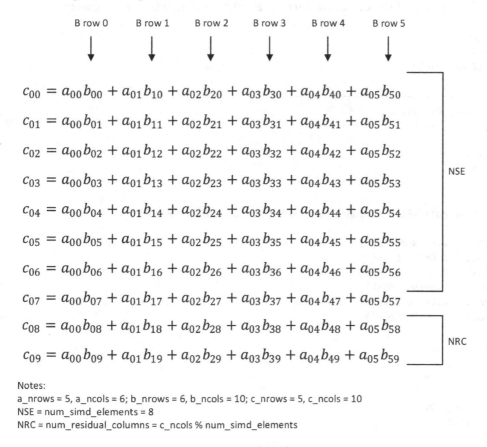

$$c_{00} = a_{00}b_{00} + a_{01}b_{10} + a_{02}b_{20} + a_{03}b_{30} + a_{04}b_{40} + a_{05}b_{50}$$

$$c_{01} = a_{00}b_{01} + a_{01}b_{11} + a_{02}b_{21} + a_{03}b_{31} + a_{04}b_{41} + a_{05}b_{51}$$

$$c_{02} = a_{00}b_{02} + a_{01}b_{12} + a_{02}b_{22} + a_{03}b_{32} + a_{04}b_{42} + a_{05}b_{52}$$

$$c_{03} = a_{00}b_{03} + a_{01}b_{13} + a_{02}b_{23} + a_{03}b_{33} + a_{04}b_{43} + a_{05}b_{53}$$

$$c_{04} = a_{00}b_{04} + a_{01}b_{14} + a_{02}b_{24} + a_{03}b_{34} + a_{04}b_{44} + a_{05}b_{54}$$

$$c_{05} = a_{00}b_{05} + a_{01}b_{15} + a_{02}b_{25} + a_{03}b_{35} + a_{04}b_{45} + a_{05}b_{55}$$

$$c_{06} = a_{00}b_{06} + a_{01}b_{16} + a_{02}b_{26} + a_{03}b_{36} + a_{04}b_{46} + a_{05}b_{56}$$

$$c_{07} = a_{00}b_{07} + a_{01}b_{17} + a_{02}b_{27} + a_{03}b_{37} + a_{04}b_{47} + a_{05}b_{57}$$

$$c_{08} = a_{00}b_{08} + a_{01}b_{18} + a_{02}b_{28} + a_{03}b_{38} + a_{04}b_{48} + a_{05}b_{58}$$

$$c_{09} = a_{00}b_{09} + a_{01}b_{19} + a_{02}b_{29} + a_{03}b_{39} + a_{04}b_{49} + a_{05}b_{59}$$

Notes:
a_nrows = 5, a_ncols = 6; b_nrows = 6, b_ncols = 10; c_nrows = 5, c_ncols = 10
NSE = num_simd_elements = 8
NRC = num_residual_columns = c_ncols % num_simd_elements

***Figure 5-2.*** *SIMD equations for a matrix product (one row)*

Listing 5-2 shows the source code for example Ch05_02. This example illustrates how to perform matrix multiplication using two matrices and FMA C++ SIMD intrinsic functions.

***Listing 5-2.*** Example Ch05_02

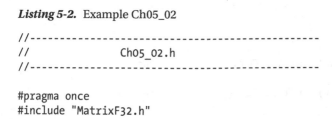

```
//-------------------------------------------------
//                  Ch05_02.h
//-------------------------------------------------

#pragma once
#include "MatrixF32.h"
```

```cpp
// Ch05_02_fcpp.cpp
void MatrixMulF32_Cpp(MatrixF32& c, const MatrixF32& a, const MatrixF32& b);
void MatrixMulF32_Iavx2(MatrixF32& c, const MatrixF32& a, const MatrixF32& b);

// Ch05_02_misc.cpp
bool CheckArgs(const MatrixF32& c, const MatrixF32& a, const MatrixF32& b);
void InitMat(MatrixF32& c1, MatrixF32& c2, MatrixF32& a, MatrixF32& b);
void SaveResults(const MatrixF32& c1, const MatrixF32& c2, const MatrixF32& a, const
MatrixF32& b);

// Ch05_02_bm.cpp
void MatrixMulF32_bm(void);

//-------------------------------------------------
//                  Ch05_02_misc.cpp
//-------------------------------------------------

#include <fstream>
#include "Ch05_02.h"
#include "MT.h"

bool CheckArgs(const MatrixF32& c, const MatrixF32& a, const MatrixF32& b)
{
    size_t a_nrows = a.GetNumRows();
    size_t a_ncols = a.GetNumCols();
    size_t b_nrows = b.GetNumRows();
    size_t b_ncols = b.GetNumCols();
    size_t c_nrows = c.GetNumRows();
    size_t c_ncols = c.GetNumCols();

    if (a_ncols != b_nrows)
        return false;
    if (c_nrows != a_nrows)
        return false;
    if (c_ncols != b_ncols)
        return false;
    return true;
}

void InitMat(MatrixF32& c1, MatrixF32& c2, MatrixF32& a, MatrixF32& b)
{
    int rng_min = 2;
    int rng_max = 50;
    unsigned int rng_seed_a = 42;
    unsigned int rng_seed_b = 43;

    MT::FillMatrix(a.Data(), a.GetNumRows(), a.GetNumCols(), rng_min, rng_max,
        rng_seed_a, true);
    MT::FillMatrix(b.Data(), b.GetNumRows(), b.GetNumCols(), rng_min, rng_max,
        rng_seed_b, true);
```

```
    const int w = 8;
    c1.SetOstreamW(w);
    c2.SetOstreamW(w);
    a.SetOstreamW(w);
    b.SetOstreamW(w);
}

void SaveResults(const MatrixF32& c1, const MatrixF32& c2, const MatrixF32& a, const
MatrixF32& b)
{
    const char nl = '\n';

    std::string fn("Ch05_02_MatrixMulF32_");
    fn += OS::GetComputerName();
    fn += std::string(".txt");

    std::ofstream ofs(fn);
    ofs << "\nMatrix a\n" << a << nl;
    ofs << "\nMatrix b\n" << b << nl;
    ofs << "\nMatrix c1\n" << c1 << nl;
    ofs << "\nMatrix c2\n" << c2 << nl;
    ofs.close();
    std::cout << "Results saved to file " << fn << nl;
}

//-------------------------------------------------
//              Ch05_02.cpp
//-------------------------------------------------

#include <iostream>
#include <iomanip>
#include "Ch05_02.h"

static void MatrixMulF32(void);

int main()
{
    try
    {
        MatrixMulF32();
        MatrixMulF32_bm();
    }

    catch (std::exception& ex)
    {
        std::cout << "Ch05_02 exception: " << ex.what() << '\n';
    }

    return 0;
}
```

```
static void MatrixMulF32()
{
    const size_t a_nrows = 11;
    const size_t a_ncols = 13;
    const size_t b_nrows = a_ncols;
    const size_t b_ncols = 19;
    const size_t c_nrows = a_nrows;
    const size_t c_ncols = b_ncols;

    MatrixF32 a(a_nrows, a_ncols);
    MatrixF32 b(b_nrows, b_ncols);
    MatrixF32 c1(c_nrows, c_ncols);
    MatrixF32 c2(c_nrows, c_ncols);

    InitMat(c1, c2, a, b);
    MatrixMulF32_Cpp(c1, a, b);
    MatrixMulF32_Iavx2(c2, a, b);

    const float epsilon = 1.0e-9f;
    bool ie12 = MatrixF32::IsEqual(c1, c2, epsilon);

    std::cout << "Results for MatrixMulF32\n";

    if (ie12)
        std::cout << "Matrix compare passed\n";
    else
        std::cout << "Matrix compare failed!\n";

    SaveResults(c1, c2, a, b);
}
//-------------------------------------------------
//                 Ch05_02_fcpp.cpp
//-------------------------------------------------

#include <stdexcept>
#include <immintrin.h>
#include "Ch05_02.h"

const uint32_t ZR = 0;
const uint32_t MV = 0x80000000;

alignas(32) const uint32_t c_Mask0[8] {ZR, ZR, ZR, ZR, ZR, ZR, ZR, ZR};
alignas(32) const uint32_t c_Mask1[8] {MV, ZR, ZR, ZR, ZR, ZR, ZR, ZR};
alignas(32) const uint32_t c_Mask2[8] {MV, MV, ZR, ZR, ZR, ZR, ZR, ZR};
alignas(32) const uint32_t c_Mask3[8] {MV, MV, MV, ZR, ZR, ZR, ZR, ZR};
alignas(32) const uint32_t c_Mask4[8] {MV, MV, MV, MV, ZR, ZR, ZR, ZR};
alignas(32) const uint32_t c_Mask5[8] {MV, MV, MV, MV, MV, ZR, ZR, ZR};
alignas(32) const uint32_t c_Mask6[8] {MV, MV, MV, MV, MV, MV, ZR, ZR};
alignas(32) const uint32_t c_Mask7[8] {MV, MV, MV, MV, MV, MV, MV, ZR};
```

```cpp
const uint32_t* c_MaskMovLUT[8]
{
    c_Mask0, c_Mask1, c_Mask2, c_Mask3, c_Mask4, c_Mask5, c_Mask6, c_Mask7
};

void MatrixMulF32_Cpp(MatrixF32& c, const MatrixF32& a, const MatrixF32& b)
{
    MatrixF32::Mul(c, a, b);
}

void MatrixMulF32_Iavx2(MatrixF32& c, const MatrixF32& a, const MatrixF32& b)
{
    if (!CheckArgs(c, a, b))
        throw std::runtime_error("MatrixMulF32_Iavx2() CheckArgs failed");

    const float* aa = a.Data();
    const float* bb = b.Data();
    float* cc = c.Data();
    size_t c_nrows = c.GetNumRows();
    size_t c_ncols = c.GetNumCols();
    size_t a_ncols = a.GetNumCols();
    size_t b_ncols = b.GetNumCols();

    const size_t num_simd_elements = 8;
    size_t num_residual_cols = c_ncols % num_simd_elements;
    __m256i res_mask = _mm256_load_si256((__m256i*)c_MaskMovLUT[num_residual_cols]);

    // Repeat for each row in c
    for (size_t i = 0; i < c_nrows; i++)
    {
        size_t j = 0;

        // Repeat while 8 or more columns remain
        while (j + num_simd_elements <= c_ncols)
        {
            __m256 c_vals = _mm256_setzero_ps();

            // Calculate products for c[i][j:j+7]
            for (size_t k = 0; k < a_ncols; k++)
            {
                __m256 a_vals = _mm256_broadcast_ss(&aa[i * a_ncols + k]);
                __m256 b_vals = _mm256_loadu_ps(&bb[k * b_ncols + j]);

                c_vals = _mm256_fmadd_ps(a_vals, b_vals, c_vals);
            }

            _mm256_storeu_ps(&cc[i * c_ncols + j], c_vals);
            j += num_simd_elements;
        }
```

```
        if (num_residual_cols)
        {
            __m256 c_vals = _mm256_setzero_ps();

            for (size_t k = 0; k < a_ncols; k++)
            {
                __m256 a_vals = _mm256_broadcast_ss(&aa[i * a_ncols + k]);
                __m256 b_vals = _mm256_maskload_ps(&bb[k * b_ncols + j], res_mask);

                c_vals = _mm256_fmadd_ps(a_vals, b_vals, c_vals);
            }

            _mm256_maskstore_ps(&cc[i * c_ncols + j], res_mask, c_vals);
        }
    }
}
```

Starting with file Ch05_02.h in Listing 5-2, note that the function declarations make use of the MatrixF32 class that was introduced in Chapter 3 (see example Ch03_08). Next in Listing 5-3 is the file Ch05_02_misc.cpp. The first function in this file is named CheckArgs(). This function verifies the sizes of the matrices used by the SIMD calculating code. The other two functions in this file, InitMat() and SaveResults(), carry out matrix initialization and file save operations. In this example, the calculated matrix products are written to a text file since this avoids any console screen size constraints when using large matrices. The file Ch05_02.cpp contains the function MatrixMulF32(), which performs test case initialization for this example. This function also invokes the matrix multiplication calculating and result saving functions.

The file Ch05_02_fcpp.cpp begins with a series of eight arrays named c_Mask0–c_Mask7. The SIMD matrix multiplication function MatrixMulF32_Iavx2() uses these arrays to perform masked load and store operations for any residual columns. More on this in a moment. The first function in Ch05_02_fcpp.cpp, MatrixMulF32_Cpp(), uses the member function MatrixF32::Mul() to carry out matrix multiplication sans any SIMD code. The code in MatrixF32::Mul() uses the conventional three for-loop construct to carry out the calculations defined in the matrix multiplication equation. The source code for this function is not shown in Listing 5-2 but is included in the software download package.

The SIMD counterpart of MatrixMulF32_Iavx2() is named MatrixMulF32_Iavx2(). Following argument validation, MatrixMulF32_Iavx2() obtains size and buffer data for matrix arguments a, b, and c. It then initializes num_simd_elements to eight and num_res_cols to c_ncols % num_simd_elements. The ensuing call to _mm256_load_si256() uses num_res_cols to initialize res_mask, which is employed in the for-loop to perform residual column masked loads and stores.

The matrix product calculation code in MatrixMulF32_Iavx2() uses three for-loops. The outer-most for-loop selects the target row in matrix c. The code block that begins with the while statement computes elements c[i][j:j+7]. Note that the while block repeats so long as j + num_simd_elements <= c_ncols is true. The inner for-loop of the while block uses SIMD C++ intrinsic functions to perform a SIMD dot product computation. The function _mm256_broadcast_ss() loads the required element from matrix a; the function _mm256_loadu_ps() loads a row from matrix b; and the function _mm256_fmadd_ps() calculates sum-of-products. Note that these three operations are the same as the ones shown Figure 5-2.

The code block that begins with the test of num_residual_cols calculates the products for any residual columns in matrix c. This block differs from the previous one in that it uses the C++ SIMD intrinsic functions _mm256_maskload_ps() and _mm256_maskstore_ps() to carry our masked load and store operations. Function _mm256_maskload_ps() only loads an element from the specified source buffer if the most significant bit of the corresponding element in res_mask is set to one; otherwise, the target element is set to zero. Figure 5-3 illustrates execution of _mm256_maskload_ps() in greater detail. The function _mm256_

maskstore_ps() performs a masked store operation and is also depicted in Figure 5-3. In MatrixMulF32_
Iavx2(), the low-order num_residual_cols elements of res_mask are set to 0x80000000, which ensures that
functions _mm256_maskload_ps() and _mm256_maskstore_ps() only access the residual columns of matrices
b and c.

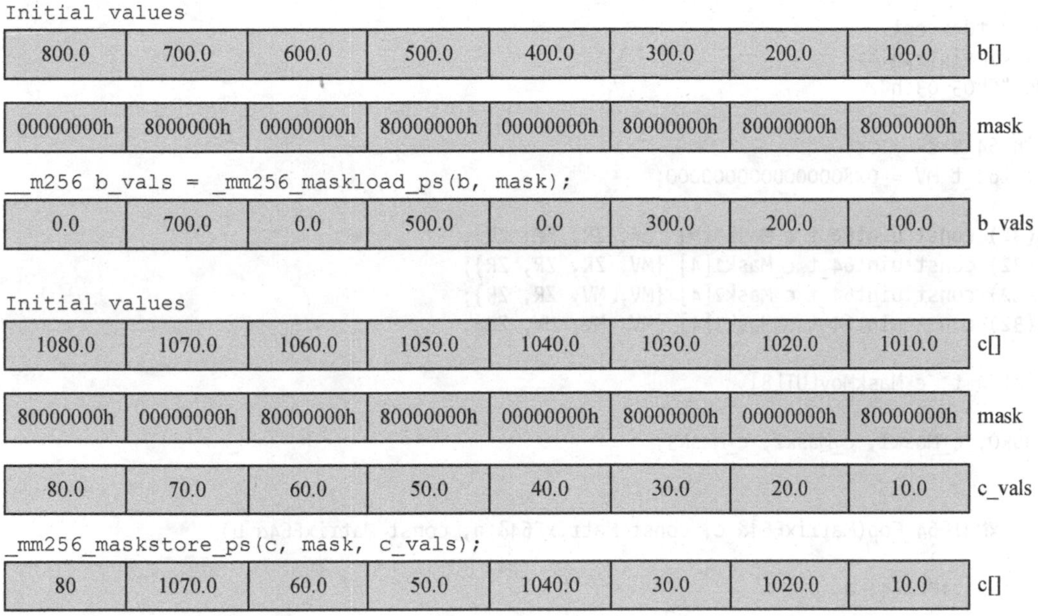

Initial values

| 800.0 | 700.0 | 600.0 | 500.0 | 400.0 | 300.0 | 200.0 | 100.0 | b[] |

| 00000000h | 8000000h | 00000000h | 80000000h | 00000000h | 80000000h | 80000000h | 80000000h | mask |

__m256 b_vals = _mm256_maskload_ps(b, mask);

| 0.0 | 700.0 | 0.0 | 500.0 | 0.0 | 300.0 | 200.0 | 100.0 | b_vals |

Initial values

| 1080.0 | 1070.0 | 1060.0 | 1050.0 | 1040.0 | 1030.0 | 1020.0 | 1010.0 | c[] |

| 80000000h | 00000000h | 80000000h | 80000000h | 00000000h | 80000000h | 00000000h | 80000000h | mask |

| 80.0 | 70.0 | 60.0 | 50.0 | 40.0 | 30.0 | 20.0 | 10.0 | c_vals |

_mm256_maskstore_ps(c, mask, c_vals);

| 80 | 1070.0 | 60.0 | 50.0 | 1040.0 | 30.0 | 1020.0 | 10.0 | c[] |

*Figure 5-3.* *Execution of _mm256_maskload_ps() and _mm256_maskstore_ps()*

Here are the results for source code example Ch05_02:

```
Results for MatrixMulF32
Matrix compare passed
Results saved to file Ch05_02_MatrixMulF32_OXYGEN4.txt

Running benchmark function MatrixMulF32_bm - please wait
Benchmark times save to file Ch05_02_MatrixMulF32_bm_OXYGEN4.csv
```

Table 5-1 shows some benchmark timing measurements for source code example Ch05_02. These
measurements were made using 250 × 250 matrices.

*Table 5-1.* *Matrix Multiplication (Single-Precision) Execution Times (Microseconds)*

| CPU | MatrixMulF32_Cpp() | MatrixMulF32_Iavx2() |
| --- | --- | --- |
| Intel Core i7-8700K | 12339 | 1606 |
| Intel Core i5-11600K | 10411 | 1380 |

Listing 5-3 shows the SIMD calculating code for source code example Ch05_03, which performs double-
precision floating-point matrix multiplication.

*Listing 5-3.* Example Ch05_03

```cpp
//-------------------------------------------------
//                 Ch05_03_fcpp.cpp
//-------------------------------------------------

#include <stdexcept>
#include <immintrin.h>
#include "Ch05_03.h"

const uint64_t ZR = 0;
const uint64_t MV = 0x8000000000000000;

alignas(32) const uint64_t c_Mask0[4] {ZR, ZR, ZR, ZR};
alignas(32) const uint64_t c_Mask1[4] {MV, ZR, ZR, ZR};
alignas(32) const uint64_t c_Mask2[4] {MV, MV, ZR, ZR};
alignas(32) const uint64_t c_Mask3[4] {MV, MV, MV, ZR};

const uint64_t* c_MaskMovLUT[8]
{
    c_Mask0, c_Mask1, c_Mask2, c_Mask3,
};

void MatrixMulF64_Cpp(MatrixF64& c, const MatrixF64& a, const MatrixF64& b)
{
    MatrixF64::Mul(c, a, b);
}

void MatrixMulF64_Iavx2(MatrixF64& c, const MatrixF64& a, const MatrixF64& b)
{
    if (!CheckArgs(c, a, b))
        throw std::runtime_error("MatrixMulF64_Iavx2() CheckArgs failed");

    const double* aa = a.Data();
    const double* bb = b.Data();
    double* cc = c.Data();
    size_t c_nrows = c.GetNumRows();
    size_t c_ncols = c.GetNumCols();
    size_t a_ncols = a.GetNumCols();
    size_t b_ncols = b.GetNumCols();

    const size_t num_simd_elements = 4;
    size_t num_residual_cols = c_ncols % num_simd_elements;
    __m256i res_mask = _mm256_load_si256((__m256i*)c_MaskMovLUT[num_residual_cols]);

    // Repeat for each row in c
    for (size_t i = 0; i < c_nrows; i++)
    {
        size_t j = 0;
```

```
    // Repeat while 4 or more columns remain
    while (j + num_simd_elements <= c_ncols)
    {
        __m256d c_vals = _mm256_setzero_pd();

        // Calculate products for c[i][j:j+3]
        for (size_t k = 0; k < a_ncols; k++)
        {
            __m256d a_vals = _mm256_broadcast_sd(&aa[i * a_ncols + k]);
            __m256d b_vals = _mm256_loadu_pd(&bb[k * b_ncols + j]);

            c_vals = _mm256_fmadd_pd(a_vals, b_vals, c_vals);
        }

        _mm256_storeu_pd(&cc[i * c_ncols + j], c_vals);
        j += num_simd_elements;
    }

    if (num_residual_cols)
    {
        __m256d c_vals = _mm256_setzero_pd();

        for (size_t k = 0; k < a_ncols; k++)
        {
            __m256d a_vals = _mm256_broadcast_sd(&aa[i * a_ncols + k]);
            __m256d b_vals = _mm256_maskload_pd(&bb[k * b_ncols + j], res_mask);

            c_vals = _mm256_fmadd_pd(a_vals, b_vals, c_vals);
        }

        _mm256_maskstore_pd(&cc[i * c_ncols + j], res_mask, c_vals);
    }
  }
}
```

The layout of `MatrixMulF64_Iavx2()` mostly parallels its single-precision counterpart `MatrixMulF32_Iavx2()`. Differences include setting `num_simd_elements` to four instead of eight and the use of the double-precision variants of the C++ SIMD intrinsic functions. Also note that 64-bit wide integers are utilized for `res_mask`. The output for source code example Ch05_03 is the same as Ch05_02.

# Matrix (4 × 4) Multiplication

Matrix multiplication using 4 × 4 matrices is another common operation in many programs. For small matrices like this, some programmers prefer to code size-optimized matrix multiplication functions to improve performance. In this section, you will learn how to code SIMD matrix multiplication functions that have been optimized for 4 × 4 matrices.

If the matrix multiplication equation is explicitly expanded for 4 × 4 matrix multiplication, the equations shown in Figure 5-4 are obtained. Just like the previous two examples, these equations are easy to implement using FMA SIMD C++ intrinsic functions. Note that these equations can be coded sans any for-loops, which often results in improved performance.

161

$$\begin{bmatrix} c_{00} & c_{01} & c_{02} & c_{03} \\ c_{10} & c_{11} & c_{12} & c_{13} \\ c_{20} & c_{21} & c_{22} & c_{23} \\ c_{30} & c_{31} & c_{32} & c_{33} \end{bmatrix} = \begin{bmatrix} a_{00} & a_{01} & a_{02} & a_{03} \\ a_{10} & a_{11} & a_{12} & a_{13} \\ a_{20} & a_{21} & a_{22} & a_{23} \\ a_{30} & a_{31} & a_{32} & a_{33} \end{bmatrix} \begin{bmatrix} b_{00} & b_{01} & b_{02} & b_{03} \\ b_{10} & b_{11} & b_{12} & b_{13} \\ b_{20} & b_{21} & b_{22} & b_{23} \\ b_{30} & b_{31} & b_{32} & b_{33} \end{bmatrix}$$

$$c_{00} = a_{00}b_{00} + a_{01}b_{10} + a_{02}b_{20} + a_{03}b_{30}$$

$$c_{01} = a_{00}b_{01} + a_{01}b_{11} + a_{02}b_{21} + a_{03}b_{31}$$

$$c_{02} = a_{00}b_{02} + a_{01}b_{12} + a_{02}b_{22} + a_{03}b_{32}$$

$$c_{03} = a_{00}b_{03} + a_{01}b_{13} + a_{02}b_{23} + a_{03}b_{33}$$

$$c_{10} = a_{10}b_{00} + a_{11}b_{10} + a_{12}b_{20} + a_{13}b_{30}$$

$$c_{11} = a_{10}b_{01} + a_{11}b_{11} + a_{12}b_{21} + a_{13}b_{31}$$

$$c_{12} = a_{10}b_{02} + a_{11}b_{12} + a_{12}b_{22} + a_{13}b_{32}$$

$$c_{13} = a_{10}b_{03} + a_{11}b_{13} + a_{12}b_{23} + a_{13}b_{33}$$

$$c_{20} = a_{20}b_{00} + a_{21}b_{10} + a_{22}b_{20} + a_{23}b_{30}$$

$$c_{21} = a_{20}b_{01} + a_{21}b_{11} + a_{22}b_{21} + a_{23}b_{31}$$

$$c_{22} = a_{20}b_{02} + a_{21}b_{12} + a_{22}b_{22} + a_{23}b_{32}$$

$$c_{23} = a_{20}b_{03} + a_{21}b_{13} + a_{22}b_{23} + a_{23}b_{33}$$

$$c_{30} = a_{30}b_{00} + a_{31}b_{10} + a_{32}b_{20} + a_{33}b_{30}$$

$$c_{31} = a_{30}b_{01} + a_{31}b_{11} + a_{32}b_{21} + a_{33}b_{31}$$

$$c_{32} = a_{30}b_{02} + a_{31}b_{12} + a_{32}b_{22} + a_{33}b_{32}$$

$$c_{33} = a_{30}b_{03} + a_{31}b_{13} + a_{32}b_{23} + a_{33}b_{33}$$

***Figure 5-4.*** *Matrix multiplication equations using 4 × 4 matrices*

Listing 5-4 shows the source code for example Ch05_04. This example illustrates 4 × 4 matrix multiplication using single-precision floating-point values.

***Listing 5-4.*** Example Ch05_04

```
//---------------------------------------------------
//                  Ch05_04.h
//---------------------------------------------------

#pragma once
#include "MatrixF32.h"

// Ch05_04_fcpp.cpp
extern void MatrixMul4x4F32_Cpp(MatrixF32& c, const MatrixF32& a,
    const MatrixF32& b);
extern void MatrixMul4x4F32_Iavx2(MatrixF32& c, const MatrixF32& a,
    const MatrixF32& b);

// Ch05_04_misc.cpp
extern void InitMat(MatrixF32& c1, MatrixF32& c2, MatrixF32& a, MatrixF32& b);

// Ch05_04_bm.cpp
extern void MatrixMul4x4F32_bm(void);

//---------------------------------------------------
//                  Ch05_04_misc.cpp
//---------------------------------------------------

#include "Ch05_04.h"

void InitMat(MatrixF32& c1, MatrixF32& c2, MatrixF32& a, MatrixF32& b)
{
    const float a_row0[] = { 10, 11, 12, 13 };
    const float a_row1[] = { 20, 21, 22, 23 };
    const float a_row2[] = { 30, 31, 32, 33 };
    const float a_row3[] = { 40, 41, 42, 43 };

    const float b_row0[] = { 100, 101, 102, 103 };
    const float b_row1[] = { 200, 201, 202, 203 };
    const float b_row2[] = { 300, 301, 302, 303 };
    const float b_row3[] = { 400, 401, 402, 403 };

    a.SetRow(0, a_row0);
    a.SetRow(1, a_row1);
    a.SetRow(2, a_row2);
    a.SetRow(3, a_row3);

    b.SetRow(0, b_row0);
    b.SetRow(1, b_row1);
    b.SetRow(2, b_row2);
    b.SetRow(3, b_row3);
```

```
    const int w = 12;
    const char* delim = "   ";
    c1.SetOstream(w, delim);
    c2.SetOstream(w, delim);
    a.SetOstream(w, delim);
    b.SetOstream(w, delim);
}
//------------------------------------------------
//                  Ch05_04.cpp
//------------------------------------------------

#include <iostream>
#include <iomanip>
#include "Ch05_04.h"

static void MatrixMul4x4F32(void);

int main()
{
    try
    {
        MatrixMul4x4F32();
        MatrixMul4x4F32_bm();
    }

    catch (std::exception& ex)
    {
        std::cout << "Ch05_04 exception: " << ex.what() << '\n';
    }

    return 0;
}

static void MatrixMul4x4F32(void)
{
    const char nl = '\n';
    const size_t nrows = 4;
    const size_t ncols = 4;
    MatrixF32 a(nrows, ncols);
    MatrixF32 b(nrows, ncols);
    MatrixF32 c1(nrows, ncols);
    MatrixF32 c2(nrows, ncols);

    InitMat(c1, c2, a, b);

    MatrixMul4x4F32_Cpp(c1, a, b);
    MatrixMul4x4F32_Iavx2(c2, a, b);

    std::cout << std::fixed << std::setprecision(1);
```

```
    std::cout << "\nResults for MatrixMul4x4F32\n";
    std::cout << "Matrix a\n" << a << nl;
    std::cout << "Matrix b\n" << b << nl;
    std::cout << "Matrix c1\n" << c1 << nl;
    std::cout << "Matrix c2\n" << c2 << nl;

    const float epsilon = 1.0e-9f;
    bool ie12 = MatrixF32::IsEqual(c1, c2, epsilon);

    if (ie12)
        std::cout << "Matrix compare passed\n";
    else
        std::cout << "Matrix compare failed!\n";
}

//-------------------------------------------------
//                  Ch05_04_fcpp.cpp
//-------------------------------------------------

#include <immintrin.h>
#include "Ch05_04.h"

void MatrixMul4x4F32_Cpp(MatrixF32& c, const MatrixF32& a, const MatrixF32& b)
{
    MatrixF32::Mul4x4(c, a, b);
}

void MatrixMul4x4F32_Iavx2(MatrixF32& c, const MatrixF32& a, const MatrixF32& b)
{
    const float* aa = a.Data();
    const float* bb = b.Data();
    float* cc = c.Data();

    // Load rows of matrix b
    __m128 b_row0 = _mm_load_ps(&bb[0]);
    __m128 b_row1 = _mm_load_ps(&bb[4]);
    __m128 b_row2 = _mm_load_ps(&bb[8]);
    __m128 b_row3 = _mm_load_ps(&bb[12]);

    // Calculate c_row0
    __m128 a_00 = _mm_broadcast_ss(&aa[0]);          // a[0][0]
    __m128 a_01 = _mm_broadcast_ss(&aa[1]);          // a[0][1]
    __m128 a_02 = _mm_broadcast_ss(&aa[2]);          // a[0][2]
    __m128 a_03 = _mm_broadcast_ss(&aa[3]);          // a[0][3]

    __m128 c_row0 = _mm_mul_ps(a_00, b_row0);
    c_row0 = _mm_fmadd_ps(a_01, b_row1, c_row0);
    c_row0 = _mm_fmadd_ps(a_02, b_row2, c_row0);
    c_row0 = _mm_fmadd_ps(a_03, b_row3, c_row0);
    _mm_store_ps(&cc[0], c_row0);
```

```
// Calculate c_row1
__m128 a_10 = _mm_broadcast_ss(&aa[4]);          // a[1][0]
__m128 a_11 = _mm_broadcast_ss(&aa[5]);          // a[1][1]
__m128 a_12 = _mm_broadcast_ss(&aa[6]);          // a[1][2]
__m128 a_13 = _mm_broadcast_ss(&aa[7]);          // a[1][3]

__m128 c_row1 = _mm_mul_ps(a_10, b_row0);
c_row1 = _mm_fmadd_ps(a_11, b_row1, c_row1);
c_row1 = _mm_fmadd_ps(a_12, b_row2, c_row1);
c_row1 = _mm_fmadd_ps(a_13, b_row3, c_row1);
_mm_store_ps(&cc[4], c_row1);

// Calculate c_row2
__m128 a_20 = _mm_broadcast_ss(&aa[8]);          // a[2][0]
__m128 a_21 = _mm_broadcast_ss(&aa[9]);          // a[2][1]
__m128 a_22 = _mm_broadcast_ss(&aa[10]);         // a[2][2]
__m128 a_23 = _mm_broadcast_ss(&aa[11]);         // a[2][3]

__m128 c_row2 = _mm_mul_ps(a_20, b_row0);
c_row2 = _mm_fmadd_ps(a_21, b_row1, c_row2);
c_row2 = _mm_fmadd_ps(a_22, b_row2, c_row2);
c_row2 = _mm_fmadd_ps(a_23, b_row3, c_row2);
_mm_store_ps(&cc[8], c_row2);

// Calculate c_row3
__m128 a_30 = _mm_broadcast_ss(&aa[12]);         // a[3][0]
__m128 a_31 = _mm_broadcast_ss(&aa[13]);         // a[3][1]
__m128 a_32 = _mm_broadcast_ss(&aa[14]);         // a[3][2]
__m128 a_33 = _mm_broadcast_ss(&aa[15]);         // a[3][3]

__m128 c_row3 = _mm_mul_ps(a_30, b_row0);
c_row3 = _mm_fmadd_ps(a_31, b_row1, c_row3);
c_row3 = _mm_fmadd_ps(a_32, b_row2, c_row3);
c_row3 = _mm_fmadd_ps(a_33, b_row3, c_row3);
_mm_store_ps(&cc[12], c_row3);
}
```

In Listing 5-4, the files Ch05_04.h and Ch05_04_misc.cpp contain function declarations and the matrix initialization function InitMat(). The function MatrixMul4x4F32(), which is located in the file Ch05_04.cpp, performs the now familiar test case setup and results streaming to std::cout. This function also compares the products generated by the matrix multiplication calculating functions.

File Ch05_04_fcpp.cpp contains the matrix multiplication functions MatrixMul4x4F32_Cpp() and MatrixMul4x4F32_Iavx2(). Function MatrixMul4x4F32_Cpp() uses the function MatrixF32::Mul4x4() to perform matrix multiplication. This function employs standard C++ statements but has been optimized for 4 × 4 matrices. Function MatrixMul4x4F32_Iavx2() implements the previously defined equations for 4 × 4 matrix multiplication using C++ SIMD intrinsic functions. Note that this function carries out its calculation sans any for-loops, which improves performance. The elimination of for-loops, especially ones where the number of iterations is a compile time constant, is called loop unrolling (or loop unwinding). Loop unrolling is frequently used in SIMD calculating functions to accelerate performance. The same technique can also be applied to standard C++ code. The drawback of loop unrolling is larger code size. Here are the results for source code example Ch05_04:

```
Results for MatrixMul4x4F32
Matrix a
        10.0          11.0          12.0          13.0
        20.0          21.0          22.0          23.0
        30.0          31.0          32.0          33.0
        40.0          41.0          42.0          43.0

Matrix b
       100.0         101.0         102.0         103.0
       200.0         201.0         202.0         203.0
       300.0         301.0         302.0         303.0
       400.0         401.0         402.0         403.0

Matrix c1
     12000.0       12046.0       12092.0       12138.0
     22000.0       22086.0       22172.0       22258.0
     32000.0       32126.0       32252.0       32378.0
     42000.0       42166.0       42332.0       42498.0

Matrix c2
     12000.0       12046.0       12092.0       12138.0
     22000.0       22086.0       22172.0       22258.0
     32000.0       32126.0       32252.0       32378.0
     42000.0       42166.0       42332.0       42498.0

Matrix compare passed

Running benchmark function MatrixMul4x4F32_bm - please wait
Benchmark times save to file Ch05_04_MatrixMul4x4F32_bm_OXYGEN4.csv
```

Table 5-2 shows some benchmark timing measurements for source code example Ch05_04.

***Table 5-2.*** *Matrix Multiplication (4 × 4, Single-Precision) Execution Times (Microseconds), 1,000,000 Multiplications*

| CPU | MatrixMul4x4F32_Cpp() | MatrixMul4x4F32_Iavx2() |
|---|---|---|
| Intel Core i7-8700K | 15101 | 3227 |
| Intel Core i5-11600K | 14273 | 2734 |

Listing 5-5 shows the SIMD calculating code for source code example Ch05_05, which illustrates 4 × 4 matrix multiplication using double-precision floating-point elements.

***Listing 5-5.*** Example Ch05_05

```cpp
//-------------------------------------------------
//                 Ch05_05_fcpp.cpp
//-------------------------------------------------

#include <immintrin.h>
#include "Ch05_05.h"

void MatrixMul4x4F64_Cpp(MatrixF64& c, const MatrixF64& a, const MatrixF64& b)
{
    MatrixF64::Mul4x4(c, a, b);
}

void MatrixMul4x4F64_Iavx2(MatrixF64& c, const MatrixF64& a, const MatrixF64& b)
{
    const double* aa = a.Data();
    const double* bb = b.Data();
    double* cc = c.Data();

    // Load rows of matrix b
    __m256d b_row0 = _mm256_load_pd(&bb[0]);
    __m256d b_row1 = _mm256_load_pd(&bb[4]);
    __m256d b_row2 = _mm256_load_pd(&bb[8]);
    __m256d b_row3 = _mm256_load_pd(&bb[12]);

    // Calculate c_row0
    __m256d a_00 = _mm256_broadcast_sd(&aa[0]);         // a[0][0]
    __m256d a_01 = _mm256_broadcast_sd(&aa[1]);         // a[0][1]
    __m256d a_02 = _mm256_broadcast_sd(&aa[2]);         // a[0][2]
    __m256d a_03 = _mm256_broadcast_sd(&aa[3]);         // a[0][3]

    __m256d c_row0 = _mm256_mul_pd(a_00, b_row0);
    c_row0 = _mm256_fmadd_pd(a_01, b_row1, c_row0);
    c_row0 = _mm256_fmadd_pd(a_02, b_row2, c_row0);
    c_row0 = _mm256_fmadd_pd(a_03, b_row3, c_row0);
    _mm256_store_pd(&cc[0], c_row0);

    // Calculate c_row1
    __m256d a_10 = _mm256_broadcast_sd(&aa[4]);         // a[1][0]
    __m256d a_11 = _mm256_broadcast_sd(&aa[5]);         // a[1][1]
    __m256d a_12 = _mm256_broadcast_sd(&aa[6]);         // a[1][2]
    __m256d a_13 = _mm256_broadcast_sd(&aa[7]);         // a[1][3]

    __m256d c_row1 = _mm256_mul_pd(a_10, b_row0);
    c_row1 = _mm256_fmadd_pd(a_11, b_row1, c_row1);
    c_row1 = _mm256_fmadd_pd(a_12, b_row2, c_row1);
    c_row1 = _mm256_fmadd_pd(a_13, b_row3, c_row1);
    _mm256_store_pd(&cc[4], c_row1);
```

```
// Calculate c_row2
__m256d a_20 = _mm256_broadcast_sd(&aa[8]);       // a[2][0]
__m256d a_21 = _mm256_broadcast_sd(&aa[9]);       // a[2][1]
__m256d a_22 = _mm256_broadcast_sd(&aa[10]);      // a[2][2]
__m256d a_23 = _mm256_broadcast_sd(&aa[11]);      // a[2][3]

__m256d c_row2 = _mm256_mul_pd(a_20, b_row0);
c_row2 = _mm256_fmadd_pd(a_21, b_row1, c_row2);
c_row2 = _mm256_fmadd_pd(a_22, b_row2, c_row2);
c_row2 = _mm256_fmadd_pd(a_23, b_row3, c_row2);
_mm256_store_pd(&cc[8], c_row2);

// Calculate c_row3
__m256d a_30 = _mm256_broadcast_sd(&aa[12]);      // a[3][0]
__m256d a_31 = _mm256_broadcast_sd(&aa[13]);      // a[3][1]
__m256d a_32 = _mm256_broadcast_sd(&aa[14]);      // a[3][2]
__m256d a_33 = _mm256_broadcast_sd(&aa[15]);      // a[3][3]

__m256d c_row3 = _mm256_mul_pd(a_30, b_row0);
c_row3 = _mm256_fmadd_pd(a_31, b_row1, c_row3);
c_row3 = _mm256_fmadd_pd(a_32, b_row2, c_row3);
c_row3 = _mm256_fmadd_pd(a_33, b_row3, c_row3);
_mm256_store_pd(&cc[12], c_row3);
}
```

The primary difference between the functions MatrixMul4x4F32_Iavx2() and MatrixMul4x4F64_Iavx2() is that the latter uses the __m256 data type and the _pd variants of the C++ SIMD calculating functions. The output for source code example Ch05_05 is the same as Ch05_04.

# Matrix (4 × 4) Vector Multiplication

Another common matrix operation is calculating the product of a 4 × 4 matrix and 4 × 1 vector. In 3D computer graphics, these types of calculations are universally employed to perform affine transformations (e.g., translation, rotation, and scaling) using homogeneous coordinates. Figure 5-5 shows the equations required to calculate the product of a 4 × 4 matrix and 4 × 1 vector. Note that these equations use the columns of the specified matrix.

$$
\begin{bmatrix} b_w \\ b_x \\ b_y \\ b_z \end{bmatrix} = \begin{bmatrix} m_{00} & m_{01} & m_{02} & m_{03} \\ m_{10} & m_{11} & m_{12} & m_{13} \\ m_{20} & m_{21} & m_{22} & m_{23} \\ m_{30} & m_{31} & m_{32} & m_{33} \end{bmatrix} \begin{bmatrix} a_w \\ a_x \\ a_y \\ a_z \end{bmatrix}
$$

$$
b_w = m_{00}a_w + m_{01}a_x + m_{02}a_y + m_{03}a_z
$$

$$
b_x = m_{10}a_w + m_{11}a_x + m_{12}a_y + m_{13}a_z
$$

$$
b_y = m_{20}a_w + m_{21}a_x + m_{22}a_y + m_{23}a_z
$$

$$
b_z = m_{30}a_w + m_{31}a_x + m_{32}a_y + m_{33}a_z
$$

$\uparrow$ M col 0  $\qquad$ $\uparrow$ M col 1  $\qquad$ $\uparrow$ M col 2  $\qquad$ $\uparrow$ M col 3

***Figure 5-5.*** *Equations required to calculate matrix (4 × 4) and vector (4 × 1) product*

Listing 5-6 shows the source code for example Ch05_06. This example demonstrates matrix-vector (4 × 4 and 4 × 1) multiplication using single-precision floating-point values.

***Listing 5-6.*** Example Ch05_06

```
//--------------------------------------------------
//                  Ch05_06.h
//--------------------------------------------------

#pragma once
#include <cstddef>
#include "MatrixF32.h"

struct Vec4x1_F32
{
    float W, X, Y, Z;
};

// Ch05_06_fcpp.cpp
extern void MatVecMulF32_Cpp(Vec4x1_F32* vec_b, const MatrixF32& m,
    const Vec4x1_F32* vec_a, size_t num_vec);
extern void MatVecMulF32_Iavx2(Vec4x1_F32* vec_b, const MatrixF32& m,
    const Vec4x1_F32* vec_a, size_t num_vec);

// Ch05_06_misc.cpp
extern bool CheckArgs(const Vec4x1_F32* vec_b, const MatrixF32& m,
    const Vec4x1_F32* vec_a, size_t num_vec);
extern void Init(MatrixF32& m, Vec4x1_F32* va, size_t num_vec);
extern bool VecCompare(const Vec4x1_F32* v1, const Vec4x1_F32* v2);
```

```cpp
// Ch05_06_bm.cpp
extern void MatrixVecMulF32_bm(void);

// Miscellaenous constants
const size_t c_Alignment = 32;
const int c_RngMinVal = 1;
const int c_RngMaxVal = 500;
const unsigned int c_RngSeedVal = 187;

//-------------------------------------------------
//                  Ch05_06_misc.cpp
//-------------------------------------------------

#include <stdexcept>
#include <random>
#include "Ch05_06.h"
#include "MatrixF32.h"
#include "AlignedMem.h"

bool CheckArgs(const Vec4x1_F32* vec_b, const MatrixF32& m,
const Vec4x1_F32* vec_a, size_t num_vec)
{
    if (num_vec == 0)
        return false;
    if (m.GetNumRows() != 4 || m.GetNumCols() != 4)
        return false;
    if (!AlignedMem::IsAligned(m.Data(), c_Alignment))
        return false;
    if (!AlignedMem::IsAligned(vec_a, c_Alignment))
        return false;
    if (!AlignedMem::IsAligned(vec_b, c_Alignment))
        return false;
    return true;
}

void Init(MatrixF32& m, Vec4x1_F32* va, size_t num_vec)
{
    const float a_row0[] = { 2.0,  7.0,  8.0,  3.0 };
    const float a_row1[] = { 11.0, 14.0, 16.0, 10.0 };
    const float a_row2[] = { 24.0, 21.0, 27.0, 29.0 };
    const float a_row3[] = { 31.0, 34.0, 38.0, 33.0 };
    m.SetRow(0, a_row0);
    m.SetRow(1, a_row1);
    m.SetRow(2, a_row2);
    m.SetRow(3, a_row3);

    std::mt19937 rng {c_RngSeedVal};
    std::uniform_int_distribution<int> dist {c_RngMinVal, c_RngMaxVal};
```

```
    for (size_t i = 0; i < num_vec; i++)
    {
        va[i].W = (float)dist(rng);
        va[i].X = (float)dist(rng);
        va[i].Y = (float)dist(rng);
        va[i].Z = (float)dist(rng);
    }

    if (num_vec >= 4)
    {
        // Use known values for test & debug
        va[0].W =  5; va[0].X =  6; va[0].Y =  7; va[0].Z =  8;
        va[1].W = 15; va[1].X = 16; va[1].Y = 17; va[1].Z = 18;
        va[2].W = 25; va[2].X = 26; va[2].Y = 27; va[2].Z = 28;
        va[3].W = 35; va[3].X = 36; va[3].Y = 37; va[3].Z = 38;
    }
}

bool VecCompare(const Vec4x1_F32* v1, const Vec4x1_F32* v2)
{
    static const float epsilon = 1.0e-12f;

    bool b0 = (fabs(v1->W - v2->W) <= epsilon);
    bool b1 = (fabs(v1->X - v2->X) <= epsilon);
    bool b2 = (fabs(v1->Y - v2->Y) <= epsilon);
    bool b3 = (fabs(v1->Z - v2->Z) <= epsilon);
    return b0 && b1 && b2 && b3;
}

//-------------------------------------------------
//                  Ch05_06.cpp
//-------------------------------------------------

#include <iostream>
#include <iomanip>
#include <stdexcept>
#include "Ch05_06.h"
#include "MatrixF32.h"
#include "AlignedMem.h"

static void MatrixVecMulF32(void);

int main()
{
    try
    {
        MatrixVecMulF32();
        MatrixVecMulF32_bm();
    }
```

```cpp
        catch (std::exception& ex)
        {
            std::cout << "Ch05_06 exception: " << ex.what() << '\n';
        }

        return 0;
}

static void MatrixVecMulF32(void)
{
    const size_t num_vec = 10;
    MatrixF32 m(4, 4);
    AlignedArray<Vec4x1_F32> vec_a_aa(num_vec, c_Alignment);
    AlignedArray<Vec4x1_F32> vec_b1_aa(num_vec, c_Alignment);
    AlignedArray<Vec4x1_F32> vec_b2_aa(num_vec, c_Alignment);
    Vec4x1_F32* vec_a = vec_a_aa.Data();
    Vec4x1_F32* vec_b1 = vec_b1_aa.Data();
    Vec4x1_F32* vec_b2 = vec_b2_aa.Data();

    Init(m, vec_a, num_vec);
    MatVecMulF32_Cpp(vec_b1, m, vec_a, num_vec);
    MatVecMulF32_Iavx2(vec_b2, m, vec_a, num_vec);

    const unsigned int w = 8;
    std::cout << "Results for MatrixVecMulF32\n";
    std::cout << std::fixed << std::setprecision(1);

    for (size_t i = 0; i < num_vec; i++)
    {
        std::cout << "Test case #" << i << '\n';

        std::cout << "vec_b1: ";
        std::cout << "  " << std::setw(w) << vec_b1[i].W << ' ';
        std::cout << "  " << std::setw(w) << vec_b1[i].X << ' ';
        std::cout << "  " << std::setw(w) << vec_b1[i].Y << ' ';
        std::cout << "  " << std::setw(w) << vec_b1[i].Z << '\n';

        std::cout << "vec_b2: ";
        std::cout << "  " << std::setw(w) << vec_b2[i].W << ' ';
        std::cout << "  " << std::setw(w) << vec_b2[i].X << ' ';
        std::cout << "  " << std::setw(w) << vec_b2[i].Y << ' ';
        std::cout << "  " << std::setw(w) << vec_b2[i].Z << '\n';

        if (!VecCompare(&vec_b1[i], &vec_b2[i]))
            throw std::runtime_error("Error - vector compare failed");
    }
}

//--------------------------------------------------
//              Ch05_06_fcpp.cpp
//--------------------------------------------------
```

```cpp
#include <stdexcept>
#include <cstdint>
#include <immintrin.h>
#include "Ch05_06.h"
#include "MatrixF32.h"
#include "AlignedMem.h"

void MatVecMulF32_Cpp(Vec4x1_F32* vec_b, const MatrixF32& m,
const Vec4x1_F32* vec_a, size_t num_vec)
{
    if (!CheckArgs(vec_b, m, vec_a, num_vec))
        throw std::runtime_error("MatVecMulF32_Cpp() - CheckArgs failed");

    const float* mm = m.Data();

    // Calculate matrix-vector products
    for (size_t i = 0; i < num_vec; i++)
    {
        vec_b[i].W =  mm[0] * vec_a[i].W + mm[1] * vec_a[i].X;
        vec_b[i].W += mm[2] * vec_a[i].Y + mm[3] * vec_a[i].Z;

        vec_b[i].X =  mm[4] * vec_a[i].W + mm[5] * vec_a[i].X;
        vec_b[i].X += mm[6] * vec_a[i].Y + mm[7] * vec_a[i].Z;

        vec_b[i].Y =  mm[8] * vec_a[i].W + mm[9] * vec_a[i].X;
        vec_b[i].Y += mm[10] * vec_a[i].Y + mm[11] * vec_a[i].Z;

        vec_b[i].Z =  mm[12] * vec_a[i].W + mm[13] * vec_a[i].X;
        vec_b[i].Z += mm[14] * vec_a[i].Y + mm[15] * vec_a[i].Z;
    }
}

void MatVecMulF32_Iavx2(Vec4x1_F32* vec_b, const MatrixF32& m,
const Vec4x1_F32* vec_a, size_t num_vec)
{
    if (!CheckArgs(vec_b, m, vec_a, num_vec))
        throw std::runtime_error("MatVecMulF32_Iavx2() - CheckArgs failed");

    // Load matrix m
    const float* mm = m.Data();
    __m128 m_row0 = _mm_load_ps(&mm[0]);
    __m128 m_row1 = _mm_load_ps(&mm[4]);
    __m128 m_row2 = _mm_load_ps(&mm[8]);
    __m128 m_row3 = _mm_load_ps(&mm[12]);

    // Transpose m to get columns
    __m128 temp0 = _mm_unpacklo_ps(m_row0, m_row1);
    __m128 temp1 = _mm_unpackhi_ps(m_row0, m_row1);
    __m128 temp2 = _mm_unpacklo_ps(m_row2, m_row3);
    __m128 temp3 = _mm_unpackhi_ps(m_row2, m_row3);
    __m128 m_col0 = _mm_movelh_ps(temp0, temp2);
```

```cpp
    __m128 m_col1 = _mm_movehl_ps(temp2, temp0);
    __m128 m_col2 = _mm_movelh_ps(temp1, temp3);
    __m128 m_col3 = _mm_movehl_ps(temp3, temp1);

    for (size_t i = 0; i < num_vec; i += 1)
    {
        // Broadcast components of next vec_a
        __m128 w_vals = _mm_broadcast_ss((float*)&vec_a[i].W);
        __m128 x_vals = _mm_broadcast_ss((float*)&vec_a[i].X);
        __m128 y_vals = _mm_broadcast_ss((float*)&vec_a[i].Y);
        __m128 z_vals = _mm_broadcast_ss((float*)&vec_a[i].Z);

        // Calculate and save matrix-vector product
        __m128 vec_b_vals = _mm_mul_ps(m_col0, w_vals);
        vec_b_vals = _mm_fmadd_ps(m_col1, x_vals, vec_b_vals);
        vec_b_vals = _mm_fmadd_ps(m_col2, y_vals, vec_b_vals);
        vec_b_vals = _mm_fmadd_ps(m_col3, z_vals, vec_b_vals);

        _mm_store_ps((float*)&vec_b[i], vec_b_vals);
    }
}
```

Near the top of Listing 5-6 is the declaration of a structure named Vec4x1_F32. This structure incorporates the components of a 4 × 1 column vector. The file Ch05_06_misc.cpp contains the auxiliary functions CheckArgs(), Init(), and VecCompare(). Function MatrixVecMulF32() in file Ch05_06.cpp includes code that allocates the requisite data structures. It also streams the results to std::cout.

The first function in Ch05_06_fcpp.cpp, MatVecMulF32_Cpp(), performs matrix-vector multiplication code using standard C++ statements. The statements inside the for-loop implement the equations shown in Figure 5-5.

Function MatVecMulF32_Iavx2() begins its execution with four _mm_load_ps() calls that load the matrix m. This is followed by a series of calls to _mm_unpacklo_ps(), _mm_unpackhi_ps(), _mm_movelh_ps(), and _mm_movelh_ps(). These C++ SIMD intrinsic functions transpose matrix m to obtain the columns as shown in Figure 5-6. In this figure, note that function _mm_unpacklo_ps() interleaves the low-order elements of m_row0 and m_row1 (or m_row2 and m_row3). Function _mm_unpackhi_ps() is similar but interleaves the high-order elements. The C++ SIMD intrinsic function _mm_movelh_ps() copies the two low-order elements of the second argument to the two high-order element positions of the first argument. Function _mm_movehl_ps() copies the two high-order elements of the second argument to the two low-order element positions of the first argument.

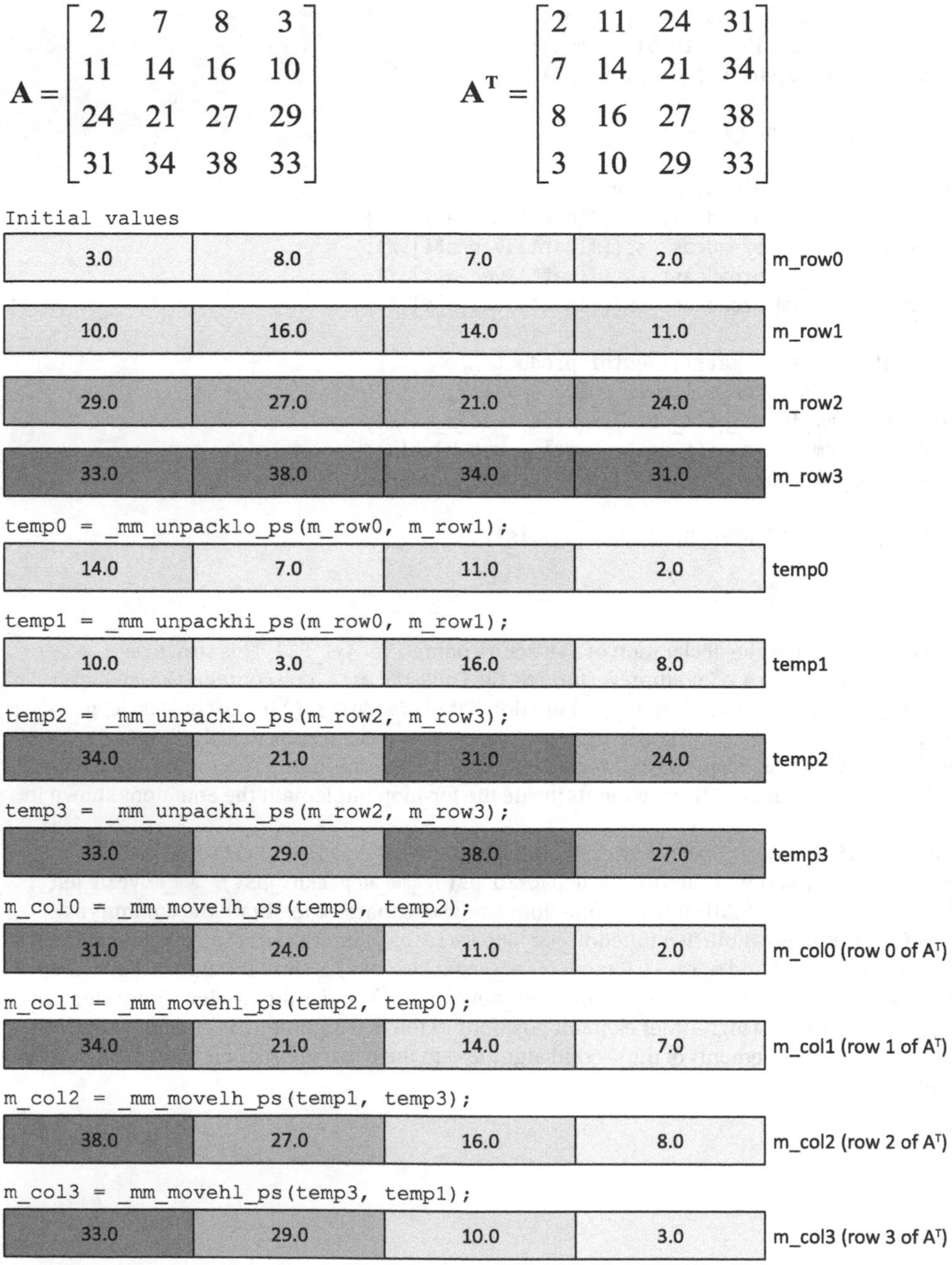

$$\mathbf{A} = \begin{bmatrix} 2 & 7 & 8 & 3 \\ 11 & 14 & 16 & 10 \\ 24 & 21 & 27 & 29 \\ 31 & 34 & 38 & 33 \end{bmatrix} \qquad \mathbf{A}^{\mathbf{T}} = \begin{bmatrix} 2 & 11 & 24 & 31 \\ 7 & 14 & 21 & 34 \\ 8 & 16 & 27 & 38 \\ 3 & 10 & 29 & 33 \end{bmatrix}$$

Initial values

| 3.0 | 8.0 | 7.0 | 2.0 | m_row0 |

| 10.0 | 16.0 | 14.0 | 11.0 | m_row1 |

| 29.0 | 27.0 | 21.0 | 24.0 | m_row2 |

| 33.0 | 38.0 | 34.0 | 31.0 | m_row3 |

temp0 = _mm_unpacklo_ps(m_row0, m_row1);

| 14.0 | 7.0 | 11.0 | 2.0 | temp0 |

temp1 = _mm_unpackhi_ps(m_row0, m_row1);

| 10.0 | 3.0 | 16.0 | 8.0 | temp1 |

temp2 = _mm_unpacklo_ps(m_row2, m_row3);

| 34.0 | 21.0 | 31.0 | 24.0 | temp2 |

temp3 = _mm_unpackhi_ps(m_row2, m_row3);

| 33.0 | 29.0 | 38.0 | 27.0 | temp3 |

m_col0 = _mm_movelh_ps(temp0, temp2);

| 31.0 | 24.0 | 11.0 | 2.0 | m_col0 (row 0 of A$^T$) |

m_col1 = _mm_movehl_ps(temp2, temp0);

| 34.0 | 21.0 | 14.0 | 7.0 | m_col1 (row 1 of A$^T$) |

m_col2 = _mm_movelh_ps(temp1, temp3);

| 38.0 | 27.0 | 16.0 | 8.0 | m_col2 (row 2 of A$^T$) |

m_col3 = _mm_movehl_ps(temp3, temp1);

| 33.0 | 29.0 | 10.0 | 3.0 | m_col3 (row 3 of A$^T$) |

**Figure 5-6.** *Transposition of a 4 × 4 matrix (single-precision floating-point)*

The for-loop in `MatVecMulF32_Iavx2()` employs the C++ SIMD intrinsic function `_mm_broadcast_ss()` to load the components of the current vector. The next code block calculates the matrix-vector products using the C++ SIMD intrinsic functions `_mm_mul_ps()` and `_mm_fmadd_ps()`. The final function call of the for-loop, `_mm_store_ps()`, saves the resultant vector. Here are the results for source code example Ch05_06:

```
Results for MatrixVecMulF32
Test case #0
vec_b1:     132.0     331.0     667.0     889.0
vec_b2:     132.0     331.0     667.0     889.0
Test case #1
vec_b1:     332.0     841.0    1677.0    2249.0
vec_b2:     332.0     841.0    1677.0    2249.0
Test case #2
vec_b1:     532.0    1351.0    2687.0    3609.0
vec_b2:     532.0    1351.0    2687.0    3609.0
Test case #3
vec_b1:     732.0    1861.0    3697.0    4969.0
vec_b2:     732.0    1861.0    3697.0    4969.0
Test case #4
vec_b1:    5950.0   14244.0   26196.0   36423.0
vec_b2:    5950.0   14244.0   26196.0   36423.0
Test case #5
vec_b1:    8287.0   19345.0   37201.0   50650.0
vec_b2:    8287.0   19345.0   37201.0   50650.0
Test case #6
vec_b1:    4595.0   13620.0   29061.0   37446.0
vec_b2:    4595.0   13620.0   29061.0   37446.0
Test case #7
vec_b1:    6669.0   16201.0   32808.0   43721.0
vec_b2:    6669.0   16201.0   32808.0   43721.0
Test case #8
vec_b1:    6027.0   15470.0   29761.0   41049.0
vec_b2:    6027.0   15470.0   29761.0   41049.0
Test case #9
vec_b1:    3161.0    9451.0   21536.0   27204.0
vec_b2:    3161.0    9451.0   21536.0   27204.0

Running benchmark function MatrixVecMulF32_bm - please wait
Benchmark times save to file Ch05_06_MatrixVecMulF32_bm_OXYGEN4.csv
```

Table 5-3 shows the benchmark timing measurements for source code example Ch05_06.

***Table 5-3.*** *Matrix-Vector (4 × 4, 4 × 1) Multiplication Execution Times (Microseconds), 1,000,000 Vectors*

| CPU | `MatVecMulF32_Cpp()` | `MatVecMulF32_Iavx2()` |
| --- | --- | --- |
| Intel Core i7-8700K | 5344 | 1588 |
| Intel Core i5-11600K | 5103 | 1155 |

Listing 5-7 shows the calculating code for source code example Ch05_07, which is the double-precision floating-point counterpart of example Ch05_06.

***Listing 5-7.*** Example Ch05_07

```
//--------------------------------------------------
//                  Ch05_07_fcpp.cpp
//--------------------------------------------------

#include <stdexcept>
#include <cstdint>
#include <immintrin.h>
#include "Ch05_07.h"
#include "MatrixF64.h"
#include "AlignedMem.h"

void MatVecMulF64_Cpp(Vec4x1_F64* vec_b, MatrixF64& m,
    Vec4x1_F64* vec_a, size_t num_vec)
{
    if (!CheckArgs(vec_b, m, vec_a, num_vec))
        throw std::runtime_error("MatVecMulF64_Cpp() - CheckArgs failed");

    const double* mm = m.Data();

    // Calculate matrix-vector products
    for (size_t i = 0; i < num_vec; i++)
    {
        vec_b[i].W =  mm[0] * vec_a[i].W + mm[1] * vec_a[i].X;
        vec_b[i].W += mm[2] * vec_a[i].Y + mm[3] * vec_a[i].Z;

        vec_b[i].X =  mm[4] * vec_a[i].W + mm[5] * vec_a[i].X;
        vec_b[i].X += mm[6] * vec_a[i].Y + mm[7] * vec_a[i].Z;

        vec_b[i].Y =  mm[8] * vec_a[i].W + mm[9] * vec_a[i].X;
        vec_b[i].Y += mm[10] * vec_a[i].Y + mm[11] * vec_a[i].Z;

        vec_b[i].Z =  mm[12] * vec_a[i].W + mm[13] * vec_a[i].X;
        vec_b[i].Z += mm[14] * vec_a[i].Y + mm[15] * vec_a[i].Z;
    }
}

void MatVecMulF64_Iavx2(Vec4x1_F64* vec_b, MatrixF64& m,
    Vec4x1_F64* vec_a, size_t num_vec)
{
    if (!CheckArgs(vec_b, m, vec_a, num_vec))
        throw std::runtime_error("MatVecMulF64_Iavx2() - CheckArgs failed");

    // Load matrix m
    const double* mm = m.Data();
    __m256d m_row0 = _mm256_load_pd(&mm[0]);
    __m256d m_row1 = _mm256_load_pd(&mm[4]);
```

```
__m256d m_row2 = _mm256_load_pd(&mm[8]);
__m256d m_row3 = _mm256_load_pd(&mm[12]);

// Transpose m to get columns
__m256d temp0 = _mm256_unpacklo_pd(m_row0, m_row1);
__m256d temp1 = _mm256_unpackhi_pd(m_row0, m_row1);
__m256d temp2 = _mm256_unpacklo_pd(m_row2, m_row3);
__m256d temp3 = _mm256_unpackhi_pd(m_row2, m_row3);
__m256d m_col0 = _mm256_permute2f128_pd(temp0, temp2, 0x20);
__m256d m_col1 = _mm256_permute2f128_pd(temp1, temp3, 0x20);
__m256d m_col2 = _mm256_permute2f128_pd(temp0, temp2, 0x31);
__m256d m_col3 = _mm256_permute2f128_pd(temp1, temp3, 0x31);

for (size_t i = 0; i < num_vec; i += 1)
{
    // Broadcast components of next vec_a
    __m256d w_vals = _mm256_broadcast_sd((double*)&vec_a[i].W);
    __m256d x_vals = _mm256_broadcast_sd((double*)&vec_a[i].X);
    __m256d y_vals = _mm256_broadcast_sd((double*)&vec_a[i].Y);
    __m256d z_vals = _mm256_broadcast_sd((double*)&vec_a[i].Z);

    // Calculate and save 2 matrix-vector products
    __m256d vec_b_vals = _mm256_mul_pd(m_col0, w_vals);
    vec_b_vals = _mm256_fmadd_pd(m_col1, x_vals, vec_b_vals);
    vec_b_vals = _mm256_fmadd_pd(m_col2, y_vals, vec_b_vals);
    vec_b_vals = _mm256_fmadd_pd(m_col3, z_vals, vec_b_vals);

    _mm256_store_pd((double*)&vec_b[i], vec_b_vals);
}
}
```

The one noteworthy difference between MatVecMulF32_Iavx2() and MatVecMulF64_Iavx2() is in the code that transposes matrix m. Since there are no double-precision variants of the C++ SIMD intrinsic functions _mm_movelh_ps() and _mm_movelh_ps(), function MatVecMulF64_Iavx2() uses the C++ SIMD intrinsic function _mm256_permute2f128_pd() instead. This function permutes the double-precision elements of the specified __m256d objects according to the specified control mask. The low nibble of the control mask specifies which 128-bit wide block (i.e., two double-precision elements) is copied to the low-order 128 bits of the destination __m256d object. Likewise, the control mask high nibble selects the 128-bit wide block for the high-order 128 bits of the destination object. Figure 5-7 illustrates these permutations in greater detail. The results for source code example Ch05_07 are the same as Ch05_06.

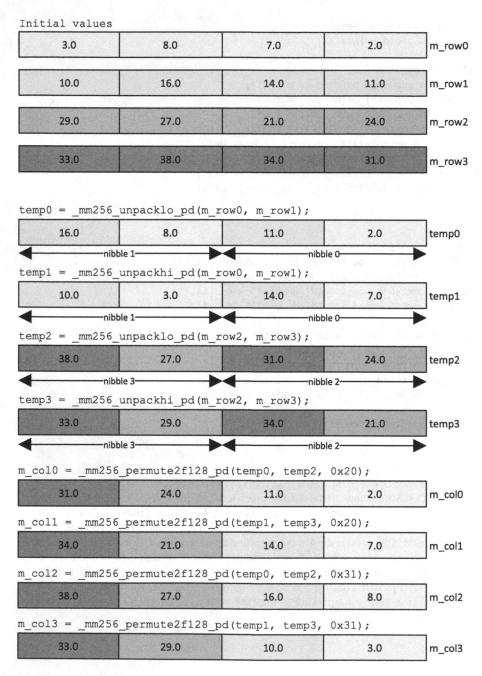

*Figure 5-7.* Packed double-precision floating-point permutation using _mm256_permute2f128_pd( )

Table 5-4 shows the benchmark timing measurements for source code example Ch05_07.

***Table 5-4.*** *Matrix-Vector (4 × 4, 4 × 1) Multiplication Execution Times (Microseconds), 1,000,000 Vectors*

| CPU | `MatVecMulF64_Cpp()` | `MatVecMulF64_Iavx2()` |
|---|---|---|
| Intel Core i7-8700K | 6025 | 3010 |
| Intel Core i5-11600K | 5277 | 2375 |

# Matrix Inverse

Another common matrix operation is the calculation of an inverse. The inverse of a matrix is defined as follows: Let **A** and **X** represent $n \times n$ matrices. Matrix **X** is an inverse of **A** if **AX** = **XA** = **I**, where **I** denotes an $n \times n$ identity matrix (i.e., a matrix of all zeros except for the main diagonal elements, which are equal to one). Figure 5-8 shows an example of an inverse matrix. It is important to note that not every $n \times n$ matrix has an inverse. A matrix without an inverse is called a singular matrix. Inverse matrices are sometimes employed to solve a system of linear equations. Many computer graphics applications also use inverse matrices to perform transformation operations.

$$\begin{bmatrix} 6.0 & 2.0 & 2.0 \\ 2.0 & -2.0 & 2.0 \\ 0.0 & 4.0 & 2.0 \end{bmatrix} \begin{bmatrix} 0.1875 & -0.0625 & -0.125 \\ 0.0625 & -0.1875 & 0.125 \\ -0.125 & 0.375 & 0.25 \end{bmatrix} = \begin{bmatrix} 1.0 & 0.0 & 0.0 \\ 0.0 & 1.0 & 0.0 \\ 0.0 & 0.0 & 1.0 \end{bmatrix}$$
$$\qquad \mathbf{A} \qquad\qquad\qquad \mathbf{X} \qquad\qquad\qquad \mathbf{I}$$

***Figure 5-8.*** *Matrix **A** and its inverse matrix **X***

The inverse of a matrix can be calculated using a variety of mathematical techniques. The source code that you will see later in this section uses a computational method based on the Cayley-Hamilton theorem. This theorem employs common matrix arithmetic operations that are straightforward to implement using SIMD arithmetic. Here are the required equations:

$$\mathbf{A}^1 = \mathbf{A}; \mathbf{A}^2 = \mathbf{AA}; \mathbf{A}^3 = \mathbf{AAA}; \cdots$$

$$trace(\mathbf{A}) = \sum_i a_{ii}$$

$$t_n = trace(\mathbf{A}^n)$$

$$c_0 = 1$$

$$c_1 = -t_1$$

$$c_2 = -\frac{1}{2}(c_1 t_1 + t_2)$$

$$c_3 = -\frac{1}{3}(c_2 t_1 + c_1 t_2 + t_3)$$

$$c_n = -\frac{1}{n}\left(c_{n-1}t_1 + c_{n-2}t_2 + \cdots + c_1 t_{n-1} + t_n\right)$$

$$\mathbf{A}^{-1} = -\frac{1}{c_n}\left(c_0 \mathbf{A}^{n-1} + c_1 \mathbf{A}^{n-2} + \cdots + c_{n-1}\mathbf{I}\right)$$

Listing 5-8 shows the source code for example Ch05_08, which demonstrates how to calculate the inverse of an $n \times n$ matrix of single-precision floating-point values using SIMD arithmetic. Note that this listing only includes the matrix inverse calculating functions MatrixInvF32_Cpp() and MatrixInvF32_Iavx2() since most of the other code (test case initialization, displaying results, etc.) is similar to the previous source code examples in this chapter. The files not shown in Listing 5-8 are included in the source code download package.

*Listing 5-8.* Example Ch05_08

```
//--------------------------------------------------
//                 Ch05_08_fcpp.cpp
//--------------------------------------------------

#include <stdexcept>
#include <vector>
#include <immintrin.h>
#include "Ch05_08.h"
#include "MatrixF32.h"

bool MatrixInvF32_Cpp(MatrixF32& a_inv, const MatrixF32& a, float epsilon)
{
    size_t n = a.GetNumRows();

    if (n != a.GetNumCols())
        throw std::runtime_error("MatrixInvF32_Cpp() - non-square matrix");

    if (n != a_inv.GetNumRows() || n != a_inv.GetNumCols())
        throw std::runtime_error("MatrixInvF32_Cpp() - non-conforming matrices");

    // Calculate matrix products and trace values
    std::vector<float> t(n + 1);
    std::vector<MatrixF32> mats(n + 1);

    mats[0] = MatrixF32::I(n);
    mats[1] = a;
    t[1] = mats[1].Trace();

    for (size_t i = 2; i <= n; i++)
    {
        mats[i] = mats[i - 1] * a;
        t[i] = mats[i].Trace();
    }
```

```cpp
        // Calculate characteristic equation coefficients
        std::vector<float> c(n + 1);
        c[0] = 1;
        c[1] = -t[1];

        for (size_t i = 2; i <= n; i++)
        {
            size_t j = 1;
            size_t k = i - 1;
            float sum = 0.0f;

            for (; j < i; j++)
            {
                sum += c[k] * t[j];
                k -= 1;
            }

            sum += t[j];
            c[i] = (-1.0f / i) * sum;
        }

        bool is_singular = (fabs(c[n]) < epsilon) ? true : false;

        if (!is_singular)
        {
            // Matrix a is non-singular, calculate the inverse
            a_inv = mats[n - 1] * c[0];
            size_t i = 1;
            size_t k = n - 2;

            for (; i <= n - 1; i++)
            {
                a_inv = a_inv + mats[k] * c[i];
                k -= 1;
            }

            MatrixF32::MulScalar(a_inv, a_inv, -1.0f / c[i]);
        }

        return is_singular;
    }

bool MatrixInvF32_Iavx2(MatrixF32& a_inv, const MatrixF32& a, float epsilon)
{
    size_t n = a.GetNumRows();

    if (n != a.GetNumCols())
        throw std::runtime_error("MatrixInvF32_Iavx2() - non-square matrix");

    if (n != a_inv.GetNumRows() || n != a_inv.GetNumCols())
        throw std::runtime_error("MatrixInvF32_Iavx2() - non-conforming matrices");
```

```cpp
    MatrixF32 temp1(n, n);

    // Calculate matrix products and trace values
    std::vector<float> t(n + 1);
    std::vector<MatrixF32> mats(n + 1);

    mats[0] = MatrixF32::I(n);
    mats[1] = a;
    t[1] = mats[1].Trace();

    for (size_t i = 2; i <= n; i++)
    {
//@@    mats[i] = mats[i - 1] * a;
        mats[i] = MatrixMulF32_Iavx2(mats[i - 1], a);
        t[i] = mats[i].Trace();
    }

    // Calculate characteristic equation coefficients
    std::vector<float> c(n + 1);
    c[0] = 1;
    c[1] = -t[1];

    for (size_t i = 2; i <= n; i++)
    {
        size_t j = 1;
        size_t k = i - 1;
        float sum = 0.0f;

        for (; j < i; j++)
        {
            sum += c[k] * t[j];
            k -= 1;
        }

        sum += t[j];
        c[i] = (-1.0f / i) * sum;
    }

    bool is_singular = (fabs(c[n]) < epsilon) ? true : false;

    if (!is_singular)
    {
        // Matrix a is non-singular, calculate the inverse
        a_inv = mats[n - 1] * c[0];
        size_t i = 1;
        size_t k = n - 2;

        for (; i <= n - 1; i++)
        {
//@@        a_inv = a_inv + mats[k] * c[i];
            MatrixMulScalarF32_Iavx2(temp1, mats[k], c[i]);
```

184

```
            a_inv = MatrixAddF32_Iavx2(a_inv, temp1);
            k -= 1;
        }

//@@     MatrixF32::MulScalar(a_inv, a_inv, -1.0f / c[i]);
        MatrixMulScalarF32_Iavx2(a_inv, a_inv, -1.0f / c[i]);
    }

    return is_singular;
}
```

Function MatrixInvF32_Cpp() calculates the inverse of a matrix using standard C++ statements. The code in this function directly executes the previously defined matrix inverse equations. Following validation of matrix arguments a and a_inv for size, MatrixInvF32_Cpp() employs a simple for-loop to calculate the required matrix products (std::vector<MatrixF32> mats) and the corresponding matrix trace values (std::vector<float> t). The matrix multiplication and trace functions used in this for-loop are defined in the C++ class MatrixF32. Function MatrixInvF32_Cpp() uses a second for-loop to calculate the various c (or characteristic equation) coefficients. Following calculation of the c coefficients, MatrixInvF32_Cpp() tests fabs(c[n]) < epsilon to see if source matrix a is singular. If source matrix a is not singular, the third for-loop gets executed, and this completes the calculation of a_inv.

Function MatrixInvF32_Iavx2() computes the inverse of a matrix using SIMD arithmetic. The arrangement of the code in this function is almost identical to the code in MatrixInvF32_Cpp(). In function MatrixInvF32_Iavx2(), lines that begin with a //@@ symbol have been replaced with statements that invoke equivalent SIMD calculating functions. If you look closely at code for MatrixInvF32_Iavx2(), you will notice that there are only three instances of the //@@ symbol. Some of the SIMD calculating functions used in MatrixInvF32_Iavx2() are defined in the file Ch05_08_fcpp2.cpp, which is not shown in Listing 5-8 since most of the code in this file was borrowed from previous source code examples.

Source code example Ch05_08 exemplifies that for many algorithms, converting a non-SIMD calculating function into a SIMD calculating function is often a straightforward undertaking. Here are the results for source code example Ch05_08:

```
Test Matrix #0
    2.000     7.000     3.000     4.000
    5.000     9.000     6.000     4.750
    6.500     3.000     4.000    10.000
    7.000     5.250     8.125     6.000

Matrix a_inv1
   -0.944     0.917     0.198    -0.426
   -0.057     0.251     0.003    -0.166
    0.545    -0.648    -0.214     0.505
    0.412    -0.412     0.056     0.124

Matrix a_I1
    1.000     0.000     0.000     0.000
    0.000     1.000     0.000     0.000
    0.000     0.000     1.000     0.000
    0.000     0.000     0.000     1.000
-------------------------------------------------------------------
```

```
Test Matrix #1
   2.000     0.000     0.000     1.000
   0.000     4.000     5.000     0.000
   0.000     0.000     0.000     7.000
   0.000     0.000     0.000     6.000

Matrix is singular
-----------------------------------------------------------------------------
Test Matrix #2
 -15.000    -4.000   -16.000   -23.000    19.000
   4.000   -14.000    18.000     2.000     3.000
  16.000    12.000   -12.000   -15.000     8.000
 -22.000     8.000   -21.000   -18.000   -19.000
   1.000   -16.000   -13.000    24.000   -16.000

Matrix a_inv1
  -0.012     0.026     0.043    -0.001     0.012
  -0.017    -0.052    -0.013    -0.009    -0.026
  -0.014     0.019    -0.014     0.002    -0.023
  -0.002    -0.046    -0.027    -0.026     0.007
   0.025    -0.030    -0.014    -0.033    -0.007

Matrix a_I1
   1.000     0.000     0.000     0.000     0.000
   0.000     1.000     0.000     0.000     0.000
   0.000     0.000     1.000     0.000     0.000
   0.000     0.000     0.000     1.000     0.000
   0.000     0.000     0.000     0.000     1.000
-----------------------------------------------------------------------------
Test Matrix #3
   2.000     0.000     0.000     1.000     0.000     3.000
   0.000     4.000     5.000     0.000     9.000    -2.000
   0.000     0.000     0.000     7.000     6.000    -7.000
   0.000     0.000     0.000     6.000    -9.000     0.000
  -6.000     0.000     0.000     0.000     0.000     0.000
  -3.000     0.000     0.000     0.000     0.000     0.000

Matrix is singular
-----------------------------------------------------------------------------
Test Matrix #4
  -9.000  -22.000  -25.000   -8.000    -4.000   -15.000   11.000  -18.000    3.000  -17.000
  12.000   13.000    9.000  -12.000    15.000    12.000   22.000   11.000  -22.000   17.000
 -22.000    5.000    8.000   25.000   -25.000   -23.000   -1.000   -3.000  -21.000   -7.000
   5.000  -11.000   -4.000    1.000    -6.000    -8.000  -13.000  -12.000   -9.000    3.000
  -6.000   17.000   -2.000    6.000    -6.000    11.000    8.000  -15.000   19.000    3.000
 -20.000  -21.000  -22.000  -18.000     4.000     9.000   16.000   -3.000    8.000    3.000
   1.000   -2.000   18.000   25.000    -8.000   -25.000    9.000    6.000  -25.000   15.000
   6.000   -6.000    8.000   -6.000   -15.000     5.000   -8.000   -4.000  -17.000    8.000
   1.000  -23.000   16.000   14.000    -6.000   -15.000   18.000    1.000   -9.000   -8.000
  -4.000   -4.000   15.000   10.000    -9.000    -7.000  -24.000  -18.000  -25.000  -24.000
```

```
Matrix a_inv1
 -0.045  0.062  0.079  0.177  -0.007 -0.041 -0.134  -0.060  0.081  -0.062
  0.041 -0.016 -0.031 -0.092   0.009 -0.014  0.057   0.033 -0.052   0.020
  0.113 -0.121 -0.191 -0.362   0.020  0.022  0.263   0.157 -0.134   0.112
 -0.168  0.135  0.216  0.433  -0.004 -0.015 -0.300  -0.203  0.186  -0.114
  0.005 -0.008 -0.044 -0.032   0.001  0.020  0.053  -0.023 -0.026   0.036
 -0.146  0.120  0.179  0.348  -0.001 -0.002 -0.270  -0.144  0.158  -0.090
  0.004  0.024  0.018  0.016   0.010 -0.006 -0.024  -0.009  0.026  -0.015
 -0.052  0.035  0.079  0.102  -0.035 -0.012 -0.104  -0.047  0.054  -0.053
  0.054 -0.071 -0.090 -0.163   0.013  0.004  0.116   0.068 -0.061   0.034
  0.021 -0.035 -0.057 -0.072   0.013  0.022  0.093   0.043 -0.051   0.020

Matrix a_I1
 1.000  0.000  0.000  0.000  0.000  0.000  0.000  0.000  0.000  0.000
 0.000  1.000  0.000  0.000  0.000  0.000  0.000  0.000  0.000  0.000
 0.000  0.000  1.000  0.000  0.000  0.000  0.000  0.000  0.000  0.000
 0.000  0.000  0.000  1.000  0.000  0.000  0.000  0.000  0.000  0.000
 0.000  0.000  0.000  0.000  1.000  0.000  0.000  0.000  0.000  0.000
 0.000  0.000  0.000  0.000  0.000  1.000  0.000  0.000  0.000  0.000
 0.000  0.000  0.000  0.000  0.000  0.000  1.000  0.000  0.000  0.000
 0.000  0.000  0.000  0.000  0.000  0.000  0.000  1.000  0.000  0.000
 0.000  0.000  0.000  0.000  0.000  0.000  0.000  0.000  1.000  0.000
 0.000  0.000  0.000  0.000  0.000  0.000  0.000  0.000  0.000  1.000

Running benchmark function CalcMatrixInvF32_bm - please wait
...................................................
Benchmark times save to file Ch05_08_CalcMatrixInvF32_bm_CHROMIUM2.csv
```

Table 5-5 shows some benchmark timing measurements for source code example Ch05_08. These measurements were made using a 10 × 10 matrix.

***Table 5-5.*** *Matrix (10 × 10) Inverse Execution Times (Microseconds), 5000 Calculations*

| CPU | `MatrixInvF32_Cpp()` | `MatrixInvF32_Iavx2()` |
|---|---|---|
| Intel Core i7-8700K | 39684 | 15746 |
| Intel Core i5-11600K | 30336 | 11121 |

Source code example Ch05_09, which is not shown here but included in the software download package, contains the double-precision counterpart of example Ch05_08. Like the earlier double-precision examples of this chapter, the primary difference between the function `MatrixInvF32_Iavx2()` and the function `MatrixInvF64_Iavx2()` is that the latter uses __m256d data types and _pd variants of the C++ SIMD intrinsic functions. The output for source code example Ch05_09 is the same as Ch05_08. Table 5-6 shows the benchmark timing measurements for source code example Ch05_09. These measurements were made using a 10 × 10 matrix.

***Table 5-6.*** *Matrix (10 × 10) Inverse Execution Times (Microseconds), 5000 Calculations*

| CPU | `MatrixInvF64_Cpp()` | `MatrixInvF64_Iavx2()` |
|---|---|---|
| Intel Core i7-8700K | 42050 | 19009 |
| Intel Core i5-11600K | 30644 | 14523 |

# Summary

Table 5-7 summarizes the C++ SIMD intrinsic functions introduced in this chapter along with other commonly used type variants. Before proceeding to the next chapter, you should understand the SIMD arithmetic calculation or data manipulation operation that is performed by each function shown in Table 5-7.

***Table 5-7.*** *C++ SIMD Intrinsic Function Summary for Chapter 5*

| C++ SIMD Function Name | Description |
|---|---|
| `_mm256_fmadd_pd, _ps` | Packed fused-multiply-add |
| `_mm256_loadu_pd, _ps` | Load (unaligned) floating-point elements |
| `_mm256_loadu_si256` | Load (unaligned) integer elements |
| `_mm256_maskload_pd, _ps` | Load (masked) floating-point elements |
| `_mm256_maskstore_pd, _ps` | Store (masked) floating-point elements |
| `_mm256_permute2f128_pd` | Permute floating-point elements |
| `_mm256_storeu_pd, _ps` | Store (unaligned) floating-point elements |
| `_mm256_unpackhi_pd, _ps` | Unpack and interleave high-order elements |
| `_mm256_unpacklo_pd, _ps` | Unpack and interleave low-order elements |
| `_mm_broadcast_ss` | Broadcast constant value to all elements |
| `_mm_fmadd_pd, _ps` | Packed fused-multiply-add |
| `_mm_movehl_ps` | Move upper single-precision elements |
| `_mm_movelh_ps` | Move lower single-precision elements |
| `_mm_mul_pd, _ps` | Packed floating-point multiplication |
| `_mm_unpackhi_pd, _ps` | Unpack and interleave high-order elements |
| `_mm_unpacklo_pd, _ps` | Unpack and interleave low-order elements |

# AVX2 C++ Programming: Part 3

The previous chapter demonstrated how to use a variety of C++ SIMD intrinsic functions to implement algorithms that performed calculations using floating-point arrays and matrices. In this chapter, you will learn how to implement some common signal processing and image processing methods using SIMD arithmetic. The chapter begins with a brief primer section that discusses signal processing fundamentals and the mathematics of convolutions. This is followed by a section that explains how to implement a 1D discrete convolution using C++ SIMD intrinsic functions. Chapter 6 concludes with an exploration of image processing algorithms that exploit 2D discrete convolutions and SIMD techniques.

Chapter 6 accentuates a specific application domain where appropriate use of AVX2 and SIMD programming techniques significantly accelerates algorithm performance. The topics and source code examples presented in this chapter are slightly more specialized and perhaps a bit more complicated than those discussed in previous chapters. If your SIMD programming interests reside elsewhere, you can either skim this chapter or skip ahead to the next one.

## Convolution Primer

A convolution is a mathematical operation that blends an input signal with a response signal to produce an output signal. Convolutions are used extensively in a wide variety of scientific and engineering applications. Many signal processing and image processing methods are founded on convolution theory. In this section, you will learn the essentials of convolution mathematics. The purpose of this section is to provide just enough background math to understand this chapter's source code examples. Numerous books have been published that explain convolution, signal processing, and image processing theory in significantly greater detail. Appendix B contains a list of references that you can consult for additional information regarding these topics.

### Convolution Math: 1D

The 1D convolution of an input signal $x$ and a response signal $g$ is defined as follows:

$$y(t) = \int_{-\infty}^{\infty} x(t-\tau) g(\tau) \, d\tau$$

where $y$ represents the output signal. The notation $x * g$ is commonly used to denote the convolution of signals (or functions) $x$ and $g$.

© Daniel Kusswurm 2022

D. Kusswurm, *Modern Parallel Programming with C++ and Assembly Language*,
https://doi.org/10.1007/978-1-4842-7918-2_6

In computer software, an array of sampled data points is frequently employed to represent the input, response, and output signals. A 1D discrete convolution can be calculated using the following equation:

$$y[i] = \sum_{k=-M}^{M} x[i-k]g[k]$$

where $i = 0, 1, \cdots, N-1$ and $M = floor(N_g/2)$. In the preceding equations, $N$ denotes the number of elements in the input and output signals, and $N_g$ symbolizes the number of elements in the response array. The ensuing discussions and source code examples in this chapter assume that $N_g$ is an odd integer greater than or equal to three. If you examine the 1D discrete convolution equation carefully, you will notice that each element of the output signal array $y$ is computed using a straightforward sum-of-products calculation that encompasses the input signal $x$ and the response signal $g$. These types of calculations are easy to implement using FMA arithmetic as you have already seen.

In digital signal processing, many applications use smoothing operators to reduce the amount of noise present in a raw data signal. For example, the top plot of Figure 6-1 shows a raw data signal that contains a fair amount of noise. The bottom plot of Figure 6-1 shows the same signal following the application of a smoothing operator. In this example, the smoothing operator convolved the original raw signal with a set of discrete coefficients that approximate a low-pass (or Gaussian) filter. These coefficients correspond to the response signal array $g$ that is included in the discrete 1D convolution equation. The response signal array is often called a convolution kernel or convolution mask. This book uses the term convolution kernel to avoid any potential confusion with SIMD masks.

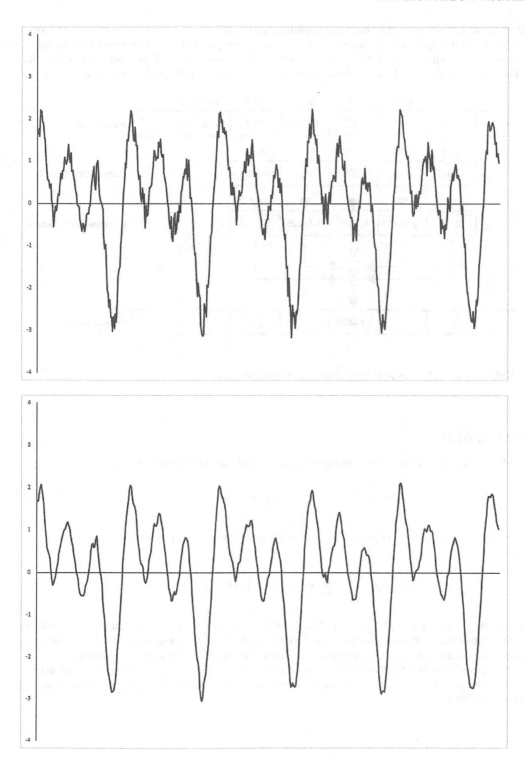

**Figure 6-1.** *Raw data signal (top plot) and its smoothed counterpart (bottom plot)*

The 1D discrete convolution equation can be implemented in source code using a couple of nested for-loops. During each outer loop iteration, the convolution kernel center point g[0] is superimposed over the current input signal array element x[i]. The inner for-loop calculates the intermediate products as shown in Figure 6-2. These intermediate products are then summed and saved to output signal array element y[i].

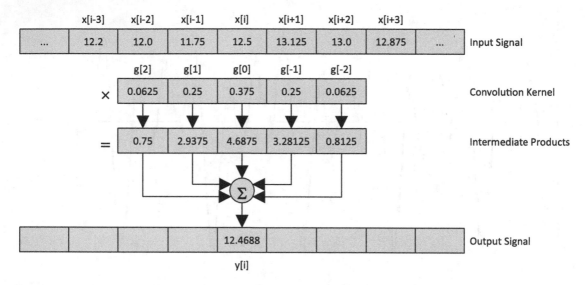

***Figure 6-2.*** *Calculation of 1D discrete convolution output signal element*

# Convolution Math: 2D

The 2D convolution of input signal *x*, response signal *g*, and output signal *y* is defined as follows:

$$y(u,v) = \int_{-\infty}^{\infty} \int_{-\infty}^{\infty} x(u - \tau_1, v - \tau_2) g(\tau_1, \tau_2) d\tau_1 d\tau_2$$

A 2D discrete convolution with a square dimensioned response signal can be calculated using the following equation:

$$y[i,j] = \sum_{k_1 = -M}^{M} \sum_{k_2 = -M}^{M} x[i - k_1, j - k_2] g[k_1, k_2]$$

where $i = 0, 1, \cdots, N_{rows} - 1, j = 0, 1, \cdots, N_{cols} - 1$, and $M = floor(N_g/2)$. In the preceding equations, $N_g$ symbolizes the height and width of the response signal (or convolution kernel) and is assumed to be an odd integer greater than or equal to three. A matrix of sampled data points is often utilized to represent the input, response, and output signals of a 2D discrete convolution. Figure 6-3 shows two images: the left image is the original grayscale image, while the right image was generated using a 2D discrete convolution kernel that performs low-pass filtering.

***Figure 6-3.*** *Application of a low-pass filter using a 2D discrete convolution*

The 2D discrete convolution equation can be implemented in source code using four nested for-loops. During each iteration of the inner-most for-loop, the convolution kernel center point g[0][0] is superimposed over the current input signal array element x[i][j] as shown in Figure 6-4. This figure also shows the equations need to calculate y[i][j].

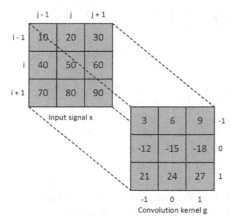

$$x[i+1, j+1] \times g[-1, -1] = 90 \times 3 = 270$$

$$x[i+1, j] \times g[-1, 0] = 80 \times 6 = 480$$

$$x[i+1, j-1] \times g[-1, 1] = 70 \times 9 = 630$$

$$x[i, j+1] \times g[0, -1] = 60 \times (-12) = -720$$

$$x[i, j] \times g[0, 0] = 50 \times (-15) = -750$$

$$x[i, j-1] \times g[0, 1] = 40 \times (-18) = -720$$

$$x[i-1, j+1] \times g[1, -1] = 30 \times 21 = 630$$

$$x[i-1, j] \times g[1, 0] = 20 \times 24 = 480$$

$$x[i-1, j-1] \times g[1, 1] = 10 \times 27 = 270$$

$$y[i, j] = 270 + 480 + 630 + (-720) + (-750) + (-720) + 630 + 480 + 270 = 570$$

***Figure 6-4.*** *Calculation of a 2D discrete convolution output signal element*

Direct implementation of the 2D discrete convolution equation is computationally expensive, even when using SIMD arithmetic. One reason for this is that the number of required arithmetic operations increases exponentially as the size of input signal gets larger. The computational costs of a 2D discrete convolution can be significantly reduced if the 2D convolution kernel is separable as shown in Figure 6-5. In this case, a 2D discrete convolution can be carried out using two independent 1D discrete convolutions.

$$
\begin{bmatrix}
1 & 4 & 6 & 4 & 1 \\
4 & 16 & 24 & 16 & 4 \\
6 & 24 & 36 & 24 & 6 \\
4 & 16 & 24 & 16 & 4 \\
1 & 4 & 6 & 4 & 1
\end{bmatrix}
=
\begin{bmatrix}
1 \\ 4 \\ 6 \\ 4 \\ 1
\end{bmatrix}
\begin{bmatrix} 1 & 4 & 6 & 4 & 1 \end{bmatrix}
$$

2D kernel     1D kernel     1D kernel
(g)         (g1)         (g2)

*Figure 6-5.* *Example of a separable 2D convolution kernel and its corresponding 1D convolution kernels*

When using a separable 2D convolution kernel, the original 2D discrete convolution equation transforms into the following:

$$
y[i,j] = \sum_{k_1=-M}^{M} \sum_{k_2=-M}^{M} x[i-k_1, j-k_2]\, g_1[k_1]\, g_2[k_2]
$$

Rearranging these terms yields the following equation:

$$
y[i,j] = \sum_{k_1=-M}^{M} g_1[k_1] \left[ \sum_{k_2=-M}^{M} x[i-k_1, j-k_2]\, g_2[k_2] \right]
$$

# 1D Convolutions

Listing 6-1 shows the source code for example Ch06_01. This example illustrates how to use C++ SIMD intrinsic functions to perform a 1D discrete convolution using single-precision floating-point values.

*Listing 6-1.* Example Ch06_01

```
//--------------------------------------------------
//              Ch06_01.h
//--------------------------------------------------

#pragma once
#include <vector>

// Ch06_01_fcpp.cpp
extern void Convolve1D_F32_Cpp(std::vector<float>& y,
    const std::vector<float>& x, const std::vector<float>& kernel);
extern void Convolve1D_F32_Iavx2(std::vector<float>& y,
    const std::vector<float>& x, const std::vector<float>& kernel);
extern void Convolve1DKs5_F32_Iavx2(std::vector<float>& y,
    const std::vector<float>& x, const std::vector<float>& kernel);
```

```cpp
// Ch06_01_misc.cpp
extern bool CheckArgs(std::vector<float>& y,
    const std::vector<float>& x, const std::vector<float>& kernel);

// Ch06_01_bm.cpp
extern void Convolve1D_F32_bm(void);

// Miscellaneous constants
const unsigned int c_RngSeed = 97;

//-------------------------------------------------
//              Ch06_01_misc.cpp
//-------------------------------------------------

#include "Ch06_01.h"

bool CheckArgs(std::vector<float>& y, const std::vector<float>& x,
    const std::vector<float>& kernel)
{
    if ((kernel.size() & 1) == 0)
        return false;
    if (y.size() != x.size())
        return false;
    if (y.size() < kernel.size())
        return false;
    return true;
}

//-------------------------------------------------
//              Ch06_01.cpp
//-------------------------------------------------

#include <iostream>
#include <iomanip>
#include <stdexcept>
#include "Ch06_01.h"
#include "MT_Convolve.h"

static void Convolve1D_F32(void);

int main()
{
    try
    {
        Convolve1D_F32();
        Convolve1D_F32_bm();
    }

    catch (std::exception& ex)
    {
        std::cout << "Ch06_01 exception: " << ex.what() << '\n';
    }
```

```cpp
    return 0;
}

static void Convolve1D_F32(void)
{
    const char nl = '\n';
    const size_t num_pts = 79;
    const char* bn_results = "Ch06_01_Convolve1D_F32_Results";
    const std::vector<float> kernel { 0.0625f, 0.25f, 0.375f, 0.25f, 0.0625f };

    // Create input and output signal arrays
    std::cout << "Executing Convolve1D_F32()" << nl;

    std::vector<float> x(num_pts);
    GenSignal1D(x, c_RngSeed);
    std::vector<float> y1(num_pts);
    std::vector<float> y2(num_pts);
    std::vector<float> y3(num_pts);

    // Perform 1D convolutions
    Convolve1D_F32_Cpp(y1, x, kernel);
    Convolve1D_F32_Iavx2(y2, x, kernel);
    Convolve1DKs5_F32_Iavx2(y3, x, kernel);

    // Save results
    std::vector<std::vector<float>*> signal_vectors { &x, &y1, &y2, &y3 };
    std::vector<std::string> titles { "x", "y1", "y2", "y3"};
    std::string results_fn = SaveResults1D(bn_results, signal_vectors, titles);
    std::cout << "Results saved to file " << results_fn << nl;
}

//-------------------------------------------------
//                Ch06_01_fcpp.cpp
//-------------------------------------------------

#include <stdexcept>
#include <immintrin.h>
#include "Ch06_01.h"
#include "MiscTypes.h"

void Convolve1D_F32_Cpp(std::vector<float>& y, const std::vector<float>& x, const
std::vector<float>& kernel)
{
    if (!CheckArgs(y, x, kernel))
        throw std::runtime_error("Convolve1D_F32_Cpp() - CheckArgs failed");

    indx_t num_pts = (indx_t)y.size();
    indx_t ks2 = kernel.size() / 2;
```

```
    for (indx_t i = ks2; i < num_pts - ks2; i++)
    {
        float y_val = 0;

        for (indx_t k = -ks2; k <= ks2; k++)
            y_val += x[i - k] * kernel[k + ks2];

        y[i] = y_val;
    }
}

void Convolve1D_F32_Iavx2(std::vector<float>& y, const std::vector<float>& x, const
std::vector<float>& kernel)
{
    if (!CheckArgs(y, x, kernel))
        throw std::runtime_error("Convolve1D_F32_Iavx2() - CheckArgs failed");

    indx_t ks2 = (indx_t)kernel.size() / 2;
    indx_t num_pts = (indx_t)y.size();
    const indx_t num_simd_elements = 8;
    const indx_t num_simd_elements2 = 4;

    indx_t i = ks2;

    while (i < num_pts - ks2)
    {
        if ((i + num_simd_elements) <= num_pts - ks2)
        {
            __m256 y_vals = _mm256_setzero_ps();

            // Calculate y[i:i+7]
            for (indx_t k = -ks2; k <= ks2; k++)
            {
                __m256 x_vals = _mm256_loadu_ps(&x[i - k]);
                __m256 kernel_vals = _mm256_set1_ps(kernel[k + ks2]);

                y_vals = _mm256_fmadd_ps(x_vals, kernel_vals, y_vals);
            }

            _mm256_storeu_ps(&y[i], y_vals);
            i += num_simd_elements;
        }
        else if ((i + num_simd_elements2) <= num_pts - ks2)
        {
            __m128 y_vals = _mm_setzero_ps();

            // Calculate y[i:i+3]
            for (indx_t k = -ks2; k <= ks2; k++)
            {
                __m128 x_vals = _mm_loadu_ps(&x[i - k]);
                __m128 kernel_vals = _mm_set1_ps(kernel[k + ks2]);
```

```cpp
                    y_vals = _mm_fmadd_ps(x_vals, kernel_vals, y_vals);
                }

                _mm_storeu_ps(&y[i], y_vals);
                i += num_simd_elements2;
            }
            else
            {
                __m128 y_val = _mm_setzero_ps();

                // Calculate y[i]
                for (indx_t k = -ks2; k <= ks2; k++)
                {
                    __m128 x_val = _mm_load_ss(&x[i - k]);
                    __m128 k_val = _mm_load_ss(&kernel[k + ks2]);
                    y_val = _mm_fmadd_ss(x_val, k_val, y_val);
                }

                _mm_store_ss(&y[i], y_val);
                i += 1;
            }
        }
    }
}

void Convolve1DKs5_F32_Iavx2(std::vector<float>& y, const std::vector<float>& x, const
std::vector<float>& kernel)
{
    if (!CheckArgs(y, x, kernel))
        throw std::runtime_error("Convolve1DKs5_F32_Iavx2() - CheckArgs failed");
    if (kernel.size() != 5)
        throw std::runtime_error("Convolve1DKs5_F32_Iavx2() - invalid kernel size");

    const indx_t ks2 = 2;
    indx_t num_pts = (indx_t)y.size();
    const indx_t num_simd_elements = 8;
    const indx_t num_simd_elements2 = 4;

    __m256 kernel256_0 = _mm256_set1_ps(kernel[0]);
    __m256 kernel256_1 = _mm256_set1_ps(kernel[1]);
    __m256 kernel256_2 = _mm256_set1_ps(kernel[2]);
    __m256 kernel256_3 = _mm256_set1_ps(kernel[3]);
    __m256 kernel256_4 = _mm256_set1_ps(kernel[4]);

    __m128 kernel128_0 = _mm_set1_ps(kernel[0]);
    __m128 kernel128_1 = _mm_set1_ps(kernel[1]);
    __m128 kernel128_2 = _mm_set1_ps(kernel[2]);
    __m128 kernel128_3 = _mm_set1_ps(kernel[3]);
    __m128 kernel128_4 = _mm_set1_ps(kernel[4]);
```

```
indx_t i = ks2;

while (i < num_pts - ks2)
{
    indx_t j = i + ks2;

    if ((i + num_simd_elements) <= num_pts - ks2)
    {
        // Calculate y[i:i+7]
        __m256 x_vals = _mm256_loadu_ps(&x[j]);
        __m256 y_vals = _mm256_mul_ps(x_vals, kernel256_0);

        x_vals = _mm256_loadu_ps(&x[j - 1]);
        y_vals = _mm256_fmadd_ps(x_vals, kernel256_1, y_vals);
        x_vals = _mm256_loadu_ps(&x[j - 2]);
        y_vals = _mm256_fmadd_ps(x_vals, kernel256_2, y_vals);
        x_vals = _mm256_loadu_ps(&x[j - 3]);
        y_vals = _mm256_fmadd_ps(x_vals, kernel256_3, y_vals);
        x_vals = _mm256_loadu_ps(&x[j - 4]);
        y_vals = _mm256_fmadd_ps(x_vals, kernel256_4, y_vals);

        _mm256_storeu_ps(&y[i], y_vals);
        i += num_simd_elements;
    }
    else if ((i + num_simd_elements2) <= num_pts - ks2)
    {
        // Calculate y[i:i+3]
        __m128 x_vals = _mm_loadu_ps(&x[j]);
        __m128 y_vals = _mm_mul_ps(x_vals, kernel128_0);

        x_vals = _mm_loadu_ps(&x[j - 1]);
        y_vals = _mm_fmadd_ps(x_vals, kernel128_1, y_vals);
        x_vals = _mm_loadu_ps(&x[j - 2]);
        y_vals = _mm_fmadd_ps(x_vals, kernel128_2, y_vals);
        x_vals = _mm_loadu_ps(&x[j - 3]);
        y_vals = _mm_fmadd_ps(x_vals, kernel128_3, y_vals);
        x_vals = _mm_loadu_ps(&x[j - 4]);
        y_vals = _mm_fmadd_ps(x_vals, kernel128_4, y_vals);

        _mm_storeu_ps(&y[i], y_vals);
        i += num_simd_elements2;
    }
    else
    {
        // Calculate y[i]
        __m128 x_val = _mm_load_ss(&x[j]);
        __m128 y_val = _mm_mul_ss(x_val, kernel128_0);

        x_val = _mm_load_ss(&x[j - 1]);
        y_val = _mm_fmadd_ss(x_val, kernel128_1, y_val);
        x_val = _mm_load_ss(&x[j - 2]);
```

```
            y_val = _mm_fmadd_ss(x_val, kernel128_2, y_val);
            x_val = _mm_load_ss(&x[j - 3]);
            y_val = _mm_fmadd_ss(x_val, kernel128_3, y_val);
            x_val = _mm_load_ss(&x[j - 4]);
            y_val = _mm_fmadd_ss(x_val, kernel128_4, y_val);

            _mm_store_ss(&y[i], y_val);
            i += 1;
        }
    }
}
```

Listing 6-1 begins with the file Ch06_01.h, which includes the function declarations for this example. Note that the function declarations use type std::vector<float> for the various signal arrays. The next file in Listing 6-1 is Ch06_01.cpp and includes the function Convolve1D_F32(). This function uses a function template named GenSignal1D() to generate a synthetic input signal. The source code for GenSignal1D() is not shown in Listing 6-1 but included in the download software package. The variable std::vector<float> kernel contains response signal coefficients that implement a simple low-pass filter. Function Convolve1D_F32() also invokes the 1D discrete convolution functions Convolve1D_F32_Cpp(), Convolve1D_F32_Iavx2(), and Convolve1DKs5_F32_Iavx2(). Following execution of these functions, Convolve1D_F32() saves the signal array data to the specified file.

The first function in file Ch06_01_fcpp.cpp is named Convolve1D_F32_Cpp(). This function is a direct implementation of the 1D discrete convolution equation using standard C++ statements. Note that the for-loop index variables in Convolve1D_F32_Cpp() are declared using the data type indx_t, which is defined in MiscTypes.h. Type indx_t is a signed integer whose size (32 or 64 bits) is platform dependent. Signed integer index variables are employed in this chapter's convolution calculating functions since this corresponds to the summation indices used in the discrete convolution equations.

Function Convolve1D_F32_Iavx2() performs a 1D discrete convolution using C++ SIMD intrinsic functions. Recall that the C++ SIMD data type __m256 can hold eight single-precision floating-point values. This type facilitates a SIMD implementation of the convolution algorithm that can process eight input signal points simultaneously. Figure 6-6 contains two graphics that illustrate a five-element convolution kernel along with an arbitrary segment of an input signal. Below the graphics are the equations that calculate output signal elements y[i:i+7]. These equations are simple expansion of the 1D discrete convolution equation that you saw earlier in this chapter. Note that each column of the SIMD convolution equation set includes a single kernel value and eight consecutive elements from the input signal array. These equations can be implemented in code using simple SIMD FMA arithmetic.

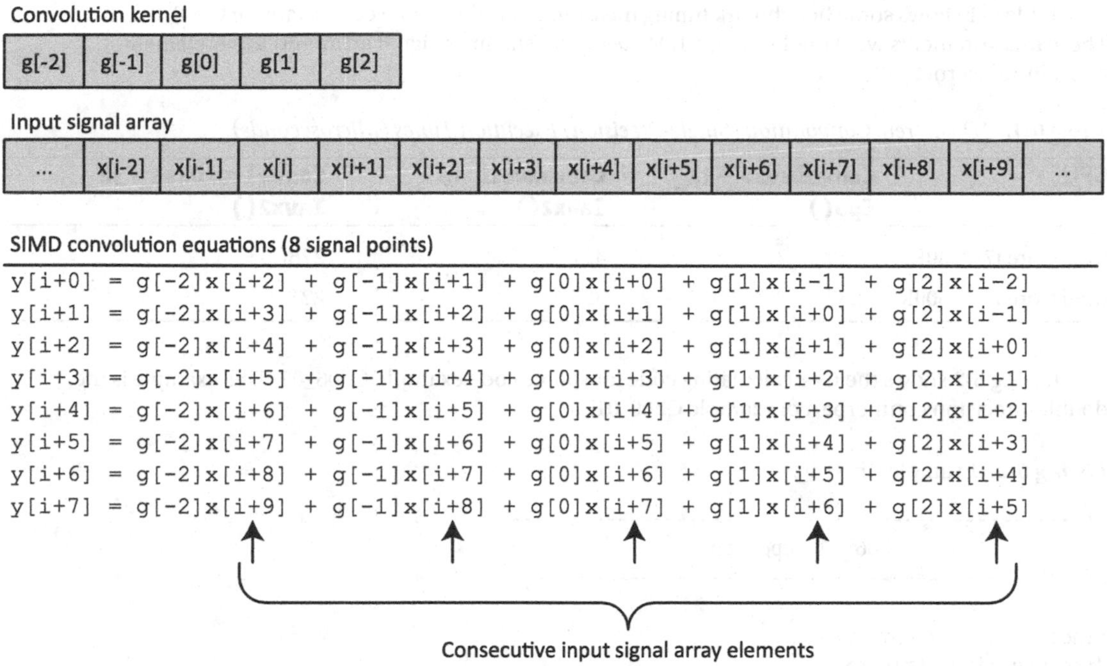

Convolution kernel

| g[-2] | g[-1] | g[0] | g[1] | g[2] |
|---|---|---|---|---|

Input signal array

| ... | x[i-2] | x[i-1] | x[i] | x[i+1] | x[i+2] | x[i+3] | x[i+4] | x[i+5] | x[i+6] | x[i+7] | x[i+8] | x[i+9] | ... |
|---|---|---|---|---|---|---|---|---|---|---|---|---|---|

SIMD convolution equations (8 signal points)

```
y[i+0] = g[-2]x[i+2] + g[-1]x[i+1] + g[0]x[i+0] + g[1]x[i-1] + g[2]x[i-2]
y[i+1] = g[-2]x[i+3] + g[-1]x[i+2] + g[0]x[i+1] + g[1]x[i+0] + g[2]x[i-1]
y[i+2] = g[-2]x[i+4] + g[-1]x[i+3] + g[0]x[i+2] + g[1]x[i+1] + g[2]x[i+0]
y[i+3] = g[-2]x[i+5] + g[-1]x[i+4] + g[0]x[i+3] + g[1]x[i+2] + g[2]x[i+1]
y[i+4] = g[-2]x[i+6] + g[-1]x[i+5] + g[0]x[i+4] + g[1]x[i+3] + g[2]x[i+2]
y[i+5] = g[-2]x[i+7] + g[-1]x[i+6] + g[0]x[i+5] + g[1]x[i+4] + g[2]x[i+3]
y[i+6] = g[-2]x[i+8] + g[-1]x[i+7] + g[0]x[i+6] + g[1]x[i+5] + g[2]x[i+4]
y[i+7] = g[-2]x[i+9] + g[-1]x[i+8] + g[0]x[i+7] + g[1]x[i+6] + g[2]x[i+5]
```

Consecutive input signal array elements

***Figure 6-6.*** *SIMD 1D discrete convolution equations for a five-element convolution kernel*

When performing a 1D discrete convolution using SIMD arithmetic, function Convolve1D_F32_Iavx2() must ensure that it does not attempt to access any elements beyond the boundaries of the input and output signal arrays. The first if code block in the while-loop verifies that a sufficient number of input signal elements are available to calculate output signal elements y[i:i+7]. If enough elements are available, the for-loop performs its calculations using the equations shown in Figure 6-6. The second if code block handles the case when there are enough input signal elements to calculate x[i:i+3]. The final else code block uses scalar arithmetic to process any residual signal elements. Note that all three code blocks in the while-loop perform unaligned load and store operations since it is impossible to guarantee that any set of consecutive input or output signal array elements will be aligned on a particular boundary.

The function Convolve1D_F32_Iavx2() carries out its calculations using a convolution kernel that can vary in size. Many real-world signal processing libraries often include convolution functions that are optimized for specific kernel sizes. Size-optimized convolution functions are often faster than their variable-width counterparts as you will soon see. The final function in Listing 6-1, Convolve1DKs5_F32_Iavx2(), is optimized for convolution kernels that contain five elements. The while and if code block arrangement of this function closely resembles the function Convolve1D_F32_Iavx2(). Note that in function Convolve1DKs5_F32_Iavx2(), the inner for-loops have been replaced with discrete calls to the appropriate C++ SIMD intrinsic functions. In this example, elimination of the inner for-loops yields results in faster code since there is no overhead code for the for-loop. Here are the results for source code example Ch06_01:

```
Executing Convolve1D_F32()
Results saved to file Ch06_01_Convolve1D_F32_Results_OXYGEN4.csv

Running benchmark function Convolve1D_F32_bm - please wait
Benchmark times saved to file Ch06_01_Convolve1D_F32_bm_OXYGEN4.csv
```

Table 6-1 shows some benchmark timing measurements for source code example Ch06_01. These measurements were made using a 1,000,000-element input signal array and a five-element convolution kernel.

***Table 6-1.*** *1D Discrete Convolution (Single-Precision) Execution Times (Microseconds)*

| CPU | Convolve1D_F32_Cpp() | Convolve1D_F32_Iavx2() | Convolve1DKs5_F32_Iavx2() |
|-----|----------------------|------------------------|---------------------------|
| Intel Core i7-8700K | 3240 | 411 | 278 |
| Intel Core i5-11600K | 2267 | 325 | 221 |

Listing 6-2 shows the C++ calculating code for source code example Ch06_02. This example is the double-precision counterpart of example Ch06_01.

***Listing 6-2.*** Example Ch06_02

```
//--------------------------------------------------
//               Ch06_02_fcpp.cpp
//--------------------------------------------------

#include <stdexcept>
#include <immintrin.h>
#include "Ch06_02.h"
#include "MiscTypes.h"

void Convolve1D_F64_Cpp(std::vector<double>& y, const std::vector<double>& x,
    const std::vector<double>& kernel)
{
    if (!CheckArgs(y, x, kernel))
        throw std::runtime_error("Convolve1D_F64_Cpp() - CheckArgs failed");

    indx_t num_pts = (indx_t)y.size();
    indx_t ks2 = kernel.size() / 2;

    for (indx_t i = ks2; i < num_pts - ks2; i++)
    {
        double y_val = 0;

        for (indx_t k = -ks2; k <= ks2; k++)
            y_val += x[i - k] * kernel[k + ks2];

        y[i] = y_val;
    }
}

void Convolve1D_F64_Iavx2(std::vector<double>& y, const std::vector<double>& x,
    const std::vector<double>& kernel)
{
    if (!CheckArgs(y, x, kernel))
        throw std::runtime_error("Convolve1D_F64_Iavx2() - CheckArgs failed");
```

```
indx_t ks2 = (indx_t)kernel.size() / 2;
indx_t num_pts = (indx_t)y.size();
const indx_t num_simd_elements = 4;
const indx_t num_simd_elements2 = 2;

indx_t i = ks2;

while (i < num_pts - ks2)
{
    if ((i + num_simd_elements) <= num_pts - ks2)
    {
        __m256d y_vals = _mm256_setzero_pd();

        // Calculate y[i:i+3]
        for (indx_t k = -ks2; k <= ks2; k++)
        {
            __m256d x_vals = _mm256_loadu_pd(&x[i - k]);
            __m256d kernel_vals = _mm256_broadcast_sd(&kernel[k + ks2]);

            y_vals = _mm256_fmadd_pd(x_vals, kernel_vals, y_vals);
        }

        _mm256_storeu_pd(&y[i], y_vals);
        i += num_simd_elements;
    }
    else if ((i + num_simd_elements2) <= num_pts - ks2)
    {
        __m128d y_vals = _mm_setzero_pd();

        // Calculate y[i:i+1]
        for (indx_t k = -ks2; k <= ks2; k++)
        {
            __m128d x_vals = _mm_loadu_pd(&x[i - k]);
            __m128d kernel_vals = _mm_set1_pd(kernel[k + ks2]);

            y_vals = _mm_fmadd_pd(x_vals, kernel_vals, y_vals);
        }

        _mm_storeu_pd(&y[i], y_vals);
        i += num_simd_elements2;
    }
    else
    {
        __m128d y_val = _mm_setzero_pd();

        // Calculate y[i]
        for (indx_t k = -ks2; k <= ks2; k++)
        {
            __m128d x_val = _mm_load_sd(&x[i - k]);
            __m128d k_val = _mm_load_sd(&kernel[k + ks2]);
            y_val = _mm_fmadd_sd(x_val, k_val, y_val);
        }
```

```
            _mm_store_sd(&y[i], y_val);
            i += 1;
        }
    }
}

void Convolve1DKs5_F64_Iavx2(std::vector<double>& y, const std::vector<double>& x,
    const std::vector<double>& kernel)
{
    if (!CheckArgs(y, x, kernel))
        throw std::runtime_error("Convolve1DKs5_F64_Iavx2() - CheckArgs failed");

    if (kernel.size() != 5)
        throw std::runtime_error("Convolve1DKs5_F64_Iavx2() - invalid kernel size");

    const indx_t ks2 = 2;
    indx_t num_pts = (indx_t)y.size();
    const indx_t num_simd_elements = 4;
    const indx_t num_simd_elements2 = 2;

    __m256d kernel256_0 = _mm256_set1_pd(kernel[0]);
    __m256d kernel256_1 = _mm256_set1_pd(kernel[1]);
    __m256d kernel256_2 = _mm256_set1_pd(kernel[2]);
    __m256d kernel256_3 = _mm256_set1_pd(kernel[3]);
    __m256d kernel256_4 = _mm256_set1_pd(kernel[4]);

    __m128d kernel128_0 = _mm_set1_pd(kernel[0]);
    __m128d kernel128_1 = _mm_set1_pd(kernel[1]);
    __m128d kernel128_2 = _mm_set1_pd(kernel[2]);
    __m128d kernel128_3 = _mm_set1_pd(kernel[3]);
    __m128d kernel128_4 = _mm_set1_pd(kernel[4]);

    indx_t i = ks2;

    while (i < num_pts - ks2)
    {
        indx_t j = i + ks2;

        if ((i + num_simd_elements) <= num_pts - ks2)
        {
            // Calculate y[i:i+3]
            __m256d x_vals = _mm256_loadu_pd(&x[j]);
            __m256d y_vals = _mm256_mul_pd(x_vals, kernel256_0);

            x_vals = _mm256_loadu_pd(&x[j - 1]);
            y_vals = _mm256_fmadd_pd(x_vals, kernel256_1, y_vals);
            x_vals = _mm256_loadu_pd(&x[j - 2]);
            y_vals = _mm256_fmadd_pd(x_vals, kernel256_2, y_vals);
            x_vals = _mm256_loadu_pd(&x[j - 3]);
            y_vals = _mm256_fmadd_pd(x_vals, kernel256_3, y_vals);
            x_vals = _mm256_loadu_pd(&x[j - 4]);
            y_vals = _mm256_fmadd_pd(x_vals, kernel256_4, y_vals);
```

```
                _mm256_storeu_pd(&y[i], y_vals);
                i += num_simd_elements;
            }
            else if ((i + num_simd_elements2) <= num_pts - ks2)
            {
                // Calculate y[i:i+1]
                __m128d x_vals = _mm_loadu_pd(&x[j]);
                __m128d y_vals = _mm_mul_pd(x_vals, kernel128_0);

                x_vals = _mm_loadu_pd(&x[j - 1]);
                y_vals = _mm_fmadd_pd(x_vals, kernel128_1, y_vals);
                x_vals = _mm_loadu_pd(&x[j - 2]);
                y_vals = _mm_fmadd_pd(x_vals, kernel128_2, y_vals);
                x_vals = _mm_loadu_pd(&x[j - 3]);
                y_vals = _mm_fmadd_pd(x_vals, kernel128_3, y_vals);
                x_vals = _mm_loadu_pd(&x[j - 4]);
                y_vals = _mm_fmadd_pd(x_vals, kernel128_4, y_vals);

                _mm_storeu_pd(&y[i], y_vals);
                i += num_simd_elements2;
            }
            else
            {
                // Calculate y[i]
                __m128d x_val = _mm_load_sd(&x[j]);
                __m128d y_val = _mm_mul_sd(x_val, kernel128_0);

                x_val = _mm_load_sd(&x[j - 1]);
                y_val = _mm_fmadd_sd(x_val, kernel128_1, y_val);
                x_val = _mm_load_sd(&x[j - 2]);
                y_val = _mm_fmadd_sd(x_val, kernel128_2, y_val);
                x_val = _mm_load_sd(&x[j - 3]);
                y_val = _mm_fmadd_sd(x_val, kernel128_3, y_val);
                x_val = _mm_load_sd(&x[j - 4]);
                y_val = _mm_fmadd_sd(x_val, kernel128_4, y_val);

                _mm_store_sd(&y[i], y_val);
                i += 1;
            }
        }
    }
}
```

Like many of the source examples presented in earlier chapters, the changes required to transform the single-precision SIMD convolutions functions into double-precision variants are relatively straightforward. In example Ch06_02, the functions Convolve1D_F64_Iavx2() and Convolve1DKs5_F64_Iavx2() use double-precision versions of the C++ SIMD intrinsic functions. Also note that the values for num_simd_elements and num_simd_elements2 have been cut in half to accommodate SIMD arithmetic using double-precision floating-point elements.

The results for source code example Ch06_02 are equivalent to the results that were obtained for source code example Ch06_01. Table 6-2 shows some benchmark timing measurements for source code example Ch06_02. These measurements were made using a 1,000,000-element input signal array and a 5-element convolution kernel.

*Table 6-2.* *1D Discrete Convolution (Double-Precision) Execution Times (Microseconds)*

| CPU | Convolve1D_F64_Cpp() | Convolve1D_F64_Iavx2() | Convolve1DKs5_F64_Iavx2() |
|---|---|---|---|
| Intel Core i7-8700K | 3383 | 956 | 660 |
| Intel Core i5-11600K | 2280 | 703 | 503 |

# 2D Convolutions

In this section, you will study source code examples that carry out 2D discrete convolutions. The first source code example demonstrates a 2D discrete convolution. The code in this example is suitable when performing a 2D discrete convolution using a nonseparable convolution kernel. The second example illustrates a 2D discrete convolution using two 1D discrete convolutions. The code in this example highlights the performance advantages of using dual 1D convolution kernels instead of a single 2D convolution kernel when the 2D kernel is separable.

## Nonseparable Kernel

Listing 6-3 shows the source code for example Ch06_03. This example demonstrates a 2D discrete convolution using a nonseparable 2D convolution kernel.

*Listing 6-3.* Example Ch06_03

```
//--------------------------------------------------
//              Ch06_03.h
//--------------------------------------------------

#pragma once
#include <array>
#include <vector>

struct CD_2D
{
    size_t m_ImH = 0;
    size_t m_ImW = 0;
    size_t m_KernelSize = 0;
    std::vector<float> m_ImSrc;
    std::vector<float> m_ImDes;
    std::vector<float> m_Kernel2D;
};
```

```
enum class KERNEL_ID : unsigned int
{
    LowPass2D_3x3, LowPass2D_5x5, LowPass2D_7x7, LowPass2D_9x9, LowPass2D_15x15
};

// Ch06_03_fcpp.cpp
extern void Convolve2D_F32_Cpp(CD_2D& cd);
extern void Convolve2D_F32_Iavx2(CD_2D& cd);

// Ch06_03_misc.cpp
extern bool CheckArgs2D(const CD_2D& cd);
extern void Init2D(std::array<CD_2D, 2>& cd, const char* fn, KERNEL_ID id);

// Ch06_03_misc2.cpp
extern void DisplayKernel2D(float sigma, size_t ks);
extern void GetKernel2D(CD_2D& cd, KERNEL_ID id);

// Ch06_03_bm.cpp
extern void Convolve2D_F32_bm(void);

// Miscellaneous constants
const KERNEL_ID c_KernelID = KERNEL_ID::LowPass2D_15x15;
const KERNEL_ID c_KernelID_BM = KERNEL_ID::LowPass2D_9x9;

//-------------------------------------------------
//                 Ch06_03_misc.cpp
//-------------------------------------------------

#include <iostream>
#include <iomanip>
#include <array>
#include <vector>
#include <stdexcept>
#include "Ch06_03.h"
#include "MT_Convolve.h"
#include "ImageMatrix.h"

bool CheckArgs2D(const CD_2D& cd)
{
    size_t im_src_size = cd.m_ImSrc.size();
    if (im_src_size != cd.m_ImDes.size())
        return false;
    if (im_src_size != cd.m_ImH * cd.m_ImW)
        return false;

    size_t ks = cd.m_KernelSize;
    if ((ks < 3) || ((ks & 0x1) == 0))
        return false;
    if (cd.m_Kernel2D.size() != ks * ks)
        return false;
    return true;
}
```

```cpp
void Init2D(std::array<CD_2D, 2>& cd, const char* fn, KERNEL_ID id)
{
    GetKernel2D(cd[0], id);
    GetKernel2D(cd[1], id);

    ImageMatrix im_src0;

    if (fn != nullptr)
    {
        ImageMatrix im_tmp(fn, PixelType::Gray8);
        im_src0 = im_tmp;
    }
    else
    {
        ImageMatrix im_tmp(101, 103, PixelType::Gray8); // test image
        im_tmp.FillRandom(0, 255, 1003);
        im_src0 = im_tmp;
    }

    ImageMatrix im_src1(im_src0);

    im_src0.FillBorder<uint8_t>(cd[0].m_KernelSize / 2, (uint8_t)0);
    cd[0].m_ImH = im_src0.GetHeight();
    cd[0].m_ImW = im_src0.GetWidth();
    cd[0].m_ImSrc = im_src0.ToVector<float>();
    cd[0].m_ImDes.resize(cd[0].m_ImSrc.size());
    std::fill(cd[0].m_ImDes.begin(), cd[0].m_ImDes.end(), 0.0f);

    im_src1.FillBorder<uint8_t>(cd[1].m_KernelSize / 2, (uint8_t)0);
    cd[1].m_ImH = im_src1.GetHeight();
    cd[1].m_ImW = im_src1.GetWidth();
    cd[1].m_ImSrc = im_src1.ToVector<float>();
    cd[1].m_ImDes.resize(cd[1].m_ImSrc.size());
    std::fill(cd[1].m_ImDes.begin(), cd[1].m_ImDes.end(), 0.0f);
}

//--------------------------------------------------
//                  Ch06_03.cpp
//--------------------------------------------------

#include <iostream>
#include <iomanip>
#include <stdexcept>
#include "Ch06_03.h"
#include "ImageMatrix.h"

static void Convolve2D_F32(void);
```

```cpp
int main()
{
    try
    {
        Convolve2D_F32();
        Convolve2D_F32_bm();
    }

    catch (std::exception& ex)
    {
        std::cout << "Ch06_03 exception: " << ex.what() << '\n';
    }

    return 0;
}

static void Convolve2D_F32(void)
{
    const char nl = '\n';
    const char* fn_src = "../../Data/ImageE.png";
    const char* fn_des0 = "Ch06_03_ImageE_Conv2D_0.png";
    const char* fn_des1 = "Ch06_03_ImageE_Conv2D_1.png";
    ImageFileType ift_des = ImageFileType::PNG;

    // Initialize convolution data structures
    std::array<CD_2D, 2> cd;
    Init2D(cd, fn_src, c_KernelID);

    // Perform convolutions
    std::cout << "Performing convolutions\n";
    Convolve2D_F32_Cpp(cd[0]);
    Convolve2D_F32_Iavx2(cd[1]);

    // Save destination image files
    std::cout << "Saving destination image files\n";
    int h0 = (int)cd[0].m_ImH, w0 = (int)cd[0].m_ImW;
    int h1 = (int)cd[1].m_ImH, w1 = (int)cd[1].m_ImW;
    ImageMatrix im_des0 = ImageMatrix::ToImage(cd[0].m_ImDes, h0, w0, PixelType::Gray8);
    ImageMatrix im_des1 = ImageMatrix::ToImage(cd[1].m_ImDes, h1, w1, PixelType::Gray8);
    im_des0.SaveImage(fn_des0, ift_des);
    im_des1.SaveImage(fn_des1, ift_des);

    // Make sure images are alike.
    size_t num_diff;
    const uint8_t max_d = 1;
    bool rc = ImageMatrix::AreAlike(im_des0, im_des1, max_d, &num_diff);
    std::cout << "rc:       " << std::boolalpha << rc << nl;
    std::cout << "num_diff: " << num_diff << nl;
}
```

```
//-------------------------------------------------
//                   Ch06_03_fcpp.cpp
//-------------------------------------------------

#include <stdexcept>
#include <immintrin.h>
#include "Ch06_03.h"
#include "MiscTypes.h"

void Convolve2D_F32_Cpp(CD_2D& cd)
{
    if (!CheckArgs2D(cd))
        throw std::runtime_error("Convolve2D_F32_Cpp() - CheckArgs failed");

    indx_t ks = (indx_t)cd.m_KernelSize;
    indx_t ks2 = ks / 2;
    indx_t im_h = (indx_t)cd.m_ImH;
    indx_t im_w = (indx_t)cd.m_ImW;
    const std::vector<float>& im_src = cd.m_ImSrc;
    std::vector<float>& im_des = cd.m_ImDes;
    std::vector<float>& im_ker = cd.m_Kernel2D;

    for (indx_t i = ks2; i < im_h - ks2; i++)
    {
        for (indx_t j = ks2; j < im_w - ks2; j++)
        {
            float im_des_val = 0;

            for (indx_t k1 = -ks2; k1 <= ks2; k1++)
            {
                for (indx_t k2 = -ks2; k2 <= ks2; k2++)
                {
                    float im_src_val = im_src[(i - k1) * im_w + j - k2];
                    float im_ker_val = im_ker[(k1 + ks2) * ks + k2 + ks2];

                    im_des_val += im_src_val * im_ker_val;
                }
            }

            im_des[i * im_w + j] = im_des_val;
        }
    }
}

void Convolve2D_F32_Iavx2(CD_2D& cd)
{
    if (!CheckArgs2D(cd))
        throw std::runtime_error("Convolve2D_F32_Iavx2() - CheckArgs failed");
```

```
indx_t ks = (indx_t)cd.m_KernelSize;
indx_t ks2 = ks / 2;
indx_t im_h = (indx_t)cd.m_ImH;
indx_t im_w = (indx_t)cd.m_ImW;
const std::vector<float>& im_src = cd.m_ImSrc;
std::vector<float>& im_des = cd.m_ImDes;
std::vector<float>& im_ker = cd.m_Kernel2D;

const indx_t num_simd_elements = 8;
const indx_t num_simd_elements2 = 4;

for (indx_t i = ks2; i < im_h - ks2; i++)
{
    indx_t j = ks2;

    while (j < im_w - ks2)
    {
        if (j + num_simd_elements <= im_w - ks2)
        {
            __m256 im_des_vals = _mm256_setzero_ps();

            for (indx_t k1 = -ks2; k1 <= ks2; k1++)
            {
                for (indx_t k2 = -ks2; k2 <= ks2; k2++)
                {
                    indx_t i_src = (i - k1) * im_w + j - k2;
                    indx_t i_ker = (k1 + ks2) * ks + k2 + ks2;

                    __m256 im_src_vals = _mm256_loadu_ps(&im_src[i_src]);
                    __m256 im_ker_vals = _mm256_set1_ps(im_ker[i_ker]);

                    im_des_vals = _mm256_fmadd_ps(im_src_vals, im_ker_vals,
                    im_des_vals);
                }
            }

            _mm256_storeu_ps(&im_des[i * im_w + j], im_des_vals);
            j += num_simd_elements;
        }
        else if (j + num_simd_elements2 <= im_w - ks2)
        {
            __m128 im_des_vals = _mm_setzero_ps();

            for (indx_t k1 = -ks2; k1 <= ks2; k1++)
            {
                for (indx_t k2 = -ks2; k2 <= ks2; k2++)
                {
                    indx_t i_src = (i - k1) * im_w + j - k2;
                    indx_t i_ker = (k1 + ks2) * ks + k2 + ks2;
```

```
                        __m128 im_src_vals = _mm_loadu_ps(&im_src[i_src]);
                        __m128 im_ker_vals = _mm_set1_ps(im_ker[i_ker]);

                        im_des_vals = _mm_fmadd_ps(im_src_vals, im_ker_vals, im_des_vals);
                    }
                }

                _mm_storeu_ps(&im_des[i * im_w + j], im_des_vals);
                j += num_simd_elements2;
            }
            else
            {
                float im_des_val = 0;

                for (indx_t k1 = -ks2; k1 <= ks2; k1++)
                {
                    for (indx_t k2 = -ks2; k2 <= ks2; k2++)
                    {
                        indx_t i_src = (i - k1) * im_w + j - k2;
                        indx_t i_ker = (k1 + ks2) * ks + k2 + ks2;

                        float im_src_val = im_src[i_src];
                        float im_ker_val = im_ker[i_ker];

                        im_des_val += im_src_val * im_ker_val;
                    }
                }

                im_des[i * im_w + j] = im_des_val;
                j += 1;
            }
        }
    }
}
```

Listing 6-3 opens with the file Ch06_03.h. Near the top of this file is the definition of a structure named CD_2D. This structure holds the input image, output image, and convolution kernel matrices, which are implemented using the C++ STL class std::vector<float>. Structure CD_2D also includes image and kernel size information. Following the definition of structure CD_2D is an enum named KERNEL_ID. The function Init2D() in Ch06_03_misc.cpp employs a KERNEL_ID argument to select a low-pass filter kernel for the convolution functions. In file Ch06_03.cpp, there is a function named Convolve2D_F32(). This function initializes the CD_2D structures, invokes the convolution calculating functions, and saves the final images.

The file Ch06_03_fcpp.cpp begins with the definition of function Convolve2D_F32_Cpp(). This non-SIMD function uses standard C++ statements to perform a 2D discrete convolution using the specified source image and convolution kernel. Note that function Convolve2D_F32_Cpp() employs four nested for-loops to implement the 2D discrete convolution equation that was defined earlier in this chapter.

The SIMD counterpart of function Convolve2D_F32_Cpp() is named Convolve2D_F32_Iavx2(). The code layout of this function is somewhat analogous to the 1D discrete convolution functions you saw earlier in this chapter. In function Convolve2D_F32_Iavx2(), the index variable i in the outer-most for-loop specifies the current image row, and the index variable j in the second-level while-loop specifies the current image column. The first if statement in the while-loop verifies that there are num_simd_elements or more columns remaining in the current row. If true, the two inner for-loops calculate im_des[i][j:j+7] using the appropriate elements from the source image im_src and the convolution kernel im_ker. Note that these C++ code variables correspond to the symbols $y$, $x$, and $g$ in the 2D discrete convolution equation.

The explicit equations required to calculate each im_des[i][j] are unwieldy to write out, especially for large convolution kernels. As an alternative, Figure 6-7 shows a table of input signal and convolution kernel (size 3 × 3) elements that are required to calculate each output signal element when using an __m256 C++ SIMD type and SIMD arithmetic. This figure uses the variable names of the 2D discrete convolution equation. To calculate y[i][j], for example, each input signal element in its row must be multiplied by the convolution kernel element that is shown at the top of each table column. These products are then summed to generate the final y[i][j]. Note that each column in the table contains consecutive input signal elements. This allows input signal element loading using the C++ SIMD intrinsic function _mm256_loadu_ps(). The function _mm256_set1_ps() broadcasts single elements from the convolution kernel, while _mm256_fmadd_ps() performs the required FMA SIMD arithmetic.

| | g[1][1] | g[1][0] | g[1][-1] | g[0][1] | g[0][0] | g[0][-1] | g[-1][1] | g[-1][0] | g[-1][-1] |
|---|---|---|---|---|---|---|---|---|---|
| y[ ][j+0] = | x[ -1][j-1] × | x[ -1][j+0] × | x[ -1][j+1] × | x[ +0][j-1] × | x[ +0][j+0] × | x[ +0][j+1] × | x[ +1][j-1] × | x[ +1][j+0] × | x[ +1][j+1] × |
| y[ ][j+1] = | x[ -1][j+0] × | x[ -1][j+1] × | x[ -1][j+2] × | x[ +0][j+0] × | x[ +0][j+1] × | x[ +0][j+2] × | x[ +1][j+0] × | x[ +1][j+1] × | x[ +1][j+2] × |
| y[ ][j+2] = | x[ -1][j+1] × | x[ -1][j+2] × | x[ -1][j+3] × | x[ +0][j+1] × | x[ +0][j+2] × | x[ +0][j+3] × | x[ +1][j+1] × | x[ +1][j+2] × | x[ +1][j+3] × |
| y[ ][j+3] = | x[ -1][j+2] × | x[ -1][j+3] × | x[ -1][j+4] × | x[ +0][j+2] × | x[ +0][j+3] × | x[ +0][j+4] × | x[ +1][j+2] × | x[ +1][j+3] × | x[ +1][j+4] × |
| y[ ][j+4] = | x[ -1][j+3] × | x[ -1][j+4] × | x[ -1][j+5] × | x[ +0][j+3] × | x[ +0][j+4] × | x[ +0][j+5] × | x[ +1][j+3] × | x[ +1][j+4] × | x[ +1][j+5] × |
| y[ ][j+5] = | x[ -1][j+4] × | x[ -1][j+5] × | x[ -1][j+6] × | x[ +0][j+4] × | x[ +0][j+5] × | x[ +0][j+6] × | x[ +1][j+4] × | x[ +1][j+5] × | x[ +1][j+6] × |
| y[ ][j+6] = | x[ -1][j+5] × | x[ -1][j+6] × | x[ -1][j+7] × | x[ +0][j+5] × | x[ +0][j+6] × | x[ +0][j+7] × | x[ +1][j+5] × | x[ +1][j+6] × | x[ +1][j+7] × |
| y[ ][j+7] = | x[ -1][j+6] × | x[ -1][j+7] × | x[ -1][j+8] × | x[ +0][j+6] × | x[ +0][j+7] × | x[ +0][j+8] × | x[ +1][j+6] × | x[ +1][j+7] × | x[ +1][j+8] × |

**Figure 6-7.** *Input signal and convolution kernel elements required to calculate an output element in a 2D discrete convolution*

Returning to the code in Listing 6-3, the second else if code block in Convolve2D_F32_Iavx2() calculates im_des[i][j:j+3] whenever the number of remaining columns in the current row is less than num_simd_elements but greater than or equal to num_simd_elements2. This facilitates the processing of signal elements using 128-bit wide SIMD operands. The final else code block handles any residual columns in the current row using scalar single-precision floating-point arithmetic. It should be noted that the convolution calculating functions Convolve2D_F32_Cpp() and Convolve2D_F32_Iavx2() ignore the border elements of the input images when performing their calculations. This is the reason for the black border in the output image of Figure 6-3. In real-word image processing, the application's functional requirements usually determine if extra processing is necessary to handle any border elements or if they can just be ignored. The image processing references listed in Appendix B contain more information regarding this topic. Here are the results for source code example Ch06_03:

```
Performing convolutions
Saving destination image files
rc:       true
num_diff: 0

Running benchmark function Convolve2D_F32_bm - please wait
.................................................
Benchmark times saved to file Ch06_03_Convolve2D_F32_bm_OXYGEN4.csv
```

Table 6-3 shows some benchmark timing measurements for source code example Ch06_03. These measurements were made using test image ImageE.png and a 9 × 9 convolution kernel that performs low-pass filtering.

*Table 6-3.* *2D Discrete Convolution (Single-Precision) Execution Times (Microseconds)*

| CPU | Convolve2D_F32_Cpp() | Convolve2D_F32_Iavx2() |
|-----|----------------------|------------------------|
| Intel Core i7-8700K | 89569 | 11241 |
| Intel Core i5-11600K | 75609 | 9266 |

# Separable Kernel

Earlier in this chapter, you learned that if a 2D convolution kernel is separable, a 2D discrete convolution can be carried out using two independent 1D discrete convolutions. Using two independent 1D discrete convolutions is significantly faster than a single 2D discrete convolution since the total number of arithmetic operations of the former is considerably less. The next source code example, Ch06_04, demonstrates using two independent 1D discrete convolutions to carry out a 2D discrete convolution. Listing 6-4 shows the source code for example Ch06_04.

*Listing 6-4.* Example Ch06_04

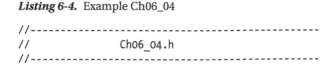

```
//-------------------------------------------------
//           Ch06_04.h
//-------------------------------------------------
```

```cpp
#pragma once
#include <array>
#include <vector>

struct CD_1Dx2
{
    size_t m_ImH;
    size_t m_ImW;
    size_t m_KernelSize;
    std::vector<float> m_ImSrc;
    std::vector<float> m_ImDes;
    std::vector<float> m_ImTmp;
    std::vector<float> m_Kernel1Dx;
    std::vector<float> m_Kernel1Dy;
};

enum class KERNEL_ID : unsigned int
{
    LowPass1Dx2_3x3, LowPass1Dx2_5x5, LowPass1Dx2_7x7,
    LowPass1Dx2_9x9, LowPass1Dx2_15x15
};

// Ch06_04_fcpp.cpp
extern void Convolve1Dx2_F32_Cpp(CD_1Dx2& cd);
extern void Convolve1Dx2_F32_Iavx2(CD_1Dx2& cd);

// Ch06_04_misc.cpp
extern bool CheckArgs1Dx2(const CD_1Dx2& cd);
extern void Init1Dx2(std::array<CD_1Dx2, 2>& cd, const char* fn, KERNEL_ID id);

// Ch06_04_misc2.cpp
extern void DisplayKernel1Dx2(float sigma, size_t ks);
extern void GetKernel1Dx2(CD_1Dx2& cd, KERNEL_ID id);

// Ch06_04_bm.cpp
extern void Convolve1Dx2_F32_bm(void);

// Miscellaneous constants
const KERNEL_ID c_KernelID = KERNEL_ID::LowPass1Dx2_15x15;
const KERNEL_ID c_KernelID_BM = KERNEL_ID::LowPass1Dx2_9x9;

//--------------------------------------------------
//                 Ch06_04_fcpp.cpp
//--------------------------------------------------

#include <stdexcept>
#include <immintrin.h>
#include "Ch06_04.h"
#include "MiscTypes.h"
```

```cpp
void Convolve1Dx2_F32_Cpp(CD_1Dx2& cd)
{
    if (!CheckArgs1Dx2(cd))
        throw std::runtime_error("Convolve1Dx2_F32_Cpp() - CheckArgs failed");

    indx_t ks = (indx_t)cd.m_KernelSize;
    indx_t ks2 = ks / 2;
    indx_t im_h = cd.m_ImH;
    indx_t im_w = cd.m_ImW;
    const std::vector<float>& im_src = cd.m_ImSrc;
    std::vector<float>& im_des = cd.m_ImDes;
    std::vector<float>& im_tmp = cd.m_ImTmp;
    const std::vector<float>& im_ker_x = cd.m_Kernel1Dx;
    const std::vector<float>& im_ker_y = cd.m_Kernel1Dy;

    // Perform 1D convolution (X)
    for (indx_t i = ks2; i < im_h - ks2; i++)
    {
        for (indx_t j = ks2; j < im_w - ks2; j++)
        {
            float im_tmp_val = 0;

            for (indx_t k = -ks2; k <= ks2; k++)
                im_tmp_val += im_src[i * im_w + j - k] * im_ker_x[k + ks2];

            im_tmp[i * im_w + j] = im_tmp_val;
        }
    }

    // Perform 1D convolution (Y)
    for (indx_t j = ks2; j < im_w - ks2; j++)
    {
        for (indx_t i = ks2; i < im_h - ks2; i++)
        {
            float im_des_val = 0;

            for (indx_t k = -ks2; k <= ks2; k++)
                im_des_val += im_tmp[(i - k) * im_w + j] * im_ker_y[k + ks2];

            im_des[i * im_w + j] = im_des_val;
        }
    }
}

void Convolve1Dx2_F32_Iavx2(CD_1Dx2& cd)
{
    if (!CheckArgs1Dx2(cd))
        throw std::runtime_error("Convolve1Dx2_F32_Iavx2() - CheckArgs failed");
```

```
indx_t ks = (indx_t)cd.m_KernelSize;
indx_t ks2 = ks / 2;
indx_t im_h = cd.m_ImH;
indx_t im_w = cd.m_ImW;
const std::vector<float>& im_src = cd.m_ImSrc;
std::vector<float>& im_des = cd.m_ImDes;
std::vector<float>& im_tmp = cd.m_ImTmp;
const std::vector<float>& im_ker_x = cd.m_Kernel1Dx;
const std::vector<float>& im_ker_y = cd.m_Kernel1Dy;

const indx_t num_simd_elements = 8;
const indx_t num_simd_elements2 = 4;

// Perform 1D convolution (X)
for (indx_t i = ks2; i < im_h - ks2; i++)
{
    indx_t j = ks2;

    while (j < im_w - ks2)
    {
        if (j + num_simd_elements <= im_w - ks2)
        {
            __m256 im_tmp_vals = _mm256_setzero_ps();

            for (indx_t k = -ks2; k <= ks2; k++)
            {
                __m256 im_src_vals = _mm256_loadu_ps(&im_src[i * im_w + j - k]);
                __m256 im_ker_vals = _mm256_set1_ps(im_ker_x[k + ks2]);

                im_tmp_vals = _mm256_fmadd_ps(im_src_vals, im_ker_vals,
                            im_tmp_vals);
            }

            _mm256_storeu_ps(&im_tmp[i * im_w + j], im_tmp_vals);
            j += num_simd_elements;
        }
        else if (j + num_simd_elements2 <= im_w - ks2)
        {
            __m128 im_tmp_vals = _mm_setzero_ps();

            for (indx_t k = -ks2; k <= ks2; k++)
            {
                __m128 im_src_vals = _mm_loadu_ps(&im_src[i * im_w + j - k]);
                __m128 im_ker_vals = _mm_set1_ps(im_ker_x[k + ks2]);

                im_tmp_vals = _mm_fmadd_ps(im_src_vals, im_ker_vals,
                            im_tmp_vals);
            }

            _mm_storeu_ps(&im_tmp[i * im_w + j], im_tmp_vals);
            j += num_simd_elements2;
        }
```

```
        else
        {
            __m128 im_tmp_vals = _mm_setzero_ps();

            for (indx_t k = -ks2; k <= ks2; k++)
            {
                __m128 im_src_vals = _mm_load_ss(&im_src[i * im_w + j - k]);
                __m128 im_ker_vals = _mm_load_ss(&im_ker_x[k + ks2]);

                im_tmp_vals = _mm_fmadd_ss(im_src_vals, im_ker_vals,
                            im_tmp_vals);
            }

            _mm_store_ss(&im_tmp[i * im_w + j], im_tmp_vals);
            j += 1;
        }
    }
}

// Perform 1D convolution (Y)
indx_t j = ks2;

while (j < im_w - ks2)
{
    if (j + num_simd_elements <= im_w - ks2)
    {
        for (indx_t i = ks2; i < im_h - ks2; i++)
        {
            __m256 im_des_vals = _mm256_setzero_ps();

            for (indx_t k = -ks2; k <= ks2; k++)
            {
                __m256 im_tmp_vals = _mm256_loadu_ps(&im_tmp[(i - k) * im_w + j]);
                __m256 im_ker_vals = _mm256_set1_ps(im_ker_y[k + ks2]);

                im_des_vals = _mm256_fmadd_ps(im_tmp_vals, im_ker_vals,
                            im_des_vals);
            }

            _mm256_storeu_ps(&im_des[i * im_w + j], im_des_vals);
        }

        j += num_simd_elements;
    }
    else if (j + num_simd_elements2 <= im_w - ks2)
    {
        for (indx_t i = ks2; i < im_h - ks2; i++)
        {
            __m128 im_des_vals = _mm_setzero_ps();
```

```
                    for (indx_t k = -ks2; k <= ks2; k++)
                    {
                        __m128 im_tmp_vals = _mm_loadu_ps(&im_tmp[(i - k) * im_w + j]);
                        __m128 im_ker_vals = _mm_set1_ps(im_ker_y[k + ks2]);

                        im_des_vals = _mm_fmadd_ps(im_tmp_vals, im_ker_vals,
                                        im_des_vals);
                    }

                    _mm_storeu_ps(&im_des[i * im_w + j], im_des_vals);
                }

            j += num_simd_elements2;
        }
        else
        {
            for (indx_t i = ks2; i < im_h - ks2; i++)
            {
                __m128 im_des_vals = _mm_setzero_ps();

                for (indx_t k = -ks2; k <= ks2; k++)
                {
                    __m128 im_tmp_vals = _mm_load_ss(&im_tmp[(i - k) * im_w + j]);
                    __m128 im_ker_vals = _mm_load_ss(&im_ker_y[k + ks2]);

                    im_des_vals = _mm_fmadd_ss(im_tmp_vals, im_ker_vals,
                                    im_des_vals);
                }

                _mm_store_ss(&im_des[i * im_w + j], im_des_vals);
            }

            j += 1;
        }
    }
}
```

In Listing 6-4, the header file Ch06_04.h begins with the definition of a structure named CD_1Dx2. This structure holds the data that is used by the convolution calculating functions. There are two noteworthy differences between the structure CD_1Dx2 and the structure CD_2D that was used in the previous example. First, structure CD_1Dx2 includes a third image buffer named m_ImTmp. This temporary buffer holds the result of the first 1D discrete convolution. The second notable change is that structure CD_1Dx2 contains two 1D convolution kernels, m_Kernel1Dx and m_Kernel1Dy, instead of a single 2D discrete convolution kernel. Not shown in Listing 6-4 are files Ch06_04_misc.cpp and Ch06_04.cpp. These files contain the functions that perform data structure initialization, image loading and saving, etc., and are very similar to the ones used in example Ch06_03. They are, of course, included in the software download package.

The first function in file Ch06_04_fcpp.cpp, Convolve1Dx2_F32_Cpp(), implements the dual 1D discrete convolution using standard C++ statements. Note that Convolve1Dx2_F32_Cpp() performs its convolutions using two separate code blocks. The first code block contains three nested for-loops that execute a 1D convolution using the x-axis of source image buffer im_src. The results of this convolution are saved to the temporary image buffer im_tmp. The second code block in function Convolve1Dx2_F32_Cpp() performs a

1D convolution using the y-axis of im_tmp. The result of this 1D convolution is saved to the output image buffer im_des.

The SIMD counterpart function of Convolve1Dx2_F32_Cpp() is named Convolve1Dx2_F32_Iavx2(). This function is also partitioned into two well-defined sections that execute independent 1D discrete convolutions. The first section carries out a 1D discrete convolution using C++ SIMD intrinsic functions and the x-axis of input image im_src. The logic used in this section is similar to the previous example in that num_simd_elements and num_simd_elements2 are tested to determine if 256-bit wide, 128-bit wide, or scalar operands should be used. The second section in Convolve1Dx2_F32_Cpp() performs a 1D discrete convolution using the y-axis of im_tmp and saves results to the output image im_des. Here are the results for source code example Ch06_04:

```
Performing convolutions
Saving destination image files
rc:       true
num_diff: 0

Running benchmark function Convolve1Dx2_F32_bm - please wait
.................................................
Benchmark times saved to file Ch06_04_Convolve1Dx2_F32_bm_OXYGEN4.csv
```

Table 6-4 shows some benchmark timing measurements for source code example Ch06_04. These measurements were made using test image ImageE.png and a 9 × 9 convolution kernel that performs low-pass filtering. If you compare the execution times in Tables 6-3 and 6-4, it was clearly worth the effort to code the functions that implement a 2D discrete convolution using two independent 1D discrete convolutions. This is true for both the standard C++ and SIMD algorithms.

***Table 6-4.*** *2D Discrete Convolution (Single-Precision) Execution Times (Microseconds)*

| CPU | Convolve1Dx2_F32_Cpp() | Convolve1Dx2_F32_Iavx2() |
|---|---|---|
| Intel Core i7-8700K | 21568 | 3623 |
| Intel Core i5-11600K | 14395 | 2467 |

Source code example Ch06_05 contains a simple function that compares the output images generated by the convolution functions in examples Ch06_03 and Ch06_04. In theory, these images should be identical. However, when comparing the images, pixel values are allowed to differ by ±1 to account for the non-associativity of floating-point arithmetic. Here are the results:

```
Comparing convolution result images
../Ch06_03/Ch06_03_ImageE_Conv2D_0.png
../Ch06_03/Ch06_03_ImageE_Conv2D_1.png
../Ch06_04/Ch06_04_ImageE_Conv2D_0.png
../Ch06_04/Ch06_04_ImageE_Conv2D_1.png

All images are alike
```

In source code file Ch06_05.cpp, changing max_d = 1 to max_d = 0 yields only a small number of pixel value discrepancies.

# Summary

Most of the C++ SIMD intrinsic functions demonstrated in the chapter were also used in previous chapters. However, some new functions were introduced, and these are summarized in Table 6-5 along with commonly used size variants. Before proceeding to the next chapter, you should understand the SIMD arithmetic calculation or data manipulation operation that is performed by each function shown in Table 6-5.

*Table 6-5.* *C++ SIMD Intrinsic Function Summary for Chapter 6*

| C++ SIMD Function Name | Description |
| --- | --- |
| _mm_fmadd_sd, _ss | Scalar fused-multiply-add |
| _mm_load_sd, _ss | Load scalar floating-point element |
| _mm_mul_pd, _ps | Packed floating-point multiplication |
| _mm_mul_sd, _ss | Scalar floating-point multiplication |
| _mm_set1_pd, _ps | Broadcast floating-point value |
| _mm_setzero_pd, _ps | Set packed floating-point elements to zero |
| _mm_store_sd, _ss | Store scalar floating-point element |

# CHAPTER 7

■ ■ ■

# AVX-512 C++ Programming: Part 1

In the five previous chapters, you learned how to code functions that exploited the computational capabilities of AVX and AVX2 using C++ SIMD intrinsic functions. The chapter you are about to read introduces AVX-512 SIMD programming. It begins with a brief overview of AVX-512 and its various instruction set extensions. This is followed by a section that explains basic packed integer arithmetic using 512-bit wide operands. The chapter concludes with a section that demonstrates a few integer-based image processing techniques using AVX-512 C++ SIMD intrinsic functions.

## AVX-512 Overview

AVX-512 is a collection of interrelated but distinct instruction set extensions. An AVX-512 compliant processor must minimally support the AVX-512 foundation (AVX512F) instruction set extension. This extension includes instructions that perform fundamental arithmetic using 512-bit wide SIMD operands of packed floating-point (single-precision or double-precision) or packed integer (32-bit or 64-bit) elements. The AVX512F extension also includes instructions that perform permutations, data conversions, and scatter operations (a scatter operation is the opposite of a gather operation). Other instructions are also available, and these are documented in the programming reference manuals listed in Appendix B.

Table 7-1 lists the AVX-512 instruction set extensions that have been incorporated into mainstream server and high-end desktop processors from Intel. This table also includes AVX-512 instruction set extensions that have been announced for inclusion in future Intel processors. Not listed in Table 7-1 are the AVX-512 instruction set extensions that are only available on specialized processors such as Intel Xeon Phi. Like other x86 instruction set extensions such as AVX, AVX2, FMA, etc., a program must never assume that its host processor supports any of the AVX-512 instruction set extensions shown in Table 7-1 based on processor name, model number, or underlying microarchitecture. To ensure software compatibility with future processors, a program should always verify at runtime that any required AVX-512 instruction set extensions are available. You will learn how to do this in Chapter 9.

© Daniel Kusswurm 2022
D. Kusswurm, *Modern Parallel Programming with C++ and Assembly Language*,
https://doi.org/10.1007/978-1-4842-7918-2_7

*Table 7-1.* *Overview of AVX-512 Instruction Set Extensions*

| Extension Name (CPUID Flag) | Description |
|---|---|
| AVX512F | Foundation instructions |
| AVX512CD | Conflict detect instructions |
| AVX512DQ | Doubleword and quadword instructions |
| AVX512BW | Byte and word instructions |
| AVX512VL | 128-bit and 256-bit vector length instructions |
| AVX512_IFMA | Integer fused-multiply-add |
| AVX512_VBMI | Vector byte manipulation instructions |
| AVX512_VNNI | Vector neural net instructions |
| AVX512_VPOPCNTDQ | Vector bit count instructions |
| AVX512_VBMI2 | Vector byte manipulation instructions |
| AVX512_BITALG | Vector bit manipulation instructions |
| AVX512_BF16 | Vector neural net instructions (BFLOAT16 format) |
| AVX512_VP2INTERSECT | Vector pair intersection instructions |
| AVX512_FP16 | Vector half-precision floating-point |

The text strings shown in the Extension Name column of Table 7-1 match the flag name that is used by the x86 cpuid (CPU Identification) instruction. A program can use this instruction to ascertain feature information about its host processor including the availability of AVX, AVX2, and AVX-512. You will learn more about the cpuid instruction in Chapter 9. The AVX-512 source code examples published in this book require a processor that supports the following AVX-512 instruction set extensions: AVX512F, AVX512BW, AVX512DQ, and AVX512VL. The host operating system must also support AVX-512. Mainstream operating systems that support AVX-512 include Windows 10 or later and Linux distributions based on the 3.15 or later kernel.

# Integer Arithmetic

In this section, you will learn how to perform basic integer arithmetic using AVX-512 C++ SIMD intrinsic functions. You will also learn how to apply merge masking and zero masking. Besides wider SIMD operands, these instruction-level operations are perhaps the most significant features that differentiate AVX-512 from its predecessor instruction set extensions AVX and AVX2.

## Basic Arithmetic

Listing 7-1 shows the source code for example Ch07_01. This example demonstrates basic arithmetic operations using 512-bit wide operands and packed integer elements. Source code example Ch07_01 also highlights some of the similarities between AVX/AVX2 and AVX-512 C++ SIMD intrinsic functions.

***Listing 7-1.*** Example Ch07_01

```
//----------------------------------------------
//              ZmmVal.h
//----------------------------------------------

#pragma once
#include <string>
#include <cstdint>
#include <sstream>
#include <iomanip>

struct  alignas(64) ZmmVal
{
public:
    union
    {
        int8_t m_I8[64];
        int16_t m_I16[32];
        int32_t m_I32[16];
        int64_t m_I64[8];
        uint8_t m_U8[64];
        uint16_t m_U16[32];
        uint32_t m_U32[16];
        uint64_t m_U64[8];
        float m_F32[16];
        double m_F64[8];
    };

//----------------------------------------------
//              Ch07_01.h
//----------------------------------------------

#pragma once
#include <cstdint>
#include "ZmmVal.h"

// Ch07_01_fcpp.cpp
extern void MathI16_Iavx512(ZmmVal c[6], const ZmmVal* a, const ZmmVal* b);
extern void MathI64_Iavx512(ZmmVal c[6], const ZmmVal* a, const ZmmVal* b);

//----------------------------------------------
//              Ch07_01.cpp
//----------------------------------------------

#include <iostream>
#include <iomanip>
#include <cstdint>
#include "Ch07_01.h"

static void MathI16(void);
static void MathI64(void);
```

```cpp
int main()
{
    MathI16();
    MathI64();
    return 0;
}

static void MathI16(void)
{
    ZmmVal a, b, c[6];

    a.m_I16[0] = 10;        b.m_I16[0] = 100;
    a.m_I16[1] = 20;        b.m_I16[1] = 200;
    a.m_I16[2] = 30;        b.m_I16[2] = 300;
    a.m_I16[3] = 40;        b.m_I16[3] = 400;
    a.m_I16[4] = 50;        b.m_I16[4] = 500;
    a.m_I16[5] = 60;        b.m_I16[5] = 600;
    a.m_I16[6] = 70;        b.m_I16[6] = 700;
    a.m_I16[7] = 80;        b.m_I16[7] = 800;

    a.m_I16[8] = 1000;      b.m_I16[8] = -100;
    a.m_I16[9] = 2000;      b.m_I16[9] = 200;
    a.m_I16[10] = 3000;     b.m_I16[10] = -300;
    a.m_I16[11] = 4000;     b.m_I16[11] = 400;
    a.m_I16[12] = 5000;     b.m_I16[12] = -500;
    a.m_I16[13] = 6000;     b.m_I16[13] = 600;
    a.m_I16[14] = 7000;     b.m_I16[14] = -700;
    a.m_I16[15] = 8000;     b.m_I16[15] = 800;

    a.m_I16[16] = -1000;    b.m_I16[16] = 100;
    a.m_I16[17] = -2000;    b.m_I16[17] = -200;
    a.m_I16[18] = 3000;     b.m_I16[18] = 303;
    a.m_I16[19] = 4000;     b.m_I16[19] = -400;
    a.m_I16[20] = -5000;    b.m_I16[20] = 500;
    a.m_I16[21] = -6000;    b.m_I16[21] = -600;
    a.m_I16[22] = -7000;    b.m_I16[22] = 700;
    a.m_I16[23] = -8000;    b.m_I16[23] = 800;

    a.m_I16[24] = 30000;    b.m_I16[24] = 3000;     // add overflow
    a.m_I16[25] = 6000;     b.m_I16[25] = 32000;    // add overflow
    a.m_I16[26] = -25000;   b.m_I16[26] = -27000;   // add overflow
    a.m_I16[27] = 8000;     b.m_I16[27] = 28700;    // add overflow
    a.m_I16[28] = 2000;     b.m_I16[28] = -31000;   // sub overflow
    a.m_I16[29] = 4000;     b.m_I16[29] = -30000;   // sub overflow
    a.m_I16[30] = -3000;    b.m_I16[30] = 32000;    // sub overflow
    a.m_I16[31] = -15000;   b.m_I16[31] = 24000;    // sub overflow

    MathI16_Iavx512(c, &a, &b);
```

```
    std::cout <<"\nResults for MathI16\n\n";
    std::cout << " i      a      b      add     adds    sub     subs    min     max\n";
    std::cout << "-----------------------------------------------------------------\n";

    for (size_t i = 0; i < 32; i++)
    {
        std::cout << std::setw(2)  << i << ' ';
        std::cout << std::setw(8) << a.m_I16[i] << ' ';
        std::cout << std::setw(8) << b.m_I16[i] << ' ';
        std::cout << std::setw(8) << c[0].m_I16[i] << ' ';
        std::cout << std::setw(8) << c[1].m_I16[i] << ' ';
        std::cout << std::setw(8) << c[2].m_I16[i] << ' ';
        std::cout << std::setw(8) << c[3].m_I16[i] << ' ';
        std::cout << std::setw(8) << c[4].m_I16[i] << ' ';
        std::cout << std::setw(8) << c[5].m_I16[i] << '\n';
    }
}

static void MathI64(void)
{
    ZmmVal a, b, c[6];

    a.m_I64[0] = 64;          b.m_I64[0] = 4;
    a.m_I64[1] = 1024;        b.m_I64[1] = 5;
    a.m_I64[2] = -2048;       b.m_I64[2] = 2;
    a.m_I64[3] = 8192;        b.m_I64[3] = 5;
    a.m_I64[4] = -256;        b.m_I64[4] = 8;
    a.m_I64[5] = 4096;        b.m_I64[5] = 7;
    a.m_I64[6] = 16;          b.m_I64[6] = 3;
    a.m_I64[7] = 512;         b.m_I64[7] = 6;

    MathI64_Iavx512(c, &a, &b);

    std::cout << "\nResults for MathI64\n\n";
    std::cout << " i      a      b      add     sub     mul     sll     sra     abs\n";
    std::cout << "------------------------------------------------------------------\n";

    for (size_t i = 0; i < 8; i++)
    {
        std::cout << std::setw(2) << i << ' ';
        std::cout << std::setw(6) << a.m_I64[i] << ' ';
        std::cout << std::setw(6) << b.m_I64[i] << ' ';
        std::cout << std::setw(8) << c[0].m_I64[i] << ' ';
        std::cout << std::setw(8) << c[1].m_I64[i] << ' ';
        std::cout << std::setw(8) << c[2].m_I64[i] << ' ';
        std::cout << std::setw(8) << c[3].m_I64[i] << ' ';
        std::cout << std::setw(8) << c[4].m_I64[i] << ' ';
        std::cout << std::setw(8) << c[5].m_I64[i] << '\n';
    }
}
```

```
//--------------------------------------------------
//                Ch07_01_fcpp.cpp
//--------------------------------------------------

#include <immintrin.h>
#include "Ch07_01.h"

void MathI16_Iavx512(ZmmVal c[6], const ZmmVal* a, const ZmmVal* b)
{
    __m512i a_vals = _mm512_load_si512((__m512i*)a);
    __m512i b_vals = _mm512_load_si512((__m512i*)b);

    __m512i c_vals0 = _mm512_add_epi16(a_vals, b_vals);
    __m512i c_vals1 = _mm512_adds_epi16(a_vals, b_vals);
    __m512i c_vals2 = _mm512_sub_epi16(a_vals, b_vals);
    __m512i c_vals3 = _mm512_subs_epi16(a_vals, b_vals);
    __m512i c_vals4 = _mm512_min_epi16(a_vals, b_vals);
    __m512i c_vals5 = _mm512_max_epi16(a_vals, b_vals);

    _mm512_store_si512((__m512i*)&c[0], c_vals0);
    _mm512_store_si512((__m512i*)&c[1], c_vals1);
    _mm512_store_si512((__m512i*)&c[2], c_vals2);
    _mm512_store_si512((__m512i*)&c[3], c_vals3);
    _mm512_store_si512((__m512i*)&c[4], c_vals4);
    _mm512_store_si512((__m512i*)&c[5], c_vals5);
}

void MathI64_Iavx512(ZmmVal c[6], const ZmmVal* a, const ZmmVal* b)
{
    __m512i a_vals = _mm512_load_si512((__m512i*)a);
    __m512i b_vals = _mm512_load_si512((__m512i*)b);

    __m512i c_vals0 = _mm512_add_epi64(a_vals, b_vals);
    __m512i c_vals1 = _mm512_sub_epi64(a_vals, b_vals);
    __m512i c_vals2 = _mm512_mullo_epi64(a_vals, b_vals);
    __m512i c_vals3 = _mm512_sllv_epi64(a_vals, b_vals);
    __m512i c_vals4 = _mm512_srav_epi64(a_vals, b_vals);
    __m512i c_vals5 = _mm512_abs_epi64(a_vals);

    _mm512_store_si512((__m512i*)&c[0], c_vals0);
    _mm512_store_si512((__m512i*)&c[1], c_vals1);
    _mm512_store_si512((__m512i*)&c[2], c_vals2);
    _mm512_store_si512((__m512i*)&c[3], c_vals3);
    _mm512_store_si512((__m512i*)&c[4], c_vals4);
    _mm512_store_si512((__m512i*)&c[5], c_vals5);
}
```

Listing 7-1 starts with the definition of the C++ structure ZmmVal, which is defined in the header file ZmmVal.h. This structure is the 512-bit wide counterpart of the XmmVal and YmmVal structures you saw in earlier chapters. Like XmmVal and YmmVal, the structure ZmmVal contains an anonymous public union that facilitates SIMD data exchange between functions. It also includes several string formatting member functions. These functions are not shown in Listing 7-1 but included in the download software package. The alignas(64) specifier that is used in the definition of ZmmVal instructs the C++ compiler to align each ZmmVal instance on a 64-byte boundary.

Following the definition of ZmmVal in Listing 7-1 is the file Ch07_01.h. This file incorporates the required function declarations for this source code example. Note that the function declarations make use of the ZmmVal structure. The file Ch07_01.cpp contains functions MathI16() and MathI64(). Function MathI16() performs test case initialization for the C++ SIMD calculating function MathI16_Iavx512(), which implements SIMD arithmetic operations using 16-bit wide integer elements. The function MathI64() is akin to MathI16() except that is uses 64-bit wide integer elements.

Function MathI16_Iavx512() begins its execution with a call to _mm512_load_si512(). This function loads the integer elements of argument value a into __m512i a_vals. An __m512i object is a C++ SIMD intrinsic data type that holds 512 bits (64 bytes) of packed integer data. The ensuing _mm512_load_si512() call loads the integer elements of argument value b into b_vals. Note that function _mm512_load_si512() requires its memory argument to be aligned on a 64-byte boundary. This is why structure ZmmVal was defined using the alignas(64) specifier.

After the two load operations, MathI16_Iavx512() employs the C++ SIMD intrinsic functions _mm512_add_epi16() and _mm512_adds_epi16() to perform packed integer addition using 16-bit wide integer elements. Note that function _mm512_adds_epi16() performs saturated addition. The next two calls, _mm512_sub_epi16() and _mm512_subs_epi16(), carry out packed integer subtraction. The ensuing calls to _mm512_min_epi16() and _mm512_max()_epi16() perform signed packed integer compares. The final code block in MathI16_Iavx512() contains a series of _mm512_store_si512() calls that save the calculated results. Like its load counterpart, the function _mm512_store_si512() requires the target memory buffer to be aligned on a 64-byte boundary.

Function MathI64_Iavx512() is similar to MathI16_Iavx512() but uses 64-bit instead of 16-bit wide integer elements. The C++ SIMD intrinsic functions _mm512_add_epi64() and _mm512_sub_epi64() carry out packed integer addition and subtraction, respectively. The C++ SIMD intrinsic function _mm512_mullo_epi64() performs packed 64-bit integer multiplication and saves the low-order 64 bits of each 128-bit product. Functions _mm512_sllv_epi64() and _mm512_srav_epi64() carry out logical left and arithmetic right shifts, respectively. Each element in a_vals is shifted left or right by the bit counts in the corresponding element positions of b_vals. The final C++ SIMD intrinsic function call in MathI64_Iavx512(), _mm512_abs_epi64(), calculates packed absolute values. Here are the results for source code example Ch07_01:

```
Results for MathI16

 i      a       b      add     adds      sub     subs      min      max
-----------------------------------------------------------------------
 0     10     100      110      110      -90      -90       10      100
 1     20     200      220      220     -180     -180       20      200
 2     30     300      330      330     -270     -270       30      300
 3     40     400      440      440     -360     -360       40      400
 4     50     500      550      550     -450     -450       50      500
 5     60     600      660      660     -540     -540       60      600
 6     70     700      770      770     -630     -630       70      700
 7     80     800      880      880     -720     -720       80      800
 8   1000    -100      900      900     1100     1100     -100     1000
 9   2000     200     2200     2200     1800     1800      200     2000
10   3000    -300     2700     2700     3300     3300     -300     3000
11   4000     400     4400     4400     3600     3600      400     4000
12   5000    -500     4500     4500     5500     5500     -500     5000
13   6000     600     6600     6600     5400     5400      600     6000
14   7000    -700     6300     6300     7700     7700     -700     7000
```

| 15 | 8000 | 800 | 8800 | 8800 | 7200 | 7200 | 800 | 8000 |
| 16 | -1000 | 100 | -900 | -900 | -1100 | -1100 | -1000 | 100 |
| 17 | -2000 | -200 | -2200 | -2200 | -1800 | -1800 | -2000 | -200 |
| 18 | 3000 | 303 | 3303 | 3303 | 2697 | 2697 | 303 | 3000 |
| 19 | 4000 | -400 | 3600 | 3600 | 4400 | 4400 | -400 | 4000 |
| 20 | -5000 | 500 | -4500 | -4500 | -5500 | -5500 | -5000 | 500 |
| 21 | -6000 | -600 | -6600 | -6600 | -5400 | -5400 | -6000 | -600 |
| 22 | -7000 | 700 | -6300 | -6300 | -7700 | -7700 | -7000 | 700 |
| 23 | -8000 | 800 | -7200 | -7200 | -8800 | -8800 | -8000 | 800 |
| 24 | 30000 | 3000 | -32536 | 32767 | 27000 | 27000 | 3000 | 30000 |
| 25 | 6000 | 32000 | -27536 | 32767 | -26000 | -26000 | 6000 | 32000 |
| 26 | -25000 | -27000 | 13536 | -32768 | 2000 | 2000 | -27000 | -25000 |
| 27 | 8000 | 28700 | -28836 | 32767 | -20700 | -20700 | 8000 | 28700 |
| 28 | 2000 | -31000 | -29000 | -29000 | -32536 | 32767 | -31000 | 2000 |
| 29 | 4000 | -30000 | -26000 | -26000 | -31536 | 32767 | -30000 | 4000 |
| 30 | -3000 | 32000 | 29000 | 29000 | 30536 | -32768 | -3000 | 32000 |
| 31 | -15000 | 24000 | 9000 | 9000 | 26536 | -32768 | -15000 | 24000 |

Results for MathI64

| i | a | b | add | sub | mul | sll | sra | abs |
|---|---|---|---|---|---|---|---|---|
| 0 | 64 | 4 | 68 | 60 | 256 | 1024 | 4 | 64 |
| 1 | 1024 | 5 | 1029 | 1019 | 5120 | 32768 | 32 | 1024 |
| 2 | -2048 | 2 | -2046 | -2050 | -4096 | -8192 | -512 | 2048 |
| 3 | 8192 | 5 | 8197 | 8187 | 40960 | 262144 | 256 | 8192 |
| 4 | -256 | 8 | -248 | -264 | -2048 | -65536 | -1 | 256 |
| 5 | 4096 | 7 | 4103 | 4089 | 28672 | 524288 | 32 | 4096 |
| 6 | 16 | 3 | 19 | 13 | 48 | 128 | 2 | 16 |
| 7 | 512 | 6 | 518 | 506 | 3072 | 32768 | 8 | 512 |

One critique of AVX-512 is the confusion that is triggered by the numerous instruction extensions listed in Table 7-1. In source code example Ch07_01, the C++ SIMD intrinsic function _mm512_add_epi64() requires a processor that supports AVX512F. However, the functions _mm512_add_epi16() and _mm512_mullo_epi64() require a processor that supports AVX512BW and AVX512DQ, respectively. Since the introduction of AVX-512, mainstream server and high-end desktop processors marketed by Intel have supported all three of these AVX-512 instruction set extensions, and this is unlikely to change in future processors. Nevertheless, as mentioned earlier in this chapter, a program should always verify at runtime that any required AVX-512 instruction set extensions are available on the host processor. The Intel Intrinsics Guide website (https://software.intel.com/sites/landingpage/IntrinsicsGuide/) contains more information about the various AVX-512 C++ SIMD intrinsic functions and their associated CPUID flags.

## Merge Masking and Zero Masking

Unlike AVX and AVX2, most AVX-512 instructions support a mask argument. This mask argument facilitates conditional merging or zeroing the results of a SIMD operation on a per-element basis.

Figure 7-1 illustrates the use of a mask argument in greater detail. In this figure, the first example illustrates execution of the AVX-512 C++ SIMD intrinsic function _mm512_add_epi32(). The result calculated by this function is akin to the functions _mm_add_epi32() and _mm256_add_epi32() that you learned about in previous chapters. The second example illustrates execution of _mm512_mask_add_epi32(), which includes the mask argument m. In this example, the processor performs addition only for those SIMD elements whose corresponding bit position in m is set to 1; otherwise, the processor copies the corresponding SIMD element from argument c into d. This is called merge masking. The final example, _mm512_maskz_add_epi32(), is similar to the second example but uses zero masking instead. With zero masking, the processor also executes addition only for those SIMD elements whose corresponding bit position in m is set to 1; otherwise, the processor sets the SIMD element to zero.

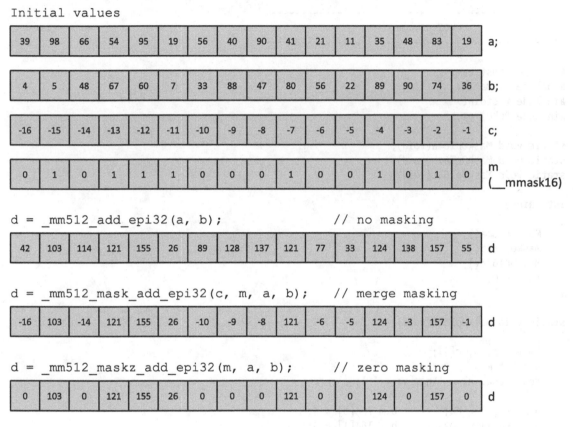

Initial values

| 39 | 98 | 66 | 54 | 95 | 19 | 56 | 40 | 90 | 41 | 21 | 11 | 35 | 48 | 83 | 19 | a; |

| 4 | 5 | 48 | 67 | 60 | 7 | 33 | 88 | 47 | 80 | 56 | 22 | 89 | 90 | 74 | 36 | b; |

| -16 | -15 | -14 | -13 | -12 | -11 | -10 | -9 | -8 | -7 | -6 | -5 | -4 | -3 | -2 | -1 | c; |

| 0 | 1 | 0 | 1 | 1 | 1 | 0 | 0 | 0 | 1 | 0 | 0 | 1 | 0 | 1 | 0 | m (__mmask16) |

`d = _mm512_add_epi32(a, b);`                    `// no masking`

| 42 | 103 | 114 | 121 | 155 | 26 | 89 | 128 | 137 | 121 | 77 | 33 | 124 | 138 | 157 | 55 | d |

`d = _mm512_mask_add_epi32(c, m, a, b);`    `// merge masking`

| -16 | 103 | -14 | 121 | 155 | 26 | -10 | -9 | -8 | 121 | -6 | -5 | 124 | -3 | 157 | -1 | d |

`d = _mm512_maskz_add_epi32(m, a, b);`        `// zero masking`

| 0 | 103 | 0 | 121 | 155 | 26 | 0 | 0 | 0 | 121 | 0 | 0 | 124 | 0 | 157 | 0 | d |

**Figure 7-1.** *Execution examples of _mm512_add_epi32(), _mm512_mask_add_epi32(), and _mm512_maskz_ add_epi32()*

Listing 7-2 shows the source code for example Ch07_02. This example demonstrates the use of various C++ SIMD intrinsic functions that use merge masking or zero masking.

**Listing 7-2.** Example Ch07_02

```
//--------------------------------------------------
//                Ch07_02.h
//--------------------------------------------------

#pragma once
#include <cstdint>
#include "ZmmVal.h"
```

```cpp
// Ch07_02_fcpp.cpp
extern void MaskOpI64a_Iavx512(ZmmVal c[5], uint8_t mask, const ZmmVal* a,
    const ZmmVal* b);
extern void MaskOpI64b_Iavx512(ZmmVal c[5], uint8_t mask, const ZmmVal* a,
    const ZmmVal* b1, const ZmmVal* b2);
extern void MaskOpI64c_Iavx512(ZmmVal* c, const ZmmVal* a, int64_t x1, int64_t x2);

//--------------------------------------------------
//                   Ch07_02.cpp
//--------------------------------------------------

#include <iostream>
#include <iomanip>
#include <cstdint>
#include "Ch07_02.h"

static void MaskOpI64a(void);
static void MaskOpI64b(void);
static void MaskOpI64c(void);

int main()
{
    MaskOpI64a();
    MaskOpI64b();
    MaskOpI64c();
    return 0;
}

static void MaskOpI64a(void)
{
    ZmmVal a, b, c[5];
    uint8_t mask = 0x7b;
    const char nl = '\n', sp = ' ';

    a.m_I64[0] = 64;          b.m_I64[0] = 4;
    a.m_I64[1] = 1024;        b.m_I64[1] = 5;
    a.m_I64[2] = -2048;       b.m_I64[2] = 2;
    a.m_I64[3] = 8192;        b.m_I64[3] = 5;
    a.m_I64[4] = -256;        b.m_I64[4] = 8;
    a.m_I64[5] = 4096;        b.m_I64[5] = 7;
    a.m_I64[6] = 16;          b.m_I64[6] = 3;
    a.m_I64[7] = 512;         b.m_I64[7] = 6;

    MaskOpI64a_Iavx512(c, mask, &a, &b);

    std::cout << "\nResults for MaskOpI64a - mask = 0x";
    std::cout << std::hex << std::setw(2) << (int)mask << std::dec << nl << nl;
    std::cout << " i      a       b       add     sub     mul     sll     sra\n";
    std::cout << "------------------------------------------------------------\n";
```

```cpp
    for (size_t i = 0; i < 8; i++)
    {
        std::cout << std::setw(2) << i << ' ';
        std::cout << std::setw(6) << a.m_I64[i] << sp;
        std::cout << std::setw(6) << b.m_I64[i] << sp;
        std::cout << std::setw(8) << c[0].m_I64[i] << sp;
        std::cout << std::setw(8) << c[1].m_I64[i] << sp;
        std::cout << std::setw(8) << c[2].m_I64[i] << sp;
        std::cout << std::setw(8) << c[3].m_I64[i] << sp;
        std::cout << std::setw(8) << c[4].m_I64[i] << nl;
    }
}

static void MaskOpI64b(void)
{
    ZmmVal a, b1, b2, c[5];
    uint8_t mask = 0xb6;
    const char nl = '\n', sp = ' ';

    a.m_I64[0] = 111111;    b1.m_I64[0] = 64;       b2.m_I64[0] = 4;
    a.m_I64[1] = 222222;    b1.m_I64[1] = 1024;     b2.m_I64[1] = 5;
    a.m_I64[2] = 333333;    b1.m_I64[2] = -2048;    b2.m_I64[2] = 2;
    a.m_I64[3] = 444444;    b1.m_I64[3] = 8192;     b2.m_I64[3] = 5;
    a.m_I64[4] = 555555;    b1.m_I64[4] = -256;     b2.m_I64[4] = 8;
    a.m_I64[5] = 666666;    b1.m_I64[5] = 4096;     b2.m_I64[5] = 7;
    a.m_I64[6] = 777777;    b1.m_I64[6] = 16;       b2.m_I64[6] = 3;
    a.m_I64[7] = 888888;    b1.m_I64[7] = 512;      b2.m_I64[7] = 6;

    MaskOpI64b_Iavx512(c, mask, &a, &b1, &b2);

    std::cout << "\nResults for MaskOpI64b - mask = 0x";
    std::cout << std::hex << std::setw(2) << (int)mask << std::dec << nl << nl;
    std::cout << " i      a      b1     b2      add      sub      mul      sll      sra\n";
    std::cout << "----------------------------------------------------------------------\n";

    for (size_t i = 0; i < 8; i++)
    {
        std::cout << std::setw(2) << i << sp;
        std::cout << std::setw(6) << a.m_I64[i] << sp;
        std::cout << std::setw(6) << b1.m_I64[i] << sp;
        std::cout << std::setw(6) << b2.m_I64[i] << sp;
        std::cout << std::setw(8) << c[0].m_I64[i] << sp;
        std::cout << std::setw(8) << c[1].m_I64[i] << sp;
        std::cout << std::setw(8) << c[2].m_I64[i] << sp;
        std::cout << std::setw(8) << c[3].m_I64[i] << sp;
        std::cout << std::setw(8) << c[4].m_I64[i] << nl;
    }
}
```

```cpp
static void MaskOpI64c(void)
{
    ZmmVal a, c;
    int64_t x1 = 0, x2 = 42;
    const char nl = '\n', sp = ' ';

    a.m_I64[0] = -100;
    a.m_I64[1] = 200;
    a.m_I64[2] = 300;
    a.m_I64[3] = -400;
    a.m_I64[4] = -500;
    a.m_I64[5] = 600;
    a.m_I64[6] = 700;
    a.m_I64[7] = -800;

    MaskOpI64c_Iavx512(&c, &a, x1, x2);

    std::cout << "\nResults for MaskOpI64c - ";
    std::cout << " x1 = " << x1 << ", x2 = " << x2 << nl << nl;
    std::cout << " i          a          c\n";
    std::cout << "--------------------\n";

    for (size_t i = 0; i < 8; i++)
    {
        std::cout << std::setw(2)  << i << ' ';
        std::cout << std::setw(8) << a.m_I64[i] << sp;
        std::cout << std::setw(8) << c.m_I64[i] << nl;
    }
}

//--------------------------------------------------
//              Ch07_02_fcpp.cpp
//--------------------------------------------------

#include <immintrin.h>
#include "Ch07_02.h"

void MaskOpI64a_Iavx512(ZmmVal c[5], uint8_t mask, const ZmmVal* a, const ZmmVal* b)
{
    __m512i a_vals = _mm512_load_si512((__m512i*)a);
    __m512i b_vals = _mm512_load_si512((__m512i*)b);

    __m512i c_vals0 = _mm512_maskz_add_epi64(mask, a_vals, b_vals);
    __m512i c_vals1 = _mm512_maskz_sub_epi64(mask, a_vals, b_vals);
    __m512i c_vals2 = _mm512_maskz_mullo_epi64(mask, a_vals, b_vals);
    __m512i c_vals3 = _mm512_maskz_sllv_epi64(mask, a_vals, b_vals);
    __m512i c_vals4 = _mm512_maskz_srav_epi64(mask, a_vals, b_vals);

    _mm512_store_si512((__m512i*)&c[0], c_vals0);
    _mm512_store_si512((__m512i*)&c[1], c_vals1);
    _mm512_store_si512((__m512i*)&c[2], c_vals2);
```

```
        _mm512_store_si512((__m512i*)&c[3], c_vals3);
        _mm512_store_si512((__m512i*)&c[4], c_vals4);
}

void MaskOpI64b_Iavx512(ZmmVal c[5], uint8_t mask, const ZmmVal* a, const ZmmVal* b1, const
ZmmVal* b2)
{
        __m512i a_vals = _mm512_load_si512((__m512i*)a);
        __m512i b1_vals = _mm512_load_si512((__m512i*)b1);
        __m512i b2_vals = _mm512_load_si512((__m512i*)b2);

        __m512i c_vals0 = _mm512_mask_add_epi64(a_vals, mask, b1_vals, b2_vals);
        __m512i c_vals1 = _mm512_mask_sub_epi64(a_vals, mask, b1_vals, b2_vals);
        __m512i c_vals2 = _mm512_mask_mullo_epi64(a_vals, mask, b1_vals, b2_vals);
        __m512i c_vals3 = _mm512_mask_sllv_epi64(a_vals, mask, b1_vals, b2_vals);
        __m512i c_vals4 = _mm512_mask_srav_epi64(a_vals, mask, b1_vals, b2_vals);

        _mm512_store_si512((__m512i*)&c[0], c_vals0);
        _mm512_store_si512((__m512i*)&c[1], c_vals1);
        _mm512_store_si512((__m512i*)&c[2], c_vals2);
        _mm512_store_si512((__m512i*)&c[3], c_vals3);
        _mm512_store_si512((__m512i*)&c[4], c_vals4);
}

void MaskOpI64c_Iavx512(ZmmVal* c, const ZmmVal* a, int64_t x1, int64_t x2)
{
        __m512i a_vals = _mm512_load_si512((__m512i*)a);
        __m512i x1_vals = _mm512_set1_epi64(x1);
        __m512i x2_vals = _mm512_set1_epi64(x2);

        // c_vals[i] = (a_vals[i] >= x1) ? a_vals[i] + x2 : a_vals[i]
        __mmask8 mask_ge = _mm512_cmpge_epi64_mask(a_vals, x1_vals);
        __m512i c_vals = _mm512_mask_add_epi64(a_vals, mask_ge, a_vals, x2_vals);

        _mm512_store_si512((__m512i*)c, c_vals);
}
```

In Listing 7-2, the file Ch07_02.h contains the function declarations for this example. The next file, Ch07_02.cpp, defines functions MaskOpI64a(), MaskOpI64b(), and MaskOpI64c(). These functions perform test case setup for the SIMD calculating functions. They also stream results to std::cout.

The first function in file Ch07_02_fcpp.cpp is named MaskOpI64a_Iavx512(). This function illustrates the use of several C++ SIMD intrinsic functions that perform zero masking. Note that argument value mask is declared as type uint8_t. This type is used here since each bit position corresponds to one element of a 512-bit wide SIMD operand of packed 64-bit integers (recall that a 512-bit wide SIMD operand can hold eight 64-bit integers). The next function, MaskOpI64b_Iavx512(), carries out the same arithmetic operations as MaskOpI64a_Iavx512() but uses merge masking instead of zero masking.

The final function in file Ch07_02_fcpp.cpp, MaskOpI64c_Iavx512(), demonstrates how to implement a SIMD ternary operator using merge masking. This function begins its execution with a call to _mm512_load_si512() that loads argument value a into a_vals. The ensuing two calls to _mm512_set1_epi64() initialize packed versions of argument values x1 and x2.

The next two C++ SIMD intrinsic functions, _mm512_cmpge_epi64_mask() and _mm512_mask_add_ epi64(), carry out the following ternary operation: c_vals[i] = (a_vals[i] >= x1) ? a_vals[i] + x2 : a_vals[i]. More specifically, the function _mm512_cmpge_epi64_mask() compares each element in a_vals against x1 and sets the corresponding bit position in mask_ge to 1 if the compare is true; otherwise, the bit is set to 0. The ensuing call to _mm512_mask_add_epi64() employs mask_ge to complete the ternary operation. This function performs addition only for those elements whose corresponding bit position in mask_ge is set to 1; otherwise, the corresponding element from a_vals is copied to c_vals. Here are the results for source code example Ch07_02:

```
Results for MaskOpI64a - mask = 0x7b

i      a      b      add      sub      mul      sll      sra
-------------------------------------------------------------
0     64      4       68       60      256     1024        4
1   1024      5     1029     1019     5120    32768       32
2  -2048      2        0        0        0        0        0
3   8192      5     8197     8187    40960   262144      256
4   -256      8     -248     -264    -2048   -65536       -1
5   4096      7     4103     4089    28672   524288       32
6     16      3       19       13       48      128        2
7    512      6        0        0        0        0        0


Results for MaskOpI64b - mask = 0xb6

i       a      b1     b2      add      sub      mul      sll      sra
--------------------------------------------------------------------
0  111111      64      4   111111   111111   111111   111111   111111
1  222222    1024      5     1029     1019     5120    32768       32
2  333333   -2048      2    -2046    -2050    -4096    -8192     -512
3  444444    8192      5   444444   444444   444444   444444   444444
4  555555    -256      8     -248     -264    -2048   -65536       -1
5  666666    4096      7     4103     4089    28672   524288       32
6  777777      16      3   777777   777777   777777   777777   777777
7  888888     512      6      518      506     3072    32768        8


Results for MaskOpI64c -  x1 = 0, x2 = 42

i       a       c
--------------------
0    -100    -100
1     200     242
2     300     342
3    -400    -400
4    -500    -500
5     600     642
6     700     742
7    -800    -800
```

# Image Processing

In Chapters 2 and 4, you learned how to code some simple image processing methods using AVX, AVX2, and C++ SIMD intrinsic functions. In this section, you will learn how to perform similar operations using AVX-512. The first example demonstrates RGB to grayscale image conversion. The second example implements a general-purpose thresholding function using AVX-512 C++ SIMD functions that lack an AVX or AVX2 counterpart. The final example of this section explains how to calculate the mean and standard deviation of a grayscale image.

## RGB to Grayscale

Listing 7-3 shows the source code for example Ch07_03. This example is an AVX-512 implementation of source code example Ch04_05, which converts an RGB image to a grayscale image. Before examining the source code, you may want to review the RGB to grayscale conversion equation that was defined for source code example Ch04_05.

*Listing 7-3.* Example Ch07_03

```
//--------------------------------------------------
//                  Ch07_03_fcpp.cpp
//--------------------------------------------------

#include <iostream>
#include <stdexcept>
#include <immintrin.h>
#include "Ch07_03.h"
#include "ImageMisc.h"

void ConvertRgbToGs_Cpp(uint8_t* pb_gs, const RGB32* pb_rgb, size_t num_pixels, const float
coef[4])
{
    if (!CheckArgs(pb_gs, pb_rgb, num_pixels, coef))
        throw std::runtime_error("ConvertRgbToGs_Cpp() - CheckArgs failed");

    for (size_t i = 0; i < num_pixels; i++)
    {
        uint8_t r = pb_rgb[i].m_R;
        uint8_t g = pb_rgb[i].m_G;
        uint8_t b = pb_rgb[i].m_B;

        float gs_temp = r * coef[0] + g * coef[1] + b * coef[2] + 0.5f;

        if (gs_temp > 255.0f)
            gs_temp = 255.0f;

        pb_gs[i] = (uint8_t)gs_temp;
    }
}
```

```
void ConvertRgbToGs_Iavx512(uint8_t* pb_gs, const RGB32* pb_rgb, size_t num_pixels, const
float coef[4])
{
    if (!CheckArgs(pb_gs, pb_rgb, num_pixels, coef))
        throw std::runtime_error("ConvertRgbToGs_Iavx512() - CheckArgs failed");

    __m512 packed_0p5_f32 = _mm512_set1_ps(0.5f);
    __m512 packed_255p0_f32 = _mm512_set1_ps(255.0f);
    __m512i u32_byte0_mask = _mm512_set1_epi32(0x000000ff);

    __m512 packed_coef_r = _mm512_set1_ps(coef[0]);
    __m512 packed_coef_g = _mm512_set1_ps(coef[1]);
    __m512 packed_coef_b = _mm512_set1_ps(coef[2]);

    const size_t num_simd_elements = 16;

    for (size_t i = 0; i < num_pixels; i += num_simd_elements)
    {
        // Load next block of sixteen RGB32 pixels
        __m512i pixel_vals = _mm512_load_si512((__m512i*)&pb_rgb[i]);

        // De-interleave color components and size promote to U32
        __m512i pixel_vals_r = pixel_vals;
        __m512i pixel_vals_g = _mm512_srli_epi32(pixel_vals, 8);
        __m512i pixel_vals_b = _mm512_srli_epi32(pixel_vals, 16);
        __m512i pixel_vals_r_u32 = _mm512_and_si512(pixel_vals_r, u32_byte0_mask);
        __m512i pixel_vals_g_u32 = _mm512_and_si512(pixel_vals_g, u32_byte0_mask);
        __m512i pixel_vals_b_u32 = _mm512_and_si512(pixel_vals_b, u32_byte0_mask);

        // Convert color components from U32 to F32
        __m512 pixel_vals_r_f32 = _mm512_cvtepi32_ps(pixel_vals_r_u32);
        __m512 pixel_vals_g_f32 = _mm512_cvtepi32_ps(pixel_vals_g_u32);
        __m512 pixel_vals_b_f32 = _mm512_cvtepi32_ps(pixel_vals_b_u32);

        // Multiply color components by conversion coefficients
        pixel_vals_r_f32 = _mm512_mul_ps(pixel_vals_r_f32, packed_coef_r);
        pixel_vals_g_f32 = _mm512_mul_ps(pixel_vals_g_f32, packed_coef_g);
        pixel_vals_b_f32 = _mm512_mul_ps(pixel_vals_b_f32, packed_coef_b);

        // Sum color components
        __m512 temp1_f32 = _mm512_add_ps(pixel_vals_r_f32, pixel_vals_g_f32);
        __m512 pixel_vals_gs_f32 = _mm512_add_ps(pixel_vals_b_f32, temp1_f32);

        // Round and clip grayscale pixel values
        pixel_vals_gs_f32 = _mm512_add_ps(pixel_vals_gs_f32, packed_0p5_f32);
        pixel_vals_gs_f32 = _mm512_min_ps(pixel_vals_gs_f32, packed_255p0_f32);

        // Convert from F32 to U8
        __m512i pixel_vals_gs_u32 = _mm512_cvtps_epi32(pixel_vals_gs_f32);
        __m128i pixel_vals_gs_u8 = _mm512_cvtusepi32_epi8(pixel_vals_gs_u32);
```

```
    // Save sixteen gray scale pixels
    _mm_store_si128((__m128i*)&pb_gs[i], pixel_vals_gs_u8);
  }
}
```

Listing 7-3 only shows the source code for file Ch07_03_fcpp.cpp since the other files (Ch07_03.h, Ch07_03_misc.cpp, and Ch07_03.cpp) for this example are essentially the same as the ones used in example Ch04_05. The first function in Ch07_03_fcpp.cpp, ConvertRgbToGs_Cpp(), converts an RGB image to grayscale using standard C++ statements. This same function was used in source code example Ch04_05 and is included again in this example for benchmarking purposes. The function ConvertRgbToGs_Iavx512() is the AVX-512 counterpart of function ConvertRgbToGs_Iavx2() that you saw in Chapter 4. The most noticeable difference between these two functions is that the former employs AVX-512 variants of the C++ SIMD intrinsic functions. Also note that num_simd_elements is initialized to 16 instead of 8 to account for the SIMD operand size difference (512 bits vs. 256 bits).

The final change in ConvertRgbToGs_Iavx512() is the code that converts floating-point grayscale values to unsigned 8-bit integers. This code is located near the end of the for-loop. Function ConvertRgbToGs_Iavx512() employs the C++ SIMD intrinsic function _mm512_cvtps_epi32() to convert the calculated grayscale values from single-precision floating-point to 32-bit integers. The ensuing call to _mm512_cvtusepi32_epi8() converts these 32-bit integer values to unsigned 8-bit integers using unsigned saturation. Note that function _mm512_cvtusepi32_epi8() returns a C++ SIMD data type of __m128i. The final for-loop function call, _mm_store_si128(), saves 16 grayscale pixels to the destination pixel buffer. Here are the results for source code example Ch07_03:

```
Results for ConvertRgbToGs
  Converting RGB image ../../Data/ImageC.png
  im_h = 960 pixels
  im_w = 640 pixels
Saving grayscale image #0 - Ch07_03_GsImage0.png
Saving grayscale image #1 - Ch07_03_GsImage1.png
Grayscale pixel buffer compare OK

Running benchmark function ConvertRgbToGs_bm - please wait
Benchmark times save to file Ch07_03_ConvertRgbToGs_bm_LITHIUM.csv
```

Source code example Ch07_03 exemplifies that with a little algorithmic forethought, it is often a straightforward task to convert an AVX or AVX2 function into one that exploits the extra computational resources of AVX-512. Table 7-2 shows some benchmark timing measurements for source code example Ch07_03. In this example, the use of AVX-512 resulted in a modest performance gain compared to the AVX2 function ConvertRgbToGs_Iavx2() of Chapter 4 (see Table 4-2). There are no benchmark timing measurements for the Intel Core i7-8700K processor since it does not support AVX-512.

***Table 7-2.*** *Pixel Clipping Algorithm Execution Times (Microseconds) Using* ImageC.png

| CPU | ConvertRgbToGs_Cpp() | ConvertRgbToGs_Iavx2() | ConvertRgbToGs_Iavx512() |
|---|---|---|---|
| Intel Core i5-11600K | 770 | 132 | 112 |

# Image Thresholding

Source code example Ch04_06 explained how to perform image thresholding using AVX2 C++ SIMD intrinsic functions. In that example, the thresholding function generated a mask image to signify which pixels in the original grayscale image were greater that a predetermined threshold. Then the next source code example, named Ch07_04, implements a general-purpose image thresholding function using AVX-512 C++ SIMD intrinsic functions. Listing 7-4 shows the source code for example Ch07_04.

*Listing 7-4.* Example Ch07_04

```
//-------------------------------------------------
//                 Ch07_04.h
//-------------------------------------------------

#pragma once
#include <cstddef>
#include <cstdint>

// Compare operators
enum class CmpOp { EQ, NE, LT, LE, GT, GE };

// Ch07_04_fcpp.cpp
extern void ComparePixels_Cpp(uint8_t* pb_des, const uint8_t* pb_src,
    size_t num_pixels, CmpOp cmp_op, uint8_t cmp_val);
extern void ComparePixels_Iavx512(uint8_t* pb_des, const uint8_t* pb_src,
    size_t num_pixels, CmpOp cmp_op, uint8_t cmp_val);

// Ch07_04_misc.cpp
extern bool CheckArgs(const uint8_t* pb_des, const uint8_t* pb_src,
    size_t num_pixels);
extern void DisplayResults(const uint8_t* pb_des1, const uint8_t* pb_des2,
    size_t num_pixels, CmpOp cmp_op, uint8_t cmp_val, size_t test_id);
extern void InitArray(uint8_t* x, size_t n, unsigned int seed);

// Miscellaneous constants
const size_t c_Alignment = 64;
const size_t c_NumPixelsMax = 16 * 1024 * 1024;


//-------------------------------------------------
//                 Ch07_04_misc.cpp
//-------------------------------------------------

#include <iostream>
#include <random>
#include <cstring>
#include <string>
#include "Ch07_04.h"
#include "MT.h"
#include "AlignedMem.h"
```

```cpp
bool CheckArgs(const uint8_t* pb_des, const uint8_t* pb_src, size_t num_pixels)
{
    if ((num_pixels == 0) || (num_pixels > c_NumPixelsMax))
        return false;
    if ((num_pixels & 0x3f) != 0)
        return false;
    if (!AlignedMem::IsAligned(pb_src, c_Alignment))
        return false;
    if (!AlignedMem::IsAligned(pb_des, c_Alignment))
        return false;
    return true;
}

void InitArray(uint8_t* x, size_t n, unsigned int rng_seed)
{
    MT::FillArray(x, n, 0, 255, rng_seed);
}

void DisplayResults(const uint8_t* pb_des1, const uint8_t* pb_des2,
    size_t num_pixels, CmpOp cmp_op, uint8_t cmp_val, size_t test_id)
{
    size_t num_non_zero = 0;
    bool are_same = memcmp(pb_des1, pb_des2, num_pixels * sizeof(uint8_t)) == 0;

    const std::string cmp_op_strings[] {"EQ", "NE", "LT", "LE", "GT", "GE"};

    if (are_same)
    {
        for (size_t i = 0; i < num_pixels; i++)
            num_non_zero += (pb_des1[i] != 0) ? 1 : 0;
    }

    std::cout << "\nTest #" << test_id << '\n';
    std::cout << "  num_pixels: " << num_pixels << '\n';
    std::cout << "  cmp_op:     " << cmp_op_strings[(int)cmp_op] << '\n';
    std::cout << "  cmp_val:    " << (int)cmp_val << '\n';

    if (are_same)
    {
        std::cout << "  Pixel masks are identical\n";
        std::cout << "  Number of non-zero mask pixels = " << num_non_zero << '\n';
    }
    else
        std::cout << "  Pixel masks are different\n";
}

//---------------------------------------------------
//              Ch07_04.cpp
//---------------------------------------------------
```

```cpp
#include <iostream>
#include <stdexcept>
#include <cassert>
#include "Ch07_04.h"
#include "AlignedMem.h"

static void ComparePixels(void);

int main()
{
    try
    {
        ComparePixels();
    }

    catch (std::exception& ex)
    {
        std::cout << "Ch07_04 exception: " << ex.what() << '\n';
    }
}

static void ComparePixels(void)
{
    const size_t num_pixels = 4 * 1024 * 1024;

    AlignedArray<uint8_t> src_aa(num_pixels, c_Alignment);
    AlignedArray<uint8_t> des1_aa(num_pixels, c_Alignment);
    AlignedArray<uint8_t> des2_aa(num_pixels, c_Alignment);
    uint8_t* pb_src = src_aa.Data();
    uint8_t* pb_des1 = des1_aa.Data();
    uint8_t* pb_des2 = des2_aa.Data();

    const uint8_t cmp_vals[] {197, 222, 43, 43, 129, 222};
    const CmpOp cmp_ops[] {CmpOp::EQ, CmpOp::NE, CmpOp::LT,
                           CmpOp::LE, CmpOp::GT, CmpOp::GE};
    const size_t num_cmp_vals = sizeof(cmp_vals) / sizeof(uint8_t);
    const size_t num_cmp_ops = sizeof(cmp_ops) / sizeof(CmpOp);
    assert(num_cmp_vals == num_cmp_ops);

    InitArray(pb_src, num_pixels, 511);

    std::cout << "Results for ComparePixels\n";

    for (size_t i = 0; i < num_cmp_ops; i++)
    {
        ComparePixels_Cpp(pb_des1, pb_src, num_pixels, cmp_ops[i], cmp_vals[i]);
        ComparePixels_Iavx512(pb_des2, pb_src, num_pixels, cmp_ops[i], cmp_vals[i]);
        DisplayResults(pb_des1, pb_des2, num_pixels, cmp_ops[i], cmp_vals[i], i + 1);
    }
}
```

```
//---------------------------------------------------
//                 Ch07_04_fcpp.cpp
//---------------------------------------------------

#include <iostream>
#include <stdexcept>
#include <immintrin.h>
#include "Ch07_04.h"

void ComparePixels_Cpp(uint8_t* pb_des, const uint8_t* pb_src,
    size_t num_pixels, CmpOp cmp_op, uint8_t cmp_val)
{
    if (!CheckArgs(pb_des, pb_src, num_pixels))
        throw std::runtime_error("ComparePixels_Cpp() - CheckArgs failed");

    const uint8_t cmp_false = 0x00;
    const uint8_t cmp_true = 0xff;

    switch (cmp_op)
    {
        case CmpOp::EQ:
            for (size_t i = 0; i < num_pixels; i++)
                pb_des[i] = (pb_src[i] == cmp_val) ? cmp_true : cmp_false;
            break;

        case CmpOp::NE:
            for (size_t i = 0; i < num_pixels; i++)
                pb_des[i] = (pb_src[i] != cmp_val) ? cmp_true : cmp_false;
            break;

        case CmpOp::LT:
            for (size_t i = 0; i < num_pixels; i++)
                pb_des[i] = (pb_src[i] < cmp_val) ? cmp_true : cmp_false;
            break;

        case CmpOp::LE:
            for (size_t i = 0; i < num_pixels; i++)
                pb_des[i] = (pb_src[i] <= cmp_val) ? cmp_true : cmp_false;
            break;

        case CmpOp::GT:
            for (size_t i = 0; i < num_pixels; i++)
                pb_des[i] = (pb_src[i] > cmp_val) ? cmp_true : cmp_false;
            break;

        case CmpOp::GE:
            for (size_t i = 0; i < num_pixels; i++)
                pb_des[i] = (pb_src[i] >= cmp_val) ? cmp_true : cmp_false;
            break;
```

```
        default:
            throw std::runtime_error("ComparePixels_Cpp() - invalid cmp_op");
    }
}

void ComparePixels_Iavx512(uint8_t* pb_des, const uint8_t* pb_src, size_t num_pixels, CmpOp
cmp_op, uint8_t cmp_val)
{
    if (!CheckArgs(pb_des, pb_src, num_pixels))
        throw std::runtime_error("ComparePixels_Iavx512() - CheckArgs failed");

    __m512i packed_255 = _mm512_set1_epi8((uint8_t)0xff);
    __m512i packed_cmp_val = _mm512_set1_epi8(cmp_val);

    __mmask64 cmp_mask;
    __m512i pixel_vals, mask_vals;
    const size_t num_simd_elements = 64;

    switch (cmp_op)
    {
        case CmpOp::EQ:
            for (size_t i = 0; i < num_pixels; i += num_simd_elements)
            {
                pixel_vals = _mm512_load_si512(&pb_src[i]);
                cmp_mask = _mm512_cmpeq_epu8_mask(pixel_vals, packed_cmp_val);
                mask_vals = _mm512_maskz_mov_epi8(cmp_mask, packed_255);
                _mm512_store_si512(&pb_des[i], mask_vals);
            }
            break;

        case CmpOp::NE:
            for (size_t i = 0; i < num_pixels; i += num_simd_elements)
            {
                pixel_vals = _mm512_load_si512(&pb_src[i]);
                cmp_mask = _mm512_cmpneq_epu8_mask(pixel_vals, packed_cmp_val);
                mask_vals = _mm512_maskz_mov_epi8(cmp_mask, packed_255);
                _mm512_store_si512(&pb_des[i], mask_vals);
            }
            break;

        case CmpOp::LT:
            for (size_t i = 0; i < num_pixels; i += num_simd_elements)
            {
                pixel_vals = _mm512_load_si512(&pb_src[i]);
                cmp_mask = _mm512_cmplt_epu8_mask(pixel_vals, packed_cmp_val);
                mask_vals = _mm512_maskz_mov_epi8(cmp_mask, packed_255);
                _mm512_store_si512(&pb_des[i], mask_vals);
            }
            break;
```

```
    case CmpOp::LE:
        for (size_t i = 0; i < num_pixels; i += num_simd_elements)
        {
            pixel_vals = _mm512_load_si512(&pb_src[i]);
            cmp_mask = _mm512_cmple_epu8_mask(pixel_vals, packed_cmp_val);
            mask_vals = _mm512_maskz_mov_epi8(cmp_mask, packed_255);
            _mm512_store_si512(&pb_des[i], mask_vals);
        }
        break;

    case CmpOp::GT:
        for (size_t i = 0; i < num_pixels; i += num_simd_elements)
        {
            pixel_vals = _mm512_load_si512(&pb_src[i]);
            cmp_mask = _mm512_cmpgt_epu8_mask(pixel_vals, packed_cmp_val);
            mask_vals = _mm512_maskz_mov_epi8(cmp_mask, packed_255);
            _mm512_store_si512(&pb_des[i], mask_vals);
        }
        break;

    case CmpOp::GE:
        for (size_t i = 0; i < num_pixels; i += num_simd_elements)
        {
            pixel_vals = _mm512_load_si512(&pb_src[i]);
            cmp_mask = _mm512_cmpge_epu8_mask(pixel_vals, packed_cmp_val);
            mask_vals = _mm512_maskz_mov_epi8(cmp_mask, packed_255);
            _mm512_store_si512(&pb_des[i], mask_vals);
        }
        break;

    default:
        throw std::runtime_error("ComparePixels_Iavx512() - invalid cmp_op");
    }
}
```

In Listing 7-4, the header file Ch07_04.h begins with the declaration of an enum named CmpOp. Unlike the example you saw in Chapter 4, the thresholding functions in this example support a complete set of compare operators. Next in Listing 7-4 is the file Ch07_04_misc.cpp, which contains the miscellaneous functions for this example. The function ComparePixels(), located in file Ch07_04.cpp, uses the C++ template class AlignedArray to instantiate simulated pixel buffers that are properly aligned for AVX-512. This function also exercises the image thresholding functions and displays results.

The first function in file Ch07_04, ComparePixels_Cpp(), implements the general-purpose thresholding algorithm using standard C++ statements. Note that inside the switch statement, each thresholding compare operator is coded using a simple for-loop and ternary expression.

The SIMD counterpart of function ComparePixels_Cpp() is named ComparePixels_Iavx512(). This function also employs a switch construct and simple for-loops to perform image thresholding. The for-loop in each case statement code block begins with a call to _mm512_load_si512() that loads 64 grayscale pixels from the source image buffer pb_src into pixel_vals. The next C++ SIMD intrinsic function call in each for-loop varies depending on the specific compare operator.

In the CmpOp::EQ code block, for example, function ComparePixels_Iavx512() uses the C++ SIMD intrinsic function _mm512_cmpeq_epu8_mask() to compare the grayscale pixels in pixel_vals and packed_cmp_vals for equality. This function returns a 64-bit wide integer mask (of type __mmask64) named cmp_mask that signifies the result of each pixel element compare (1 = true, 0 = false). The variable cmp_mask is then used by the function _mm512_maskz_mov_epi8() to generate a two-color (0x00 or 0xff) pixel mask. The final C++ SIMD intrinsic function call of the for-loop, _mm512_store_si512(), saves the calculated pixel mask to the destination image buffer pb_des. The other case statement code blocks are identical to the CmpOp::EQ code block except for the function that performs the actual compare. Here are the results for source code example Ch07_04:

```
Results for ComparePixels

Test #1
  num_pixels: 4194304
  cmp_op:    EQ
  cmp_val:   197
  Pixel masks are identical
  Number of non-zero mask pixels = 16424

Test #2
  num_pixels: 4194304
  cmp_op:    NE
  cmp_val:   222
  Pixel masks are identical
  Number of non-zero mask pixels = 4177927

Test #3
  num_pixels: 4194304
  cmp_op:    LT
  cmp_val:   43
  Pixel masks are identical
  Number of non-zero mask pixels = 703652

Test #4
  num_pixels: 4194304
  cmp_op:    LE
  cmp_val:   43
  Pixel masks are identical
  Number of non-zero mask pixels = 719787

Test #5
  num_pixels: 4194304
  cmp_op:    GT
  cmp_val:   129
  Pixel masks are identical
  Number of non-zero mask pixels = 2065724
```

```
Test #6
  num_pixels: 4194304
  cmp_op:     GE
  cmp_val:    222
  Pixel masks are identical
  Number of non-zero mask pixels = 556908
```

## Image Statistics

The final source code example of this chapter, Ch07_05, illustrates how to calculate the mean and standard deviation of a grayscale image. The mean and standard deviation of the pixels in a grayscale image can be calculated using the following equations:

$$\bar{x} = \frac{1}{n}\sum_i x_i$$

$$s = \sqrt{\frac{n\sum_i x_i^2 - \left(\sum_i x_i\right)^2}{n(n-1)}}$$

In this equation, the symbol $x_i$ represents an image pixel, and $n$ denotes the total number of pixels. If you study these equations carefully, you will notice that two sum quantities must be calculated: the sum of all pixels and the sum of pixel values squared. Once these sums are calculated, the mean and standard deviation can be computed using scalar floating-point arithmetic. It should be noted that the standard deviation equation defined here is suitable for this source code example since integer arithmetic is employed to calculate the required sums. However, this same equation is often unsuitable for other standard deviation calculations especially those that involve floating-point values (a loss of precision can occur if the sums in the numerator are approximately the same). You may want to consult one of the statistical variance references listed in Appendix B before using this equation in your own programs.

To make the source code in example Ch07_05 a bit more interesting, the mean and standard deviation calculating functions only use pixel values that reside between two threshold limits. Listing 7-5 shows the source code for example Ch07_05.

**Listing 7-5.** Example Ch07_05

```
//--------------------------------------------------
//                  Ch07_05.h
//--------------------------------------------------

#pragma once
#include <cstddef>
#include <cstdint>

struct ImageStats
{
    uint8_t* m_PixelBuffer;
    uint32_t m_PixelMinVal;
```

```
        uint32_t m_PixelMaxVal;
        size_t m_NumPixels;
        size_t m_NumPixelsInRange;
        uint64_t m_PixelSum;
        uint64_t m_PixelSumSquares;
        double m_PixelMean;
        double m_PixelStDev;
};

// Ch07_05.cpp
extern const char* c_ImageFileName;

// Ch07_05_fcpp.cpp
extern void CalcImageStats_Cpp(ImageStats& im_stats);
extern void CalcImageStats_Iavx512(ImageStats& im_stats);

// Ch07_05_misc.cpp
extern bool CheckArgs(const ImageStats& im_stats);

// Ch07_05_bm.cpp
extern void CalcImageStats_bm(void);

// Miscellaneous constants
const size_t c_Alignment = 64;
const size_t c_NumPixelsMax = 64 * 1024 * 1024;
const uint32_t c_PixelMinVal = 40;
const uint32_t c_PixelMaxVal = 230;

//--------------------------------------------------
//                  Ch07_05_misc.cpp
//--------------------------------------------------

#include "Ch07_05.h"
#include "AlignedMem.h"

bool CheckArgs(const ImageStats& im_stats)
{
    if (im_stats.m_NumPixels == 0)
        return false;
    if (im_stats.m_NumPixels % 64 != 0)
        return false;
    if (im_stats.m_NumPixels > c_NumPixelsMax)
        return false;
    if (!AlignedMem::IsAligned(im_stats.m_PixelBuffer, c_Alignment))
        return false;
    return true;
}

//--------------------------------------------------
//                  Ch07_05.cpp
//--------------------------------------------------
```

```cpp
#include <iostream>
#include <iomanip>
#include <stdexcept>
#include "Ch07_05.h"
#include "ImageMatrix.h"

const char* c_ImageFileName = "../../Data/ImageB.png";
static void CalcImageStats(void);

int main()
{
    try
    {
        CalcImageStats();
        CalcImageStats_bm();
    }

    catch (std::exception& ex)
    {
        std::cout << "Ch07_05 exception: " << ex.what() << '\n';
    }
}

static void CalcImageStats(void)
{
    const char* image_fn = c_ImageFileName;

    ImageStats is1, is2;
    ImageMatrix im(image_fn, PixelType::Gray8);
    size_t num_pixels = im.GetNumPixels();
    uint8_t* pb = im.GetPixelBuffer<uint8_t>();

    is1.m_PixelBuffer = pb;
    is1.m_NumPixels = num_pixels;
    is1.m_PixelMinVal = c_PixelMinVal;
    is1.m_PixelMaxVal = c_PixelMaxVal;

    is2.m_PixelBuffer = pb;
    is2.m_NumPixels = num_pixels;
    is2.m_PixelMinVal = c_PixelMinVal;
    is2.m_PixelMaxVal = c_PixelMaxVal;

    const char nl = '\n';
    const char* s = " | ";
    const unsigned int w1 = 22;
    const unsigned int w2 = 12;

    std::cout << std::fixed << std::setprecision(6) << std::left;
    std::cout << "\nResults for CalcImageStats\n";
    std::cout << std::setw(w1) << "image_fn:" << std::setw(w2) << image_fn << nl;
    std::cout << std::setw(w1) << "num_pixels:" << std::setw(w2) << num_pixels << nl;
```

249

```
        std::cout << std::setw(w1) << "c_PixelMinVal:" << std::setw(w2) << c_PixelMinVal << nl;
        std::cout << std::setw(w1) << "c_PixelMaxVal:" <<   std::setw(w2) << c_PixelMaxVal << nl;
        std::cout << nl;

        CalcImageStats_Cpp(is1);
        CalcImageStats_Iavx512(is2);

        std::cout << std::setw(w1) << "m_NumPixelsInRange: ";
        std::cout << std::setw(w2) << is1.m_NumPixelsInRange << s;
        std::cout << std::setw(w2) << is2.m_NumPixelsInRange << nl;
        std::cout << std::setw(w1) << "m_PixelSum:";
        std::cout << std::setw(w2) << is1.m_PixelSum << s;
        std::cout << std::setw(w2) << is2.m_PixelSum << nl;

        std::cout << std::setw(w1) << "m_PixelSumSquares:";
        std::cout << std::setw(w2) << is1.m_PixelSumSquares << s;
        std::cout << std::setw(w2) << is2.m_PixelSumSquares << nl;
        std::cout << std::setw(w1) << "m_PixelMean:";
        std::cout << std::setw(w2) << is1.m_PixelMean << s;
        std::cout << std::setw(w2) << is2.m_PixelMean << nl;

        std::cout << std::setw(w1) << "m_PixelStDev:";
        std::cout << std::setw(w2) << is1.m_PixelStDev << s;
        std::cout << std::setw(w2) << is2.m_PixelStDev << nl;
}

//------------------------------------------------
//                  Ch07_05_fcpp.cpp
//------------------------------------------------

#include <iostream>
#include <stdexcept>
#include <cmath>
#include <immintrin.h>
#include "Ch07_05.h"

inline void CalcMeanStDev(ImageStats& im_stats)
{
    // Calculate mean and standard deviation
    double temp0 = (double)im_stats.m_NumPixelsInRange * im_stats.m_PixelSumSquares;
    double temp1 = (double)im_stats.m_PixelSum * im_stats.m_PixelSum;
    double var_num = temp0 - temp1;
    double var_den = (double)im_stats.m_NumPixelsInRange * (im_stats.
        m_NumPixelsInRange - 1);
    double var = var_num / var_den;

    im_stats.m_PixelMean = (double)im_stats.m_PixelSum / im_stats.m_NumPixelsInRange;
    im_stats.m_PixelStDev = sqrt(var);
}
```

```cpp
void CalcImageStats_Cpp(ImageStats& im_stats)
{
    if (!CheckArgs(im_stats))
        throw std::runtime_error("CalcImageStats_Cpp() - CheckArgs failed");

    im_stats.m_PixelSum = 0;
    im_stats.m_PixelSumSquares = 0;
    im_stats.m_NumPixelsInRange = 0;

    size_t num_pixels = im_stats.m_NumPixels;
    const uint8_t* pb = im_stats.m_PixelBuffer;

    // Calculate intermediate sums
    for (size_t i = 0; i < num_pixels; i++)
    {
        uint32_t pval = pb[i];

        if (pval >= im_stats.m_PixelMinVal && pval <= im_stats.m_PixelMaxVal)
        {
            im_stats.m_PixelSum += pval;
            im_stats.m_PixelSumSquares += (uint64_t)pval * pval;
            im_stats.m_NumPixelsInRange++;
        }
    }

    CalcMeanStDev(im_stats);
}

inline uint64_t Sum_u64x8(__m512i x)
{
    return _mm512_reduce_add_epi64(x);
}

inline __m512i Add_u64x8_u32x16(__m512i x_u64x8, __m512i y_u32x16)
{
    // Add 32-bit integers in y to 64-bit integers in x
    __m256i temp0 = _mm512_extracti32x8_epi32(y_u32x16, 0);
    __m256i temp1 = _mm512_extracti32x8_epi32(y_u32x16, 1);
    __m256i temp2 = _mm256_add_epi32(temp0, temp1);
    __m512i temp3 = _mm512_cvtepu32_epi64(temp2);
    __m512i temp4 = _mm512_add_epi64(x_u64x8, temp3);
    return temp4;
}

void CalcImageStats_Iavx512(ImageStats& im_stats)
{
    if (!CheckArgs(im_stats))
        throw std::runtime_error("CalcImageStats_Iavx512() - CheckArgs failed");

    size_t num_pixels = im_stats.m_NumPixels;
    const uint8_t* pb = im_stats.m_PixelBuffer;
```

```
    __m512i pixel_min_vals = _mm512_set1_epi8((uint8_t)im_stats.m_PixelMinVal);
    __m512i pixel_max_vals = _mm512_set1_epi8((uint8_t)im_stats.m_PixelMaxVal);

    __m512i pixel_sums_u64x8 = _mm512_setzero_si512();
    __m512i pixel_sum_squares_u64x8 = _mm512_setzero_si512();

    uint64_t num_pixels_in_range = 0;
    const size_t num_simd_elements = 64;

    for (size_t i = 0; i < num_pixels; i += num_simd_elements)
    {
        // Load next block of 64 pixels
        __m512i pixel_vals = _mm512_load_si512(&pb[i]);

        // Calculate in-range pixels
        __mmask64 mask_ge_min = _mm512_cmpge_epu8_mask(pixel_vals, pixel_min_vals);
        __mmask64 mask_le_max = _mm512_cmple_epu8_mask(pixel_vals, pixel_max_vals);
        __mmask64 mask_in_range = _kand_mask64(mask_ge_min, mask_le_max);
        __m512i pixel_vals_in_range = _mm512_maskz_mov_epi8(mask_in_range, pixel_vals);

        num_pixels_in_range += _mm_popcnt_u64(mask_in_range);

        // Calculate pixel_sums and pixel_sum_squares for current block
        __m128i pixel_vals_u8x16;
        __m512i pixel_vals_u32x16;
        __m512i pixel_sums_u32x16 = _mm512_setzero_si512();
        __m512i pixel_sum_squares_u32x16 = _mm512_setzero_si512();

        pixel_vals_u8x16 = _mm512_extracti64x2_epi64(pixel_vals_in_range, 0);
        pixel_vals_u32x16 = _mm512_cvtepu8_epi32(pixel_vals_u8x16);
        pixel_sums_u32x16 = _mm512_add_epi32(pixel_sums_u32x16, pixel_vals_u32x16);
        pixel_vals_u32x16 = _mm512_mullo_epi32(pixel_vals_u32x16, pixel_vals_u32x16);
        pixel_sum_squares_u32x16 = _mm512_add_epi32(pixel_sum_squares_u32x16, pixel_vals_
        u32x16);

        pixel_vals_u8x16 = _mm512_extracti64x2_epi64(pixel_vals_in_range, 1);
        pixel_vals_u32x16 = _mm512_cvtepu8_epi32(pixel_vals_u8x16);
        pixel_sums_u32x16 = _mm512_add_epi32(pixel_sums_u32x16, pixel_vals_u32x16);
        pixel_vals_u32x16 = _mm512_mullo_epi32(pixel_vals_u32x16, pixel_vals_u32x16);
        pixel_sum_squares_u32x16 = _mm512_add_epi32(pixel_sum_squares_u32x16, pixel_vals_
        u32x16);

        pixel_vals_u8x16 = _mm512_extracti64x2_epi64(pixel_vals_in_range, 2);
        pixel_vals_u32x16 = _mm512_cvtepu8_epi32(pixel_vals_u8x16);
        pixel_sums_u32x16 = _mm512_add_epi32(pixel_sums_u32x16, pixel_vals_u32x16);
        pixel_vals_u32x16 = _mm512_mullo_epi32(pixel_vals_u32x16, pixel_vals_u32x16);
        pixel_sum_squares_u32x16 = _mm512_add_epi32(pixel_sum_squares_u32x16, pixel_vals_
        u32x16);
```

```
    pixel_vals_u8x16 = _mm512_extracti64x2_epi64(pixel_vals_in_range, 3);
    pixel_vals_u32x16 = _mm512_cvtepu8_epi32(pixel_vals_u8x16);
    pixel_sums_u32x16 = _mm512_add_epi32(pixel_sums_u32x16, pixel_vals_u32x16);
    pixel_vals_u32x16 = _mm512_mullo_epi32(pixel_vals_u32x16, pixel_vals_u32x16);
    pixel_sum_squares_u32x16 = _mm512_add_epi32(pixel_sum_squares_u32x16, pixel_vals_
    u32x16);

    // Update uint64_t sums and sum_squares
    pixel_sums_u64x8 = Add_u64x8_u32x16(pixel_sums_u64x8, pixel_sums_u32x16);
    pixel_sum_squares_u64x8 = Add_u64x8_u32x16(pixel_sum_squares_u64x8, pixel_sum_
    squares_u32x16);
  }

  // Perform reductions
  im_stats.m_PixelSum = Sum_u64x8(pixel_sums_u64x8);
  im_stats.m_PixelSumSquares = Sum_u64x8(pixel_sum_squares_u64x8);
  im_stats.m_NumPixelsInRange = num_pixels_in_range;

  // Calculate mean and SD
  CalcMeanStDev(im_stats);
}
```

Listing 7-5 begins with the declaration of a structure named ImageStats, which is located in the header file Ch07_05.h. This structure contains the required data for the mean and standard deviation calculating functions. In file Ch07_05.cpp, the function CalcImageStats() uses the C++ class ImageMatrix to load a test PNG image file. This function also invokes the statistical calculating functions CalcImageStats_Cpp() and CalcImageStats_Iavx512(). Note that both functions require an argument of type ImageStats.

Next in Listing 7-5 is the file Ch07_05_fcpp.cpp. This file begins with the definition of an inline function named CalcMeanStDev(). Function CalcMeanStDev() calculates the final mean and standard deviation using the sum values in an ImageStats structure. The next function, CalcImageStats_Cpp(), calculates the required sum values using standard C++ statements. Note that for-loop includes a block of code that tests each pixel value to ensure that it is in range before updating m_PixelSum, m_PixelSumSquares, and m_NumPixelsInRange. Following calculation of the required sums, CalcImageStats_Cpp() calls CalcMeanStDev() to compute the final mean and standard deviation.

Following CalcImageStats_Cpp() is the definition of an inline function named Sum_u64x8(), which sums the 64-bit integer elements of an __m512i data type. Function Sum_u64x8() uses the AVX-512 C++ SIMD intrinsic function _mm512_reduce_add_epi64() to sum the eight 64-bit integer elements of argument value x. It should be noted that the AVX-512 C++ intrinsic library includes dozens of other functions that perform reduction operations. The use of these functions is often much easier than coding sequences of intrinsic functions to perform a reduction, which is usually required on systems that lack AVX-512. Immediately after Sum_u64x8() is another inline function named Add_u64x8_u32x16(). This function sums 32-bit integer elements of argument value y_u32x16. It then size-promotes these intermediate sums to 64 bits and adds them to the 64-bit integer values in argument value x_u64x8. Note that Add_u64x8_u32x16() uses the C++ SIMD intrinsic function _mm512_extracti32x8_epi32() twice to extract eight low- and high-order 32-bit integers from y_u32x16.

The final function in the file Ch07_05_fcpp.cpp is named CalcImageStats_Iavx512(). This function uses C++ SIMD intrinsic functions to calculate the sums needed to compute the pixel mean and standard deviation. Near the beginning of this function are two calls to _mm512_set1_epi8(), which create packed versions of m_PixelMinVal and m_PixelMaxVal. Function CalcImageStats_Iavx512() then uses two calls to _mm512_setzero_si512() to initialize pixel_sums_u64x8 and pixel_sum_squares_u64x8 to zero.

Each iteration of the for-loop in `CalcImageStats_Iavx512()` begins with a call to `_mm512_load_si512()` that loads a block of 64 pixels from pixel buffer pb. The next code block uses the C++ SIMD intrinsic functions `_mm512_cmpge_epu8_mask()`, `_mm512_cmple_epu8_mask()`, `_kand_mask64()`, and `_mm512_maskz_mov_epi8()` to remove any pixel values less than m_PixelMinVal or greater than m_PixelMaxVal. Figure 7-2 illustrates execution of this function call sequence in greater detail. Note that the C++ SIMD intrinsic function `_kand_mask64()` performs a bitwise logical AND using the specified _mask64 operands. Following removal of any out-of-range pixels, `CalcImageStats_Iavx512()` uses the non-SIMD C++ intrinsic function `_mm_popcnt_u64()` to count the number of in-range pixels in the current pixel block. This function counts the number of bits set to 1 in mask_in_range.

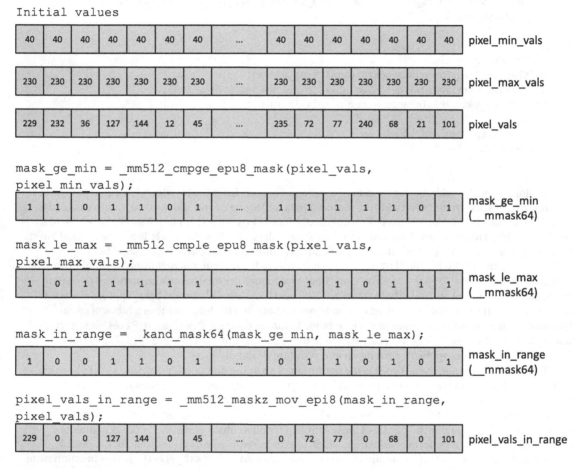

*Figure 7-2.* Removal of out-of-range pixels using _mm512_cmpge_epu8_mask(), _mm512_cmple_epu8_mask(), _kand_mask64(), and _mm512_maskz_mov_epi8()

Following out-of-range pixel removal, `CalcImageStats_Iavx512()` initializes pixel_sums_u32x16 and pixel_sum_squares_u32x16 to all zeros using the C++ SIMD intrinsic function `_mm512_setzero_si512()`. The ensuing code in the for-loop uses these variables to maintain intermediate results. Function `CalcImageStats_Iavx512()` then uses the C++ SIMD intrinsic function `_mm512_extracti64x2_epi64()` to extract the low-order 16 8-bit integers from pixel_vals_in_range. These integer values are then size-promoted to 32 bits using the function _mm512_cvtepu8_epi32(). The subsequent calls to _mm512_add_epi32(), _mm512_mullo_epi32(), and _mm512_add_epi32() update the intermediate sums maintained in pixel_sums_u32x16 and pixel_sum_squares_u32x16. The remaining pixel values in pixel_vals_in_range are processed using similar sequences of C++ SIMD intrinsic functions.

The final two statements of the for-loop employ the previously defined inline function Add_u64x8_u32x16 to update pixel_sums_u64x8 and pixel_sum_squares_u64x8. Following completion of the for-loop, CalcImageStats_Iavx512() uses inline function Sum_u64x8() to reduce both pixel_sums_u64x8 and pixel_sum_squares_u64x8 to 64-bit integers. It then calls CalcMeanStDev() to calculate the final mean and standard deviation. Here are the results for source code example Ch07_05:

```
Results for CalcImageStats
image_fn:                ../../Data/ImageB.png
num_pixels:              2457600
c_PixelMinVal:           40
c_PixelMaxVal:           230

m_NumPixelsInRange:      2039471        | 2039471
m_PixelSum:              252932299      | 252932299
m_PixelSumSquares:       37534652095    | 37534652095
m_PixelMean:             124.018581     | 124.018581
m_PixelStDev:            54.986406      | 54.986406

Running benchmark function CalcImageStats_bm - please wait
Benchmark times save to file Ch07_05_CalcImageStats_bm_LITHIUM.csv
```

Table 7-3 shows some benchmark timing measurements for source code example Ch07_05.

***Table 7-3.*** *Image Statistics Execution Times (Microseconds) Using ImageB.png*

| CPU | CalcImageStats_Cpp() | CalcImageStats_Iavx512() |
|---|---|---|
| Intel Core i5-11600K | 3201 | 201 |

# Summary

Table 7-4 summarizes the C++ SIMD intrinsic functions introduced in this chapter along with other commonly used size variants. AVX-512 C++ SIMD intrinsic functions that perform merge (_mask_) masking and zero (_maskz_) masking are also available for most of the functions listed in Table 7-4, but these are not shown. Before proceeding to the next chapter, you should understand the SIMD arithmetic calculation or data manipulation operation that is performed by each function shown in Table 7-4.

*Table 7-4.* C++ *SIMD Intrinsic Function Summary for Chapter 7*

| C++ SIMD Function Name | Description |
| --- | --- |
| _kand_mask8, _mask16, _mask32, _mask64 | Bitwise logical AND for __mmask8, __mask16, __mmask32, and __mmask64 |
| _kor_mask8, _mask16, _mask32, _mask64 | Bitwise logical OR for __mmask8, __mask16, __mmask32, and __mmask64 |
| _kxor_mask8, _mask16, _mask32, _mask64 | Bitwise logical exclusive OR __mmask8, __mask16, __mmask32, and __mmask64 |
| _mm512_abs_epi8, _epi16, _epi32, _epi64 | Packed integer absolute value |
| _mm512_add_epi8, _epi16, _epi32, _epi64 | Packed integer addition |
| _mm512_adds_epi8, _epi16 | Packed signed integer addition (saturated) |
| _mm512_adds_epu8, _epu16 | Packed unsigned integer addition (saturated) |
| _mm512_add_pd, _ps | Packed floating-point addition |
| _mm512_and_si512 | Bitwise logical AND |
| _mm512_cmpeq_epi8_mask, _epi16_, _epi32_, _epi64_ | Packed signed integer compare (equal) |
| _mm512_cmpge_epi8_mask, _epi16_, _epi32_, _epi64_ | Packed signed integer compare (greater than or equal) |
| _mm512_cmpgt_epi8_mask, _epi16_, _epi32_, _epi64_ | Packed signed integer compare (greater than) |
| _mm512_cmple_epi8_mask, _epi16_, _epi32_, _epi64_ | Packed signed integer compare (less than or equal) |
| _mm512_cmplt_epi8_mask, _epi16_, _epi32_, _epi64_ | Packed signed integer compare (less than) |
| _mm512_cmpneq_epi8_mask, _epi16_, _epi32_, _epi64_ | Packed signed integer compare (not equal) |
| _mm512_cmpeq_epu8_mask, _epu16_, _epu32_, _epu64_ | Packed unsigned integer compare (equal) |
| _mm512_cmpge_epu8_mask, _epu16_, _epu32_, _epu64_ | Packed unsigned integer compare (greater than or equal) |
| _mm512_cmpgt_epu8_mask, _epu16_, _epu32_, _epu64_ | Packed unsigned integer compare (greater than) |
| _mm512_cmple_epu8_mask, _epu16_, _epu32_, _epu64_ | Packed unsigned integer compare (less than or equal) |
| _mm512_cmplt_epu8_mask, _epu16_, _epu32_, _epu64_ | Packed unsigned integer compare (less than) |

*(continued)*

***Table 7-4.*** (*continued*)

| C++ SIMD Function Name | Description |
|---|---|
| _mm512_cmpneq_epu8_mask, _epu16_, _epu32_, _epu64_ | Packed unsigned integer compare (not equal) |
| _mm512_cvtepi32_pd, _ps | Convert packed signed integers to floating-point |
| _mm512_cvtepu32_epi64 | Convert packed unsigned 32-bit integers to 64-bit integers |
| _mm512_cvtepu8_epi16, _epi32, _epi64 | Convert packed unsigned 8-bit integers to 16-, 32-, or 64-bit integers |
| _mm512_cvtps_epi32, _epi64 | Convert packed floating-point to packed signed integers |
| _mm512_cvtps_epu32, _epu64 | Convert packed floating-point to packed unsigned integers |
| _mm512_cvtusepi32_epi8, _epi16 | Convert packed unsigned integers using unsigned saturation |
| _mm512_extracti32x4_epi32, 32x8_epi32 | Extract packed 32-bit integers |
| _mm512_extracti64x2_epi64, 64x4_epi64 | Extract packed 64-bit integers |
| _mm512_load_si512 | Load (aligned) 512-bit wide packed integers |
| _mm512_maskz_mov_epi8, _epi16, _epi32, _epi64 | Packed integer move (zero masking) |
| _mm512_mask_mov_epi8, _epi16, _epi32, _epi64 | Packed integer move (merge masking) |
| _mm512_max_epi8, _epi16, _epi32, _epi64 | Packed signed integer maximum |
| _mm512_max_epu8, _epu16, _epu32, _epu64 | Packed unsigned integer maximum |
| _mm512_min_epi8, _epi16, _epi32, _epi64 | Packed signed integer minimum |
| _mm512_min_epu8, _epu16, _epu32, _epu64 | Packed unsigned integer minimum |
| _mm512_min_pd, _ps | Packed floating-point minimum |
| _mm512_mul_pd, _ps | Packed floating-point multiplication |
| _mm512_mullo_epi16, _epi32, _epi64 | Packed signed integer multiplication (low result) |
| _mm512_reduce_add_epi64 | Sum 64-bit integer elements |
| _mm512_set1_epi8, _epi16, _epi32, _epi64 | Broadcast integer value to all elements |
| _mm512_set1_pd, _ps | Broadcast floating-point value to all elements |
| _mm512_setzero_si512 | Set packed integers to zero |
| _mm512_sllv_epi16, _epi32, _epi64 | Packed integer shift left logical |
| _mm512_srav_epi16, _epi32, _epi64 | Packed integer shift right arithmetic |

(*continued*)

***Table 7-4.*** (*continued*)

| C++ SIMD Function Name | Description |
|---|---|
| _mm512_srli_epi16, _epi32, _epi64 | Packed integer shift right logical |
| _mm512_store_si512 | Store (aligned) 512-bit wide packed integers |
| _mm512_sub_epi8, _epi16, _epi32, _epi64 | Packed integer subtraction |
| _mm512_subs_epi8, _epi16 | Packed signed integer subtraction (saturated) |
| _mm512_subs_epu8, _epu16 | Packed unsigned integer subtraction (saturated) |
| _mm_popcnt_u32, _u64 | Count number of bits set to 1 |

# CHAPTER 8

■ ■ ■

# AVX-512 C++ Programming: Part 2

In earlier chapters, you studied a variety of source code examples that demonstrated floating-point calculations and algorithms using AVX and AVX2 C++ SIMD intrinsic functions. In this chapter, you will examine similar source code examples that highlight the use of AVX-512 C++ SIMD intrinsic functions that perform floating-point operations. The first section contains two source code examples that illustrate simple floating-point arithmetic using 512-bit wide operands. The next two sections focus on using AVX-512 to perform computations with floating-point arrays and matrices. The final section explains how to perform discrete convolutions using AVX-512.

## Floating-Point Arithmetic

In this section, you will learn how to perform elementary floating-point arithmetic using AVX-512 C++ SIMD intrinsic functions. You will also learn how to carry out merge masking and zero masking using floating-point operands.

### Basic Arithmetic

Listing 8-1 contains the source code for example Ch08_01. This example demonstrates basic arithmetic operations using 512-bit wide packed floating-point operands.

**Listing 8-1.** Example Ch08_01

```
//-------------------------------------------------
//              Ch08_01.h
//-------------------------------------------------

#pragma once
#include "ZmmVal.h"

// Ch08_01_fcpp.cpp
extern void PackedMathF32_Iavx512(ZmmVal c[8], const ZmmVal* a, const ZmmVal* b);
extern void PackedMathF64_Iavx512(ZmmVal c[8], const ZmmVal* a, const ZmmVal* b);

//-------------------------------------------------
//              Ch08_01.cpp
//-------------------------------------------------
```

© Daniel Kusswurm 2022
D. Kusswurm, *Modern Parallel Programming with C++ and Assembly Language*,
https://doi.org/10.1007/978-1-4842-7918-2_8

```cpp
#include <iostream>
#define _USE_MATH_DEFINES
#include <math.h>
#include "Ch08_01.h"

static void PackedMathF32(void);
static void PackedMathF64(void);

int main()
{
    PackedMathF32();
    PackedMathF64();
}

static void PackedMathF32(void)
{
    ZmmVal a, b, c[8];
    const char nl = '\n';

    a.m_F32[0] = 36.0f;                 b.m_F32[0] = -0.1111111f;
    a.m_F32[1] = 0.03125f;              b.m_F32[1] = 64.0f;
    a.m_F32[2] = 2.0f;                  b.m_F32[2] = -0.0625f;
    a.m_F32[3] = 42.0f;                 b.m_F32[3] = 8.666667f;
    a.m_F32[4] = 7.0f;                  b.m_F32[4] = -18.125f;
    a.m_F32[5] = 20.5f;                 b.m_F32[5] = 56.0f;
    a.m_F32[6] = 36.125f;               b.m_F32[6] = 24.0f;
    a.m_F32[7] = 0.5f;                  b.m_F32[7] = -158.6f;

    a.m_F32[8] = 136.0f;                b.m_F32[8] = -9.1111111f;
    a.m_F32[9] = 2.03125f;              b.m_F32[9] = 864.0f;
    a.m_F32[10] = 32.0f;                b.m_F32[10] = -70.0625f;
    a.m_F32[11] = 442.0f;               b.m_F32[11] = 98.666667f;
    a.m_F32[12] = 57.0f;                b.m_F32[12] = -518.125f;
    a.m_F32[13] = 620.5f;               b.m_F32[13] = 456.0f;
    a.m_F32[14] = 736.125f;             b.m_F32[14] = 324.0f;
    a.m_F32[15] = 80.5f;                b.m_F32[15] = -298.6f;

    PackedMathF32_Iavx512(c, &a, &b);

    std::cout << ("\nResults for PackedMathF32\n");

    for (unsigned int i = 0; i < 4; i++)
    {
        std::cout << "Group #" << i << nl;
        std::cout << "  a:      " << a.ToStringF32(i) << nl;
        std::cout << "  b:      " << b.ToStringF32(i) << nl;
        std::cout << "  addps:  " << c[0].ToStringF32(i) << nl;
        std::cout << "  subps:  " << c[1].ToStringF32(i) << nl;
        std::cout << "  mulps:  " << c[2].ToStringF32(i) << nl;
        std::cout << "  divps:  " << c[3].ToStringF32(i) << nl;
        std::cout << "  minps:  " << c[4].ToStringF32(i) << nl;
```

```
            std::cout << "   maxps:    " << c[5].ToStringF32(i) << nl;
            std::cout << "   sqrtps:   " << c[6].ToStringF32(i) << nl;
            std::cout << "   absps:    " << c[7].ToStringF32(i) << nl;
            std::cout << nl;
    }
}

static void PackedMathF64(void)
{
    ZmmVal a, b, c[8];
    const char nl = '\n';

    a.m_F64[0] = 2.0;           b.m_F64[0] = M_PI;
    a.m_F64[1] = 4.875;         b.m_F64[1] = M_E;
    a.m_F64[2] = 7.5;           b.m_F64[2] = -9.125;
    a.m_F64[3] = 3.0;           b.m_F64[3] = -M_PI;

    a.m_F64[4] = 12.3333;       b.m_F64[4] = M_PI / 2;
    a.m_F64[5] = 24.0;          b.m_F64[5] = M_E / 2;
    a.m_F64[6] = 37.5;          b.m_F64[6] = -9.125 / 2;
    a.m_F64[7] = 43.0;          b.m_F64[7] = -M_PI / 2;

    PackedMathF64_Iavx512(c, &a, &b);
    std::cout << ("\nResults for PackedMathF64\n");

    for (unsigned int i = 0; i < 4; i++)
    {
        std::cout << "Group #" << i << nl;

        std::cout << "   a:        " << a.ToStringF64(i) << nl;
        std::cout << "   b:        " << b.ToStringF64(i) << nl;
        std::cout << "   addpd:    " << c[0].ToStringF64(i) << nl;
        std::cout << "   subpd:    " << c[1].ToStringF64(i) << nl;
        std::cout << "   mulpd:    " << c[2].ToStringF64(i) << nl;
        std::cout << "   divpd:    " << c[3].ToStringF64(i) << nl;
        std::cout << "   minpd:    " << c[4].ToStringF64(i) << nl;
        std::cout << "   maxpd:    " << c[5].ToStringF64(i) << nl;
        std::cout << "   sqrtpd:   " << c[6].ToStringF64(i) << nl;
        std::cout << "   abspd:    " << c[7].ToStringF64(i) << nl;
        std::cout << nl;
    }
}

//--------------------------------------------------
//                Ch08_01_fcpp.cpp
//--------------------------------------------------

#include <immintrin.h>
#include "Ch08_01.h"
```

```
void PackedMathF32_Iavx512(ZmmVal c[8], const ZmmVal* a, const ZmmVal* b)
{
    __m512 a_vals = _mm512_load_ps(a);
    __m512 b_vals = _mm512_load_ps(b);

    __m512 c_vals0 = _mm512_add_ps(a_vals, b_vals);
    __m512 c_vals1 = _mm512_sub_ps(a_vals, b_vals);
    __m512 c_vals2 = _mm512_mul_ps(a_vals, b_vals);
    __m512 c_vals3 = _mm512_div_ps(a_vals, b_vals);
    __m512 c_vals4 = _mm512_min_ps(a_vals, b_vals);
    __m512 c_vals5 = _mm512_max_ps(a_vals, b_vals);
    __m512 c_vals6 = _mm512_sqrt_ps(a_vals);
    __m512 c_vals7 = _mm512_abs_ps(b_vals);

    _mm512_store_ps(&c[0], c_vals0);
    _mm512_store_ps(&c[1], c_vals1);
    _mm512_store_ps(&c[2], c_vals2);
    _mm512_store_ps(&c[3], c_vals3);
    _mm512_store_ps(&c[4], c_vals4);
    _mm512_store_ps(&c[5], c_vals5);
    _mm512_store_ps(&c[6], c_vals6);
    _mm512_store_ps(&c[7], c_vals7);
}

void PackedMathF64_Iavx512(ZmmVal c[8], const ZmmVal* a, const ZmmVal* b)
{
    __m512d a_vals = _mm512_load_pd(a);
    __m512d b_vals = _mm512_load_pd(b);

    __m512d c_vals0 = _mm512_add_pd(a_vals, b_vals);
    __m512d c_vals1 = _mm512_sub_pd(a_vals, b_vals);
    __m512d c_vals2 = _mm512_mul_pd(a_vals, b_vals);
    __m512d c_vals3 = _mm512_div_pd(a_vals, b_vals);
    __m512d c_vals4 = _mm512_min_pd(a_vals, b_vals);
    __m512d c_vals5 = _mm512_max_pd(a_vals, b_vals);
    __m512d c_vals6 = _mm512_sqrt_pd(a_vals);
    __m512d c_vals7 = _mm512_abs_pd(b_vals);

    _mm512_store_pd(&c[0], c_vals0);
    _mm512_store_pd(&c[1], c_vals1);
    _mm512_store_pd(&c[2], c_vals2);
    _mm512_store_pd(&c[3], c_vals3);
    _mm512_store_pd(&c[4], c_vals4);
    _mm512_store_pd(&c[5], c_vals5);
    _mm512_store_pd(&c[6], c_vals6);
    _mm512_store_pd(&c[7], c_vals7);
}
```

Toward the top of Listing 8-1 are the function declarations for example Ch08_01. Note that these declarations use the ZmmVal structure that you learned about in Chapter 7. The file Ch08_01.cpp contains two functions named PackedMathF32() and PackedMathF64(). These functions perform test case initialization for the SIMD calculating functions PackedMathF32_Iavx512() and PackedMathF64_Iavx512(). They also stream results to std::cout.

The file Ch08_01_fcpp.cpp begins with the definition of function PackedMathF32_Iavx512(). This function uses the C++ SIMD intrinsic function _mm512_load_ps() to initialize a_vals and b_vals. The next code block consists of C++ SIMD intrinsic function calls that perform various AVX-512 arithmetic operations using packed single-precision floating-point operands. This is followed by a series of _mm512_store_ps() calls that save the calculated results. Note that both _mm512_load_ps() and _mm512_store_ps() require their memory operands to be aligned on a 64-byte boundary.

Function PackedMathF64_Iavx512() is the double-precision floating-point counterpart of PackedMathF32_Iavx512(). Note that this function uses the double-precision (_pd) variants of the same C++ SIMD intrinsic functions. Here are the results for source code example Ch08_01:

```
Results for PackedMathF32
Group #0
   a:        36.000000       0.031250  |      2.000000      42.000000
   b:        -0.111111      64.000000  |     -0.062500       8.666667
   addps:    35.888889      64.031250  |      1.937500      50.666668
   subps:    36.111111     -63.968750  |      2.062500      33.333332
   mulps:    -4.000000       2.000000  |     -0.125000     364.000000
   divps:  -324.000031       0.000488  |    -32.000000       4.846154
   minps:    -0.111111       0.031250  |     -0.062500       8.666667
   maxps:    36.000000      64.000000  |      2.000000      42.000000
   sqrtps:    6.000000       0.176777  |      1.414214       6.480741
   absps:     0.111111      64.000000  |      0.062500       8.666667

Group #1
   a:         7.000000      20.500000  |     36.125000       0.500000
   b:       -18.125000      56.000000  |     24.000000    -158.600006
   addps:   -11.125000      76.500000  |     60.125000    -158.100006
   subps:    25.125000     -35.500000  |     12.125000     159.100006
   mulps:  -126.875000    1148.000000  |    867.000000     -79.300003
   divps:    -0.386207       0.366071  |      1.505208      -0.003153
   minps:   -18.125000      20.500000  |     24.000000    -158.600006
   maxps:     7.000000      56.000000  |     36.125000       0.500000
   sqrtps:    2.645751       4.527693  |      6.010407       0.707107
   absps:    18.125000      56.000000  |     24.000000     158.600006

Group #2
   a:       136.000000       2.031250  |     32.000000     442.000000
   b:        -9.111111     864.000000  |    -70.062500      98.666664
   addps:   126.888885     866.031250  |    -38.062500     540.666687
   subps:   145.111115    -861.968750  |    102.062500     343.333344
   mulps: -1239.111084    1755.000000  |  -2242.000000   43610.664062
   divps:   -14.926830       0.002351  |     -0.456735       4.479730
   minps:    -9.111111       2.031250  |    -70.062500      98.666664
   maxps:   136.000000     864.000000  |     32.000000     442.000000
   sqrtps:   11.661903       1.425219  |      5.656854      21.023796
   absps:     9.111111     864.000000  |     70.062500      98.666664
```

Group #3
```
a:           57.000000       620.500000    |     736.125000       80.500000
b:         -518.125000       456.000000    |     324.000000     -298.600006
addps:     -461.125000      1076.500000    |    1060.125000     -218.100006
subps:      575.125000       164.500000    |     412.125000      379.100006
mulps:   -29533.125000    282948.000000    |  238504.500000   -24037.300781
divps:       -0.110012         1.360746    |       2.271991       -0.269591
minps:     -518.125000       456.000000    |     324.000000     -298.600006
maxps:       57.000000       620.500000    |     736.125000       80.500000
sqrtps:       7.549834        24.909838    |      27.131624        8.972179
absps:      518.125000       456.000000    |     324.000000      298.600006
```

Results for PackedMathF64
Group #0
```
a:             2.000000000000    |       4.875000000000
b:             3.141592653590    |       2.718281828459
addpd:         5.141592653590    |       7.593281828459
subpd:        -1.141592653590    |       2.156718171541
mulpd:         6.283185307180    |      13.251623913738
divpd:         0.636619772368    |       1.793412275711
minpd:         2.000000000000    |       2.718281828459
maxpd:         3.141592653590    |       4.875000000000
sqrtpd:        1.414213562373    |       2.207940216582
abspd:         3.141592653590    |       2.718281828459
```

Group #1
```
a:             7.500000000000    |       3.000000000000
b:            -9.125000000000    |      -3.141592653590
addpd:        -1.625000000000    |      -0.141592653590
subpd:        16.625000000000    |       6.141592653590
mulpd:       -68.437500000000    |      -9.424777960769
divpd:        -0.821917808219    |      -0.954929658551
minpd:        -9.125000000000    |      -3.141592653590
maxpd:         7.500000000000    |       3.000000000000
sqrtpd:        2.738612787526    |       1.732050807569
abspd:         9.125000000000    |       3.141592653590
```

Group #2
```
a:            12.333300000000    |      24.000000000000
b:             1.570796326795    |       1.359140914230
addpd:        13.904096326795    |      25.359140914230
subpd:        10.762503673205    |      22.640859085770
mulpd:        19.373102337259    |      32.619381941509
divpd:         7.851622638541    |      17.658213176229
minpd:         1.570796326795    |       1.359140914230
maxpd:        12.333300000000    |      24.000000000000
sqrtpd:        3.511879838491    |       4.898979485566
abspd:         1.570796326795    |       1.359140914230
```

```
Group #3
  a:                 37.500000000000    |              43.000000000000
  b:                 -4.562500000000    |              -1.570796326795
  addpd:             32.937500000000    |              41.429203673205
  subpd:             42.062500000000    |              44.570796326795
  mulpd:            -171.093750000000   |             -67.544242052181
  divpd:             -8.219178082192    |             -27.374650211806
  minpd:             -4.562500000000    |              -1.570796326795
  maxpd:             37.500000000000    |              43.000000000000
  sqrtpd:             6.123724356958    |               6.557438524302
  abspd:              4.562500000000    |               1.570796326795
```

## Compare Operations

The next source code example is named Ch08_02. This example demonstrates packed floating-point compare operations using 512-bit wide SIMD operands. It also highlights mask merging operations using floating-point elements. Listing 8-2 shows the source code for example Ch08_02.

*Listing 8-2.* Example Ch08_02

```cpp
//-----------------------------------------------
//                Ch08_02.h
//-----------------------------------------------

#pragma once
#include <cstdint>
#include "ZmmVal.h"

// Ch08_02_fcpp.cpp
extern void PackedCompareF32_Iavx512(uint16_t c[8], const ZmmVal* a, const ZmmVal* b);
extern void PackedCompareF64_Iavx512(ZmmVal* c, const ZmmVal* a, const ZmmVal* b,
    double x1, double x2, double x3);


//-----------------------------------------------
//                Ch08_02.cpp
//-----------------------------------------------

#include <iostream>
#include <iomanip>
#include <limits>
#define _USE_MATH_DEFINES
#include <math.h>
#include "Ch08_02.h"

static void PackedCompareF32(void);
static void PackedCompareF64(void);
static const char* c_CmpStr[8] = { "EQ", "NE", "LT", "LE", "GT", "GE", "OD", "UO" };
```

```cpp
int main()
{
    PackedCompareF32();
    PackedCompareF64();
    return 0;
}

static void PackedCompareF32(void)
{
    ZmmVal a, b;
    uint16_t c[8];
    const char nl = '\n';
    constexpr float qnan_f32 = std::numeric_limits<float>::quiet_NaN();

    a.m_F32[0] = 2.0f;                      b.m_F32[0] = 1.0f;
    a.m_F32[1] = 7.0f;                      b.m_F32[1] = 12.0f;
    a.m_F32[2] = -6.0f;                     b.m_F32[2] = -6.0f;
    a.m_F32[3] = 3.0f;                      b.m_F32[3] = 8.0f;
    a.m_F32[4] = -16.0f;                    b.m_F32[4] = -36.0f;
    a.m_F32[5] = 3.5f;                      b.m_F32[5] = 3.5f;
    a.m_F32[6] = (float)M_PI;               b.m_F32[6] = -6.0f;
    a.m_F32[7] = (float)M_SQRT2;            b.m_F32[7] = qnan_f32;
    a.m_F32[8] = 102.0f;                    b.m_F32[8] = (float)M_SQRT1_2;
    a.m_F32[9] = 77.0f;                     b.m_F32[9] = 77.0f;
    a.m_F32[10] = 187.0f;                   b.m_F32[10] = 33.0f;
    a.m_F32[11] = -5.1f;                    b.m_F32[11] = -87.0f;
    a.m_F32[12] = 16.0f;                    b.m_F32[12] = 936.0f;
    a.m_F32[13] = 0.5f;                     b.m_F32[13] = 0.5f;
    a.m_F32[14] = (float)(M_PI * 2);        b.m_F32[14] = 66.6667f;
    a.m_F32[15] = (float)(1.0/M_SQRT2);     b.m_F32[15] = 100.7f;

    PackedCompareF32_Iavx512(c, &a, &b);

    const size_t w1 = 10;
    const size_t w2 = 6;
    std::cout << ("\nResults for PackedCompareF32\n");
    std::cout << std::fixed << std::setprecision(4);
    std::cout << "       a          b       ";

    for (unsigned int j = 0; j < 8; j++)
        std::cout << std::setw(w2) << c_CmpStr[j];
    std::cout << nl << std::string(70, '-') << nl;

    for (unsigned int i = 0; i < 16; i++)
    {
        std::cout << std::setw(w1) << a.m_F32[i];
        std::cout << std::setw(w1) << b.m_F32[i];
```

```cpp
        for (unsigned int j = 0; j < 8; j++)
            std::cout << std::setw(w2) << ((c[j] & (1 << i)) ? 1 : 0);

        std::cout << nl;
    }
}

static void PackedCompareF64(void)
{
    ZmmVal a, b, c;
    const double x1 = -20.0, x2 = 20.0, x3 = 999.0;
    const char nl = '\n';

    a.m_F64[0] = 5.0;           b.m_F64[0] = -1.0;
    a.m_F64[1] = 21.0;          b.m_F64[1] =  2.0;
    a.m_F64[2] = 3.0;           b.m_F64[2] = 14.0;
    a.m_F64[3] = 4.0;           b.m_F64[3] = -9.0;
    a.m_F64[4] = 52.0;          b.m_F64[4] = -5.0;
    a.m_F64[5] = 6.0;           b.m_F64[5] = 6.0;
    a.m_F64[6] = 7.0;           b.m_F64[6] = -37.0;
    a.m_F64[7] = 8.0;           b.m_F64[7] = -9.0;

    PackedCompareF64_Iavx512(&c, &a, &b, x1, x2, x3);

    const size_t w1 = 8;
    const size_t w2 = 12;
    std::cout << std::fixed << std::setprecision(4);
    std::cout << ("\nResults for PackedCompareF64 ");
    std::cout << "(x1 = " << std::setw(w1) << x1;
    std::cout << " x2 = " << std::setw(w1) << x2 << ")\n";

    for (unsigned int i = 0; i < 8; i++)
    {
        std::cout << std::setw(w2) << a.m_F64[i];
        std::cout << std::setw(w2) << b.m_F64[i];
        std::cout << std::setw(w2) << c.m_F64[i];
        std::cout << nl;
    }
}

//-------------------------------------------------
//             Ch08_02_fcpp.cpp
//-------------------------------------------------

#include <immintrin.h>
#include "Ch08_02.h"

void PackedCompareF32_Iavx512(uint16_t c[8], const ZmmVal* a, const ZmmVal* b)
{
    __m512 a_vals = _mm512_load_ps(a);
    __m512 b_vals = _mm512_load_ps(b);
```

```
    // Perform packed F32 compares
    c[0] = _mm512_cmp_ps_mask(a_vals, b_vals, _CMP_EQ_OQ);
    c[1] = _mm512_cmp_ps_mask(a_vals, b_vals, _CMP_NEQ_OQ);
    c[2] = _mm512_cmp_ps_mask(a_vals, b_vals, _CMP_LT_OQ);
    c[3] = _mm512_cmp_ps_mask(a_vals, b_vals, _CMP_LE_OQ);
    c[4] = _mm512_cmp_ps_mask(a_vals, b_vals, _CMP_GT_OQ);
    c[5] = _mm512_cmp_ps_mask(a_vals, b_vals, _CMP_GE_OQ);
    c[6] = _mm512_cmp_ps_mask(a_vals, b_vals, _CMP_ORD_Q);
    c[7] = _mm512_cmp_ps_mask(a_vals, b_vals, _CMP_UNORD_Q);
}

void PackedCompareF64_Iavx512(ZmmVal* c, const ZmmVal* a, const ZmmVal* b,
    double x1, double x2, double x3)
{
    __m512d a_vals = _mm512_load_pd(a);
    __m512d b_vals = _mm512_load_pd(b);
    __m512d x1_vals = _mm512_set1_pd(x1);
    __m512d x2_vals = _mm512_set1_pd(x2);
    __m512d x3_vals = _mm512_set1_pd(x3);

    __mmask8 m;
    m  = _mm512_cmp_pd_mask(a_vals, x1_vals, _CMP_GE_OQ);
    m &= _mm512_cmp_pd_mask(a_vals, x2_vals, _CMP_LE_OQ);
    m &= _mm512_cmp_pd_mask(b_vals, x1_vals, _CMP_GE_OQ);
    m &= _mm512_cmp_pd_mask(b_vals, x2_vals, _CMP_LE_OQ);

    __m512d temp0 = _mm512_mask_mul_pd(x3_vals, m, a_vals, b_vals);
    _mm512_store_pd(c, temp0);
}
```

In Listing 8-2, the files Ch08_02.h and Ch08_02.cpp contain function declarations and test case initialization code for this source code example. The first function in file Ch08_02_fcpp.cpp, PackedCompareF32_Iavx512(), performs SIMD compare operations using packed single-precision floating-point operands. Unlike AVX and AVX2, AVX-512 SIMD floating-point compare operations return scalar integers that signify the results. In the current example, the C++ SIMD intrinsic function _mm512_cmp_ps_mask() returns an integer value of type __mmask16. Each bit position of this 16-bit wide mask value reports the compare result for the corresponding SIMD operand element position (1 = compare predicate true, 0 = compare predicate false). Function _mm512_cmp_ps_mask() uses the same compare predicates that _mm256_cmp_ps() uses (see example Ch03_02).

The next function in file Ch08_02_fcpp.cpp is named PackedCompareF64_Iavx512(). This function demonstrates execution of the C++ SIMD intrinsic function _mm512_cmp_pd_mask(). Note that the mask value calculated by the four _mm512_cmp_pd_mask() calls is used in the ensuing call to _mm512_mask_mul_pd(), which carries out multiplication using only those element pairs whose values are greater than or equal to x1 and less than or equal to x2. Element pairs whose values do not meet these criteria are set to x3. This (somewhat contrived) computation illustrates how to perform merge masking using packed double-precision floating-point operands. Most AVX-512 floating-point C++ SIMD intrinsic functions support both merge masking and zero masking variants. Here are the results for source code example Ch08_02:

```
Results for PackedCompareF32
       a          b      EQ   NE   LT   LE   GT   GE   OD   UO
--------------------------------------------------------------
    2.0000    1.0000     0    1    0    0    1    1    1    0
    7.0000   12.0000     0    1    1    1    0    0    1    0
   -6.0000   -6.0000     1    0    0    1    0    1    1    0
    3.0000    8.0000     0    1    1    1    0    0    1    0
  -16.0000  -36.0000     0    1    0    0    1    1    1    0
    3.5000    3.5000     1    0    0    1    0    1    1    0
    3.1416   -6.0000     0    1    0    0    1    1    1    0
    1.4142      nan      0    0    0    0    0    0    0    1
  102.0000    0.7071     0    1    0    0    1    1    1    0
   77.0000   77.0000     1    0    0    1    0    1    1    0
  187.0000   33.0000     0    1    0    0    1    1    1    0
   -5.1000  -87.0000     0    1    0    0    1    1    1    0
   16.0000  936.0000     0    1    1    1    0    0    1    0
    0.5000    0.5000     1    0    0    1    0    1    1    0
    6.2832   66.6667     0    1    1    1    0    0    1    0
    0.7071  100.7000     0    1    1    1    0    0    1    0

Results for PackedCompareF64 (x1 = -20.0000 x2 =   20.0000)
    5.0000     -1.0000      -5.0000
   21.0000      2.0000     999.0000
    3.0000     14.0000      42.0000
    4.0000     -9.0000     -36.0000
   52.0000     -5.0000     999.0000
    6.0000      6.0000      36.0000
    7.0000    -37.0000     999.0000
    8.0000     -9.0000     -72.0000
```

# Floating-Point Arrays

In Chapter 3, you learned how to calculate the mean and standard deviation of an array of single-precision floating-point values using AVX (see example Ch03_04). The next source example, Ch08_03, explains how to perform these same calculations using AVX-512. Listing 8-3 shows the only mean and standard deviation calculating code for example Ch08_03. Not shown is the test case initialization and error checking code since it is almost identical to the code that you saw in example Ch03_04.

*Listing 8-3.* Example Ch08_03

```
//--------------------------------------------------
//              Ch08_03_fcpp.cpp
//--------------------------------------------------

#include <cmath>
#include <stdexcept>
#include <immintrin.h>
```

```cpp
#include "Ch08_03.h"
#include "AlignedMem.h"

void CalcMeanF32_Cpp(float* mean, const float* x, size_t n)
{
    if (!CheckArgs(x, n))
        throw std::runtime_error("CalcMeanF32_Cpp() - CheckArgs failed");

    float sum = 0.0f;

    for (size_t i = 0; i < n; i++)
        sum += x[i];

    *mean = sum / n;
}

void CalcStDevF32_Cpp(float* st_dev, const float* x, size_t n, float mean)
{
    if (!CheckArgs(x, n))
        throw std::runtime_error("CalcStDevF32_Cpp() - CheckArgs failed");

    float sum_squares = 0.0f;

    for (size_t i = 0; i < n; i++)
    {
        float temp = x[i] - mean;
        sum_squares += temp * temp;
    }

    *st_dev = sqrt(sum_squares / (n - 1));
}

void CalcMeanF32_Iavx512(float* mean, const float* x, size_t n)
{
    if (!CheckArgs(x, n))
        throw std::runtime_error("CalcMeanF32_Iavx512() - CheckArgs failed");

    __m512 sums = _mm512_setzero_ps();

    size_t i = 0;
    const size_t num_simd_elements = 16;

    for (; n - i >= num_simd_elements; i += num_simd_elements)
    {
        __m512 x_vals = _mm512_load_ps(&x[i]);
        sums = _mm512_add_ps(x_vals, sums);
    }
```

```
    // Reduce packed sums to scalar value, then process remaining elements
    float sum = _mm512_reduce_add_ps(sums);

    for (; i < n; i++)
        sum += x[i];

    *mean = sum / n;
}

void CalcStDevF32_Iavx512(float* st_dev, const float* x, size_t n, float mean)
{
    if (!CheckArgs(x, n))
        throw std::runtime_error("CalcStDevF32_Iavx512() - CheckArgs failed");

    __m512 packed_mean = _mm512_set1_ps(mean);
    __m512 packed_sum_squares = _mm512_setzero_ps();

    size_t i = 0;
    const size_t num_simd_elements = 16;

    for (; n - i >= num_simd_elements; i += num_simd_elements)
    {
        __m512 x_vals = _mm512_load_ps(&x[i]);
        __m512 temp1 = _mm512_sub_ps(x_vals, packed_mean);

        packed_sum_squares = _mm512_fmadd_ps(temp1, temp1, packed_sum_squares);
    }

    // Reduce packed_sum_squares to scalar value, then process remaining elements
    float sum_squares =_mm512_reduce_add_ps(packed_sum_squares);

    for (; i < n; i++)
    {
        float temp1 = x[i] - mean;
        sum_squares += temp1 * temp1;
    }

    *st_dev = sqrt(sum_squares / (n - 1));
}
```

The first two functions in file Ch08_03_fcpp.cpp, CalcMeanF32_Cpp() and CalcStDevF32_Cpp(), calculate the mean and standard deviation using standard C++ statements. These functions are included in this example for comparison purposes. The next function, CalcMeanF32_Iavx512(), calculates the array mean using AVX-512 C++ SIMD intrinsic functions. Following argument validation, function CalcMeanF32_Iavx512() uses _mm512_setzero_ps() to initialize sums to zero. The variable sums contains 16 intermediate single-precision floating-point sum values. These values are updated during each iteration of the ensuing for-loop. Following execution of the for-loop, CalcMeanF32_Iavx512() uses the C++ SIMD intrinsic function _mm512_reduce_add_ps() to reduce the 16 single-precision floating-point values in sums to a single scalar value. Recall that the AVX code in example Ch03_04 employed a sequence of C++ SIMD intrinsic function calls to perform this same reduction. Following the reduction of sums, the second for-loop in CalcMeanF32_Iavx512() processes any residual elements using scalar arithmetic.

The standard deviation calculating code in function `CalcStDevF32_Iavx512()` uses the C++ SIMD intrinsic function `_mm512_set1_ps()` to initialize `packed_means`. This is followed by a call to `_mm512_setzero_ps()`, which initializes `packed_sum_squares` to zero. During each iteration, the first for-loop in `CalcStDevF32_Iavx512()` updates this value using 16 elements from array x. Following execution of the for-loop, `packed_sum_squares` is reduced to a scalar value using the C++ SIMD intrinsic function `_mm512_reduce_add_ps()`. The second for-loop in `CalcStDevF32_Iavx512()` processes any residual elements using scalar arithmetic. Here are the results for source code example Ch08_03:

```
Results for CalcMeanF32_Cpp and CalcStDevF32_Cpp
mean1:    49.602146  st_dev1:  27.758242

Results for CalcMeanF32_Iavx512 and CalcStDevF32_Iavx512
mean2:    49.602158  st_dev2:  27.758244
```

Like example Ch03_04, the results for source code example Ch08_03 contain some slight discrepancy values due to the non-associativity of floating-point arithmetic. Whether these discrepancies are of any consequence depends on the specific application.

# Floating-Point Matrices

In Chapter 5, you studied several source code examples that explained how to perform common matrix operations using AVX2 C++ SIMD intrinsic functions. In this section, you will learn how to carry out some of the same matrix operations using AVX-512 C++ SIMD intrinsic functions. The first source code example highlights the use of AVX-512 to calculate a covariance matrix. This is followed by two source code examples that spotlight matrix multiplication. The final source code example of this section explicates matrix-vector multiplication. As you will soon see, it is often a straightforward programming task to adapt an algorithm originally written using AVX2 C++ SIMD intrinsic functions to one that exploits the computational resources of AVX-512.

## Covariance Matrix

Mathematicians often use a statistical measure called covariance to quantify the extent to which two random variables vary together. When multiple random variables are being analyzed, it is common to calculate a matrix of all possible covariances. This matrix is called, unsurprisingly, a covariance matrix. Once calculated, a covariance matrix can be employed to perform a wide variety of advanced statistical analyses. Appendix B contains several references that you can consult if you are interested in learning more about covariance and covariance matrices.

The calculation of a covariance matrix begins with a sample data matrix as shown in Figure 8-1. In this figure, each row of matrix $\mathbf{X}$ represents one random variable (or feature). Each column in $\mathbf{X}$ is a multivariate observation. The elements $c_{ij}$ in covariance matrix $\mathbf{C}$ are calculated using the following equation:

$$c_{ij} = \frac{\sum_{k=0}^{n_{obv}-1}\left(x_{ik} - \overline{x}_i\right)\left(x_{jk} - \overline{x}_j\right)}{n_{obv} - 1}$$

where $i = 0, 1, \cdots, n_{var} - 1$ and $j = 0, 1, \cdots, n_{var} - 1$. In these equations, the symbols $n_{obv}$ and $n_{var}$ signify the number of observations and variables, respectively. A covariance matrix is always a square $(n_{var} \times n_{var})$ symmetric $(c_{ij} = c_{ji})$ matrix as shown in Figure 8-1. Each covariance matrix element $c_{ij}$ represents the covariance between random variables $x_i$ and $x_j$, and each main diagonal element $c_{ii}$ is the variance for variable $x_i$.

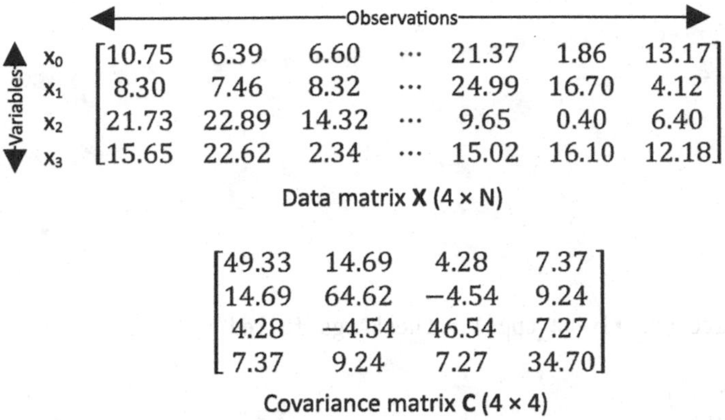

Data matrix **X** (4 × N)

$$\begin{bmatrix} 49.33 & 14.69 & 4.28 & 7.37 \\ 14.69 & 64.62 & -4.54 & 9.24 \\ 4.28 & -4.54 & 46.54 & 7.27 \\ 7.37 & 9.24 & 7.27 & 34.70 \end{bmatrix}$$

Covariance matrix **C** (4 × 4)

***Figure 8-1.*** *Example data matrix and covariance matrix*

Listing 8-4 shows the source code for example Ch08_04. This example demonstrates how to calculate a covariance matrix using AVX-512 SIMD arithmetic.

***Listing 8-4.*** Example Ch08_04

```
//--------------------------------------------------
//              Ch08_04.h
//--------------------------------------------------

#pragma once
#include <vector>
#include "MatrixF64.h"

// Note: In this example, CMD stands for covariance matrix data
struct CMD
{
    MatrixF64 m_X;                      // Data matrix
    MatrixF64 m_CovMat;                 // Covariance matrix
    std::vector<double> m_VarMeans;     // Variable (row) means

    CMD(size_t n_vars, size_t n_obvs) :
        m_X(n_vars, n_obvs), m_CovMat(n_vars, n_vars), m_VarMeans(n_vars) { }
};

// Ch08_04_fcpp.cpp
extern void CalcCovMatF64_Cpp(CMD& cmd);
extern void CalcCovMatF64_Iavx512(CMD& cmd);

// Ch08_04_misc.cpp
extern bool CheckArgs(const CMD& cmd);
extern bool CompareResults(CMD& cmd1, CMD& cmd2);
extern void InitCMD(CMD& cmd1, CMD& cmd2);

// Ch08_04_misc2.cpp
extern void DisplayData(const CMD& cmd);
```

```cpp
//--------------------------------------------------
//                  Ch08_04_fcpp.cpp
//--------------------------------------------------

#include <immintrin.h>
#include "Ch08_04.h"

void CalcCovMatF64_Cpp(CMD& cmd)
{
    if (!CheckArgs(cmd))
        throw std::runtime_error("CalcCovMatrixF64_Cpp() - CheckArgs failed");

    size_t n_vars = cmd.m_X.GetNumRows();
    size_t n_obvs = cmd.m_X.GetNumCols();
    double* cov_mat = cmd.m_CovMat.Data();
    double* x = cmd.m_X.Data();
    double* var_means = cmd.m_VarMeans.data();

    // Calculate variable means (rows of cmd.m_X)
    for (size_t i = 0; i < n_vars; i++)
    {
        var_means[i] = 0.0;
        for (size_t j = 0; j < n_obvs; j++)
            var_means[i] += x[i * n_obvs + j];
        var_means[i] /= n_obvs;
    }

    // Calculate covariance matrix
    for (size_t i = 0; i < n_vars; i++)
    {
        for (size_t j = 0; j < n_vars; j++)
        {
            if (i <= j)
            {
                double sum = 0.0;

                for (size_t k = 0; k < n_obvs; k++)
                {
                    double temp1 = x[i * n_obvs + k] - var_means[i];
                    double temp2 = x[j * n_obvs + k] - var_means[j];
                    sum += temp1 * temp2;
                }

                cov_mat[i * n_vars + j] = sum / (n_obvs - 1);
            }
            else
                cov_mat[i * n_vars + j] = cov_mat[j * n_vars + i];
        }
    }
}
```

```
inline double ReduceAddF64(__m512d a, __m256d b, __m128d c)
{
    // Sum double precision values of arguments a, b, and c
    __m256d temp0 = _mm256_setzero_pd();
    __m256d temp1 = _mm256_insertf64x2(temp0, c, 0);
    __m256d temp2 = _mm256_add_pd(temp1, b);
    __m512d temp3 = _mm512_setzero_pd();
    __m512d temp4 = _mm512_insertf64x4(temp3, temp2, 0);
    __m512d temp5 = _mm512_add_pd(temp4, a);

    return _mm512_reduce_add_pd(temp5);
}

void CalcCovMatF64_Iavx512(CMD& cmd)
{
    if (!CheckArgs(cmd))
        throw std::runtime_error("CalcCovMatrixF64_Iavx512() - CheckArgs failed");

    size_t n_vars = cmd.m_X.GetNumRows();
    size_t n_obvs = cmd.m_X.GetNumCols();
    double* cov_mat = cmd.m_CovMat.Data();
    double* x = cmd.m_X.Data();
    double* var_means = cmd.m_VarMeans.data();
    const size_t num_simd_elements8 = 8;
    const size_t num_simd_elements4 = 4;
    const size_t num_simd_elements2 = 2;

    // Calculate variable means (rows of cmd.m_X)
    for (size_t i = 0; i < n_vars; i++)
    {
        size_t j = 0;
        __m512d sums_512 = _mm512_setzero_pd();
        __m256d sums_256 = _mm256_setzero_pd();
        __m128d sums_128 = _mm_setzero_pd();

        while (j < n_obvs)
        {
            if (n_obvs - j >= num_simd_elements8)
            {
                __m512d x_vals = _mm512_loadu_pd(&x[i * n_obvs + j]);
                sums_512 = _mm512_add_pd(x_vals, sums_512);
                j += num_simd_elements8;
            }
            else if (n_obvs - j >= num_simd_elements4)
            {
                __m256d x_vals = _mm256_loadu_pd(&x[i * n_obvs + j]);
                sums_256 = _mm256_add_pd(x_vals, sums_256);
                j += num_simd_elements4;
            }
```

```
            else if (n_obvs - j >= num_simd_elements2)
            {
                __m128d x_vals = _mm_loadu_pd(&x[i * n_obvs + j]);
                sums_128 = _mm_add_pd(x_vals, sums_128);
                j += num_simd_elements2;
            }
            else
            {
                __m128d x_val = _mm_load_sd(&x[i * n_obvs + j]);
                sums_128 = _mm_add_pd(x_val, sums_128);
                j += 1;
            }
        }
    }

    double sum = ReduceAddF64(sums_512, sums_256, sums_128);
    var_means[i] = sum / n_obvs;
}

// Calculate covariance matrix
for (size_t i = 0; i < n_vars; i++)
{
    for (size_t j = 0; j < n_vars; j++)
    {
        if (i <= j)
        {
            size_t k = 0;
            __m512d sums_512 = _mm512_setzero_pd();
            __m256d sums_256 = _mm256_setzero_pd();
            __m128d sums_128 = _mm_setzero_pd();

            while (k < n_obvs)
            {
                if (n_obvs - k >= num_simd_elements8)
                {
                    __m512d var_means1_512 = _mm512_set1_pd(var_means[i]);
                    __m512d var_means2_512 = _mm512_set1_pd(var_means[j]);
                    __m512d x_vals1 = _mm512_loadu_pd(&x[i * n_obvs + k]);
                    __m512d x_vals2 = _mm512_loadu_pd(&x[j * n_obvs + k]);
                    __m512d temp1 = _mm512_sub_pd(x_vals1, var_means1_512);
                    __m512d temp2 = _mm512_sub_pd(x_vals2, var_means2_512);

                    sums_512 = _mm512_fmadd_pd(temp1, temp2, sums_512);
                    k += num_simd_elements8;
                }
                else if (n_obvs - k >= num_simd_elements4)
                {
                    __m256d var_means1_256 = _mm256_set1_pd(var_means[i]);
                    __m256d var_means2_256 = _mm256_set1_pd(var_means[j]);
                    __m256d x_vals1 = _mm256_loadu_pd(&x[i * n_obvs + k]);
                    __m256d x_vals2 = _mm256_loadu_pd(&x[j * n_obvs + k]);
                    __m256d temp1 = _mm256_sub_pd(x_vals1, var_means1_256);
                    __m256d temp2 = _mm256_sub_pd(x_vals2, var_means2_256);
```

```
                    sums_256 = _mm256_fmadd_pd(temp1, temp2, sums_256);
                    k += num_simd_elements4;
                }
                else if (n_obvs - k >= num_simd_elements2)
                {
                    __m128d var_means1_128 = _mm_set1_pd(var_means[i]);
                    __m128d var_means2_128 = _mm_set1_pd(var_means[j]);
                    __m128d x_vals1 = _mm_loadu_pd(&x[i * n_obvs + k]);
                    __m128d x_vals2 = _mm_loadu_pd(&x[j * n_obvs + k]);
                    __m128d temp1 = _mm_sub_pd(x_vals1, var_means1_128);
                    __m128d temp2 = _mm_sub_pd(x_vals2, var_means2_128);

                    sums_128 = _mm_fmadd_pd(temp1, temp2, sums_128);
                    k += num_simd_elements2;
                }
                else
                {
                    __m128d var_means1_64 = _mm_load_sd(&var_means[i]);
                    __m128d var_means2_64 = _mm_load_sd(&var_means[j]);
                    __m128d x_vals1 = _mm_load_sd(&x[i * n_obvs + k]);
                    __m128d x_vals2 = _mm_load_sd(&x[j * n_obvs + k]);
                    __m128d temp1 = _mm_sub_pd(x_vals1, var_means1_64);
                    __m128d temp2 = _mm_sub_pd(x_vals2, var_means2_64);

                    sums_128 = _mm_fmadd_pd(temp1, temp2, sums_128);
                    k += 1;
                }
            }

            double sum = ReduceAddF64(sums_512, sums_256, sums_128);
            cov_mat[i * n_vars + j] = sum / (n_obvs - 1);
        }
        else
            cov_mat[i * n_vars + j] = cov_mat[j * n_vars + i];
        }
    }
}
```

Near the top of Listing 8-4 is the file Ch08_04.h, which begins with the definition of structure CMD (CMD = covariance matrix data). This structure contains the data matrix, the variable means vector, and the covariance matrix. Note that CMD also includes a simple constructor that allocates space for the three container objects using the specified n_vars and n_obvs. The source code that performs argument validation, test data initialization, and result comparisons is not shown in Listing 8-4 but included in the download software package.

The core calculating functions of source code example are in Ch08_08_fcpp.cpp, which begins with the definition of function CalcCovMatF64_Cpp(). This function uses standard C++ statements to calculate the covariance matrix and is included for comparison purposes. The code in CalcCovMatF64_Cpp() is split into two major sections. The first section calculates the mean for each variable (or row) in data matrix x. The second section calculates the covariances. Note that function CalcCovMatF64_Cpp() exploits the fact that a covariance matrix is symmetric and only carries out a complete calculation when i <= j is true. If i <= j is false, CalcCovMatF64_Cpp() executes cov_mat[i][j] = cov_mat[j][j].

The next function in Ch08_04_fcpp.cpp is a SIMD inline function named ReduceAddF64(). This function reduces the double-precision floating-point elements of arguments a (__m512d), b (__m256d), and c (__m128d) to a scalar double-precision value. Note that ReduceAddF64() employs several C++ SIMD intrinsic functions to size-extend argument values b and c to packed 512-bit wide SIMD values. Doing this facilitates the use of the AVX-512 C++ SIMD intrinsic function _mm512_reduce_add_pd() to perform the reduction.

The final function in Listing 8-4 is named CalcCovMatF64_Iavx512(). Like its standard C++ counterpart, function CalcCovMatF64_Iavx512() uses distinct sections of code to calculate the variable means and the covariance matrix. The mean calculating while-loop employs __m512d, __m256d, __m128d, or scalar objects to perform its computations. Note that each if section verifies that enough elements are available in the current row before carrying out any SIMD calculations. Following the while-loop, CalcCovMatF64_Iavx512() invokes ReduceAddF64() to reduce sums_512, sums_256, and sums_128 to a scalar value. It then calculates var_means[i].

Function CalcCovMatF64_Iavx512() uses a similar while-loop construct to calculate the elements of the covariance matrix. Like the function CalcCovMatF64_Cpp(), function CalcCovMatF64_Iavx512() calculates a covariance matrix element only if i <= j is true; otherwise, a covariance matrix element copy is performed. Note that the four covariance-matrix-element calculating code blocks in CalcCovMatF64_Iavx512() employ FMA arithmetic to carry out their computations. Here are the results for source code example Ch08_04:

```
Results for CalcCovMatF64
n_vars = 12, n_obvs = 111
Variable means
    0:      13.37       13.37
    1:      12.34       12.34
    2:      12.62       12.62
    3:      13.25       13.25
    4:      11.89       11.89
    5:      12.10       12.10
    6:      11.65       11.65
    7:      12.13       12.13
    8:      12.49       12.49
    9:      12.53       12.53
   10:      12.08       12.08
   11:      12.33       12.33


cmd1.m_CovMat
  50.61    2.00    0.60    1.41  -1.57    3.15   -2.68    4.36   -0.70    3.04    5.16   -4.16
   2.00   48.45   -6.96    2.20   5.23    1.45    0.62   -4.88   -0.52    9.59    1.86   -1.76
   0.60   -6.96   48.26  -13.01   1.15   -2.10    5.47   -5.81    3.22    0.46   -0.75    7.50
   1.41    2.20  -13.01   51.71   2.05    1.76   -5.01    7.45   -2.03    4.34   -5.41    7.26
  -1.57    5.23    1.15    2.05  55.88   -6.90   -7.11    0.17    4.78    4.57   -0.03   -3.01
   3.15    1.45   -2.10    1.76  -6.90   54.28   10.10    4.07    0.17   -0.99    1.24    3.15
  -2.68    0.62    5.47   -5.01  -7.11   10.10   56.98   -4.95   -2.19   -2.47  -10.59    1.63
   4.36   -4.88   -5.81    7.45   0.17    4.07   -4.95   52.51    3.89    1.76    4.04    1.80
  -0.70   -0.52    3.22   -2.03   4.78    0.17   -2.19    3.89   52.56    3.16   -2.82    5.82
   3.04    9.59    0.46    4.34   4.57   -0.99   -2.47    1.76    3.16   42.41    8.35    1.28
   5.16    1.86   -0.75   -5.41  -0.03    1.24  -10.59    4.04   -2.82    8.35   58.25  -11.63
  -4.16   -1.76    7.50    7.26  -3.01    3.15    1.63    1.80    5.82    1.28  -11.63   49.79
```

```
cmd2.m_CovMat
  50.61    2.00    0.60    1.41   -1.57    3.15   -2.68    4.36   -0.70    3.04    5.16   -4.16
   2.00   48.45   -6.96    2.20    5.23    1.45    0.62   -4.88   -0.52    9.59    1.86   -1.76
   0.60   -6.96   48.26  -13.01    1.15   -2.10    5.47   -5.81    3.22    0.46   -0.75    7.50
   1.41    2.20  -13.01   51.71    2.05    1.76   -5.01    7.45   -2.03    4.34   -5.41    7.26
  -1.57    5.23    1.15    2.05   55.88   -6.90   -7.11    0.17    4.78    4.57   -0.03   -3.01
   3.15    1.45   -2.10    1.76   -6.90   54.28   10.10    4.07    0.17   -0.99    1.24    3.15
  -2.68    0.62    5.47   -5.01   -7.11   10.10   56.98   -4.95   -2.19   -2.47  -10.59    1.63
   4.36   -4.88   -5.81    7.45    0.17    4.07   -4.95   52.51    3.89    1.76    4.04    1.80
  -0.70   -0.52    3.22   -2.03    4.78    0.17   -2.19    3.89   52.56    3.16   -2.82    5.82
   3.04    9.59    0.46    4.34    4.57   -0.99   -2.47    1.76    3.16   42.41    8.35    1.28
   5.16    1.86   -0.75   -5.41   -0.03    1.24  -10.59    4.04   -2.82    8.35   58.25  -11.63
  -4.16   -1.76    7.50    7.26   -3.01    3.15    1.63    1.80    5.82    1.28  -11.63   49.79

CompareResults - passed
```

## Matrix Multiplication

In Chapter 5, you learned how to perform single-precision floating-point matrix multiplication using C++ SIMD intrinsic functions and AVX2 (see example Ch05_02). The next source code example, named Ch08_05, illustrates single-precision floating-point matrix multiplication using C++ SIMD intrinsic functions and AVX-512. Listing 8-5 shows the matrix multiplication calculating code for source code example Ch08_05. Before examining this source code, you may want to review the matrix multiplication equations that were discussed in Chapter 5.

*Listing 8-5.* Example Ch08_05

```cpp
//--------------------------------------------------
//              Ch08_05_fcpp.cpp
//--------------------------------------------------

#include <stdexcept>
#include <immintrin.h>
#include "Ch08_05.h"

void MatrixMulF32_Cpp(MatrixF32& c, const MatrixF32& a, const MatrixF32& b)
{
    MatrixF32::Mul(c, a, b);
}

void MatrixMulF32_Iavx512(MatrixF32& c, const MatrixF32& a, const MatrixF32& b)
{
    if (!CheckArgs(c, a, b))
        throw std::runtime_error("MatrixMulF32_Iavx512() CheckArgs failed");

    const float* aa = a.Data();
    const float* bb = b.Data();
    float* cc = c.Data();
```

```
    size_t c_nrows = c.GetNumRows();
    size_t c_ncols = c.GetNumCols();
    size_t a_ncols = a.GetNumCols();
    size_t b_ncols = b.GetNumCols();
    size_t m = a_ncols;

    const size_t num_simd_elements = 16;
    size_t num_residual_cols = c_ncols % num_simd_elements;

    // res_mask = 2 ** num_residual_cols - 1
    __mmask16 res_mask = (__mmask16)((1 << num_residual_cols) - 1);
    for (size_t i = 0; i < c_nrows; i++)
    {
        size_t j = 0;

        while (j + num_simd_elements <= c_ncols)
        {
            __m512 c_vals = _mm512_setzero_ps();

            for (size_t k = 0; k < m; k++)
            {
                __m512 a_vals = _mm512_set1_ps(aa[i * a_ncols + k]);
                __m512 b_vals = _mm512_loadu_ps(&bb[k * b_ncols + j]);

                c_vals = _mm512_fmadd_ps(a_vals, b_vals, c_vals);
            }

            _mm512_storeu_ps(&cc[i * c_ncols + j], c_vals);
            j += num_simd_elements;
        }

        if (num_residual_cols != 0)
        {
            __m512 c_vals = _mm512_setzero_ps();

            for (size_t k = 0; k < m; k++)
            {
                __m512 a_vals = _mm512_set1_ps(aa[i * a_ncols + k]);
                __m512 b_vals = _mm512_maskz_loadu_ps(res_mask, &bb[k * b_ncols + j]);

                c_vals = _mm512_fmadd_ps(a_vals, b_vals, c_vals);
            }

            _mm512_mask_storeu_ps(&cc[i * c_ncols + j], res_mask, c_vals);
        }
    }
}
```

Near the top of Listing 8-5 is the source code for function MatrixMulF32_Iavx512(), which performs single-precision floating-point matrix multiplication. The primary difference between this function and the function MatrixMulF32_Iavx2() that you studied in example Ch05_02 is in the code that calculates the residual column mask for the current row. In example Ch05_02, function MatrixMulF32_Iavx2() used a SIMD integer (__m256i) mask. In this example, function MatrixMulF32_Iavx512() uses a scalar integer (__mmask16) mask since these are directly supported by AVX-512.

Following its initialization tasks, function MatrixMulF32_Iavx512() calculates num_residual_cols. This value is then used to compute the mask needed to process any residual columns in the current row. The layout of MatrixMulF32_Iavx512() is akin to the Ch05_02's layout of MatrixMulF32_Iavx2(). For nonresidual columns, function MatrixMulF32_Iavx512() uses the C++ SIMD intrinsic functions _mm512_set1_ps(), _mm512_loadu_ps(), _mm512_fmadd_ps(), and _mm512_storeu_ps() to calculate products c[i][j:j+15]. Calculation of residual column products is similar except that this code block uses the C++ SIMD intrinsic functions _mm512_maskz_loadu_ps() and _mm512_mask_storeu_ps() to perform masked load and store operations. Here are the results for source code example Ch08_05:

```
Results for MatrixMulF32
Matrix compare passed
Results saved to file Ch08_05_MatrixMulF32_LITHIUM.txt

Running benchmark function MatrixMulF32_bm - please wait
Benchmark times save to file Ch08_05_MatrixMulF32_bm_LITHIUM.csv
```

Table 8-1 shows some benchmark timing measurements for source code example Ch08_05. These measurements were made using 250 × 250 matrices.

*Table 8-1.* *Matrix Multiplication (Single-Precision) Execution Times (Microseconds)*

| CPU | MatrixMulF32_Cpp() | MatrixMulF32_Iavx512() |
|---|---|---|
| Intel Core i5-11600K | 11432 | 713 |

Listing 8-6 shows the calculating code for source code example Ch08_06, which performs double-precision floating-point matrix multiplication.

*Listing 8-6.* Example Ch08_06

```
//--------------------------------------------------
//              Ch08_06_fcpp.cpp
//--------------------------------------------------

#include <stdexcept>
#include <immintrin.h>
#include "Ch08_06.h"

void MatrixMulF64_Cpp(MatrixF64& c, const MatrixF64& a, const MatrixF64& b)
{
    MatrixF64::Mul(c, a, b);
}
```

```cpp
void MatrixMulF64_Iavx512(MatrixF64& c, const MatrixF64& a, const MatrixF64& b)
{
    if (!CheckArgs(c, a, b))
        throw std::runtime_error("MatrixMulF64_Iavx512() CheckArgs failed");

    const double* aa = a.Data();
    const double* bb = b.Data();
    double* cc = c.Data();

    size_t m = a.GetNumCols();
    size_t c_nrows = c.GetNumRows();
    size_t c_ncols = c.GetNumCols();
    size_t a_ncols = a.GetNumCols();
    size_t b_ncols = b.GetNumCols();

    const size_t num_simd_elements = 8;
    size_t num_residual_cols = c_ncols % num_simd_elements;

    // res_mask = 2 ** num_residual_cols - 1
    __mmask8 res_mask = (__mmask8)((1 << num_residual_cols) - 1);
    for (size_t i = 0; i < c_nrows; i++)
    {
        size_t j = 0;

        while (j + num_simd_elements <= c_ncols)
        {
            __m512d c_vals = _mm512_setzero_pd();

            for (size_t k = 0; k < m; k++)
            {
                __m512d a_vals = _mm512_set1_pd(aa[i * a_ncols + k]);
                __m512d b_vals = _mm512_loadu_pd(&bb[k * b_ncols + j]);

                c_vals = _mm512_fmadd_pd(a_vals, b_vals, c_vals);
            }

            _mm512_storeu_pd(&cc[i * c_ncols + j], c_vals);
            j += num_simd_elements;
        }

        if (num_residual_cols != 0)
        {
            __m512d c_vals = _mm512_setzero_pd();

            for (size_t k = 0; k < m; k++)
            {
                __m512d a_vals = _mm512_set1_pd(aa[i * a_ncols + k]);
                __m512d b_vals = _mm512_maskz_loadu_pd(res_mask, &bb[k * b_ncols + j]);

                c_vals = _mm512_fmadd_pd(a_vals, b_vals, c_vals);
            }
```

```
        _mm512_mask_storeu_pd(&cc[i * c_ncols + j], res_mask, c_vals);
      }
    }
}
```

The primary difference between functions `MatrixMulF32_Iavx512()` and `MatrixMulF64_Iavx512()` is that the latter uses the `__m512d` data type and `_pd` variants of the C++ SIMD calculating functions. It also uses a mask of type `__mmask8` instead of `__mmask16`. The results for Ch08_06 are the same as Ch08_05. Table 8-2 shows the benchmark timing measurements for source code example Ch08_06. These measurements were made using 250 × 250 matrices.

*Table 8-2.* *Matrix Multiplication (Double-Precision) Execution Times (Microseconds)*

| CPU | MatrixMulF64_Cpp() | MatrixMulF64_Iavx512() |
|---|---|---|
| Intel Core i5-11600K | 11972 | 1518 |

## Matrix (4 x 4) Vector Multiplication

Listing 8-7 shows the calculating code for source code example Ch08_07. This example, which is an AVX-512 implementation of source code example Ch05_06, illustrates matrix-vector (4 × 4, 4 × 1) multiplication using single-precision floating-point values. Before examining the source code in Listing 8-7, you may want to review the matrix-vector multiplication equations shown in Figure 5-5.

*Listing 8-7.* Example Ch08_07

```
//------------------------------------------------
//                Ch08_07_fcpp.cpp
//------------------------------------------------

#include <stdexcept>
#include <cstdint>
#include <immintrin.h>
#include "Ch08_07.h"
#include "MatrixF32.h"
#include "AlignedMem.h"

// Permutation indices for matrix columns
alignas(64) const uint32_t c_MatIndCol0[] { 0, 4, 8, 12, 0, 4, 8, 12,
                                            0, 4, 8, 12, 0, 4, 8, 12 };
alignas(64) const uint32_t c_MatIndCol1[] { 1, 5, 9, 13, 1, 5, 9, 13,
                                            1, 5, 9, 13, 1, 5, 9, 13 };
alignas(64) const uint32_t c_MatIndCol2[] { 2, 6, 10, 14, 2, 6, 10, 14,
                                            2, 6, 10, 14, 2, 6, 10, 14 };
alignas(64) const uint32_t c_MatIndCol3[] { 3, 7, 11, 15, 3, 7, 11, 15,
                                            3, 7, 11, 15, 3, 7, 11, 15 };

// Permutation indices for vector components
alignas(64) const uint32_t c_VecIndW[] { 0, 0, 0, 0, 4, 4, 4, 4,
                                         8, 8, 8, 8, 12, 12, 12, 12 };
```

```
alignas(64) const uint32_t c_VecIndX[] { 1, 1, 1, 1, 5, 5, 5, 5,
                                         9, 9, 9, 9, 13, 13, 13, 13 };
alignas(64) const uint32_t c_VecIndY[] { 2, 2, 2, 2, 6, 6, 6, 6,
                                         10, 10, 10, 10, 14, 14, 14, 14 };
alignas(64) const uint32_t c_VecIndZ[] { 3, 3, 3, 3, 7, 7, 7, 7,
                                         11, 11, 11, 11, 15, 15, 15, 15 };

void MatVecMulF32_Cpp(Vec4x1_F32* vec_b, MatrixF32& m, Vec4x1_F32* vec_a,
    size_t num_vec)
{
    if (!CheckArgs(vec_b, m, vec_a, num_vec))
        throw std::runtime_error("MatVecMulF32_Cpp() - CheckArgs failed");

    const float* mm = m.Data();

    // Calculate matrix-vector products
    for (size_t i = 0; i < num_vec; i++)
    {
        vec_b[i].W =  mm[0] * vec_a[i].W + mm[1] * vec_a[i].X;
        vec_b[i].W += mm[2] * vec_a[i].Y + mm[3] * vec_a[i].Z;

        vec_b[i].X =  mm[4] * vec_a[i].W + mm[5] * vec_a[i].X;
        vec_b[i].X += mm[6] * vec_a[i].Y + mm[7] * vec_a[i].Z;

        vec_b[i].Y =  mm[8] * vec_a[i].W + mm[9] * vec_a[i].X;
        vec_b[i].Y += mm[10] * vec_a[i].Y + mm[11] * vec_a[i].Z;

        vec_b[i].Z =  mm[12] * vec_a[i].W + mm[13] * vec_a[i].X;
        vec_b[i].Z += mm[14] * vec_a[i].Y + mm[15] * vec_a[i].Z;
    }
}

void MatVecMulF32a_Iavx512(Vec4x1_F32* vec_b, MatrixF32& m, Vec4x1_F32* vec_a, size_t
num_vec)
{
    if (!CheckArgs(vec_b, m, vec_a, num_vec))
        throw std::runtime_error("MatVecMulF32a_Iavx512() - CheckArgs failed");

    // Load indices for matrix and vector permutations
    __m512i m_ind_col0 = _mm512_load_epi32(c_MatIndCol0);
    __m512i m_ind_col1 = _mm512_load_epi32(c_MatIndCol1);
    __m512i m_ind_col2 = _mm512_load_epi32(c_MatIndCol2);
    __m512i m_ind_col3 = _mm512_load_epi32(c_MatIndCol3);

    __m512i v_ind_w = _mm512_load_epi32(c_VecIndW);
    __m512i v_ind_x = _mm512_load_epi32(c_VecIndX);
    __m512i v_ind_y = _mm512_load_epi32(c_VecIndY);
    __m512i v_ind_z = _mm512_load_epi32(c_VecIndZ);

    // Load source matrix and permute 4 copies of each column
    __m512 m_vals = _mm512_load_ps(m.Data());
    __m512 m_col0_vals = _mm512_permutexvar_ps(m_ind_col0, m_vals);
```

```cpp
    __m512 m_col1_vals = _mm512_permutexvar_ps(m_ind_col1, m_vals);
    __m512 m_col2_vals = _mm512_permutexvar_ps(m_ind_col2, m_vals);
    __m512 m_col3_vals = _mm512_permutexvar_ps(m_ind_col3, m_vals);

    // Calculate matrix-vector products
    size_t i = 0;
    const size_t num_vec_per_iteration = 4;

    for (; num_vec - i >= num_vec_per_iteration; i += num_vec_per_iteration)
    {
        // Load next block of 4 vectors
        __m512 va_vals = _mm512_load_ps(&vec_a[i]);

        // Permute vectors into W, X, Y, Z components
        __m512 va_w_vals = _mm512_permutexvar_ps(v_ind_w, va_vals);
        __m512 va_x_vals = _mm512_permutexvar_ps(v_ind_x, va_vals);
        __m512 va_y_vals = _mm512_permutexvar_ps(v_ind_y, va_vals);
        __m512 va_z_vals = _mm512_permutexvar_ps(v_ind_z, va_vals);

        // Calculate and save matrix-vector products
        __m512 vb_vals = _mm512_mul_ps(m_col0_vals, va_w_vals);
        vb_vals = _mm512_fmadd_ps(m_col1_vals, va_x_vals, vb_vals);
        vb_vals = _mm512_fmadd_ps(m_col2_vals, va_y_vals, vb_vals);
        vb_vals = _mm512_fmadd_ps(m_col3_vals, va_z_vals, vb_vals);

        _mm512_store_ps(&vec_b[i], vb_vals);
    }

    if (i < num_vec)
    {
        __m128 m_col0_vals2 = _mm512_extractf32x4_ps(m_col0_vals, 0);
        __m128 m_col1_vals2 = _mm512_extractf32x4_ps(m_col1_vals, 1);
        __m128 m_col2_vals2 = _mm512_extractf32x4_ps(m_col2_vals, 2);
        __m128 m_col3_vals2 = _mm512_extractf32x4_ps(m_col3_vals, 3);

        for (; i < num_vec; i++)
        {
            __m128 va_w_vals = _mm_broadcast_ss(&vec_a[i].W);
            __m128 va_x_vals = _mm_broadcast_ss(&vec_a[i].X);
            __m128 va_y_vals = _mm_broadcast_ss(&vec_a[i].Y);
            __m128 va_z_vals = _mm_broadcast_ss(&vec_a[i].Z);

            __m128 vb_vals = _mm_mul_ps(m_col0_vals2, va_w_vals);
            vb_vals = _mm_fmadd_ps(m_col1_vals2, va_x_vals, vb_vals);
            vb_vals = _mm_fmadd_ps(m_col2_vals2, va_y_vals, vb_vals);
            vb_vals = _mm_fmadd_ps(m_col3_vals2, va_z_vals, vb_vals);

            _mm_store_ps((float*)&vec_b[i], vb_vals);
        }
    }
}
```

The source code in file Ch08_07_fcpp.cpp begins with a series of arrays that contain permutation indices. The AVX-512 implementation of the matrix-vector multiplication algorithm uses these indices to reorder the elements of the source matrix and vectors. The reason for this reordering is to facilitate the calculation of four matrix-vector products during each iteration of the for-loop. The definition of function MatVecMulF32_Cpp() follows the permutation indices. This function calculates matrix-vector (4 × 4, 4 × 1) products using standard C++ statements.

Following argument validation, function MatVecMulF32a_Iavx512() loads the permutation indices using a series of _mm512_load_epi32() calls. The ensuing call to _mm512_load_ps() loads matrix m into m_vals. This is followed by a series of four calls to _mm512_permutexvar_ps() that permute the elements in m_vals to generate four copies of each column in matrix m as shown in Figure 8-2.

```
Matrix permutation indices
```

| 12 | 8 | 4 | 0 | 12 | 8 | 4 | 0 | 12 | 8 | 4 | 0 | 12 | 8 | 4 | 0 | m_ind_col0 |

| 13 | 9 | 5 | 1 | 13 | 9 | 5 | 1 | 13 | 9 | 5 | 1 | 13 | 9 | 5 | 1 | m_ind_col1 |

| 14 | 10 | 6 | 2 | 14 | 10 | 6 | 2 | 14 | 10 | 6 | 2 | 14 | 10 | 6 | 2 | m_ind_col2 |

| 15 | 11 | 7 | 3 | 15 | 11 | 7 | 3 | 15 | 11 | 7 | 3 | 15 | 11 | 7 | 3 | m_ind_col3 |

```
Matrix          m[3][0]              m[2][0]              m[1][0]              m[0][0]
```

| 43.0 | 42.0 | 41.0 | 40.0 | 33.0 | 32.0 | 31.0 | 30.0 | 23.0 | 22.0 | 21.0 | 20.0 | 13.0 | 12.0 | 11.0 | 10.0 | m_vals |

```
m_col0_vals = _mm512_permutexvar_ps(m_ind_col0, m_vals);
```

| 40.0 | 30.0 | 20.0 | 10.0 | 40.0 | 30.0 | 20.0 | 10.0 | 40.0 | 30.0 | 20.0 | 10.0 | 40.0 | 30.0 | 20.0 | 10.0 | m_col0_vals |

```
m_col1_vals = _mm512_permutexvar_ps(m_ind_col1, m_vals);
```

| 41.0 | 31.0 | 21.0 | 11.0 | 41.0 | 31.0 | 21.0 | 11.0 | 41.0 | 31.0 | 21.0 | 11.0 | 41.0 | 31.0 | 21.0 | 11.0 | m_col1_vals |

```
m_col2_vals = _mm512_permutexvar_ps(m_ind_col2, m_vals);
```

| 42.0 | 32.0 | 22.0 | 12.0 | 42.0 | 32.0 | 22.0 | 12.0 | 42.0 | 32.0 | 22.0 | 12.0 | 42.0 | 32.0 | 22.0 | 12.0 | m_col2_vals |

```
m_col3_vals = _mm512_permutexvar_ps(m_ind_col3, m_vals);
```

| 43.0 | 33.0 | 23.0 | 13.0 | 43.0 | 33.0 | 23.0 | 13.0 | 43.0 | 33.0 | 23.0 | 13.0 | 43.0 | 33.0 | 23.0 | 13.0 | m_col3_vals |

*Figure 8-2.* Permutation of matrix columns using _mm512_permutexvar_ps()

Each iteration of the first for-loop in MatVecMulF32a_Iavx512() begins with a call to _mm512_load_ps() that loads a block of four vectors into va_vals. The next code block employs the C++ SIMD intrinsic function _mm512_permutexvar_ps() to reorder vector components W, X, Y, and Z. Figure 8-3 illustrates this operation in greater detail. Following the permutation, MatVecMulF32a_Iavx512() invokes _mm512_mul_ps() and _mm512_fmadd_ps() to calculate four matrix-vector products. The final call of the for-loop, _mm512_store_ps(), saves the just calculated matrix-vector products. The second for-loop in MatVecMulF32a_Iavx512() calculates any residual matrix-vector products if num_vec is not an integral multiple of num_vec_per_iteration.

Vector permutation indices

| 12 | 12 | 12 | 12 | 8 | 8 | 8 | 8 | 4 | 4 | 4 | 4 | 0 | 0 | 0 | 0 | v_ind_w |
|----|----|----|----|----|----|----|----|----|----|----|----|----|----|----|----|---------|

| 13 | 13 | 13 | 13 | 9 | 9 | 9 | 9 | 5 | 5 | 5 | 5 | 1 | 1 | 1 | 1 | v_ind_x |
|----|----|----|----|----|----|----|----|----|----|----|----|----|----|----|----|---------|

| 14 | 14 | 14 | 14 | 10 | 10 | 10 | 10 | 6 | 6 | 6 | 6 | 2 | 2 | 2 | 2 | v_ind_y |
|----|----|----|----|----|----|----|----|----|----|----|----|----|----|----|----|---------|

| 15 | 15 | 15 | 15 | 11 | 11 | 11 | 11 | 7 | 7 | 7 | 7 | 3 | 3 | 3 | 3 | v_ind_z |
|----|----|----|----|----|----|----|----|----|----|----|----|----|----|----|----|---------|

| a[3].Z | a[3].Y | a[3].X | a[3].W | a[2].Z | a[2].Y | a[2].X | a[2].W | a[1].Z | a[1].Y | a[1].X | a[1].W | a[0].Z | a[0].Y | a[0].X | a[0].W | |
|--------|--------|--------|--------|--------|--------|--------|--------|--------|--------|--------|--------|--------|--------|--------|--------|---------|
| 38.0 | 37.0 | 36.0 | 35.0 | 28.0 | 27.0 | 26.0 | 25.0 | 18.0 | 17.0 | 16.0 | 15.0 | 8.0 | 7.0 | 6.0 | 5.0 | va_vals |

va_w_vals = _mm512_permutexvar_ps(v_ind_w, va_vals);

| 35.0 | 35.0 | 35.0 | 35.0 | 25.0 | 25.0 | 25.0 | 25.0 | 15.0 | 15.0 | 15.0 | 15.0 | 5.0 | 5.0 | 5.0 | 5.0 | va_w_vals |
|------|------|------|------|------|------|------|------|------|------|------|------|-----|-----|-----|-----|-----------|

va_x_vals = _mm512_permutexvar_ps(v_ind_x, va_vals);

| 36.0 | 36.0 | 36.0 | 36.0 | 26.0 | 26.0 | 26.0 | 26.0 | 16.0 | 16.0 | 16.0 | 16.0 | 6.0 | 6.0 | 6.0 | 6.0 | va_x_vals |
|------|------|------|------|------|------|------|------|------|------|------|------|-----|-----|-----|-----|-----------|

va_y_vals = _mm512_permutexvar_ps(v_ind_y, va_vals);

| 37.0 | 37.0 | 37.0 | 37.0 | 27.0 | 27.0 | 27.0 | 27.0 | 17.0 | 17.0 | 17.0 | 17.0 | 7.0 | 7.0 | 7.0 | 7.0 | va_y_vals |
|------|------|------|------|------|------|------|------|------|------|------|------|-----|-----|-----|-----|-----------|

va_z_vals = _mm512_permutexvar_ps(v_ind_z, va_vals);

| 38.0 | 38.0 | 38.0 | 38.0 | 28.0 | 28.0 | 28.0 | 28.0 | 18.0 | 18.0 | 18.0 | 18.0 | 8.0 | 8.0 | 8.0 | 8.0 | va_z_vals |
|------|------|------|------|------|------|------|------|------|------|------|------|-----|-----|-----|-----|-----------|

*Figure 8-3.* *Permutation of vector components using_mm512_permutexvar_ps()*

Not shown in Listing 8-7 is the function MatVecMulF32b_Iavx512(). This function differs slightly from MatVecMulF32a_Iavx512() in that it uses the C++ SIMD intrinsic function _mm512_stream_ps() to save the calculated matrix-vector products. Unlike function _mm512_store_ps(), function _mm512_stream_ps() saves the specified data SIMD value using a nontemporal memory hint. A nontemporal memory hint notifies the processor that the data being saved will not be immediately referenced again. This allows the processor to (optionally) bypass its normal memory cache hierarchy, which minimizes cache pollution and often results in better performance as you will soon see. It is, however, important to note that improper use of _mm512_ stream_ps() can result in slower performance. Appendix B contains a list of AMD and Intel programming reference manuals that you can consult for more information about nontemporal memory hints. Here are the results for source code example Ch08_07:

```
Results for MatrixVecMulF32
Test case #0
vec_b1:     304.0      564.0      824.0     1084.0
vec_b2:     304.0      564.0      824.0     1084.0
vec_b3:     304.0      564.0      824.0     1084.0
Test case #1
vec_b1:     764.0     1424.0     2084.0     2744.0
```

```
vec_b2:      764.0     1424.0     2084.0      2744.0
vec_b3:      764.0     1424.0     2084.0      2744.0
Test case #2
vec_b1:     1224.0     2284.0     3344.0      4404.0
vec_b2:     1224.0     2284.0     3344.0      4404.0
vec_b3:     1224.0     2284.0     3344.0      4404.0
Test case #3
vec_b1:     1684.0     3144.0     4604.0      6064.0
vec_b2:     1684.0     3144.0     4604.0      6064.0
vec_b3:     1684.0     3144.0     4604.0      6064.0
Test case #4
vec_b1:    11932.0    22452.0    32972.0     43492.0
vec_b2:    11932.0    22452.0    32972.0     43492.0
vec_b3:    11932.0    22452.0    32972.0     43492.0
Test case #5
vec_b1:    17125.0    31705.0    46285.0     60865.0
vec_b2:    17125.0    31705.0    46285.0     60865.0
vec_b3:    17125.0    31705.0    46285.0     60865.0
Test case #6
vec_b1:    12723.0    23873.0    35023.0     46173.0
vec_b2:    12723.0    23873.0    35023.0     46173.0
vec_b3:    12723.0    23873.0    35023.0     46173.0
Test case #7
vec_b1:    15121.0    27871.0    40621.0     53371.0
vec_b2:    15121.0    27871.0    40621.0     53371.0
vec_b3:    15121.0    27871.0    40621.0     53371.0
Test case #8
vec_b1:    13789.0    26039.0    38289.0     50539.0
vec_b2:    13789.0    26039.0    38289.0     50539.0
vec_b3:    13789.0    26039.0    38289.0     50539.0
Test case #9
vec_b1:     9663.0    17873.0    26083.0     34293.0
vec_b2:     9663.0    17873.0    26083.0     34293.0
vec_b3:     9663.0    17873.0    26083.0     34293.0

Running benchmark function MatrixVecMulF32_bm - please wait
Benchmark times save to file Ch08_07_MatrixVecMulF32_bm_LITHIUM.csv
```

Table 8-3 shows the benchmark timing measurements for source code example Ch08_07. Note that use of the C++ intrinsic function _mm512_stream_ps() in MatVecMulF32b_Iavx512() yielded an appreciable improvement in performance.

***Table 8-3.*** *Matrix-Vector (4 × 4, 4 × 1) Multiplication Execution Times (Microseconds), 1,000,000 Vectors*

| CPU | MatVecMulF32_Cpp() | MatVecMulF32a_Iavx512() | MatVecMulF32b_Iavx512() |
|---|---|---|---|
| Intel Core i5-11600K | 5069 | 1111 | 708 |

# Convolutions

In Chapter 6, you learned how to compute 1D and 2D discrete convolutions using C++ intrinsic functions and AVX2. In this section, you will examine two source code examples that illustrate convolutions using AVX-512. Like Chapter 6, the source code examples discussed in this section are somewhat more specialized than those covered in the previous sections. If your SIMD programming interests reside elsewhere, you can either skim this section or skip ahead to the next chapter. If you decide to continue, you may want to review the sections in Chapter 6 that explained the mathematics of a discrete convolution before examining the source code.

## 1D Convolutions

The next source code example, Ch08_08, implements a 1D discrete convolution using C++ SIMD intrinsic functions and AVX-512. Listing 8-8 shows the calculating code for this source code example, which is a modified version of source code example Ch06_01.

***Listing 8-8.*** Example Ch08_08

```
//--------------------------------------------------
//                  Ch08_08_fcpp.cpp
//--------------------------------------------------

#include <stdexcept>
#include <immintrin.h>
#include "Ch08_08.h"
#include "MiscTypes.h"

void Convolve1D_F32_Cpp(std::vector<float>& y, const std::vector<float>& x, const
std::vector<float>& kernel)
{
    if (!CheckArgs(y, x, kernel))
        throw std::runtime_error("Convolve1D_F32_Cpp() - CheckArgs failed");

    indx_t num_pts = (indx_t)y.size();
    indx_t ks2 = kernel.size() / 2;

    for (indx_t i = ks2; i < num_pts - ks2; i++)
    {
        float y_val = 0;

        for (indx_t k = -ks2; k <= ks2; k++)
            y_val += x[i - k] * kernel[k + ks2];

        y[i] = y_val;
    }
}
```

```cpp
void Convolve1D_F32_Iavx512(std::vector<float>& y, const std::vector<float>& x, const
std::vector<float>& kernel)
{
    if (!CheckArgs(y, x, kernel))
        throw std::runtime_error("Convolve1D_F32_Iavx512() - CheckArgs failed");

    indx_t ks2 = (indx_t)kernel.size() / 2;
    indx_t num_pts = (indx_t)y.size();
    const indx_t num_simd_elements = 16;
    const indx_t num_simd_elements2 = 8;
    const indx_t num_simd_elements3 = 4;

    indx_t i = ks2;

    while (i < num_pts - ks2)
    {
        if ((i + num_simd_elements) <= num_pts - ks2)
        {
            __m512 y_vals = _mm512_setzero_ps();

            for (indx_t k = -ks2; k <= ks2; k++)
            {
                __m512 x_vals = _mm512_loadu_ps(&x[i - k]);
                __m512 kernel_vals = _mm512_set1_ps(kernel[k + ks2]);

                y_vals = _mm512_fmadd_ps(x_vals, kernel_vals, y_vals);
            }

            _mm512_storeu_ps(&y[i], y_vals);
            i += num_simd_elements;
        }
        else if ((i + num_simd_elements2) <= num_pts - ks2)
        {
            __m256 y_vals = _mm256_setzero_ps();

            for (indx_t k = -ks2; k <= ks2; k++)
            {
                __m256 x_vals = _mm256_loadu_ps(&x[i - k]);
                __m256 kernel_vals = _mm256_set1_ps(kernel[k + ks2]);

                y_vals = _mm256_fmadd_ps(x_vals, kernel_vals, y_vals);
            }

            _mm256_storeu_ps(&y[i], y_vals);
            i += num_simd_elements2;
        }
        else if ((i + num_simd_elements3) <= num_pts - ks2)
        {
            __m128 y_vals = _mm_setzero_ps();
```

```
                for (indx_t k = -ks2; k <= ks2; k++)
                {
                    __m128 x_vals = _mm_loadu_ps(&x[i - k]);
                    __m128 kernel_vals = _mm_set1_ps(kernel[k + ks2]);

                    y_vals = _mm_fmadd_ps(x_vals, kernel_vals, y_vals);
                }

                _mm_storeu_ps(&y[i], y_vals);
                i += num_simd_elements3;
            }
            else
            {
                __m128 y_val = _mm_setzero_ps();

                for (indx_t k = -ks2; k <= ks2; k++)
                {
                    __m128 x_val = _mm_load_ss(&x[i - k]);
                    __m128 k_val = _mm_load_ss(&kernel[k + ks2]);
                    y_val = _mm_fmadd_ss(x_val, k_val, y_val);
                }

                _mm_store_ss(&y[i], y_val);
                i += 1;
            }
        }
    }
}

void Convolve1DKs5_F32_Iavx512(std::vector<float>& y, const std::vector<float>& x, const
std::vector<float>& kernel)
{
    if (!CheckArgs(y, x, kernel))
        throw std::runtime_error("Convolve1DKs5_F32_Iavx2() - CheckArgs failed");
    if (kernel.size() != 5)
        throw std::runtime_error("Convolve1DKs5_F32_Iavx2() - invalid kernel size");

    indx_t ks2 = (indx_t)kernel.size() / 2;
    indx_t num_pts = (indx_t)y.size();
    const indx_t num_simd_elements = 16;  // number of F32 elements (__m512)
    const indx_t num_simd_elements2 = 8;  // number of F32 elements (__m256)
    const indx_t num_simd_elements3 = 4;  // number of F32 elements (__m128)

    __m512 kernel512_0 = _mm512_set1_ps(kernel[0]);
    __m512 kernel512_1 = _mm512_set1_ps(kernel[1]);
    __m512 kernel512_2 = _mm512_set1_ps(kernel[2]);
    __m512 kernel512_3 = _mm512_set1_ps(kernel[3]);
    __m512 kernel512_4 = _mm512_set1_ps(kernel[4]);

    __m256 kernel256_0 = _mm256_set1_ps(kernel[0]);
    __m256 kernel256_1 = _mm256_set1_ps(kernel[1]);
    __m256 kernel256_2 = _mm256_set1_ps(kernel[2]);
```

```
    __m256 kernel256_3 = _mm256_set1_ps(kernel[3]);
    __m256 kernel256_4 = _mm256_set1_ps(kernel[4]);

    __m128 kernel128_0 = _mm_set1_ps(kernel[0]);
    __m128 kernel128_1 = _mm_set1_ps(kernel[1]);
    __m128 kernel128_2 = _mm_set1_ps(kernel[2]);
    __m128 kernel128_3 = _mm_set1_ps(kernel[3]);
    __m128 kernel128_4 = _mm_set1_ps(kernel[4]);

    indx_t i = ks2;

    while (i < num_pts - ks2)
    {
        indx_t j = i + ks2;

        if ((i + num_simd_elements) <= num_pts - ks2)
        {
            __m512 x_vals = _mm512_loadu_ps(&x[j]);
            __m512 y_vals = _mm512_mul_ps(x_vals, kernel512_0);

            x_vals = _mm512_loadu_ps(&x[j - 1]);
            y_vals = _mm512_fmadd_ps(x_vals, kernel512_1, y_vals);
            x_vals = _mm512_loadu_ps(&x[j - 2]);
            y_vals = _mm512_fmadd_ps(x_vals, kernel512_2, y_vals);
            x_vals = _mm512_loadu_ps(&x[j - 3]);
            y_vals = _mm512_fmadd_ps(x_vals, kernel512_3, y_vals);
            x_vals = _mm512_loadu_ps(&x[j - 4]);
            y_vals = _mm512_fmadd_ps(x_vals, kernel512_4, y_vals);

            _mm512_storeu_ps(&y[i], y_vals);
            i += num_simd_elements;
        }
        else if ((i + num_simd_elements2) <= num_pts - ks2)
        {
            __m256 x_vals = _mm256_loadu_ps(&x[j]);
            __m256 y_vals = _mm256_mul_ps(x_vals, kernel256_0);

            x_vals = _mm256_loadu_ps(&x[j - 1]);
            y_vals = _mm256_fmadd_ps(x_vals, kernel256_1, y_vals);
            x_vals = _mm256_loadu_ps(&x[j - 2]);
            y_vals = _mm256_fmadd_ps(x_vals, kernel256_2, y_vals);
            x_vals = _mm256_loadu_ps(&x[j - 3]);
            y_vals = _mm256_fmadd_ps(x_vals, kernel256_3, y_vals);
            x_vals = _mm256_loadu_ps(&x[j - 4]);
            y_vals = _mm256_fmadd_ps(x_vals, kernel256_4, y_vals);

            _mm256_storeu_ps(&y[i], y_vals);
            i += num_simd_elements2;
        }
```

```
    else if ((i + num_simd_elements3) <= num_pts - ks2)
    {
        __m128 x_vals = _mm_loadu_ps(&x[j]);
        __m128 y_vals = _mm_mul_ps(x_vals, kernel128_0);

        x_vals = _mm_loadu_ps(&x[j - 1]);
        y_vals = _mm_fmadd_ps(x_vals, kernel128_1, y_vals);
        x_vals = _mm_loadu_ps(&x[j - 2]);
        y_vals = _mm_fmadd_ps(x_vals, kernel128_2, y_vals);
        x_vals = _mm_loadu_ps(&x[j - 3]);
        y_vals = _mm_fmadd_ps(x_vals, kernel128_3, y_vals);
        x_vals = _mm_loadu_ps(&x[j - 4]);
        y_vals = _mm_fmadd_ps(x_vals, kernel128_4, y_vals);

        _mm_storeu_ps(&y[i], y_vals);
        i += num_simd_elements3;
    }
    else
    {
        __m128 x_val = _mm_load_ss(&x[j]);
        __m128 y_val = _mm_mul_ss(x_val, kernel128_0);

        x_val = _mm_load_ss(&x[j - 1]);
        y_val = _mm_fmadd_ss(x_val, kernel128_1, y_val);
        x_val = _mm_load_ss(&x[j - 2]);
        y_val = _mm_fmadd_ss(x_val, kernel128_2, y_val);
        x_val = _mm_load_ss(&x[j - 3]);
        y_val = _mm_fmadd_ss(x_val, kernel128_3, y_val);
        x_val = _mm_load_ss(&x[j - 4]);
        y_val = _mm_fmadd_ss(x_val, kernel128_4, y_val);

        _mm_store_ss(&y[i], y_val);
        i += 1;
    }
  }
}
```

The first function in Listing 8-8, Convolve1D_F32_Cpp(), implements a 1D discrete convolution using standard C++ statements. This function is identical to the one you saw in source code example Ch06_01 and is included again here for benchmarking purposes. The next function in Listing 8-8, named Convolve1D_F32_Iavx512(), uses AVX-512 C++ SIMD intrinsic functions to implement a 1D discrete convolution. This function is similar to the function Convolve1D_F32_Iavx2() that was presented in source example Ch06_01. The primary difference is that Convolve1D_F32_Iavx512() includes an extra code block near the top of the while-loop that processes signal elements y[i:i+15] using __m512 data types and the following C++ SIMD intrinsic functions: _mm512_loadu_ps(), _mm512_set1_ps(), _mm512_fmadd_ps(), and _mm512_storeu_ps(). The other code blocks in the while-loop process signal elements y[i:i+7], y[i:i+3], or y[i] using C++ SIMD intrinsic functions and data types just like function Convolve1D_F32_Iavx2() did in example Ch06_01.

Following Convolve1D_F32_Iavx512() in Listing 8-8 is the function Convolve1DKs5_F32_Iavx512(). This function implements a 1D discrete convolution using AVX-512 and is optimized for a five-element convolution kernel. Recall from the discussions in Chapter 6 that many real-world signal processing applications frequently employ size-optimized convolution functions since they are often faster than their variable-width counterparts. Note that the principal modification between the code in `Convolve1DKs5_F32_Iavx512()` and the Ch06_01 function `Convolve1DKs5_F32_Iavx2()` is that the former includes a code block near the top of the while-loop that processes signal elements y[i:i+15] using _m512 data types and AVX-512 C++ SIMD intrinsic functions.

Source code example Ch08_08 exemplifies that it is often a straightforward programming exercise to port an AVX2 calculating function to one that can exploit the additional computational resources of AVX-512. Here are the results for source code example Ch08_08:

```
Executing Convolve1D_F32()
Results saved to file Ch08_08_Convolve1D_F32_Results_LITHIUM.csv

Running benchmark function Convolve1D_F32_bm - please wait
Benchmark times saved to file Ch08_08_Convolve1D_F32_bm_LITHIUM.csv
```

Table 8-4. shows some benchmark timing measurements for source code example Ch08_08. These measurements were made using a 1,000,000-element input signal array and a five-element convolution kernel.

**Table 8-4.** *1D Discrete Convolution (Single-Precision) Execution Times (Microseconds)*

| CPU | Convolve1D_F32_Cpp() | Convolve1D_F32_Iavx512() | Convolve1DKs5_F32_Iavx512 |
|---|---|---|---|
| Intel Core i5-11600K 2268 | | 242 | 200 |

## 2D Convolutions

The final source code example of this chapter, Ch08_09, demonstrates how to employ AVX-512 C++ SIMD intrinsic functions to calculate a 2D discrete convolution. This example is a modified version of source code example Ch06_04, which carried out a 2D discrete convolution using two 1D discrete convolutions. Listing 8-9 shows the calculating code for example Ch08_09. Before examining the code in Listing 8-9, you may want to review the definition of structure CD_1Dx2 that is shown in Listing 6-4 since the same structure is used in example Ch08_09.

**Listing 8-9.** Example Ch08_09

```
//------------------------------------------------
//              Ch08_09_fcpp.cpp
//------------------------------------------------

#include <stdexcept>
#include <immintrin.h>
#include "Ch08_09.h"
#include "MiscTypes.h"

void Convolve1Dx2_F32_Cpp(CD_1Dx2& cd)
{
    if (!CheckArgs1Dx2(cd))
        throw std::runtime_error("Convolve1Dx2_F32_Cpp() - CheckArgs failed");
```

```
        indx_t ks = (indx_t)cd.m_KernelSize;
        indx_t ks2 = ks / 2;
        indx_t im_h = cd.m_ImH;
        indx_t im_w = cd.m_ImW;
        const std::vector<float>& im_src = cd.m_ImSrc;
        std::vector<float>& im_des = cd.m_ImDes;
        std::vector<float>& im_tmp = cd.m_ImTmp;
        const std::vector<float>& im_ker_x = cd.m_Kernel1Dx;
        const std::vector<float>& im_ker_y = cd.m_Kernel1Dy;

        // Perform 1D convolution (X)
        for (indx_t i = ks2; i < im_h - ks2; i++)
        {
            for (indx_t j = ks2; j < im_w - ks2; j++)
            {
                float im_tmp_val = 0;

                for (indx_t k = -ks2; k <= ks2; k++)
                    im_tmp_val += im_src[i * im_w + j - k] * im_ker_x[k + ks2];

                im_tmp[i * im_w + j] = im_tmp_val;
            }
        }

        // Perform 1D convolution (Y)
        for (indx_t j = ks2; j < im_w - ks2; j++)
        {
            for (indx_t i = ks2; i < im_h - ks2; i++)
            {
                float im_des_val = 0;

                for (indx_t k = -ks2; k <= ks2; k++)
                    im_des_val += im_tmp[(i - k) * im_w + j] * im_ker_y[k + ks2];

                im_des[i * im_w + j] = im_des_val;
            }
        }
    }

void Convolve1Dx2_F32_Iavx512(CD_1Dx2& cd)
{
    if (!CheckArgs1Dx2(cd))
        throw std::runtime_error("Convolve1Dx2_F32_Iavx512() - CheckArgs failed");

    indx_t ks = (indx_t)cd.m_KernelSize;
    indx_t ks2 = ks / 2;
    indx_t im_h = cd.m_ImH;
    indx_t im_w = cd.m_ImW;
```

```cpp
const std::vector<float>& im_src = cd.m_ImSrc;
std::vector<float>& im_des = cd.m_ImDes;
std::vector<float>& im_tmp = cd.m_ImTmp;
const std::vector<float>& im_ker_x = cd.m_Kernel1Dx;
const std::vector<float>& im_ker_y = cd.m_Kernel1Dy;

const indx_t num_simd_elements = 16;
const indx_t num_simd_elements2 = 8;
const indx_t num_simd_elements3 = 4;

// Perform 1D convolution (X)
for (indx_t i = ks2; i < im_h - ks2; i++)
{
    indx_t j = ks2;

    while (j < im_w - ks2)
    {
        if (j + num_simd_elements <= im_w - ks2)
        {
            __m512 im_tmp_vals = _mm512_setzero_ps();

            for (indx_t k = -ks2; k <= ks2; k++)
            {
                __m512 im_src_vals = _mm512_loadu_ps(&im_src[i * im_w + j - k]);
                __m512 im_ker_vals = _mm512_set1_ps(im_ker_x[k + ks2]);

                im_tmp_vals = _mm512_fmadd_ps(im_src_vals, im_ker_vals,
                                im_tmp_vals);
            }

            _mm512_storeu_ps(&im_tmp[i * im_w + j], im_tmp_vals);
            j += num_simd_elements;
        }
        else if (j + num_simd_elements2 <= im_w - ks2)
        {
            __m256 im_tmp_vals = _mm256_setzero_ps();

            for (indx_t k = -ks2; k <= ks2; k++)
            {
                __m256 im_src_vals = _mm256_loadu_ps(&im_src[i * im_w + j - k]);
                __m256 im_ker_vals = _mm256_set1_ps(im_ker_x[k + ks2]);

                im_tmp_vals = _mm256_fmadd_ps(im_src_vals, im_ker_vals,
                                im_tmp_vals);
            }

            _mm256_storeu_ps(&im_tmp[i * im_w + j], im_tmp_vals);
            j += num_simd_elements2;
        }
```

```
            else if (j + num_simd_elements3 <= im_w - ks2)
            {
                __m128 im_tmp_vals = _mm_setzero_ps();

                for (indx_t k = -ks2; k <= ks2; k++)
                {
                    __m128 im_src_vals = _mm_loadu_ps(&im_src[i * im_w + j - k]);
                    __m128 im_ker_vals = _mm_set1_ps(im_ker_x[k + ks2]);

                    im_tmp_vals = _mm_fmadd_ps(im_src_vals, im_ker_vals,
                                   im_tmp_vals);
                }

                _mm_storeu_ps(&im_tmp[i * im_w + j], im_tmp_vals);
                j += num_simd_elements3;
            }
            else
            {
                __m128 im_tmp_vals = _mm_setzero_ps();

                for (indx_t k = -ks2; k <= ks2; k++)
                {
                    __m128 im_src_vals = _mm_load_ss(&im_src[i * im_w + j - k]);
                    __m128 im_ker_vals = _mm_load_ss(&im_ker_x[k + ks2]);

                    im_tmp_vals = _mm_fmadd_ss(im_src_vals, im_ker_vals,      .
                                   im_tmp_vals);
                }

                _mm_store_ss(&im_tmp[i * im_w + j], im_tmp_vals);
                j += 1;
            }
        }
    }
}

// Perform 1D convolution (Y)
indx_t j = ks2;

while (j < im_w - ks2)
{
    if (j + num_simd_elements <= im_w - ks2)
    {
        for (indx_t i = ks2; i < im_h - ks2; i++)
        {
            __m512 im_des_vals = _mm512_setzero_ps();

            for (indx_t k = -ks2; k <= ks2; k++)
            {
                __m512 im_tmp_vals = _mm512_loadu_ps(&im_tmp[(i - k) * im_w + j]);
                __m512 im_ker_vals = _mm512_set1_ps(im_ker_y[k + ks2]);
```

```
                    im_des_vals = _mm512_fmadd_ps(im_tmp_vals, im_ker_vals,
                                  im_des_vals);
            }

            _mm512_storeu_ps(&im_des[i * im_w + j], im_des_vals);
        }

        j += num_simd_elements;
    }
    else if (j + num_simd_elements2 <= im_w - ks2)
    {
        for (indx_t i = ks2; i < im_h - ks2; i++)
        {
            __m256 im_des_vals = _mm256_setzero_ps();

            for (indx_t k = -ks2; k <= ks2; k++)
            {
                __m256 im_tmp_vals = _mm256_loadu_ps(&im_tmp[(i - k) * im_w + j]);
                __m256 im_ker_vals = _mm256_set1_ps(im_ker_y[k + ks2]);

                im_des_vals = _mm256_fmadd_ps(im_tmp_vals, im_ker_vals,
                                  im_des_vals);
            }

            _mm256_storeu_ps(&im_des[i * im_w + j], im_des_vals);
        }

        j += num_simd_elements2;
    }
    else if (j + num_simd_elements3 <= im_w - ks2)
    {
        for (indx_t i = ks2; i < im_h - ks2; i++)
        {
            __m128 im_des_vals = _mm_setzero_ps();

            for (indx_t k = -ks2; k <= ks2; k++)
            {
                __m128 im_tmp_vals = _mm_loadu_ps(&im_tmp[(i - k) * im_w + j]);
                __m128 im_ker_vals = _mm_set1_ps(im_ker_y[k + ks2]);

                im_des_vals = _mm_fmadd_ps(im_tmp_vals, im_ker_vals,
                                  im_des_vals);
            }

            _mm_storeu_ps(&im_des[i * im_w + j], im_des_vals);
        }

        j += num_simd_elements3;
    }
```

```
    else
    {
        for (indx_t i = ks2; i < im_h - ks2; i++)
        {
            __m128 im_des_vals = _mm_setzero_ps();

            for (indx_t k = -ks2; k <= ks2; k++)
            {
                __m128 im_tmp_vals = _mm_load_ss(&im_tmp[(i - k) * im_w + j]);
                __m128 im_ker_vals = _mm_load_ss(&im_ker_y[k + ks2]);

                im_des_vals = _mm_fmadd_ss(im_tmp_vals, im_ker_vals,
                                    im_des_vals);
            }

            _mm_store_ss(&im_des[i * im_w + j], im_des_vals);
        }

        j += 1;
    }
}
}
```

The source code for file Ch08_09_fcpp.cpp that is shown in Listing 8-9 is somewhat lengthy but (hopefully) relatively straightforward to comprehend. It begins with the function Convolve1Dx2_F32_Cpp(), which implements a 2D discrete convolution using standard C++ statements. This function is identical to the one you studied in source code example Ch06_04 and is included again in this example for benchmarking purposes.

Also shown in Listing 8-9 is the SIMD calculating function Convolve1Dx2_F32_Iavx512(). This function, which is a modified version of function Convolve1Dx2_F32_Iavx2() (see Listing 6-4), performs a 2D discrete convolution using AVX-512 C++ SIMD intrinsic functions. In function Convolve1Dx2_F32_Iavx512(), note the inclusion of an extra if block in the x-axis section that processes image pixels using __m512 data types and the following C++ SIMD intrinsic functions: _mm512_loadu_ps(), _mm512_set1_ps(), _mm512_fmadd_ps(), and _mm512_storeu_ps(). A similar if block was also added to the y-axis section of Convolve1Dx2_F32_Iavx512().

Source code example Ch08_09 exemplifies again that with a little forethought, it is often relatively easy to transform a calculating function that employs AVX2 to one that exploits AVX-512. When developing SIMD calculating functions that perform calculations using AVX or AVX2, you should always keep in mind that you may want to create an AVX-512 variant sometime in the future. Here are the results for source code example Ch08_09:

```
Performing convolutions
Saving destination image files
rc:        true
num_diff: 0

Running benchmark function Convolve1Dx2_F32_bm - please wait
...............................................
Benchmark times saved to file Ch08_09_Convolve1Dx2_F32_bm_LITHIUM.csv
```

Table 8-5 shows some benchmark timing measurements for source code example Ch08_09. These measurements were made using test image ImageE.png and a 9 × 9 convolution kernel that performs low-pass filtering.

*Table 8-5.* *2D Discrete Convolution (Single-Precision) Execution Times (Microseconds)*

| CPU | Convolve1Dx2_F32_Cpp() | Convolve1Dx2_F32_Iavx512() |
|---|---|---|
| Intel Core i5-11600K | 14373 | 2065 |

# Summary

Table 8-6 summarizes the C++ SIMD intrinsic functions that were introduced in this chapter. This table also includes commonly used size variants. AVX-512 C++ SIMD intrinsic functions that perform merge (_mask_) masking and zero (_maskz_) masking are also available for most of the functions listed in Table 8-6, but these are not shown. Before proceeding to the next chapter, you should understand the SIMD arithmetic calculation or data manipulation operation that is performed by each function shown in Table 8-6.

*Table 8-6.* *C++ SIMD Intrinsic Function Summary for Chapter 8*

| C++ SIMD Function Name | Description |
|---|---|
| _mm256_insertf64x2 | Insert double-precision elements |
| _mm512_abs_pd, _ps | Packed floating-point absolute value |
| _mm512_add_pd, _ps | Packed floating-point addition |
| _mm512_cmp_pd_mask, _ps_mask | Packed floating-point compare |
| _mm512_div_pd, _ps | Packed floating-point division |
| _mm512_extractf32x4_ps, f32x8_ps | Extract floating-point elements |
| _mm512_fmadd_pd, ps | Packed floating-point fused-multiple-add |
| _mm512_insertf64x2, f64x4 | Insert double-precision elements |
| _mm512_load_epi8, _epi16, _epi32, _epi64 | Load packed integer elements |
| _mm512_load_pd, _ps | Load (aligned) floating-point elements |
| _mm512_loadu_pd, _ps | Load (unaligned) floating-point elements |
| _mm512_max_pd, _ps | Packed floating-point maximum |
| _mm512_min_pd, _ps | Packed floating-point minimum |
| _mm512_permutexvar_pd, _ps | Permute floating-point elements |
| _mm512_reduce_add_pd, _ps | Reduce (sum) floating-point elements |
| _mm512_set1_pd, _ps | Broadcast floating-point value to all elements |
| _mm512_setzero_pd, _ps | Set floating-point elements to zero |

(*continued*)

***Table 8-6*** (*continued*)

| C++ SIMD Function Name | Description |
| --- | --- |
| _mm512_sqrt_pd, _ps | Packed floating-point square root |
| _mm512_store_pd, _ps | Store (aligned) floating-point elements |
| _mm512_storeu_pd, _ps | Store (unaligned) floating-point elements |
| _mm512_stream_pd, _ps | Store (nontemporal) floating-point elements |
| _mm512_sub_pd, _ps | Packed floating-point subtraction |
| _mm_stream_pd, _ps | Store (nontemporal) floating-point elements |

# CHAPTER 9

■ ■ ■

# Supplemental C++ SIMD Programming

In the previous eight chapters, you learned critical programming details about AVX, AVX2, and AVX-512. You also discovered how to create SIMD calculating functions that exploited the computational resources of these x86 instruction set extensions. This chapter focuses on supplemental x86 C++ SIMD programming topics. It begins with a source code example that demonstrates utilization of the cpuid instruction and how to exercise this instruction to detect x86 instruction set extensions such as AVX, AVX2, and AVX-512. This is followed by a section that explains how to use SIMD versions of common C++ math library routines.

## Using CPUID

It has been mentioned several times already in this book, but it bears repeating one more time: a program should *never* assume that a specific instruction set extension such as FMA, AVX, AVX2, or AVX-512 is available on its host processor. To ensure software compatibility with both current and future x86 processors, a program should *always* use the x86 cpuid instruction (or an equivalent C++ intrinsic function) to verify that any required x86 instruction set extensions are available. An application program will crash or be terminated by the host operating system if it attempts to execute a nonsupported x86-AVX instruction. Besides x86 instruction set extensions, the cpuid instruction can also be directed to obtain supplemental feature information about a processor. The focus of this section is the use of cpuid to detect the presence of x86 instruction set extensions and a few basic processor features. If you are interested in learning how to use cpuid to detect other processor features, you should consult the AMD and Intel programming reference manuals listed in Appendix B.

   Source code example Ch09_01 demonstrates how to use the cpuid instruction to detect x86 processor instruction set extensions. It also illustrates using cpuid to obtain useful processor feature information including vendor name, vendor brand, and cache sizes. Listing 9-1 includes the principal C++ data structures and software functions for source code for example Ch09_01. The complete source code for this example is included as part of the software download package.

*Listing 9-1.* Example Ch09_01

```
//------------------------------------------------
//              Cpuid__.h
//------------------------------------------------

#pragma once
#include <cstdint>
```

© Daniel Kusswurm 2022
D. Kusswurm, *Modern Parallel Programming with C++ and Assembly Language*,
https://doi.org/10.1007/978-1-4842-7918-2_9

```cpp
struct CpuidRegs
{
    uint32_t EAX;
    uint32_t EBX;
    uint32_t ECX;
    uint32_t EDX;
};

// Cpuid__.cpp
extern uint32_t Cpuid__(uint32_t r_eax, uint32_t r_ecx, CpuidRegs* r_out);
extern void Xgetbv__(uint32_t r_ecx, uint32_t* r_eax, uint32_t* r_edx);

//------------------------------------------------
//                  Cpuid__.cpp
//------------------------------------------------

#include <string>
#include <cassert>
#include <immintrin.h>
#include "Cpuid__.h"

#if defined(_MSC_VER)
#include <intrin.h>
#elif defined (__GNUG__)
#include <cpuid.h>
#include <x86intrin.h>
#else
#error Unknown target in Cpuid__.cpp
#endif

uint32_t Cpuid__(uint32_t r_eax, uint32_t r_ecx, CpuidRegs* r_out)
{
#if defined(_MSC_VER)
    int cpuid_info[4];

    cpuid_info[0] = cpuid_info[1] = cpuid_info[2] = cpuid_info[3] = 0;

    __cpuidex(cpuid_info, r_eax, r_ecx);
#endif

#if defined (__GNUG__)
    uint32_t cpuid_info[4];

    cpuid_info[0] = cpuid_info[1] = cpuid_info[2] = cpuid_info[3] = 0;

    __get_cpuid_count(r_eax, r_ecx, &cpuid_info[0], &cpuid_info[1],
                                    &cpuid_info[2], &cpuid_info[3]);
#endif
```

```
        r_out->EAX = cpuid_info[0];
        r_out->EBX = cpuid_info[1];
        r_out->ECX = cpuid_info[2];
        r_out->EDX = cpuid_info[3];

        uint32_t rc = cpuid_info[0] | cpuid_info[1] | cpuid_info[2] | cpuid_info[3];
        return rc;
}

void Xgetbv_(uint32_t r_ecx, uint32_t* r_eax, uint32_t* r_edx)
{
        uint64_t x = _xgetbv(r_ecx);

        *r_eax = (uint32_t)(x & 0xFFFFFFFF);
        *r_edx = (uint32_t)((x & 0xFFFFFFFF00000000) >> 32);
}

//------------------------------------------------
//                CpuidInfo.h
//------------------------------------------------

#pragma once
#include <cstdint>
#include <vector>
#include <string>
#include "Cpuid__.h"

class CpuidInfo
{
public:
    class CacheInfo
    {
    public:
        enum class Type
        {
            Unknown, Data, Instruction, Unified
        };

    private:
        uint32_t m_Level = 0;
        Type m_Type = Type::Unknown;
        uint32_t m_Size = 0;

    public:
        uint32_t GetLevel(void) const           { return m_Level; }
        uint32_t GetSize(void) const            { return m_Size; }
        Type GetType(void) const                { return m_Type; }

        // These are defined in CacheInfo.cpp
        CacheInfo(uint32_t level, uint32_t type, uint32_t size);
        std::string GetTypeString(void) const;
    };
```

```
private:
    uint32_t m_MaxEax;                                  // Max EAX for basic CPUID
    uint32_t m_MaxEaxExt;                               // Max EAX for extended CPUID
    uint64_t m_FeatureFlags;                            // Processor feature flags
    std::vector<CpuidInfo::CacheInfo> m_CacheInfo;      // Processor cache information
    char m_VendorId[13];                               // Processor vendor ID string
    char m_ProcessorBrand[49];                         // Processor brand string
    bool m_OsXsave;                                     // XSAVE is enabled for app use
    bool m_OsAvxState;                                  // AVX state is enabled by OS
    bool m_OsAvx512State;                               // AVX-512 state is enabled by OS

    void Init(void);
    void InitProcessorBrand(void);
    void LoadInfo0(void);
    void LoadInfo1(void);
    void LoadInfo2(void);
    void LoadInfo3(void);
    void LoadInfo4(void);
    void LoadInfo5(void);

public:
    enum class FF : uint64_t
    {
        FXSR            = (uint64_t)1 << 0,
        MMX             = (uint64_t)1 << 1,
        MOVBE           = (uint64_t)1 << 2,
        SSE             = (uint64_t)1 << 3,
        SSE2            = (uint64_t)1 << 4,
        SSE3            = (uint64_t)1 << 5,
        SSSE3           = (uint64_t)1 << 6,
        SSE4_1          = (uint64_t)1 << 7,
        SSE4_2          = (uint64_t)1 << 8,
        PCLMULQDQ       = (uint64_t)1 << 9,
        POPCNT          = (uint64_t)1 << 10,
        PREFETCHW       = (uint64_t)1 << 11,
        PREFETCHWT1     = (uint64_t)1 << 12,
        RDRAND          = (uint64_t)1 << 13,
        RDSEED          = (uint64_t)1 << 14,
        ERMSB           = (uint64_t)1 << 15,
        AVX             = (uint64_t)1 << 16,
        AVX2            = (uint64_t)1 << 17,
        F16C            = (uint64_t)1 << 18,
        FMA             = (uint64_t)1 << 19,
        BMI1            = (uint64_t)1 << 20,
        BMI2            = (uint64_t)1 << 21,
        LZCNT           = (uint64_t)1 << 22,
        ADX             = (uint64_t)1 << 23,
        AVX512F         = (uint64_t)1 << 24,
        AVX512ER        = (uint64_t)1 << 25,
        AVX512PF        = (uint64_t)1 << 26,
        AVX512DQ        = (uint64_t)1 << 27,
```

306

```cpp
        AVX512CD            = (uint64_t)1 << 28,
        AVX512BW            = (uint64_t)1 << 29,
        AVX512VL            = (uint64_t)1 << 30,
        AVX512_IFMA         = (uint64_t)1 << 31,
        AVX512_VBMI         = (uint64_t)1 << 32,
        AVX512_4FMAPS       = (uint64_t)1 << 33,
        AVX512_4VNNIW       = (uint64_t)1 << 34,
        AVX512_VPOPCNTDQ    = (uint64_t)1 << 35,
        AVX512_VNNI         = (uint64_t)1 << 36,
        AVX512_VBMI2        = (uint64_t)1 << 37,
        AVX512_BITALG       = (uint64_t)1 << 38,
        AVX512_BF16         = (uint64_t)1 << 39,
        AVX512_VP2INTERSECT = (uint64_t)1 << 40,
        CLWB                = (uint64_t)1 << 41,
        GFNI                = (uint64_t)1 << 42,
        AESNI               = (uint64_t)1 << 43,
        VAES                = (uint64_t)1 << 44,
        VPCLMULQDQ          = (uint64_t)1 << 45,
        AVX_VNNI            = (uint64_t)1 << 46,
        AVX512_FP16         = (uint64_t)1 << 47,
    };

    CpuidInfo(void) { Init(); };
    ~CpuidInfo() {};

    const std::vector<CpuidInfo::CacheInfo>& GetCacheInfo(void) const
    {
        return m_CacheInfo;
    }

    bool GetFF(FF flag) const
    {
        return (m_FeatureFlags & (uint64_t)flag) != 0;
    }

    std::string GetProcessorBrand(void) const   { return std::string(m_ProcessorBrand); }
    std::string GetProcessorVendor(void) const  { return std::string(m_VendorId); }

    void LoadInfo(void);
};

//-------------------------------------------------
//                Ch09_01.cpp
//-------------------------------------------------

#include <iostream>
#include <string>
#include "CpuidInfo.h"

static void DisplayProcessorInfo(const CpuidInfo& ci);
static void DisplayCacheInfo(const CpuidInfo& ci);
```

```cpp
static void DisplayFeatureFlags(const CpuidInfo& ci);

int main()
{
    CpuidInfo ci;
    ci.LoadInfo();

    DisplayProcessorInfo(ci);
    DisplayCacheInfo(ci);
    DisplayFeatureFlags(ci);
    return 0;
}

static void DisplayProcessorInfo(const CpuidInfo& ci)
{
    const char nl = '\n';
    std::cout << "\n----- Processor Info  -----" << nl;
    std::cout << "Processor vendor: " << ci.GetProcessorVendor() << nl;
    std::cout << "Processor brand:  " << ci.GetProcessorBrand() << nl;
}

static void DisplayCacheInfo(const CpuidInfo& ci)
{
    const char nl = '\n';
    const std::vector<CpuidInfo::CacheInfo>& cache_info = ci.GetCacheInfo();

    std::cout << "\n----- Cache Info  -----" << nl;

    for (const CpuidInfo::CacheInfo& x : cache_info)
    {
        uint32_t cache_size = x.GetSize();
        uint32_t cache_size_kb = cache_size / 1024;

        std::cout << "Cache L" << x.GetLevel() << ": ";
        std::cout << cache_size_kb << " KB - ";
        std::cout << x.GetTypeString() << nl;
    }
}

static void DisplayFeatureFlags(const CpuidInfo& ci)
{
    const char nl = '\n';

    std::cout << "\n----- Processor CPUID Feature Flags -----" << nl;
    std::cout << "FMA:                " << ci.GetFF(CpuidInfo::FF::FMA) << nl;
    std::cout << "AVX:                " << ci.GetFF(CpuidInfo::FF::AVX) << nl;
    std::cout << "AVX2:               " << ci.GetFF(CpuidInfo::FF::AVX2) << nl;
    std::cout << "AVX512F:            " << ci.GetFF(CpuidInfo::FF::AVX512F) << nl;
    std::cout << "AVX512CD:           " << ci.GetFF(CpuidInfo::FF::AVX512CD) << nl;
    std::cout << "AVX512DQ:           " << ci.GetFF(CpuidInfo::FF::AVX512DQ) << nl;
    std::cout << "AVX512BW:           " << ci.GetFF(CpuidInfo::FF::AVX512BW) << nl;
```

```
    std::cout << "AVX512VL:            " << ci.GetFF(CpuidInfo::FF::AVX512VL) << nl;
    std::cout << "AVX512_IFMA:         " << ci.GetFF(CpuidInfo::FF::AVX512_IFMA) << nl;
    std::cout << "AVX512_VBMI:         " << ci.GetFF(CpuidInfo::FF::AVX512_VBMI) << nl;
    std::cout << "AVX512_VNNI:         " << ci.GetFF(CpuidInfo::FF::AVX512_VNNI) << nl;
    std::cout << "AVX512_VPOPCNTDQ:    " << ci.GetFF(CpuidInfo::FF::AVX512_VPOPCNTDQ) << nl;
    std::cout << "AVX512_VBMI2:        " << ci.GetFF(CpuidInfo::FF::AVX512_VBMI2) << nl;
    std::cout << "AVX512_BITALG:       " << ci.GetFF(CpuidInfo::FF::AVX512_BITALG) << nl;
    std::cout << "AVX512_BF16:         " << ci.GetFF(CpuidInfo::FF::AVX512_BF16) << nl;
    std::cout << "AVX512_VP2INTERSECT: " << ci.GetFF(CpuidInfo::FF::AVX512_
                                            VP2INTERSECT) << nl;
    std::cout << "AVX512_FP16:         " << ci.GetFF(CpuidInfo::FF::AVX512_FP16) << nl;
}


//-------------------------------------------------
//                  CpuidInfo.cpp
//-------------------------------------------------

#include <string>
#include <cstring>
#include <vector>
#include "CpuidInfo.h"

void CpuidInfo::LoadInfo(void)
{
    // Note: LoadInfo0 must be called first
    LoadInfo0();
    LoadInfo1();
    LoadInfo2();
    LoadInfo3();
    LoadInfo4();
    LoadInfo5();
}

void CpuidInfo::LoadInfo4(void)
{
    CpuidRegs r_eax01h;
    CpuidRegs r_eax07h;
    CpuidRegs r_eax07h_ecx01h;

    if (m_MaxEax < 7)
        return;

    Cpuid__(1, 0, &r_eax01h);
    Cpuid__(7, 0, &r_eax07h);
    Cpuid__(7, 1, &r_eax07h_ecx01h);

    // Test CPUID.(EAX=01H, ECX=00H):ECX.OSXSAVE[bit 27] to verify use of XGETBV
    m_OsXsave = (r_eax01h.ECX & (0x1 << 27)) ? true : false;

    if (m_OsXsave)
    {
```

```cpp
    // Use XGETBV to obtain following information
    // AVX state is enabled by OS if (XCR0[2:1] == '11b') is true
    // AVX-512 state is enabled by OS if (XCR0[7:5] == '111b') is true

    uint32_t xgetbv_eax, xgetbv_edx;

    Xgetbv__(0, &xgetbv_eax, &xgetbv_edx);
    m_OsAvxState = (((xgetbv_eax >> 1) & 0x03) == 0x03) ? true : false;

    if (m_OsAvxState)
    {
        // CPUID.(EAX=01H, ECX=00H):ECX.AVX[bit 28]
        if (r_eax01h.ECX & (0x1 << 28))
        {
            m_FeatureFlags |= (uint64_t)FF::AVX;

            //
            // Decode ECX flags
            //

            // CPUID.(EAX=07H, ECX=00H):EBX.AVX2[bit 5]
            if (r_eax07h.EBX & (0x1 << 5))
                m_FeatureFlags |= (uint64_t)FF::AVX2;

            // CPUID.(EAX=07H, ECX=00H):ECX.VAES[bit 9]
            if (r_eax07h.ECX & (0x1 << 9))
                m_FeatureFlags |= (uint64_t)FF::VAES;

            // CPUID.(EAX=07H, ECX=00H):ECX.VPCLMULQDQ[bit 10]
            if (r_eax07h.ECX & (0x1 << 10))
                m_FeatureFlags |= (uint64_t)FF::VPCLMULQDQ;

            // CPUID.(EAX=01H, ECX=00H):ECX.FMA[bit 12]
            if (r_eax01h.ECX & (0x1 << 12))
                m_FeatureFlags |= (uint64_t)FF::FMA;

            // CPUID.(EAX=01H, ECX=00H):ECX.F16C[bit 29]
            if (r_eax01h.ECX & (0x1 << 29))
                m_FeatureFlags |= (uint64_t)FF::F16C;

            //
            // Decode EAX flags (subleaf 1)
            //

            // CPUID.(EAX=07H, ECX=01H):EAX.AVX_VNNI[bit 4]
            if (r_eax07h_ecx01h.EAX & (0x1 << 4))
                m_FeatureFlags |= (uint64_t)FF::AVX_VNNI;

            m_OsAvx512State = (((xgetbv_eax >> 5) & 0x07) == 0x07) ? true : false;

            if (m_OsAvx512State)
```

```cpp
{
    // CPUID.(EAX=07H, ECX=00H):EBX.AVX512F[bit 16]
    if (r_eax07h.EBX & (0x1 << 16))
    {
        m_FeatureFlags |= (uint64_t)FF::AVX512F;

        //
        // Decode EBX flags
        //

        // CPUID.(EAX=07H, ECX=00H):EBX.AVX512DQ[bit 17]
        if (r_eax07h.EBX & (0x1 << 17))
            m_FeatureFlags |= (uint64_t)FF::AVX512DQ;

        // CPUID.(EAX=07H, ECX=00H):EBX.AVX512_IFMA[bit 21]
        if (r_eax07h.EBX & (0x1 << 21))
            m_FeatureFlags |= (uint64_t)FF::AVX512_IFMA;

        // CPUID.(EAX=07H, ECX=00H):EBX.AVX512PF[bit 26]
        if (r_eax07h.EBX & (0x1 << 26))
            m_FeatureFlags |= (uint64_t)FF::AVX512PF;

        // CPUID.(EAX=07H, ECX=00H):EBX.AVX512ER[bit 27]
        if (r_eax07h.EBX & (0x1 << 27))
            m_FeatureFlags |= (uint64_t)FF::AVX512ER;

        // CPUID.(EAX=07H, ECX=00H):EBX.AVX512CD[bit 28]
        if (r_eax07h.EBX & (0x1 << 28))
            m_FeatureFlags |= (uint64_t)FF::AVX512CD;

        // CPUID.(EAX=07H, ECX=00H):EBX.AVX512BW[bit 30]
        if (r_eax07h.EBX & (0x1 << 30))
            m_FeatureFlags |= (uint64_t)FF::AVX512BW;

        // CPUID.(EAX=07H, ECX=00H):EBX.AVX512VL[bit 31]
        if (r_eax07h.EBX & (0x1 << 31))
            m_FeatureFlags |= (uint64_t)FF::AVX512VL;

        //
        // Decode ECX flags
        //

        // CPUID.(EAX=07H, ECX=00H):ECX.AVX512_VBMI[bit 1]
        if (r_eax07h.ECX & (0x1 << 1))
            m_FeatureFlags |= (uint64_t)FF::AVX512_VBMI;

        // CPUID.(EAX=07H, ECX=00H):ECX.AVX512_VBMI2[bit 6]
        if (r_eax07h.ECX & (0x1 << 6))
            m_FeatureFlags |= (uint64_t)FF::AVX512_VBMI2;

        // CPUID.(EAX=07H, ECX=00H):ECX.AVX512_VNNI[bit 11]
```

```
                    if (r_eax07h.ECX & (0x1 << 11))
                        m_FeatureFlags |= (uint64_t)FF::AVX512_VNNI;

                    // CPUID.(EAX=07H, ECX=00H):ECX.AVX512_BITALG[bit 12]
                    if (r_eax07h.ECX & (0x1 << 12))
                        m_FeatureFlags |= (uint64_t)FF::AVX512_BITALG;

                    // CPUID.(EAX=07H, ECX=00H):ECX.AVX512_VPOPCNTDQ[bit 14]
                    if (r_eax07h.ECX & (0x1 << 14))
                        m_FeatureFlags |= (uint64_t)FF::AVX512_VPOPCNTDQ;

                    //
                    // Decode EDX flags
                    //

                    // CPUID.(EAX=07H, ECX=00H):EDX.AVX512_4FMAPS[bit 2]
                    if (r_eax07h.EDX & (0x1 << 2))
                        m_FeatureFlags |= (uint64_t)FF::AVX512_4FMAPS;

                    // CPUID.(EAX=07H, ECX=00H):EDX.AVX512_4VNNIW[bit 3]
                    if (r_eax07h.EDX & (0x1 << 3))
                        m_FeatureFlags |= (uint64_t)FF::AVX512_4VNNIW;

                    // CPUID.(EAX=07H, ECX=00H):EDX.AVX512_VP2INTERSECT[bit 8]
                    if (r_eax07h.EDX & (0x1 << 8))
                        m_FeatureFlags |= (uint64_t)FF::AVX512_VP2INTERSECT;

                    // CPUID.(EAX=07H, ECX=00H):EDX.AVX512_FP16[bit 23]
                    if (r_eax07h.EDX & (0x1 << 23))
                        m_FeatureFlags |= (uint64_t)FF::AVX512_FP16;

                    //
                    // Decode EAX flags (subleaf 1)
                    //

                    // CPUID.(EAX=07H, ECX=01H):EAX.AVX512_BF16[bit 5]
                    if (r_eax07h_ecx01h.EAX & (0x1 << 5))
                        m_FeatureFlags |= (uint64_t)FF::AVX512_BF16;
                }
            }
        }
    }
  }
}
```

Before examining the source code in Listing 9-1, a few words regarding x86 registers and cpuid instruction usage are necessary. A register is a storage area within a processor that contains data. Most x86 processor instructions carry out their operations using one or more registers as operands. A register can also be used to temporarily store an intermediate result instead of saving it to memory. The cpuid instruction uses four 32-bit wide x86 registers named EAX, EBX, ECX, and EDX to query and return processor feature information. You will learn more about x86 processor registers in Chapter 10.

Prior to using the cpuid instruction, the calling function must load a "leaf" value into the processor's EAX register. The leaf value specifies what information the cpuid instruction should return. The function may also need to load a "sub-leaf" value into register ECX before using cpuid. The cpuid instruction returns its results in registers EAX, EBX, ECX, and EDX. The calling function must then decipher the values in these registers to ascertain processor feature or instruction set availability. It is often necessary for a program to use cpuid multiple times. Most programs typically exercise the cpuid instruction during initialization and save the results for later use. The reason for this is that cpuid is a serializing instruction. A serializing instruction forces the processor to finish executing all previously fetched instructions and perform any pending memory writes before fetching the next instruction. In other words, it takes the processor a long time to execute a cpuid instruction.

Listing 9-1 begins with the definition of a simple C++ structure named CpuidRegs, which is located in file Cpuid__.h. This structure contains four uint32_t members named EAX, EBX, ECX, and EDX. Source code example Ch09_01 uses the CpuidRegs structure to hold cpuid instruction leaf and sub-leaf values. It also uses CpuidRegs to obtain and process the information returned from cpuid.

The next file in Listing 9-1 is named Cpuid__.cpp. The first function in this file, Cpuid__(), is a wrapper function that hides implementation differences between Windows and Linux. This function uses C++ compiler preprocessor definitions to select which cpuid intrinsic function, __cpuidex (Windows) or __get_cpuid_count (Linux), to use. The other function in Cpuid__.cpp is named Xgetbv__(). This is a wrapper function for the x86 xgetbv (Get Value of Extended Control Register) instruction. Function Xgetbv__() obtains state information from the processor that indicates whether the host operating system has enabled support for AVX, AVX2, or AVX-512.

Following Cpuid__.cpp in Listing 9-1 is a file named CpuidInfo.h. This file contains the declaration of class CpuidInfo. Class CpuidInfo begins with the declaration of a subclass named CacheInfo. As implied by its name, CpuidInfo::CacheInfo includes a public interface that provides information about the processor's on-chip memory caches. Following the declaration of CpuidInfo::CacheInfo are the private data values for class CpuidInfo. These values maintain the data that is returned by various executions of the cpuid instruction.

Class CpuidInfo also includes a public interface that a program can use to obtain information returned by the cpuid instruction. The type CpuidInfo::FF defines symbolic names for x86 instruction set extensions that are commonly used in application programs. Note that the public function CpuidInfo::GetFF() requires a single argument value of type CpuidInfo::FF. This function returns a bool value that signifies whether the host processor (and host operating system) supports the specified instruction set extension. Class CpuidInfo also includes other useful public member functions. The functions CpuidInfo::GetProc essorBrand() and CpuidInfo::GetProcessorVendor() return text strings that report processor brand and vendor information. The member function CpuidInfo::GetCacheInfo() obtains information about the processor's memory caches. Finally, the member function CpuidInfo::LoadInfo() performs one-time data initialization tasks. Calling this function triggers multiple executions of the cpuid instruction.

The next file in Listing 9-1 is Ch09_01.cpp. The code in this file demonstrates how to properly use class CpuidInfo. Function main() begins with the instantiation of a CpuidInfo object named ci. The ci. LoadInfo() call that follows initializes the private data members of ci. Note that CpuidInfo::LoadInfo() must be called prior to calling any other public member functions of class CpuidInfo. A program typically requires only one CpuidInfo instance, but multiple instances can be created. Following the ci.LoadInfo() call, function main() calls DisplayProcessorInfo(), DisplayCacheInfo(), and DisplayFeatureFlags(). These functions stream processor feature information obtained during the execution of CpuidInfo::LoadInfo() to std::cout.

The final file in Listing 9-1 is CpuidInfo.cpp. Near the top of this file is the definition of member function CpuidInfo::LoadInfo(). Recall that function main() calls CpuidInfo::LoadInfo() to initialize the private members of CpuidInfo instance ci. During its execution, CpuidInfo::LoadInfo() calls six private member functions named CpuidInfo::LoadInfo0() – CpuidInfo::LoadInfo5(). These functions exercise the previously described functions Cpuid__() and Xgetbv__() to determine processor support for the various x86 instruction set extensions enumerated by CpuidInfo::FF. Listing 9-1 only shows the source code for CpuidInfo::LoadInfo4(), which ascertains processor support for FMA, AVX, AVX2, AVX-512, and several other recent x86 instruction set extensions. Due to their length, the source code for the five other CpuidInfo::LoadInfoX() functions is not shown in Listing 9-1, but this code is included in the download software package.

Function CpuidInfo::LoadInfo4() begins its execution with three calls to Cpuid__(). Note that Cpuid__() requires three arguments: a leaf value, a sub-leaf value, and a pointer to a CpuidRegs structure. The specific leaf and sub-leaf values employed here direct Cpuid__() to obtain status flags that facilitate detection of x86-AVX instruction set extensions. The AMD and Intel programming reference manuals contain additional details regarding permissible cpuid instruction leaf and sub-leaf values.

Following execution of the three Cpuid__() calls, CpuidInfo::LoadInfo4() determines if the host operating system allows an application program to use the xgetbv instruction (or _xgetbv() intrinsic function), which is used in Xgetbv__(). Function Xgetbv__() sets status flags in xgetbv_eax that indicate whether the host operating system has enabled the internal processor states necessary for AVX and AVX2. If m_OsAvxState is true, function CpuidInfo::LoadInfo4() initiates a series of brute-force flag checks that test for AVX, AVX2, FMA, and several other x86 instruction set extensions. Note that each successful test sets a status flag in CpuidInfo::m_FeatureFlags to indicate availability of a specific x86 instruction set extension. These flags are the same ones returned by CpuidInfo::GetFF().

If m_OsAvxState is true, CpuidInfo::LoadInfo4() also checks additional status bits in xgetbv_eax to ascertain host operating system support for AVX-512. If m_OsAvx512State is true, CpuidInfo::LoadInfo4() initiates another series of brute-force flag tests to determine which AVX-512 instruction set extensions (see Table 7-1) are available. These tests also update CpuidInfo::m_FeatureFlags to indicate processor support for specific AVX-512 instruction set extensions. Here are the results for source code Ch09_01 that were obtained using Intel Core i7-8700K and Intel Core i5-11600K:

```
----- Processor Info  -----
Processor vendor: GenuineIntel
Processor brand:  Intel(R) Core(TM) i7-8700K CPU @ 3.70GHz

----- Cache Info  -----
Cache L1: 32 KB - Data
Cache L1: 32 KB - Instruction
Cache L2: 256 KB - Unified
Cache L3: 12288 KB - Unified

----- Processor CPUID Feature Flags -----
FMA:                1
AVX:                1
AVX2:               1
AVX512F:            0
AVX512CD:           0
AVX512DQ:           0
AVX512BW:           0
AVX512VL:           0
AVX512_IFMA:        0
AVX512_VBMI:        0
AVX512_VNNI:        0
AVX512_VPOPCNTDQ:   0
AVX512_VBMI2:       0
AVX512_BITALG:      0
AVX512_BF16:        0
AVX512_VP2INTERSECT: 0
```

```
AVX512_FP16:           0

----- Processor Info  -----
Processor vendor: GenuineIntel
Processor brand:  11th Gen Intel(R) Core(TM) i5-11600K @ 3.90GHz

----- Cache Info  -----
Cache L1: 48 KB - Data
Cache L1: 32 KB - Instruction
Cache L2: 512 KB - Unified
Cache L3: 12288 KB - Unified

----- Processor CPUID Feature Flags -----
FMA:                   1
AVX:                   1
AVX2:                  1
AVX512F:               1
AVX512CD:              1
AVX512DQ:              1
AVX512BW:              1
AVX512VL:              1
AVX512_IFMA:           1
AVX512_VBMI:           1
AVX512_VNNI:           1
AVX512_VPOPCNTDQ:      1
AVX512_VBMI2:          1
AVX512_BITALG:         1
AVX512_BF16:           0
AVX512_VP2INTERSECT:   0
AVX512_FP16:           0
```

Source code example Ch09_01 illustrates how to code a comprehensive x86 instruction set extension detection class. Code fragments from this example can be extracted to create a streamlined x86 instruction set detection class with fewer detection capabilities (e.g., only AVX, AVX2, and FMA). Finally, it should also be noted that many AVX-512 instructions (and their corresponding C++ SIMD intrinsic functions) can only be used if the host processor supports multiple AVX-512 instruction set extensions. For example, the AVX-512 C++ SIMD intrinsic function _mm256_mask_sub_epi16() will only execute on a processor that supports AVX512F, AVX512BW, and AVX512VL. One programming strategy to overcome the inconvenience of having to test multiple AVX-512 instruction set extensions is to create a single application-level status flag that logically ANDs any required AVX-512 instruction-set-extension status flags into a single Boolean variable. The Intel programming reference manuals listed in Appendix B contain additional information about this topic. Appendix B also contains a list of open-source libraries that you can use to determine x86 processor instruction set availability.

# Short Vector Math Library

Many numerically oriented algorithms use standard C++ math library routines such as exp(), log(), log10(), pow(), sin(), cos(), and tan(). These functions carry out their calculations using scalar single-precision or double-precision floating-point values. The Short Vector Math Library (SVML), originally developed by Intel for their C/C++ compilers, contains SIMD versions of most standard C++ math library routines. SVML functions can also be used in application programs that are developed using Visual Studio 2019 or later. In this section, you will learn how to code some SIMD calculating functions that exploit SVML. The first example demonstrates converting an array of rectangular coordinates into polar coordinates. This is followed by an example that calculates body surface areas using arrays of patient heights and weights.

## Rectangular to Polar Coordinates

A point on a two-dimensional plane can be uniquely specified using an ordered $(x, y)$ pair. The values $x$ and $y$ represent signed distances from an origin point, which is located at the intersection of two perpendicular axes. An ordered $(x, y)$ pair is called a rectangular (or Cartesian) coordinate. A point on a two-dimensional plane can also be uniquely specified using a radius vector $r$ and angle $\theta$ as illustrated in Figure 9-1. An ordered $(r, \theta)$ pair is called a polar coordinate.

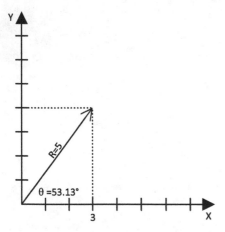

**Figure 9-1.** *Specification of a point using rectangular and polar coordinates*

A rectangular coordinate can be converted to a polar coordinate using the following equations:

$$r = \sqrt{x^2 + y^2}$$

$$\theta = atan2\left(\frac{y}{x}\right) \text{ where } \theta = [-\pi, \pi]$$

A polar coordinate can be converted to a rectangular coordinate using the following equations:

$$x = r\cos\theta$$

$$y = r\sin\theta$$

Listing 9-2 shows the source code for example Ch09_02. This example illustrates how to use several SVML functions to convert arrays of rectangular coordinates to polar coordinates and vice versa.

*Listing 9-2.* Example Ch09_02

```
//--------------------------------------------------
//                  Ch09_02.h
//--------------------------------------------------

#pragma once
#include <vector>

// Ch09_02_fcpp.cpp
extern void ConvertRectToPolarF32_Cpp(std::vector<float>& r, std::vector<float>& a,
    const std::vector<float>& x, const std::vector<float>& y);
extern void ConvertRectToPolarF32_Iavx(std::vector<float>& r, std::vector<float>& a,
    const std::vector<float>& x, const std::vector<float>& y);
extern void ConvertPolarToRectF32_Cpp(std::vector<float>& x, std::vector<float>& y,
    const std::vector<float>& r, const std::vector<float>& a);
extern void ConvertPolarToRectF32_Iavx(std::vector<float>& x, std::vector<float>& y, const
std::vector<float>& r, const std::vector<float>& a);

// Ch09_02_misc.cpp
extern bool CheckArgs(const std::vector<float>& v1, const std::vector<float>& v2,
    const std::vector<float>& v3, const std::vector<float>& v4);
extern bool CompareResults(const std::vector<float>& v1,
    const std::vector<float>& v2);
extern void FillVectorsRect(std::vector<float>& x, std::vector<float>& y);
extern void FillVectorsPolar(std::vector<float>& r, std::vector<float>& a);

//--------------------------------------------------
//                  Ch09_02_misc.cpp
//--------------------------------------------------

#include <vector>
#include <stdexcept>
#include <cmath>
#include "Ch09_02.h"
#include "MT.h"

bool CheckArgs(const std::vector<float>& v1, const std::vector<float>& v2,
    const std::vector<float>& v3, const std::vector<float>& v4)
{
    size_t n = v1.size();
    return (n == v2.size() && n == v3.size() && n == v4.size());
}

bool CompareResults(const std::vector<float>& v1, const std::vector<float>& v2)
{
    float epsilon = 1.0e-4f;

    if (v1.size() != v2.size())
        return false;

    size_t n = v1.size();
```

```cpp
    for (size_t i = 0; i < n; i++)
    {
        if (fabs(v1[i] - v2[i]) > epsilon)
            return false;
    }

    return true;
}

void FillVectorsRect(std::vector<float>& x, std::vector<float>& y)
{
    if (x.size() != y.size())
        throw std::runtime_error("FillVectorsRect() - non-conforming vectors");

    const int rng_min = -25;
    const int rng_max =  25;
    const unsigned int rng_seed_x = 699;
    const unsigned int rng_seed_y = 701;

    MT::FillArray(x.data(), x.size(), rng_min, rng_max, rng_seed_x, true);
    MT::FillArray(y.data(), y.size(), rng_min, rng_max, rng_seed_y, true);
}

void FillVectorsPolar(std::vector<float>& r, std::vector<float>& a)
{
    if (r.size() != a.size())
        throw std::runtime_error("FillVectorsPolar() - non-conforming vectors");

    const int rng_min_r = 1;
    const int rng_max_r =  50;
    const int rng_min_a = -359;
    const int rng_max_a =  359;
    const unsigned int rng_seed_r = 703;
    const unsigned int rng_seed_a = 707;

    MT::FillArray(r.data(), r.size(), rng_min_r, rng_max_r, rng_seed_r, true);
    MT::FillArray(a.data(), a.size(), rng_min_a, rng_max_a, rng_seed_a, true);
}

//--------------------------------------------------
//                  Ch09_02.cpp
//--------------------------------------------------

#include <iostream>
#include <iomanip>
#include <vector>
#include <stdexcept>
#include "Ch09_02.h"

static void ConvertRectToPolar(void);
static void ConvertPolarToRect(void);
```

```cpp
int main()
{
    try
    {
        ConvertRectToPolar();
        ConvertPolarToRect();
    }

    catch (std::exception& ex)
    {
        std::cout << "Ch09_02 exception: " << ex.what() << '\n';
    }

    return 0;
}

static void ConvertRectToPolar(void)
{
    const size_t n = 19;
    std::vector<float> x(n), y(n);
    std::vector<float> r1(n), a1(n);
    std::vector<float> r2(n), a2(n);

    FillVectorsRect(x, y);
    ConvertRectToPolarF32_Cpp(r1, a1, x, y);
    ConvertRectToPolarF32_Iavx(r2, a2, x, y);

    size_t w = 10;
    std::cout << std::fixed << std::setprecision(4);
    std::cout << "\n----- Results for ConvertRectToPolar -----\n";

    for (size_t i = 0; i < n; i++)
    {
        std::cout << std::setw(4) << i << ": ";
        std::cout << std::setw(w) << x[i] << ", ";
        std::cout << std::setw(w) << y[i] << " | ";
        std::cout << std::setw(w) << r1[i] << ", ";
        std::cout << std::setw(w) << a1[i] << " | ";
        std::cout << std::setw(w) << r2[i] << ", ";
        std::cout << std::setw(w) << a2[i] << '\n';
    }

    if (!CompareResults(r1, r2) || !CompareResults(a1, a2))
        throw std::runtime_error("CompareResults() failed");
}

static void ConvertPolarToRect(void)
{
    const size_t n = 19;
    std::vector<float> r(n), a(n);
    std::vector<float> x1(n), y1(n);
    std::vector<float> x2(n), y2(n);
```

```
    FillVectorsPolar(r, a);
    ConvertPolarToRectF32_Cpp(x1, y1, r, a);
    ConvertPolarToRectF32_Iavx(x2, y2, r, a);

    size_t w = 10;
    std::cout << std::fixed << std::setprecision(4);
    std::cout << "\n----- Results for ConvertPolarToRect -----\n";

    for (size_t i = 0; i < n; i++)
    {
        std::cout << std::setw(4) << i << ": ";
        std::cout << std::setw(w) << r[i] << ", ";
        std::cout << std::setw(w) << a[i] << " | ";
        std::cout << std::setw(w) << x1[i] << ", ";
        std::cout << std::setw(w) << y1[i] << " | ";
        std::cout << std::setw(w) << x2[i] << ", ";
        std::cout << std::setw(w) << y2[i] << '\n';
    }

    if (!CompareResults(x1, x2) || !CompareResults(y1, y2))
        throw std::runtime_error("CompareResults() failed");
}

//--------------------------------------------------
//                  SimdMath.h
//--------------------------------------------------

#if _MSC_VER >= 1921          // VS 2019 or later
#include <cmath>
#include <immintrin.h>
#elif defined(__GNUG__)
#include <cmath>
#include <immintrin.h>
#else
#error Unknown target in SimdMath.h
#endif

inline __m256 atan2_f32x8(__m256 y, __m256 x)
{
#if _MSC_VER >= 1921
    return _mm256_atan2_ps(y, x);
#endif

#if defined(__GNUG__)
    __m256 atan2_vals;
    for (size_t i = 0; i < 8; i++)
        atan2_vals[i] = atan2(y[i], x[i]);
    return atan2_vals;
#endif
}
```

```cpp
inline __m256 cos_f32x8(__m256 x)
{
#if _MSC_VER >= 1921
    return _mm256_cos_ps(x);
#endif

#if defined(__GNUG__)
    __m256 cos_vals;
    for (size_t i = 0; i < 8; i++)
        cos_vals[i] = cos(x[i]);
    return cos_vals;
#endif
}

inline __m256d pow_f64x4(__m256d x, __m256d y)
{
#if _MSC_VER >= 1921
    return _mm256_pow_pd(x, y);
#endif

#if defined(__GNUG__)
    __m256d pow_vals;
    for (size_t i = 0; i < 4; i++)
        pow_vals[i] = pow(x[i], y[i]);
    return pow_vals;
#endif
}

inline __m256 sin_f32x8(__m256 x)
{
#if _MSC_VER >= 1921
    return _mm256_sin_ps(x);
#endif

#if defined(__GNUG__)
    __m256 sin_vals;
    for (size_t i = 0; i < 8; i++)
        sin_vals[i] = sin(x[i]);
    return sin_vals;
#endif
}

//--------------------------------------------------
//                 Ch09_02_fcpp.cpp
//--------------------------------------------------

#include <iostream>
#include <stdexcept>
#include <immintrin.h>
#define _USE_MATH_DEFINES
#include <math.h>
```

```cpp
#include "Ch09_02.h"
#include "SimdMath.h"

const float c_DegToRad = (float)(M_PI / 180.0);
const float c_RadToDeg = (float)(180.0 / M_PI);

void ConvertRectToPolarF32_Cpp(std::vector<float>& r, std::vector<float>& a,
    const std::vector<float>& x, const std::vector<float>& y)
{
    if (!CheckArgs(r, a, x, y))
        throw std::runtime_error("ConvertRectToPolarF32_Cpp() - CheckArgs failed");

    size_t n = r.size();

    for (size_t i = 0; i < n; i++)
    {
        r[i] = sqrt(x[i] * x[i] + y[i] * y[i]);
        a[i] = atan2(y[i], x[i]) * c_RadToDeg;
    }
}

void ConvertPolarToRectF32_Cpp(std::vector<float>& x, std::vector<float>& y,
    const std::vector<float>& r, const std::vector<float>& a)
{
    if (!CheckArgs(x, y, r, a))
        throw std::runtime_error("ConvertPolarToRectF32_Cpp() - CheckArgs failed");

    size_t n = x.size();

    for (size_t i = 0; i < n; i++)
    {
        x[i] = r[i] * cos(a[i] * c_DegToRad);
        y[i] = r[i] * sin(a[i] * c_DegToRad);
    }
}

void ConvertRectToPolarF32_Iavx(std::vector<float>& r, std::vector<float>& a,
    const std::vector<float>& x, const std::vector<float>& y)
{
    if (!CheckArgs(r, a, x, y))
        throw std::runtime_error("ConvertRectToPolarF32_Iavx() - CheckArgs failed");

    size_t n = r.size();

    __m256 rad_to_deg = _mm256_set1_ps(c_RadToDeg);

    size_t i = 0;
    const size_t num_simd_elements = 8;
```

```
    for (; n - i >= num_simd_elements; i += num_simd_elements)
    {
        __m256 x_vals = _mm256_loadu_ps(&x[i]);
        __m256 y_vals = _mm256_loadu_ps(&y[i]);
        __m256 x_vals2 = _mm256_mul_ps(x_vals, x_vals);
        __m256 y_vals2 = _mm256_mul_ps(y_vals, y_vals);

        __m256 temp = _mm256_add_ps(x_vals2, y_vals2);
        __m256 r_vals = _mm256_sqrt_ps(temp);
        _mm256_storeu_ps(&r[i], r_vals);

        __m256 a_vals_rad = atan2_f32x8(y_vals, x_vals);
        __m256 a_vals_deg = _mm256_mul_ps(a_vals_rad, rad_to_deg);
        _mm256_storeu_ps(&a[i], a_vals_deg);
    }

    for (; i < n; i++)
    {
        r[i] = sqrt(x[i] * x[i] + y[i] * y[i]);
        a[i] = atan2(y[i], x[i]) * c_RadToDeg;
    }
}

void ConvertPolarToRectF32_Iavx(std::vector<float>& x, std::vector<float>& y,
    const std::vector<float>& r, const std::vector<float>& a)
{
    if (!CheckArgs(x, y, r, a))
        throw std::runtime_error("ConvertPolarToRectF32_Iavx() - CheckArgs failed");

    size_t n = x.size();

    __m256 deg_to_rad = _mm256_set1_ps(c_DegToRad);

    size_t i = 0;
    const size_t num_simd_elements = 8;

    for (; n - i >= num_simd_elements; i += num_simd_elements)
    {
        __m256 r_vals = _mm256_loadu_ps(&r[i]);
        __m256 a_vals_deg = _mm256_loadu_ps(&a[i]);
        __m256 a_vals_rad = _mm256_mul_ps(a_vals_deg, deg_to_rad);

        __m256 x_vals_temp = cos_f32x8(a_vals_rad);
        __m256 x_vals = _mm256_mul_ps(r_vals, x_vals_temp);
        _mm256_storeu_ps(&x[i], x_vals);

        __m256 y_vals_temp = sin_f32x8(a_vals_rad);
        __m256 y_vals = _mm256_mul_ps(r_vals, y_vals_temp);
        _mm256_storeu_ps(&y[i], y_vals);
    }
```

```
    for (; i < n; i++)
    {
        x[i] = r[i] * cos(a[i] * c_DegToRad);
        y[i] = r[i] * sin(a[i] * c_DegToRad);
    }
}
```

Listing 9-2 starts with the file Ch09_02.h. Note that the function declarations in this file use arguments of type std::vector<float> for the various coordinate arrays. The next file in Listing 9-2, Ch09_02_misc. cpp, contains assorted functions that perform argument checking and vector initialization. Also shown in Listing 9-2 is the file Ch09_02.cpp. This file contains a function named ConvertRectToPolar(), which performs test case initialization. Function ConvertRectToPolar() also exercises the SIMD rectangular to polar coordinate conversion function and streams results to std::cout. The polar to rectangular counterpart of function ConvertRectToPolar() is named ConvertPolarToRect() and is also located in file Ch09_02.cpp.

The next file in Listing 9-2, SimdMath.h, defines several inline functions that perform common math operations using SIMD arguments of type __m256 or __m256d. Note that this file includes preprocessor definitions that enable different code blocks for Visual C++ and GNU C++. The Visual C++ sections emit SVML library function calls since these are directly supported in Visual Studio 2019 and later. The GNU C++ sections substitute simple for-loops for the SVML functions since SVML is not directly supported. If you are interested in using SVML with GNU C++ and Linux, you should consult the Intel C++ compiler and GNU C++ compiler references listed in Appendix B.

The final file in Listing 9-2, Ch09_02_fcpp.cpp, begins with the definitions of functions ConvertRectToPolarF32_Cpp() and ConvertPolarToRectF32_Cpp(). These functions perform rectangular to polar and polar to rectangular coordinate conversions using standard C++ statements and math library functions. The next function, ConvertRectToPolarF32_Iavx(), performs rectangular to polar coordinate conversions using AVX and C++ SIMD intrinsic functions. Following argument validation, ConvertRectToPolarF32_Iavx() employs _mm256_set1_ps() to create a packed version of the constant 180.0 / M_PI for radian to degree conversions. The first for-loop in ConvertRectToPolarF32_Iavx() uses C++ SIMD intrinsic functions that you have already seen. Note the use of atan2_f32x8(), which is defined in SimdMath.h. This function calculates eight polar coordinate angle components. The second for-loop in ConvertRectToPolarF32_Iavx() process any residual coordinates using standard C++ math library functions.

Also included in file Ch09_02_fcpp.cpp is the polar to rectangular coordinate conversion function ConvertPolarToRectF32_Iavx(). The layout of this function is akin to ConvertRectToPolarF32_Iavx(). Note that the first for-loop in ConvertPolarToRectF32_Iavx() uses the SIMD math functions cos_f32x8() and sin_f32x8(), also defined in SimdMath.h. It is important to keep in mind that minor value discrepancies may exist between a standard C++ math library function and its SVML counterpart. Here are the results for source code example Ch09_02:

```
----- Results for ConvertRectToPolar -----
  0:  -1.0000,  13.0000 |  13.0384,   94.3987 |  13.0384,   94.3987
  1:   5.0000,  -6.0000 |   7.8102,  -50.1944 |   7.8102,  -50.1944
  2:  21.0000,  -6.0000 |  21.8403,  -15.9454 |  21.8403,  -15.9454
  3: -16.0000,  -4.0000 |  16.4924, -165.9638 |  16.4924, -165.9638
  4:  11.0000,  20.0000 |  22.8254,   61.1892 |  22.8254,   61.1892
  5:  22.0000, -14.0000 |  26.0768,  -32.4712 |  26.0768,  -32.4712
  6:  24.0000,  -2.0000 |  24.0832,   -4.7636 |  24.0832,   -4.7636
  7:  -9.0000,  -5.0000 |  10.2956, -150.9454 |  10.2956, -150.9454
  8: -23.0000,   3.0000 |  23.1948,  172.5686 |  23.1948,  172.5686
  9:  23.0000,  17.0000 |  28.6007,   36.4692 |  28.6007,   36.4692
 10:  -2.0000,  -4.0000 |   4.4721, -116.5650 |   4.4721, -116.5650
```

```
11:   23.0000,   21.0000 |   31.1448,    42.3974 |   31.1448,    42.3974
12:   25.0000,  -17.0000 |   30.2324,   -34.2157 |   30.2324,   -34.2157
13:   -4.0000,  -12.0000 |   12.6491,  -108.4350 |   12.6491,  -108.4350
14:   21.0000,   -2.0000 |   21.0950,    -5.4403 |   21.0950,    -5.4403
15:   17.0000,   -7.0000 |   18.3848,   -22.3801 |   18.3848,   -22.3801
16:   -3.0000,  -19.0000 |   19.2354,   -98.9726 |   19.2354,   -98.9726
17:  -25.0000,   21.0000 |   32.6497,   139.9697 |   32.6497,   139.9697
18:    5.0000,   16.0000 |   16.7631,    72.6460 |   16.7631,    72.6460

----- Results for ConvertPolarToRect -----
 0:   43.0000,  -64.0000 |   18.8500,   -38.6481 |   18.8500,   -38.6481
 1:   22.0000,  194.0000 |  -21.3465,    -5.3223 |  -21.3465,    -5.3223
 2:   11.0000,  -81.0000 |    1.7208,   -10.8646 |    1.7208,   -10.8646
 3:   47.0000,  149.0000 |  -40.2869,    24.2068 |  -40.2869,    24.2068
 4:   34.0000, -217.0000 |  -27.1536,    20.4617 |  -27.1536,    20.4617
 5:    8.0000,  194.0000 |   -7.7624,    -1.9354 |   -7.7624,    -1.9354
 6:   12.0000,  158.0000 |  -11.1262,     4.4953 |  -11.1262,     4.4953
 7:   11.0000,   90.0000 |   -0.0000,    11.0000 |   -0.0000,    11.0000
 8:   46.0000,  111.0000 |  -16.4849,    42.9447 |  -16.4849,    42.9447
 9:   34.0000,   92.0000 |   -1.1866,    33.9793 |   -1.1866,    33.9793
10:   14.0000,   84.0000 |    1.4634,    13.9233 |    1.4634,    13.9233
11:   17.0000,  -37.0000 |   13.5768,   -10.2309 |   13.5768,   -10.2309
12:   26.0000,  -61.0000 |   12.6050,   -22.7401 |   12.6050,   -22.7401
13:   14.0000,  -76.0000 |    3.3869,   -13.5841 |    3.3869,   -13.5841
14:   27.0000,  197.0000 |  -25.8202,    -7.8940 |  -25.8202,    -7.8940
15:    3.0000,  -36.0000 |    2.4271,    -1.7634 |    2.4271,    -1.7634
16:    5.0000,  196.0000 |   -4.8063,    -1.3782 |   -4.8063,    -1.3782
17:   40.0000, -149.0000 |  -34.2867,   -20.6015 |  -34.2867,   -20.6015
18:   27.0000,  354.0000 |   26.8521,    -2.8223 |   26.8521,    -2.8223
```

# Body Surface Area

Healthcare professionals often use body surface area (BSA) to establish chemotherapy dosages for cancer patients. Table 9-1 lists three well-known equations that calculate BSA. In this table, each equation uses the symbol $H$ for patient height in centimeters, $W$ for patient weight in kilograms, and $BSA$ for patient body surface area in square meters.

**Table 9-1.** *Body Surface Area Equations*

| Method | Equation |
|---|---|
| DuBois and DuBois | $BSA = 0.007184 \times H^{0.725} \times W^{0.425}$ |
| Gehan and George | $BSA = 0.0235 \times H^{0.42246} \times W^{0.51456}$ |
| Mosteller | $BSA = \sqrt{H \times W / 3600}$ |

Listing 9-3 shows the source code for example Ch09_03. This example implements the three BSA equations shown in Table 9-1 using SIMD arithmetic and arrays of double-precision floating-point heights and weights.

*Listing 9-3.* Example Ch09_03

```
//--------------------------------------------------
//                  Ch09_03.h
//--------------------------------------------------

#pragma once
#include <vector>

// Ch09_03_fcpp.cpp
extern void CalcBSA_F64_Cpp(std::vector<double>& bsa, const std::vector<double>& ht,
    const std::vector<double>& wt);
extern void CalcBSA_F64_Iavx(std::vector<double>& bsa, const std::vector<double>& ht,
    const std::vector<double>& wt);

// Ch09_03_misc.cpp
extern bool CheckArgs(const std::vector<double>& bsa,
    const std::vector<double>& ht, const std::vector<double>& wt);
extern bool CompareResults(const std::vector<double>& bsa1,
    const std::vector<double>& bsa2);
extern void FillHeightWeightVectors(std::vector<double>& ht,
    std::vector<double>& wt);

// Ch09_03_bm.cpp
void CalcBSA_bm(void);

//--------------------------------------------------
//                  Ch09_03_misc.cpp
//--------------------------------------------------

#include <vector>
#include <algorithm>
#include <stdexcept>
#include <cmath>
#include "Ch09_03.h"
#include "MT.h"

bool CheckArgs(const std::vector<double>& bsa, const std::vector<double>& ht,
    const std::vector<double>& wt)
{
    if (ht.size() != wt.size())
        return false;

    if (bsa.size() != ht.size() * 3)
        return false;

    return true;
}
```

```cpp
bool CompareResults(const std::vector<double>& bsa1,
    const std::vector<double>& bsa2)
{
    double epsilon = 1.0e-9;

    if (bsa1.size() != bsa2.size())
        return false;

    size_t n = bsa1.size();

    for (size_t i = 0; i < n; i++)
    {
        if (fabs(bsa1[i] - bsa2[i]) > epsilon)
            return false;
    }

    return true;
}

void FillHeightWeightVectors(std::vector<double>& ht, std::vector<double>& wt)
{
    const int rng_min_ht = 140;            // cm
    const int rng_max_ht =  204;           // cm
    const int rng_min_wt = 40;             // kg
    const int rng_max_wt = 140;            // kg
    const unsigned int rng_seed_ht = 803;
    const unsigned int rng_seed_wt = 807;

    MT::FillArray(ht.data(), ht.size(), rng_min_ht, rng_max_ht, rng_seed_ht);
    MT::FillArray(wt.data(), wt.size(), rng_min_wt, rng_max_wt, rng_seed_wt);
}

//--------------------------------------------------
//                  Ch09_03.cpp
//--------------------------------------------------

#include <iostream>
#include <iomanip>
#include <vector>
#include <string>
#include "Ch09_03.h"

static void CalcBSA(void);

int main()
{
    try
    {
        CalcBSA();
        CalcBSA_bm();
    }
```

```cpp
    catch (std::exception& ex)
    {
        std::cout << "Ch09_03 exception: " << ex.what() << '\n';
    }

    return 0;
}

static void CalcBSA(void)
{
    const size_t n = 19;
    std::vector<double> heights(n);
    std::vector<double> weights(n);
    std::vector<double> bsa1(n * 3);
    std::vector<double> bsa2(n * 3);

    FillHeightWeightVectors(heights, weights);

    CalcBSA_F64_Cpp(bsa1, heights, weights);
    CalcBSA_F64_Iavx(bsa2, heights, weights);

    size_t w = 8;
    std::cout << std::fixed;
    std::cout << "----- Results for CalcBSA -----\n\n";

    std::cout << "           ht(cm)    wt(kg)";
    std::cout << "    CppAlg0    CppAlg1    CppAlg2";
    std::cout << "    AvxAlg0    AvxAlg1    AvxAlg2";
    std::cout << '\n' << std::string(86, '-') << '\n';

    for (size_t i = 0; i < n; i++)
    {
        std::cout << std::setw(4) << i << ": ";

        std::cout << std::setprecision(2);
        std::cout << std::setw(w) << heights[i] << "  ";
        std::cout << std::setw(w) << weights[i] << " | ";

        std::cout << std::setprecision(4);
        std::cout << std::setw(w) << bsa1[(n * 0) + i] << "  ";
        std::cout << std::setw(w) << bsa1[(n * 1) + i] << "  ";
        std::cout << std::setw(w) << bsa1[(n * 2) + i] << " | ";
        std::cout << std::setw(w) << bsa2[(n * 0) + i] << "  ";
        std::cout << std::setw(w) << bsa2[(n * 1) + i] << "  ";
        std::cout << std::setw(w) << bsa2[(n * 2) + i] << '\n';
    }

    if (!CompareResults(bsa1, bsa2))
        throw std::runtime_error("CompareResults() failed");
}
```

```cpp
//---------------------------------------------------
//                 Ch09_03_fcpp.cpp
//---------------------------------------------------

#include <iostream>
#include <immintrin.h>
#include <cmath>
#include "Ch09_03.h"
#include "SimdMath.h"

void CalcBSA_F64_Cpp(std::vector<double>& bsa, const std::vector<double>& ht,
    const std::vector<double>& wt)
{
    if (!CheckArgs(bsa, ht, wt))
        throw std::runtime_error("CalcBSA_F64_Cpp() - CheckArgs failed");

    size_t n = ht.size();

    for (size_t i = 0; i < n; i++)
    {
        bsa[(n * 0) + i] = 0.007184 * pow(ht[i], 0.725) * pow(wt[i], 0.425);
        bsa[(n * 1) + i] = 0.0235 * pow(ht[i], 0.42246) * pow(wt[i], 0.51456);
        bsa[(n * 2) + i] = sqrt(ht[i] * wt[i] / 3600.0);
    }
}

void CalcBSA_F64_Iavx(std::vector<double>& bsa, const std::vector<double>& ht,
    const std::vector<double>& wt)
{
    if (!CheckArgs(bsa, ht, wt))
        throw std::runtime_error("CalcBSA_F64_Iavx() - CheckArgs failed");

    __m256d f64_0p007184 = _mm256_set1_pd(0.007184);
    __m256d f64_0p725 = _mm256_set1_pd(0.725);
    __m256d f64_0p425 = _mm256_set1_pd(0.425);
    __m256d f64_0p0235 = _mm256_set1_pd(0.0235);
    __m256d f64_0p42246 = _mm256_set1_pd(0.42246);
    __m256d f64_0p51456 = _mm256_set1_pd(0.51456);
    __m256d f64_3600p0 = _mm256_set1_pd(3600.0);

    size_t i = 0;
    size_t n = ht.size();
    const size_t num_simd_elements = 4;

    for (; n - i >= num_simd_elements; i += num_simd_elements)
    {
        __m256d ht_vals = _mm256_loadu_pd(&ht[i]);
        __m256d wt_vals = _mm256_loadu_pd(&wt[i]);

        __m256d temp1 = pow_f64x4(ht_vals, f64_0p725);
        __m256d temp2 = pow_f64x4(wt_vals, f64_0p425);
```

329

```
        __m256d temp3 = _mm256_mul_pd(temp1, temp2);
        __m256d bsa_vals = _mm256_mul_pd(f64_0p007184, temp3);
        _mm256_storeu_pd(&bsa[(n * 0) + i], bsa_vals);

        temp1 = pow_f64x4(ht_vals, f64_0p42246);
        temp2 = pow_f64x4(wt_vals, f64_0p51456);
        temp3 = _mm256_mul_pd(temp1, temp2);
        bsa_vals = _mm256_mul_pd(f64_0p0235, temp3);
        _mm256_storeu_pd(&bsa[(n * 1) + i], bsa_vals);

        temp1 = _mm256_mul_pd(ht_vals, wt_vals);
        temp2 = _mm256_div_pd(temp1, f64_3600p0);
        bsa_vals = _mm256_sqrt_pd(temp2);
        _mm256_storeu_pd(&bsa[(n * 2) + i], bsa_vals);
    }

    for (; i < n; i++)
    {
        bsa[(n * 0) + i] = 0.007184 * pow(ht[i], 0.725) * pow(wt[i], 0.425);
        bsa[(n * 1) + i] = 0.0235 * pow(ht[i], 0.42246) * pow(wt[i], 0.51456);
        bsa[(n * 2) + i] = sqrt(ht[i] * wt[i] / 3600.0);
    }
}
```

The first file in Listing 9-1, Ch09_03.h, includes the requisite function declarations for this example. Note that the BSA calculating functions require arrays of type std::vector<double> for the heights, weights, and BSAs. File Ch09_03_misc.cpp contains functions that validate arguments and initialize test data vectors. In function CheckArgs(), note that the size of array bsa must be three times the size of array ht since the results for all three BSA equations are saved in bsa. The function CalcBSA(), located in file Ch09_03.cpp, allocates the test data vectors, invokes the BSA calculating functions, and displays results.

The first function in file Ch09_03_fcpp.cpp, CalcBSA_F64_Cpp(), calculates BSA values using standard C++ statements and is included for comparison purposes. The SIMD counterpart of function CalcBSA_F64_Cpp() is named CalcBSA_F64_Iavx(). This function begins its execution with a series of _mm256_set1_pd() calls that initialize packed versions of the constants used in the BSA equations. In the first for-loop, each iteration begins with two calls to _mm256_loadu_pd() that load four pairs of heights and weights from arrays ht and wt, respectively. The next three code blocks calculate the equations shown in Table 9-1 using C++ SIMD intrinsic functions that you have already seen. Note that function pow_f64x4() is defined in the header file SimdMath.h. Following calculation of each BSA equation, CalcBSA_F64_Iavx() uses the C++ SIMD intrinsic function _mm256_storeu_pd() to save the computed BSAs in array bsa. Here is the output for source code example Ch09_03:

```
----- Results for CalcBSA -----

   ht(cm)  wt(kg)   CppAlg0  CppAlg1  CppAlg2   AvxAlg0  AvxAlg1  AvxAlg2
--------------------------------------------------------------------------
 0: 151.00  116.00 |  2.0584   2.2588   2.2058 |  2.0584   2.2588   2.2058
 1: 192.00  136.00 |  2.6213   2.7133   2.6932 |  2.6213   2.7133   2.6932
 2: 175.00   84.00 |  1.9970   2.0362   2.0207 |  1.9970   2.0362   2.0207
 3: 187.00   52.00 |  1.7090   1.6361   1.6435 |  1.7090   1.6361   1.6435
 4: 165.00   51.00 |  1.5480   1.5364   1.5289 |  1.5480   1.5364   1.5289
 5: 184.00   44.00 |  1.5734   1.4911   1.4996 |  1.5734   1.4911   1.4996
```

```
 6: 145.00   59.00 |  1.4996   1.5681   1.5416 |  1.4996   1.5681   1.5416
 7: 154.00   56.00 |  1.5321   1.5659   1.5478 |  1.5321   1.5659   1.5478
 8: 154.00   59.00 |  1.5665   1.6085   1.5887 |  1.5665   1.6085   1.5887
 9: 167.00  127.00 |  2.3012   2.4695   2.4272 |  2.3012   2.4695   2.4272
10: 142.00  119.00 |  1.9901   2.2301   2.1665 |  1.9901   2.2301   2.1665
11: 183.00   65.00 |  1.8498   1.8185   1.8177 |  1.8498   1.8185   1.8177
12: 186.00  132.00 |  2.5293   2.6364   2.6115 |  2.5293   2.6364   2.6115
13: 154.00  117.00 |  2.0955   2.2878   2.2372 |  2.0955   2.2878   2.2372
14: 185.00   85.00 |  2.0896   2.0973   2.0900 |  2.0896   2.0973   2.0900
15: 191.00  103.00 |  2.3204   2.3466   2.3377 |  2.3204   2.3466   2.3377
16: 148.00   97.00 |  1.8801   2.0428   1.9969 |  1.8801   2.0428   1.9969
17: 192.00   62.00 |  1.8773   1.8112   1.8184 |  1.8773   1.8112   1.8184
18: 198.00   93.00 |  2.2806   2.2606   2.2616 |  2.2806   2.2606   2.2616

Running benchmark function CalcBSA_bm - please wait

Benchmark times save to file Ch09_03_CalcBSA_bm_OXYGEN4.csv
```

Table 9-2 shows some benchmark timing measurements for source code example Ch09_03.

***Table 9-2.*** *BSA Execution Times (Microseconds), 200,000 Heights and Weights*

| CPU | CalcBSA_F64_Cpp() | CalcBSA_F64_Iavx() |
|-----|-------------------|--------------------|
| Intel Core i7-8700K | 19628 | 3173 |
| Intel Core i5-11600K | 13347 | 2409 |

# Summary

In this chapter, you learned how to exercise the cpuid instruction to ascertain availability of x86 processor extensions such as AVX, AVX2, and AVX-512. The AMD and Intel programming reference manuals listed in Appendix B contain additional information regarding proper use of the cpuid instruction. You are strongly encouraged to consult these guides before using the cpuid instruction (or an equivalent C++ intrinsic function) in your own programs.

The SVML includes hundreds of functions that implement SIMD versions of common C++ math library routines. It also includes dozens of other useful SIMD functions. You can obtain more information about SVML at https://software.intel.com/sites/landingpage/IntrinsicsGuide/#!=undefined&t echs=SVML.

# CHAPTER 10

■ ■ ■

# X86-64 Processor Architecture

In the previous nine chapters, you learned about AVX, AVX2, and AVX-512. You also acquired the programming skills necessary to code C++ SIMD functions that exploited these x86 instruction set extensions to significantly accelerate the performance of a wide variety of algorithms. The chapter that you are about to read commences the second half of this book, which covers x86-AVX SIMD programming using x86-64 assembly language.

Unlike higher-level languages such as C and C++, a software developer must understand critical architectural details about the target processor before attempting to write any assembly language code. The goal of this chapter is to impart enough architectural information that will enable you to code x86-64 assembly language functions that utilize the computational capabilities of AVX, AVX2, and AVX-512. It begins with a section that explains x86 data types. This is followed by a section that succinctly describes the internal architecture of an x86-64 processor. The final three sections cover x86-64 instruction operands, memory addressing modes, and condition codes.

The goal of the next nine chapters is to teach you how to code x86-AVX SIMD functions using x86-64 assembly language. This is an ambitious objective given the breadth and legacy of the x86 platform. To keep the forthcoming explanations and source code examples focused on the stated goal, I have intentionally excluded some secondary topics (e.g., advanced string processing, bit manipulation instructions, and x86 microarchitectures) that are normally examined in an x86 assembly language programming book. You can read about these topics in my earlier book, *Modern X86 Assembly Language Programming, Second Edition*. You can also consult the AMD and Intel programming reference manuals listed in Appendix B for more information regarding the minutiae of x86 processor architecture and assembly language programming.

Like the earlier chapters, the remainder of this book uses the acronyms AVX, AVX2, and AVX-512 when explaining features or instructions exclusive to these technologies. The term x86-AVX is used as an umbrella expression for SIMD capabilities or resources common to all three instruction set extensions. The expressions x86-32 and x86-64 signify 32-bit and 64-bit processors or execution environments, while the term x86 applies to both. The remaining discussions in this and all subsequent chapters assume that you have a basic understanding of SIMD principles and are versed with AVX, AVX2, and AVX-512 programming using C++ SIMD intrinsic functions. If you feel your comprehension of these topics is lacking, you may want to review the relevant chapters in the first half of this book before proceeding.

## Data Types

Functions written in x86-64 assembly language can use a wide variety of data types. Most of these types originate from a small set of fundamental data types that are intrinsic to the x86 platform. A programmer can employ these fundamental data types to perform arithmetic and data manipulation operations using signed and unsigned integers, single-precision and double-precision floating-point values, text strings, or SIMD operands. The remainder of this section describes the x86 data types that are used in x86-64 assembly language functions.

© Daniel Kusswurm 2022
D. Kusswurm, *Modern Parallel Programming with C++ and Assembly Language*,
https://doi.org/10.1007/978-1-4842-7918-2_10

## Fundamental Data Types

A fundamental data type is an elementary unit of data that the processor manipulates during program execution. The x86-64 platform supports fundamental data type ranging from 8 bits (1 byte) to 128 bits (16 bytes). Table 10-1 shows these types along with typical usages.

**Table 10-1.** *Fundamental Data Types*

| Data Type | Size (Bits) | Typical Use |
| --- | --- | --- |
| Byte | 8 | Characters, small integers |
| Word | 16 | Characters, integers |
| Doubleword | 32 | Integers, single-precision floating-point |
| Quadword | 64 | Integers, double-precision floating-point, memory address |
| Double Quadword | 128 | Integers, packed integers, packed floating-point |

The fundamental data types shown in Table 10-1 are, unsurprisingly, sized using integer powers of two. The bits of a fundamental data type are numbered from right to left with *0* and *size - 1* used to identify the least and most significant bits, respectively. Fundamental data types larger than a single byte are stored in memory using little-endian byte ordering. Recall from the discussions in Chapter 1 that little-endian byte ordering stores the least significant byte of a multibyte value at the lowest memory address. Figure 10-1 illustrates the bit numbering and byte ordering schemes used by the fundamental data types shown in Table 10-1.

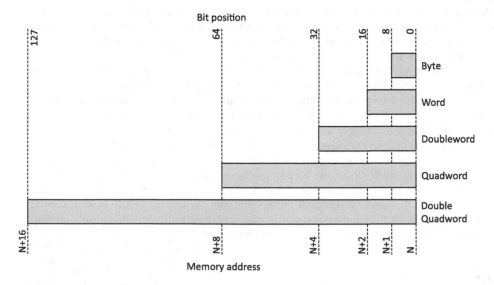

**Figure 10-1.** *Bit-numbering and byte-ordering schemes for x86-64 fundamental data types*

A fundamental data type is properly aligned in memory when its address is an integral multiple of its size in bytes. For example, a doubleword is properly aligned when it is stored at a memory address that is an integral multiple of four. Similarly, a quadword is properly aligned when it is stored at a memory address that is evenly divisible by eight. Unless enabled by the host operating system, an x86-64 processor does not require fundamental data types to be properly aligned in memory. However, it is standard programming practice to properly align all values whenever possible to avoid potential performance penalties that can occur when the processor accesses an improperly aligned data value in memory.

## Numerical Data Types

A numerical data type is an elementary scalar value such as an integer or floating-point number. All x86 numerical data types are represented using one of the fundamental data types discussed in the previous section. Table 10-2 shows valid x86-64 numerical data types and their corresponding C++ data types. The x86-64 instruction set supports arithmetic and logical operations using 8-, 16-, 32-, and 64-bit integers, both signed and unsigned. It also supports arithmetic calculations and data manipulation operations using scalar single-precision and double-precision floating-point values.

***Table 10-2.*** *X86-64 Numerical Data Types*

| Type | Size (bits) | C++ Type | <cstdint> |
|------|-------------|----------|-----------|
| Signed integer | 8 | char | int8_t |
| | 16 | short | int16_t |
| | 32 | int, long | int32_t |
| | 64 | long, long long | int64_t |
| Unsigned integer | 8 | unsigned char | uint8_t |
| | 16 | unsigned short | uint16_t |
| | 32 | unsigned int, unsigned long | uint32_t |
| | 64 | unsigned long, unsigned long long | uint64_t |
| Floating point | 32 | float | n/a |
| | 64 | double | n/a |

In Table 10-2, note that the size of a C++ long and unsigned long varies. 64-bit versions of Linux use 64-bit wide integers for both long and unsigned long, while 64-bit versions of Windows use 32-bit wide integers for these same types.

## SIMD Data Types

The X86 SIMD data types are described in Chapter 1. You can refer to this chapter if you need to refresh your understanding of these types.

## Strings

An x86 string is a contiguous block of bytes, words, doublewords, or quadwords. The x86-64 instruction set includes instructions that perform string compare, load, move, scan, and store operations. X86-64 string instructions also can be employed to carry out processing operations using arrays, bitmaps, or similar contiguous-block data structures. For example, the instruction movsb (Move Data from String to String) is often used to copy data bytes from one buffer to another, while the instruction stosb (Store String) can be used to set each element in an array to zero or some other constant value.

# Internal Architecture

From the perspective of an executing application program, the internal architecture of an x86-64 processor can be partitioned into the following sections:

- General-purpose registers

- Instruction pointer

- RFLAGS register

- Floating-point and SIMD registers

- MXCSR register

Figure 10-2 illustrates the logical architecture of an x86-64 processor from the perspective of an application (i.e., lowest privilege level) program. The remainder of this section will describe the components of this diagram in greater detail.

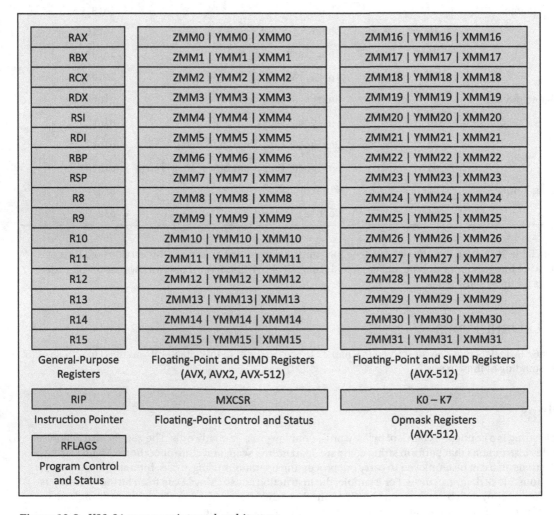

*Figure 10-2. X86-64 processor internal architecture*

# General-Purpose Registers

All x86-64 processors contain 16 64-bit wide general-purpose registers. Functions use these registers to perform integer arithmetic, bitwise logical operations, comparisons, address calculations, and data transfers. A function can also store a temporary result in a general-purpose register instead of saving it to memory. Figure 10-3 shows the complete set of x86-64 general-purpose registers along with their operand names.

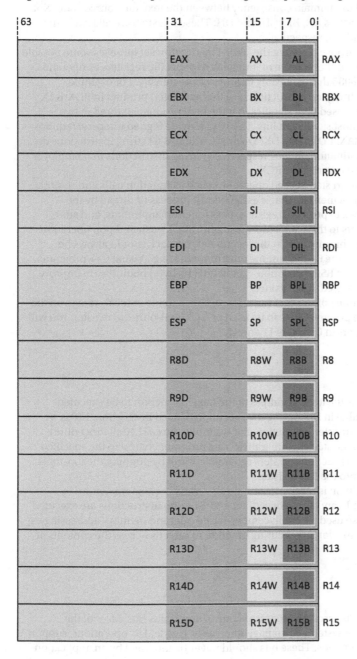

***Figure 10-3.*** *X86-64 general-purpose registers*

The low-order doubleword, word, and byte of each 64-bit general-purpose register are independently accessible and can be used to carry out operations using 32-, 16-, or 8-bit wide operands. For example, a function can use registers EAX, EBX, ECX, and EDX to perform 32-bit integer arithmetic in the low-order doublewords of RAX, RBX, RCX, and RDX, respectively. Similarly, registers AL, BL, CL, and DL can be used to perform 8-bit calculations in the low-order bytes. It should be noted that the Intel programming reference manuals use different names for some of the byte registers. This book uses the same register names as the Microsoft 64-bit macro assembler (MASM) to maintain consistency between the text and source code. Not shown in Figure 10-3 are the legacy byte registers AH, BH, CH, and DH. These registers are aliased to the high-order bytes of registers AX, BX, CX, and DX, respectively.

Despite their designation as general-purpose registers, the x86-64 instruction set imposes some notable restrictions on their use. Several instructions either require or implicitly use specific registers as operands. This is a legacy scheme inherited from the 8086 that ostensibly improves code density. For example, some variants of the imul (Multiply Signed Integers) instruction save the calculated product in RDX:RAX, EDX:EAX, DX:AX, or AX. The colon notation used here signifies that the final product is stored in two registers with the first register holding the most significant bits. The idiv (Divide Signed integers) requires the integer dividend to be loaded in RDX:RAX, EDX:EAX, DX:AX, or AX. The x86-64 string instructions use registers RSI and RDI for the source and destination buffers, respectively; string instructions that employ a repeat (or length) count must load this value into register RCX.

The processor uses register RSP to support stack-based operations such as function calls and returns. The stack itself is simply a contiguous block of memory that is assigned to a process or thread by the operating system. Programs can use the stack to preserve registers, pass function arguments, and store temporary results. Register RSP always points to the stack's top-most item. Stack push and pop operations are performed using 64-bit wide operands. This means that the location of the stack should always be aligned on a quadword (8-byte) boundary. Some 64-bit runtime environments (e.g., Visual C++ programs running on Windows) align stack memory and RSP to a double quadword (16-byte) boundary to improve performance when loading or storing stack-based SIMD values.

Register RBP is frequently used as a frame pointer that can reference data items or local storage on the stack. If a function does not require a frame pointer, RBP can be used as a general-purpose register. You will learn more about the stack and frame pointers in Chapters 11 and 12.

## Instruction Pointer

The instruction pointer register RIP contains the logical address of the next instruction to be executed. The processor automatically updates the value in RIP during the execution of each instruction. RIP is also updated during execution of a control-transfer instruction. For example, the call (Call Procedure) instruction pushes the contents of RIP onto the stack before transferring program control to the specified address. The ret (Return from Procedure) instruction transfers program control by popping the top-most eight bytes off the stack and loading them into the RIP register.

The jmp (Jump) and jcc (Jump if Condition is Met) instructions also transfer program control by modifying the contents of RIP. Unlike the call and ret instructions, x86-64 jump instructions are executed independent of the stack. Register RIP is also used for displacement-based operand memory addressing as explained later in this chapter. It is not possible for an executing function to directly access the contents of register RIP.

## RFLAGS Register

RFLAGS is a 64-bit wide register that contains assorted processor control and status bits. Most of the control bits in RFLAGS are used by operating systems to manage interrupts, restrict I/O operations, support program debugging, and handle virtual operations. These bits should never be modified by an application program. The status bits (or flags) in RFLAGS report results of arithmetic, bitwise logical, and compare operations. Table 10-3 summarizes the purpose of each control and status bit in the RFLAGS register.

*Table 10-3.* RFLAGS Register

| Bit Position | Name | RFLAGS Symbol | Use |
| --- | --- | --- | --- |
| 0 | Carry Flag | CF | Status |
| 1 | Reserved | | 1 |
| 2 | Parity Flag | PF | Status |
| 3 | Reserved | | 0 |
| 4 | Auxiliary Carry Flag | AF | Status |
| 5 | Reserved | | 0 |
| 6 | Zero Flag | ZF | Status |
| 7 | Sign Flag | SF | Status |
| 8 | Trap Flag | TF | System |
| 9 | Interrupt Enable Flag | IF | System |
| 10 | Direction Flag | DF | Control |
| 11 | Overflow Flag | OF | Status |
| 12 | I/O Privilege Level Bit 0 | IOPL | System |
| 13 | I/O Privilege Level Bit 1 | IOPL | System |
| 14 | Nested Task | NT | System |
| 15 | Reserved | | 0 |
| 16 | Resume Flag | RF | System |
| 17 | Virtual 8086 Mode | VM | System |
| 18 | Alignment Check | AC | System |
| 19 | Virtual Interrupt Flag | VIF | System |
| 20 | Virtual Interrupt Pending | VIP | System |
| 21 | ID Flag | ID | System |
| 22–63 | Reserved | | 0 |

For application programs, the most important status bits in RFLAGS are the following flags: carry flag (RFLAGS.CF), overflow flag (RFLAGS.OF), parity flag (RFLAGS.PF), sign flag (RFLAGS.SF), and zero flag (RFLAGS.ZF). Some arithmetic instructions use the carry flag to signify an overflow condition when performing unsigned integer arithmetic. It is also used by some rotate and shift instructions. The overflow flag signals that the result of a signed integer operation is too small or too large. The processor sets the parity flag to indicate whether the least-significant byte of an arithmetic, compare, or logical operation contains an even number of "1" bits (parity bits are used by some communication protocols to detect transmission errors). The sign and zero flags are set by arithmetic and logical instructions to signify a negative, zero, or positive result.

RFLAGS contains a control bit called the direction flag (RFLAGS.DF) that is used by x86 string instructions. An application program can set or clear the direction flag, which defines the auto increment direction (0 = low to high addresses, 1 = high to low addresses) of the RDI and RSI registers during execution of a string instruction. Reserved bits in RFLAGS should never be modified, and no assumptions should ever be made regarding the state of any reserved bit.

## Floating-Point and SIMD Registers

X86-64 processors that support AVX and AVX2 include 16 256-bit wide registers named YMM0–YMM15. The low-order 128 bits of each YMM register is aliased to a 128-bit wide XMM register as shown in Figure 10-4. The YMM and XMM registers can be used as operands with most AVX and AVX2 instructions to carry out either packed integer or packed floating-point operations.

| Bit position | | |
|---|---|---|
| 255 | 128 127 | 0 |
| | XMM0 | YMM0 |
| | XMM1 | YMM1 |
| | XMM2 | YMM2 |
| | XMM3 | YMM3 |
| | XMM4 | YMM4 |
| | XMM5 | YMM5 |
| | XMM6 | YMM6 |
| | XMM7 | YMM7 |
| | XMM8 | YMM8 |
| | XMM9 | YMM9 |
| | XMM10 | YMM10 |
| | XMM11 | YMM11 |
| | XMM12 | YMM12 |
| | XMM13 | YMM13 |
| | XMM14 | YMM14 |
| | XMM15 | YMM15 |

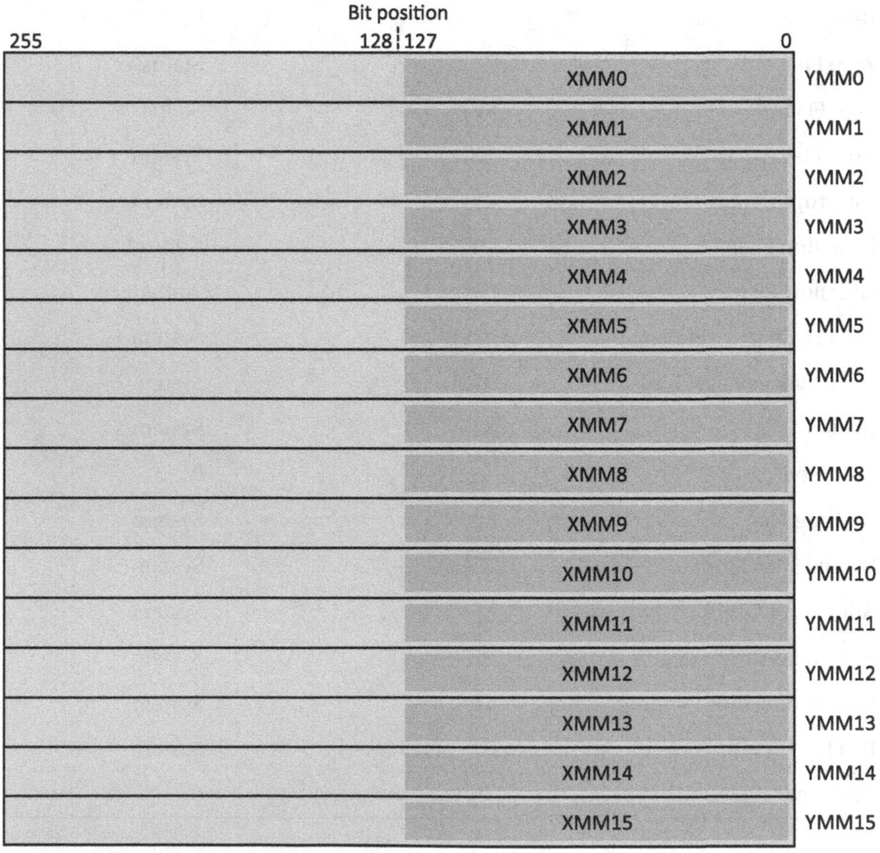

*Figure 10-4. AVX/AVX2 register set*

The XMM register set also supports scalar floating-point operations including basic arithmetic, comparisons, and type conversions. The processor uses the low-order 32 bits of an XMM register to perform scalar single-precision floating-point operations as illustrated in Figure 10-5. Similarly, the processor uses the low-order 64 bits of an XMM register to carry out scalar double-precision floating-point operations.

When performing scalar floating-point operations, the processor does not directly manipulate the high-order 96 bits (single precision) or 64 bits (double precision) of an XMM register. However, some x86-AVX scalar floating-point instructions modify these bits in a destination operand. You will learn more about this in Chapter 12.

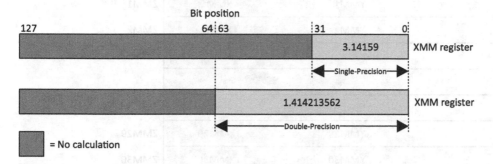

***Figure 10-5.*** *Scalar floating-point values in an XMM register*

Not shown in Figure 10-2 is the legacy x87 floating-point unit (FPU). An x86-64 program can still use the x87 FPU to perform scalar floating-point arithmetic. However, the x87 FPU is normally not used in x86-64 programs since it is more efficient code-wise to use the XMM register set to carry out scalar floating-point arithmetic.

AVX-512 extends the width of each YMM register from 256 bits to 512 bits. The 512-bit wide registers are named ZMM0–ZMM15. AVX-512 also adds 16 new SIMD registers named ZMM16–ZMM31. These new registers include aliased 256-bit wide YMM and 128-bit wide XMM registers as illustrated in Figure 10-6. Also shown in Figure 10-6 are eight opmask registers. AVX-512 instructions use these registers to perform merge masking and zero masking. The opmask registers are also employed to store the results of AVX-512 SIMD compare operations. You will learn more about the opmask registers in Chapters 17 and 18.

Bit position

| 511 | 256 | 255 | 128 | 127 | 0 | |
|---|---|---|---|---|---|---|
| | | YMM0 | | XMM0 | | ZMM0 |
| | | YMM1 | | XMM1 | | ZMM1 |
| | | YMM2 | | XMM2 | | ZMM2 |
| | | | | | | . |
| | | | | | | . |
| | | | | | | . |
| | | YMM29 | | XMM29 | | ZMM29 |
| | | YMM30 | | XMM30 | | ZMM30 |
| | | YMM31 | | XMM31 | | ZMM31 |

AVX-512 SIMD Register Set

Bit position

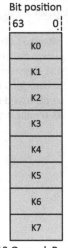

| 63 | 0 |
|---|---|
| K0 | |
| K1 | |
| K2 | |
| K3 | |
| K4 | |
| K5 | |
| K6 | |
| K7 | |

AVX-512 Opmask Register Set

***Figure 10-6.*** *AVX-512 register sets*

## MXCSR Register

An x86 processor includes a 32-bit control-status register named MXCSR. This register contains a series of control flags that enable a program to configure options for floating-point operations and exceptions. It also includes a set of status flags that a program can test to detect floating-point error conditions. Table 10-4 describes the purpose of each MXCSR bit field.

*Table 10-4.* *MXCSR Register Bit Fields*

| Bits | Symbol | Name | Description |
|------|--------|------|-------------|
| 0 | IE | Invalid operation flag | Floating-point invalid operation error flag |
| 1 | DE | Denormal flag | Floating-point denormal error flag |
| 2 | ZE | Divide-by-zero flag | Floating-point division-by-zero error flag |
| 3 | OE | Overflow flag | Floating-point overflow error flag |
| 4 | UE | Underflow flag | Floating-point underflow error flag |
| 5 | PE | Precision flag | Floating-point precision error flag |
| 6 | DAZ | Denormals are zero | Enables automatic conversion of a denormal to zero |
| 7 | IM | Invalid operation mask | Floating-point invalid operation error exception mask |
| 8 | DM | Denormal mask | Floating-point denormal error exception mask |
| 9 | ZM | Divide-by-zero mask | Floating-point divide-by-zero error exception mask |
| 10 | OM | Overflow mask | Floating-point overflow error exception mask |
| 11 | UM | Underflow mask | Floating-point underflow error exception mask |
| 12 | PM | Precision mask | Floating-point precision error exception mask |
| 13–14 | RC | Rounding control | Specifies the method for rounding floating-point results; valid options include round to nearest (00b), round down toward $-\infty$ (01b), round up toward $+\infty$ (10b), and round toward zero (11b) |
| 15 | FZ | Flush to zero | Forces a zero result if the underflow exception is masked and a floating-point underflow error occurs |
| 16–31 | --- | Reserved | Reserved for future use |

Application programs normally do not directly modify the floating-point exception mask bits in MXCSR. However, most C++ runtime environments provide a library function that allows an application program to designate a callback function that gets invoked whenever a floating-point exception occurs. Application programs can modify the MXCSR's rounding control bits, and you will learn how to do this in Chapter 12.

# Instruction Operands

Nearly all x86-64 instructions use operands, which designate the specific values that an instruction will act upon. Most instructions require one or more source operands along with a single destination operand. Most instructions also require the programmer to explicitly specify the source and destination operands. There are, however, several instructions where register operands are either implicitly specified or required by an instruction as discussed earlier in this chapter.

There are three basic types of operands: immediate, register, and memory. An immediate operand is a constant value that is explicitly coded. A register operand is the value in a general-purpose or SIMD register. A memory operand specifies a location in memory, which can contain any of the previously described data types. An instruction can specify a location in memory for either the source or destination operand but not both. Table 10-5 contains several examples of instructions that employ various x86-64 operand types.

*Table 10-5. Examples of X86-64 Instructions and Operands*

| Type | Example | Analogous C++ Statement |
|------|---------|------------------------|
| Immediate | mov rax,42 | rax = 42 |
| | imul r12,-47 | r12 *= -47 |
| | shl r15,8 | r15 <<= 8 |
| | xor ecx,80000000h | ecx ^= 0x80000000 |
| | sub r9b,14 | r9b -= 14 |
| Register | mov rax,rbx | rax = rbx |
| | add rbx,r10 | rbx += r10 |
| | mul rbx | rdx:rax = rax * rbx |
| | and r8w,0ff00h | r8w &= 0xff00 |
| Memory | mov rax,[r13] | rax = *r13 |
| | or rcx,[rbx+rsi*8] | rcx \|= *(rbx+rsi*8) |
| | mov qword ptr [r8],17 | *(long long*)r8 = 17 |
| | shl word ptr [r12],2 | *(short*)r12 <<= 2 |

The mul rbx (Multiply Unsigned Integers) instruction that is shown in Table 10-5 is an example of an instruction that uses an implicit operand. In this example, implicit register RAX and explicit register RBX are used as the source operands, and implicit register pair RDX:RAX is the destination operand. The multiplicative product's high-order and low-order quadwords are stored in RDX and RAX, respectively.

The qword ptr text that is used in Table 10-5's penultimate example is an assembler operator that acts like a C++ cast operator. In this instruction, the value 17 is subtracted from the 64-bit value whose memory location is specified by the contents of register R8. Without the qword ptr operator, the assembly language statement is ambiguous since the assembler cannot ascertain the size of the operand pointed to by R8; the destination operand in memory could also be an 8-, 16-, or 32-bit value. The final example in Table 10-5 uses the word ptr operator in a similar manner. You will learn more about assembler operators and directives in subsequent chapters.

# Memory Addressing

An x86 instruction requires up to four separate components to specify the location of an operand in memory. The four components include a constant displacement value, a base register, an index register, and a scale factor. Using these components, the processor calculates an effective address for a memory operand as follows:

EffectiveAddress = BaseReg + IndexReg * ScaleFactor + Disp

The base register (BaseReg) can be any general-purpose register. The index register (IndexReg) can be any general-purpose register except RSP. Valid scale factor (ScaleFactor) values include 2, 4, and 8. Finally, the displacement (Disp) is an 8-, 16-, or 32-bit signed offset that is encoded within the instruction. Table 10-6 illustrates x86-64 memory addressing using different forms of the mov (Move) instruction. In these examples, register RAX (the destination operand) is loaded with the quadword value that is specified by the source operand. Note that it is not necessary for an instruction to explicitly specify a complete set of effective address components. For example, a default value of zero is used for the displacement if an explicit value is not specified. The final size of an effective address calculation is always 64 bits.

**Table 10-6.** *Memory Operand Addressing*

| Addressing Form | Example |
| --- | --- |
| RIP + Disp | mov rax,[Val] |
| BaseReg | mov rax,[rbx] |
| BaseReg + Disp | mov rax,[rbx+16] |
| IndexReg * SF + Disp | mov rax,[r15*8+48] |
| BaseReg + IndexReg | mov rax,[rbx+r15] |
| BaseReg + IndexReg + Disp | mov rax,[rbx+r15+32] |
| BaseReg + IndexReg * SF | mov rax,[rbx+r15*8] |
| BaseReg + IndexReg * SF + Disp | mov rax,[rbx+r15*8+64] |

The memory addressing forms shown in Table 10-6 facilitate the referencing of simple variables, elements in an array, or members in a data structure. For example, the simple displacement form is often used to access a single global or static value. The base register form is analogous to a C++ pointer and is used to indirectly reference a single value. Individual fields within a data structure can be retrieved using a base register and a displacement. The index register forms are useful for accessing a specific element in an array or matrix. Scale factors can reduce the amount code needed to access elements in an array or matrix. Elements in more elaborate data structures can be referenced using a base register together with an index register, scale factor, and displacement.

The mov rax,[Val] instruction that's shown in the first row of Table 10-6 is an example of RIP-relative (or instruction pointer relative) addressing. With RIP-relative addressing, the processor calculates an effective address using the contents of the RIP register and a signed 32-bit displacement value that is encoded within the instruction. Figure 10-7 illustrates this calculation in greater detail. Note the little-endian ordering of the displacement value that's embedded in the mov rax,[Val] instruction. RIP-relative addressing allows the processor to reference global or static operands using a 32-bit displacement instead of a 64-bit displacement, which reduces code space. It also facilitates position-independent code.

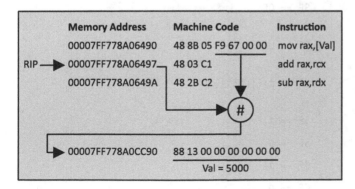

**Figure 10-7.** *RIP-relative effective address calculation*

One minor constraint of RIP-relative addressing is that the target operand must reside with a ± 2GB address window of the value in RIP. For most programs, this limitation is rarely a concern. The calculation of a RIP-relative displacement value is usually determined automatically by the assembler or linker. This means that you can use a mov rax,[Val] or similar instruction without having to worry about the details of the displacement value calculation.

# Condition Codes

Most arithmetic and logical instructions update one or more of the status flags in the RFLAGS register. As discussed earlier in this chapter, the status flags provide additional information about the results of an operation. The jcc, cmovcc (Conditional Move), and setcc (Set Byte on Condition) instructions use what are called condition codes to test the status flags either individually or logically combined. Table 10-7 lists the condition codes, mnemonic suffixes, and the corresponding RFLAGS tested by these instructions.

***Table 10-7.*** *Condition Codes, Mnemonic Suffixes, and Test Conditions*

| Condition Code | Mnemonic Suffix | RFLAGS Test Condition |
|---|---|---|
| Above<br>Neither below nor equal | A<br>NBE | `CF == 0 && ZF == 0` |
| Above or equal<br>Not below | AE<br>NB | `CF == 0` |
| Below<br>Neither above nor equal | B<br>NAE | `CF == 1` |
| Below or equal<br>Not above | BE<br>NA | `CF == 1 \|\| ZF == 1` |
| Equal<br>Zero | E<br>Z | `ZF == 1` |
| Not equal<br>Not zero | NE<br>NZ | `ZF == 0` |
| Greater<br>Neither less nor equal | G<br>NLE | `ZF == 0 && SF == OF` |
| Greater or equal<br>Not less | GE<br>NL | `SF == OF` |
| Less<br>Neither greater nor equal | L<br>NGE | `SF != OF` |
| Less or equal<br>Not greater | LE<br>NG | `ZF == 1 \|\| SF != OF` |
| Sign | S | `SF == 1` |
| Not sign | NS | `SF == 0` |
| Carry | C | `CF == 1` |
| Not carry | NC | `CF == 0` |

*(continued)*

*Table 10-7.* (*continued*)

| Condition Code | Mnemonic Suffix | RFLAGS Test Condition |
|---|---|---|
| Overflow | O | OF == 1 |
| Not overflow | NO | OF == 0 |
| Parity | P | PF == 1 |
| Parity even | PE | |
| Not parity | NP | PF == 0 |
| Parity odd | PO | |

Note that Table 10-7 shows alternate forms for most mnemonic suffixes. These are defined to provide algorithmic flexibility or improve program readability. When using a conditional instruction such as jcc in source code, condition codes containing the words "above" and "below" are employed for unsigned integer operands, while the words "greater" and "less" are used for signed integer operands. If Table 10-7 seems a little confusing or abstract, don't worry. You will see a plethora of condition code examples in the assembly language programming chapters of this book.

# Summary

Here are the key learning points for Chapter 10:

- The fundamental data types of the x86-64 platform include bytes, words, doublewords, quadwords, and double quadwords. Programming language primitive data types such as characters, text strings, integers, and floating-point values are derived from the fundamental data types.

- An x86-64 processor includes 16 64-bit general-purpose registers that are used to perform arithmetic, logical, and data transfer operations using 8-bit, 16-bit, 32-bit, and 64-bit operands.

- An x86-64 processor also includes an instruction pointer (RIP) and control and status (RFLAGS) register. The former points to the next executable instruction; the latter contains processor control bits and status flags. Most arithmetic and logical instructions update one or more of the status flags in RFLAGS. These flags can be tested to alter program flow or conditionally assign values to variables.

- X86-64 processors that support AVX/AVX2 include 16 256-bit wide registers named YMM0–YMM15. The low-order 128 bits of each YMM register can be referenced as XMM0–XMM15.

- X86-64 processors that support AVX-512 include 32 512-bit wide registers named ZMM0–ZMM31. The low-order 256 bits/128 bits of each ZMM register is aliased to a corresponding YMM/XMM register. AVX-512-compliant processors also include eight opmask registers that facilitate merge masking and zero masking.

- A function can use the ZMM, YMM, and XMM registers to carry out SIMD operations using packed integers or packed floating-point values. The XMM registers can also be used to perform scalar floating-point arithmetic using single-precision or double-precision values.

- The MXCSR register contains control bits that select options for floating-point operations and exceptions. This register also contains status bits that report floating-point error conditions.

- An operand in memory can be referenced using a variety of addressing modes that include one or more of the following components: fixed displacement, base register, index register, and/or scale factor.

- Most x86-64 assembly language instructions can be used with the following explicit operand types: immediate, register, and memory. Some instructions employ implicit registers as their operands.

■ ■ ■

# Core Assembly Language Programming: Part 1

Chapter 11 introduces core x86-64 assembly language programming and basic instruction use. In this chapter, you will learn how to code simple x86-64 assembly language functions that are callable from C++. You will also learn about the semantics and syntax of an x86-64 assembly language source code file. The purpose of this chapter and the next one is to provide the necessary foundation that will enable you to code x86-AVX functions using x86-64 assembly language.

The content of Chapter 11 is organized as follows: The first section contains source code examples that explain how to perform simple integer arithmetic. These source code examples also illustrate passing argument values to and return values from an assembly language function. The second section highlights important x86-64 assembly language programming concepts including memory addressing modes, for-loops, and condition codes. The final section describes the use of several x86-64 string instructions.

The source code examples discussed in this chapter are intended to elucidate proper use of the x86-64 instruction set and basic assembly language programming techniques. The assembly language code is straightforward, but not necessarily optimal since understanding optimized assembly language code can be challenging especially for beginners. The source code presented in later chapters places more emphasis on efficient x86-64 assembly language coding techniques.

Some of the x86-64 assembly language source code examples published in this book are adaptations of those previously published in *Modern X86 Assembly Language Programming, Second Edition*. The reworked source code examples and accompanying explanations are designed to accentuate essential x86-64 assembly language programming topics that one must comprehend before attempting to code x86-AVX assembly language functions.

The x86 instruction set is lengthy and intricate, which is not surprising given its extensive history. This means is that when developing x86 assembly language code, you should always verify proper instruction usage using the programming reference manuals published by AMD or Intel. These manuals contain comprehensive information for every x86 processor instruction including detailed operational descriptions, lists of valid operands, affected status flags, and potential exceptions. A list of these manual can be found in Appendix B.

## Integer Arithmetic

In this section, you will learn the basics of x86-64 assembly language programming. It begins with a simple program that demonstrates integer addition and subtraction. This is followed by a source code example that illustrates integer multiplication. The final source code example in this section explains how to perform integer division.

© Daniel Kusswurm 2022
D. Kusswurm, *Modern Parallel Programming with C++ and Assembly Language*,
https://doi.org/10.1007/978-1-4842-7918-2_11

As mentioned in the Introduction, the x86-64 assembly language source code examples published in this book were created using Microsoft's Visual C++ compiler and Macro Assembler (MASM), which are included with Visual Studio. Appendix A contains more information regarding the use of these development tools. This appendix also includes instructions for downloading the example source code. Depending on your personal preference, you may want to download and set up the source code first before proceeding with the remainder of this chapter.

---

■ **Note**   Each source code example in this and subsequent chapters employs a single listing that incorporates all relevant files. This is done to minimize the number of listing references in the main text. The actual source code uses separate files for the C++ (.h, .cpp) and assembly language (.asm) code. The assembly language source code examples also use the file and function naming conventions that were described in Chapter 1.

---

## Addition and Subtraction

The first source code example is named Ch11_01. This example demonstrates how to use the x86-64 assembly language instructions add (Integer Add) and sub (Integer Subtract). It also illustrates some basic assembly language programming concepts including argument passing, returning values, and how to use a few MASM assembler directives. Listing 11-1 shows the source code for example Ch11_01.

*Listing 11-1.*  Example Ch11_01

```
//--------------------------------------------------
//              Ch11_01.h
//--------------------------------------------------

#pragma once

// Ch11_01_misc.cpp
extern void DisplayResultsAddI32(int a, int b, int c, int d);
extern void DisplayResultsSubI64(long long a, long long b, long long c, long long d);

// Ch11_01_fasm.asm
extern "C" int AddI32_A(int a, int b, int c);
extern "C" long long SubI64_A(long long a, long long b, long long c);

//--------------------------------------------------
//              Ch11_01_misc.cpp
//--------------------------------------------------

#include <iostream>
#include "Ch11_01.h"

void DisplayResultsAddI32(int a, int b, int c, int d)
{
    const char nl = '\n';
    std::cout << "Results for AddI32_A()\n";
    std::cout << "a = " << a << nl;
    std::cout << "b = " << b << nl;
```

```cpp
    std::cout << "c = " << c << nl;
    std::cout << "d = " << d << nl;
    std::cout << nl;
}

void DisplayResultsSubI64(long long a, long long b, long long c, long long d)
{
    const char nl = '\n';
    std::cout << "Results for SubI64_A()\n";
    std::cout << "a = " << a << nl;
    std::cout << "b = " << b << nl;
    std::cout << "c = " << c << nl;
    std::cout << "d = " << d << nl;
    std::cout << nl;
}

//---------------------------------------------------
//                   Ch11_01.cpp
//---------------------------------------------------

#include <iostream>
#include "Ch11_01.h"

static void AddI32(void);
static void SubI64(void);

int main()
{
    AddI32();
    SubI64();
    return 0;
}

static void AddI32(void)
{
    int a = 10;
    int b = 20;
    int c = 30;
    int d = AddI32_A(a, b, c);

    DisplayResultsAddI32(a, b, c, d);
}

static void SubI64(void)
{
    long long a = 10;
    long long b = 20;
    long long c = 30;
    long long d = SubI64_A(a, b, c);

    DisplayResultsSubI64(a, b, c, d);
}
```

```
;-----------------------------------------------
;                 Ch11_01_fasm.asm
;-----------------------------------------------

;---------------------------------------------------------------------
; extern "C" int AddI32_A(int a, int b, int c);
;---------------------------------------------------------------------

        .code
AddI32_A proc

; Calculate a + b + c
        add ecx,edx                     ;ecx = a + b
        add ecx,r8d                     ;ecx = a + b + c
        mov eax,ecx                     ;eax = final result

        ret                             ;return to caller
AddI32_A endp

;---------------------------------------------------------------------
; extern "C" long long SubI64_A(long long a, long long b, long long c);
;---------------------------------------------------------------------

SubI64_A proc

; Calculate a - b - c
        sub rcx,rdx                     ;rcx = a - b
        sub rcx,r8                      ;rcx = a - b - c
        mov rax,rcx                     ;rax = final result

        ret                             ;return to caller
SubI64_A endp
        end
```

Listing 11-1 begins with the file Ch11_01.h, which contains the requisite function declarations for this example. Note that the declaration statements for x86-64 assembly language functions AddI32_A() and SubI64_A() include a "C" modifier. This modifier instructs the C++ compiler to use C-style naming for these functions instead of C++ decorated names (a C++ decorated name includes extra characters that facilitate function overloading). Note that it is possible to call an assembly language function that uses a C++ decorated name, but this is normally not done due to the extra effort required to ascertain the decorated name. The next file in Listing 11-1, Ch11_01_misc.cpp, incorporates functions that stream this example's results to std::cout. This is followed by the file Ch11_01.cpp, which contains the function main(). File Ch11_01.cpp also includes two function definitions named AddI32() and SubI64().

The C++ function AddI32() performs test case initialization for the assembly language function AddI32_A(). This function requires three argument values of type int. Function AddI32_A() calculates a + b + c and returns this value as an int. Like many programming languages, Visual C++ uses a combination of processor registers and the stack to pass argument values to a function. In the current example, the C++ compiler generates code that loads a, b, and c into registers ECX, EDX, and R8D, respectively, prior to calling function AddI32_A(). The C++ function SubI64() performs test case initialization for the assembly language function SubI64_A(), which calculates a - b - c. Note that this function uses argument values of type long long instead of int. Argument values a, b, and c are passed to SubI64_A() via registers RCX, RDX, and R8, respectively. The C++ compiler's use of registers RCX, RDX, and R8 (or ECX, EDX, and R8D) is defined in a binary protocol known as a calling convention. You will learn more about this later.

The final file in Listing 11-1 is Ch11_01_fasm.asm. The first thing to notice in this file are the top-most lines that begin with a semicolon. These are comment lines. MASM treats any text that follows a semicolon as comment text. The .code statement that follows is a MASM directive that defines the start of an assembly language code section. A MASM directive is a statement that instructs the assembler how to perform an action during assembly of the source code. You will learn how to use additional directives throughout this book.

The statement AddI32_A proc defines the start of function AddI32_A(). If you scan forward a few lines, you will see the statement AddI32_A endp. This line signifies the end of function AddI32_A(). The first executable instruction of AddI32_A(), add ecx,edx, calculates ecx += edx (or a + b). Recall that argument values a and b were passed to AddI32_A() via registers ECX and EDX, respectively. Following execution of this instruction, register ECX contains the value a + b, and register EDX contains b. The next instruction, add ecx,r8d, adds argument value c to the contents of register ECX, which yields the sum a + b + c. An x86-64 assembly language function must return a single 32-bit integer (or C++ int) value to its calling function in register EAX. In function AddI32_A(), the mov eax,ecx (Move) instruction copies the value in ECX (a + b + c) to EAX. The mov instruction does not modify the contents of source operand ECX. The final ret (Return from Procedure) instruction transfers program control back to the calling function, which is main() in the current example.

The layout of assembly language SubI64_A() is similar to AddI32_A() but uses long long integers to illustrate the passing of 64-bit argument values. It also performs subtraction instead of addition. The first instruction of this function, sub rcx,rdx, calculates a - b and saves this result in register RCX. Recall that long long argument values a and b were passed to SubI64_A() in registers RCX and RDX, respectively. The next instruction, sub rcx,r8, calculates a - b - c. This is followed by a mov rax,rcx instruction that copies the contents to RCX into RAX. An x86-64 assembly language function must use register RAX to return a single 64-bit integer (or C++ long long) value. The ret instruction transfers control back to the calling function. The final statement, end, is a required assembler directive that indicates the completion of statements for the assembly language file Ch11_01_fasm.asm. The assembler ignores any text that appears after the end directive. Here are the results for source code example Ch11_01:

```
Results for AddI32_A()
a = 10
b = 20
c = 30
d = 60

Results for SubI64_A()
a = 10
b = 20
c = 30
d = -40
```

# Multiplication

Listing 11-2 shows the source code for example Ch11_02. This example illustrates how to perform integer multiplication in an x86-64 assembly language function.

*Listing 11-2.* Example Ch11_02

```
//-------------------------------------------------
//                  Ch11_02.h
//-------------------------------------------------

#pragma once
#include <cstdint>

// Ch11_02_misc.cpp
extern void DisplayResultsMulI32(int32_t a, int32_t b, int32_t c, int32_t d);
extern void DisplayResultsMulU64(uint64_t a, uint64_t b, uint64_t c, uint64_t d);

// Ch11_02_fasm.asm
extern "C" int32_t MulI32_A(int32_t a, int32_t b, int32_t c);
extern "C" uint64_t MulU64_A(uint64_t a, uint64_t b, uint64_t c);

//-------------------------------------------------
//                  Ch11_02_misc.cpp
//-------------------------------------------------

#include <iostream>
#include "Ch11_02.h"

void DisplayResultsMulI32(int32_t a, int32_t b, int32_t c, int32_t d)
{
    const char nl = '\n';
    std::cout << "Results for MulI32_A()\n";
    std::cout << "a = " << a << nl;
    std::cout << "b = " << b << nl;
    std::cout << "c = " << c << nl;
    std::cout << "d = " << d << nl;
    std::cout << nl;
}

void DisplayResultsMulU64(uint64_t a, uint64_t b, uint64_t c, uint64_t d)
{
    const char nl = '\n';
    std::cout << "Results for MulU64_A()\n";
    std::cout << "a = " << a << nl;
    std::cout << "b = " << b << nl;
    std::cout << "c = " << c << nl;
    std::cout << "d = " << d << nl;
    std::cout << nl;
}

//-------------------------------------------------
//                  Ch11_02.cpp
//-------------------------------------------------

#include <iostream>
#include <cstdint>
```

```c
#include "Ch11_02.h"

static void MulI32(void);
static void MulU64(void);

int main()
{
    MulI32();
    MulU64();
    return 0;
}

static void MulI32(void)
{
    int32_t a = 10;
    int32_t b = -20;
    int32_t c = 30;
    int32_t d = MulI32_A(a, b, c);

    DisplayResultsMulI32(a, b, c, d);
}

static void MulU64(void)
{
    uint64_t a = 10;
    uint64_t b = 20;
    uint64_t c = 1000000000;
    uint64_t d = MulU64_A(a, b, c);

    DisplayResultsMulU64(a, b, c, d);
}
```

```asm
;-------------------------------------------------
;                 Ch11_02_fasm.asm
;-------------------------------------------------

;------------------------------------------------------------------------
; extern "C" int32_t MulI32_A(int32_t a, int32_t b, int32_t c);
;------------------------------------------------------------------------

        .code
MulI32_A proc

; Calculate a * b * c * 42
        imul ecx,edx                    ;ecx = a * b
        imul eax,r8d,42                 ;eax = c * 42
        imul eax,ecx                    ;eax = a * b * c * 42

        ret                             ;return to caller
MulI32_A endp
```

```
;-------------------------------------------------------------------------
; extern "C" uint64_t MulU64_A(uint64_t a, uint64_t b, uint64_t c);
;-------------------------------------------------------------------------

MulU64_A proc

; Calculate a * b * c * 42
        mov  rax,rcx                 ;rax = a
        mul  rdx                     ;rdx:rax = a * b
        mov  r10,rax                 ;r10 = a * b (low-order 64-bits)

        mov  rax,42                  ;rax = 42
        mul  r8                      ;rdx:rax = c * 42
        mul  r10                     ;rdx:rax = a * b * c * 42

        ret                          ;return to caller
MulU64_A endp
        end
```

The first file in Listing 11-2, Ch11_02.h, contains the function declarations for this example. Unlike the previous example, these declarations use the standard integer types that are declared in the C++ header file <cstdint> instead of int and unsigned long long. Some assembly language programmers prefer to use fixed-sized integer types for assembly language function declarations since it accentuates the exact size and type of the argument. The next file in Listing 11-2, Ch11_02_misc.cpp, contains two functions that stream results to std::cout. The file Ch11_02.cpp includes two functions named MulI32() and MulU64(). These functions perform test case initialization for 32-bit signed and 64-bit unsigned integer multiplication.

File Ch11_02_fasm.asm begins with the definition of function MulI32_A(), which calculates a * b * c * 42. Like the previous example, argument values a, b, and c are passed to MulI32_A() in registers ECX, EDX, and R8D. The first instruction of this function, imul ecx,edx (Multiply Signed Integers), calculates a * b and saves the low-order 32 bits of the product in register ECX. The next instruction, imul eax,r8d,42, calculates c * 42 and saves the low-order 32 bits of the product in register EAX. The ensuing imul eax,ecx instruction completes the calculation of a * b * c * 42. Since register EAX already has the final return value, no other instructions are necessary. The final instruction of MulI32_A(), ret, transfers program control back to the calling function.

The next function in Ch11_02_fasm.asm is named MulU64_A(). This function calculates a * b * c * 42 using unsigned 64-bit integers. The first instruction of MulU64_A(), mov rax,rcx, copies argument value a into register RAX. This copy operation is performed to prepare for the upcoming mul instruction. The next instruction, mul rdx (Multiply Unsigned Integers), calculates a * b. More specifically, this instruction performs 64-bit unsigned integer multiplication using the values in registers RAX and RDX; it then saves the complete 128-bit product in register pair RDX:RAX. It is important to note that the mul instruction can only specify a single source operand, either a register or a memory location. The second (implicit) source operand is always register RAX, EAX, AX, or AL when performing 64-, 32-, 16-, or 8-bit unsigned integer multiplication (the assembler automatically determines the width of the multiplication using the size of the mul instruction operand).

The next instruction, mov r10,rax, copies the low-order 64 bits of the 128-bit product a * b into register R10. This is followed by a mov rax,42 that loads 42 into register RAX. The ensuing instruction, mul r8, calculates c * 42, and the instruction mul r10 completes the calculation of a * b * c * 42.

Note again that the required return value is already in register RAX. Function Mul64U_A() concludes with a ret instruction. Here are the results for source code example Ch11_02:

---

```
Results for MulI32_A()
a = 10
b = -20
c = 30
d = -252000

Results for MulU64_A()
a = 10
b = 20
c = 1000000000
d = 8400000000000
```

---

# Division

The next example, named Ch11_03, explains how to perform integer division. This example also demonstrates how to reference a memory location in an assembly language function and the use of several bitwise logical instructions. Listing 11-3 shows the source code for example Ch11_03.

***Listing 11-3.*** Example Ch11_03

```cpp
//--------------------------------------------------
//              Ch11_03.h
//--------------------------------------------------

#pragma once
#include <cstdint>

// Ch11_03_misc.cpp
extern void DisplayResultsDivI32(size_t test_id, int32_t rc, int32_t a,
int32_t b, int32_t quo, int32_t rem);
extern void DisplayResultsDivU64(size_t test_id, int32_t rc, uint64_t a,
uint64_t b, uint64_t quo, uint64_t rem);

// Ch11_03_fasm.asm
extern "C" int32_t DivI32_A(int32_t a, int32_t b, int32_t* quo, int32_t* rem);
extern "C" int32_t DivU64_A(uint64_t a, uint64_t b, uint64_t* quo, uint64_t* rem);

//--------------------------------------------------
//              Ch11_03_misc.cpp
//--------------------------------------------------

#include <iostream>
#include "Ch11_03.h"

void DisplayResultsDivI32(size_t test_id, int rc, int32_t a,
    int32_t b, int32_t quo, int32_t rem)
{
```

```cpp
    const char nl = '\n';
    std::cout << "Test #" << test_id << " | ";
    std::cout << "a: " << a << "  b: " << b << nl;

    if (rc != 0)
        std::cout << "quo: " << quo << "  rem: " << rem << nl;
    else
        std::cout << "quo: undefined  rem: undefined" << nl;

    std::cout << nl;
}

void DisplayResultsDivU64(size_t test_id, int rc, uint64_t a,
uint64_t b, uint64_t quo, uint64_t rem)
{
    const char nl = '\n';
    std::cout << "Test #" << test_id << " | ";
    std::cout << "a: " << a << "  b: " << b << nl;

    if (rc != 0)
        std::cout << "quo: " << quo << "  rem: " << rem << nl;
    else
        std::cout << "quo: undefined  rem: undefined" << nl;

    std::cout << nl;
}

//----------------------------------------------
//                Ch11_03.cpp
//----------------------------------------------

#include <iostream>
#include <cstdint>
#include "Ch11_03.h"

static void DivI32(void);
static void DivU64(void);

int main()
{
    DivI32();
    DivU64();
    return 0;
}

static void DivI32(void)
{
    const size_t n = 4;
    const int32_t a[n] = { 47, -291, 19, 247 };
    const int32_t b[n] = { 13, 7, 0, 85 };
```

```cpp
    std::cout << "----- Results for DivI32() -----\n";

    for (size_t i = 0; i < n; i++)
    {
        int32_t quo = 0, rem = 0;
        int32_t rc = DivI32_A(a[i], b[i], &quo, &rem);

        DisplayResultsDivI32(i, rc, a[i], b[i], quo, rem);
    }
}

static void DivU64(void)
{
    const size_t n = 4;
    const uint64_t a[4] = { 147, 300, 2000, 9876543210 };
    const uint64_t b[4] = { 17, 15, 0, 1011 };

    std::cout << "----- Results for Div64U() -----\n";

    for (size_t i = 0; i < n; i++)
    {
        uint64_t quo = 0, rem = 0;
        int32_t rc = DivU64_A(a[i], b[i], &quo, &rem);

        DisplayResultsDivU64(i, rc, a[i], b[i], quo, rem);
    }
}
```

```asm
;-------------------------------------------------
;                 Ch11_03_fasm.asm
;-------------------------------------------------

;-------------------------------------------------------------------------
; extern int32_t DivI32_A(int32_t a, int32_t b, int32_t* quo, int32_t* rem);
;-------------------------------------------------------------------------

        .code
DivI32_A proc

; Make sure divisor b is not zero
        or edx,edx                          ;bitwise OR (sets status flags)
        jz InvalidDivisor                   ;jump if b is zero

; Calculate quotient and remainder of a / b
        mov eax,ecx                         ;eax = a
        mov r10d,edx                        ;r10d = b
        cdq                                 ;edx:eax = 64-bit signed dividend
        idiv r10d                           ;eax = quotient, edx = remainder

; Save results
        mov [r8],eax                        ;save quotient
```

```
        mov [r9],edx                        ;save remainder
        mov eax,1                           ;set success return code
        ret

InvalidDivisor:
        xor eax,eax                         ;set error return code (eax = 0)
        ret
DivI32_A endp

;-----------------------------------------------------------------------
; extern int32_t DivU64_A(uint64_t a, uint64_t b, uint64_t* quo, uint64_t* rem);
;-----------------------------------------------------------------------

DivU64_A proc

; Make sure divisor b is not zero
        or rdx,rdx                          ;bitwise OR (sets status flags)
        jz InvalidDivisor                   ;jump if b is zero

; Calculate quotient and remainder of a / b
        mov r10,rdx                         ;r10 = b
        mov rax,rcx                         ;rax = a
        xor rdx,rdx                         ;rdx:rax = 128-bit unsigned dividend
        div r10                             ;rax = quotient, rdx = remainder

; Save results
        mov [r8],rax                        ;save quotient
        mov [r9],rdx                        ;save remainder
        mov eax,1                           ;set success return code
        ret

InvalidDivisor:
        xor eax,eax                         ;set error return code (eax = 0)
        ret

DivU64_A endp
        end
```

Near the top of Listing 11-3 are the function declarations for DivI32_A() and DivU64(), which perform 32-bit signed and 64-bit unsigned integer division. Note that both functions include two pointer arguments named quo and rem. Functions DivI32_A() and DivU64_A() use these pointers to return the calculated quotient and remainder. Like the previous two examples, the file Ch11_03_misc.cpp includes functions that display results. File Ch11_03.cpp contains two functions named DivI32() and DivI64(). These functions perform test case initialization for the assembly language functions DivI32_A() and DivU64_A().

File Ch11_03_fasm.asm opens with the function DivI32_A(). The first instruction of this function, or edx,edx (Bitwise Logical OR), performs a bitwise logical OR of register EDX (which contains argument value b) with itself. Execution of this instruction sets RFLAGS.ZF (zero flag) to 1 if argument value b is zero; otherwise, RFLAGS.ZF is set to 0. The next instruction, jz InvalidDivisor, is a conditional jump instruction that transfers program control to the first assembly language instruction that follows the label InvalidDivisor if RFLAGS.ZF is set to 1. If you look ahead a few lines, you will notice a statement with the text InvalidDivisior:. This text is called a label. A label can be used as a stand-alone statement or on the same line as an assembly language instruction. The colon is required in both cases. To summarize, the instruction pair or edx,edx and jz InvalidDivisor verifies that argument value b is not equal to zero and skips over the idiv (Divide Signed Integers) instruction if b == 0 is true.

Following the jz InvalidDivisor instruction, DivI32_A() employs two mov instructions that load argument values a and b into registers EAX and R10D, respectively. Then the next instruction, cdq (Sign-Extend Doubleword to Quadword), sign-extends the 32-bit integer in EAX to 64 bits. Following execution of cdq, register pair EDX:EAX contains the 64-bit dividend, and register R10D contains the 32-bit divisor. The idiv r10d instruction divides the contents of register pair EDX:EAX by the value in R10D. Execution of the idiv instruction yields a 32-bit quotient and a 32-bit remainder that reside in registers EAX and EDX, respectively.

The next instruction, mov [r8],eax, saves the calculated quotient to the memory location pointed to by register R8, which contains argument value quo. This is followed by a mov [r9],edx instruction that saves the calculated remainder to the memory location specified by rem. The ensuing instruction pair, mov eax,1 and ret, loads 1 into EAX and returns program control to the calling function. The code block that follows label InvalidDivisor uses an xor eax,eax (Bitwise Logical XOR) to load zero into EAX, which signifies an error condition.

The arrangement of function DivU64_A(), which performs 64-bit unsigned integer division, is similar to DivI32_A(). The most obvious difference between these two functions is that DivU64_A() uses 64-bit registers to perform its calculations. The other item of note is the use of the xor rdx,rdx instruction. This instruction zero-extends 64-bit argument value a in RAX to 128 bits in RDX:RAX for use with the ensuing div r10 (Divide Unsigned Integers) instruction. During execution of div r10, the processor divides RDX:RAX by R10; it then saves the calculated quotient and remainder in registers RAX and RDX, respectively. Here are the results for source code example Ch11_03:

```
----- Results for DivI32() -----
Test #0 | a: 47  b: 13
quo: 3  rem: 8

Test #1 | a: -291  b: 7
quo: -41  rem: -4

Test #2 | a: 19  b: 0
quo: undefined  rem: undefined

Test #3 | a: 247  b: 85
quo: 2  rem: 77

----- Results for Div64U() -----
Test #0 | a: 147  b: 17
quo: 8  rem: 11

Test #1 | a: 300  b: 15
quo: 20  rem: 0

Test #2 | a: 2000  b: 0
quo: undefined  rem: undefined

Test #3 | a: 9876543210  b: 1011
quo: 9769083  rem: 297
```

It should be noted that both idiv and div require the dividend to be loaded into register pair RDX:RAX, EDX:EAX, DX:AX, or AX; an explicit dividend operand cannot be specified. The divisor operand can be another register (e.g., RCX, ECX, CX, or CL) or a value in memory.

# Calling Convention: Part 1

A calling convention is a binary protocol that describes how arguments and return values are exchanged between a called function and its caller. As you have already seen, the Visual C++ calling convention for x86-64 programs on Windows requires a calling function to pass its first four integer (or pointer) arguments using registers RCX, RDX, R8, and R9. The low-order portions of these registers are used for argument values smaller than 64 bits (e.g., ECX, CX, or CL for a 32-, 16-, or 8-bit integer). Any additional arguments are passed using the stack. The calling convention also defines additional requirements including rules for volatile and nonvolatile registers, floating-point values, and stack frames. You will learn more about these requirements later in this chapter and in Chapter 12.

---

■ **Caution**   The Visual C++ calling convention requirements that are described in this and subsequent chapters may be different for other high-level programming languages and operating systems. If you plan on using x86-64 assembly language with a different high-level programming language or operating system, you should consult the appropriate documentation for more information regarding the target platform's calling convention requirements.

---

Listing 11-4 shows the source code for example Ch11_04. This example illustrates how to use integer arguments that are passed via the stack. It also demonstrates the use of additional x86-64 move instructions.

*Listing 11-4.*  Example Ch11_04

```
//--------------------------------------------------
//              Ch11_04.h
//--------------------------------------------------

#pragma once
#include <cstdint>

// Ch11_04_fasm.asm
extern "C" int64_t CalcResultI64_A(int8_t a, int16_t b, int32_t c, int64_t d,
    int8_t e, int16_t f, int32_t g, int64_t h);

extern "C" int32_t CalcResultU64_A(uint8_t a, uint16_t b, uint32_t c, uint64_t d,
    uint8_t e, uint16_t f, uint32_t g, uint64_t h, uint64_t* quo, uint64_t* rem);

//--------------------------------------------------
//              Ch11_04.cpp
//--------------------------------------------------

#include <iostream>
#include <cstdint>
#include "Ch11_04.h"
```

```cpp
static void CalcResultI64(void);
static void CalcResultU64(void);

int main()
{
    CalcResultI64();
    CalcResultU64();
    return 0;
}

static void CalcResultI64(void)
{
    int8_t a = 2;
    int16_t b = -3;
    int32_t c = 8;
    int64_t d = 4;
    int8_t e = 3;
    int16_t f = -7;
    int32_t g = -5;
    int64_t h = 10;

    // Calculate (a * b * c * d) + (e * f * g * h)
    int64_t result1 = ((int64_t)a * b * c * d) + ((int64_t)e * f * g * h);
    int64_t result2 = CalcResultI64_A(a, b, c, d, e, f, g, h);

    std::cout << "\n----- Results for CalcResultI64 -----\n";
    std::cout << "a = " << (int)a << ", b = " << b << ", c = " << c << ' ';
    std::cout << "d = " << d << ", e = " << (int)e << ", f = " << f << ' ';
    std::cout << "g = " << g << ", h = " << h << '\n';
    std::cout << "result1 = " << result1 << '\n';
    std::cout << "result2 = " << result2 << '\n';
}

static void CalcResultU64(void)
{
    uint8_t a = 12;
    uint16_t b = 17;
    uint32_t c = 71000000;
    uint64_t d = 90000000000;
    uint8_t e = 101;
    uint16_t f = 37;
    uint32_t g = 25;
    uint64_t h = 5;
    uint64_t quo1, rem1;
    uint64_t quo2, rem2;

    quo1 = ((uint64_t)a + b + c + d) / ((uint64_t)e + f + g + h);
    rem1 = ((uint64_t)a + b + c + d) % ((uint64_t)e + f + g + h);
    CalcResultU64_A(a, b, c, d, e, f, g, h, &quo2, &rem2);

    std::cout << "\n----- Results for CalcResultU64 -----\n";
```

```cpp
    std::cout << "a = " << (unsigned)a << ", b = " << b << ", c = " << c << ' ';
    std::cout << "d = " << d << ", e = " << (unsigned)e << ", f = " << f << ' ';
    std::cout << "g = " << g << ", h = " << h << '\n';
    std::cout << "quo1 = " << quo1 << ", rem1 = " << rem1 << '\n';
    std::cout << "quo2 = " << quo2 << ", rem2 = " << rem2 << '\n';
}
```

```asm
;--------------------------------------------------
;                   Ch11_04_fasm.asm
;--------------------------------------------------


;-------------------------------------------------------------------------
; extern "C" int64_t CalcResultI64_A(int8_t a, int16_t b, int32_t c, int64_t d,
;   int8_t e, int16_t f, int32_t g, int64_t h);
;-------------------------------------------------------------------------


        .code
CalcResultI64_A proc

; Calculate a * b * c * d
        movsx rax,cl                    ;rax = a
        movsx rdx,dx                    ;rdx = b
        imul rax,rdx                    ;rax = a * b
        movsxd rcx,r8d                  ;rcx = c
        imul rcx,r9                     ;rcx = c * d
        imul rax,rcx                    ;rax = a * b * c * d

; Calculate e * f * g * h
        movsx rcx,byte ptr [rsp+40]     ;rcx = e
        movsx rdx,word ptr [rsp+48]     ;rdx = f
        imul rcx,rdx                    ;rcx = e * f
        movsxd rdx,dword ptr [rsp+56]   ;rdx = g
        imul rdx,qword ptr [rsp+64]     ;rdx = g * h
        imul rcx,rdx                    ;rcx = e * f * g * h

; Calculate final result
        add rax,rcx                     ;rax = result
        ret
CalcResultI64_A endp

;-------------------------------------------------------------------------
; extern "C" int32_t CalcResultU64_A(uint8_t a, uint16_t b, uint32_t c, uint64_t d,
;   uint8_t e, uint16_t f, uint32_t g, uint64_t h, uint64_t* quo, uint64_t* rem);
;-------------------------------------------------------------------------


CalcResultU64_A proc

; Calculate a + b + c + d
        movzx rax,cl                    ;rax = a
        movzx rdx,dx                    ;rdx = b
        add rax,rdx                     ;rax = a + b
```

```
        mov r8d,r8d                     ;r8 = c
        add r8,r9                       ;r8 = c + d
        add rax,r8                      ;rax = a + b + c + d
        xor rdx,rdx                     ;rdx:rax = a + b + c + d

; Calculate e + f + g + h
        movzx r8,byte ptr [rsp+40]      ;r8 = e
        movzx r9,word ptr [rsp+48]      ;r9 = f
        add r8,r9                       ;r8 = e + f
        mov r10d,[rsp+56]               ;r10 = g
        add r10,[rsp+64]                ;r10 = g + h;
        add r8,r10                      ;r8 = e + f + g + h
        jnz DivOK                       ;jump if divisor is not zero

        xor eax,eax                     ;set error return code
        ret

; Calculate (a + b + c + d) / (e + f + g + h)
DivOK:  div r8                          ;unsigned divide rdx:rax / r8
        mov rcx,[rsp+72]
        mov [rcx],rax                   ;save quotient
        mov rcx,[rsp+80]
        mov [rcx],rdx                   ;save remainder

        mov eax,1                       ;set success return code
        ret
CalcResultU64_A endp
        end
```

Toward the top of Listing 11-4 are the function declarations for CalcResultI64_A() and CalcResultU64_A(). Note that these functions require eight integer arguments of varying sizes. The declaration for function CalcResultU64_A() also incorporates two additional pointer arguments. The file Ch11_04.cpp includes a function named CalcResultI64(). This function performs test case initialization for the assembly language function CalcResultI64_A(). It also includes code that streams results to std::cout. The other function in Ch11_04.cpp, CalcResultU64(), contains similar code for the assembly language function CalcResultU64_A().

Figure 11-1 illustrates the state of the stack and argument value registers at entry to function CalcResultsI64_A() but prior to execution of its first instruction. Like the examples that you have seen thus far, the first four integer arguments (a, b, c, and d) are passed to CalcResultsI64_A() using registers RCX, RDX, R8, and R9. Note that the high-order bits of registers RCX, RDX, and R8 are undefined since argument values a, b, and c are smaller than 64 bits. The remaining four integer arguments (e, f, g, and h) are passed via the stack. The stack also includes areas that are undefined since each argument value that is passed via the stack must be aligned on a quadword (8-byte) boundary.

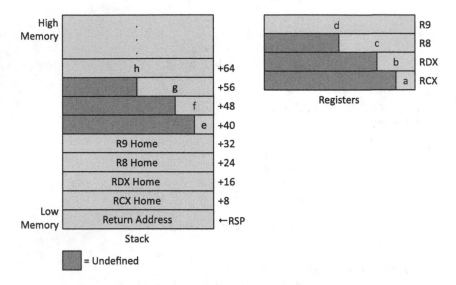

*Figure 11-1.* *Argument registers and stack at entry to* `CalcResultI64_A()`

Note in Figure 11-1 that register RSP points to the caller's return address on the stack. During execution of a `ret` instruction, the processor copies this value from the stack and stores it in register RIP. The `ret` instruction also removes the caller's return address from the stack by adding 8 to the value in RSP. The stack locations labeled RCX Home, RDX Home, R8 Home, and R9 Home are storage areas that can be used to temporarily save the corresponding argument registers. A called function can also use these areas to store other transient data. You will learn more about the home area in Chapter 12.

Function `CalcResultI64_A()` calculates (a * b * c * d) + (e * f * g * h). The first instruction of this function, `movsx rax,cl` (Move with Sign Extension), copies the value in register CL, sign-extends it to 64 bits, and saves the result in register RAX. Following execution of this instruction, register RAX contains argument value a signed-extended to 64 bits. The ensuing `movsx rdx,dx` instruction sign-extends a copy of the 16-bit integer in register DX (argument value b) to 64 bits and saves this value in register RDX. This is followed by an `imul rax,rdx` instruction that calculates a * b. Following the calculation of a * b, `CalcResultI64_A()` uses a `movsxd rcx,r8d` instruction to sign-extend argument value c from 32 to 64 bits. The instruction pair that follows, `imul rcx,r9` and `imul rax,rcx`, completes the calculation of a * b * c * d.

The second code block in `CalcResultI64_A()` calculates e * f * g * h. The first instruction of this block, `movsx rcx,byte ptr [rsp+40]`, copies argument value e from its location on the stack, sign-extends it to 64 bits, and saves the result in register RCX. The text `byte ptr` is a MASM operator that acts like a C++ cast operator and conveys to the assembler the size of the source operand. Without the `byte ptr` operator, the `movsx` instruction is ambiguous since several different sizes are possible for the source operand.

Argument value f is loaded next using a `movsx rdx,word ptr [rsp+48]` instruction. Following calculation of the intermediate product e * f using an `imul rcx,rdx` instruction, the `movsxd rdx,dword ptr [rsp+56]` instruction loads a sign-extended copy of g into RDX. This is followed by an `imul rdx,qword ptr [rsp+64]` instruction that calculates the intermediate product g * h. Note that the use of the `qword ptr` operator is optional here, but size operators are often employed in this manner to improve code readability. The final two `imul` instructions complete the calculation of the intermediate product e * f * g * h. The `add rax,rcx` instruction that appears just before the `ret` instruction finishes the calculation of (a * b * c * d) + (e * f * g * h).

Figure 11-2 illustrates the contents of the stack at entry to the function CalcResultU64_A(). This function calculates the quotient and remainder of the expression (a + b + c + d) / (e + f + g + h). Function CalcResultU64_A() uses unsigned integer arguments of different sizes and performs unsigned integer division. To calculate the correct result, all integer arguments smaller than 64 bits must be zero-extended prior to any arithmetic calculations. The movzx rax,cl (Move with Zero-Extend) and movzx rdx,dx instructions load zero-extended copies of argument values a and b into their respective destination registers. The add rax,rdx instruction that immediately follows calculates the intermediate sum a + b. At first glance, the mov r8d,r8d instruction that follows seems superfluous, but it is actually performing a necessary operation. When an x86 processor is executing 64-bit code, instructions that employ 32-bit operands produce 32-bit results. If the destination operand is a 32-bit register, the high-order 32 bits (i.e., bits 63–32) of the corresponding 64-bit register are set to zero. The mov r8d,r8d instruction used here zero-extends argument value c from 32 bits to 64 bits and saves this value in R8. The next two add instructions calculate the intermediate sum a + b + c + d and save the result to RAX. The ensuing xor rdx,rdx instruction yields a 128-bit wide zero-extended dividend value in register pair RDX:RAX.

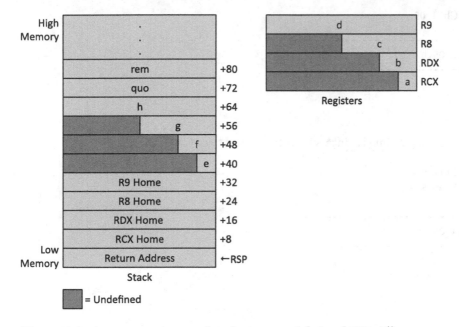

**Figure 11-2.** *Argument registers and stack at entry to CalcResultU64_A()*

A similar sequence of instructions is used to calculate the intermediate sum e + f + g + h, with the main difference being that these arguments are loaded from the stack. Note that the add r8,r10 instruction, which completes the calculation of e + f + g + h, updates RFLAGS.ZF. If the divisor value in R8 is not zero, the div r8 instruction performs unsigned integer division using register pair RDX:RAX as the dividend and register R8 as the divisor. The resulting quotient (RAX) and remainder (RDX) are then saved to the memory locations specified by the pointers quo and rem, which were passed to CalcResultU64_A() via the stack as shown in Figure 11-2. Here are the results for source example Ch11_04:

```
----- Results for CalcResultI64 -----
a = 2, b = -3, c = 8 d = 4, e = 3, f = -7 g = -5, h = 10
result1 = 858
result2 = 858
```

```
----- Results for CalcResultU64 -----
a = 12, b = 17, c = 71000000 d = 90000000000, e = 101, f = 37 g = 25, h = 5
quo1 = 536136904, rem1 = 157
quo2 = 536136904, rem2 = 157
```

# Memory Addressing Modes

You learned in Chapter 1 that the x86-64 instruction set supports a variety of addressing modes that can be used to reference an operand in memory. In this section, you will examine an assembly language function that illustrates how to use some of these modes. You will also learn how to initialize an assembly language lookup table (LUT) and reference assembly language global variables in a C++ function. Listing 11-5 shows the source code for example Ch11_05.

*Listing 11-5.* Example Ch11_05

```cpp
//-------------------------------------------------
//               Ch11_05.h
//-------------------------------------------------

#pragma once

// Ch11_05_fasm.asm
extern "C" int MemAddressing_A(int i, int* v1, int* v2, int* v3, int* v4);

extern "C" int g_NumPrimes_A;
extern "C" int g_SumPrimes_A;

//-------------------------------------------------
//               Ch11_05.cpp
//-------------------------------------------------

#include <iostream>
#include <iomanip>
#include <cstdint>
#include "Ch11_05.h"

static void MemAddressing(void);

int main()
{
    MemAddressing();
    return 0;
}

static void MemAddressing()
{
    const int w = 5;
    const char nl = '\n';
    const char* delim = ", ";
```

```
    int n = g_NumPrimes_A;

    g_SumPrimes_A = 0;

    for (int i = -1; i < n + 1; i++)
    {
        int v1 = -1, v2 = -1, v3 = -1, v4 = -1;
        int rc = MemAddressing_A(i, &v1, &v2, &v3, &v4);

        std::cout << "i = " << std::setw(w - 1) << i << delim;
        std::cout << "rc = " << std::setw(w - 1) << rc << delim;
        std::cout << "v1 = " << std::setw(w) << v1 << delim;
        std::cout << "v2 = " << std::setw(w) << v2 << delim;
        std::cout << "v3 = " << std::setw(w) << v3 << delim;
        std::cout << "v4 = " << std::setw(w) << v4 << delim;
        std::cout << nl;
    }

    std::cout << "\ng_SumPrimes_A = " << g_SumPrimes_A << nl;
}

;---------------------------------------------------
;                    Ch11_05_fasm.asm
;---------------------------------------------------

; Simple LUT (.const section data is read only)
                .const
PrimeNums       dword 2, 3, 5, 7, 11, 13, 17, 19, 23
                dword 29, 31, 37, 41, 43, 47, 53, 59
                dword 61, 67, 71, 73, 79, 83, 89, 97

g_NumPrimes_A   dword ($ - PrimeNums) / sizeof dword
                public g_NumPrimes_A

; Data section (data is read/write)
                .data
g_SumPrimes_A   dword ?
                public g_SumPrimes_A


;-------------------------------------------------------------------------
; extern "C" int MemAddressing_A(int i, int* v1, int* v2, int* v3, int* v4);
;-------------------------------------------------------------------------

        .code
MemAddressing_A proc

; Make sure 'i' is valid
        cmp ecx,-1
        jle InvalidIndex                ;jump if i <= -1
        cmp ecx,[g_NumPrimes_A]
        jge InvalidIndex                ;jump if i >= g_NumPrimes_A
```

```
; Sign extend i for use in address calculations
        movsxd rcx,ecx                          ;sign extend i
        mov [rsp+8],rcx                         ;save copy of i (in rcx home area)

; Memory addressing - base register
        mov r11,offset PrimeNums                ;r11 = PrimeNums
        shl rcx,2                               ;rcx = i * 4
        add r11,rcx                             ;r11 = PrimeNums + i * 4
        mov eax,[r11]                           ;eax = PrimeNums[i]
        mov [rdx],eax                           ;save to v1

; Memory addressing - base register + index register
        mov r11,offset PrimeNums                ;r11 = PrimeNums
        mov rcx,[rsp+8]                         ;rcx = i
        shl rcx,2                               ;rcx = i * 4
        mov eax,[r11+rcx]                       ;eax = PrimeNums[i]
        mov [r8],eax                            ;save to v2

; Memory addressing - base register + index register * scale factor
        mov r11,offset PrimeNums                ;r11 = PrimeNums
        mov rcx,[rsp+8]                         ;rcx = i
        mov eax,[r11+rcx*4]                     ;eax = PrimeNums[i]
        mov [r9],eax                            ;save to v3

; Memory addressing - base register + index register * scale factor + disp
        mov r11,offset PrimeNums-42             ;r11 = PrimeNums - 42
        mov rcx,[rsp+8]                         ;rcx = i
        mov eax,[r11+rcx*4+42]                  ;eax = PrimeNums[i]
        mov r10,[rsp+40]                        ;r10 = ptr to v4
        mov [r10],eax                           ;save to v4

; Mmeory addressing - RIP relative
        add [g_SumPrimes_A],eax                 ;update sum
        mov eax,1                               ;set success return code
        ret

InvalidIndex:
        xor eax,eax                             ;set error return code
        ret


MemAddressing_A endp
        end
```

Listing 11-5 begins with the file Ch11_05.h. Near the top of Ch11_05.h is the declaration of assembly language function MemAddressing_A(). This is followed by the declaration of two global variables, g_NumPrimes_A and g_SumPrimes_A. Note that both declaration statements include the "C" modifier, which instructs the C++ compiler to use C-style variable names instead of C++ decorated names. The reason for using the "C" modifier is that both g_NumPrimes_A and g_SumPrimes_A are defined in the assembly language file Ch11_05_fasm.asm. More about this in a moment.

The file Ch11_05.cpp includes a function named MemAddressing(). This function includes a simple for-loop that exercises the assembly language function MemAddressing_A(). Note that the for-loop index variable i is initialized to -1. This is done to test the error checking code in MemAddressing_A(). The for-loop index variable i is also allowed to exceed the value of g_NumPrimes_A for the same reason.

The assembly language function MemAddresing_A() uses argument value i as an index into a simple LUT of constant integers, while the four pointer arguments are used to save values loaded from the LUT using different addressing modes.

Near the top of Listing 11-5 is a .const directive. This directive signifies the start of a block of memory that contains read-only data. Immediately following the .const directive, a LUT named PrimeNums is defined. The LUT PrimeNums contains 25 doubleword integer values. The text dword is an assembler directive that allocates storage space and optionally initializes a doubleword value. Other assembler space storage directives include byte, word, and qword. You can also use the storage space synonyms dd, db, dw, and dq.

The statement g_NumPrimes_A dword ($ - PrimeNums) / sizeof dword allocates storage space for a single doubleword value and initializes it with the number of doubleword elements in PrimeNums. The $ character is an assembler symbol that equals the current value of the location counter (or offset from the beginning of the current memory block). Subtracting the offset of PrimeNums from $ yields the size of the LUT in bytes. Dividing this result by the size in bytes of a doubleword value generates the correct number of elements. These statements emulate a commonly used technique in C++ to define and initialize a variable with the number of elements in an array:

```
const int Values[] = {10, 20, 30, 40, 50};
const int NumValues = sizeof(Values) / sizeof(int);
```

The final statement of the .const section, public g_NumPrimes_A, declares g_NumPrimes_A as a public symbol so that it can be referenced in other functions. In the current example, g_NumPrimes is used in the C++ function MemAddressing(). The .data directive denotes the start of a memory block that contains modifiable data. The g_SumPrimes_A dword ? statement defines an uninitialized (signified by the ? symbol) doubleword variable; the subsequent statement public g_SumPrimes_A makes it accessible in other functions.

Upon entry into function MemAddressing_A(), argument value i is checked for validity since it will be used as an index into the LUT PrimeNums. The cmp ecx,-1 (Compare) instruction compares the contents of ECX, which contains i, to the immediate value -1. When the processor executes a cmp instruction, it subtracts the second operand from the first operand, sets the status flags based on the results of this operation, and discards the result. If i <= -1 is true, the ensuing jle InvalidIndex (Jump if Less or Equal) instruction transfers program control to the first instruction that follows the label InvalidIndex. A similar sequence of instructions is used to determine if i is too large. The cmp ecx,[g_NumPrimes_A] instruction compares ECX against the number of elements in the lookup table. If i >= g_NumPrimes_A is true, program control is transferred to the target location that is specified by the jge (Jump if Greater or Equal) instruction.

Immediately following the validation of i, a movsxd rcx,ecx sign-extends the table index value to 64 bits. Sign-extending or zero-extending a 32-bit integer to a 64-bit integer is often necessary when using an addressing mode that employs an index register as you'll soon see. The subsequent mov [rsp+8],rcx saves a copy of the signed-extended table index value to the RCX home area on the stack and is done primarily to exemplify the use of the stack home area.

The remaining code blocks in MemAddressing_A() illustrate accessing items in the LUT using various memory addressing modes. The first example uses a single base register to read an item from the table. To use a single base register, MemAddressing_A() must explicitly calculate the address of the i-th table element, which is achieved by adding the starting address of PrimeNums and the value i * 4. The mov r11,offset PrimeNums instruction loads the address of PrimeNums into R11. Note that the offset directive is required; without it, the mov instruction would load the value of PrimeNums instead of its address. This is followed by a shl rcx,2 (Shift Left) instruction that determines the offset of the i-th item relative to the start of the LUT. A two-bit shift is used here since PrimeNums contains doubleword elements. The add r11,rcx instruction calculates the final address. Once this is complete, the specified LUT value is read using a mov eax,[r11] instruction. It is then saved to the memory location specified by the argument value v1.

In the second example, the LUT value is read using BaseReg+IndexReg memory addressing. This example is similar to the first one except that the processor computes the final effective address during execution of the mov eax,[r11+rcx] instruction. Note that recalculation of the LUT element offset using the mov rcx,[rsp+8] and shl rcx,2 instructions is superfluous but included to illustrate the use of the stack home area.

The third example demonstrates the use of BaseReg+IndexReg*ScaleFactor memory addressing. In this example, the address of PrimeNums and the value i are loaded into registers R11 and RCX, respectively. The correct LUT value is loaded into EAX using a mov eax,[r11+rcx*4] instruction. In the fourth (and somewhat contrived) example, BaseReg+IndexReg*ScaleFactor+Disp memory addressing is demonstrated. The fifth and final memory addressing mode example uses an add [g_SumPrimes_A],eax instruction to demonstrate RIP-relative addressing. This instruction, which uses a memory location as a destination operand, updates a running sum that is ultimately displayed by the C++ code. Here are the results for source code example Ch11_05:

```
i =   -1, rc =   0, v1 =   -1, v2 =   -1, v3 =   -1, v4 =   -1,
i =    0, rc =   1, v1 =    2, v2 =    2, v3 =    2, v4 =    2,
i =    1, rc =   1, v1 =    3, v2 =    3, v3 =    3, v4 =    3,
i =    2, rc =   1, v1 =    5, v2 =    5, v3 =    5, v4 =    5,
i =    3, rc =   1, v1 =    7, v2 =    7, v3 =    7, v4 =    7,
i =    4, rc =   1, v1 =   11, v2 =   11, v3 =   11, v4 =   11,
i =    5, rc =   1, v1 =   13, v2 =   13, v3 =   13, v4 =   13,
i =    6, rc =   1, v1 =   17, v2 =   17, v3 =   17, v4 =   17,
i =    7, rc =   1, v1 =   19, v2 =   19, v3 =   19, v4 =   19,
i =    8, rc =   1, v1 =   23, v2 =   23, v3 =   23, v4 =   23,
i =    9, rc =   1, v1 =   29, v2 =   29, v3 =   29, v4 =   29,
i =   10, rc =   1, v1 =   31, v2 =   31, v3 =   31, v4 =   31,
i =   11, rc =   1, v1 =   37, v2 =   37, v3 =   37, v4 =   37,
i =   12, rc =   1, v1 =   41, v2 =   41, v3 =   41, v4 =   41,
i =   13, rc =   1, v1 =   43, v2 =   43, v3 =   43, v4 =   43,
i =   14, rc =   1, v1 =   47, v2 =   47, v3 =   47, v4 =   47,
i =   15, rc =   1, v1 =   53, v2 =   53, v3 =   53, v4 =   53,
i =   16, rc =   1, v1 =   59, v2 =   59, v3 =   59, v4 =   59,
i =   17, rc =   1, v1 =   61, v2 =   61, v3 =   61, v4 =   61,
i =   18, rc =   1, v1 =   67, v2 =   67, v3 =   67, v4 =   67,
i =   19, rc =   1, v1 =   71, v2 =   71, v3 =   71, v4 =   71,
i =   20, rc =   1, v1 =   73, v2 =   73, v3 =   73, v4 =   73,
i =   21, rc =   1, v1 =   79, v2 =   79, v3 =   79, v4 =   79,
i =   22, rc =   1, v1 =   83, v2 =   83, v3 =   83, v4 =   83,
i =   23, rc =   1, v1 =   89, v2 =   89, v3 =   89, v4 =   89,
i =   24, rc =   1, v1 =   97, v2 =   97, v3 =   97, v4 =   97,
i =   25, rc =   0, v1 =   -1, v2 =   -1, v3 =   -1, v4 =   -1,

g_SumPrimes_A = 1060
```

Factors that you should consider when selecting a memory addressing mode include the number of free registers, data structure type (e.g., array, matrix, C++ struct, etc.), memory access patterns, and the algorithmic particulars of a function. It would not be unreasonable to apply the KISS (keep it simple, stupid) principle here since simplicity often results in better performance.

# For-Loops

In many programming languages, the ubiquitous for-loop is perhaps the most important programming construct. The next source code example, Ch11_06, illustrates how to code an assembly language for-loop using x86-64 instructions. Listing 11-6 shows the source code for this example.

*Listing 11-6.* Example Ch11_06

```
//-------------------------------------------------
//                 Ch11_06.h
//-------------------------------------------------

#pragma once

// Ch11_06_fcpp.cpp
extern int SumElementsI32_Cpp(const int* x, size_t n);

// Ch11_06_fasm.asm
extern "C" int SumElementsI32_A(const int* x, size_t n);

// Ch11_06_misc.cpp
extern void FillArray(int* x, size_t n);
extern void DisplayResults(const int* x, size_t n, int sum1, int sum2);

//-------------------------------------------------
//               Ch11_06_misc.cpp
//-------------------------------------------------

#include <iostream>
#include <iomanip>
#include "Ch11_06.h"
#include "MT.h"

void FillArray(int* x, size_t n)
{
    const int min_val = -2000;
    const int max_val = 2000;
    const unsigned int rng_seed = 1337;

    MT::FillArray(x, n, min_val, max_val, rng_seed, true);
}

void DisplayResults(const int* x, size_t n, int sum1, int sum2)
{
    const char nl = '\n';
    std::cout << "----- Results for SumElementsI32() -----\n";

    for (size_t i = 0; i < n; i++)
        std::cout << "x[" << i << "] = " << std::setw(4) << x[i] << nl;

    std::cout << nl;
```

```cpp
    std::cout << "sum1 = " << sum1 << nl;
    std::cout << "sum2 = " << sum2 << nl;
}
//-------------------------------------------------
//                  Ch11_06.cpp
//-------------------------------------------------

#include <iostream>
#include <cstdint>
#include "Ch11_06.h"

static void SumElementsI32(void);

int main()
{
    SumElementsI32();
    return 0;
}

static void SumElementsI32(void)
{
    const size_t n = 20;
    int x[n];

    FillArray(x, n);

    int sum1 = SumElementsI32_Cpp(x, n);
    int sum2 = SumElementsI32_A(x, n);

    DisplayResults(x, n, sum1, sum2);
}


//-------------------------------------------------
//                  Ch11_06_fcpp.cpp
//-------------------------------------------------

#include "Ch11_06.h"

int SumElementsI32_Cpp(const int* x, size_t n)
{
    int sum = 0;

    for (size_t i = 0; i < n; i++)
        sum += x[i];

    return sum;
}
```

```
;--------------------------------------------------
;                 Ch11_06_fasm.asm
;--------------------------------------------------


;----------------------------------------------------------------------
; extern "C" int SumElementsI32_A(const int* x, size_t n);
;----------------------------------------------------------------------

            .code
SumElementsI32_A proc

; Initialize sum to zero
        xor eax,eax                     ;sum = 0
        mov r10,-1                      ;i = -1

; Sum the elements of the array
Loop1:  inc r10                         ;i += 1
        cmp r10,rdx                     ;is i >= n?
        jae Done                        ;jump if i >= n

        add eax,[rcx+r10*4]             ;sum += x[i]
        jmp Loop1                       ;perform next iteration

Done:   ret                             ;return to caller

SumElementsI32_A endp
        end
```

Listing 11-6 begins with the files Ch11_06.h and Ch11_06_misc.cpp. Like the earlier examples, these files contain function declarations and miscellaneous functions. The file Ch11_06.cpp includes a function named SumElementsI32(). This function exercises two functions, SumElementsI32_Cpp() and SumElementsI32_A(), that sum the elements of an integer array. Function SumElementsI32_Cpp() is located in file Ch11_06_fcpp.cpp and is included in this example for comparison purposes.

The final file in Listing 11-6, Ch11_06_fasm.asm, contains the function SumElementsI32_A(). Note that this function requires two argument values: a pointer to an array of int values and an element count of type size_t. Type size_t is an ISO C++–defined type that corresponds to a 64-bit unsigned integer in 64-bit Visual C++ programs. The first instruction of SumElementsI32_A(), xor eax,eax, sets sum = 0. This is followed by a mov r10,-1 instruction that sets i = -1.

The next code block sums the elements of array x using an assembly language for-loop. The first instruction of the for-loop, inc r10 (Increment by 1), adds 1 to the value in R10 (or variable i). It should be noted that unlike most x86 arithmetic instructions, execution of an inc instruction does not update RFLAGS. CF (carry flag). The ensuing instruction pair, cmp r10,rdx and jae Done, checks if i >= n is true. If i >= n is true, program control is transferred to the ret instruction. The add eax,[rcx+r10*4] instruction that follows calculates sum += x[i]. In this instruction, RCX points to array x and R10 contains index i. A scale factor 4 is used since the size of each element in array x is four bytes. The final instruction of the for-loop, jmp Loop1, performs an unconditional jump to Loop1. Here are the results for source code example Ch11_06:

```
----- Results for SumElementsI32() -----
x[0]  =   139
x[1]  = 1244
x[2]  = -1851
x[3]  = -1207
x[4]  = -266
x[5]  =   771
x[6]  =   -49
x[7]  = -457
x[8]  =   249
x[9]  =   407
x[10] = 1732
x[11] =   503
x[12] = 1109
x[13] = -356
x[14] =   589
x[15] = -1417
x[16] = 1895
x[17] = -178
x[18] = 1266
x[19] = -1407

sum1 = 2716
sum2 = 2716
```

## Condition Codes

When developing code to implement a particular algorithm, it is often necessary to determine the minimum or maximum value of two numbers. The standard C++ library defines two template functions named std::min() and std::max() to perform these operations. The assembly language code that is shown in Listing 11-7 contains several three-argument versions of signed-integer minimum and maximum functions. The purpose of these functions is to illustrate the use of the jcc (Conditional Jump) and cmovcc (Conditional Move) instructions.

*Listing 11-7.* Example Ch11_07

```
//-------------------------------------------------
//                 Ch11_07.h
//-------------------------------------------------

#pragma once

// Ch11_07_fasm.asm
extern "C" int SignedMin1_A(int a, int b, int c);
extern "C" int SignedMin2_A(int a, int b, int c);
extern "C" int SignedMax1_A(int a, int b, int c);
extern "C" int SignedMax2_A(int a, int b, int c);
```

```cpp
// Ch11_07_misc.cpp
void DisplayResult(const char* s1, int a, int b, int c, int result);

//--------------------------------------------------
//                 Ch11_07_misc.cpp
//--------------------------------------------------

#include <iostream>
#include <iomanip>
#include "Ch11_07.h"

void DisplayResult(const char* s1, int a, int b, int c, int result)
{
    const size_t w = 4;

    std::cout << s1 << "(";
    std::cout << std::setw(w) << a << ", ";
    std::cout << std::setw(w) << b << ", ";
    std::cout << std::setw(w) << c << ") = ";
    std::cout << std::setw(w) << result << '\n';
}

//--------------------------------------------------
//                 Ch11_07.cpp
//--------------------------------------------------

#include <iostream>
#include <cstdint>
#include "Ch11_07.h"

static void SignedMinI32(void);
static void SignedMaxI32(void);

int main()
{
    SignedMinI32();
    SignedMaxI32();
    return 0;
}

static void SignedMinI32()
{
    const char nl = '\n';
    int a, b, c, smin1, smin2;

    // SignedMin examples
    a = 2; b = 15; c = 8;
    smin1 = SignedMin1_A(a, b, c);
    smin2 = SignedMin2_A(a, b, c);
    DisplayResult("SignedMin1_A", a, b, c, smin1);
    DisplayResult("SignedMin2_A", a, b, c, smin2);
    std::cout << nl;
```

```cpp
    a = -3; b = -22; c = 28;
    smin1 = SignedMin1_A(a, b, c);
    smin2 = SignedMin2_A(a, b, c);
    DisplayResult("SignedMin1_A", a, b, c, smin1);
    DisplayResult("SignedMin2_A", a, b, c, smin2);
    std::cout << nl;

    a = 17; b = 37; c = -11;
    smin1 = SignedMin1_A(a, b, c);
    smin2 = SignedMin2_A(a, b, c);
    DisplayResult("SignedMin1_A", a, b, c, smin1);
    DisplayResult("SignedMin2_A", a, b, c, smin2);
    std::cout << nl;
}

static void SignedMaxI32()
{
    const char nl = '\n';
    int a, b, c, smax1, smax2;

    // SignedMax examples
    a = 10; b = 5; c = 3;
    smax1 = SignedMax1_A(a, b, c);
    smax2 = SignedMax2_A(a, b, c);
    DisplayResult("SignedMax1_A", a, b, c, smax1);
    DisplayResult("SignedMax2_A", a, b, c, smax2);
    std::cout << nl;

    a = -3; b = 28; c = 15;
    smax1 = SignedMax1_A(a, b, c);
    smax2 = SignedMax2_A(a, b, c);
    DisplayResult("SignedMax1_A", a, b, c, smax1);
    DisplayResult("SignedMax2_A", a, b, c, smax2);
    std::cout << nl;

    a = -25; b = -37; c = -17;
    smax1 = SignedMax1_A(a, b, c);
    smax2 = SignedMax2_A(a, b, c);
    DisplayResult("SignedMax1_A", a, b, c, smax1);
    DisplayResult("SignedMax2_A", a, b, c, smax2);
    std::cout << nl;
}

;----------------------------------------------------
;                 Ch11_07_fasm.asm
;----------------------------------------------------

;------------------------------------------------------------------------
; extern "C" int SignedMin1_A(int a, int b, int c);
;------------------------------------------------------------------------
```

```
        .code
SignedMin1_A proc
        mov eax,ecx
        cmp eax,edx                     ;compare a and b
        jle @F                          ;jump if a <= b
        mov eax,edx                     ;eax = b

@@:     cmp eax,r8d                     ;compare min(a, b) and c
        jle @F
        mov eax,r8d                     ;eax = min(a, b, c)

@@:     ret
SignedMin1_A endp

;-------------------------------------------------------------------------
; extern "C" int SignedMin2_A(int a, int b, int c);
;-------------------------------------------------------------------------

SignedMin2_A proc
        cmp ecx,edx
        cmovg ecx,edx                   ;ecx = min(a, b)
        cmp ecx,r8d
        cmovg ecx,r8d                   ;ecx = min(a, b, c)
        mov eax,ecx
        ret
SignedMin2_A endp

;-------------------------------------------------------------------------
; extern "C" int SignedMax1_A(int a, int b, int c);
;-------------------------------------------------------------------------

SignedMax1_A proc
        mov eax,ecx
        cmp eax,edx                     ;compare a and b
        jge @F                          ;jump if a >= b
        mov eax,edx                     ;eax = b

@@:     cmp eax,r8d                     ;compare max(a, b) and c
        jge @F
        mov eax,r8d                     ;eax = max(a, b, c)

@@:     ret
SignedMax1_A endp

;-------------------------------------------------------------------------
; extern "C" int SignedMax2_A(int a, int b, int c);
;-------------------------------------------------------------------------

SignedMax2_A proc
        cmp ecx,edx
        cmovl ecx,edx                   ;ecx = max(a, b)
```

```
        cmp ecx,r8d
        cmovl ecx,r8d                        ;ecx = max(a, b, c)
        mov eax,ecx
        ret
SignedMax2_A endp
        end
```

In Listing 11-7, the files Ch11_07.h, Ch11_07_misc.cpp, and Ch11_07.cpp contain function declarations, test case initialization code, and miscellaneous functions. The first function in file Ch11_07_fasm.asm, SignedMin1_A(), finds the minimum value of three signed integers. The initial code block determines min(a, b) using two instructions: cmp eax,ecx and jle @F. Recall that the cmp instruction, which you saw earlier in this chapter, subtracts the source operand from the destination operand and sets the status flags based on the result; the result is not saved. The operand of the jle (Jump if Less or Equal) instruction, @F, is an assembler symbol that designates nearest forward @@ label as the target of the conditional jump (the symbol @B can be used for backward jumps). Following calculation of min(a, b), the next code block determines min(min(a, b), c) using the same technique. Note that register EAX contains the final minimum prior to execution of the ret instruction.

The next function in Listing 11-7, SignedMin2_A(), determines the minimum value of three signed integers using conditional move instructions. The cmovcc instruction tests the specified condition, and if true, the source operand is copied to the destination operand. If the specified condition is false, the destination operand is not altered. If you examine SignedMin2_A() closely, you will notice that following the cmp ecx,edx instruction is a cmovg ecx,edx instruction. The cmovg (Move if Greater) instruction copies the contents of EDX to ECX if ECX is greater than EDX. In this example, registers ECX and EDX contain argument values a and b, respectively. Following execution of the cmovg instruction, register ECX contains min(a, b). Another cmp and cmovg instruction sequence follows, which yields min(min(a, b), c).

The functions SignedMax1_A() and SignedMax2_A() calculate signed maximum values. The only difference between these functions and SignedMin1_A() and SignedMin2_A() is the exercised condition codes. Function SignedMax1_A() uses jge (Jump if Greater or Equal) instead of jle, while SignedMax2_A() employs cmovl (Move if Less) instead of cmovg.

Unsigned versions of this example's minimum and maximum functions can be easily created using the following instruction substitutions: jbe (Jump if Below or Equal) for jle, jae (Jump if Above or Equal) for jge, cmova (Move if Above) for cmovg, and cmovb (Move if Below) for cmovl. Here are the results for source code example Ch11_07:

```
SignedMin1_A(    2,    15,     8) =     2
SignedMin2_A(    2,    15,     8) =     2

SignedMin1_A(   -3,   -22,    28) =   -22
SignedMin2_A(   -3,   -22,    28) =   -22

SignedMin1_A(   17,    37,   -11) =   -11
SignedMin2_A(   17,    37,   -11) =   -11

SignedMax1_A(   10,     5,     3) =    10
SignedMax2_A(   10,     5,     3) =    10

SignedMax1_A(   -3,    28,    15) =    28
SignedMax2_A(   -3,    28,    15) =    28

SignedMax1_A( -25,   -37,   -17) =   -17
SignedMax2_A( -25,   -37,   -17) =   -17
```

# Strings

The x86-64 instruction set includes several useful instructions that process and manipulate strings. In x86 parlance, a string is a contiguous sequence of bytes, words, doublewords, or quadwords. Programs can use the x86 string instructions to process conventional text strings such as "Hello, World." They also can be employed to perform operations using the elements of an array or a similarly ordered data structure in memory. Listing 11-8 shows the source code for example Ch11_08. This example demonstrates the use of the movsd (Move Data from String to String, Doubleword) and stosd (Store String, Doubleword) instructions. Source code example Ch11_08 also introduces some new assembler directives.

***Listing 11-8.*** Example Ch11_08

```
//-------------------------------------------------
//              Ch11_08.h
//-------------------------------------------------

#pragma once

// Ch11_08_fasm.asm
extern "C" void CopyArrayI32_A(int32_t* b, const int32_t* a, size_t n);
extern "C" void FillArrayI32_A(const int32_t* a, int32_t val, size_t n);

//-------------------------------------------------
//              Ch11_08.cpp
//-------------------------------------------------

#include <iostream>
#include <iomanip>
#include <cstdint>
#include "Ch11_08.h"

static void CopyArray(void);
static void FillArray(void);

int main()
{
    CopyArray();
    FillArray();
    return 0;
}

static void CopyArray(void)
{
    const size_t n = 10;
    const int32_t a[n] = {100, -200, 300, 400, -500, 600, 700, -800, 900, 1000};
    int32_t b[n] = {0, 0, 0, 0, 0, 0, 0, 0, 0, 0};

    CopyArrayI32_A(b, a, n);

    std::cout << "\n----- Results for CopyArrayI32_A -----\n";
```

```cpp
    for (size_t i = 0; i < n; i++)
    {
        std::cout << std::setw(5) << i << ": ";
        std::cout << std::setw(5) << a[i] << " ";
        std::cout << std::setw(5) << b[i] << '\n';
    }
}

static void FillArray(void)
{
    const int32_t val = -7;
    const size_t n = 10;
    const int32_t a[n] = {0, 0, 0, 0, 0, 0, 0, 0, 0, 0};

    FillArrayI32_A(a, val, n);

    std::cout << "\n----- Results for FillArrayI32_A -----\n";

    for (size_t i = 0; i < n; i++)
    {
        std::cout << std::setw(5) << i << ": ";
        std::cout << std::setw(5) << a[i] << '\n';
    }
}
```

```asm
;-------------------------------------------------
;                  Ch11_08_fasm.asm
;-------------------------------------------------


;-----------------------------------------------------------------------
;extern "C" void CopyArrayI32_A(int32_t* b, const int32_t* a, size_t n);
;-----------------------------------------------------------------------

        .code
CopyArrayI32_A proc frame

; Save non-volatile registers on stack
        push rsi                        ;save rsi
        .pushreg rsi
        push rdi                        ;save rdi
        .pushreg rdi
        .endprolog

; Copy the array
        mov rsi,rdx                     ;rsi = source array
        mov rdi,rcx                     ;rdi = destination array
        mov rcx,r8                      ;rcx = element count

        rep movsd                       ;copy the array
```

```
; Restore non-volatile registers and return
        pop rdi                          ;restore rdi
        pop rsi                          ;restore rsi
        ret
CopyArrayI32_A endp

;-------------------------------------------------------------------
; extern "C" void FillArrayI32_A(const int32_t* a, int32_t val, size_t n);
;-------------------------------------------------------------------

FillArrayI32_A proc frame

; Save non-volatile registers on stack
        push rdi                         ;save rdi
        .pushreg rdi
        .endprolog

; Fill the array
        mov rdi,rcx                      ;rdi = destination array
        mov eax,edx                      ;eax = fill value
        mov rcx,r8                       ;rcx = element count

        rep stosd                        ;fill the array

; Restore non-volatile registers and return
        pop rdi                          ;restore rdi
        ret
FillArrayI32_A endp
        end
```

Before examining the source code in Listing 11-8, a few more words regarding the Visual C++ calling convention are warranted. You may have noticed that the previous source code examples in this chapter used only a subset of the complete general-purpose register set. The reason for this is that the Visual C++ calling convention designates each general-purpose register as either volatile or nonvolatile. A function is permitted to alter the contents of any volatile register but must not modify the value in a nonvolatile register unless it preserves the caller's original value. The Visual C++ calling convention designates registers RAX, RCX, RDX, R8, R9, R10, and R11 as volatile; the remaining general-purpose registers are classified as nonvolatile.

The x86-64 string instructions use nonvolatile registers RSI and RDI, which means that their values must be preserved. A function typically saves the values of any nonvolatile registers it modifies on the stack in a section of code called the function prologue. A function epilogue contains code that restores the values of any saved nonvolatile registers. Function prologues and epilogues are also used to perform other calling convention initialization tasks, and you will learn about these in Chapter 12.

In Listing 11-8, the file Ch11_08.cpp includes a function named CopyArray(). This function performs test case initialization for the assembly language function CopyArrayI32_A(), which copies the elements of an integer array. Similarly, the C++ function FillArray() performs test case initialization for the assembly language function FillArrayI64_A(). This function sets each element in an array of 64-bit integers to the same value.

The first function in file Ch11_08_fasm.asm is named CopyArrayI32_A(). Note that this function includes a frame attribute in its proc directive. The frame attribute indicates that CopyArrayI32_A() uses a formal function prologue. It also enables additional directives that must be used whenever a general-purpose register is saved on the stack or whenever a function employs a stack frame pointer. Chapter 12 discusses the frame attribute and stack frame pointers in greater detail.

Function CopyArrayI32_A() begins its execution with a push rsi (Push Value onto Stack) instruction that saves the current value in register RSI on the stack. Immediately following the push rsi instruction is the assembler directive .pushreg rsi. This directive instructs the assembler to save information about the push rsi instruction in an assembler-maintained table that is used to unwind the stack during exception processing. Using exceptions with assembly language code is not discussed in this book, but the calling convention requirements for saving registers on the stack must still be observed. Register RDI is also saved on the stack using a push rdi instruction. The obligatory .pushreg rdi directive follows next, and the subsequent .endprolog directive signifies the end of the function prologue for CopyArrayI32_A(). Figure 11-3 illustrates the contents of the stack following execution of the push rdi instruction.

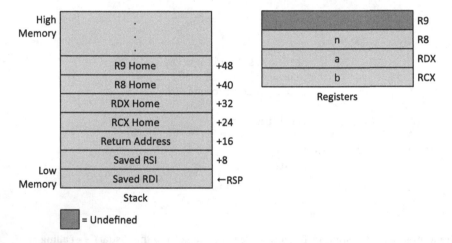

*Figure 11-3.* *Argument registers and stack in CopyArrayI32_A() following execution of push rdi*

Following its prologue, CopyArrayI32_A() uses a mov rsi,rdx instruction that loads source array pointer a into register RSI. The ensuing mov rdi,rcx instruction loads destination array pointer b into register RDI. This is followed by a mov rcx,r8 instruction that copies the element count n to RCX. Following initialization of registers RSI, RDI, and RCX, CopyArrayI32_A() uses the x86 instruction rep movsd to copy the doubleword elements in array a to array b. This is a two-part instruction. The movsd instruction copies the doubleword value pointed to by register RSI into the buffer pointed to by register RDI. If RFLAGS.DF is zero (the default for Visual C++ programs), movsd then adds 4 to both RSI and RDI, which updates both pointers for the next doubleword element move. If RFLAGS.DF is 1, movsd subtracts 4 from both RSI and RDI. The rep (Repeat String Operation) is an instruction repeat prefix that subtracts 1 from register RCX; it then repeats execution of the movsd instruction until RCX == 0 is true.

Recall that in its prologue, CopyArrayI32_A() saved the caller's RSI and RDI registers on the stack using two push instructions. The epilogue of CopyArrayI32_A() uses the instructions pop rdi (Pop Value from Stack) and pop rsi to restore the caller's RDI and RSI registers. The order in which nonvolatile registers are popped from the stack in an epilogue *must be the reverse* of how they were saved in the prologue. Following nonvolatile register restoration is a ret instruction that transfers program control back to the calling function.

■ **Caution**   Given the stack operations that occur in a function's prologue and epilogue, it should be readily apparent that failure to properly save or restore a nonvolatile register is likely to cause a program crash if the return address is incorrect or an obscure software bug that may be difficult to pinpoint.

The other function in Ch11_08_fasm.asm is named FillArrayI32_A(). This function uses the rep stosd instruction to set each element of a doubleword array to a constant value. Function FillArrayI32_A() begins its execution with a push rdi instruction that saves the caller's RDX register on the stack. Following the required assembler directives, FillArrayI32_A() uses a mov rdi,rcx instruction to load the address of array a into register RDI. The next instruction, mov eax,edx, loads the fill value val into register EAX. This is followed by a mov rcx,r8 instruction that loads the element count into register RCX. The stosd instruction copies the contents of register EAX to the memory location pointed to by register RDI. It then adds 4 (RFLAGS.DF = 0) to RDI or subtracts 4 (RFLAGS.DF = 1) from RDI. The rep prefix subtracts 1 from RCX and repeats execution of the stosd instruction until RCX == 0 is true. Here are the results for source code example Ch11_08:

```
----- Results for CopyArrayI32_A -----
    0:    100    100
    1:   -200   -200
    2:    300    300
    3:    400    400
    4:   -500   -500
    5:    600    600
    6:    700    700
    7:   -800   -800
    8:    900    900
    9:   1000   1000

----- Results for FillArrayI32_A -----
    0:     -7
    1:     -7
    2:     -7
    3:     -7
    4:     -7
    5:     -7
    6:     -7
    7:     -7
    8:     -7
    9:     -7
```

Source code example Ch11_08 demonstrated doubleword element moves and stores using the movsd and stosd instructions. You can also perform x86 string moves and stores using byte (movsb and stosb), word (movsw and stosw), or quadword (movsq and stosq) elements. The x86 instruction set also includes instructions that perform string compares (cmpsX), loads (lodsX), and scans (scasX). The X that is used in the preceding mnemonics is a place holder for b (byte), w (word), d (doubleword), or q (quadword). The cmpsX and scasX instructions can be used with a repe (Repeat Until RCX == 0 || RFLAGS.ZF == 0) prefix or repne (Repeat Until RCX == 0 || RFLAGS.ZF == 1) prefix. You can consult the AMD and Intel programming reference manuals listed in Appendix B for more information about x86 string instructions.

# Summary

Table 11-1 summarizes the x86 assembly language instructions introduced in this chapter. This table also includes closely related instructions. Before proceeding to the next chapter, make sure you understand the operation that is performed by each instruction shown in Table 11-1. You may also want to review the AMD and Intel programming reference manuals listed in Appendix B for additional information regarding these instructions. These documents contain important particulars regarding valid operands, memory addressing modes, and status flags for each x86 assembly language instruction.

*Table 11-1.* *X86 Assembly Language Instruction Summary for Chapter 11*

| Instruction Mnemonic | Description |
| --- | --- |
| add | Integer addition |
| and | Bitwise logical AND |
| call | Call procedure/function |
| cbw | Sign-extend byte to word |
| cdq | Sign-extend doubleword to quadword |
| cwd | Sign-extend word to doubleword |
| cqo | Sign-extend quadword to double quadword |
| cmovcc | Conditional move |
| cmps[b\|w\|d\|q] | Compare string |
| cmp | Compare integers |
| dec | Decrement integer by 1 |
| div | Integer division (unsigned) |
| inc | Increment integer by 1 |
| idiv | Integer division (signed) |
| imul | Integer multiplication (signed) |
| lods[b\|w\|d\|q] | Load string |
| jcc | Jump (conditional) |
| jmp | Jump (unconditional) |
| mov | Move data |
| movs[b\|w\|d\|q] | Move string |
| movsx[d] | Move with sign extension |
| movzx | Move with zero extension |
| mul | Integer multiplication (unsigned) |

*(continued)*

**Table 11-1.** (*continued*)

| Instruction Mnemonic | Description |
| --- | --- |
| neg | Negate integer (2's complement) |
| not | Negate integer (1's complement) |
| or | Bitwise logical inclusive OR |
| pop | Pop value from stack |
| push | Push value onto stack |
| rep, rep[e\|z\|ne\|nz] | String repeat prefix |
| ret | Return from procedure/function |
| sar | Shift right arithmetic |
| scas[b\|w\|d\|q] | Scan string |
| shl | Shift left logical |
| shr | Shift right logical |
| stos[b\|w\|d\|q] | Store string |
| sub | Integer subtraction |
| xor | Bitwise logical exclusive OR |

# CHAPTER 12

■ ■ ■

# Core Assembly Language Programming: Part 2

In the previous chapter, you were introduced to the fundamentals of x86-64 assembly language programming. You learned how to use elementary instructions that performed integer addition, subtraction, multiplication, and division. You also acquired valuable knowledge regarding memory addressing modes, condition codes, and assembly language programming syntax. The chapter that you are about to read is a continuation of the previous chapter. Topics discussed include scalar floating-point arithmetic, compares, and conversions. This chapter also provides additional details regarding the Visual C++ calling convention including volatile and nonvolatile registers, stack frames, and function prologues and epilogues.

## Scalar Floating-Point Arithmetic

Besides its SIMD capabilities, AVX also includes instructions that perform scalar floating-point operations including basic arithmetic, compares, and conversions. Many modern programs use AVX scalar floating-point instructions instead of legacy SSE2 or x87 FPU instructions. The primary reason for this is that most AVX instructions employ three operands: two nondestructive source operands and one destination operand. The use of nondestructive source operands often reduces the number of register-to-register transfers that a function must perform, which yields more efficient code. In this section, you will learn how to code functions that perform scalar floating-point operations using AVX. You will also learn how to pass floating-point arguments and return values between a C++ and assembly language function.

### Single-Precision Arithmetic

Listing 12-1 shows the source code for example Ch12_01. This example illustrates how to perform temperature conversions between Fahrenheit and Celsius using AVX and single-precision floating-point values. It also explains how to define and use floating-point constants in an assembly language function.

© Daniel Kusswurm 2022

D. Kusswurm, *Modern Parallel Programming with C++ and Assembly Language*,
https://doi.org/10.1007/978-1-4842-7918-2_12

***Listing 12-1.*** Example Ch12_01

```
//---------------------------------------------------
//                  Ch12_01.h
//---------------------------------------------------

#pragma once

// Ch12_01_fasm.asm
extern "C" float ConvertFtoC_Aavx(float deg_f);
extern "C" float ConvertCtoF_Aavx(float deg_c);


//---------------------------------------------------
//                  Ch12_01.cpp
//---------------------------------------------------

#include <iostream>
#include <iomanip>
#include "Ch12_01.h"

static void ConvertFtoC(void);
static void ConvertCtoF(void);

int main()
{
    ConvertFtoC();
    ConvertCtoF();
    return 0;
}

static void ConvertFtoC(void)
{
    const size_t w = 10;
    float deg_fvals[] = {-459.67f, -40.0f, 0.0f, 32.0f, 72.0f, 98.6f, 212.0f};
    size_t n = sizeof(deg_fvals) / sizeof(float);

    std::cout << "\n-------- ConvertFtoC Results --------\n";
    std::cout << std::fixed << std::setprecision(4);

    for (size_t i = 0; i < n; i++)
    {
        float deg_c = ConvertFtoC_Aavx(deg_fvals[i]);

        std::cout << "  i: " << i << "  ";
        std::cout << "f: " << std::setw(w) << deg_fvals[i] << "   ";
        std::cout << "c: " << std::setw(w) << deg_c << '\n';
    }
}

static void ConvertCtoF(void)
{
    const size_t w = 10;
```

```cpp
    float deg_cvals[] = {-273.15f, -40.0f, -17.777778f, 0.0f, 25.0f, 37.0f, 100.0f};
    size_t n = sizeof(deg_cvals) / sizeof(float);

    std::cout << "\n-------- ConvertCtoF Results --------\n";
    std::cout << std::fixed << std::setprecision(4);

    for (size_t i = 0; i < n; i++)
    {
        float deg_f = ConvertCtoF_Aavx(deg_cvals[i]);

        std::cout << "  i: " << i << " ";
        std::cout << "c: " << std::setw(w) << deg_cvals[i] << "  ";
        std::cout << "f: " << std::setw(w) << deg_f << '\n';
    }
}
```

```asm
;---------------------------------------------------
;                Ch12_01_fasm.asm
;---------------------------------------------------

            .const
r4_ScaleFtoC    real4 0.55555556            ; 5 / 9
r4_ScaleCtoF    real4 1.8                   ; 9 / 5
r4_32p0         real4 32.0

;-----------------------------------------------------------------------
; extern "C" float ConvertFtoC_Aavx(float deg_f);
;-----------------------------------------------------------------------

            .code
ConvertFtoC_Aavx proc
        vmovss xmm1,[r4_32p0]               ;xmm1 = 32
        vsubss xmm2,xmm0,xmm1               ;xmm2 = f - 32

        vmovss xmm1,[r4_ScaleFtoC]          ;xmm1 = 5 / 9
        vmulss xmm0,xmm2,xmm1               ;xmm0 = (f - 32) * 5 / 9

        ret
ConvertFtoC_Aavx endp

;-----------------------------------------------------------------------
; extern "C" float ConvertCtoF_Aavx(float deg_c);
;-----------------------------------------------------------------------

ConvertCtoF_Aavx proc
        vmulss xmm0,xmm0,[r4_ScaleCtoF]     ;xmm0 = c * 9 / 5
        vaddss xmm0,xmm0,[r4_32p0]          ;xmm0 = c * 9 / 5 + 32

        ret
ConvertCtoF_Aavx endp
        end
```

In Listing 12-1, the header file Ch12_01.h includes declaration statements for the functions ConvertFtoC_Aavx() and ConvertCtoF_Aavx(). Note that these functions require a single argument value of type float. Both functions also return a value of type float. The file Ch12_01.cpp includes a function named ConvertFtoC() that performs test case initialization for ConvertFtoC_Aavx() and displays the calculated results. File Ch12_01.cpp also includes the function ConvertCtoF(), which is the Celsius to Fahrenheit counterpart of ConvertFtoC().

The assembly language code in Ch12_01_fasm.asm starts with a .const section that defines the constants needed to convert a temperature value from Fahrenheit to Celsius and vice versa. The text real4 is a MASM directive that allocates storage space for single-precision floating-point value (the directive real8 can be used for double-precision floating-point values). Following the .const section is the code for function ConvertFtoC_Aavx(). The first instruction of this function, vmovss xmm1,[r4_32p0] (Move or Merge Scalar SPFP[1] Value), loads the single-precision floating-point value 32.0 from memory into register XMM1 (more precisely into XMM1[31:0]). A memory operand is used here since AVX does not support using immediate operands for scalar floating-point constants.

Per the Visual C++ calling convention, the first four floating-point argument values are passed to a function using registers XMM0, XMM1, XMM2, and XMM3. This means that upon entry to function ConvertFtoC_Aavx(), register XMM0 contains argument value deg_f. Following execution of the vmovss instruction, the vsubss xmm2,xmm0,xmm1 (Subtract Scalar SPFP Value) instruction calculates deg_f - 32.0 and saves the result in XMM2[31:0]. Execution of vsubss does not modify the contents of source operands XMM0 and XMM1. However, this instruction copies bits XMM0[127:32] to XMM2[127:32] (other AVX scalar arithmetic instructions also perform this copy operation). The ensuing vmovss xmm1,[r4_ScaleFtoC] loads the constant value 0.55555556 (or 5 / 9) into register XMM1. This is followed by a vmulss xmm0,xmm2,xmm1 (Multiply Scalar SPFP Value) instruction that computes (deg_f - 32.0) * 0.55555556 and saves the result (i.e., the converted temperature in Celsius) in XMM0. The Visual C++ calling convention designates register XMM0 for floating-point return values. Since the return value is already in XMM0, no additional vmovss instructions are necessary.

The assembly language function ConvertCtoF_Aavx() follows next. The code for this function differs slightly from ConvertFtoC_Aavx() in that the AVX scalar floating-point arithmetic instructions use memory operands to reference the required conversion constants. At entry to ConvertCtoF_Aavx(), register XMM0 contains argument value deg_c. The instruction vmulss xmm0,xmm0,[r4_ScaleCtoF] calculates deg_c * 1.8. This is followed by a vaddss xmm0,xmm0,[r4_32p0] (Add Scalar SPFP Value) instruction that calculates deg_c * 1.8 + 32.0. It should be noted at this point that neither ConvertFtoC_Aavx() nor ConvertCtoF_Aavx() perform any validity checks for argument values that are physically impossible (e.g., a temperature of -1000 degrees Fahrenheit). Such checks require floating-point compare instructions, and you will learn about these instructions later in this chapter. Here are the results for source code example Ch12_01:

```
-------- ConvertFtoC Results --------
 i: 0  f:  -459.6700  c:  -273.1500
 i: 1  f:   -40.0000  c:   -40.0000
 i: 2  f:     0.0000  c:   -17.7778
 i: 3  f:    32.0000  c:     0.0000
 i: 4  f:    72.0000  c:    22.2222
 i: 5  f:    98.6000  c:    37.0000
 i: 6  f:   212.0000  c:   100.0000
```

---

[1] Single-precision floating-point

```
-------- ConvertCtoF Results --------
  i: 0  c:   -273.1500  f:   -459.6700
  i: 1  c:    -40.0000  f:    -40.0000
  i: 2  c:    -17.7778  f:      0.0000
  i: 3  c:      0.0000  f:     32.0000
  i: 4  c:     25.0000  f:     77.0000
  i: 5  c:     37.0000  f:     98.6000
  i: 6  c:    100.0000  f:    212.0000
```

## Double-Precision Arithmetic

Listing 12-2 shows the source code for example Ch12_02. This example calculates 3D distances using AVX scalar arithmetic and double-precision floating-point values.

*Listing 12-2.* Example Ch12_02

```
//--------------------------------------------------
//              Ch12_02.h
//--------------------------------------------------

#pragma once

// Ch12_02_fcpp.cpp
extern double CalcDistance_Cpp(double x1, double y1, double z1, double x2,
    double y2, double z2);

// Ch12_02_fasm.asm
extern "C" double CalcDistance_Aavx(double x1, double y1, double z1, double x2,
    double y2, double z2);

// Ch12_02_misc.cpp
extern void InitArrays(double* x, double* y, double* z, size_t n,
    unsigned int rng_seed);

//--------------------------------------------------
//              Ch12_02.cpp
//--------------------------------------------------

#include <iostream>
#include <iomanip>
#include "Ch12_02.h"

static void CalcDistance(void);

int main()
{
    CalcDistance();
    return 0;
}
```

```
static void CalcDistance(void)
{
    const size_t n = 20;
    double x1[n], y1[n], z1[n], dist1[n];
    double x2[n], y2[n], z2[n], dist2[n];

    InitArrays(x1, y1, z1, n, 29);
    InitArrays(x2, y2, z2, n, 37);

    for (size_t i = 0; i < n; i++)
    {
        dist1[i] = CalcDistance_Cpp(x1[i], y1[i], z1[i], x2[i], y2[i], z2[i]);
        dist2[i] = CalcDistance_Aavx(x1[i], y1[i], z1[i], x2[i], y2[i], z2[i]);
    }

    size_t w1 = 3, w2 = 8;
    std::cout << std::fixed;

    for (size_t i = 0; i < n; i++)
    {
        std::cout << "i: " << std::setw(w1) << i << "   ";

        std::cout << std::setprecision(0);

        std::cout << "p1(";
        std::cout << std::setw(w1) << x1[i] << ",";
        std::cout << std::setw(w1) << y1[i] << ",";
        std::cout << std::setw(w1) << z1[i] << ") | ";

        std::cout << "p2(";
        std::cout << std::setw(w1) << x2[i] << ",";
        std::cout << std::setw(w1) << y2[i] << ",";
        std::cout << std::setw(w1) << z2[i] << ") | ";

        std::cout << std::setprecision(4);
        std::cout << "dist1: " << std::setw(w2) << dist1[i] << " | ";
        std::cout << "dist2: " << std::setw(w2) << dist2[i] << '\n';
    }
}

;----------------------------------------------------
;                 Ch12_02_fasm.asm
;----------------------------------------------------


;--------------------------------------------------------------------------
; extern "C" double CalcDistance_Aavx(double x1, double y1, double z1, double x2,
;   double y2, double z2);
;--------------------------------------------------------------------------
```

```
        .code
CalcDistance_Aavx proc

; Load arguments from stack
        vmovsd xmm4,real8 ptr [rsp+40]      ;xmm4 = y2
        vmovsd xmm5,real8 ptr [rsp+48]      ;xmm5 = z2

; Calculate squares of coordinate distances
        vsubsd xmm0,xmm3,xmm0               ;xmm0 = x2 - x1
        vmulsd xmm0,xmm0,xmm0               ;xmm0 = (x2 - x1) * (x2 - x1)

        vsubsd xmm1,xmm4,xmm1               ;xmm1 = y2 - y1
        vmulsd xmm1,xmm1,xmm1               ;xmm1 = (y2 - y1) * (y2 - y1)

        vsubsd xmm2,xmm5,xmm2               ;xmm2 = z2 - z1
        vmulsd xmm2,xmm2,xmm2               ;xmm2 = (z2 - z1) * (z2 - z1)

; Calculate final distance
        vaddsd xmm3,xmm0,xmm1
        vaddsd xmm4,xmm2,xmm3               ;xmm4 = sum of squares
        vsqrtsd xmm0,xmm0,xmm4              ;xmm0 = final distance value
        ret

CalcDistance_Aavx endp
        end
```

The Euclidian distance between two 3D points can be calculated using the following equation:

$$dist = \sqrt{\left(x_2 - x_1\right)^2 + \left(y_2 - y_1\right)^2 + \left(z_2 - z_1\right)^2}$$

If you examine the declaration of function CalcDistance_Aavx(), you will notice that it specifies six argument values of type double. Argument values x1, y1, z1, and x2 are passed in registers XMM0, XMM1, XMM2, and XMM3, respectively. The final two argument values, y2 and z2, are passed on the stack as illustrated in Figure 12-1. Note that this figure shows only the low-order quadword (bits 63:0) of each XMM register; the high-order quadword (bits 127:64) of each XMM register is undefined. Registers RCX, RDX, R8, and R9 are also undefined since CalcDistance_Aavx() does not utilize any integer or pointer arguments.

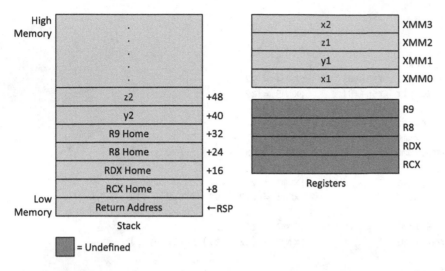

**Figure 12-1.** *Stack layout and argument registers at entry to* CalcDistance_Aavx()

The function CalcDistance_Aavx() begins with a vmovsd xmm4,real8 ptr [rsp+40] (Move or Merge Scalar DPFP[2] Value) instruction that loads argument value y2 from the stack into register XMM4 (more precisely into XMM4[63:0]). This is followed by a vmovsd xmm5,real8 ptr [rsp+48] instruction that loads argument value z2 into register XMM5. The next two instructions, vsubsd xmm0,xmm3,xmm0 (Subtract Scalar DPFP Value) and vmulsd xmm0,xmm0,xmm0 (Multiply Scalar DPFP Value), calculate (x2 - x1) * (x2 - x1). Similar sequences of instructions are then employed to calculate (y2 - y1) * (y2 - y1) and (z2 - z1) * (z2 - z1). This is followed by two vaddsd (Add Scalar DPFP Value) instructions that sum the three coordinate squares. A vsqrtsd xmm0,xmm0,xmm4 (Compute Square Root of Scalar DPFP Value) instruction computes the final distance. It is important to note that vsqrtsd computes the square root of its *second* source operand. Like other scalar double-precision floating-point arithmetic instructions, vsqrtsd also copies bits 127:64 of its first source operand to the same bit positions of the destination operand. Here are the results for source example Ch12_02:

```
i:   0  p1( 24,  4, 45) | p2(  8, 45, 20) | dist1:  50.6162 | dist2:  50.6162
i:   1  p1( 54, 59, 33) | p2( 22, 20, 81) | dist1:  69.6348 | dist2:  69.6348
i:   2  p1( 25, 23, 61) | p2( 83, 20, 44) | dist1:  60.5145 | dist2:  60.5145
i:   3  p1( 83,  4, 22) | p2( 98, 20, 62) | dist1:  45.6180 | dist2:  45.6180
i:   4  p1( 81, 21, 12) | p2( 73, 49, 64) | dist1:  59.5987 | dist2:  59.5987
i:   5  p1( 81, 97, 22) | p2( 70, 48, 45) | dist1:  55.2359 | dist2:  55.2359
i:   6  p1( 24, 62, 77) | p2( 20, 32, 15) | dist1:  68.9928 | dist2:  68.9928
i:   7  p1( 97, 81, 45) | p2( 20, 79, 18) | dist1:  81.6211 | dist2:  81.6211
i:   8  p1( 94, 81, 17) | p2(  8, 89, 87) | dist1: 111.1755 | dist2: 111.1755
i:   9  p1( 53, 82, 62) | p2( 43, 31, 84) | dist1:  56.4358 | dist2:  56.4358
i:  10  p1( 90, 72, 88) | p2( 25, 27, 30) | dist1:  98.0510 | dist2:  98.0510
i:  11  p1( 32,  4, 46) | p2( 62, 33, 53) | dist1:  42.3084 | dist2:  42.3084
i:  12  p1(  7, 88, 13) | p2( 12, 75, 30) | dist1:  21.9773 | dist2:  21.9773
i:  13  p1(  3, 90, 97) | p2( 89, 52, 38) | dist1: 111.0000 | dist2: 111.0000
```

---

[2] Double-precision floating-point

```
i:  14  p1( 60, 95, 54) | p2( 91, 51, 33) | dist1:  57.7754 | dist2:  57.7754
i:  15  p1( 16, 10, 52) | p2(  2, 32, 50) | dist1:  26.1534 | dist2:  26.1534
i:  16  p1( 87,  2, 68) | p2( 53, 20, 75) | dist1:  39.1024 | dist2:  39.1024
i:  17  p1( 32, 10, 37) | p2(  8, 41, 13) | dist1:  45.9674 | dist2:  45.9674
i:  18  p1( 62, 29, 84) | p2( 62, 37, 35) | dist1:  49.6488 | dist2:  49.6488
i:  19  p1( 16, 32, 31) | p2( 85, 19, 17) | dist1:  71.5961 | dist2:  71.5961
```

The final two letters of many x86-AVX arithmetic instruction mnemonics denote the operand type. You have already seen the instructions vaddss and vaddsd, which perform scalar single-precision and double-precision floating-point addition. In these instructions, the suffixes ss and sd denote scalar single-precision and double-precision values, respectively. X86-AVX instructions also use the mnemonic suffixes ps and pd to signify packed single-precision and double-precision values. X86-AVX instructions that manipulate more than one data type often include multiple data type characters in their mnemonics.

## Compares

Listing 12-3 shows the source code for example Ch12_03, which demonstrates the use of the floating-point compare instruction vcomiss (Compare Scalar SPFP Values). The vcomiss instruction compares two single-precision floating-point values and sets status flags in RFLAGS to signify a result of less than, equal, greater than, or unordered. The vcomisd (Compare Scalar DPFP Values) instruction is the double counterpart of vcomiss.

*Listing 12-3.* Example Ch12_03

```cpp
//-------------------------------------------------
//              Ch12_03.h
//-------------------------------------------------

#pragma once
#include <cstdint>

// Ch12_03_fasm.asm
extern "C" void CompareF32_Aavx(float a, float b, uint8_t* results);

// Ch12_03_misc.cpp
extern void DisplayResults(float a, float b, const uint8_t* cmp_results);

// Miscellaenous constants
const size_t c_NumCmpOps = 7;

//-------------------------------------------------
//              Ch12_03.cpp
//-------------------------------------------------

#include <iostream>
#include <iomanip>
#include <limits>
#include <string>
#include "Ch12_03.h"
```

```
static void CompareF32(void);

int main()
{
    CompareF32();
    return 0;
}

static void CompareF32(void)
{
    const size_t n = 6;
    float a[n] {120.0, 250.0, 300.0, -18.0, -81.0, 42.0};
    float b[n] {130.0, 240.0, 300.0, 32.0, -100.0, 0.0};

    // Set NAN test value
    b[n - 1] = std::numeric_limits<float>::quiet_NaN();

    std::cout << "\n----- Results for CompareF32 -----\n";

    for (size_t i = 0; i < n; i++)
    {
        uint8_t cmp_results[c_NumCmpOps];

        CompareF32_Aavx(a[i], b[i], cmp_results);
        DisplayResults(a[i], b[i], cmp_results);
    }
}

;--------------------------------------------------
;                  Ch12_03_fasm.asm
;--------------------------------------------------

;-----------------------------------------------------------------------
; extern "C" void CompareF32_Aavx(float a, float b, uint8_t* results);
;-----------------------------------------------------------------------

        .code
CompareF32_Aavx proc

; Set result flags based on compare status
        vcomiss xmm0,xmm1
        setp byte ptr [r8]                  ;RFLAGS.PF = 1 if unordered
        jnp @F
        xor al,al
        mov byte ptr [r8+1],al              ;set remaining elements in array
        mov byte ptr [r8+2],al              ;result[] to 0
        mov byte ptr [r8+3],al
        mov byte ptr [r8+4],al
        mov byte ptr [r8+5],al
        mov byte ptr [r8+6],al
        ret
```

```
@@:     setb byte ptr [r8+1]          ;set byte if a < b
        setbe byte ptr [r8+2]         ;set byte if a <= b
        sete byte ptr [r8+3]          ;set byte if a == b
        setne byte ptr [r8+4]         ;set byte if a != b
        seta byte ptr [r8+5]          ;set byte if a > b
        setae byte ptr [r8+6]         ;set byte if a >= b
        ret

CompareF32_Aavx endp
        end
```

The function CompareF32_Aavx() accepts three argument values: two of type float and a pointer to an array of uint8_t values for the results. The first instruction of CompareF32_Aavx(), vcomiss xmm0,xmm1, performs a single-precision floating-point compare of argument values a and b Note that these values were passed to CompareF32_Aavx() in registers XMM0 and XMM1, respectively. Execution of vcomiss sets RFLAGS.ZF, RFLAGS.PF, and RFLAGS.CF as shown in Table 12-1. The setting of these status flags facilitates the use of the conditional instructions cmovcc, jcc, and setcc (Set Byte on Condition) as shown in Table 12-2.

**Table 12-1.** *Status Flags Set by* vcomis[d|s]

| Condition | RFLAGS.ZF | RFLAGS.PF | RFLAGS.CF |
|---|---|---|---|
| XMM0 > XMM1 | 0 | 0 | 0 |
| XMM0 == XMM1 | 1 | 0 | 0 |
| XMM0 < XMM1 | 0 | 0 | 1 |
| Unordered | 1 | 1 | 1 |

**Table 12-2.** *Condition Codes Following Execution of* vcomis[d|s]

| Relational Operator | Condition Code | RFLAGS Test Condition |
|---|---|---|
| XMM0 < XMM1 | Below (b) | CF == 1 |
| XMM0 <= XMM1 | Below or equal (be) | CF == 1 \|\| ZF == 1 |
| XMM0 == XMM1 | Equal (e or z) | ZF == 1 |
| XMM0 != XMM1 | Not Equal (ne or nz) | ZF == 0 |
| XMM0 > XMM1 | Above (a) | CF == 0 && ZF == 0 |
| XMM0 >= XMM1 | Above or Equal (ae) | CF == 0 |
| Unordered | Parity (p) | PF == 1 |

It should be noted that the status flags shown in Table 12-1 are set only if floating-point exceptions are masked (the default state for Visual C++ and most other C++ compilers). If floating-point invalid operation or denormal exceptions are unmasked (MXCSR.IM = 0 or MXCSR.DM = 0) and one of the compare operands is a QNaN, SNaN, or denormal, the processor will generate an exception without updating the status flags in RFLAGS.

Following execution of the vcomiss xmm0,xmm1 instruction, CompareF32_Aavx() uses a series of setcc instructions to highlight the relational operators shown in Table 12-2. The setp byte ptr [r8] instruction sets the destination operand byte pointed to by R8 to 1 if RFLAGS.PF is set (i.e., one of the operands is a QNaN or SNaN); otherwise, the destination operand byte is set to 0. If the compare was ordered, the remaining setcc instructions in CompareF32_Aavx() save all possible compare outcomes by setting each entry in array results to 0 or 1. As previously mentioned, a function can also use a jcc or cmovcc instruction following execution of a vcomis[d|s] instruction to perform conditional jumps or moves based on the outcome of a floating-point compare. Here is the output for source code example Ch12_03:

```
----- Results for CompareF32 -----
a = 120, b = 130
UO=0       LT=1       LE=1       EQ=0       NE=1       GT=0       GE=0

a = 250, b = 240
UO=0       LT=0       LE=0       EQ=0       NE=1       GT=1       GE=1

a = 300, b = 300
UO=0       LT=0       LE=1       EQ=1       NE=0       GT=0       GE=1

a = -18, b = 32
UO=0       LT=1       LE=1       EQ=0       NE=1       GT=0       GE=0

a = -81, b = -100
UO=0       LT=0       LE=0       EQ=0       NE=1       GT=1       GE=1

a = 42, b = nan
UO=1       LT=0       LE=0       EQ=0       NE=0       GT=0       GE=0
```

## Conversions

Most C++ programs perform type conversions. For example, it is often necessary to cast a single-precision or double-precision floating-point value to an integer or vice versa. A function may also need to size-promote a single-precision floating-point value to double precision or narrow a double-precision floating-point value to single precision. AVX includes several instructions that perform conversions using either scalar or packed operands. Listing 12-4 shows the source code for example Ch12_04. This example illustrates the use of AVX scalar conversion instructions. Source code example Ch12_04 also introduces macros and explains how to change the rounding control bits in the MXCSR register.

*Listing 12-4.* Example Ch12_04

```
//-------------------------------------------------
//              Ch12_04.h
//-------------------------------------------------

#pragma once

// Simple union for data exchange
union Uval
{
    int32_t m_I32;
```

```cpp
    int64_t m_I64;
    float m_F32;
    double m_F64;
};

// The order of values in enum CvtOp must match the jump table
// that's defined in the .asm file.
enum class CvtOp : unsigned int
{
    I32_F32,        // int32_t to float
    F32_I32,        // float to int32_t
    I32_F64,        // int32_t to double
    F64_I32,        // double to int32_t
    I64_F32,        // int64_t to float
    F32_I64,        // float to int64_t
    I64_F64,        // int64_t to double
    F64_I64,        // double to int64_t
    F32_F64,        // float to double
    F64_F32,        // double to float
};

// Enumerated type for rounding control
enum class RC : unsigned int
{
    Nearest, Down, Up, Zero      // Do not change order
};

// Ch12_04_fasm.asm
extern "C" bool ConvertScalar_Aavx(Uval* a, Uval* b, CvtOp cvt_op, RC rc);

//--------------------------------------------------
//              Ch12_04.cpp
//--------------------------------------------------

#include <iostream>
#include <iomanip>
#include <cstdint>
#include <string>
#include <limits>
#define _USE_MATH_DEFINES
#include <math.h>
#include "Ch12_04.h"

const std::string c_RcStrings[] = {"Nearest", "Down", "Up", "Zero"};
const RC c_RcVals[] = {RC::Nearest, RC::Down, RC::Up, RC::Zero};
const size_t c_NumRC = sizeof(c_RcVals) / sizeof (RC);

static void ConvertScalars(void);

int main()
{
```

```cpp
    ConvertScalars();
    return 0;
}

static void ConvertScalars(void)
{
    const char nl = '\n';
    Uval src1, src2, src3, src4, src5, src6, src7;

    src1.m_F32 = (float)M_PI;
    src2.m_F32 = (float)-M_E;
    src3.m_F64 = M_SQRT2;
    src4.m_F64 = M_SQRT1_2;
    src5.m_F64 = 1.0 + DBL_EPSILON;
    src6.m_I32 = std::numeric_limits<int>::max();
    src7.m_I64 = std::numeric_limits<long long>::max();

std::cout << "----- Results for ConvertScalars() -----\n";

    for (size_t i = 0; i < c_NumRC; i++)
    {
        RC rc = c_RcVals[i];
        Uval des1, des2, des3, des4, des5, des6, des7;

        ConvertScalar_Aavx(&des1, &src1, CvtOp::F32_I32, rc);
        ConvertScalar_Aavx(&des2, &src2, CvtOp::F32_I64, rc);
        ConvertScalar_Aavx(&des3, &src3, CvtOp::F64_I32, rc);
        ConvertScalar_Aavx(&des4, &src4, CvtOp::F64_I64, rc);
        ConvertScalar_Aavx(&des5, &src5, CvtOp::F64_F32, rc);
        ConvertScalar_Aavx(&des6, &src6, CvtOp::I32_F32, rc);
        ConvertScalar_Aavx(&des7, &src7, CvtOp::I64_F64, rc);

        std::cout << std::fixed;
        std::cout << "\nRounding control = " << c_RcStrings[(int)rc] << nl;

        std::cout << "  F32_I32: " << std::setprecision(8);
        std::cout << src1.m_F32 << " --> " << des1.m_I32 << nl;

        std::cout << "  F32_I64: " << std::setprecision(8);
        std::cout << src2.m_F32 << " --> " << des2.m_I64 << nl;

        std::cout << "  F64_I32: " << std::setprecision(8);
        std::cout << src3.m_F64 << " --> " << des3.m_I32 << nl;

        std::cout << "  F64_I64: " << std::setprecision(8);
        std::cout << src4.m_F64 << " --> " << des4.m_I64 << nl;

        std::cout << "  F64_F32: ";
        std::cout << std::setprecision(16) << src5.m_F64 << " --> ";
        std::cout << std::setprecision(8) << des5.m_F32 << nl;

        std::cout << "  I32_F32: " << std::setprecision(8);
```

```
        std::cout << src6.m_I32 << " --> " << des6.m_F32 << nl;

        std::cout << "  I64_F64: " << std::setprecision(8);
        std::cout << src7.m_I64 << " --> " << des7.m_F64 << nl;
    }
}


;-------------------------------------------------
;                Ch12_04_fasm.asm
;-------------------------------------------------

MxcsrRcMask       equ 9fffh                   ;bit mask for MXCSR.RC
MxcsrRcShift      equ 13                      ;shift count for MXCSR.RC


;----------------------------------------------------------------------------
; Macro GetRC_M - copies MXCSR.RC to r10d[1:0]
;----------------------------------------------------------------------------

GetRC_M macro
        vstmxcsr dword ptr [rsp+8]            ;save mxcsr register
        mov r10d,[rsp+8]

        shr r10d,MxcsrRcShift                 ;r10d[1:0] = MXCSR.RC bits
        and r10d,3                            ;clear unused bits
        endm

;----------------------------------------------------------------------------
; Macro SetRC_M - sets MXCSR.RC to rm_reg[1:0]
;----------------------------------------------------------------------------

SetRC_M macro RcReg
        vstmxcsr dword ptr [rsp+8]            ;save current MXCSR
        mov eax,[rsp+8]

        and RcReg,3                           ;clear unusned bits
        shl RcReg,MxcsrRcShift                ;rc_reg[14:13] = rc

        and eax,MxcsrRcMask                   ;clear non MXCSR.RC bits
        or eax,RcReg                          ;insert new MXCSR.RC

        mov [rsp+8],eax
        vldmxcsr dword ptr [rsp+8]            ;load updated MXCSR
        endm

;----------------------------------------------------------------------------
; extern "C" bool ConvertScalar_Aavx(Uval* des, const Uval* src, CvtOp cvt_op, RC rc)
;
; Note:    This function requires linker option /LARGEADDRESSAWARE:NO
;----------------------------------------------------------------------------

        .code
ConvertScalar_Aavx proc
```

403

```
; Make sure cvt_op is valid
        cmp r8d,CvtOpTableCount              ;is cvt_op >= CvtOpTableCount
        jae BadCvtOp                         ;jump if cvt_op is invalid

; Save current MSCSR.RC
        GetRC_M                              ;r10d = current RC

; Set new rounding mode
        SetRC_M r9d                          ;set new MXCSR.RC

; Jump to target conversion code block
        mov eax,r8d                          ;rax = cvt_op
        jmp [CvtOpTable+rax*8]

; Conversions between int32_t and float/double

I32_F32:
        mov eax,[rdx]                        ;load integer value
        vcvtsi2ss xmm0,xmm0,eax              ;convert to float
        vmovss real4 ptr [rcx],xmm0          ;save result
        jmp Done

F32_I32:
        vmovss xmm0,real4 ptr [rdx]          ;load float value
        vcvtss2si eax,xmm0                   ;convert to integer
        mov [rcx],eax                        ;save result
        jmp Done

I32_F64:
        mov eax,[rdx]                        ;load integer value
        vcvtsi2sd xmm0,xmm0,eax              ;convert to double
        vmovsd real8 ptr [rcx],xmm0          ;save result
        jmp Done

F64_I32:
        vmovsd xmm0,real8 ptr [rdx]          ;load double value
        vcvtsd2si eax,xmm0                   ;convert to integer
        mov [rcx],eax                        ;save result
        jmp Done

; Conversions between int64_t and float/double

I64_F32:
        mov rax,[rdx]                        ;load integer value
        vcvtsi2ss xmm0,xmm0,rax              ;convert to float
        vmovss real4 ptr [rcx],xmm0          ;save result
        jmp Done

F32_I64:
        vmovss xmm0,real4 ptr [rdx]          ;load float value
        vcvtss2si rax,xmm0                   ;convert to integer
```

```
        mov [rcx],rax                     ;save result
        jmp Done

I64_F64:
        mov rax,[rdx]                     ;load integer value
        vcvtsi2sd xmm0,xmm0,rax           ;convert to double
        vmovsd real8 ptr [rcx],xmm0       ;save result
        jmp Done

F64_I64:
        vmovsd xmm0,real8 ptr [rdx]       ;load double value
        vcvtsd2si rax,xmm0                ;convert to integer
        mov [rcx],rax                     ;save result
        jmp Done

; Conversions between float and double

F32_F64:
        vmovss xmm0,real4 ptr [rdx]       ;load float value
        vcvtss2sd xmm1,xmm1,xmm0          ;convert to double
        vmovsd real8 ptr [rcx],xmm1       ;save result
        jmp Done

F64_F32:
        vmovsd xmm0,real8 ptr [rdx]       ;load double value
        vcvtsd2ss xmm1,xmm1,xmm0          ;convert to float
        vmovss real4 ptr [rcx],xmm1       ;save result
        jmp Done

BadCvtOp:
        xor eax,eax                       ;set error return code
        ret

Done:   SetRC_M r10d                      ;restore original MXCSR.RC
        mov eax,1                         ;set success return code
        ret

; The order of values in following table must match enum CvtOp
; that's defined in the .h file.

        align 8
CvtOpTable equ $
        qword I32_F32, F32_I32
        qword I32_F64, F64_I32
        qword I64_F32, F32_I64
        qword I64_F64, F64_I64
        qword F32_F64, F64_F32
CvtOpTableCount equ ($ - CvtOpTable) / size qword

ConvertScalar_Aavx endp
        end
```

Near the top of Listing 12-4 is the definition of a union named Uval. Source code example Ch12_04 uses this union to simplify data exchange between the C++ and assembly language code. Following Uval is an enum named CvtOp, which defines symbolic names for the conversions. Also included in file Ch12_04.h is the enum RC. This type defines symbolic names for the floating-point rounding modes. Recall from the discussions in Chapter 10 that the MXCSR register contains a two-bit field that specifies the rounding method for floating-point operations (see Table 10-4).

Also shown in Listing 12-4 is the file Ch12_04.cpp. This file includes the driver function ConvertScalars(), which performs test case initialization and streams results to std::cout. Note that each use of the assembly language function ConvertScalar_Aavx() requires two argument values of type Uval, one argument of type CvtOp, and one argument of type RC.

Assembly language source code files often employ the equ (equate) directive to define symbolic names for numerical expressions. The equ directive is somewhat analogous to a C++ const definition (e.g., const int x = 100;). The first noncomment statement in Ch12_04_fasm.asm, MxcsrRcMask equ 9fffh, defines a symbolic name for a mask that will be used to modify bits MXCSR.RC. This is followed by another equ directive MxcsrRcShift equ 13 that defines a shift count for bits MXCSR.RC.

Immediately following the two equate statements is the definition of a macro named GetRC_M. A macro is a text substitution mechanism that enables a programmer to represent a sequence of assembly language instructions, data, or other statements using a single text string. Assembly language macros are typically employed to generate sequences of instructions that will be used more than once. Macros are also frequently exercised to factor out and reuse code without the performance overhead of a function call.

Macro GetRC_M emits a sequence of assembly language instructions that obtain the current value of MXCSR.RC. The first instruction of this macro, vstmxcsr dword ptr [rsp+8] (Store MXCSR Register State), saves the contents of register MXCSR on the stack. The reason for saving MXCSR on the stack is that vstmxcsr only supports memory operands. The next instruction, mov r10d,[rsp+8], copies this value from the stack and loads it into register R10D. The ensuing instruction pair, shr r10d,MxcsrRcShift and and r10d,3, relocates the rounding control bits to bits 1:0 of register R10D; all other bits in R10D are set to zero. The text endm is an assembler directive that signifies the end of macro GetRC_M.

Following the definition of macro GetRC_M is another macro named SetRC_M. This macro emits instructions that modify MXCSR.RC. Note that macro SetRC_M includes an argument named RcReg. This is a symbolic name for the general-purpose register that contains the new value for MXCSR.RC. More on this in a moment. Macro SetRC_M also begins with the instruction sequence vstmxcsr dword ptr [rsp+8] and mov eax,[rsp+8] to obtain the current contents of MXCSR. It then employs the instruction pair and RcReg,3 and shl RcReg,MxcsrRcShift. These instructions shift the new bits for MXCSR.RC into the correct position. During macro expansion, the assembler replaces macro argument RcReg with the actual register name as you will soon see. The ensuing and eax,MxcsrRcMask and or eax,RcReg instructions update MXCSR.RC with the new rounding mode. The next instruction pair, mov [rsp+8],eax and vldmxcsr dword ptr [rsp+8] (Load MXCSR Register State), loads the new RC control bits into MXCSR.RC. Note that the instruction sequence used in SetRC_M preserves all other bits in the MXCSR register.

Function ConvertScalar_Aavx() begins its execution with the instruction pair cmp r8d,CvtOpTableCount and jae BadCvtOp that validates argument value cvt_op. If cvt_op is valid, ConvertScalar_Aavx() uses GetRC_M and SetRC_M r9d to modify MXCSR.RC. Note that register R9D contains the new rounding mode. Figure 12-2 contains a portion of the MASM listing file (with some minor edits to improve readability) that shows the expansion of macros GetRC_M and SetRC_M. The MASM listing file denotes macro expanded instructions with a '1' in a column located to the left of each instruction mnemonic. Note that in the expansion of macro SetRC_M, register r9d is substituted for macro argument RcReg.

```
00000000                                        .code
00000000                          ConvertScalar_Aavx proc

                                  ; Make sure cvt_op is valid
00000000  41/ 81 F8                              cmp r8d,CvtOpTableCount    ;is cvt_op >= CvtOpTableCount
          0000000A
00000007  0F 83 000000C5                         jae BadCvtOp               ;jump if cvt_op is invalid

                                  ; Save current MSCSR.RC
                                        GetRC_M                            ;r10d = current RC
0000000D  C5 F8/ AE 5C 24    1                   vstmxcsr dword ptr [rsp+8] ;save mxcsr register
          08
00000013  44/ 8B 54 24       1                   mov r10d,[rsp+8]
          08
00000018  41/ C1 EA 0D       1                   shr r10d,MxcsrRcShift      ;r10d[1:0] = MXCSR.RC bits
0000001C  41/ 83 E2 03       1                   and r10d,3                 ;clear unused bits

                                  ; Set new rounding mode
                                        SetRC_M r9d                        ;set new MXCSR.RC
00000020  C5 F8/ AE 5C 24    1                   vstmxcsr dword ptr [rsp+8] ;save current MXCSR
          08
00000026  8B 44 24 08        1                   mov eax,[rsp+8]
0000002A  41/ 83 E1 03       1                   and r9d,3                  ;clear unusned bits
0000002E  41/ C1 E1 0D       1                   shl r9d,MxcsrRcShift       ;rc_reg[14:13] = rc
00000032  25 00009FFF        1                   and eax,MxcsrRcMask        ;clear non MXCSR.RC bits
00000037  41/ 0B C1          1                   or eax,r9d                 ;insert new MXCSR.RC
0000003A  89 44 24 08        1                   mov [rsp+8],eax
0000003E  C5 F8/ AE 54 24    1                   vldmxcsr dword ptr [rsp+8] ;load updated MXCSR
          08

                                  ; Jump to target conversion code block
00000044  41/ 8B C0                              mov eax,r8d                ;rax = cvt_op
00000047  FF 24 C5                               jmp [CvtOpTable+rax*8]
          00000100 R
```

**Figure 12-2.** *Expansion of macros GetRC_M and SetRC_M*

Function ConvertScalar_Aavx() uses argument value cvt_op and a jump table to select a conversion code block. This construct is akin to a C++ switch statement. Immediately after the ret instruction is a jump table named CvtOpTable. The align 8 statement that appears just before the start of CvtOpTable is an assembler directive that instructs the assembler to align the start of CvtOpTable on a quadword boundary. The align 8 directive is used here since CvtOpTable contains quadword elements of labels defined in ConvertScalar_Aavx(). The labels correspond to code blocks that perform a specific numerical conversion. The instruction jmp [CvtOpTable+rax*8] transfers program control to the code block specified by cvt_op, which was copied into RAX. More specifically, execution of the jmp [CvtOpTable+rax*8] instruction loads RIP with the quadword value stored in memory location CvtOpTable + rax * 8.

Each conversion code block in ConvertScalar_Aavx() uses a different AVX instruction to carry out a specific conversion operation. For example, the code block that follows label I32_F32 uses the instruction vcvtsi2ss (Convert Doubleword Integer to SPFP Value) to convert a 32-bit signed integer to single-precision floating-point. Table 12-3 summarizes the scalar floating-point conversion instructions used in example Ch12_04.

*Table 12-3.* *AVX Scalar Floating-Point Conversion Instructions*

| Instruction Mnemonic | Description |
| --- | --- |
| vcvtsi2ss | Convert 32- or 64-bit signed integer to SPFP |
| vcvtsi2sd | Convert 32- or 64-bit signed integer to DPFP |
| vcvtss2si | Convert SPFP to 32- or 64-bit signed integer |
| vcvtsd2si | Convert DPFP to 32- or 64-bit signed integer |
| vcvtss2sd | Convert SPFP to DPFP |
| vcvtsd2ss | Convert DPFP to SPFP |

The last instruction of each conversion code block is a jmp Done instruction. The label Done is located near the end of function ConvertScalar_Aavx(). At label Done, function ConvertScalar_Aavx() uses SetRC_M r10d to restore the original value of MXCSR.RC. The Visual C++ calling convention requires MXCSR.RC to be preserved across function boundaries. You will learn more about this later in this chapter. Here are the results for source code example Ch12_04:

```
----- Results for ConvertScalars() -----
Rounding control = Nearest
  F32_I32: 3.14159274 → 3
  F32_I64: -2.71828175 --> -3
  F64_I32: 1.41421356 --> 1
  F64_I64: 0.70710678 --> 1
  F64_F32: 1.0000000000000002 --> 1.00000000
  I32_F32: 2147483647 --> 2147483648.00000000
  I64_F64: 9223372036854775807 --> 9223372036854775808.00000000

Rounding control = Down
  F32_I32: 3.14159274 --> 3
  F32_I64: -2.71828175 --> -3
  F64_I32: 1.41421356 --> 1
  F64_I64: 0.70710678 --> 0
  F64_F32: 1.0000000000000002 --> 1.00000000
  I32_F32: 2147483647 --> 2147483520.00000000
  I64_F64: 9223372036854775807 --> 9223372036854774784.00000000

Rounding control = Up
  F32_I32: 3.14159274 --> 4
  F32_I64: -2.71828175 --> -2
  F64_I32: 1.41421356 --> 2
  F64_I64: 0.70710678 --> 1
  F64_F32: 1.0000000000000002 --> 1.00000012
  I32_F32: 2147483647 --> 2147483648.00000000
  I64_F64: 9223372036854775807 --> 9223372036854775808.00000000

Rounding control = Zero
  F32_I32: 3.14159274 --> 3
  F32_I64: -2.71828175 --> -2
```

```
F64_I32: 1.41421356 --> 1
F64_I64: 0.70710678 --> 0
F64_F32: 1.0000000000000002 --> 1.00000000
I32_F32: 2147483647 --> 2147483520.00000000
I64_F64: 9223372036854775807 --> 9223372036854774784.00000000
```

# Scalar Floating-Point Arrays

Listing 12-5 shows the source code for example Ch12_05. This example illustrates how to calculate the mean and standard deviation of an array of single-precision floating-point values. Listing 12-5 only shows the assembly language code for example Ch12_05 since most of the other code is identical to what you saw in example Ch03_04. The equations used to calculate the mean and standard deviation are also the same.

***Listing 12-5.*** Example Ch12_05

```
;---------------------------------------------------
;               Ch12_05_fasm.asm
;---------------------------------------------------


;--------------------------------------------------------------------------
; exte"n""C" bool CalcMeanF32_Aavx(float* mean, const float* x, size_t n);
;--------------------------------------------------------------------------

        .code
CalcMeanF32_Aavx proc

; Make sure n is valid
        cmp r8,2                        ;is n >= 2?
        jae @F                          ;jump if yes
        xor eax,eax                     ;set error return code
        ret

; Initialize
@@:     vxorps xmm0,xmm0,xmm0           ;sum = 0.0f
        mov rax,-1                      ;i = -1

; Sum the elements of x
Loop1:  inc rax                         ;i += 1
        cmp rax,r8                      ;is i >= n?
        jae CalcM                       ;jump if yes

        vaddss xmm0,xmm0,real4 ptr [rdx+rax*4]  ;sum += x[i]
        jmp Loop1

; Calculate and save the mean
CalcM:  vcvtsi2ss xmm1,xmm1,r8          ;convert n to SPFP
        vdivss xmm1,xmm0,xmm1           ;xmm2 = mean = sum / n
        vmovss real4 ptr [rcx],xmm1     ;save mean
```

```
        mov eax,1                               ;set success return code
        ret

CalcMeanF32_Aavx endp

;-------------------------------------------------------------------------
; exte"n""C" bool CalcStDevF32_Aavx(float* st_dev, const float* x, size_t n, float mean);
;-------------------------------------------------------------------------

CalcStDevF32_Aavx proc

; Make sure n is valid
        cmp r8,2                                ;is n >= 2?
        jae @F                                  ;jump if yes
        xor eax,eax                             ;set error return code
        ret

; Initialize
@@:     vxorps xmm0,xmm0,xmm0                   ;sum_squares = 0.0f
        mov rax,-1                              ;i = -1

; Sum the elements of x
Loop1:  inc rax                                 ;i += 1
        cmp rax,r8                              ;is i >= n?
        jae CalcSD                              ;jump if yes

        vmovss xmm1,real4 ptr [rdx+rax*4]       ;xmm1 = x[i]
        vsubss xmm2,xmm1,xmm3                    ;xmm2 = x[-] - mean
        vmulss xmm2,xmm2,xmm2                    ;xmm2 = (x[-] - mean) ** 2
        vaddss xmm0,xmm0,xmm2                    ;update sum_squares
        jmp Loop1

; Calculate and save standard deviation
CalcSD: dec r8                                  ;r8 =-n - 1
        vcvtsi2ss xmm1,xmm1,r8                   ;convert-n - 1 to SPFP
        vdivss xmm0,xmm0,xmm1                    ;xmm0 = sum_squares / -n - 1)
        vsqrtss xmm0,xmm0,xmm0                   ;xmm0 = st_dev
        vmovss real4 ptr [rcx],xmm0              ;save st_dev

        mov eax,1                               ;set success return code
        ret
CalcStDevF32_Aavx endp
        end
```

Listing 12-5 begins with the definition of assembly language function CalcMeanF32_Aavx(). The first code block of this function verifies that n >= 2 is true. Following validation of n, CalcMeanF32_Aavx() uses a vxorps xmm0,xmm0,xmm0 (Bitwise Logical XOR of Packed SPFP Values) instruction to set sum = 0.0. The next instruction, mov rax,-1, initializes loop index variable i to -1. Each iteration of Loop1 begins with an inc rax instruction that calculates i += 1. The ensuing instruction pair, cmp rax,r8 and jae CalcM, terminates Loop1 when i >= n is true. The vaddss xmm0,xmm0,real4 ptr [rdx+rax*4] instruction computes sum += x[i]. Following the calculation of sum, CalcMeanF32_Aavx() converts n to a single-precision floating-point value using the AVX instruction vcvtsi2ss  xmm1,xmm1,r8. The next two instructions, vdivss xmm1,xmm0,xmm1 and vmovss real4 ptr [rcx],xmm1, calculate and save mean.

Function CalcStDev_Aavx() uses a similar for-loop construct to calculate the standard deviation. Inside Loop1, CalcStDev_Aavx() calculates sum_squares using the AVX instructions vsubss, vmulss, and vaddss. Note that argument value mean was passed in register XMM3. Following execution of Loop1, CalcStDev_ Aavx() calculates the standard deviation using the instructions dec r8 (to calculate n - 1), vcvtsi2ss, vdivss, and vsqrtss.

The assembly language code in Listing 12-5 can be easily modified to create the double-precision counterpart functions CalcMeanF64_Aavx() and CalcStDevF64_Aavx(). Simply switch the single-precision (ss suffix) instructions to their double-precision (sd suffix) counterparts. Instructions that reference operands in memory will also need to use real8 ptr and a scale factor of 8 instead of real4 ptr and 4. Here are the results for source code example Ch12_05:

```
Results for CalcMeanF32_Cpp and CalcStDevF32_Cpp
mean1:    49.602146  st_dev1:  27.758242

Results for CalcMeanF32_Aavx and CalcStDevF32_Aavx
mean2:    49.602146  st_dev2:  27.758242
```

# Calling Convention: Part 2

The source code presented thus far has informally discussed various aspects of the Visual C++ calling convention. In this section, the calling convention is formally explained. It reiterates some earlier elucidations and introduces new requirements that have not been discussed. A basic understanding of the calling convention is necessary since it is used extensively in subsequent chapters that explain x86-AVX SIMD programming using x86-64 assembly language.

---

■ **Note** As a reminder, if you are reading this book to learn x86-64 assembly language programming and plan on using it with a different operating system or high-level language, you should consult the appropriate documentation for more information regarding the particulars of that calling convention.

---

The Visual C++ calling convention designates each x86-64 processor general-purpose register as volatile or nonvolatile. It also applies a volatile or nonvolatile classification to each XMM register. An x86-64 assembly language function can modify the contents of any volatile register but *must* preserve the contents of any nonvolatile register it uses. Table 12-4 lists the volatile and nonvolatile general-purpose and XMM registers.

**Table 12-4.** *Visual C++ 64-Bit Volatile and Nonvolatile Registers*

| Register Group | Volatile Registers | Nonvolatile Registers |
| --- | --- | --- |
| General-purpose | RAX, RCX, RDX, R8, R9, R10, R11 | RBX, RSI, RDI, RBP, RSP, R12, R13, R14, R15 |
| Floating point and SIMD | XMM0–XMM5 | XMM6–XMM15 |

On systems that support AVX or AVX2, the high-order 128 bits of registers YMM0–YMM15 are classified as volatile. Similarly, the high-order 384 bits of registers ZMM0–ZMM15 are classified as volatile on systems that support AVX-512. Registers ZMM16–ZMM31 and their corresponding YMM and XMM registers are also designated as volatile and need not be preserved. The legacy x87 FPU register stack is classified as volatile. All control bits in RFLAGS and MXCSR must be preserved across function boundaries. For example, assume function Foo() changes MXCSR.RC prior to performing a floating-point calculation. It then needs to call the C++ library function cos() to perform another calculation. Function Foo() must restore the original contents of MXCSR.RC before calling cos().

The programming requirements imposed on an x86-64 assembly language function by the Visual C++ calling convention vary depending on whether the function is a leaf or nonleaf function. Leaf functions are functions that

- Do not call any other functions

- Do not modify the contents of register RSP

- Do not allocate any local stack space

- Do not modify any of the nonvolatile general-purpose or XMM registers

- Do not use exception handling

X86-64-bit assembly language leaf functions are easier to code, but they are only suitable for relatively simple computations. A nonleaf function can use the entire x86-64 register set, create a stack frame, or allocate local stack space. The preservation of nonvolatile registers and local stack space allocation is typically performed at the beginning of a function in a code block known as the prologue. Functions that utilize a prologue must also include a corresponding epilogue. A function epilogue releases any locally allocated stack space and restores any prologue preserved nonvolatile registers.

In the remainder of this section, you will examine four source code examples. The first three examples illustrate how to code nonleaf functions using explicit x86-64 assembly language instructions and assembler directives. These examples also convey critical programming information regarding the organization of a nonleaf function stack frame. The fourth example demonstrates how to use several prologue and epilogue macros. These macros help automate most of the programming labor that is associated with a nonleaf function. The source code listings in this section include only the C++ header file and the x86-64 assembly language code. The C++ code that performs test case initialization, argument checking, displaying of results, etc., is not shown to streamline the elucidations. The software download package includes the complete source code for each example.

## Stack Frames

Listing 12-6 shows the source code for example Ch12_06. This example demonstrates how to create and use a stack frame pointer in an assembly language function. Source code example Ch12_06 also illustrates some of the programming protocols that an assembly language function prologue and epilogue must observe.

***Listing 12-6.*** Example Ch12_06

```
//-------------------------------------------------
//                 Ch12_06.h
//-------------------------------------------------

#pragma once
#include <cstdint>

// Ch12_06_fasm.asm
```

```
extern "C" int64_t SumIntegers_A(int8_t a, int16_t b, int32_t c, int64_t d,
    int8_t e, int16_t f, int32_t g, int64_t h);

;-------------------------------------------------
;                 Ch12_06_fasm.asm
;-------------------------------------------------

;---------------------------------------------------------------------------
; extern "C" int64_t SumIntegers_A(int8_t a, int16_t b, int32_t c, int64_t d,
;   int8_t e, int16_t f, int32_t g, int64_t h);
;---------------------------------------------------------------------------

; Named expressions for constant values:
;
; RBP_RA       = number of bytes between RBP and return address on stack
; STK_LOCAL    = size of local stack space

RBP_RA = 24
STK_LOCAL = 16


        .code
SumIntegers_A proc frame

; Function prologue
        push rbp                        ;save caller's rbp register
        .pushreg rbp
        sub rsp,STK_LOCAL               ;allocate local stack space
        .allocstack STK_LOCAL
        mov rbp,rsp                     ;set frame pointer
        .setframe rbp,0
        .endprolog                      ;mark end of prologe
; Save argument registers to home area (optional)
        mov [rbp+RBP_RA+8],rcx
        mov [rbp+RBP_RA+16],rdx
        mov [rbp+RBP_RA+24],r8
        mov [rbp+RBP_RA+32],r9

; Calculate a + b + c + d
        movsx rcx,cl                    ;rcx = a
        movsx rdx,dx                    ;rdx = b
        movsxd r8,r8d                   ;r8 = c;
        add rcx,rdx                     ;rcx = a + b
        add r8,r9                       ;r8 = c + d
        add r8,rcx                      ;r8 = a + b + c + d
        mov [rbp],r8                    ;save a + b + c + d on stack

; Calculate e + f + g + h
        movsx rcx,byte ptr [rbp+RBP_RA+40]   ;rcx = e
        movsx rdx,word ptr [rbp+RBP_RA+48]   ;rdx = f
        movsxd r8,dword ptr [rbp+RBP_RA+56]  ;r8 = g
```

413

```
        add rcx,rdx                             ;rcx = e + f
        add r8,qword ptr [rbp+RBP_RA+64]        ;r8 = g + h
        add r8,rcx                              ;r8 = e + f + g + h

; Compute final sum
        mov rax,[rbp]                           ;rax = a + b + c + d
        add rax,r8                              ;rax = final sum

; Function epilogue
        add rsp,16                              ;release local stack space
        pop rbp                                 ;restore caller's rbp register
        ret


SumIntegers_A endp
        end
```

Functions that need to reference both argument values and local variables on the stack often create a stack frame during execution of their prologues. During creation of a stack frame, register RBP is typically initialized as a stack frame pointer. Following stack frame initialization, the remaining code in a function can access items on the stack using RBP as a base register.

Near the top of file Ch12_06_fasm.asm are the statements RBP_RA = 24 and STK_LOCAL = 16. The = symbol is an assembler directive that defines a symbolic name for a numerical value. Unlike the equ directive, symbolic names defined using the = directive can be redefined. RBP_RA denotes the number of bytes between RBP and the return address on stack (it also equals the number of extra bytes needed to reference the stack home area). STK_LOCAL represents the number of bytes allocated on the stack for local storage. More on these values in a moment.

Following definition of RBP_RA and STK_LOCAL is the statement SumIntegers_A proc frame, which defines the beginning of function SumIntegers_A(). The frame attribute notifies the assembler that the function SumIntegers_A uses a stack frame pointer. It also instructs the assembler to generate static table data that the Visual C++ runtime environment uses to process exceptions. The ensuing push rbp instruction saves the caller's RBP register on the stack since function SumIntegers_A() uses this register as its stack frame pointer. The .pushreg rbp statement that follows is an assembler directive that saves offset information about the push rbp instruction in an assembler-maintained exception handling table (see example Ch11_08 for more information about why this is necessary). It is important to keep in mind that assembler directives are not executable instructions; they are directions to the assembler on how to perform specific actions during assembly of the source code.

The sub rsp,STK_LOCAL instruction allocates STK_LOCAL bytes of space on the stack for local variables. Function SumIntegers_A() only uses eight bytes of this space, but the Visual C++ calling convention for 64-bit programs requires nonleaf functions to maintain double quadword (16-byte) alignment of the stack pointer outside of the prologue. You will learn more about stack pointer alignment requirements later in this section. The next statement, .allocstack STK_LOCAL, is an assembler directive that saves local stack size allocation information in the Visual C++ runtime exception handling tables.

The mov rbp,rsp instruction initializes register RBP as the stack frame pointer, and the .setframe rbp,0 directive notifies the assembler of this action. The offset value 0 that is included in the .setframe directive is the difference in bytes between RSP and RBP. In function SumIntegers_A(), registers RSP and RBP are the same, so the offset value is zero. Later in this section, you learn more about the .setframe directive. It should be noted that x86-64 assembly language functions can use any nonvolatile register as a stack frame pointer. Using RBP provides consistency between x86-64 and x86-32 assembly language code, which uses register EBP. The final assembler directive, .endprolog, signifies the end of the prologue for function SumIntegers_A(). Figure 12-3 shows the stack layout and argument registers following execution of the prologue.

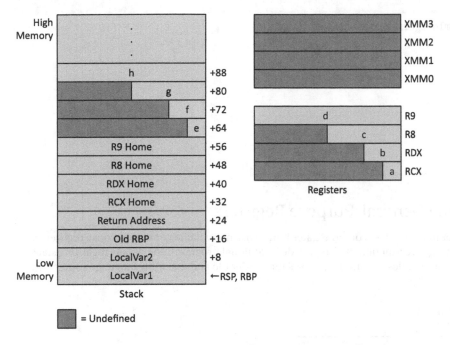

**Figure 12-3.** *Stack layout and registers of function SumIntegers_A() following execution of the prologue*

The next code block contains a series of mov instructions that save registers RCX, RDX, R8, and R9 to their respective home areas on this stack. This step is optional and included in SumIntegers_A() for demonstration purposes. Note that the offset of each mov instruction includes the symbolic constant RBP_RA. Another option allowed by the Visual C++ calling convention is to save an argument register to its corresponding home area *prior* to the push rbp instruction using RSP as a base register (e.g., mov [rsp+8],rcx, mov [rsp+16],rdx, and so on). Also keep in mind that a function can use its home area to store other temporary values. When used for alternative storage purposes, the home area should not be referenced by an assembly language instruction until after the .endprolog directive per the Visual C++ calling convention.

Following the home area save operation, the function SumIntegers_A() sums argument values a, b, c, and d. It then saves this intermediate sum to LocalVar1 on the stack using a mov [rbp],r8 instruction. Note that the summation calculation sign-extends argument values a, b, and c using a movsx or movsxd instruction. A similar sequence of instructions is used to sum argument values e, f, g, and h, which are located on the stack and referenced using the stack frame pointer RBP and a constant offset. The symbolic name RBP_RA is also used here to account for the extra stack space needed to reference argument values on the stack. The two intermediate sums are then added to produce the final sum in register RAX.

A function epilogue must release any local stack storage space that was allocated in the prologue, restore any nonvolatile registers that were saved on the stack, and execute a function return. The add rsp,16 instruction releases the 16 bytes of stack space that SumIntegers_A() allocated in its prologue. This is followed by a pop rbp instruction, which restores the caller's RBP register. The obligatory ret instruction is next. Here are the results for source code example Ch12_06:

```
----- Results for SumIntegers_A -----
a:          10
b:        -200
c:        -300
d:        4000
e:         -20
f:         400
g:        -600
h:       -8000
sum:     -4710
```

# Using Nonvolatile General-Purpose Registers

The next source code example, Ch12_07, demonstrates how to use nonvolatile general-purpose registers in an x86-64-bit assembly language function. It also provides additional programming details regarding stack frames and the use of local variables. Listing 12-7 shows the header file and assembly language source code for source code example Ch12_07.

***Listing 12-7.*** Example Ch12_07

```
//-------------------------------------------------
//                 Ch12_07.h
//-------------------------------------------------

#pragma once
#include <cstdint>

// Ch12_07_fasm.asm
extern "C" void CalcSumProd_A(const int64_t* a, const int64_t* b, int32_t n,
    int64_t* sum_a, int64_t* sum_b, int64_t* prod_a, int64_t* prod_b);

;-------------------------------------------------
;                 Ch12_07_fasm.asm
;-------------------------------------------------

;----------------------------------------------------------------------
; extern "C" void CalcSumProd_A(const int64_t* a, const int64_t* b, int32_t n,
;     int64_t* sum_a, int64_t* sum_b, int64_t* prod_a, int64_t* prod_b);
;----------------------------------------------------------------------

; Named expressions for constant values:
;
; NUM_PUSHREG    = number of prolog non-volatile register pushes
; STK_LOCAL1     = size in bytes of STK_LOCAL1 area (see figure in text)
; STK_LOCAL2     = size in bytes of STK_LOCAL2 area (see figure in text)
; STK_PAD        = extra bytes (0 or 8) needed to 16-byte align RSP
```

```
; STK_TOTAL        = total size in bytes of local stack
; RBP_RA           = number of bytes between RBP and return address on stack

NUM_PUSHREG       = 4
STK_LOCAL1        = 32
STK_LOCAL2        = 16
STK_PAD           = ((NUM_PUSHREG AND 1) XOR 1) * 8
STK_TOTAL         = STK_LOCAL1 + STK_LOCAL2 + STK_PAD
RBP_RA            = NUM_PUSHREG * 8 + STK_LOCAL1 + STK_PAD

        .const
TestVal db 0, 1, 2, 3, 4, 5, 6, 7, 8, 9, 10, 11, 12, 13, 14, 15

        .code
CalcSumProd_A proc frame

; Function prologue
        push rbp                            ;save non-volatile register RBP
        .pushreg rbp
        push rbx                            ;save non-volatile register RBX
        .pushreg rbx
        push r12                            ;save non-volatile register R12
        .pushreg r12
        push r13                            ;save non-volatile register R13
        .pushreg r13

        sub rsp,STK_TOTAL                   ;allocate local stack space
        .allocstack STK_TOTAL
        lea rbp,[rsp+STK_LOCAL2]            ;set frame pointer
        .setframe rbp,STK_LOCAL2
        .endprolog                          ;end of prologue

; Initialize local variables on the stack (demonstration only)
        vmovdqu xmm5, xmmword ptr [TestVal]
        vmovdqa xmmword ptr [rbp-16],xmm5   ;save xmm5 to LocalVar2A/2B
        mov qword ptr [rbp],0aah            ;save 0xaa to LocalVar1A
        mov qword ptr [rbp+8],0bbh          ;save 0xbb to LocalVar1B
        mov qword ptr [rbp+16],0cch         ;save 0xcc to LocalVar1C
        mov qword ptr [rbp+24],0ddh         ;save 0xdd to LocalVar1D

; Save argument values to home area (optional)
        mov qword ptr [rbp+RBP_RA+8],rcx
        mov qword ptr [rbp+RBP_RA+16],rdx
        mov qword ptr [rbp+RBP_RA+24],r8
        mov qword ptr [rbp+RBP_RA+32],r9

; Perform required initializations for processing loop
        test r8d,r8d                        ;is n <= 0?
        jle Done                            ;jump if n <= 0
```

```
        mov rbx,-8                        ;rbx = offset to array elements
        xor r10,r10                       ;r10 = sum_a
        xor r11,r11                       ;r11 = sum_b
        mov r12,1                         ;r12 = prod_a
        mov r13,1                         ;r13 = prod_b

; Compute the array sums and products
@@:     add rbx,8                         ;rbx = offset to next elements
        mov rax,[rcx+rbx]                 ;rax = a[i]
        add r10,rax                       ;update sum_a
        imul r12,rax                      ;update prod_a
        mov rax,[rdx+rbx]                 ;rax = b[i]
        add r11,rax                       ;update sum_b
        imul r13,rax                      ;update prod_b

        dec r8d                           ;adjust count
        jnz @B                            ;repeat until done

; Save the final results
        mov [r9],r10                      ;save sum_a
        mov rax,[rbp+RBP_RA+40]           ;rax = ptr to sum_b
        mov [rax],r11                     ;save sum_b
        mov rax,[rbp+RBP_RA+48]           ;rax = ptr to prod_a
        mov [rax],r12                     ;save prod_a
        mov rax,[rbp+RBP_RA+56]           ;rax = ptr to prod_b
        mov [rax],r13                     ;save prod_b

; Function epilogue
Done:   lea rsp,[rbp+STK_LOCAL1+STK_PAD]  ;restore rsp
        pop r13                           ;restore non-volatile GP registers
        pop r12
        pop rbx
        pop rbp
        ret


CalcSumProd_A endp
        end
```

Toward the top of the assembly language code is a series of named constants that control how much stack space is allocated in the prologue of function CalcSumProd_A(). Like the previous example, the function CalcSumProd_A() includes the frame attribute as part of its proc statement to indicate that it uses a stack frame pointer. A series of push instructions saves nonvolatile registers RBP, RBX, R12, and R13 on the stack. Note that a .pushreg directive follows each x86-64 push instruction, which instructs the assembler to add information about each push instruction to the Visual C++ runtime exception handling tables.

A sub rsp,STK_TOTAL instruction allocates space on the stack for local variables, and the required .allocstack STK_TOTAL directive follows next. Register RBP is then initialized as the function's stack frame pointer using a lea rbp,[rsp+STK_LOCAL2] (Load Effective Address) instruction, which loads rsp + STK_LOCAL2 into register RBP. Figure 12-4 illustrates the layout of the stack following execution of the lea instruction. Positioning RBP so that it "splits" the local stack area into two sections enables the assembler to generate machine code that is slightly more efficient since a larger portion of the local stack area can be referenced using 8-bit signed instead of 32-bit signed displacements. It also simplifies the saving and restoring of nonvolatile XMM registers, which is discussed later in this chapter. Following the lea instruction is a .setframe rbp,STK_LOCAL2 directive that enables the assembler to properly configure the runtime exception handling tables. The size parameter of a .setframe directive must be an even multiple of 16 and less than or equal to 240. The .endprolog directive signifies the end of the prologue for function CalcSumProd_A().

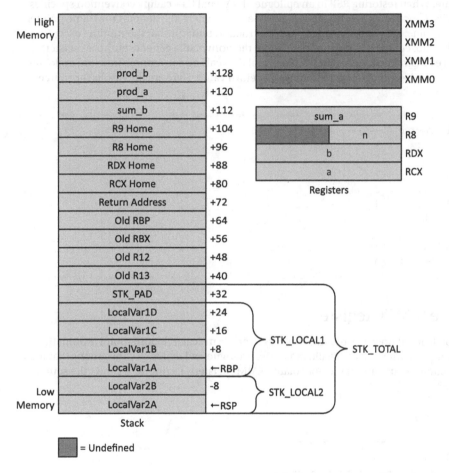

*Figure 12-4. Stack layout and argument registers following execution of* lea rbp,[rsp+STK_LOCAL2] *in function CalcSumProd_A()*

The next code block contains instructions that initialize several local variables on the stack. These instructions are for demonstration purposes only. Note that the vmovdqa [rbp-16],xmm5 (Move Aligned Packed Integer Values) instruction requires its destination operand to be aligned on a 16-byte boundary. Following initialization of the local variables, the argument registers are saved to their home locations, also just for demonstration purposes.

Function CalcSumProd_A() computes sums and products using the elements of two integer arrays. Prior to the start of the for-loop, the instruction pair test r8d,r8d (Logical Compare) and jle Done skips over the for-loop if n <= 0 is true. The test instruction performs a bitwise logical AND of its two operands and updates the status flags in RFLAGS; the result of the bitwise and operation is discarded. Following validation of argument value n, the function CalcSumProd_A() initializes the intermediate values sum_a (R10) and sum_b (R11) to zero and prod_a (R12) and prod_b (R13) to one. It then calculates the sum and product of the input arrays a and b. The results are saved to the memory locations specified by the caller. Note that the pointers for sum_b, prod_a, and prod_b were passed to CalcSumProd_A() via the stack as shown in Figure 12-4.

The epilogue of function CalcSumProd_A() begins with a lea rsp,[rbp+STK_LOCAL1+STK_PAD] instruction that restores register RSP to the value it had immediately after execution of the push r13 instruction in the prologue. When restoring RSP in an epilogue, the Visual C++ calling convention specifies that either a lea rsp,[RFP+X] or add rsp,X instruction must be used, where RFP denotes the frame pointer register and X is a constant value. This limits the number of instruction patterns that the runtime exception handler must identify. The subsequent pop instructions restore the nonvolatile general-purpose registers prior to execution of the ret instruction. According to the Visual C++ calling convention, function epilogues *must* be void of any processing logic including the setting of a return value. Here are the results for source code example Ch12_07:

```
----- Results for CalcSumProd_A -----
i:      0   a:      2   b:      3
i:      1   a:     -2   b:      5
i:      2   a:     -6   b:     -7
i:      3   a:      7   b:      8
i:      4   a:     12   b:      4
i:      5   a:      5   b:      9

sum_a =      18    sum_b =      22
prod_a =  10080    prod_b = -30240
```

# Using Nonvolatile SIMD Registers

Earlier in this chapter, you learned how to use XMM registers to perform scalar floating-point arithmetic. The next source code example, named Ch12_08, illustrates the prologue and epilogue conventions that must be observed before a function can use any of the nonvolatile XMM registers. Listing 12-8 shows the source code for example Ch12_08.

***Listing 12-8.*** Example Ch12_08

```
//--------------------------------------------------
//                  Ch12_08.h
//--------------------------------------------------

#pragma once

// Ch12_08_fcpp.cpp
extern bool CalcConeAreaVol_Cpp(const double* r, const double* h, int n,
    double* sa_cone, double* vol_cone);

// Ch12_08_fasm.asm
extern "C" bool CalcConeAreaVol_A(const double* r, const double* h, int n,
    double* sa_cone, double* vol_cone);

;--------------------------------------------------
;                  Ch12_08_fasm.asm
;--------------------------------------------------
```

```
;-----------------------------------------------------------------------
; extern "C" bool CalcConeAreaVol_A(const double* r, const double* h, int n,
; double* sa_cone, double* vol_cone);
;-----------------------------------------------------------------------

; Named expressions for constant values
;
; NUM_PUSHREG    = number of prolog non-volatile register pushes
; STK_LOCAL1     = size in bytes of STK_LOCAL1 area (see figure in text)
; STK_LOCAL2     = size in bytes of STK_LOCAL2 area (see figure in text)
; STK_PAD        = extra bytes (0 or 8) needed to 16-byte align RSP
; STK_TOTAL      = total size in bytes of local stack
; RBP_RA         = number of bytes between RBP and ret addr on stack

NUM_PUSHREG      = 7
STK_LOCAL1       = 16
STK_LOCAL2       = 64
STK_PAD          = ((NUM_PUSHREG AND 1) XOR 1) * 8
STK_TOTAL        = STK_LOCAL1 + STK_LOCAL2 + STK_PAD
RBP_RA           = NUM_PUSHREG * 8 + STK_LOCAL1 + STK_PAD

            .const
r8_3p0      real8 3.0
r8_pi       real8 3.14159265358979323846

        .code
CalcConeAreaVol_A proc frame

; Save non-volatile general-purpose registers
        push rbp
        .pushreg rbp
        push rbx
        .pushreg rbx
        push rsi
        .pushreg rsi
        push r12
        .pushreg r12
        push r13
        .pushreg r13
        push r14
        .pushreg r14
        push r15
        .pushreg r15

; Allocate local stack space and initialize frame pointer
        sub rsp,STK_TOTAL                ;allocate local stack space
        .allocstack STK_TOTAL
        lea rbp,[rsp+STK_LOCAL2]         ;rbp = stack frame pointer
        .setframe rbp,STK_LOCAL2

; Save non-volatile registers XMM12 - XMM15. Note that STK_LOCAL2 must
```

```
; be greater than or equal to the number of XMM register saves times 16.
        vmovdqa xmmword ptr [rbp-STK_LOCAL2+48],xmm12
        .savexmm128 xmm12,48
        vmovdqa xmmword ptr [rbp-STK_LOCAL2+32],xmm13
        .savexmm128 xmm13,32
        vmovdqa xmmword ptr [rbp-STK_LOCAL2+16],xmm14
        .savexmm128 xmm14,16
        vmovdqa xmmword ptr [rbp-STK_LOCAL2],xmm15
        .savexmm128 xmm15,0
        .endprolog

; Access local variables on the stack (demonstration only)
        mov qword ptr [rbp],-1                  ;LocalVar1A = -1
        mov qword ptr [rbp+8],-2                ;LocalVar1B = -2

; Initialize the processing loop variables. Note that many of the
; register initializations below are performed merely to illustrate
; use of the non-volatile GP and XMM registers.
        mov esi,r8d                            ;esi = n
        test esi,esi                           ;is n > 0?
        jg @F                                  ;jump if n > 0

        xor eax,eax                            ;set error return code
        jmp Done

@@:     mov rbx,-8                             ;rbx = offset to array elements
        mov r12,rcx                            ;r12 = ptr to r
        mov r13,rdx                            ;r13 = ptr to h
        mov r14,r9                             ;r14 = ptr to sa_cone
        mov r15,[rbp+RBP_RA+40]                ;r15 = ptr to vol_cone
        vmovsd xmm14,real8 ptr [r8_pi]         ;xmm14 = pi
        vmovsd xmm15,real8 ptr [r8_3p0]        ;xmm15 = 3.0

; Calculate cone surface areas and volumes
; sa = pi * r * (r + sqrt(r * r + h * h))
; vol = pi * r * r * h / 3
@@:     add rbx,8                              ;rbx = offset to next elements
        vmovsd xmm0,real8 ptr [r12+rbx]        ;xmm0 = r
        vmovsd xmm1,real8 ptr [r13+rbx]        ;xmm1 = h
        vmovsd xmm12,xmm12,xmm0                ;xmm12 = r
        vmovsd xmm13,xmm13,xmm1                ;xmm13 = h

        vmulsd xmm0,xmm0,xmm0                  ;xmm0 = r * r
        vmulsd xmm1,xmm1,xmm1                  ;xmm1 = h * h
        vaddsd xmm0,xmm0,xmm1                  ;xmm0 = r * r + h * h

        vsqrtsd xmm0,xmm0,xmm0                 ;xmm0 = sqrt(r * r + h * h)
        vaddsd xmm0,xmm0,xmm12                 ;xmm0 = r + sqrt(r * r + h * h)
        vmulsd xmm0,xmm0,xmm12                 ;xmm0 = r * (r + sqrt(r * r + h * h))
        vmulsd xmm0,xmm0,xmm14                 ;xmm0 = pi * r * (r + sqrt(r * r + h * h))
```

```
        vmulsd  xmm12,xmm12,xmm12      ;xmm12 = r * r
        vmulsd  xmm13,xmm13,xmm14      ;xmm13 = h * pi
        vmulsd  xmm13,xmm13,xmm12      ;xmm13 = pi * r * r * h
        vdivsd  xmm13,xmm13,xmm15      ;xmm13 = pi * r * r * h / 3

        vmovsd  real8 ptr [r14+rbx],xmm0      ;save surface area
        vmovsd  real8 ptr [r15+rbx],xmm13     ;save volume

        dec esi                               ;update counter
        jnz @B                                ;repeat until done

        mov eax,1                             ;set success return code

; Restore non-volatile XMM registers
Done:   vmovdqa xmm12,xmmword ptr [rbp-STK_LOCAL2+48]
        vmovdqa xmm13,xmmword ptr [rbp-STK_LOCAL2+32]
        vmovdqa xmm14,xmmword ptr [rbp-STK_LOCAL2+16]
        vmovdqa xmm15,xmmword ptr [rbp-STK_LOCAL2]

; Restore non-volatile general-purpose registers
        lea rsp,[rbp+STK_LOCAL1+STK_PAD]      ;restore rsp
        pop r15
        pop r14
        pop r13
        pop r12
        pop rsi
        pop rbx
        pop rbp
        ret
CalcConeAreaVol_A endp
        end
```

The assembly language function CalcConeAreaVol_A() calculates surface areas and volumes of right-circular cones. The following formulas are used to calculate these values:

$$sa = \pi\, r\left(r + \sqrt{r^2 + h^2}\right)$$

$$vol = \pi\, r^2 h / 3$$

The function CalcConeAreaVol_A() begins by saving the nonvolatile general-purpose registers that it uses on the stack. It then allocates the specified amount of local stack space and initializes RBP as the stack frame pointer. The next code block saves nonvolatile registers XMM12-XMM15 on the stack using a series of vmovdqa instructions. A .savexmm128 directive must be used after each vmovdqa instruction. Like the other prologue directives, the .savexmm128 directive instructs the assembler to store information regarding the preservation of a nonvolatile XMM register in its exception handling tables. The offset argument of a .savexmm128 directive represents the displacement of the saved XMM register on the stack relative to register RSP. Note that the size of STK_LOCAL2 must be greater than or equal to the number of saved XMM registers multiplied by 16. Figure 12-5 illustrates the layout of the stack following execution of the vmovdqa xmmword ptr [rbp-STK_LOCAL2],xmm15 instruction.

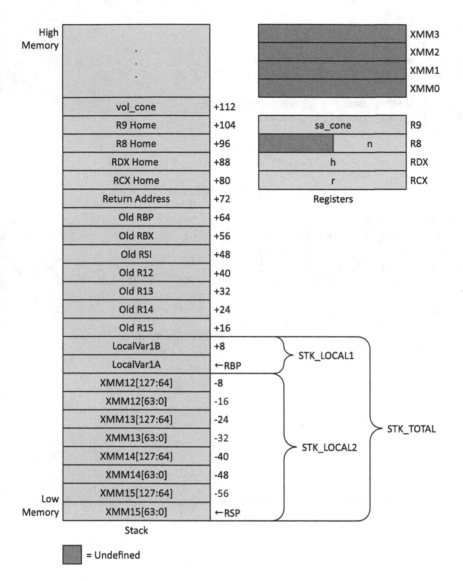

**Figure 12-5.** *Stack layout and argument registers following execution of* vmovdqa xmmword ptr [rbp-STK_LOCAL2],xmm15 *in function* CalcConeAreaVol_A()

Following the prologue, local variables LocalVar1A and LocalVar1B are accessed for demonstration purposes. Initialization of the registers used by the main processing loop occurs next. Note that many of these initializations are either suboptimal or superfluous; they are performed merely to highlight the use of nonvolatile registers, both general purpose and XMM. Calculation of the cone surface areas and volumes is then carried out using AVX double-precision floating-point arithmetic.

Upon completion of the processing loop, the nonvolatile XMM registers are restored using a series of vmovdqa instructions. The function CalcConeAreaVol_A() then releases its local stack space and restores the previously saved nonvolatile general-purpose registers that it used. Here are the results for source code example Ch12_08:

```
----- Results for CalcConeAreaVol -----
r/h:          1.00              1.00
sa:        7.584476          7.584476
vol:       1.047198          1.047198

r/h:          1.00              2.00
sa:       10.166407         10.166407
vol:       2.094395          2.094395

r/h:          2.00              3.00
sa:       35.220717         35.220717
vol:      12.566371         12.566371

r/h:          2.00              4.00
sa:       40.665630         40.665630
vol:      16.755161         16.755161

r/h:          3.00              5.00
sa:       83.229761         83.229761
vol:      47.123890         47.123890

r/h:          3.00             10.00
sa:      126.671905        126.671905
vol:      94.247780         94.247780

r/h:          4.25             12.50
sa:      233.025028        233.025028
vol:     236.437572        236.437572
```

## Macros for Function Prologues and Epilogues

The purpose of the three previous source code examples was to explicate the requirements of the Visual C++ calling convention for 64-bit nonleaf functions. The calling convention's rigid requisites for function prologues and epilogues are somewhat lengthy and a potential source of programming errors. It is important to recognize that the stack layout of a nonleaf function is primarily determined by the number of nonvolatile (both general-purpose and XMM) registers that must be preserved and the amount of local stack space that is needed. A method is needed to automate most of the coding drudgery associated with the calling convention.

Listing 12-9 shows the assembly language source code for example Ch12_09. This source code example demonstrates how to use several macros that I have written to simplify prologue and epilogue coding in a nonleaf function. This example also illustrates how to call a C++ library function from an x86-64 assembly language function.

*Listing 12-9.* Example Ch12_09

```
//--------------------------------------------------
//                  Ch12_09.h
//--------------------------------------------------

#pragma once

// Ch12_09_fcpp.cpp
extern bool CalcBSA_Cpp(const double* ht, const double* wt, int n,
    double* bsa1, double* bsa2, double* bsa3);

// Ch12_09_fasm.asm
extern "C" bool CalcBSA_Aavx(const double* ht, const double* wt, int n,
    double* bsa1, double* bsa2, double* bsa3);


;--------------------------------------------------
;                 Ch12_09_fasm.asm
;--------------------------------------------------

        include <MacrosX86-64-AVX.asmh>


;-----------------------------------------------------------------------
; extern "C" bool CalcBSA_Aavx(const double* ht, const double* wt, int n,
;   double* bsa1, double* bsa2, double* bsa3);
;-----------------------------------------------------------------------

                .const
r8_0p007184     real8 0.007184
r8_0p725        real8 0.725
r8_0p425        real8 0.425
r8_0p0235       real8 0.0235
r8_0p42246      real8 0.42246
r8_0p51456      real8 0.51456
r8_3600p0       real8 3600.0

        .code
        extern pow:proc

CalcBSA_Aavx proc frame
        CreateFrame_M BSA_,16,64,rbx,rsi,r12,r13,r14,r15
        SaveXmmRegs_M xmm6,xmm7,xmm8,xmm9
        EndProlog_M

; Save argument registers to home area (optional). Note that the home
; area can also be used to store other transient data values.
        mov qword ptr [rbp+BSA_OffsetHomeRCX],rcx
        mov qword ptr [rbp+BSA_OffsetHomeRDX],rdx
        mov qword ptr [rbp+BSA_OffsetHomeR8],r8
        mov qword ptr [rbp+BSA_OffsetHomeR9],r9
```

```
; Initialize processing loop pointers. Note that the pointers are
; maintained in non-volatile registers, which eliminates reloads after
; the calls to pow().
            test r8d,r8d                            ;is n > 0?
            jg @F                                   ;jump if n > 0

            xor eax,eax                             ;set error return code
            jmp Done

@@:         mov [rbp],r8d                           ;save n to local var
            mov r12,rcx                             ;r12 = ptr to ht
            mov r13,rdx                             ;r13 = ptr to wt
            mov r14,r9                              ;r14 = ptr to bsa1
            mov r15,[rbp+BSA_OffsetStackArgs]       ;r15 = ptr to bsa2
            mov rbx,[rbp+BSA_OffsetStackArgs+8]     ;rbx = ptr to bsa3
            mov rsi,-8                              ;rsi = array element offset

; Allocate home space on stack for use by pow()
            sub rsp,32

; Calculate bsa1 = 0.007184 * pow(ht, 0.725) * pow(wt, 0.425);
@@:         add rsi,8                               ;rsi = next offset
            vmovsd xmm0,real8 ptr [r12+rsi]         ;xmm0 = ht
            vmovsd xmm8,xmm8,xmm0
            vmovsd xmm1,real8 ptr [r8_0p725]
            call pow                                ;xmm0 = pow(ht, 0.725)
            vmovsd xmm6,xmm6,xmm0

            vmovsd xmm0,real8 ptr [r13+rsi]         ;xmm0 = wt
            vmovsd xmm9,xmm9,xmm0
            vmovsd xmm1,real8 ptr [r8_0p425]
            call pow                                ;xmm0 = pow(wt, 0.425)
            vmulsd xmm6,xmm6,real8 ptr [r8_0p007184]
            vmulsd xmm6,xmm6,xmm0                   ;xmm6 = bsa1

; Calculate bsa2 = 0.0235 * pow(ht, 0.42246) * pow(wt, 0.51456);
            vmovsd xmm0,xmm0,xmm8                   ;xmm0 = ht
            vmovsd xmm1,real8 ptr [r8_0p42246]
            call pow                                ;xmm0 = pow(ht, 0.42246)
            vmovsd xmm7,xmm7,xmm0

            vmovsd xmm0,xmm0,xmm9                   ;xmm0 = wt
            vmovsd xmm1,real8 ptr [r8_0p51456]
            call pow                                ;xmm0 = pow(wt, 0.51456)
            vmulsd xmm7,xmm7,real8 ptr [r8_0p0235]
            vmulsd xmm7,xmm7,xmm0                   ;xmm7 = bsa2

; Calculate bsa3 = sqrt(ht * wt / 3600.0);
            vmulsd xmm8,xmm8,xmm9                   ;xmm8 = ht * wt
            vdivsd xmm8,xmm8,real8 ptr [r8_3600p0]  ;xmm8 = ht * wt / 3600
            vsqrtsd xmm8,xmm8,xmm8                  ;xmm8 = bsa3
```

```
; Save BSA results
        vmovsd real8 ptr [r14+rsi],xmm6          ;save bsa1 result
        vmovsd real8 ptr [r15+rsi],xmm7          ;save bsa2 result
        vmovsd real8 ptr [rbx+rsi],xmm8          ;save bsa3 result

        dec dword ptr [rbp]                      ;n -= 1
        jnz @B
        mov eax,1                                ;set success return code

Done:   RestoreXmmRegs_M xmm6,xmm7,xmm8,xmm9
        DeleteFrame_M rbx,rsi,r12,r13,r14,r15
        ret

CalcBSA_Aavx endp
        end
```

In Listing 12-9, the assembly language code begins with the statement include <MacrosX86-64-AVX. asmh>, which incorporates the contents of file MacrosX86-64-AVX.asmh into Ch12_09_fasm.asm during assembly. This file (source code not shown but included in the software download package) contains several macros that help automate much of the coding grunt work associated with the Visual C++ calling convention. Using an assembly language include file is analogous to using a C++ include file. The angled brackets that surround the file name can be omitted in some cases, but it is usually simpler and more consistent to just always use them. Note that there is no standard file name extension for x86 assembly language header files; I use .asmh but .inc is also used.

Figure 12-6 shows a generic stack layout diagram for a nonleaf function. Note the similarities between this figure and the more detailed stack layouts of Figures 12-4 and 12-5. The macros defined in MacrosX86-64-AVX.asmh assume that a function's stack layout will conform to what is shown in Figure 12-6. They enable a function to tailor a custom stack frame by specifying the amount of local stack space that is needed and which nonvolatile registers must be preserved. The macros also perform most of the critical stack offset calculations, which reduces the risk of a programming error in a function prologue or epilogue.

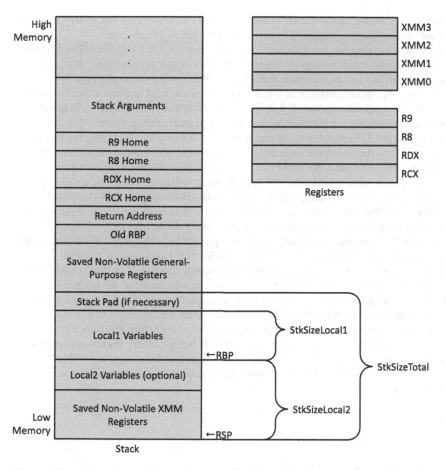

**Figure 12-6.** *Generic stack layout for a nonleaf function*

Function CalcBSA_A() computes body surface areas (BSA) using the same equations that were used in example Ch09_03 (see Table 9-1). Following the include statement in Listing 12-9 is .const section that contains definitions for the various floating-point constant values used in the BSA equations. The line extern pow:proc enables the use of the external C++ library function pow(). Following the CalcBSA_A proc frame statement, the macro CreateFrame_M emits assembly language code that initializes the stack frame. It also saves the specified nonvolatile general-purpose registers on the stack. Macro CreateFrame_M requires several parameters including a prefix string and the size in bytes of StkSizeLocal1 and StkSizeLocal2 (see Figure 12-6). Macro CreateFrame_M uses the specified prefix string to generate symbolic names that can be employed to reference items on the stack. It is somewhat convenient to use a shortened version of the function name as the prefix string, but any file-unique text string can be used. Both StkSizeLocal1 and StkSizeLocal2 must be evenly divisible by 16. StkSizeLocal2 must also be less than or equal to 240 and greater than or equal to the number of saved XMM registers multiplied by 16.

The next statement makes use of the SaveXmmRegs_M macro to save the specified nonvolatile XMM registers to the XMM save area on the stack. This is followed by the EndProlog_M macro, which signifies the end of the function's prologue. At this point, register RBP is configured as the function's stack frame pointer. It is also safe to use any of the saved nonvolatile general-purpose or XMM registers.

The code block that follows EndProlog_M saves argument registers RCX, RDX, R8, and R9 to their home locations on the stack. Note that each mov instruction includes a symbolic name that equates to the offset of the register's home area on the stack relative to the RBP register. The symbolic names and the corresponding offset values were automatically generated by the CreateFrame_M macro. The home area can also be used to store temporary data instead of the argument registers, as mentioned earlier in this chapter.

Initialization of the processing for-loop variables occurs next. Argument value n in register R8D is checked for validity and then saved on the stack as a local variable. Several nonvolatile registers are then initialized as pointer registers. Nonvolatile registers are used to avoid register reloads following each call to the C++ library function pow(). Note that the pointer to array bsa2 is loaded from the stack using a mov r15,[rbp+BSA_OffsetStackArgs] instruction. The symbolic constant BSA_OffsetStackArgs also was automatically generated by the macro CreateFrame_M and equates to the offset of the first stack argument relative to the RBP register. A mov rbx,[rbp+BSA_OffsetStackArgs+8] instruction loads argument bsa3 into register RBX; the constant 8 is included as part of the source operand displacement since bsa3 is the second argument passed via the stack.

The Visual C++ calling convention requires the caller of a function to allocate that function's home area on the stack. The sub rsp,32 instruction performs this operation for function pow(). The ensuing code block calculates BSA values using the equations shown in Table 9-1. Note that registers XMM0 and XMM1 are loaded with the necessary argument values prior to each call to pow(). Also note that some of the return values from pow() are preserved in nonvolatile XMM registers prior to their actual use.

Following completion of the BSA processing for-loop is the epilogue for CalcBSA_A(). Before execution of the ret instruction, function CalcBSA_A() must restore all nonvolatile XMM and general-purpose registers that it saved in the prologue. The stack frame must also be properly deleted. The RestoreXmmRegs_M macro restores the nonvolatile XMM registers. Note that this macro *requires* the order of the registers in its argument list to match the register list that was used with the SaveXmmRegs_M macro. Stack frame cleanup and general-purpose register restores are handled by the DeleteFrame_M macro. The order of the registers specified in this macro's argument list *must* be identical to the prologue's CreateFrame_M macro. The DeleteFrame_M macro also restores RSP from RBP, which means that it is not necessary to code an explicit add rsp,32 instruction to release the home area that was allocated on the stack for pow(). You will see additional examples of function prologue and epilogue macro usage in subsequent chapters. Here are the results for source code example Ch12_09:

```
----- Results for CalcBSA -----
height:  150.0 (cm)
weight:   50.0 (kg)
BSA (C++):  1.432500   1.460836   1.443376 (sq. m)
BSA (AVX):  1.432500   1.460836   1.443376 (sq. m)

height:  160.0 (cm)
weight:   60.0 (kg)
BSA (C++):  1.622063   1.648868   1.632993 (sq. m)
BSA (AVX):  1.622063   1.648868   1.632993 (sq. m)

height:  170.0 (cm)
weight:   70.0 (kg)
BSA (C++):  1.809708   1.831289   1.818119 (sq. m)
BSA (AVX):  1.809708   1.831289   1.818119 (sq. m)

height:  180.0 (cm)
weight:   80.0 (kg)
BSA (C++):  1.996421   2.009483   2.000000 (sq. m)
BSA (AVX):  1.996421   2.009483   2.000000 (sq. m)

height:  190.0 (cm)
weight:   90.0 (kg)
BSA (C++):  2.182809   2.184365   2.179449 (sq. m)
BSA (AVX):  2.182809   2.184365   2.179449 (sq. m)
```

```
height:  200.0 (cm)
weight:  100.0 (kg)
BSA (C++):  2.369262   2.356574   2.357023 (sq. m)
BSA (AVX):  2.369262   2.356574   2.357023 (sq. m)
```

If the discussions of this section have left you feeling a little bewildered, don't worry. In this book's remaining chapters, you will see an abundance of x86-64 assembly language source code that demonstrates proper use of the Visual C++ calling convention and its programming requirements.

# Summary

Table 12-5 summarizes the x86 assembly language instructions introduced in this chapter. This table also includes closely related instructions. Before proceeding to the next chapter, make sure you understand the operation that is performed by each instruction shown in Table 12-5.

***Table 12-5.*** *X86 Assembly Language Instruction Summary for Chapter 12*

| Instruction Mnemonic | Description |
|---|---|
| call | Call procedure/function |
| lea | Load effective address |
| setcc | Set byte if condition is true; clear otherwise |
| test | Logical compare (bitwise logical AND to set RFLAGS) |
| vadds[d\|s] | Scalar floating-point addition |
| vcvtsd2ss | Convert scalar DPFP value to SPFP |
| vcomis[d\|s] | Scalar floating-point compare |
| vcvts[d\|s]2si | Convert scalar floating-point to signed integer |
| vcvtsi2s[d\|s] | Convert signed integer to scalar floating-point |
| vcvtss2sd | Convert scalar SPFP to scalar DPFP |
| vdivs[d\|s] | Scalar floating-point division |
| vldmxcsr | Load MXCSR register |
| vmovdqa | Move double quadword (aligned) |
| vmovdqu | Move double quadword (unaligned) |
| vmovs[d\|s] | Move scalar floating-point value |
| vmuls[d\|s] | Scalar floating-point multiplication |
| vsqrts[d\|s] | Scalar floating-point square root |
| vstmxcsr | Store MXCSR register |
| vsubs[d\|s] | Scalar floating-point subtraction |
| vxorp[d\|s] | Packed floating-point bitwise logical exclusive OR |

# CHAPTER 13

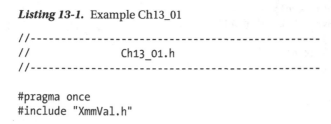

# AVX Assembly Language Programming: Part 1

The previous two chapters explored the basics of x86-64 assembly language programing. In these chapters, you learned how to perform simple integer arithmetic using x86-64 instructions. You also learned how to carry out scalar floating-point calculations using AVX instructions. Finally, you studied important x86-64 assembly language programming constructs and concepts including for-loop coding, memory addressing modes, use of condition codes, and function calling convention requirements.

In this chapter, you will discover how to code x86-64 assembly language functions that perform packed integer operations using AVX instructions and 128-bit wide operands. The first section covers basic packed integer arithmetic. The second section details a few image processing algorithms. The source code examples presented in this chapter are adaptations of examples that you saw in Chapter 2. This was done intentionally to highlight the programming similarities that exist between C++ SIMD intrinsic functions and AVX instructions.

## Integer Arithmetic

In this section, you will learn how to perform elementary packed integer arithmetic using x86-64 assembly language and AVX instructions. The first example explains packed integer addition and subtraction using 128-bit wide SIMD operands. This is followed by an example that demonstrates packed integer multiplication. The final two examples illustrate packed integer bitwise logical and shift operations.

### Addition and Subtraction

Listing 13-1 shows the source code for example Ch13_01. This example explicates packed integer addition and subtraction using AVX instructions and 128-bit wide operands.

***Listing 13-1.*** Example Ch13_01

```
//--------------------------------------------------
//              Ch13_01.h
//--------------------------------------------------

#pragma once
#include "XmmVal.h"
```

© Daniel Kusswurm 2022
D. Kusswurm, *Modern Parallel Programming with C++ and Assembly Language,*
https://doi.org/10.1007/978-1-4842-7918-2_13

```cpp
// Ch13_01_fasm.asm
extern "C" void AddI16_Aavx(XmmVal* c1, XmmVal* c2, const XmmVal* a, const XmmVal* b);
extern "C" void SubI16_Aavx(XmmVal* c1, XmmVal* c2, const XmmVal* a, const XmmVal* b);

//-------------------------------------------------
//                  Ch13_01.cpp
//-------------------------------------------------

#include <iostream>
#include <iomanip>
#include "Ch13_01.h"

static void AddI16(void);
static void SubI16(void);

int main()
{
    AddI16();
    SubI16();
    return 0;
}

static void AddI16(void)
{
    const char nl = '\n';
    XmmVal a, b, c1, c2;

    // Packed int16_t addition
    a.m_I16[0] = 10;          b.m_I16[0] = 100;
    a.m_I16[1] = 200;         b.m_I16[1] = -200;
    a.m_I16[2] = 30;          b.m_I16[2] = 32760;
    a.m_I16[3] = -32766;      b.m_I16[3] = -400;
    a.m_I16[4] = 50;          b.m_I16[4] = 500;
    a.m_I16[5] = 60;          b.m_I16[5] = -600;
    a.m_I16[6] = 32000;       b.m_I16[6] = 1200;
    a.m_I16[7] = -32000;      b.m_I16[7] = -950;

    AddI16_Aavx(&c1, &c2, &a, &b);

    std::cout << "\nResults for AddI16_Aavx - Wraparound Addition\n";
    std::cout << "a:  " << a.ToStringI16() << nl;
    std::cout << "b:  " << b.ToStringI16() << nl;
    std::cout << "c1: " << c1.ToStringI16() << nl;
    std::cout << "\nResults for AddI16_Aavx - Saturated Addition\n";
    std::cout << "a:  " << a.ToStringI16() << nl;
    std::cout << "b:  " << b.ToStringI16() << nl;
    std::cout << "c2: " << c2.ToStringI16() << nl;

}
```

```
static void SubI16(void)
{
    const char nl = '\n';
    XmmVal a, b, c1, c2;

    a.m_I16[0] = 10;          b.m_I16[0] = 100;
    a.m_I16[1] = 200;         b.m_I16[1] = -200;
    a.m_I16[2] = -30;         b.m_I16[2] = 32760;
    a.m_I16[3] = -32766;      b.m_I16[3] = 400;
    a.m_I16[4] = 50;          b.m_I16[4] = 500;
    a.m_I16[5] = 60;          b.m_I16[5] = -600;
    a.m_I16[6] = 32000;       b.m_I16[6] = 1200;
    a.m_I16[7] = -32000;      b.m_I16[7] = 950;

    SubI16_Aavx(&c1, &c2, &a, &b);

    std::cout << "\nResults for SubI16_Aavx - Wraparound Subtraction\n";
    std::cout << "a:  " << a.ToStringI16() << nl;
    std::cout << "b:  " << b.ToStringI16() << nl;
    std::cout << "c1: " << c1.ToStringI16() << nl;
    std::cout << "\nResults for SubI16_Aavx - Saturated Subtraction\n";
    std::cout << "a:  " << a.ToStringI16() << nl;
    std::cout << "b:  " << b.ToStringI16() << nl;
    std::cout << "c2: " << c2.ToStringI16() << nl;
}

;--------------------------------------------------
;                Ch13_01_fasm.asm
;--------------------------------------------------

;----------------------------------------------------------------------------
; extern "C" void AddI16_Aavx(XmmVal* c1, XmmVal* c2, const XmmVal* a, const XmmVal* b);
;----------------------------------------------------------------------------

        .code
AddI16_Aavx proc
        vmovdqa xmm0,xmmword ptr [r8]        ;xmm0 = a
        vmovdqa xmm1,xmmword ptr [r9]        ;xmm1 = b

        vpaddw xmm2,xmm0,xmm1                ;packed add - wraparound
        vpaddsw xmm3,xmm0,xmm1               ;packed add - saturated

        vmovdqa xmmword ptr [rcx],xmm2       ;save c1
        vmovdqa xmmword ptr [rdx],xmm3       ;save c2
        ret
AddI16_Aavx endp

;----------------------------------------------------------------------------
; extern "C" void SubI16_Aavx(XmmVal* c1, XmmVal* c2, const XmmVal* a, const XmmVal* b);
;----------------------------------------------------------------------------
```

```
SubI16_Aavx proc
        vmovdqa xmm0,xmmword ptr [r8]        ;xmm0 = a
        vmovdqa xmm1,xmmword ptr [r9]        ;xmm1 = b

        vpsubw xmm2,xmm0,xmm1                ;packed sub - wraparound
        vpsubsw xmm3,xmm0,xmm1               ;packed sub - saturated

        vmovdqa xmmword ptr [rcx],xmm2       ;save c1
        vmovdqa xmmword ptr [rdx],xmm3       ;save c2
        ret
SubI16_Aavx endp
        end
```

The first file in Listing 13-1, Ch13_01.h, contains the function declarations for this example. Note that functions AddI16_Aavx() and SubI16_Aavx() both require pointer arguments of type XmmVal. This is the same C++ SIMD data structure that was introduced in Chapter 2. The file Ch13_01.cpp contains code that performs test case initialization and streams results to std::cout.

The first function in file Ch13_01_fasm.asm, AddI16_Aavx(), illustrates packed integer addition using 16-bit wide elements. Function AddI16_Aavx() begins with a vmovdqa xmm0,xmmword ptr [r8] that loads argument value a into register XMM0. The text xmmword ptr is an assembler operator that conveys the size (128 bits) of the source operand pointed to by R8. The next instruction, vmovdqa xmm1,xmmword ptr [r9], loads argument value b into register XMM1. The ensuing instruction pair, vpaddw xmm2,xmm0,xmm1 (Add Packed Integers) and vpaddsw xmm3,xmm0,xmm1 (Add Packed Integers with Signed Saturation), performs packed integer addition of word elements using wraparound and saturated arithmetic, respectively. The final two AVX instructions of AddI16_Aavx(), vmovdqa xmmword ptr [rcx],xmm2 and vmovdqa xmmword ptr [rdx],xmm3, save the calculated results to the XmmVal buffers pointed to by c1 and c2.

Recall that source code example Ch02_01 included a C++ function named AddI16_Iavx(). This function employed _mm_load_si128() and _mm_store_si128() to perform SIMD load and store operations. In the current example, the assembly language function AddI16_Aavx() (which performs the same operations as AddI16_Iavx()) uses the vmovdqa instruction to perform SIMD loads and stores. Function AddI16_Iavx() also used _mm_add_epi16() and _mm_adds_epi16() to carry out packed integer addition using 16-bit wide integer elements. These C++ SIMD intrinsic functions are the counterparts of the AVX instructions vpaddw and vpaddsw. Most of the C++ SIMD intrinsic functions that you learned about in the first half of this book are essentially wrapper functions for x86-AVX instructions.

The second function in file Ch13_01_fasm.asm, named SubI16_Aavx(), performs packed subtraction using 16-bit wide integer elements. The code arrangement of this function is identical to AddI16_Aavx() except for the use of vpsubw (Subtract Packed Integers) and vpsubsw (Subtract Packed Integers with Signed Saturation) to carry out packed integer subtraction. X86-AVX also includes other size variants of the addition and subtraction instructions demonstrated in this example. These are listed in the summary table (Table 13-3) located at the end of this chapter. Here are the results for source code example Ch13_01:

```
Results for AddI16_Aavx - Wraparound Addition
a:         10      200        30   -32766   |     50       60    32000   -32000
b:        100     -200     32760     -400   |    500     -600     1200     -950
c1:       110        0    -32746    32370   |    550     -540   -32336    32586

Results for AddI16_Aavx - Saturated Addition
a:         10      200        30   -32766   |     50       60    32000   -32000
b:        100     -200     32760     -400   |    500     -600     1200     -950
c2:       110        0     32767   -32768   |    550     -540    32767   -32768
```

```
Results for SubI16_Aavx - Wraparound Subtraction
a:        10     200     -30  -32766  |     50      60   32000  -32000
b:       100    -200   32760     400  |    500    -600    1200     950
c1:      -90     400   32746   32370  |   -450     660   30800   32586

Results for SubI16_Aavx - Saturated Subtraction
a:        10     200     -30  -32766  |     50      60   32000  -32000
b:       100    -200   32760     400  |    500    -600    1200     950
c2:      -90     400  -32768  -32768  |   -450     660   30800  -32768
```

# Multiplication

The next source code example, named Ch13_02, demonstrates how to perform packed integer multiplication. This example is the assembly language counterpart of source example Ch02_03. Listing 13-2 shows the assembly language code for example Ch13_02. The C++ test case initialization code for this example is not shown in Listing 13-2 since it is identical to the code used in example Ch02_03.

***Listing 13-2.*** Example Ch13_02

```
;-------------------------------------------------
;                  Ch13_02_fasm.asm
;-------------------------------------------------


;-----------------------------------------------------------------------
; extern "C" void MulI16_Aavx(XmmVal c[2], const XmmVal* a, const XmmVal* b);
;-----------------------------------------------------------------------

        .code
MulI16_Aavx proc
        vmovdqa xmm0,xmmword ptr [rdx]        ;xmm0 = a
        vmovdqa xmm1,xmmword ptr [r8]         ;xmm1 = b

        vpmullw xmm2,xmm0,xmm1                ;packed mul - low result
        vpmulhw xmm3,xmm0,xmm1                ;packed mul - high result

        vpunpcklwd xmm4,xmm2,xmm3             ;packed low-order dwords
        vpunpckhwd xmm5,xmm2,xmm3             ;packed high-order dwords

        vmovdqa xmmword ptr [rcx],xmm4        ;save c[0]
        vmovdqa xmmword ptr [rcx+16],xmm5     ;save c[1]
        ret
MulI16_Aavx endp

;-----------------------------------------------------------------------
; extern "C" void MulI32a_Aavx(XmmVal* c, const XmmVal* a, const XmmVal* b);
;-----------------------------------------------------------------------

MulI32a_Aavx proc
        vmovdqa xmm0,xmmword ptr [rdx]        ;xmm0 = a
        vmovdqa xmm1,xmmword ptr [r8]         ;xmm1 = b
```

```
        vpmulld xmm2,xmm0,xmm1               ;packed mul - low result

        vmovdqa xmmword ptr [rcx],xmm2       ;save c
        ret
MulI32a_Aavx endp

;-------------------------------------------------------------------------
; extern "C" void MulI32b_Aavx(XmmVal c[2], const XmmVal* a, const XmmVal* b);
;-------------------------------------------------------------------------

MulI32b_Aavx proc
        vmovdqa xmm0,xmmword ptr [rdx]       ;xmm0 = a
        vmovdqa xmm1,xmmword ptr [r8]        ;xmm1 = b

        vpmuldq xmm2,xmm0,xmm1               ;packed mul - a & b even dwords
        vpsrldq xmm3,xmm0,4                  ;shift a_vals right 4 bytes
        vpsrldq xmm4,xmm1,4                  ;shift b_vals right 4 bytes
        vpmuldq xmm5,xmm3,xmm4               ;packed mul - a & b odd dwords

        vpextrq qword ptr [rcx],xmm2,0       ;save qword product 0
        vpextrq qword ptr [rcx+8],xmm5,0     ;save qword product 1
        vpextrq qword ptr [rcx+16],xmm2,1    ;save qword product 2
        vpextrq qword ptr [rcx+24],xmm5,1    ;save qword product 3
        ret
MulI32b_Aavx endp
        end
```

The file Ch13_02_fasm.asm contains three functions that perform packed integer multiplication. The first function, MulI16_Aavx(), begins its execution with two vmovdqa instructions that load argument values a and b into registers XMM0 and XMM1, respectively. This is followed by a vpmullw xmm2,xmm0,xmm1 (Multiply Packed Signed Integers and Store Low Result) instruction that performs packed signed integer multiplication using the 16-bit wide elements of XMM0 and XMM1. The vpmullw instruction saves the low-order 16 bits of each 32-bit product in register XMM2. The vpmulhw xmm3,xmm0,xmm1 (Multiply Packed Signed Integers and Store High Result) that follows calculates and saves the high-order 16 bits of each 32-bit product in register XMM3. The ensuing instruction pair, vpunpcklwd xmm4,xmm2,xmm3 (Unpack Low Data) and vpunpckhwd xmm5,xmm2,xmm3 (Unpack High Data), interleaves the low- and high-order word elements of their respective source operands to form the final doubleword products as shown in Figure 13-1. The last two AVX instructions of MulI16_Aavx(), vmovdqa xmmword ptr [rcx],xmm4 and vmovdqa xmmword ptr [rcx+16],xmm5, save the calculated products to c[0] and c[1]. Note that the second vmovdqa instruction uses a displacement value of 16 since each XmmVal structure instance in array c is 16 bytes wide.

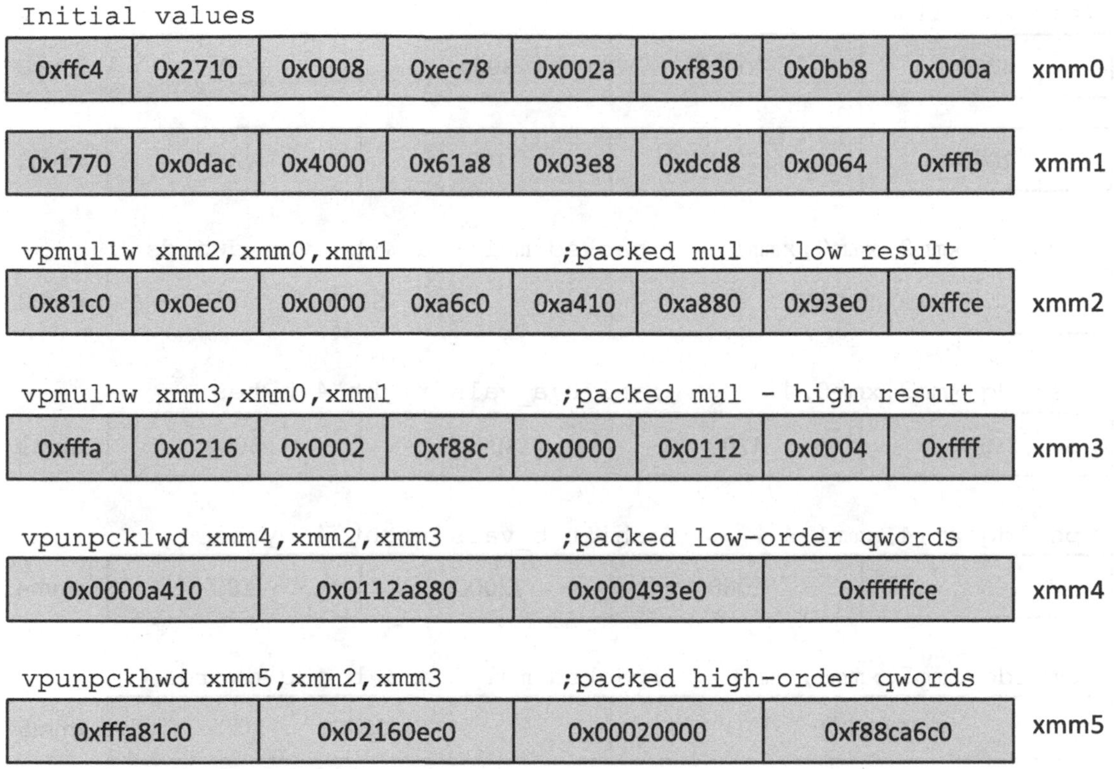

```
Initial values
```

| 0xffc4 | 0x2710 | 0x0008 | 0xec78 | 0x002a | 0xf830 | 0x0bb8 | 0x000a | xmm0 |

| 0x1770 | 0x0dac | 0x4000 | 0x61a8 | 0x03e8 | 0xdcd8 | 0x0064 | 0xfffb | xmm1 |

```
vpmullw xmm2,xmm0,xmm1                    ;packed mul - low result
```

| 0x81c0 | 0x0ec0 | 0x0000 | 0xa6c0 | 0xa410 | 0xa880 | 0x93e0 | 0xffce | xmm2 |

```
vpmulhw xmm3,xmm0,xmm1                    ;packed mul - high result
```

| 0xfffa | 0x0216 | 0x0002 | 0xf88c | 0x0000 | 0x0112 | 0x0004 | 0xffff | xmm3 |

```
vpunpcklwd xmm4,xmm2,xmm3                 ;packed low-order qwords
```

| 0x0000a410 | 0x0112a880 | 0x000493e0 | 0xfffffce | xmm4 |

```
vpunpckhwd xmm5,xmm2,xmm3                 ;packed high-order qwords
```

| 0xfffa81c0 | 0x02160ec0 | 0x00020000 | 0xf88ca6c0 | xmm5 |

*Figure 13-1.* *Packed 16-bit signed integer multiplication using vpmullw, vpmulhw, vpunpcklwd, and vpunpckhwd*

The next function in Ch13_02_fasm.asm, MulI32a_Aavx(), performs packed signed integer multiplication using 32-bit wide elements. Note that this function only saves the low-order 32 bits of each 64-bit product. The final function in Listing 13-2, MulI32b_Aavx(), performs packed signed integer multiplication using 32-bit wide elements and saves complete 64-bit products. Function MulI32b_Aavx() begins its execution with two vmovdqa instructions that load argument values a and b into registers XMM0 and XMM1. The next instruction, vpmuldq xmm2,xmm0,xmm1 (Multiple Packed Doubleword Integers), performs packed 32-bit signed integer multiplication using the even-numbered elements of XMM0 and XMM1 and saves the resultant 64-bit products in register XMM2. The ensuing vpsrldq xmm3,xmm0,4 (Shift Double Quadword Right) and vpsrldq xmm4,xmm1,4 instructions right shift registers XMM0 (a) and XMM1 (b) by 4 bytes. This facilitates the use of the next instruction, vpmuldq xmm5,xmm3,xmm4, which calculates products using the odd-numbered elements of a and b as illustrated in Figure 13-2.

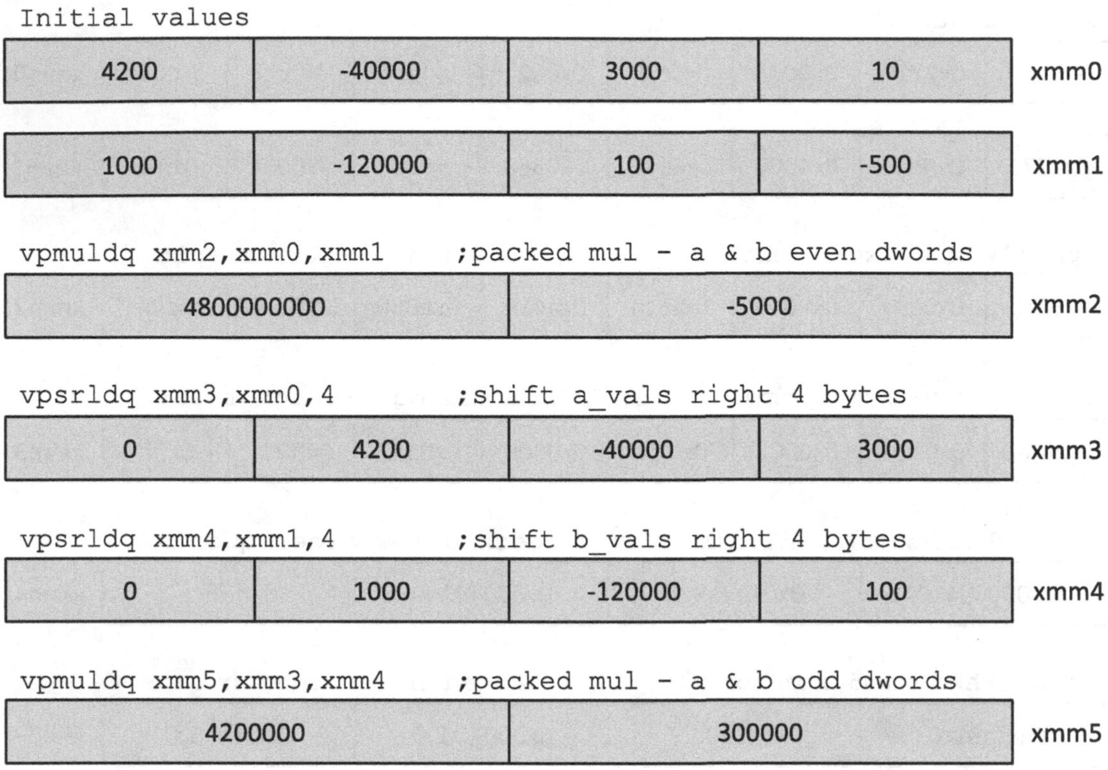

Initial values

| 4200 | -40000 | 3000 | 10 | xmm0 |
|------|--------|------|----|----|

| 1000 | -120000 | 100 | -500 | xmm1 |
|------|---------|-----|------|----|

vpmuldq xmm2,xmm0,xmm1      ;packed mul - a & b even dwords

| 4800000000 | -5000 | xmm2 |
|------------|-------|----|

vpsrldq xmm3,xmm0,4        ;shift a_vals right 4 bytes

| 0 | 4200 | -40000 | 3000 | xmm3 |
|---|------|--------|------|----|

vpsrldq xmm4,xmm1,4        ;shift b_vals right 4 bytes

| 0 | 1000 | -120000 | 100 | xmm4 |
|---|------|---------|-----|----|

vpmuldq xmm5,xmm3,xmm4     ;packed mul - a & b odd dwords

| 4200000 | 300000 | xmm5 |
|---------|--------|----|

*Figure 13-2.* *Packed 32-bit signed integer multiplication using* vpmuldq *and* vpsrldq

Following calculation of the quadword products, MulI32b_Aavx() uses four vpextrq (Extract Quadword) instructions to save the results. Note that the immediate constant used with each vpextrq instruction selects which quadword element to extract from the first source operand. Also note that each vpextrq instruction specifies a destination operand in memory. This is different than most x86-AVX instructions, which require the destination operand to be an XMM, YMM, or ZMM register. Here are the results for source code example Ch13_02:

```
Results for MulI16_Aavx
a[0]:       10   b[0]:      -5   c[0][0]:          -50
a[1]:     3000   b[1]:     100   c[0][1]:       300000
a[2]:    -2000   b[2]:   -9000   c[0][2]:     18000000
a[3]:       42   b[3]:    1000   c[0][3]:        42000
a[4]:    -5000   b[4]:   25000   c[1][0]:   -125000000
a[5]:        8   b[5]:   16384   c[1][1]:       131072
a[6]:    10000   b[6]:    3500   c[1][2]:     35000000
a[7]:      -60   b[7]:    6000   c[1][3]:      -360000
```

```
-------------------------------------------------------------------------
Results for MulI32a_Aavx
a[0]:          10  b[0]:         -500  c[0]:        -5000
a[1]:        3000  b[1]:          100  c[1]:       300000
a[2]:       -2000  b[2]:       -12000  c[2]:     24000000
a[3]:        4200  b[3]:         1000  c[3]:      4200000


-------------------------------------------------------------------------

Results for MulI32b_Aavx
a[0]:          10  b[0]:         -500  c[0][0]:        -5000
a[1]:        3000  b[1]:          100  c[0][1]:       300000
a[2]:      -40000  b[2]:      -120000  c[1][0]:   4800000000
a[3]:        4200  b[3]:         1000  c[1][1]:      4200000
```

# Bitwise Logical Operations

Listing 13-3 shows the assembly language code for source code example Ch13_03. This example spotlights the use of the AVX bitwise logical instructions vpand (Bitwise Logical AND), vpor (Bitwise Logical OR), and vpxor (Bitwise Logical Exclusive OR).

***Listing 13-3.*** Example Ch13_03

```
;--------------------------------------------------
;                Ch13_03_fasm.asm
;--------------------------------------------------


;-------------------------------------------------------------------------
; extern "C" void AndU16_Aavx(XmmVal* c, const XmmVal* a, const XmmVal* b);
;-------------------------------------------------------------------------

        .code
AndU16_Aavx proc
        vmovdqa xmm0,xmmword ptr [rdx]      ;xmm0 = a
        vmovdqa xmm1,xmmword ptr [r8]       ;xmm1 = b

        vpand xmm2,xmm0,xmm1                ;bitwise and

        vmovdqa xmmword ptr [rcx],xmm2      ;save result
        ret
AndU16_Aavx endp

;-------------------------------------------------------------------------
; extern "C" void OrU16_Aavx(XmmVal* c, const XmmVal* a, const XmmVal* b);
;-------------------------------------------------------------------------


OrU16_Aavx proc
        vmovdqa xmm0,xmmword ptr [rdx]      ;xmm0 = a
        vmovdqa xmm1,xmmword ptr [r8]       ;xmm1 = b
```

```
        vpor xmm2,xmm0,xmm1                  ;bitwise or

        vmovdqa xmmword ptr [rcx],xmm2       ;save result
        ret
OrU16_Aavx endp

;-----------------------------------------------------------------------
; extern "C" void XorU16_Aavx(XmmVal* c, const XmmVal* a, const XmmVal* b);
;-----------------------------------------------------------------------

XorU16_Aavx proc
        vmovdqa xmm0,xmmword ptr [rdx]       ;xmm0 = a
        vmovdqa xmm1,xmmword ptr [r8]        ;xmm1 = b

        vpxor xmm2,xmm0,xmm1                 ;bitwise xor

        vmovdqa xmmword ptr [rcx],xmm2       ;save result
        ret
XorU16_Aavx endp
        end
```

The functions shown in Listing 13-3 are the assembly language counterparts of the C++ SIMD calculating functions used in source code example Ch02_04. Function AndU16_Aavx() uses the vpand xmm2,xmm0,xmm1 instruction to perform a bitwise logical AND using the values in registers XMM0 and XMM1. Functions OrU16_Aavx() and XorU16_Aavx() are similar to AndU16_Aavx() but carry out bitwise logical OR and bitwise logical exclusive OR operations, respectively. Recall that when performing AVX (or AVX2) packed integer bitwise logical operations, the notion of distinct elements (e.g., byte, word, doubleword, or quadword) is not applicable. This explains why the instruction mnemonics vpand, vpor, and vpxor lack a size suffix letter. Here are the results for source code example Ch13_03:

```
Results for AndU16_Aavx
a:    1234    ABDC    AA55    1111    |    FFFF    7F7F    9876    7F00
b:    FF00    00FF    AAAA    5555    |    8000    7FFF    F0F0    0880
c:    1200    00DC    AA00    1111    |    8000    7F7F    9070    0800

Results for OrU16_Aavx
a:    1234    ABDC    AA55    1111    |    FFFF    7F7F    9876    7F00
b:    FF00    00FF    AAAA    5555    |    8000    7FFF    F0F0    0880
c:    FF34    ABFF    AAFF    5555    |    FFFF    7FFF    F8F6    7F80

Results for XorU16_Aavx
a:    1234    ABDC    AA55    1111    |    FFFF    7F7F    9876    7F00
b:    FF00    00FF    AAAA    5555    |    8000    7FFF    F0F0    0880
c:    ED34    AB23    00FF    4444    |    7FFF    0080    6886    7780
```

## Arithmetic and Logical Shifts

The final source code example of this section, Ch13_04, highlights the use of the AVX instructions `vpsllw` (Shift Packed Data Left Logical), `vpsrlw` (Shift Packed Data Right Logical), and `vpsraw` (Shift Packed Data Right Arithmetic). Listing 13-4 shows the assembly language source code for example Ch13_04.

***Listing 13-4.*** Example Ch13_04

```
;------------------------------------------------
;               Ch13_04_fasm.asm
;------------------------------------------------

;-------------------------------------------------------------------------
; extern void SllU16_Aavx(XmmVal* c, const XmmVal* a, int count);
;-------------------------------------------------------------------------

        .code
SllU16_Aavx proc
        vmovdqa xmm0,xmmword ptr [rdx]          ;xmm0 = a
        vmovd xmm1,r8d                          ;xmm1[31:0] = count

        vpsllw xmm2,xmm0,xmm1                   ;left shift word elements of a

        vmovdqa xmmword ptr [rcx],xmm2          ;save result
        ret
SllU16_Aavx endp

;-------------------------------------------------------------------------
; extern void SrlU16_Aavx(XmmVal* c, const XmmVal* a, int count);
;-------------------------------------------------------------------------

SrlU16_Aavx proc
        vmovdqa xmm0,xmmword ptr [rdx]          ;xmm0 = a
        vmovd xmm1,r8d                          ;xmm1[31:0] = count

        vpsrlw xmm2,xmm0,xmm1                   ;right shift word elements of a

        vmovdqa xmmword ptr [rcx],xmm2          ;save result
        ret
SrlU16_Aavx endp

;-------------------------------------------------------------------------
; extern void SraU16_Aavx(XmmVal* c, const XmmVal* a, int count);
;-------------------------------------------------------------------------

SraU16_Aavx proc
        vmovdqa xmm0,xmmword ptr [rdx]          ;xmm0 = a
        vmovd xmm1,r8d                          ;xmm1[31:0] = count

        vpsraw xmm2,xmm0,xmm1                   ;right shift word elements of a
```

```
        vmovdqa xmmword ptr [rcx],xmm2      ;save result
        ret
SraU16_Aavx endp
        end
```

Function SllU16_Aavx() begins its execution with a vmovdqa xmm0,xmmword ptr [rdx] instruction that loads argument value a into register XMM0. The next instruction, vmovd xmm1,r8d (Move Doubleword), copies the doubleword value in register R8D (argument value count) to XMM1[31:0]. Execution of this instruction also zeros bits YMM1[255:32]; bits ZMM1[511:256] are likewise zeroed if the processor supports AVX-512. The ensuing vpsllw xmm2,xmm0,xmm1 instruction left shifts each word element in XMM0 using the shift count in XMM1[31:0].

Functions SrlU16_Aavx() and SraU16_Aavx() use a code arrangement that is similar to SllU16_Aavx(). Function SrlU16_Aavx() demonstrates the use of the vpsrlw instruction, while SraU16_Aavx() highlights the use of the vpsraw instruction. The AVX instructions vpsllw, vpsrlw, and vpsraw can also be used with an immediate operand that specifies the shift count. X86-AVX also includes instructions that perform shifts using doubleword and quadword elements. These are listed in the end-of-chapter summary table (Table 13-3). Here are the results for source code example Ch13_04:

```
Results for SllU16_Aavx - count = 8
a:    1234    FFB0    00CC    8080   |   00FF    AAAA    0F0F    0101
c:    3400    B000    CC00    8000   |   FF00    AA00    0F00    0100

Results for SrlU16_Aavx - count = 4
a:    1234    FFB0    00CC    8080   |   00FF    AAAA    0F0F    0101
c:    0123    0FFB    000C    0808   |   000F    0AAA    00F0    0010

Results for SraU16_Aavx - count = 4
a:    1234    FFB0    00CC    8080   |   00FF    AAAA    0F0F    0101
c:    0123    FFFB    000C    F808   |   000F    FAAA    00F0    0010
```

# Image Processing Algorithms

In the first part of this book, several source code examples were presented that explained how to exploit C++ SIMD intrinsic functions to perform common image processing techniques. In this section, you will learn how to code a few image processing methods using x86-64 assembly language and AVX. The first source code example illustrates using AVX instructions to find the minimum and maximum values in a pixel buffer. The second source code example describes how to calculate a pixel buffer mean. Note that the AVX instructions and SIMD processing computations demonstrated in this section are also appropriate for use in other functions that carry out calculations using arrays or matrices of integer elements.

## Pixel Minimum and Maximum

Listing 13-5 shows the x86-64 assembly language source code for example Ch13_05. This example, which is a modified version of example Ch02_06, finds the minimum and maximum value in a pixel buffer of 8-bit unsigned integers. The non-assembly language source code for example Ch13_05 is not shown in Listing 13-5 since it is almost identical to the code you saw in example Ch02_06. However, the complete code for example Ch13_05 is included in the download software package.

***Listing 13-5.*** Example Ch13_05

```
;-------------------------------------------------
;               Ch13_05_fasm.asm
;-------------------------------------------------


;------------------------------------------------------------------------
; extern "C" bool CalcMinMaxU8_Aavx(uint8_t* x_min, uint8_t* x_max,
;   const uint8_t* x, size_t n);
;------------------------------------------------------------------------


NSE     equ 16                          ;num_simd_elements

        .code
CalcMinMaxU8_Aavx proc

; Make sure n and x are valid
        test r9,r9                      ;is n == 0?
        jz BadArg                       ;jump if yes
        test r9,0fh                     ;is n even multiple of 16?
        jnz BadArg                      ;jump if no

        test r8,0fh                     ;is x aligned to 16b boundary?
        jnz BadArg                      ;jump if no

; Initialize packed min and max values
        vpcmpeqb xmm4,xmm4,xmm4          ;packed minimums (all 0xff)
        vpxor xmm5,xmm5,xmm5            ;packed maximums (all 0x00)
        mov rax,-NSE                    ;initialize i

Loop1:  add rax,NSE                     ;i += NSE
        cmp rax,r9                      ;is i >= n?
        jae @F                          ;jump if yes

        vmovdqa xmm0,xmmword ptr [r8+rax]  ;xmm0 = block of 16 pixels
        vpminub xmm4,xmm4,xmm0          ;update packed min values
        vpmaxub xmm5,xmm5,xmm0          ;update packed max values

        jmp Loop1                       ;repeat until done

; Reduce packed min values
@@:     vpsrldq xmm0,xmm4,8
        vpminub xmm0,xmm0,xmm4          ;xmm0[63:0] = final 8 min vals
        vpsrldq xmm1,xmm0,4
        vpminub xmm1,xmm0,xmm1          ;xmm1[31:0] = final 4 min vals
        vpsrldq xmm2,xmm1,2
        vpminub xmm2,xmm2,xmm1          ;xmm2[15:0] = final 2 min vals
        vpsrldq xmm3,xmm2,1
        vpminub xmm3,xmm3,xmm2          ;xmm3[7:0] = final min val
        vpextrb byte ptr [rcx],xmm3,0   ;save final min val
```

```
; Reduce packed max values
        vpsrldq xmm0,xmm5,8
        vpmaxub xmm0,xmm0,xmm5          ;xmm0[63:0] = final 8 max vals
        vpsrldq xmm1,xmm0,4
        vpmaxub xmm1,xmm0,xmm1          ;xmm1[31:0] = final 4 max vals
        vpsrldq xmm2,xmm1,2
        vpmaxub xmm2,xmm2,xmm1          ;xmm2[15:0] = final 2 max vals
        vpsrldq xmm3,xmm2,1
        vpmaxub xmm3,xmm3,xmm2          ;xmm3[7:0] = final max val
        vpextrb byte ptr [rdx],xmm3,0  ;save final max val

        mov eax,1                      ;set success return code
        ret

BadArg: xor eax,eax                    ;set error return code
        ret


CalcMinMaxU8_Aavx endp
        end
```

Near the top of Listing 13-5, function CalcMinMaxU8_Aavx() employs two test instructions to confirm that argument value n is not equal to zero and an integral multiple of 16. The third test instruction verifies that pixel buffer x is aligned on a 16-byte boundary. Following argument validation, CalcMinMaxU8_Aavx() uses a vpcmpeqb xmm4,xmm4,xmm4 (Compare Packed Data for Equal) instruction to load 0xFF into each byte element of register XMM4. More specifically, vpcmpeqb performs byte element compares using its two source operands and sets the corresponding byte element in the destination operand to 0xFF if source operand elements are equal. Function CalcMinMaxU8_Aavx() uses vpcmpeqb xmm4,xmm4,xmm4 to set each byte element of XMM4 to 0xFF since this is faster than using vmovdqa instruction to load a 128-bit constant of all ones from memory. The ensuing vpxor xmm5,xmm5,xmm5 instruction sets each byte element in register XMM5 to 0x00.

The next instruction, mov rax,-NSE, initializes loop index variable i. Register RAX is loaded with -NSE since each iteration of Loop1 begins with an add RAX,NSE instruction that calculates i += NSE. This is followed by the instruction pair cmp rax,r9 and jae @F, which terminates Loop1 when i >= n is true. Note that the order of instructions used to initialize and update i in Loop1 precludes a loop-carried dependency condition from occurring. A loop-carried dependency condition arises when calculations in a for-loop are dependent on values computed during a prior iteration. Having a loop-carried dependency in a for-loop sometimes results in slower performance. A for-loop sans any loop-carried dependencies provides better opportunities for the processor to perform calculations of successive iterations simultaneously.

During execution of Loop1, function CalcMinMaxU8_Aavx() maintains packed minimums and maximums in registers XMM4 and XMM5, respectively. The first AVX instruction of Loop1, vmovdqa xmm0,xmmword ptr [r8+rax], loads a block of 16 pixels (x[i:i+15]) into register XMM0. This is followed by a vpminub xmm4,xmm4,xmm0 (Minimum of Packed Unsigned Integers) instruction that updates the packed minimum pixel values in XMM4. The ensuing vpmaxub xmm5,xmm5,xmm0 (Maximum of Packed Unsigned Integers) instruction updates the packed maximum values in XMM5.

Following execution of Loop1, CalcMinMaxU8_Aavx() reduces the 16 minimum values in XMM4 to a single scalar value. The code block that performs this operation uses a series of vpsrldq and vpminub instructions as shown in Figure 13-3.

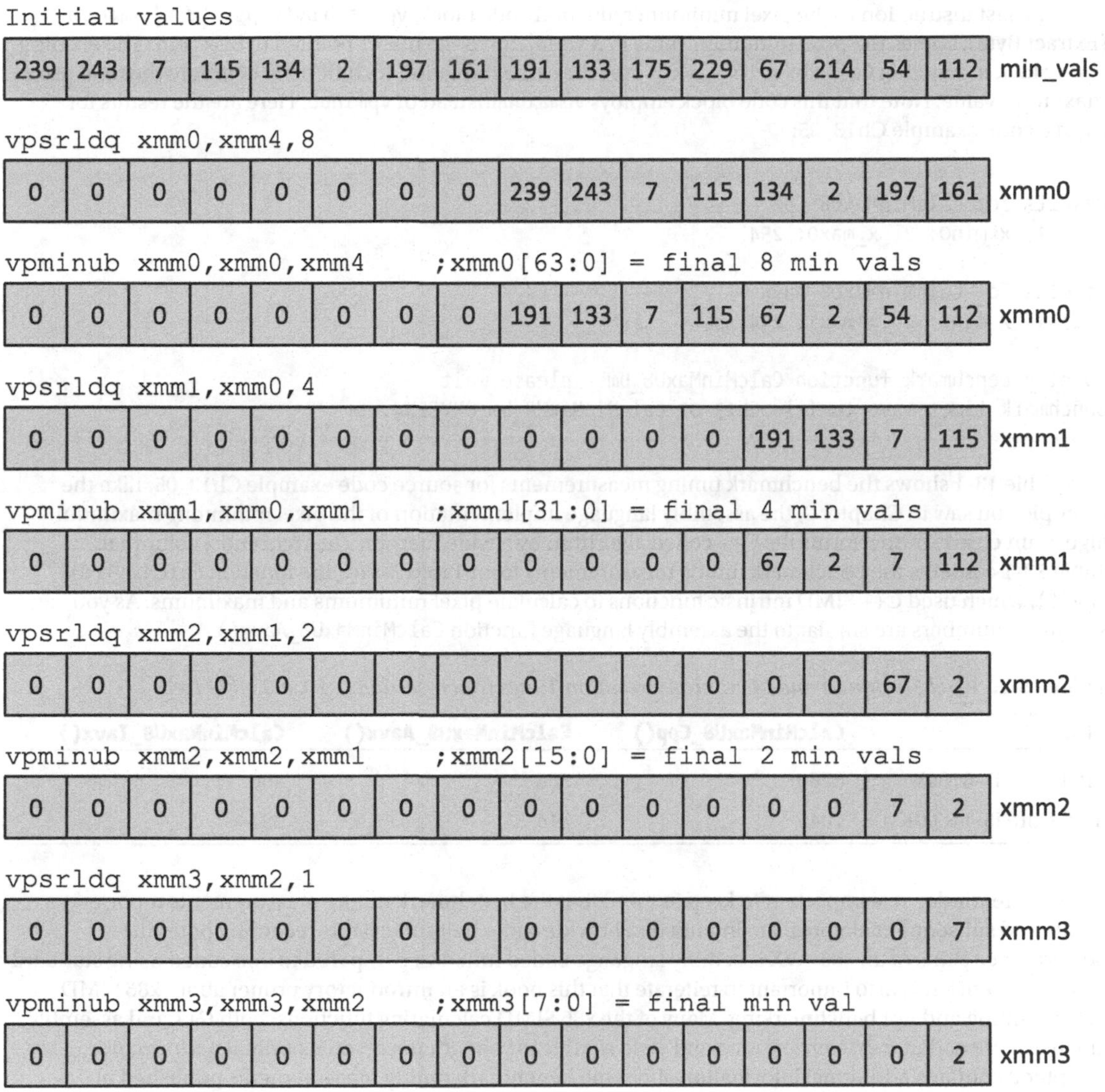

Initial values

| 239 | 243 | 7 | 115 | 134 | 2 | 197 | 161 | 191 | 133 | 175 | 229 | 67 | 214 | 54 | 112 | min_vals |

vpsrldq xmm0,xmm4,8

| 0 | 0 | 0 | 0 | 0 | 0 | 0 | 0 | 239 | 243 | 7 | 115 | 134 | 2 | 197 | 161 | xmm0 |

vpminub xmm0,xmm0,xmm4      ;xmm0[63:0] = final 8 min vals

| 0 | 0 | 0 | 0 | 0 | 0 | 0 | 0 | 191 | 133 | 7 | 115 | 67 | 2 | 54 | 112 | xmm0 |

vpsrldq xmm1,xmm0,4

| 0 | 0 | 0 | 0 | 0 | 0 | 0 | 0 | 0 | 0 | 0 | 0 | 191 | 133 | 7 | 115 | xmm1 |

vpminub xmm1,xmm0,xmm1      ;xmm1[31:0] = final 4 min vals

| 0 | 0 | 0 | 0 | 0 | 0 | 0 | 0 | 0 | 0 | 0 | 0 | 67 | 2 | 7 | 112 | xmm1 |

vpsrldq xmm2,xmm1,2

| 0 | 0 | 0 | 0 | 0 | 0 | 0 | 0 | 0 | 0 | 0 | 0 | 0 | 0 | 67 | 2 | xmm2 |

vpminub xmm2,xmm2,xmm1      ;xmm2[15:0] = final 2 min vals

| 0 | 0 | 0 | 0 | 0 | 0 | 0 | 0 | 0 | 0 | 0 | 0 | 0 | 0 | 7 | 2 | xmm2 |

vpsrldq xmm3,xmm2,1

| 0 | 0 | 0 | 0 | 0 | 0 | 0 | 0 | 0 | 0 | 0 | 0 | 0 | 0 | 0 | 7 | xmm3 |

vpminub xmm3,xmm3,xmm2      ;xmm3[7:0] = final min val

| 0 | 0 | 0 | 0 | 0 | 0 | 0 | 0 | 0 | 0 | 0 | 0 | 0 | 0 | 0 | 2 | xmm3 |

*Figure 13-3.* *Reduction of packed 8-bit unsigned integers using* vpsrldq *and* vpminub

The last instruction in the pixel minimum reduction code block, vpextrb byte ptr [rcx],xmm3,0 (Extract Byte), copies the pixel minimum value in XMM3[7:0] to the buffer pointed to by x_min. The ensuing code block in function CalcMinMaxU8_Aavx() uses the same reduction technique to compute the final pixel maximum value. Note that this code block employs vpmaxub instead of vpminub. Here are the results for source code example Ch13_05:

```
Results for CalcMinMaxU8_Cpp
rc0: 1  x_min0: 2  x_max0: 254

Results for CalcMinMaxU8_Aavx
rc1: 1  x_min1: 2  x_max1: 254

Running benchmark function CalcMinMaxU8_bm - please wait
Benchmark times save to file Ch13_05_CalcMinMaxU8_bm_OXYGEN4.csv
```

Table 13-1 shows the benchmark timing measurements for source code example Ch13_05. Like the example you saw in Chapter 2, the assembly language implementation of the pixel minimum-maximum algorithm clearly outperforms the C++ coded algorithm by a wide margin. The right-most column in Table 13-1 contains the benchmark timing measurements from Table 2-3 for the function CalcMinMaxU8_Iavx(), which used C++ SIMD intrinsic functions to calculate pixel minimums and maximums. As you can see, these numbers are similar to the assembly language function CalcMinMaxU8_Aavx().

*Table 13-1.* *Pixel Minimum and Maximum Execution Times (Microseconds), 10,000,000 Pixels*

| CPU | CalcMinMaxU8_Cpp() | CalcMinMaxU8_Aavx() | CalcMinMaxU8_Iavx() |
|---|---|---|---|
| Intel Core i7-8700K | 6760 | 388 | 406 |
| Intel Core i5-11600K | 7045 | 314 | 304 |

As a reminder, it is important to keep in mind that the benchmark timing measurements reported in this and subsequent chapters are intended to provide some helpful insights regarding potential performance gains of an x86-AVX assembly language coded function compared to one coded using standard C++ statements. It is also important to reiterate that this book is an introductory primer about x86 SIMD programming and not benchmarking. Many of the x86 SIMD calculating functions, both C++ and assembly language, are coded to hasten learning and yield significant but not necessarily optimal performance. Chapter 2 contains additional information about the benchmark timing measurements published in this book.

## Pixel Mean Intensity

In source code example Ch02_07, you learned how to calculate the arithmetic mean of an array of 8-bit unsigned integers using C++ SIMD intrinsic functions. The final source example of this chapter, named Ch13_06, illustrates how to perform this same calculation using x86-64 assembly language and AVX instructions. Listing 13-6 shows the assembly language source code for example Ch13_06.

**Listing 13-6.** Example Ch13_06

```
;--------------------------------------------------
;               Ch13_06_fasm.asm
;--------------------------------------------------


;------------------------------------------------------------------------
; extern "C" bool CalcMeanU8_Aavx(double* mean_x, uint64_t* sum_x, const uint8_t* x,
;   size_t n);
;------------------------------------------------------------------------


NSE       equ 64                          ;num_simd_elements

          .code
          extern g_NumElementsMax:qword

CalcMeanU8_Aavx proc
; Make sure n and x are valid
          test r9,r9                      ;is n == 0?
          jz BadArg                       ;jump if yes
          cmp r9,[g_NumElementsMax]       ;is n > g_NumElementsMax?
          ja BadArg                       ;jump if yes
          test r9,3fh                     ;is n even multiple of 64?
          jnz BadArg                      ;jump if no

          test r8,0fh                     ;is x aligned to 16b boundary?
          jnz BadArg                      ;jump if no

; Initialize
          vpxor xmm4,xmm4,xmm4            ;packed zero
          vpxor xmm5,xmm5,xmm5            ;packed sums (4 dwords)
          mov rax,-NSE                    ;initialize i

; Calculate sum of all pixels
Loop1:    add rax,NSE                     ;i += NSE
          cmp rax,r9                      ;is i >= n?
          jae @F                          ;jump if yes

          vpxor xmm3,xmm3,xmm3            ;loop packed sums (8 words)

          vmovdqa xmm0,xmmword ptr [r8+rax]    ;load block of 16 pixels
          vpunpcklbw xmm1,xmm0,xmm4       ;promote bytes to words
          vpunpckhbw xmm2,xmm0,xmm4
          vpaddw xmm3,xmm3,xmm1           ;update loop packed sums
          vpaddw xmm3,xmm3,xmm2

          vmovdqa xmm0,xmmword ptr [r8+rax+16] ;load block of 16 pixels
          vpunpcklbw xmm1,xmm0,xmm4       ;promote bytes to words
          vpunpckhbw xmm2,xmm0,xmm4
          vpaddw xmm3,xmm3,xmm1           ;update loop packed sums
          vpaddw xmm3,xmm3,xmm2
```

```
        vmovdqa xmm0,xmmword ptr [r8+rax+32]    ;load block of 16 pixels
        vpunpcklbw xmm1,xmm0,xmm4               ;promote bytes to words
        vpunpckhbw xmm2,xmm0,xmm4
        vpaddw xmm3,xmm3,xmm1                   ;update loop packed sums
        vpaddw xmm3,xmm3,xmm2

        vmovdqa xmm0,xmmword ptr [r8+rax+48]    ;load block of 16 pixels
        vpunpcklbw xmm1,xmm0,xmm4               ;promote bytes to words
        vpunpckhbw xmm2,xmm0,xmm4
        vpaddw xmm3,xmm3,xmm1                   ;update loop packed sums
        vpaddw xmm3,xmm3,xmm2

        vpunpcklwd xmm0,xmm3,xmm4               ;promote loop packed sums
        vpunpckhwd xmm1,xmm3,xmm4
        vpaddd xmm5,xmm5,xmm0                   ;update packed dword sums
        vpaddd xmm5,xmm5,xmm1

        jmp Loop1                               ;repeat until done

; Reduce packed sums (4 dwords) to single qword
@@:     vpextrd eax,xmm5,0                      ;rax = xmm5[31:0]
        vpextrd r10d,xmm5,1                     ;r10 = xmm5[63:32]
        add rax,r10                             ;update qword sum
        vpextrd r10d,xmm5,2                     ;r10 = xmm5[95:64]
        add rax,r10                             ;update qword sum
        vpextrd r10d,xmm5,3                     ;r10 = xmm5[127:96]
        add rax,r10                             ;update qword sum
        mov qword ptr [rdx],rax                 ;save final qword sum

; Calculate mean
        vcvtsi2sd xmm0,xmm0,rax                 ;convert sum to DPFP
        vcvtsi2sd xmm1,xmm1,r9                  ;convert n to DPFP
        vdivsd xmm2,xmm0,xmm1                   ;mean = sum / n
        vmovsd real8 ptr [rcx],xmm2             ;save mean

        mov eax,1                               ;set success return code
        ret

BadArg: xor eax,eax                            ;set error return code
        ret

CalcMeanU8_Aavx endp
        end
```

Near the top of file Ch13_06_fasm.asm is the statement extern g_NumElementsMax:qword, which declares g_NumElementsMax as an external quadword variable (the definition of g_NumElementsMax is located in the file Ch13_06_Misc.cpp). The first code block of CalcMeanU8_Aavx() uses a test r9,r9 and jz BadArg to ensure that argument value n is not equal to zero. The next instruction pair, cmp r9,[g_NumElementsMax] and ja BadArg, bypasses the calculating code if n > g_NumElementsMax is true. This is followed by the instruction pair test r9,3fh and jnz BadArg, which confirms that n is an even multiple of 64 (in later examples, you will learn how to process residual pixels). The final check of the first code block, test r8,0fh and jnz BadArg, confirms that pixel buffer x is aligned on a 16-byte boundary.

Following argument validation, `CalcMeanU8_Aavx()` sums the elements of pixel buffer x using SIMD arithmetic. The technique used in for-loop `Loop1` is identical to the one used in source code example `Ch02_07` and begins with a `vpxor xmm3,xmm3,xmm3` instruction that initializes eight word sums to zero. The `vmovdqa xmm0,xmmword ptr [r8+rax]` instruction that follows loads pixel values x[i:i+15] into register XMM0. The ensuing instruction pair, `vpunpcklbw xmm1,xmm0,xmm4` and `vpunpckhbw xmm2,xmm0,xmm4`, size-promotes the pixel values to 16 bits. These values are then added to the intermediate word sums in register XMM3 using the instructions `vpaddw xmm3,xmm3,xmm1` and `vpaddw xmm3,xmm3,xmm2` as shown in Figure 13-4. The next three code blocks in `Loop1` add pixel values x[i+16:i+31], x[i+32:i+47], and x[i+48:i+63] to the intermediate sums in register XMM3. The final code block in `Loop1` employs the instruction pair `vpunpcklwd xmm0,xmm3,xmm4` and `vpunpckhwd xmm1,xmm3,xmm4` to size-promote the packed word sums in XMM3 to doublewords. It then exercises two `vpaddd` instructions to add the current iteration sums to the intermediate packed doubleword sums maintained in register XMM5.

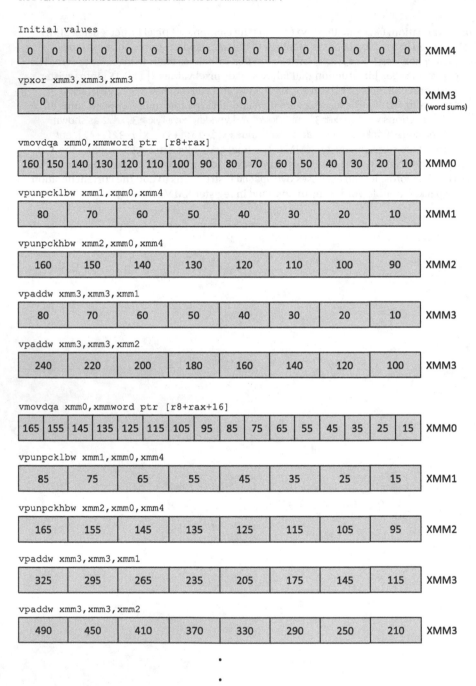

*Figure 13-4.* *Summing of pixel values using* vpunpcklbw, vpunpckhbw, *and* vpaddw *in Loop1 of CalcMeanU8_Aavx()*

Following execution of Loop1, CalcMeanU8_Aavx() uses a series of vpextrd and add instructions to reduce the packed doubleword sums to a single quadword value. Function CalcMeanU8_Aavx() then employs the instruction vcvtsi2sd xmm0,xmm0,rax to convert sum to a double-precision floating-point value. The next instruction, vcvtsi2sd xmm1,xmm1,r9, converts n to double-precision floating-point. This is followed by a vdivsd xmm2,xmm0,xmm1 instruction that calculates the mean. The ensuing vmovsd real8 ptr [rcx],xmm2 instruction saves the calculated mean. Here are the results for source code example Ch13_06:

---

```
Results for CalcMeanU8_Cpp
rc0: 1  sum_x0: 1275046509  mean_x0: 127.504651

Results for CalcMeanU8_Aavx
rc1: 1  sum_x1: 1275046509  mean_x1: 127.504651

Running benchmark function CalcMeanU8_bm - please wait
Benchmark times save to file Ch13_06_CalcMeanU8_bm_OXYGEN4.csv
```

---

Table 13-2 shows some benchmark timing measurements for source code example Ch13_05. This table also shows the timing measurements from Table 2-4 for CalcMeanU8_Iavx(), which used C++ SIMD intrinsic functions. Like the previous example, the benchmark timing measurements for the assembly language and C++ SIMD intrinsic function implementations are similar.

***Table 13-2.*** *Pixel Array Arithmetic Mean Execution Times (Microseconds), 10,000,000 Pixels*

| CPU | CalcMeanU8_Cpp() | CalcMeanU8_Aavx() | CalcMeanU8_Iavx() |
|---|---|---|---|
| Intel Core i7-8700K | 2289 | 461 | 462 |
| Intel Core i5-11600K | 1856 | 301 | 288 |

# Summary

Table 13-3 summarizes the x86 assembly language instructions introduced in this chapter. This table also includes closely related instructions. Before proceeding to the next chapter, make sure you understand the operation that is performed by each instruction shown in Table 13-3.

*Table 13-3.* *X86 Assembly Language Instruction Summary for Chapter 13*

| Instruction Mnemonic | Description |
|---|---|
| vmov[d\|q] | Move doubleword or quadword into XMM register |
| vpadd[b\|w\|d\|q] | Packed integer addition |
| vpadds[b\|w] | Packed signed integer addition (saturated) |
| vpaddus[b\|w] | Packed unsigned integer addition (saturated) |
| vpand | Bitwise logical AND |
| vpcmpeq[b\|w\|d\|q] | Packed integer compare for equality |
| vpextr[b\|w\|d\|q] | Extract integer |
| vpmaxs[b\|w\|d\|q] | Packed signed integer maximum |
| vpmaxu[b\|w\|d\|q] | Packed unsigned integer maximum |
| vpmins[b\|w\|d\|q] | Packed signed integer minimum |
| vpminu[b\|w\|d\|q] | Packed unsigned integer minimum |
| vpmuldq | Packed signed integer multiplication (quadword results) |
| vpmulhw | Packed signed integer multiplication (high results) |
| vpmull[w\|d\|q] | Packed signed integer multiplication (low results) |
| vpor | Bitwise logical OR |
| vpsll[w\|d\|q] | Packed integer shift left logical |
| vpsra[w\|d\|q] | Packed integer shift right arithmetic |
| vpsrl[w\|d\|q] | Packed integer shift right logical |
| vpslldq | Shift double quadword left logical |
| vpsrldq | Shift double quadword right logical |
| vpsub[b\|w\|d\|q] | Packed integer subtraction |
| vpsubs[b\|w] | Packed signed integer subtraction (saturated) |
| vpsubus[b\|w] | Packed unsigned integer subtraction (saturated) |
| vpunpckh[bw\|wd\|dq\|qdq] | Unpack and interleave high-order integers |
| vpunpckl[bw\|wd\|dq\|qdq] | Unpack and interleave low-order integers |
| vpxor | Bitwise logical exclusive OR |

# CHAPTER 14

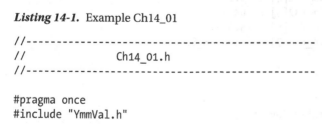

# AVX Assembly Language Programming: Part 2

In the previous chapter, you learned how to use AVX instructions to perform calculations using packed integer operands. The chapter you are about to read is similar to the previous chapter but uses packed floating-point instead of packed integer operands. It begins with a section that demonstrates standard floating-point arithmetic operations using AVX instructions. This is followed by a section that explains how to use AVX instructions to perform SIMD calculations using floating-point arrays. The final section illustrates the use of AVX instructions to carry out computations using floating-point matrices.

Like the previous chapter, some of the code examples presented in this chapter are adaptations of examples you saw in Chapter 3. Doing this allows you to better grasp the programming similarities that exist between AVX assembly language instructions and their corresponding C++ SIMD intrinsic functions.

## Floating-Point Operations

In this section, you will examine two source code examples that explain floating-point operations using AVX instructions and packed single-precision and double-precision floating-point operands. The first example covers basic arithmetic including addition, subtraction, multiplication, and division. The second example describes the use of the AVX instructions that carry out packed floating-point compares.

### Floating-Point Arithmetic

Listing 14-1 shows the source code for example Ch14_01. This example illustrates common arithmetic operations using 256-bit wide SIMD operands that contain single-precision or double-precision floating-point elements. Source code example Ch14_01 also explains how to properly use the vzeroupper (Zero Upper Bits of YMM and ZMM Registers) instruction.

***Listing 14-1.*** Example Ch14_01

```
//-------------------------------------------------
//                  Ch14_01.h
//-------------------------------------------------

#pragma once
#include "YmmVal.h"
```

```cpp
// Ch14_01_fcpp.cpp
extern "C" void PackedMathF32_Aavx(YmmVal c[8], const YmmVal* a, const YmmVal* b);
extern "C" void PackedMathF64_Aavx(YmmVal c[8], const YmmVal* a, const YmmVal* b);

//-------------------------------------------------
//                Ch14_01.cpp
//-------------------------------------------------

#include <iostream>
#include <iomanip>
#include <string>
#define _USE_MATH_DEFINES
#include <math.h>
#include "Ch14_01.h"

static void PackedMathF32();
static void PackedMathF64();

static const char* c_OprStr[8] =
{
    "Add", "Sub", "Mul", "Div", "Min", "Max", "Sqrt a", "Abs b"
};

int main()
{
    const char nl = '\n';

    PackedMathF32();
    std::cout << nl << std::string(78, '-') << nl;
    PackedMathF64();
}

static void PackedMathF32(void)
{
    YmmVal a, b, c[8];
    const char nl = '\n';

    a.m_F32[0] = 36.0f;                  b.m_F32[0] = -(float)(1.0 / 9.0);
    a.m_F32[1] = (float)(1.0 / 32.0);    b.m_F32[1] = 64.0f;
    a.m_F32[2] = 2.0f;                   b.m_F32[2] = -0.0625f;
    a.m_F32[3] = 42.0f;                  b.m_F32[3] = 8.666667f;
    a.m_F32[4] = (float)M_PI;            b.m_F32[4] = -4.0;
    a.m_F32[5] = 18.6f;                  b.m_F32[5] = -64.0f;
    a.m_F32[6] = 3.0f;                   b.m_F32[6] = -5.95f;
    a.m_F32[7] = 142.0f;                 b.m_F32[7] = (float)M_SQRT2;

    PackedMathF32_Aavx(c, &a, &b);

    size_t w = 9;
    std::cout << ("\nResults for PackedMathF32_Aavx\n");
```

```cpp
    for (unsigned int i = 0; i < 2; i++)
    {
        std::string s0 = (i == 0) ? "a lo:    " : "a hi:    ";
        std::string s1 = (i == 0) ? "b lo:    " : "b hi:    ";

        std::cout << s0 << a.ToStringF32(i) << nl;
        std::cout << s1 << b.ToStringF32(i) << nl;

        for (unsigned int j = 0; j < 8; j++)
        {
            std::cout << std::setw(w) << std::left << c_OprStr[j];
            std::cout << c[j].ToStringF32(i) << nl;
        }

        if (i == 0)
            std::cout << nl;
    }
}

static void PackedMathF64(void)
{
    YmmVal a, b, c[8];
    const char nl = '\n';

    a.m_F64[0] = 2.0;           b.m_F64[0] = M_PI;
    a.m_F64[1] = 4.0 ;          b.m_F64[1] = M_E;
    a.m_F64[2] = 7.5;           b.m_F64[2] = -9.125;
    a.m_F64[3] = 3.0;           b.m_F64[3] = -M_PI;

    PackedMathF64_Aavx(c, &a, &b);

    size_t w = 9;
    std::cout << ("\nResults for PackedMathF64_Aavx\n");

    for (unsigned int i = 0; i < 2; i++)
    {
        std::string s0 = (i == 0) ? "a lo:    " : "a hi:    ";
        std::string s1 = (i == 0) ? "b lo:    " : "b hi:    ";

        std::cout << s0 << a.ToStringF64(i) << nl;
        std::cout << s1 << b.ToStringF64(i) << nl;

        for (unsigned int j = 0; j < 8; j++)
        {
            std::cout << std::setw(w) << std::left << c_OprStr[j];
            std::cout << c[j].ToStringF64(i) << nl;
        }

        if (i == 0)
            std::cout << nl;
    }
}
```

```
;-------------------------------------------------
;                Ch14_01_fasm.asm
;-------------------------------------------------

            .const
r8_AbsMask   qword 07fffffffffffffffh
r4_AbsMask   dword 07fffffffh


;----------------------------------------------------------------------------
; extern void PackedMathF32_Aavx(YmmVal c[8], const YmmVal* a, const YmmVal* b);
;----------------------------------------------------------------------------

            .code
PackedMathF32_Aavx proc
        vmovaps ymm0,ymmword ptr [rdx]      ;ymm0 = a
        vmovaps ymm1,ymmword ptr [r8]       ;ymm1 = b

        vaddps ymm2,ymm0,ymm1                ;SPFP addition
        vmovaps ymmword ptr[rcx],ymm2

        vsubps ymm2,ymm0,ymm1                ;SPFP subtraction
        vmovaps ymmword ptr[rcx+32],ymm2

        vmulps ymm2,ymm0,ymm1                ;SPFP multiplication
        vmovaps ymmword ptr[rcx+64],ymm2

        vdivps ymm2,ymm0,ymm1                ;SPFP division
        vmovaps ymmword ptr[rcx+96],ymm2

        vminps ymm2,ymm0,ymm1                ;SPFP min
        vmovaps ymmword ptr[rcx+128],ymm2

        vmaxps ymm2,ymm0,ymm1                ;SPFP max
        vmovaps ymmword ptr[rcx+160],ymm2

        vsqrtps ymm2,ymm0                    ;SPFP sqrt(a)
        vmovaps ymmword ptr[rcx+192],ymm2

        vbroadcastss ymm3,real4 ptr [r4_AbsMask]  ;load abs mask
        vandps ymm2,ymm3,ymm1                      ;SPFP abs(b)
        vmovaps ymmword ptr[rcx+224],ymm2

        vzeroupper                          ;clear upper YMM/ZMM bits
        ret
PackedMathF32_Aavx endp

;----------------------------------------------------------------------------
; extern void PackedMathF64_Aavx(YmmVal c[8], const YmmVal* a, const YmmVal* b);
;----------------------------------------------------------------------------
```

```
PackedMathF64_Aavx proc
        vmovapd ymm0,ymmword ptr [rdx]          ;ymm0 = a
        vmovapd ymm1,ymmword ptr [r8]           ;ymm1 = b

        vaddpd ymm2,ymm0,ymm1                    ;DPFP addition
        vmovapd ymmword ptr[rcx],ymm2

        vsubpd ymm2,ymm0,ymm1                    ;DPFP subtraction
        vmovapd ymmword ptr[rcx+32],ymm2

        vmulpd ymm2,ymm0,ymm1                    ;DPFP multiplication
        vmovapd ymmword ptr[rcx+64],ymm2

        vdivpd ymm2,ymm0,ymm1                    ;DPFP division
        vmovapd ymmword ptr[rcx+96],ymm2

        vminpd ymm2,ymm0,ymm1                    ;DPFP min
        vmovapd ymmword ptr[rcx+128],ymm2

        vmaxpd ymm2,ymm0,ymm1                    ;DPFP max
        vmovapd ymmword ptr[rcx+160],ymm2

        vsqrtpd ymm2,ymm0                        ;DPFP sqrt(a)
        vmovapd ymmword ptr[rcx+192],ymm2

        vbroadcastsd ymm3,real8 ptr [r8_AbsMask] ;load abs mask
        vandpd ymm2,ymm3,ymm1                    ;DPFP abs(b)
        vmovapd ymmword ptr[rcx+224],ymm2

        vzeroupper                               ;clear upper YMM/ZMM bits
        ret
PackedMathF64_Aavx endp
        end
```

The first file in Listing 14-1, Ch14_01.h, contains the function declarations for this example. Note that both PackedMathF32_Aavx() and PackedMathF64_Aavx() require arguments of type YmmVal. Recall from the discussions in Chapter 3 that a YmmVal object contains a simple C++ union whose members correspond to the packed data types of a 256-bit wide x86-AVX operand (see Listing 3-1). Next in Listing 14-1 is the file Ch14_01.cpp. This function contains two functions named PackedMathF32() and PackedMathF64(). These functions perform test case initialization for the assembly language functions PackedMathF32_Aavx() and PackedMathF64_Aavx(), respectively. They also format and stream the results to std::cout.

The file Ch14_01_fasm.asm begins with a .const section that defines masks for calculating floating-point absolute values. Note that the most significant bit of both r8_AbsMask and r4_AbsMask is set to zero while all other bits are set to one. The most significant bit in each mask corresponds to the floating-point sign bit. Also note that both r8_AbsMask and r4_AbsMask are properly aligned since the assembler automatically aligns the start of each .const section on a double quadword (16-byte) boundary.

Function PackedMathF32_Aavx() begins with a vmovaps ymm0,ymmword ptr [rdx] (Move Aligned Packed SPFP Values) instruction that loads argument value a into register YMM0. This is followed by a vmovaps ymm1,ymmword ptr [r8] instruction that loads argument value b into YMM1. When loading a YMM register, the vmovaps instruction requires its source operand in memory to be aligned on a 32-byte boundary (recall that the declaration of YmmVal included an alignas(32) specifier). Then the next instruction, vaddps ymm2,ymm0,ymm1 (Add Packed SPFP Values), adds the floating-point elements in registers YMM0 (a) and YMM1 (b) and saves the result in register YMM2. The vmovaps ymmword ptr[rcx],ymm2 instruction that follows saves the resultant packed sums in YMM2 to c[0].

The ensuing code blocks illustrate other packed arithmetic operations using 256-bit wide operands and single-precision floating-point elements. The vsubps (Subtract Packed SPFP values), vmulps (Multiply Packed SPFP Values), and vdivps (Divide Packed SPFP Values) perform packed subtraction, multiplication, and division. The instructions vminps (Minimum of SPFP Values), vmaxps (Maximum of SPFP Values), and vsqrtps (Square Root of SPFP values) calculate packed minimums, maximums, and square roots, respectively.

Following calculation of the square roots, PackedMathF32_Aavx() uses a vbroadcastss ymm3,real4 ptr [r4_AbsMask] (Load with Broadcast Floating-Point Data) instruction, which loads r4_AbsMask (0x7FFFFFFF) into each doubleword element of YMM3. The next instruction, vandps ymm2,ymm3,ymm1 (Bitwise Logical AND of Packed SPFP Values), performs a bitwise logical AND of registers YMM3 and YMM1 and saves the result in YMM2. This ANDing operation zeros the sign bit of each single-precision floating-point element in YMM1, which yields the absolute values.

Prior to its ret instruction, function PackedMathF32_Aavx() uses a vzeroupper instruction. Operationally, this instruction zeros the upper 128 (384) bits of registers YMM0–YMM15 (ZMM0–ZMM15); vzeroupper does not modify registers XMM0–XMM15. The real reason for using a vzeroupper instruction is to avoid potential delays that can occur whenever the processor transitions from executing x86-AVX instructions to executing legacy x86-SSE instructions. Any function that uses a YMM or ZMM register operand should always include a vzeroupper instruction prior to executing a ret instruction or calling any function that might use x86-SSE legacy instructions including C++ library functions. A function can also use the vzeroall (Zero XMM, YMM, and ZMM Registers) instruction as an alternative to vzeroupper. The vzeroall instruction zeros all bits in registers XMM0–XMM15, YMM0–YMM15, and ZMM0–ZMM15; it does not modify any bits in registers ZMM16–ZMM31.

Following PackedMathF32_Aavx() in Listing 14-1 is the function PackedMathF64_Aavx. This function illustrates common arithmetic operations using 256-bit wide operands and double-precision floating-point elements. Note that the instruction mnemonics for the double-precision variants use a "pd" suffix instead of "ps." Here are the results for source code example Ch14_01:

```
Results for PackedMathF32_Aavx
a lo:       36.000000        0.031250   |     2.000000       42.000000
b lo:       -0.111111       64.000000   |    -0.062500        8.666667
Add         35.888889       64.031250   |     1.937500       50.666668
Sub         36.111111      -63.968750   |     2.062500       33.333332
Mul         -4.000000        2.000000   |    -0.125000      364.000000
Div       -324.000000        0.000488   |   -32.000000        4.846154
Min         -0.111111        0.031250   |    -0.062500        8.666667
Max         36.000000       64.000000   |     2.000000       42.000000
Sqrt a       6.000000        0.176777   |     1.414214        6.480741
Abs b        0.111111       64.000000   |     0.062500        8.666667


a hi:        3.141593       18.600000   |     3.000000      142.000000
b hi:       -4.000000      -64.000000   |    -5.950000        1.414214
Add         -0.858407      -45.400002   |    -2.950000      143.414215
Sub          7.141593       82.599998   |     8.950000      140.585785
Mul        -12.566371    -1190.400024   |   -17.849998      200.818329
Div         -0.785398       -0.290625   |    -0.504202      100.409164
Min         -4.000000      -64.000000   |    -5.950000        1.414214
```

```
Max             3.141593       18.600000    |     3.000000      142.000000
Sqrt a          1.772454        4.312772    |     1.732051       11.916375
Abs b           4.000000       64.000000    |     5.950000        1.414214


---------------------------------------------------------------------------


Results for PackedMathF64_Aavx
a lo:                      2.000000000000   |               4.000000000000
b lo:                      3.141592653590   |               2.718281828459
Add                        5.141592653590   |               6.718281828459
Sub                       -1.141592653590   |               1.281718171541
Mul                        6.283185307180   |              10.873127313836
Div                        0.636619772368   |               1.471517764686
Min                        2.000000000000   |               2.718281828459
Max                        3.141592653590   |               4.000000000000
Sqrt a                     1.414213562373   |               2.000000000000
Abs b                      3.141592653590   |               2.718281828459

a hi:                      7.500000000000   |               3.000000000000
b hi:                     -9.125000000000   |              -3.141592653590
Add                       -1.625000000000   |              -0.141592653590
Sub                       16.625000000000   |               6.141592653590
Mul                      -68.437500000000   |              -9.424777960769
Div                       -0.821917808219   |              -0.954929658551
Min                       -9.125000000000   |              -3.141592653590
Max                        7.500000000000   |               3.000000000000
Sqrt a                     2.738612787526   |               1.732050807569
Abs b                      9.125000000000   |               3.141592653590
```

## Floating-Point Compares

In Chapter 3, you learned how to perform compare operations using packed single-precision and double-precision floating-point operands (see example Ch03_02). The next source code example, Ch14_02, demonstrates packed floating-point compare operations using the AVX instructions vcmpps (Compare Packed SPFP values) and vcmppd (Compare Packed DPFP Values). Listing 14-2 shows the assembly language code for example Ch14_02. Not shown in Listing 14-2 is the C++ code that performs test case initialization since this code is the same as the code used in example Ch03_02.

*Listing 14-2.* Example Ch14_02

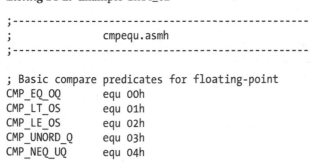

```
;---------------------------------------------------
;               cmpequ.asmh
;---------------------------------------------------

; Basic compare predicates for floating-point
CMP_EQ_OQ          equ 00h
CMP_LT_OS          equ 01h
CMP_LE_OS          equ 02h
CMP_UNORD_Q        equ 03h
CMP_NEQ_UQ         equ 04h
```

```
CMP_NLT_US         equ 05h
CMP_GE_US          equ 05h
CMP_NLE_US         equ 06h
CMP_GT_US          equ 06h
CMP_ORD_Q          equ 07h

; Extended compare predicates for floating-point
CMP_EQ_UQ          equ 08h
CMP_NGE_US         equ 09h
CMP_NGT_US         equ 0ah
CMP_FALSE_OQ       equ 0bh
CMP_NEQ_OQ         equ 0ch
CMP_GE_OS          equ 0dh
CMP_GT_OS          equ 0eh
CMP_TRUE_UQ        equ 0fh
CMP_EQ_OS          equ 10h
CMP_LT_OQ          equ 11h
CMP_LE_OQ          equ 12h
CMP_UNORD_S        equ 13h
CMP_NEQ_US         equ 14h
CMP_NLT_UQ         equ 15h
CMP_NLE_UQ         equ 16h
CMP_ORD_S          equ 17h
CMP_EQ_US          equ 18h
CMP_NGE_UQ         equ 19h
CMP_NGT_UQ         equ 1ah
CMP_FALSE_OS       equ 1bh
CMP_NEQ_OS         equ 1ch
CMP_GE_OQ          equ 1dh
CMP_GT_OQ          equ 1eh
CMP_TRUE_US        equ 1fh

; Compare predicates for packed integers
CMP_EQ             equ 00h
CMP_LT             equ 01h
CMP_LE             equ 02h
CMP_FALSE          equ 03h
CMP_NEQ            equ 04h
CMP_NLT            equ 05h
CMP_GE             equ 05h
CMP_NLE            equ 06h
CMP_GT             equ 06h
CMP_TRUE           equ 07h

;-------------------------------------------------
;                 Ch14_02_fasm.asm
;-------------------------------------------------

        include <cmpequ.asmh>
```

```asm
;-----------------------------------------------------------------------
; extern "C" void PackedCompareF32_Aavx(YmmVal c[8], const YmmVal* a, const YmmVal* b);
;-----------------------------------------------------------------------

        .code
PackedCompareF32_Aavx proc
        vmovaps ymm0,ymmword ptr [rdx]          ;ymm0 = a
        vmovaps ymm1,ymmword ptr [r8]           ;ymm1 = b

        vcmpps ymm2,ymm0,ymm1,CMP_EQ_OQ         ;packed compare for EQ
        vmovaps ymmword ptr[rcx],ymm2

        vcmpps ymm2,ymm0,ymm1,CMP_NEQ_OQ        ;packed compare for NEQ
        vmovaps ymmword ptr[rcx+32],ymm2

        vcmpps ymm2,ymm0,ymm1,CMP_LT_OQ         ;packed compare for LT
        vmovaps ymmword ptr[rcx+64],ymm2

        vcmpps ymm2,ymm0,ymm1,CMP_LE_OQ         ;packed compare for LE
        vmovaps ymmword ptr[rcx+96],ymm2

        vcmpps ymm2,ymm0,ymm1,CMP_GT_OQ         ;packed compare for GT
        vmovaps ymmword ptr[rcx+128],ymm2

        vcmpps ymm2,ymm0,ymm1,CMP_GE_OQ         ;packed compare for GE
        vmovaps ymmword ptr[rcx+160],ymm2

        vcmpps ymm2,ymm0,ymm1,CMP_ORD_Q         ;packed compare for ORD
        vmovaps ymmword ptr[rcx+192],ymm2

        vcmpps ymm2,ymm0,ymm1,CMP_UNORD_Q       ;packed compare for UNORD
        vmovaps ymmword ptr[rcx+224],ymm2

        vzeroupper
        ret
PackedCompareF32_Aavx endp

;-----------------------------------------------------------------------
; extern "C" void PackedCompareF64_Aavx(YmmVal c[8], const YmmVal* a, const YmmVal* b);
;-----------------------------------------------------------------------

PackedCompareF64_Aavx proc
        vmovapd ymm0,ymmword ptr [rdx]          ;ymm0 = a
        vmovapd ymm1,ymmword ptr [r8]           ;ymm1 = b

        vcmppd ymm2,ymm0,ymm1,CMP_EQ_OQ         ;packed compare for EQ
        vmovapd ymmword ptr[rcx],ymm2

        vcmppd ymm2,ymm0,ymm1,CMP_NEQ_OQ        ;packed compare for NEQ
        vmovapd ymmword ptr[rcx+32],ymm2
```

```
        vcmppd ymm2,ymm0,ymm1,CMP_LT_OQ        ;packed compare for LT
        vmovapd ymmword ptr[rcx+64],ymm2

        vcmppd ymm2,ymm0,ymm1,CMP_LE_OQ        ;packed compare for LE
        vmovapd ymmword ptr[rcx+96],ymm2

        vcmppd ymm2,ymm0,ymm1,CMP_GT_OQ        ;packed compare for GT
        vmovapd ymmword ptr[rcx+128],ymm2

        vcmppd ymm2,ymm0,ymm1,CMP_GE_OQ        ;packed compare for GE
        vmovapd ymmword ptr[rcx+160],ymm2

        vcmppd ymm2,ymm0,ymm1,CMP_ORD_Q        ;packed compare for ORD
        vmovapd ymmword ptr[rcx+192],ymm2

        vcmppd ymm2,ymm0,ymm1,CMP_UNORD_Q      ;packed compare for UNORD
        vmovapd ymmword ptr[rcx+224],ymm2


        vzeroupper
        ret
PackedCompareF64_Aavx endp
        end
```

Listing 14-2 commences with the assembly language header file cmpequ.asmh. This file contains a series of assembler equate directives that define symbolic names for the compare predicates used by the instructions vcmpps and vcmppd. The same equates can also be used with the AVX instructions vcmpss (Compare Scalar SPFP Value) and vcmpsd (Compare Scalar DPFP Value). Chapter 3 contains additional information regarding the meaning of the suffixes used in these equates.

Function PackedCompareF32_Aavx() begins its execution with two vmovaps instructions that load argument values a and b into registers YMM0 and YMM1, respectively. The next instruction, vcmpps ymm2,ymm0,ymm1,CMP_EQ_OQ, compares corresponding single-precision floating-point elements in YMM0 and YMM1 for equality. If the elements are equal, the corresponding element position in YMM2 is set to 0xFFFFFFFF; otherwise, it is set to 0x00000000. The ensuing vmovaps ymmword ptr[rcx],ymm2 instruction saves the vcmpps result to c[0].

The remaining instructions in PackedCompareF32_Aavx() perform other common compare operations. Note that each vcmpps instruction uses a different compare predicate. Like the previous example, PackedCompareF32_Aavx() employs a vzeroupper instruction prior to its ret instruction. Also shown in Listing 14-2 is function PackedCompareF64_Aavx(), which demonstrates packed double-precision floating-point compares. Here are the results for source code example Ch14_02:

```
Results for PackedCompareF32_Aavx
a lo:          2.000000      7.000000   |    -6.000000     3.000000
b lo:          1.000000     12.000000   |    -6.000000     8.000000
EQ             00000000      00000000   |     FFFFFFFF     00000000
NE             FFFFFFFF      FFFFFFFF   |     00000000     FFFFFFFF
LT             00000000      FFFFFFFF   |     00000000     FFFFFFFF
LE             00000000      FFFFFFFF   |     FFFFFFFF     FFFFFFFF
GT             FFFFFFFF      00000000   |     00000000     00000000
GE             FFFFFFFF      00000000   |     FFFFFFFF     00000000
ORDERED        FFFFFFFF      FFFFFFFF   |     FFFFFFFF     FFFFFFFF
UNORDERED      00000000      00000000   |     00000000     00000000
```

```
a hi:        -16.000000      3.500000   |     3.141593       1.414214
b hi:        -36.000000      3.500000   |    -6.000000            nan
EQ            00000000      FFFFFFFF    |    00000000       00000000
NE            FFFFFFFF      00000000    |    FFFFFFFF       00000000
LT            00000000      00000000    |    00000000       00000000
LE            00000000      FFFFFFFF    |    00000000       00000000
GT            FFFFFFFF      00000000    |    FFFFFFFF       00000000
GE            FFFFFFFF      FFFFFFFF    |    FFFFFFFF       00000000
ORDERED       FFFFFFFF      FFFFFFFF    |    FFFFFFFF       00000000
UNORDERED     00000000      00000000    |    00000000       FFFFFFFF


-----------------------------------------------------------------------

Results for PackedCompareF64_Aavx
a lo:              2.000000000000   |        3.141592653590
b lo:              2.718281828459   |       -0.318309886184
EQ          0000000000000000       |    0000000000000000
NE          FFFFFFFFFFFFFFFF       |    FFFFFFFFFFFFFFFF
LT          FFFFFFFFFFFFFFFF       |    0000000000000000
LE          FFFFFFFFFFFFFFFF       |    0000000000000000
GT          0000000000000000       |    FFFFFFFFFFFFFFFF
GE          0000000000000000       |    FFFFFFFFFFFFFFFF
ORDERED     FFFFFFFFFFFFFFFF       |    FFFFFFFFFFFFFFFF
UNORDERED   0000000000000000       |    0000000000000000

a hi:             12.000000000000   |                   nan
b hi:             42.000000000000   |        1.414213562373
EQ          0000000000000000       |    0000000000000000
NE          FFFFFFFFFFFFFFFF       |    0000000000000000
LT          FFFFFFFFFFFFFFFF       |    0000000000000000
LE          FFFFFFFFFFFFFFFF       |    0000000000000000
GT          0000000000000000       |    0000000000000000
GE          0000000000000000       |    0000000000000000
ORDERED     FFFFFFFFFFFFFFFF       |    0000000000000000
UNORDERED   0000000000000000       |    FFFFFFFFFFFFFFFF
```

Some x86 assemblers, including MASM, support pseudo-op forms of the vcmpps and vcmppd instructions. Pseudo-op forms are simulated instruction mnemonics that contain an embedded compare predicate. For example, vcmpeqps ymm2,ymm0,ymm1 could have been used in PackedCompareF32_Aavx() instead of vcmpps ymm2,ymm0,ymm1,CMP_EQ_OQ. I personally prefer the latter style since it is much easier to discern the compare predicate.

# Floating-Point Arrays

In this section, you will learn how to use AVX instructions to perform SIMD calculations using the elements of a floating-point array. The first source example explains how to calculate the sample mean and sample standard deviation of a floating-point array. This is followed by a source code example that illustrates packed square root and compare operations using the elements of a floating-point array.

# Mean and Standard Deviation

In Chapter 3, you learned how to calculate the mean and standard deviation of an array of single-precision floating-point values using C++ SIMD intrinsic functions (see example Ch03_04). Then the next source code example, named Ch14_03, demonstrates how to perform these same calculations using x86-64 assembly language and AVX SIMD instructions. Listing 14-3 shows the assembly language source code for example Ch14_03.

*Listing 14-3.* Example Ch14_03

```
;--------------------------------------------------
;                 Ch14_03_fasm.asm
;--------------------------------------------------


;-----------------------------------------------------------------------
; extern "C" bool CalcMeanF32_Aavx(float* mean, const float* x, size_t n);
;-----------------------------------------------------------------------

NSE       equ 8                             ;num_simd_elements

          .code
CalcMeanF32_Aavx proc

; Validate arguments
          cmp r8,2                          ;is n >= 2?
          jb BadArg                         ;jump if no
          test rdx,01fh                     ;is x 32b aligned?
          jnz BadArg                        ;jump if no

; Initialize
          mov rax,-NSE                      ;initialize i
          vxorps ymm5,ymm5,ymm5             ;packed sums = 0.0;

Loop1:    add rax,NSE                       ;i += NSE
          mov r10,r8                        ;r10 = n
          sub r10,rax                       ;r10 = n - i
          cmp r10,NSE                       ;is n - i >= NSE?
          jb @F                             ;jump if no

          vaddps ymm5,ymm5,ymmword ptr [rdx+rax*4]    ;add elements x[i:i+7]
          jmp Loop1                         ;repeat loop until done

; Reduce packed sums to single value
@@:       vextractf128 xmm1,ymm5,1          ;extract upper 4 packed sums
          vaddps xmm2,xmm1,xmm5             ;xmm2 = 4 packed sums
          vhaddps xmm3,xmm2,xmm2            ;xmm3[63:0] = 2 packed sums
          vhaddps xmm5,xmm3,xmm3            ;xmm5[31:0] = sum

Loop2:    cmp rax,r8                        ;is i >= n?
          jae @F                            ;jump if yes
          vaddss xmm5,xmm5,real4 ptr[rdx+rax*4]    ;sum += x[i]
```

```
        inc rax                                ;i += 1
        jmp Loop2                              ;repeat loop until done

; Calculate mean
@@:     vcvtsi2ss xmm0,xmm0,r8                 ;convert n to SPFP
        vdivss xmm1,xmm5,xmm0                  ;mean = sum / n
        vmovss real4 ptr [rcx],xmm1            ;save mean

        mov eax,1                              ;set success code
        vzeroupper                             ;clear upper YMM/ZMM bits
        ret

BadArg: xor eax,eax                            ;set error return code
        ret


CalcMeanF32_Aavx endp

;--------------------------------------------------------------------------
; extern "C" bool CalcStDevF32_Aavx(float* st_dev, const float* x, size_t n,
;   float mean);
;--------------------------------------------------------------------------

CalcStDevF32_Aavx proc
        cmp r8,2                               ;is n >= 2?
        jb BadArg                              ;jump if no
        test rdx,01fh                          ;is x 32b aligned?
        jnz BadArg                             ;jump if no

; Initialize
        mov rax,-NSE                           ;initialize i
        vxorps ymm5,ymm5,ymm5                  ;packed sum_sqs = 0.0;

        vmovss real4 ptr [rsp+8],xmm3          ;save mean
        vbroadcastss ymm4,real4 ptr [rsp+8]    ;ymm4 = packed mean

Loop1:  add rax,NSE                            ;i += NSE
        mov r10,r8                             ;r10 = n
        sub r10,rax                            ;r10 = n - i
        cmp r10,NSE                            ;is n - i >= NSE?
        jb @F                                  ;jump if no

        vmovaps ymm0,ymmword ptr [rdx+rax*4]   ;load elements x[i:i+7]
        vsubps ymm1,ymm0,ymm4                  ;ymm1 = packed x[i] - mean
        vmulps ymm2,ymm1,ymm1                  ;ymm2 = packed (x[i] - mean) ** 2
        vaddps ymm5,ymm5,ymm2                  ;update packed sum_sqs
        jmp Loop1                              ;repeat loop until done
```

```
; Reduce packed sum_sqs to single value
@@:       vextractf128 xmm1,ymm5,1                    ;extract upper 4 packed sum_sqs
          vaddps xmm2,xmm1,xmm5                       ;xmm2 = 4 packed sum_sqs
          vhaddps xmm3,xmm2,xmm2                      ;xmm3[63:0] = 2 sums_sqs
          vhaddps xmm5,xmm3,xmm3                      ;xmm5[31:0] = sum_sqs


Loop2:    cmp rax,r8                                  ;is i >= n?
          jae @F                                      ;jump if yes
          vmovss xmm0,real4 ptr [rdx+rax*4]           ;load x[i]
          vsubss xmm1,xmm0,xmm4                        ;xmm1 = x[i] - mean
          vmulss xmm2,xmm1,xmm1                        ;xmm2 = (x[i] - mean) ** 2
          vaddss xmm5,xmm5,xmm2                        ;update sum_sqs
          inc rax                                      ;i += 1
          jmp Loop2                                    ;repeat loop until done


; Calculate standard deviation
@@:       dec r8                                       ;r8 = n - 1
          vcvtsi2ss xmm0,xmm0,r8                        ;convert n - 1 to SPFP
          vdivss xmm1,xmm5,xmm0                          ;var = sum_sqs / (n - 1)
          vsqrtss xmm2,xmm2,xmm1                         ;sd = sqrt(var)
          vmovss real4 ptr [rcx],xmm2                    ;save sd


          mov eax,1                                       ;set success code
          vzeroupper                                      ;clear upper YMM/ZMM bits
          ret


BadArg: xor eax,eax                                       ;set error return code
        ret
CalcStDevF32_Aavx endp
        end
```

The first function in Listing 14-3, CalcMeanF32_Aavx(), calculates the mean of an array of single-precision floating-point values using AVX SIMD instructions. This function begins its execution with a code block that ensures n >= 2 is true and array pointer x is aligned on a 32-byte boundary. The next code block uses a mov rax,-NSE instruction to initialize loop index variable i and a vxorps ymm5,ymm5,ymm5 instruction that initializes eight intermediate single-precision floating-point sums in YMM5 to zero.

Each iteration of Loop1 begins with an add rax,NSE instruction that calculates i += NSE. The next two instructions, mov r10,r8 and sub r10,rax, calculate n - i. This is followed by a cmp r10,NSE instruction that compares n - i to NSE. If n - i < NSE is true, the subsequent jb @F instruction terminates Loop1 since fewer than NSE elements are available. The ensuing instruction vaddps ymm5,ymm5,ymmword ptr [rdx+rax*4] adds elements x[i:i+7] to the intermediate sums maintained in register YMM5.

The code block that follows Loop1 reduces the eight intermediate sums in register YMM5 to a scalar value. The first instruction of this block, vextractf128 xmm1,ymm5,1 (Extract Floating-Point Values), copies the upper four single-precision floating-point elements in YMM5 to register XMM1. The next instruction, vaddps xmm2,xmm1,xmm5, reduces the number of intermediate sums from eight to four. The following two instructions, vhaddps xmm3,xmm2,xmm2 and vhaddps xmm5,xmm3,xmm3 (Packed SPFP Horizontal Add), reduce the four intermediate sums to a single scalar value as illustrated in Figure 14-1.

Initial values

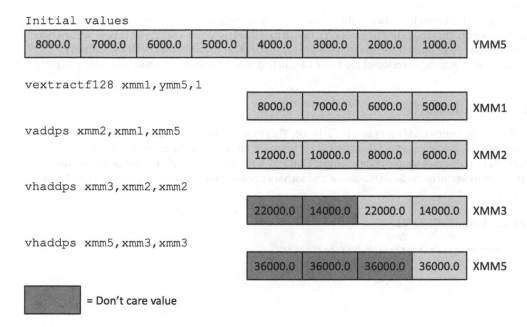

*Figure 14-1.* *Reduction of eight single-precision floating-point values in* CalcMeanF32a_Aavx()

After the reduction operation, CalcMeanF32_Aavx() employs another for-loop (Loop2) that adds any residual elements from array x to sum using a vaddss xmm5,xmm5,real4 ptr[rdx+rax*4] instruction. The final mean is calculated using the instructions vcvtsi2ss xmm0,xmm0,r8, which converts n to a single-precision floating-point value, and vdivss xmm1,xmm5,xmm0.

Also shown in Listing 14-3 is function CalcStDevF32_Aavx(), which calculates the standard deviation. The arrangement of this function is similar to CalcMeanF32_Aavx() but with a few minor changes. In the initialization code block, CalcStDevF32_Aavx() employs the instruction pair vmovss real4 ptr [rsp+8],xmm3 and vbroadcastss ymm4,real4 ptr [rsp+8] to copy argument value mean (XMM3) into each element position of YMM4. The reason for temporarily copying mean onto the stack prior to the broadcast operation is that the AVX vbroadcastss instruction requires a source operand in memory (on systems that support AVX2, vbroadcastss can also be used with an XMM register source operand).

Each iteration of Loop1 in CalcStDevF32_Aavx() calculates packed sums of squares using elements x[i:i+7]. The code that updates i and terminates Loop1 is identical to the code used in CalcMeanF32_Aavx(). The vmovaps ymm0,ymmword ptr [rdx+rax*4] instruction loads elements x[i:i+7] into register YMM0. This is followed by the instruction triplet vsubps ymm1,ymm0,ymm4, vmulps ymm2,ymm1,ymm1, and vaddps ymm5,ymm5,ymm2 that updates the sums of squares maintained in YMM5.

The reduction of the packed sums of squares also uses the same series of vextractf128, vaddps, and vhaddps instructions. Following the reduction, Loop2 processes any residual elements in array x. The final code block in CalcStDevF32_Aavx() calculates the standard deviation using AVX scalar arithmetic. Here are the results for source code example Ch14_03:

```
Results for CalcMeanF32_Cpp and CalcStDevF32_Cpp
mean1:    49.602146  st_dev1:  27.758242

Results for CalcMeanF32_Aavx and CalcStDevF32_Aavx
mean2:    49.602154  st_dev2:  27.758245
```

The slight value discrepancies between the C++ and assembly language functions are a consequence of different sequences of floating-point instructions. Recall that floating-point arithmetic is non-associative. This is something to keep in mind if you are developing an application that includes both a standard C++ and x86-AVX assembly language version of the same calculating function since the results may vary slightly.

## Distance Calculations

Listing 14-4 shows the source code for example Ch14_04. This example employs double-precision floating-point AVX instructions to calculate Euclidean distances between two points on a 2D grid. Source code example Ch14_04 is a repeat of source code example Ch03_07 with the primary difference being the use of assembly language to perform the SIMD distance and ternary operator computations instead of C++ SIMD intrinsic functions.

***Listing Ch14-4..*** Example Ch14_04

```
//--------------------------------------------------
//                 Ch14_04.h
//--------------------------------------------------

#pragma once

// The members of PA below must match the PA structure
// that's declared in Ch14_04_fasm.asm

struct PA
{
    double* X1;
    double* Y1;
    double* X2;
    double* Y2;
    double* Dist1;
    double* Dist2;
    double* DistCmp1;
    double* DistCmp2;
    size_t NumPoints;
};

// Ch14_04_fcpp.cpp
extern bool CalcDistancesF64(PA& pa);
extern void CompareDistancesF64(PA& pa, double cmp_val);

// Ch14_04_fasm.asm
extern "C" bool CalcDistancesF64_Aavx(PA& pa);
extern "C" void CompareDistancesF64_Aavx(PA& pa, const double* cmp_val);

// Ch14_04_misc.cpp
extern "C" bool CheckArgs(PA& pa);
extern void FillPAF64(PA& pa, double min_val, double max_val, unsigned int rng_seed);

// Miscellaneous constants
const size_t c_NumPoints = 21;
```

```
const unsigned int c_RngSeed = 39;
const double c_ArrayFillMin = 1.0;
const double c_ArrayFillMax = 75.0;
const double c_CmpVal = 50.0;
const size_t c_Alignment = 32;


;-------------------------------------------------
;                   Ch14_04_fasm.asm
;-------------------------------------------------

            include <cmpequ.asmh>
            include <MacrosX86-64-AVX.asmh>

; The members of PA below must match the PA structure
; that's declared in Ch14_04.h

PA          struct
X1          qword ?
Y1          qword ?
X2          qword ?
Y2          qword ?
Dist1       qword ?
Dist2       qword ?
DistCmp1    qword ?
DistCmp2    qword ?
NumPoints   qword ?
PA          ends

NSE         equ 4                           ;num_simd_elements

            .const
r8_minus2   real8 -2.0


;-----------------------------------------------------------------------
; extern "C" bool CalcDistancesF64_Aavx(PA& pa);
;-----------------------------------------------------------------------

        extrn CheckArgs:proc

        .code
CalcDistancesF64_Aavx proc frame
        CreateFrame_M CDIS_,0,0,r12,r13
        EndProlog_M

; Make sure all PA pointers are properly aligned
        mov r12,rcx                         ;save pa
        sub rsp,32                          ;allocate home area for CheckArgs
        call CheckArgs                      ;validate pointers in pa
        or eax,eax
        jz Error                           ;jump if CheckArgs failed
```

```
; Initialize
        mov rdx,qword ptr [r12+PA.NumPoints]     ;rdx = NumPoints

        mov r8,qword ptr  [r12+PA.X1]            ;r8 = X1 array pointer
        mov r9,qword ptr  [r12+PA.X2]            ;r9 = X2 array pointer
        mov r10,qword ptr [r12+PA.Y1]            ;r10 = Y1 array pointer
        mov r11,qword ptr [r12+PA.Y2]            ;r11 = Y2 array pointer
        mov r12,qword ptr [r12+PA.Dist2]         ;r12 = Dist2 array pointer

        mov rax,-NSE                             ;initialize i

; Calculate distances using packed arithmetic
Loop1:  add rax,NSE                              ;i += NSE
        mov r13,rdx                              ;r13 = NumPoints
        sub r13,rax                              ;r13 = NumPoints - i
        cmp r13,NSE                              ;is NumPoints - i >= NSE?
        jb Loop2                                 ;jump if no

        vmovdqa ymm0,ymmword ptr [r8+rax*8]      ;X1 vals
        vsubpd ymm0,ymm0,ymmword ptr [r9+rax*8]  ;X1[i:i+3] - X2[i:i+3]
        vmulpd ymm0,ymm0,ymm0                    ;calc squares

        vmovdqa ymm1,ymmword ptr [r10+rax*8]     ;Y1 vals
        vsubpd ymm1,ymm1,ymmword ptr [r11+rax*8] ;Y1[i:i+3] - Y2[i:i+3]
        vmulpd ymm1,ymm1,ymm1                    ;calc squares

        vaddpd ymm2,ymm0,ymm1                    ;packed sum of squares
        vsqrtpd ymm3,ymm2                        ;packed distances
        vmovdqa ymmword ptr [r12+rax*8],ymm3     ;save to Dist2[i:i+3]
        jmp Loop1

; Calculate distances for final few points
Loop2:  cmp rax,rdx                              ;is i >= n
        jae Done                                 ;jump if yes

        vmovsd xmm0,real8 ptr [r8+rax*8]         ;xmm0 = X1[i]
        vsubsd xmm0,xmm0,real8 ptr [r9+rax*8]    ;xmm0 = X1[i] - X2[i]
        vmulsd xmm0,xmm0,xmm0                     ;xmm0 = (X1[i] - X2[i]) ** 2

        vmovsd xmm1,real8 ptr [r10+rax*8]        ;xmm1 = Y1[i]
        vsubsd xmm1,xmm1,real8 ptr [r11+rax*8]   ;xmm1 = Y1[i] - Y2[i]
        vmulsd xmm1,xmm1,xmm1                     ;xmm1 = (Y1[i] - Y2[i]) ** 2

        vaddsd xmm2,xmm0,xmm1                     ;sum of squares
        vsqrtsd xmm3,xmm3,xmm2                    ;distance
        vmovsd real8 ptr[r12+rax*8],xmm3         ;save to Dist2[i]
        inc rax                                   ;i += 1
        jmp Loop2

Done:   mov eax,1                                ;set success return code
        vzeroupper
```

```
@@::    DeleteFrame_M r12,r13
        ret

Error:  xor eax,eax                              ;set errror return code
        jmp @B

CalcDistancesF64_Aavx endp

;-------------------------------------------------------------------------
; extern "C" void CompareDistancesF64_Aavx(PA& pa, const double* cmp_val);
;-------------------------------------------------------------------------

CompareDistancesF64_Aavx proc frame
        CreateFrame_M CD_,0,32
        SaveXmmRegs_M xmm6,xmm7
        EndProlog_M

; Initalize
        vbroadcastsd ymm6,real8 ptr [rdx]       ;packed cmp_val
        vbroadcastsd ymm7,real8 ptr [r8_minus2] ;packed -2.0

        mov r8,qword ptr [rcx+PA.Dist2]         ;r8 = Dist2 array pointer
        mov r9,qword ptr [rcx+PA.DistCmp2]      ;r9 = DistCmp2 array pointer
        mov r10,qword ptr [rcx+PA.NumPoints]    ;r10 = NumPoints

        mov rax,-NSE                            ;initialize i

; Calculate DistCmp2 values
Loop1:  add rax,NSE                             ;i += NSE
        mov r11,r10                             ;r11 = NumPoints
        sub r11,rax                             ;r11 = NumPoints - i
        cmp r11,NSE                             ;is NumPoints - i >= NSE?
        jb Loop2                                ;jump if no

        vmovdqa ymm0,ymmword ptr [r8+rax*8]     ;ymm0 = Dist2[i:i+3]
        vcmppd ymm1,ymm0,ymm6,CMP_GE_OQ         ;compare Dist2[i:i+3] to cmp_val

        vandpd ymm2,ymm1,ymm7                   ;ymm2 = -2.0 or 0.0
        vmulpd ymm3,ymm2,ymm0                   ;ymm3 = -2.0 * Dist2[i] or 0.0
        vandnpd ymm4,ymm1,ymm0                  ;ymm4 = 0.0 or Dist2[i]
        vorpd ymm5,ymm3,ymm4                    ;ymm5 = final result

        vmovdqa ymmword ptr[r9+rax*8],ymm5      ;save DistCmp2[i:i+3]
        jmp Loop1

; Calculate DistCmp2 values for residual elements
Loop2:  cmp rax,r10                             ;is i >= n?
        jae Done                                ;jump if yes

        vmovsd xmm0,real8 ptr [r8+rax*8]        ;xmm0 = Dist2[i]
        vcmpsd xmm1,xmm0,xmm6,CMP_GE_OQ         ;compare Dist2[i] to cmp_val
```

```
        vandpd  xmm2,xmm1,xmm7              ;xmm2 = -2.0 or 0.0
        vmulsd  xmm3,xmm2,xmm0              ;xmm3 = -2.0 * Dist2[i] or 0.0
        vandnpd xmm4,xmm1,xmm0              ;xmm4  = 0.0 or Dist2[i]
        vorpd   xmm5,xmm3,xmm4              ;xmm5 = final result

        vmovsd  real8 ptr[r9+rax*8],xmm5    ;save DistCmp2[i]
        inc rax                            ;i += 1
        jmp Loop2

Done:   vzeroupper
        RestoreXmmRegs_M xmm6,xmm7
        DeleteFrame_M
        ret


CompareDistancesF64_Aavx endp
        end
```

Listing 14-4 begins with the declaration of a structure named PA, which contains pointers to the arrays that are used by the SIMD distance calculating functions. Note that the function declarations in file Ch14_04.h use a C++ reference for argument value pa. From the perspective of an assembly language function, there is no difference between a C++ reference and a pointer argument. Both types correspond to an address. Not shown in Listing 14-4 is the code that performs test case initialization, results formatting, etc., since this code is almost identical to the code you saw in Chapter 3.

Near the top of file Ch14_04_fasm.asm is the assembly language declaration of structure PA. This declaration contains the same members as the corresponding C++ structure PA. Note that the structure name PA is used on both the struct and ends assembler directives. The ? symbol that follows each qword directive notifies the assembler to perform *uninitialized* storage allocation. While not used in this example, you can also define instances of an assembly language structure in a .const or .data section. In these cases, an initialization constant can be used instead of the ? operator.

Using an assembly language structure is analogous to using a C++ structure as you will soon see. There are, however, a few points that warrant further explanation. First, it is not possible to define a single structure in a common header file that can be included in both C++ and assembly language code. If you want to use the same data structure in both C++ and assembly language code, the structure must be declared twice as shown in this example, and the two declarations must be semantically equivalent. Second, this example uses the name PA for both the C++ and assembly langue structure definitions, but it is acceptable to use different names so long as the two structure declarations are semantically equivalent. The final and most important point involves the padding of structure members. The default action for most C++ compilers is to align each structure member on its natural boundary. Most assemblers, however, *do not* automatically align structure members on their natural boundaries. This means that an assembly language structure declaration must sometimes incorporate additional pad bytes to ensure equivalence to a counterpart C++ structure. In file Ch14_04_fasm.asm, the structure PA does not require any pad bytes since the size of each member is eight bytes, which matches the corresponding member sizes in the C++ PA structure.

Source code example Ch14_04 mimics the earlier Ch03_07 example in that it includes two assembly language functions. The first function, CalcDistancesF64_Aavx(), calculates 2D Euclidean distances using packed double-precision floating-point arithmetic. The second function, CompareDistancesF64_Aavx(), performs packed compare operations and illustrates how to implement a SIMD ternary operator using AVX instructions.

Following its prologue, CalcDistancesF64_Aavx() calls the C++ function CheckArgs() to validate the pointers in the PA structure for proper alignment. Note that CalcDistancesF64_Aavx() uses a mov r12,rcx instruction before calling CheckArgs(), which saves argument value pa in a nonvolatile register (recall that function CheckArgs() can modify RCX but must preserve R12). Also note that immediately before the call

CheckArgs instruction is a sub rsp,32 instruction. Execution of this instruction allocates the home area for CheckArgs() as required by the Visual C++ calling convention.

Following the call to CheckArgs(), function CalcDistancesF64_Aavx() uses a series of mov instructions to load the required array pointers into registers R8–R12. A mov instruction is also used to load pa.NumPoints into register RDX. Note that each mov instruction uses a symbolic displacement identifier that incorporates both the structure name and member name. This illustrates the syntax that must be used to reference a member in an assembly language structure.

The first for-loop (Loop1) in CalcDistancesF64_Aavx() uses packed double-precision AVX instructions to calculate 2D distances. Note that CalcDistancesF64_Aavx() uses the same logic that was employed in source code example Ch14_03 to terminate Loop1 if fewer than NSE points are remaining. The second for-loop Loop2 uses scalar AVX double-precision arithmetic to calculate the final few distances if pa.NumPoints is not an integral multiple of NSE. Note that both for-loops save their calculated distances to the array pa.Dist2.

Function CompareDistancesF64_Aavx() compares each distance value in pa.Dist2[i] to cmp_val. If pa.Dist2[i] >= cmp_val is true, pa.Dist2[i] is multiplied by -2.0, which is an arbitrary constant for demonstration purposes. The initialization code block in CompareDistancesF64_Aavx() begins with two vbroadcastsd instructions that initialize YMM6 and YMM7 with packed versions of cmp_val and -2.0, respectively. The next two mov instructions load array pointers pa.Dist2 and pa.Dist2Cmp into registers R8 and R9. The final two mov instructions load pa.NumPoints into R10 and -NSE into RAX.

Figure 14-2 illustrates execution of the AVX instructions that perform the SIMD ternary operation in Loop1. The first instruction, vmovdqa ymm0,ymmword ptr [r8+rax*8], loads elements pa.Dist2[i:i+3] into register YMM0. The ensuing vcmppd ymm1,ymm0,ymm6,CMP_GE_OQ instruction compares each element in YMM0 to cmp_val and sets the corresponding element in YMM1 to 0xFFFFFFFFFFFFFFFF if pa.Dist2[i] >= cmp_val is true; otherwise, the element is set to 0x0000000000000000. The vandpd ymm2,ymm1,ymm7 instruction loads -2.0 or 0.0 into each element of YMM2, and the subsequent vmulpd ymm3,ymm2,ymm0 instruction loads -2.0 * pa.Dist2[i] or 0.0 into each element of YMM3. Execution of the vandnpd ymm4,ymm1,ymm0 (Bitwise Logical AND NOT of Packed DPFP Values) instruction loads 0.0 or pa.Dist2[i] into each element of YMM4 (the vandnpd instruction calculates ~ymm1 & ymm0). This is followed by a vorpd ymm5,ymm3,ymm4 instruction that completes the SIMD ternary operator.

Initial values

| 50.0 | 50.0 | 50.0 | 50.0 | YMM6 |

| -2.0 | -2.0 | -2.0 | -2.0 | YMM7 |

`vmovdqa ymm0,ymmword ptr [r8+rax*8]`

| 63.158 | 54.071 | 56.728 | 28.513 | YMM0 |

`vcmppd ymm1,ymm0,ymm6,CMP_GE_OQ`

| 0xFFFFFFFFFFFFFFFF | 0xFFFFFFFFFFFFFFFF | 0xFFFFFFFFFFFFFFFF | 0x0000000000000000 | YMM1 |

`vandpd ymm2,ymm1,ymm7`

| -2.0 | -2.0 | -2.0 | 0.0 | YMM2 |

`vmulpd ymm3,ymm2,ymm0`

| -126.315 | -108.141 | -113.457 | 0.0 | YMM3 |

`vandnpd ymm4,ymm1,ymm0`

| 0.0 | 0.0 | 0.0 | 28.513 | YMM4 |

`vorpd ymm5,ymm3,ymm4`

| -126.315 | -108.141 | -113.457 | 28.513 | YMM5 |

***Figure 14-2.*** *SIMD ternary calculation performed by* `CompareDistancesF64_Aavx()`

The second for-loop in `CompareDistancesF64_Aavx()` processes any residual elements if `pa.NumPoints` is not an integral multiple of NSE. Note that `Loop2` uses the AVX scalar instruction `vcmpsd xmm1,xmm0,xmm6,CMP_GE_OQ` to perform the compare. This instruction sets bits XMM1[63:0] to all ones if the double-precision value in XMM0[63:0] is greater than or equal to the value in XMM6[63:0]; otherwise, XMM1[63:0] is set to all zeros. The `vcmps[d|s]` instructions are sometimes employed as alternatives to the scalar floating-point compare instructions `vcomis[d|s]` that you learned about in Chapter 12 since the use of the former facilitates subsequent Boolean operations as illustrated in this example. Note that unlike `vcomis[d|s]`, execution of a `vcmps[d|s]` instruction *does not* update any of the status flags in RFLAGS.

Following the `vcmpsd` instruction, `Loop2` also uses the instructions `vandpd`, `vmulsd`, `vandnpd`, and `vorpd` to carry out the required scalar floating-point ternary operation. The reason for using packed floating-point Boolean instructions here is that AVX does not include scalar versions of these instructions. In the current example, the high-order double-precision element in each XMM register operand is simply ignored. Here are the results for source code example Ch14_04:

| X1 | Y1 | X2 | Y2 | Dist1 | Dist2 | DistCmp1 | DistCmp2 |
|---|---|---|---|---|---|---|---|
| 41.470 | 60.045 | 1.419 | 60.938 | 40.060 | 40.060 | 40.060 | 40.060 |
| 61.710 | 10.032 | 28.150 | 62.320 | 62.132 | 62.132 | -124.264 | -124.264 |
| 45.548 | 39.888 | 45.621 | 31.345 | 8.544 | 8.544 | 8.544 | 8.544 |
| 35.329 | 35.887 | 17.867 | 52.203 | 23.898 | 23.898 | 23.898 | 23.898 |
| 47.821 | 69.499 | 19.309 | 69.724 | 28.513 | 28.513 | 28.513 | 28.513 |
| 61.347 | 70.889 | 40.176 | 18.259 | 56.728 | 56.728 | -113.457 | -113.457 |
| 69.049 | 31.697 | 35.764 | 74.309 | 54.071 | 54.071 | -108.141 | -108.141 |
| 62.110 | 71.023 | 25.831 | 19.325 | 63.158 | 63.158 | -126.315 | -126.315 |
| 47.475 | 19.668 | 26.502 | 28.675 | 22.826 | 22.826 | 22.826 | 22.826 |
| 44.834 | 64.670 | 27.339 | 51.671 | 21.796 | 21.796 | 21.796 | 21.796 |
| 4.585 | 64.255 | 22.440 | 68.924 | 18.455 | 18.455 | 18.455 | 18.455 |
| 54.296 | 22.902 | 8.905 | 19.004 | 45.558 | 45.558 | 45.558 | 45.558 |
| 36.920 | 63.476 | 64.079 | 12.002 | 58.200 | 58.200 | -116.400 | -116.400 |
| 45.584 | 12.629 | 37.245 | 66.029 | 54.048 | 54.048 | -108.096 | -108.096 |
| 39.932 | 14.882 | 25.214 | 24.382 | 17.518 | 17.518 | 17.518 | 17.518 |
| 50.613 | 41.607 | 53.261 | 18.449 | 23.309 | 23.309 | 23.309 | 23.309 |
| 12.576 | 70.005 | 33.699 | 39.280 | 37.286 | 37.286 | 37.286 | 37.286 |
| 41.179 | 49.289 | 15.620 | 56.153 | 26.464 | 26.464 | 26.464 | 26.464 |
| 50.680 | 61.602 | 51.222 | 26.242 | 35.364 | 35.364 | 35.364 | 35.364 |
| 2.003 | 63.741 | 21.990 | 17.102 | 50.740 | 50.740 | -101.481 | -101.481 |
| 33.195 | 36.332 | 49.349 | 62.033 | 30.357 | 30.357 | 30.357 | 30.357 |

# Floating-Point Matrices

The final example of this chapter, named Ch14_05, explains how to use AVX instructions to calculate the column means of a matrix that contains double-precision floating-point elements. This example is a redo of example Ch03_09 that uses assembly language to calculate the column means instead of C++ SIMD intrinsic functions. Listing 14-5 shows the assembly language source code for example Ch14_05.

***Listing 14-5.*** Example Ch14_05

```
;------------------------------------------------
;                 Ch14_05_fasm.asm
;------------------------------------------------


;-----------------------------------------------------------------------
; extern "C" void CalcColumnMeansF64_Aavx(double* col_means, const double* x,
;   size_t nrows, size_t ncols);
;-----------------------------------------------------------------------

NSE     equ 4                           ;num_simd_elements
NSE2    equ 2                           ;num_simd_elements2

        .code
CalcColumnMeansF64_Aavx proc frame

; Function prologue
        push rbx
```

```
        .pushreg rbx
        push rdi
        .pushreg rdi
        .endprolog

; Validate nrows and ncols
        test r8,r8
        jz Done                         ;jump if nrows == 0
        test r9,r9
        jz Done                         ;jump if ncols == 0

; Initialize all elements in col_means to 0.0
        mov r10,rcx                     ;save col_means for later
        mov rdi,rcx                     ;rdi = col_means
        mov rcx,r9                      ;number of elements in ncol_means
        xor eax,eax                     ;rax = fill value
        rep stosq                       ;fill col_means with 0

;   Register use in code below
;
;   rbx = &x[i][j]          r8  = nrows      rax = scratch register
;   rcx = &x[0][0]          r9  = ncols
;   rdx = &col_means[j]     r10 = i
;   rdi = &col_means[0]     r11 = j

; Initialize
        mov rcx,rdx                     ;rcx = &x[0][0]
        mov rdi,r10                     ;rdi = &col_means[0]
        xor r10d,r10d                   ;i = 0

; Repeat Loop1 while i < nrows
Loop1:  cmp r10,r8
        jae CalcCM                      ;jump if i >= nrows

        xor r11d,r11d                   ;j = 0

; Repeat Loop2 while j < ncols
Loop2:  cmp r11,r9
        jb @F                           ;jump if j < ncols

        inc r10                         ;i += 1
        jmp Loop1

; Calculate &x[i][j] and &col_means[j]
@@:     mov rax,r10                     ;rax = i
        mul r9                          ;rax = i * ncols
        add rax,r11                     ;rax = i * ncols + j
        lea rbx,[rcx+rax*8]             ;rbx = &x[i][j]
        lea rdx,[rdi+r11*8]             ;rdx = &col_means[j]

        mov rax,r11                     ;rax = j
```

```
        add rax,NSE                             ;rax = j + NSE
        cmp rax,r9
        ja @F                                   ;jump if j + NSE > ncols

; Update sums (4 columns)
        vmovupd ymm0,ymmword ptr [rdx]          ;ymm0 = col_means[j:j+3]
        vaddpd ymm1,ymm0,ymmword ptr [rbx]      ;col_means[j:j+3] += x[i][j:j+3]
        vmovupd ymmword ptr [rdx],ymm1          ;save result

        add r11,NSE                             ;j += NSE
        jmp Loop2

@@:     mov rax,r11                             ;rax = j
        add rax,NSE2                            ;rax = j + NSE2
        cmp rax,r9
        ja @F                                   ;jump if j + NSE2 > ncols

; Update sums (2 columns)
        vmovupd xmm0,xmmword ptr [rdx]          ;xmm0 = col_means[j:j+1]
        vaddpd xmm1,xmm0,xmmword ptr [rbx]      ;col_means[j:j+1] += x[i][j:j+1]
        vmovupd xmmword ptr [rdx],xmm1          ;save result

        add r11,NSE2                            ;j += NSE2
        jmp Loop2

; Update sums (1 column)
@@:     vmovsd xmm0,real8 ptr [rdx]             ;xmm0 = col_means[j]
        vaddsd xmm1,xmm0,real8 ptr [rbx]        ;col_means[j] += x[i][j]
        vmovsd real8 ptr [rdx],xmm1             ;save result

        inc r11                                 ;j += 1
        jmp Loop2

; Calculate column means
CalcCM: xor eax,eax                             ;j = 0;
        vcvtsi2sd xmm2,xmm2,r8                  ;xmm2 = nrows (DPFP)

Loop3:  vmovsd xmm0,real8 ptr [rdi+rax*8]       ;col_means[j]
        vdivsd xmm1,xmm0,xmm2                   ;mean = col_means[j] / nrows
        vmovsd real8 ptr [rdi+rax*8],xmm1       ;save result

        inc rax                                 ;j += 1
        cmp rax,r9
        jb Loop3                                ;jump if j < ncols

Done:   vzeroupper
        pop rdi
        pop rbx
        ret
CalcColumnMeansF64_Aavx endp
        end
```

Following its prologue, function `CalcColumnMeansF64_Aavx()` tests argument values `nrows` and `ncols` to make sure that neither value is equal to zero. The next code block uses the x86-64 string instruction `stosq` to initialize each element in array `col_means` to 0.0. Note that registers RDI, RCX, and RAX are loaded with `col_means`, `ncols`, and zero (which also corresponds to 0.0) prior to execution of the `stosq` instruction. To calculate the column means, `CalcColumnMeansF64_Aavx()` must sum the elements of each column and then divide each column sum by the number of rows. The summing calculations are performed in the nested for-loops `Loop1` and `Loop2`. The outer for-loop `Loop1` simply cycles through each row of the matrix. Note that prior to the start of `Loop2`, `CalcColumnMeansF64_Aavx()` employs an `xor r11d,r11d` instruction to initialize `j = 0`.

The summing code in for-loop `Loop2` is partitioned to three code blocks. If four or more columns are available, `CalcColumnMeansF64_Aavx()` uses the instruction triplet `vmovupd ymm0,ymmword ptr [rdx]`, `vaddpd ymm1,ymm0,ymmword ptr [rbx]`, and `vmovupd ymmword ptr [rdx],ymm1` to calculate `col_means[j:j+3]` += `x[i][j:j+3]`. The `vmovupd` (Move Unaligned Packed DPFP Values) instruction is used here since for most matrices, elements `x[i][j:j+3]` will not be properly aligned on a 32-byte boundary. If two or more columns are available, the same instruction triplet with XMM register operands is used to calculate `col_means[j:j+1]` += `x[i][j:j+1]`. The final code block uses scalar double-precision arithmetic to compute `col_means[j]` += `x[i][j]`.

Following calculation of the column sums, `CalcColumnMeansF64_Aavx()` employs a simple for-loop (`Loop3`) that utilizes floating-point scalar arithmetic to calculate the column means. Packed arithmetic could also be used to calculate the final column means, but this is a one-time calculation so simpler scalar arithmetic is used. Note the use of the `vcvtsi2sd xmm2,xmm2,r8` instruction, which converts `nrows` from a 64-bit integer to a double-precision floating-point value. Here are the results for source code example Ch14_05:

```
Results for CalcColumnMeansF64
 54.8 26.4  13.3 48.4  74.0 63.2  61.3 56.5  66.9 64.4  15.1 37.4  56.1 70.0 41.5
 19.9  3.9  11.5 32.3  58.2 41.0  55.0 45.9  34.4 20.4  56.1  9.7  56.3 75.9 50.2
 26.7  7.1  44.2 37.9  61.3 16.3  38.2 62.0  47.7 61.7  72.9 70.0   8.9 55.7 44.4
 30.3  5.3  64.4  7.8  33.8 51.6  20.4 30.3  61.3 14.1  50.0 37.8  14.4 43.0 63.0
 20.8 51.8   7.2 12.1  38.8 38.4  27.7 46.5  66.0 61.9  11.2 11.4  41.1 59.7 77.5
 54.6 62.5  59.7 61.8  18.3 34.0  60.6 68.8  78.4 33.1  74.9 50.0   7.8 29.4 35.2
 11.9 41.3   7.7 19.9  31.5 37.8  35.8 19.4  32.6 56.4  27.3  5.3  27.5 10.5 53.1
 32.5 23.3  14.7 19.1  69.2  8.2  65.0 42.6  27.8 30.8  36.1 29.9  37.5 78.0 10.8
 75.7 43.1  16.5 77.1  17.6 72.3  35.1 17.6  27.9 46.7  72.3 68.0  72.3 44.4 38.3
 68.8 46.8  32.0 36.8  43.7 66.8  45.7 77.1  15.9 33.5  59.2 76.0  15.4 32.4 56.1
 64.0 56.1  39.8 74.0  31.6 43.6   4.1 29.1  42.8 27.7  41.7  6.2  43.5 29.0 61.5
 31.0 33.6  62.9 58.9  30.4 66.2  63.6 27.1  64.7 11.6   3.5 77.1  75.3 25.5 53.2
 22.9 48.4  35.7  6.8   7.3 33.5  40.8 20.5  61.5  3.4  76.4  9.3  69.9 62.4 78.8
 71.5 13.6  55.1 15.7  79.7 63.9  40.0 66.5  39.0 75.3  63.1 51.8  10.1 25.5  4.1
 68.3 34.4  44.7 69.5  39.4 13.9   6.0 78.6  52.4 20.3  62.1 22.4  44.9 48.1 14.2
 75.6 77.4  24.9 16.7  12.5 61.4  59.2 65.7  34.4 21.9  77.8 45.6  13.3 57.7 56.8
 66.1 48.6  57.7 77.4  11.9 53.2  50.6 24.4  58.1 58.9  29.7 19.1  57.0  9.5 42.4
 61.7 68.2  21.5 52.3  43.1 25.3  37.3 77.9  67.1 11.6  30.9 21.8  74.5 34.9 76.0
 55.0 42.5   8.8  3.6  72.3 48.6  26.8 62.8  24.7 42.6  22.9 19.7   7.0 45.5 11.6
 23.1 37.2  21.6 77.1  16.4 59.3  60.4 46.7  43.5 61.2  10.6 68.9  23.7 41.6 24.2
 22.3 20.9  36.8 17.4  30.8 24.8   4.3 21.2  55.6 20.2  40.1 51.5  78.4 13.1 26.0

 45.6 37.7  32.4 39.2  39.1 44.0  39.9 47.0  47.8 37.0  44.5 37.6  39.8 42.5 43.8
 45.6 37.7  32.4 39.2  39.1 44.0  39.9 47.0  47.8 37.0  44.5 37.6  39.8 42.5 43.8
```

# Summary

Table 14-1 summarizes the x86 assembly language instructions introduced in this chapter. This table also includes closely related instructions. Before proceeding to the next chapter, make sure you understand the operation that is performed by each instruction shown in Table 14-1.

**Table 14-1.** *X86 Assembly Language Instruction Summary for Chapter 14*

| Instruction Mnemonic | Description |
| --- | --- |
| vaddp[d\|s] | Packed floating-point addition |
| vandnp[d\|s] | Packed floating-point bitwise logical AND NOT |
| vandp[d\|s] | Packed floating-point bitwise logical AND |
| vbroadcasts[d\|s] | Broadcast floating-point data |
| vcmpp[d\|s] | Packed floating-point compare |
| vdivp[d\|s] | Packed floating-point division |
| vextractf128 | Extract packed floating-point values |
| vhaddp[d\|s] | Packed floating-point horizontal addition |
| vmaxp[d\|s] | Packed floating-point maximums |
| vminp[d\|s] | Packed floating-point minimums |
| vmovap[d\|s] | Move packed floating-point values (aligned) |
| vmovup[d\|s] | Move packed floating-point values (unaligned) |
| vmulp[d\|s] | Packed floating-point multiplication |
| vorp[d\|s] | Packed floating-point bitwise logical OR |
| vsqrtp[d\|s] | Packed floating-point square root |
| vsubp[d\|s] | Packed floating-point subtraction |
| vxorp[d\|s] | Packed floating-point bitwise logical exclusive OR |
| vzeroall | Zero all bits in registers XMM0–XMM15, YMM0–YMM15, ZMM0–ZMM15 |
| vzeroupper | Zero upper 128 (384) bits of registers YMM0–YMM15 (ZMM0–ZMM15) |

# CHAPTER 15

■ ■ ■

# AVX2 Assembly Language Programming: Part 1

In Chapter 13, you learned how to code x86-64 assembly language functions that performed packed integer operations using 128-bit wide operands. In this chapter, you will learn how to perform similar operations using AVX2 instructions and 256-bit wide operands. The first section illustrates basic integer arithmetic. The second section spotlights familiar image processing techniques.

Using AVX2 instructions and 256-bit wide integer operands is not much different than using AVX instructions and 128-bit wide integer operands. The primary reason for this is that the same assembly language mnemonics are used for both operand types. AVX2 contains some new packed integer instructions that are not available on processors that only support AVX. However, on processors that support AVX2, most packed integer instructions can be used with either XMM or YMM register operands as you will soon see.

## Integer Arithmetic

In this section, you will learn how to perform fundamental integer arithmetic using AVX2 instructions and 256-bit wide integer operands. The first source code example highlights basic operations using packed operands. This is followed by an example that demonstrates packed integer size promotions. The source code examples examined in this section are designed to provide you with the necessary foundation for understanding the more sophisticated x86-64 assembly language source code presented later in this and subsequent chapters.

### Basic Operations

Listing 15-1 shows the assembly language source for example Ch15_01. This example, which is the assembly language counterpart of example Ch04_01, demonstrates how to perform basic arithmetic operations using AVX2 instructions and 256-bit wide packed integer operands.

© Daniel Kusswurm 2022
D. Kusswurm, *Modern Parallel Programming with C++ and Assembly Language*,
https://doi.org/10.1007/978-1-4842-7918-2_15

***Listing 15-1.*** Example Ch15_01

```
;--------------------------------------------------
;                  Ch15_01_fasm.asm
;--------------------------------------------------


;------------------------------------------------------------------------
; extern "C" void MathI16_Aavx2(YmmVal c[6], const YmmVal* a, const YmmVal* b);
;------------------------------------------------------------------------

        .code
MathI16_Aavx2 proc
        vmovdqa ymm0,ymmword ptr [rdx]          ;ymm0 = a
        vmovdqa ymm1,ymmword ptr [r8]           ;ymm1 = b

        vpaddw ymm2,ymm0,ymm1                   ;packed addition - wraparound
        vmovdqa ymmword ptr [rcx],ymm2

        vpaddsw ymm2,ymm0,ymm1                  ;packed addition - saturated
        vmovdqa ymmword ptr [rcx+32],ymm2

        vpsubw ymm2,ymm0,ymm1                   ;packed subtraction - wraparound
        vmovdqa ymmword ptr [rcx+64],ymm2

        vpsubsw ymm2,ymm0,ymm1                  ;packed subtraction - saturated
        vmovdqa ymmword ptr [rcx+96],ymm2

        vpminsw ymm2,ymm0,ymm1                  ;packed minimum
        vmovdqa ymmword ptr [rcx+128],ymm2

        vpmaxsw ymm2,ymm0,ymm1                  ;packed maximum
        vmovdqa ymmword ptr [rcx+160],ymm2

        vzeroupper
        ret
MathI16_Aavx2 endp

;------------------------------------------------------------------------
; extern "C" void MathI32_Aavx2(YmmVal c[6], const YmmVal* a, const YmmVal* b);
;------------------------------------------------------------------------

MathI32_Aavx2 proc
        vmovdqa ymm0,ymmword ptr [rdx]          ;ymm0 = a
        vmovdqa ymm1,ymmword ptr [r8]           ;ymm1 = b

        vpaddd ymm2,ymm0,ymm1                   ;packed addition
        vmovdqa ymmword ptr [rcx],ymm2

        vpsubd ymm2,ymm0,ymm1                   ;packed subtraction
        vmovdqa ymmword ptr [rcx+32],ymm2
```

```
        vpmulld ymm2,ymm0,ymm1                  ;packed multiplication (low result)
        vmovdqa ymmword ptr [rcx+64],ymm2

        vpsllvd ymm2,ymm0,ymm1                  ;packed shift left logical
        vmovdqa ymmword ptr [rcx+96],ymm2

        vpsravd ymm2,ymm0,ymm1                  ;packed shift right arithmetic
        vmovdqa ymmword ptr [rcx+128],ymm2

        vpabsd ymm2,ymm0                        ;packed absolute value
        vmovdqa ymmword ptr [rcx+160],ymm2


        vzeroupper
        ret
MathI32_Aavx2 endp
        end
```

The first function in Listing 15-1, MathI16_Aavx2(), begins its execution with a vmovdqa ymm0,ymmword ptr [rdx] instruction that loads argument value a into register YMM0. The next instruction, vmovdqa ymm1,ymmword ptr [r8], loads argument value b into register YMM1. Note that registers RDX and R8 both point to buffers of type YmmVal, which means that they are aligned on a 32-byte boundary. The ensuing instruction pair, vpaddw ymm2,ymm0,ymm1 and vmovdqa ymmword ptr [rcx],ymm2, performs packed integer addition using 16-bit integer elements and saves the calculated sums to c[0]. This is followed by the instruction pair vpaddsw ymm2,ymm0,ymm1 and vmovdqa ymmword ptr [rcx+32],ymm2, which performs packed saturated addition using 16-bit signed integer elements. The resulting sums are saved to c[1]. The remaining code blocks in MathI16_Aavx2() illustrate the use of the vpsubw, vpsubsw, vpminsw, and vpmaxsw instructions using 256-bit wide SIMD operands and 16-bit integer elements. Note that the displacements used in the vmovdqa instructions that save results to array c are integral multiples of 32 since the size of a YmmVal is 32 bytes.

The second function in Listing 15-1, MathI32_Aavx2(), highlights common packed operations using 256-bit wide operands and 32-bit integer elements. In this function, the vpsllvd ymm2,ymm0,ymm1 (Variable Bit Shift Left Logical) instruction left shifts each 32-bit element of YMM0 using the bit count of the corresponding element in YMM1. The vpsravd ymm2,ymm0,ymm1 (Variable Bit Shift Right Arithmetic) instruction performs arithmetic right shifts using the 32-bit integer elements in YMM0 and the corresponding element bit counts in YMM1. The vpabsd ymm2,ymm0 (Packed Absolute Value) instruction calculates absolute values of the 32-bit signed integer elements in YMM0. Note that both MathI16_Aavx2() and MathI32_Aavx2() include a vzeroupper instruction just before their respective ret instructions. Recall from the discussions in Chapter 14 that the vzeroupper instruction should be used to avoid potential performance penalties that can occur when the processor transitions from executing x86-AVX instructions to x86-SSE instructions. Here are the results for source code example Ch15_01:

```
Results for MathI16_Aavx2

i        a        b      add     adds      sub     subs      min      max
-------------------------------------------------------------------------
0       10     1000     1010     1010     -990     -990       10     1000
1       20     2000     2020     2020    -1980    -1980       20     2000
2     3000       30     3030     3030     2970     2970       30     3000
3     4000       40     4040     4040     3960     3960       40     4000
4    30000     3000   -32536    32767    27000    27000     3000    30000
5     6000    32000   -27536    32767   -26000   -26000     6000    32000
```

| 6 | 2000 | -31000 | -29000 | -29000 | -32536 | 32767 | -31000 | 2000 |
| 7 | 4000 | -30000 | -26000 | -26000 | -31536 | 32767 | -30000 | 4000 |
| 8 | 4000 | -2500 | 1500 | 1500 | 6500 | 6500 | -2500 | 4000 |
| 9 | 3600 | -1200 | 2400 | 2400 | 4800 | 4800 | -1200 | 3600 |
| 10 | 6000 | 9000 | 15000 | 15000 | -3000 | -3000 | 6000 | 9000 |
| 11 | -20000 | -20000 | 25536 | -32768 | 0 | 0 | -20000 | -20000 |
| 12 | -25000 | -27000 | 13536 | -32768 | 2000 | 2000 | -27000 | -25000 |
| 13 | 8000 | 28700 | -28836 | 32767 | -20700 | -20700 | 8000 | 28700 |
| 14 | 3 | -32766 | -32763 | -32763 | -32767 | 32767 | -32766 | 3 |
| 15 | -15000 | 24000 | 9000 | 9000 | 26536 | -32768 | -15000 | 24000 |

Results for MathI32_Aavx2

| i | a | b | add | sub | mull | sll | sra | abs |
|---|---|---|-----|-----|------|-----|-----|-----|
| 0 | 64 | 4 | 68 | 60 | 256 | 1024 | 4 | 64 |
| 1 | 1024 | 5 | 1029 | 1019 | 5120 | 32768 | 32 | 1024 |
| 2 | -2048 | 2 | -2046 | -2050 | -4096 | -8192 | -512 | 2048 |
| 3 | 8192 | 5 | 8197 | 8187 | 40960 | 262144 | 256 | 8192 |
| 4 | -256 | 8 | -248 | -264 | -2048 | -65536 | -1 | 256 |
| 5 | 4096 | 7 | 4103 | 4089 | 28672 | 524288 | 32 | 4096 |
| 6 | 16 | 3 | 19 | 13 | 48 | 128 | 2 | 16 |
| 7 | 512 | 6 | 518 | 506 | 3072 | 32768 | 8 | 512 |

# Size Promotions

The next source code example, Ch15_02, explains how to size-promote packed integers using AVX2 instructions. This example is the assembly language counterpart of source code example Ch04_03. Listing 15-2 shows the assembly language source code for example Ch15_02.

*Listing 15-2.* Example Ch15_02

```
;--------------------------------------------------
;              Ch15_02_fasm.asm
;--------------------------------------------------


;---------------------------------------------------------------------
; extern "C" void ZeroExtU8_U16_Aavx2(YmmVal c[2], YmmVal* a);
;---------------------------------------------------------------------

        .code
ZeroExtU8_U16_Aavx2 proc
        vmovdqa ymm0,ymmword ptr [rdx]      ;ymm0 = a (32 byte values)
        vextracti128 xmm1,ymm0,1            ;xmm1 = high-order byte values

        vpmovzxbw ymm2,xmm0                 ;zero extend a[0:15] to word
        vpmovzxbw ymm3,xmm1                 ;zero extend a[16:31] to words

        vmovdqa ymmword ptr [rcx],ymm2      ;save words c[0:15]
        vmovdqa ymmword ptr [rcx+32],ymm3   ;save words c[16:31]
```

```
        vzeroupper
        ret
ZeroExtU8_U16_Aavx2 endp


;---------------------------------------------------------------------------
; extern "C" void ZeroExtU8_U32_Aavx2(YmmVal c[4], YmmVal* a);
;---------------------------------------------------------------------------

ZeroExtU8_U32_Aavx2 proc
        vmovdqa ymm0,ymmword ptr [rdx]        ;ymm0 = a (32 bytes values)
        vextracti128 xmm1,ymm0,1              ;xmm1 = high-order byte values

        vpmovzxbd ymm2,xmm0                    ;zero extend a[0:7] to dword
        vpsrldq xmm0,xmm0,8                    ;xmm0[63:0] = a[8:15]
        vpmovzxbd ymm3,xmm0                    ;zero extend a[8:15] to dword

        vpmovzxbd ymm4,xmm1                    ;zero extend a[16:23] to dword
        vpsrldq xmm1,xmm1,8                    ;xmm1[63:0] = a[24:31]
        vpmovzxbd ymm5,xmm1                    ;zero extend a[24:31] to dword

        vmovdqa ymmword ptr [rcx],ymm2        ;save dwords c[0:7]
        vmovdqa ymmword ptr [rcx+32],ymm3     ;save dwords c[8:15]
        vmovdqa ymmword ptr [rcx+64],ymm4     ;save dwords c[16:23]
        vmovdqa ymmword ptr [rcx+96],ymm5     ;save dwords c[24:31]

        vzeroupper
        ret
ZeroExtU8_U32_Aavx2 endp

;---------------------------------------------------------------------------
; extern "C" void SignExtI16_I32_Aavx2(YmmVal c[2], YmmVal* a);
;---------------------------------------------------------------------------

SignExtI16_I32_Aavx2 proc
        vmovdqa ymm0,ymmword ptr [rdx]        ;ymm0 = a (16 word values)
        vextracti128 xmm1,ymm0,1              ;xmm1 = high-order word values

        vpmovsxwd ymm2,xmm0                    ;sign extend a[0:7] to dword
        vpmovsxwd ymm3,xmm1                    ;sign extend a[8:15] to dwords

        vmovdqa ymmword ptr [rcx],ymm2        ;save dwords c[0:7]
        vmovdqa ymmword ptr [rcx+32],ymm3     ;save dwords c[8:15]

        vzeroupper
        ret
SignExtI16_I32_Aavx2 endp


;---------------------------------------------------------------------------
; extern "C" void SignExtI16_I64_Aavx2(YmmVal c[4], YmmVal* a);
;---------------------------------------------------------------------------
```

```
SignExtI16_I64_Aavx2 proc
        vmovdqa ymm0,ymmword ptr [rdx]      ;ymm0 = a (16 word values)
        vextracti128 xmm1,ymm0,1            ;xmm1 = high-order word values

        vpmovsxwq ymm2,xmm0                 ;sign extend a[0:3] to qword
        vpsrldq xmm0,xmm0,8                 ;xmm0[63:0] = a[4:7]
        vpmovsxwq ymm3,xmm0                 ;sign extend a[4:7] to qword

        vpmovsxwq ymm4,xmm1                 ;sign extend a[8:11] to qword
        vpsrldq xmm1,xmm1,8                 ;xmm1[63:0] = a[12:15]
        vpmovsxwq ymm5,xmm1                 ;sign extend a[12:15] to qword

        vmovdqa ymmword ptr [rcx],ymm2      ;save qwords c[0:3]
        vmovdqa ymmword ptr [rcx+32],ymm3   ;save qwords c[4:7]
        vmovdqa ymmword ptr [rcx+64],ymm4   ;save qwords c[8:11]
        vmovdqa ymmword ptr [rcx+96],ymm5   ;save qwords c[12:16]

        vzeroupper
        ret
SignExtI16_I64_Aavx2 endp
        end
```

The first function in file Ch15_02_fasm.asm, ZeroExtU8_U16_Aavx2(), zero-extends 8-bit integer elements to 16 bits. This function begins with a vmovdqa ymm0,ymmword ptr [rdx] instruction that loads argument value a into register YMM0. The next instruction, vextracti128 xmm1,ymm0,1 (Extract Packed Integer Values), copies the high-order 128 bits of register YMM0 into register XMM0. Note that the immediate operand of the vextracti128 instruction specifies which 128-bit lane (0 = lower, 1 = upper) to copy. The ensuing instruction pair, vpmovzxbw ymm2,xmm0 (Packed Move with Zero Extend) and vpmovzxbw ymm3,xmm1, zero-extends the 8-bit wide elements of registers XMM0 and XMM1 (a[0:15] and a[16:31]) and saves the resultant 16-bit values in registers YMM2 and YMM3, respectively.

Function ZeroExtU8_U32_Aavx2() illustrates the zero-extension of 8-bit integer elements to 32 bits. This function uses sequences of the vpmovzxbd and vpsrldq instructions to carry out its operations as shown in Figure 15-1. Note that each vpmovzxbd instruction zero-extends the low-order eight elements of the specified XMM register operand.

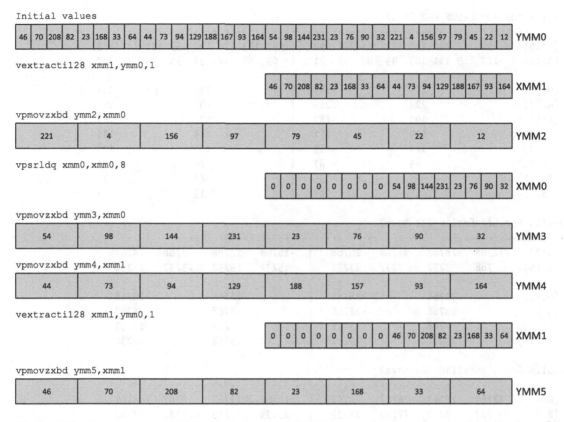

***Figure 15-1.*** *Zero-extension of 8-bit integer elements to 32-bit integer elements using* vpmovzxbd *and* vpsrldq

The final two functions in Listing 15-2, SignExtI16_I32_Aavx2() and SignExtI16_I64_Aavx2(), illustrate how to sign-extend 16-bit integer elements to 32- and 64-bit elements, respectively. Note that these functions use instructions vpmovsxwd (Packed Move with Sign Extend) and vpmovsxwq to carry out signed word to doubleword and word to quadword extensions. Here are the results for source code example Ch15_02:

```
Results for ZeroExtU8_U16_Aavx2
----------------------------------------------------------------------
a (0:15):     0   8  16  24  32  40  48  56  |  64  72  80  88  96 104 112 120
a (16:31):  128 136 144 152 160 168 176 184  | 192 200 208 216 224 232 240 248

c (0:7):       0      8     16     24  |    32     40     48     56
c (8:15):     64     72     80     88  |    96    104    112    120
c (16:23):   128    136    144    152  |   160    168    176    184
c (24:31):   192    200    208    216  |   224    232    240    248
```

```
Results for ZeroExtU8_U32_Aavx2
------------------------------------------------------------------------
a (0:15):   255 247 239 231 223 215 207 199  | 191 183 175 167 159 151 143 135
a (16:31):  127 119 111 103  95  87  79  71  |  63  55  47  39  31  23  15   7

c (0:3):             255            247  |            239            231
c (4:7):             223            215  |            207            199
c (8:11):            191            183  |            175            167
c (12:15):           159            151  |            143            135
c (16:19):           127            119  |            111            103
c (20:23):            95             87  |             79             71
c (24:27):            63             55  |             47             39
c (28:31):            31             23  |             15              7

Results for SignExtI16_I32_Aavx2
------------------------------------------------------------------------
a (0:7):  -32768   -28768   -24768   -20768  | -16768  -12768   -8768   -4768
a (8:15):   -768     3232     7232    11232  |  15232   19232   23232   27232

c (0:3):           -32768           -28768  |          -24768          -20768
c (4:7):           -16768           -12768  |           -8768           -4768
c (8:11):            -768             3232  |            7232           11232
c (12:15):          15232            19232  |           23232           27232

Results for SignExtI16_I64_Aavx2
------------------------------------------------------------------------
a (0:7):   32767    28767    24767    20767  |  16767   12767    8767    4767
a (8:15):    767    -3233    -7233   -11233  | -15233  -19233  -23233  -27233

c (0:1):                      32767  |                           28767
c (2:3):                      24767  |                           20767
c (4:5):                      16767  |                           12767
c (6:7):                       8767  |                            4767
c (8:9):                        767  |                           -3233
c (10:11):                    -7233  |                          -11233
c (12:13):                   -15233  |                          -19233
c (14:15):                   -23233  |                          -27233
```

# Image Processing

The source code examples presented in this section demonstrate a few common image processing techniques using AVX2 instructions and 256-bit wide SIMD operands. The first example explains how to clip the pixel values of a grayscale image. The second example demonstrates converting an RGB image to grayscale. This is followed by a source code example that performs unsigned 8-bit integer to single-precision floating-point pixel conversions.

As mentioned in Chapter 2, SIMD techniques are suitable for many types of image processing algorithms. While the focus of this section is image processing algorithms, you should keep in mind that the same techniques can also be employed to carry out similar operations in any algorithm that uses large arrays or matrices of integer data.

# Pixel Clipping

In Chapter 4, you learned how to use C++ SIMD intrinsic functions to clip the pixels of a grayscale image (see example Ch04_04). Then the next example of this chapter, named Ch15_03, illustrates the use of AVX2 instructions to perform pixel clipping. Listing 15-3 shows the source code for example Ch15_03.

***Listing 15-3.*** Example Ch15_03

```
//-------------------------------------------------
//                  Ch15_03.h
//-------------------------------------------------

#pragma once
#include <cstddef>
#include <cstdint>

// The members of ClipData must match the corresponding structure
// that's declared in Ch15_03_fasm.asm

struct ClipData
{
    uint8_t* m_PbSrc;               // source buffer pointer
    uint8_t* m_PbDes;               // destination buffer pointer
    size_t m_NumPixels;             // number of pixels
    size_t m_NumClippedPixels;      // number of clipped pixels
    uint8_t m_ThreshLo;             // low threshold
    uint8_t m_ThreshHi;             // high threshold
};

// Ch15_03_fcpp.cpp
extern void ClipPixels_Cpp(ClipData* clip_data);

// Ch15_03_fasm.asm
extern "C" void ClipPixels_Aavx2(ClipData* clip_data);

// Ch15_03_misc.cpp
extern bool CheckArgs(const ClipData* clip_data);

// Ch15_03_bm.cpp
extern void ClipPixels_bm(void);

// Miscellaneous constants
const size_t c_Alignment = 32;
const int c_RngMinVal = 0;
const int c_RngMaxVal = 255;
const unsigned int c_RngSeed = 157;
const uint8_t c_ThreshLo = 10;
const uint8_t c_ThreshHi = 245;
const size_t c_NumPixels = 8 * 1024 * 1024 + 31;
const size_t c_NumPixelsBM = 10000000;
```

```
;----------------------------------------------------
;                 Ch15_03_fasm.asm
;----------------------------------------------------

; The members of CD must match the corresponding structure
; that's declared in Ch15_03.h

CD                struct
PbSrc             qword ?
PbDes             qword ?
NumPixels         qword ?
NumClippedPixels  qword ?
ThreshLo          byte ?
ThreshHi          byte ?
CD                ends

;-----------------------------------------------------------------------
; extern "C" void ClipPixels_Aavx2(ClipData* clip_data);
;-----------------------------------------------------------------------

NSE       equ 32                             ;num_simd_elements

          .code
ClipPixels_Aavx2 proc frame
          push rsi
          .pushreg rsi
          push rdi
          .pushreg rdi
          .endprolog

; Initialize
          xor r11,r11                        ;r11 = NumClippedPixels

          mov r8,qword ptr [rcx+CD.PbSrc]    ;r8 = PbSrc
          test r8,1fh
          jnz Done                           ;jump if PbSrc not 32b aligned

          mov r9,qword ptr [rcx+CD.PbDes]    ;r9 = PbDes
          test r9,1fh
          jnz Done                           ;jump if PbDes not 32b aligned

          mov r10,qword ptr [rcx+CD.NumPixels]  ;r10 = NumPixels
          test r10,r10
          jz Done                            ;jump if NumPixels is zero

          mov rax,-NSE                             ;initialize i
          vpbroadcastb ymm4,byte ptr [rcx+CD.ThreshLo]    ;packed ThreshLo
          vpbroadcastb ymm5,byte ptr [rcx+CD.ThreshHi]    ;packed ThreshHi
```

```
; Main for-loop
Loop1:  add rax,NSE                         ;i += NSE
        mov rdx,r10                         ;rdx = NumPixels
        sub rdx,rax                         ;rdx = NumPixels - i
        cmp rdx,NSE                         ;NumPixels - i < NSE?
        jb @F                               ;jump if yes

        vmovdqa ymm0,ymmword ptr [r8+rax]   ;load PbSrc[i:i+31]
        vpmaxub ymm1,ymm0,ymm4              ;clip to ThreshLo
        vpminub ymm2,ymm1,ymm5              ;clip to ThreshHi
        vmovdqa ymmword ptr [r9+rax],ymm2   ;save PbDes[i:i+31] (clipped pixels)

        vpcmpeqb ymm3,ymm2,ymm0             ;compare clipped to original
        vpmovmskb edx,ymm3                  ;edx = mask of non-clipped pixels
        not edx                             ;edx = mask of clipped pixels
        popcnt esi,edx                      ;esi = num clipped this iteration
        add r11,rsi                         ;update NumClippedPixels

        jmp Loop1                           ;repeat until done

@@:     cmp rax,r10                         ;is i >= NumPixels?
        jae Done                            ;jump if yes

        dec rax                             ;adjust for Loop2
        mov sil,byte ptr [rcx+CD.ThreshLo]  ;sil = ThreshLo
        mov dil,byte ptr [rcx+CD.ThreshHi]  ;dil = ThreshHi

; Second for-loop for residual pixels (if any)
Loop2:  inc rax                             ;i += 1
        cmp rax,r10                         ;is i >= NumPixels
        jae Done                            ;jump if yes

        mov dl,byte ptr [r8+rax]            ;load next PbSrc[i]
        cmp dl,sil                          ;PbSrc[i] < ThreshLo?
        jb TH_LT                            ;jump is yes
        cmp dl,dil                          ;PbSrc[i] > ThreshHi?
        ja TH_GT                            ;jump if yes

        mov byte ptr [r9+rax],dl            ;save non-clipped pixel to PbDes[i]
        jmp Loop2

TH_LT:  inc r11                             ;NumClippedPixels += 1
        mov byte ptr [r9+rax],sil           ;save clipped pixel to PbDes[i]
        jmp Loop2

TH_GT:  inc r11                             ;NumClippedPixels += 1
        mov byte ptr [r9+rax],dil           ;save clipped pixel to PbDes[i]
        jmp Loop2

Done:   mov qword ptr [rcx+CD.NumClippedPixels],r11 ;save NumClippedPixels
```

```
        vzeroupper
        pop rdi
        pop rsi
        ret
ClipPixels_Aavx2 endp
        end
```

Listing 15-3 begins with the declaration of a C++ structure named ClipData. This is the same structure that was used in example Ch04_04. The assembly language file Ch15_03_fasm.asm that is shown in Listing 15-3 starts with the declaration of a structure named CD, which is the assembly language counterpart of ClipData. Following its prologue, function ClipPixels_Aavx2() performs its requisite initializations. Note that pointers PbSrc (R8) and PbDes (R9) are tested to ensure that they are properly aligned on a 32-byte boundary. Also note the use of the vpbroadcastb (Load Integer and Broadcast) instruction to initialize packed versions of ThreshLo (YMM4) and ThreshHi (YMM5).

Each iteration of Loop1 begins with a check to ensure that at least 32 (NSE) pixels are available to process. Following this check, the vmovdqa ymm0,ymmword ptr [r8+rax] instruction loads pixels PbSrc[i:i+31] into register YMM0. The ensuing instruction pair, vpmaxub ymm1,ymm0,ymm4 and vpminub ymm2,ymm1,ymm5, clips any pixel values less than ThreshLo or greater than ThreshHi. The next instruction, vmovdqa ymmword ptr [r9+rax],ymm2, saves the clipped pixels to PbDes[i:i+31].

The subsequent code block in ClipPixels_Aavx2() counts the number of pixels that were clipped during the current iteration. This block begins with a vpcmpeqb ymm3,ymm2,ymm0 instruction that compares the original pixel values in YMM0 to the clipped values in YMM2 for equality. The vpcmpeqb instruction sets each corresponding byte element in YMM3 to 0xFF if PbSrc[i] == PbDes[i] is true (i.e., the pixel was not clipped); otherwise, the byte element in YMM3 is set to 0x00. Then the next instruction, vpmovmskb edx,ymm3 (Move Byte Mask), copies the most significant bit of each byte element in YMM3 to its corresponding bit position in register EDX. This is followed by a not edx instruction whose execution yields a mask of clipped pixels. The next instruction, popcnt esi,edx (Return the Count of Number of Bits Set to 1), counts the number of bits set to 1 in EDX, which equals the number of pixels clipped during the current iteration. The ensuing add r11,rsi instruction adds this value to NumClippedPixels in register R11.

Following execution of Loop1, ClipPixels_Aavx2() employs a simple for-loop to process any residual pixels. Note that Loop2 uses x86 byte registers to carry out its compare operations. The mov qword ptr [rcx+CD.NumClippedPixels],r11 instruction saves the total number of clipped pixels. Here are the results for source code example Ch15_03:

```
Results for ClipPixels_Cpp
  cd0.m_NumClippedPixels: 654950

Results for ClipPixels_Aavx2
  cd1.m_NumClippedPixels: 654950

Result compare checks passed

Running benchmark function ClipPixels_bm - please wait
Benchmark times save to file Ch15_03_ClipPixels_bm_OXYGEN4.csv
```

Table 15-1 shows the benchmark timing measurements for source code example Ch15_03. The rightmost column of this table shows the benchmark timing measurements for function ClipPixels_Iavx2() from source code example Ch04_04 (see Table 4-1). As you can see, the measurements for both the assembly language and C++ SIMD intrinsic function implementations of the pixel clipping algorithm are essentially the same.

**Table 15-1.** *Pixel Clipping Algorithm Execution Times (Microseconds), 10,000,000 Pixels*

| CPU | ClipPixels_Cpp() | ClipPixels_Aavx2() | ClipPixels_Iavx2() |
| --- | --- | --- | --- |
| Intel Core i7-8700K | 12212 | 806 | 810 |
| Intel Core i5-11600K | 9656 | 649 | 665 |

## RGB to Grayscale

Listing 15-4 shows the assembly language source code for example Ch15_04, which illustrates how to convert an RGB color image to grayscale using AVX2 instructions. This example uses the same RGB to grayscale pixel conversion technique as source example Ch04_05. It also uses the same RGB32 data structure (see Listing 4-5).

***Listing 15-4.*** Example Ch15_04

```
;-----------------------------------------------------
;                 Ch15_04_fasm.asm
;-----------------------------------------------------

            include <MacrosX86-64-AVX.asmh>

;-------------------------------------------------------------------------
; extern "C" void ConvertRgbToGs_Aavx2(uint8_t* pb_gs, const RGB32* pb_rgb,
;    size_t num_pixels, const float coef[4]);
;-------------------------------------------------------------------------

            .const
r4_0p5      real4 0.5
r4_255p0    real4 255.0
i4_0xff     dword 0ffh

NSE         equ 8                         ;num_simd_elements

        extern g_NumPixelsMax:qword

        .code
ConvertRgbToGs_Aavx2 proc frame
        CreateFrame_M CD_,0,64
        SaveXmmRegs_M xmm12,xmm13,xmm14,xmm15
        EndProlog_M

; Validate argument values
        test rcx,1fh
        jnz Done                        ;jump if pb_gs not 32b aligned
        test rdx,1fh
        jnz Done                        ;jump if pb_rgb not 32b aligned

        cmp r8,[g_NumPixelsMax]
        ja Done                         ;jump if num_pixels > g_NumPixelsMax
```

495

```
        test r8,07h
        jnz Done                            ;jump if num_pixels not multiple of 8

        vxorps xmm0,xmm0,xmm0               ;xmm0 = 0.0

        vmovss xmm13,real4 ptr [r9]         ;xmm13 = coef[0]
        vcomiss xmm13,xmm0
        jb Done                             ;jump if coef[0] < 0.0

        vmovss xmm14,real4 ptr [r9+4]       ;xmm14 = coef[1]
        vcomiss xmm14,xmm0
        jb Done                             ;jump if coef[1] < 0.0

        vmovss xmm15,real4 ptr [r9+8]       ;xmm15 = coef[2]
        vcomiss xmm15,xmm0
        jb  Done                            ;jump if coef[2] < 0.0

; Initialize
        vbroadcastss ymm4,real4 ptr [r4_0p5]    ;packed 0.5
        vbroadcastss ymm5,real4 ptr [r4_255p0]  ;packed 255.0

        vpbroadcastd ymm12,[i4_0xff]             ;packed 0x000000ff

        vbroadcastss ymm13,xmm13                 ;packed coef[0]
        vbroadcastss ymm14,xmm14                 ;packed coef[1]
        vbroadcastss ymm15,xmm15                 ;packed coef[2]

        mov rax,-NSE                             ;initialize i

; Convert pixels from RGB to gray scale
Loop1:  add rax,NSE                         ;i += NSE
        cmp rax,r8
        jae Done                            ;jump if i >= num_pixels

        vmovdqa ymm0,ymmword ptr [rdx+rax*4]    ;load next block of 8 RGB32 pixels

        vpand ymm1,ymm0,ymm12               ;ymm1 = r values (dwords)
        vpsrld ymm0,ymm0,8
        vpand ymm2,ymm0,ymm12               ;ymm2 = g values (dwords)
        vpsrld ymm0,ymm0,8
        vpand ymm3,ymm0,ymm12               ;ymm3 = b values (dwords)

        vcvtdq2ps ymm1,ymm1                 ;ymm1 = r values (F32)
        vcvtdq2ps ymm2,ymm2                 ;ymm2 = g values (F32)
        vcvtdq2ps ymm3,ymm3                 ;ymm3 = b values (F32)

        vmulps ymm1,ymm1,ymm13              ;ymm1 = r values * coef[0]
        vmulps ymm2,ymm2,ymm14              ;ymm2 = g values * coef[1]
        vmulps ymm3,ymm3,ymm15              ;ymm3 = b values * coef[2]

        vaddps ymm0,ymm1,ymm2               ;ymm0 = sum of r and g values
```

```
        vaddps  ymm1,ymm3,ymm4          ;ymm1 = sum of b values and 0.5
        vaddps  ymm0,ymm0,ymm1          ;ymm0 = sum of r, g, b, and 0.5

        vminps  ymm1,ymm0,ymm5          ;clip grayscale values to 255.0

        vcvtps2dq ymm0,ymm1             ;convert F32 values to dword
        vpackusdw ymm1,ymm0,ymm0        ;convert dwords to words
        vpermq  ymm2,ymm1,10001000b     ;ymm2[127:0] = 8 grayscale words
        vpackuswb ymm3,ymm2,ymm2        ;ymm3[63:0] = 8 grayscale bytes

        vmovq   qword ptr [rcx+rax],xmm3  ;save pb_gs[i:i+7]
        jmp Loop1

Done:   vzeroupper
        RestoreXmmRegs_M xmm12,xmm13,xmm14,xmm15
        DeleteFrame_M
        ret
ConvertRgbToGs_Aavx2 endp
        end
```

In Listing 15-4, file Ch15_04_fasm.asm opens with a .const section that defines the constants needed for this example. Function ConvertRgbToGs_Aavx2() begins its execution with a prologue that preserves nonvolatile SIMD registers XMM12–XMM15 on the stack using the macro SaveXmmRegs_M. Following its prologue, ConvertRgbToGs_Aavx2() verifies that pb_gs (RCX) and pb_rgb (RDX) are properly aligned on a 32-byte boundary. It also checks num_pixels (R8) and the color conversion coefficients for validity.

Following argument validation, ConvertRgbToGs_Aavx2() employs the instruction pair vbroadcastss ymm4,real4 ptr [r4_0p5] and vbroadcastss ymm5,real4 ptr [r4_255p0] to create packed versions of the floating-point constants 0.5 and 255.0, respectively. The next instruction, vpbroadcastd ymm12,[i4_0xff], sets each doubleword element in YMM12 to 0x000000FF. This packed mask will be used during RGB de-interleaving as you will soon see. The ensuing instruction triplet, vbroadcastss ymm13,xmm13, vbroadcastss ymm14,xmm14, and vbroadcastss ymm15,xmm15, creates packed versions of the color conversions coefficients. Note that the source operand for these vbroadcastss instructions is an XMM register. Unlike AVX, the AVX2 vbroadcasts[d|s] instruction can be used with either a memory or register source operand.

Each iteration of Loop1 begins with an add rax,NSE instruction that updates i. If i >= num_pixels is false, the ensuing vmovdqa ymm0,ymmword ptr [rdx+rax*4] instruction loads a block of eight RGB32 pixels into register YMM0. The next code block uses a series of vpand and vpsrld instructions to de-interleave the 8-bit color components of each RGB32 pixel as shown in Figure 15-2. These values are then converted to single-precision floating point using the vcvtdq2ps instruction, also shown in Figure 15-2.

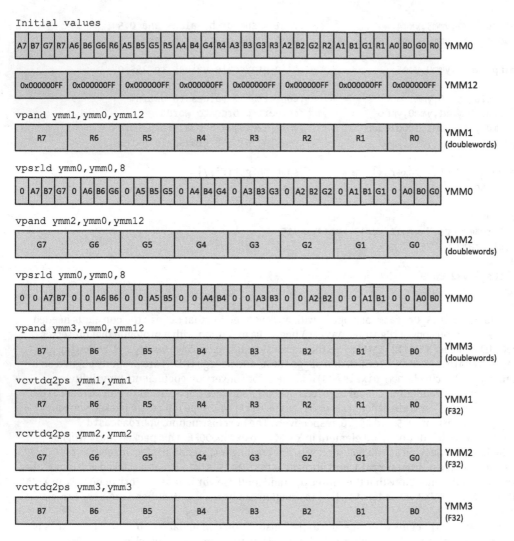

***Figure 15-2.*** *RGB32 pixel de-interleaving and conversion to floating point*

Following the conversion operation, ConvertRgbToGs_Aavx2() uses a series of vmulps instructions to multiply each color component by its corresponding color conversion coefficient. This is followed by a series of vaddps instructions that sum the color component values as shown in Figure 15-3. The vminps ymm1,ymm0,ymm5 instruction ensures that each grayscale pixel value is not greater than 255.0.

```
Initial values
```

| 0.5 | 0.5 | 0.5 | 0.5 | 0.5 | 0.5 | 0.5 | 0.5 | YMM4 |
|---|---|---|---|---|---|---|---|---|
| 0.2126 | 0.2126 | 0.2126 | 0.2126 | 0.2126 | 0.2126 | 0.2126 | 0.2126 | YMM13 |
| 0.7152 | 0.7152 | 0.7152 | 0.7152 | 0.7152 | 0.7152 | 0.7152 | 0.7152 | YMM14 |
| 0.0722 | 0.0722 | 0.0722 | 0.0722 | 0.0722 | 0.0722 | 0.0722 | 0.0722 | YMM15 |
| 222.0 | 218.0 | 212.0 | 202.0 | 199.0 | 224.0 | 227.0 | 229.0 | YMM1 |
| 162.0 | 158.0 | 156.0 | 165.0 | 155.0 | 159.0 | 161.0 | 164.0 | YMM2 |
| 88.0 | 84.0 | 83.0 | 79.0 | 82.0 | 86.0 | 89.0 | 87.0 | YMM3 |

```
vmulps  ymm1,ymm1,ymm13              ;ymm1 = r values * coef[0]
```

| 47.20 | 46.35 | 45.07 | 42.95 | 42.31 | 47.62 | 48.26 | 48.69 | YMM1 |
|---|---|---|---|---|---|---|---|---|

```
vmulps  ymm2,ymm2,ymm14              ;ymm2 = g values * coef[1]
```

| 115.86 | 113.00 | 111.57 | 118.01 | 110.86 | 113.72 | 115.15 | 117.29 | YMM2 |
|---|---|---|---|---|---|---|---|---|

```
vmulps  ymm3,ymm3,ymm15              ;ymm3 = b values * coef[2]
```

| 6.35 | 6.06 | 5.99 | 5.70 | 5.92 | 6.21 | 6.43 | 6.28 | YMM3 |
|---|---|---|---|---|---|---|---|---|

```
vaddps  ymm0,ymm1,ymm2               ;ymm0 = sum of r and g values
```

| 163.06 | 159.35 | 156.64 | 160.96 | 153.17 | 161.34 | 163.41 | 165.98 | YMM0 |
|---|---|---|---|---|---|---|---|---|

```
vaddps  ymm1,ymm3,ymm4               ;ymm1 = sum of b values and 0.5
```

| 6.85 | 6.56 | 6.49 | 6.20 | 6.42 | 6.71 | 6.93 | 6.78 | YMM1 |
|---|---|---|---|---|---|---|---|---|

```
vaddps  ymm0,ymm0,ymm1               ;ymm0 = sum of r, g, b, and 0.5
```

| 169.91 | 165.91 | 163.13 | 167.16 | 159.59 | 168.05 | 170.34 | 172.76 | YMM0 |
|---|---|---|---|---|---|---|---|---|

***Figure 15-3.*** *RGB to grayscale calculation*

Figure 15-4 illustrates the final sequence of instructions used by ConvertRgbToGs_Aavx2() in Loop1. The vcvtps2dq ymm0,ymm1 (Convert Packed SPFP Values to Packed Signed Doubleword Values) instruction converts each single-precision floating-point element in YMM1 to a doubleword integer. Note that vcvtps2dq performs its conversions using the MXCSR rounding mode (the default MXCSR rounding mode for Visual C++ programs is round to nearest). The ensuing vpackusdw ymm1,ymm0,ymm0 (Pack with Unsigned Saturation) instruction size reduces the doubleword values in YMM0 to words. Note that vpackusdw performs two independent operations using the upper and lower lanes of YMM0. The next instruction, vpermq ymm2,ymm1,10001000b (Qwords Element Permutation), reorders the word elements of YMM1 as shown in Figure 15-4. In this instruction, bit positions 0 and 1 of the immediate operand

10001000b select the quadword that gets copied into YMM2[63:0] (00 = YMM1[63:0]; a function can also use 01 = YMM1[127:64], 10 = YMM1[191:128], and 11 = YMM1[255:192]). Similarly, bit positions 2 and 3 of the immediate operand select the quadword that gets copied into YMM2[127:64]. Following execution of the vpermq instruction, ConvertRgbToGs_Aavx2() employs a vpackuswb ymm3,ymm2,ymm2 instruction to size-reduce the word elements of YMM2 to bytes.

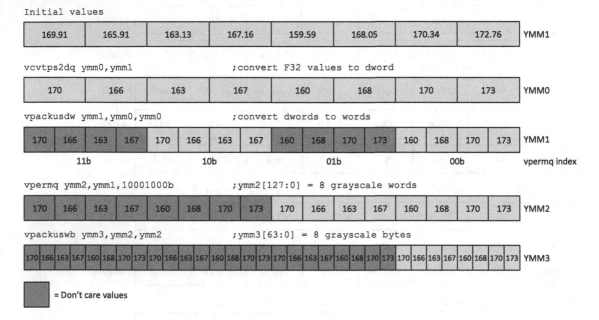

*Figure 15-4.* *Grayscale floating-point to 8-bit unsigned integer conversion*

The penultimate instruction of Loop1, vmovq qword ptr [rcx+rax],xmm3 (Move Quadword) instruction, saves the converted pixel values to pb_des[i:i+7]. More specifically, the vmovq instruction copies XMM3[63:0] to the memory location specified by its destination operand. Here are the results for source code example Ch15_04:

```
Results for ConvertRgbToGs
  Converting RGB image ../../Data/ImageC.png
  im_h = 960 pixels
  im_w = 640 pixels
Saving grayscale image #0 - Ch15_04_GsImage0.png
Saving grayscale image #1 - Ch15_04_GsImage1.png
Grayscale pixel buffer compare OK

Running benchmark function ConvertRgbToGs_bm - please wait
Benchmark times save to file Ch15_04_ConvertRgbToGs_bm_OXYGEN4.csv
```

Table 15-2 shows some benchmark timing measurements for source code example Ch15_04. In this table, the measurements for function ConvertRgbToGs_Iavx2() were copied from Table 4-2. As you can see, the timing benchmark measurements for the assembly language and C++ SIMD implementations are about the same.

***Table 15-2.*** *RGB to Grayscale Algorithm Execution Times (Microseconds) Using ImageC.png*

| CPU | ConvertRgbToGs_Cpp() | ConvertRgbToGs_Aavx2() | ConvertRgbToGs_Iavx2() |
|---|---|---|---|
| Intel Core i7-8700K | 884 | 167 | 162 |
| Intel Core i5-11600K | 773 | 137 | 132 |

## Pixel Conversions

The final example of this chapter, Ch15_05, demonstrates how to convert the pixels of a grayscale image from 8-bit unsigned integers [0, 255] to single-precision floating-point [0.0, 1.0] using a LUT and the vgatherdps (Gather Packed SPFP with DWORD) instruction. This example is the assembly language counterpart of source example Ch04_07. Listing 15-5 shows the assembly language source code for example Ch15_05.

***Listing 15-5.*** Example Ch15_05

```
;------------------------------------------------
;               Ch15_05_fasm.asm
;------------------------------------------------

            .const
r4_1p0      real4 1.0
r4_255p0    real4 255.0


;-------------------------------------------------------------------
; extern "C" void ConvertU8ToF32_Aavx2(float* pb_des, const uint8_t* pb_src,
;    size_t num_pixels);
;-------------------------------------------------------------------

        extern g_NumPixelsMax:qword
        extern g_LUT_U8ToF32:qword
NSE     equ 32                          ;num_simd_elements

        .code
ConvertU8ToF32_Aavx2 proc

; Validate arguments
        test r8,r8
        jz Done                         ;jump if num_pixels == 0
        cmp r8,[g_NumPixelsMax]
        ja Done                         ;jump if num_pixels > g_NumPixelsMax

        test rcx,1fh
        jnz Done                        ;jump if pb_des not 32b aligned
        test rdx,1fh
        jnz Done                        ;jump if pb_src not 32b aligned

; Initialize
        mov rax,-NSE                    ;initialize i
        lea r9,[g_LUT_U8ToF32]          ;r9 = pointer to LUT
        vpcmpeqb ymm5,ymm5,ymm5         ;ymm5 = all ones
```

501

```
; Main processing loop
Loop1:  add rax,NSE                              ;i += NSE
        mov r10,r8                               ;r10 = num_pixels
        sub r10,rax                              ;r10 = num_pixels - i
        cmp r10,NSE                              ;num_pixels - i < NSE?
        jb @F                                    ;jump if yes

; Convert pixels from U8 to F32 using LUT
        vpmovzxbd ymm0,qword ptr [rdx+rax]       ;ymm0 = pb_src[i:i+7] (U32)
        vmovdqa ymm1,ymm5                        ;ymm1 = vgatherdps load mask
        vgatherdps ymm2,[r9+ymm0*4],ymm1         ;ymm2 = pb_src[i:i+7] (F32)
        vmovaps ymmword ptr [rcx+rax*4],ymm2     ;save pb_des[i:i+7]

        vpmovzxbd ymm0,qword ptr [rdx+rax+8]     ;ymm0 = pb_src[i+8:i+15] (U32)
        vmovdqa ymm1,ymm5                        ;ymm1 = vgatherdps load mask
        vgatherdps ymm2,[r9+ymm0*4],ymm1         ;ymm2 = pb_src[i_8:i+15] (F32)
        vmovaps ymmword ptr [rcx+rax*4+32],ymm2  ;save pb_des[i+8:i+15]

        vpmovzxbd ymm0,qword ptr [rdx+rax+16]    ;ymm0 = pb_src[i+16:i+23] (U32)
        vmovdqa ymm1,ymm5                        ;ymm1 = vgatherdps load mask
        vgatherdps ymm2,[r9+ymm0*4],ymm1         ;ymm2 = pb_src[i+16:i+23] (F32)
        vmovaps ymmword ptr [rcx+rax*4+64],ymm2  ;save pb_des[i+16:i+23]

        vpmovzxbd ymm0,qword ptr [rdx+rax+24]    ;ymm0 = pb_src[i+24:i+31] (U32)
        vmovdqa ymm1,ymm5                        ;ymm1 = vgatherdps load mask
        vgatherdps ymm2,[r9+ymm0*4],ymm1         ;ymm2 = pb_src[i+24:i+31] (F32)
        vmovaps ymmword ptr [rcx+rax*4+96],ymm2  ;save pb_des[i+24:i+31]

        jmp Loop1

; Process any residual pixels
@@:     cmp rax,r8
        jae Done                                 ;jump if i >= num_pixels

Loop2:  movzx r10d,byte ptr [rdx+rax]            ;load pb_src[i]
        vmovss xmm0,real4 ptr [r9+r10*4]         ;convert to F32 using LUT
        vmovss real4 ptr [rcx+rax*4],xmm0        ;save pb_des[i]

        inc rax                                  ;i += 1
        cmp rax,r8
        jb Loop2                                 ;jump if i < num_pixels

Done:   vzeroupper
        ret
ConvertU8ToF32_Aavx2 endp
        end
```

Function ConvertU8ToF32_Aavx2() begins its execution with a code block that validates argument value num_pixels (R8) for size. It then checks array pointers pb_des (RCX) and pb_src (RDX) for proper alignment. Following argument validation, ConvertU8ToF32_Aavx2() performs its required initialization operations. Note that the lea r9,[g_LUT_U8ToF32] instruction loads the address of the pixel conversion LUT g_LUT_U8ToF32 into R9.

Each iteration of Loop1 begins with the now familiar code block that verifies at least NSE pixels are available. If NSE pixels are available, ConvertU8ToF32_Aavx2() employs a vpmovzxbd ymm0,qword ptr [rdx+rax] instruction to load pixel values pb_src[i:i+7] into register YMM0. Note that the vpmovzxbd instruction zero-extends each byte pixel value to a doubleword. The ensuing vmovdqa ymm1,ymm5 instruction loads register YMM1 with a mask. The most significant bit of each doubleword element in YMM1 is used by the subsequent vgatherdps instruction to perform conditional loads. More on this in a moment. The vgatherdps ymm2,[r9+ymm0*4],ymm1 instruction loads single-precision floating-point elements from the array pointed to by R9 (g_LUT_U8ToF32) into register YMM1. The elements loaded into YMM2 are designated by the doubleword indices in register YMM0 as illustrated in Figure 15-5.

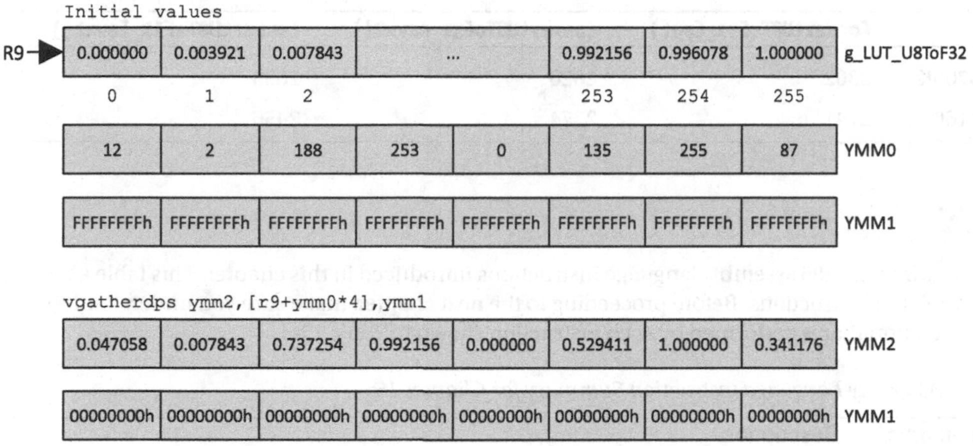

**Figure 15-5.** *Execution of vgatherdps instruction*

The vgatherdps ymm2,[r9+ymm0*4],ymm1 instruction will load an element from the specified array into YMM2 only if the most significant bit of the corresponding doubleword element in YMM1 (the mask operand) is set to 1. If this bit is set to 0, the doubleword element in destination operand YMM2 is not altered. Following each successful element gather, the vgatherdps instruction zeros the corresponding doubleword element in the mask operand (YMM1); otherwise, the doubleword mask element remains unaltered. This mask operand zeroing scheme allows the host operating system to resume execution of a vgatherdps instruction should a page fault occur when gathering an element from the specified array. It is important to note that this sequence of events occurs automatically; no action is required by the function that uses the vgatherdps instruction.

The next three code blocks employ the same sequence of instructions to convert pixels pb_src[i+8:i+15], pb_src[i+16:i+23], and pb_src[i+24:i+31]. Note that ConvertU8ToF32_Aavx2() uses a vmovdqa ymm1,ymm5 instruction prior to each vgatherdps, which reloads the mask operand since execution of the previous vgatherdps instruction zeroed all doubleword elements in YMM1. Following execution of Loop1, the for-loop Loop2 processes any residual pixels using scalar AVX instructions. Here are the results for source code example Ch15_05:

```
Results for ConvertU8ToF32
  num_pixels:   1048595
  num_diff:     0

Running benchmark function ConvertU8ToF32_bm - please wait
Benchmark times save to file Ch15_05_ConvertU8ToF32_bm_OXYGEN4.csv
```

It is important to note that the vgatherdps instruction does not perform any checks for invalid indices. The use of an invalid index will cause the processor to load an erroneous data value or generate an exception if vgatherdps references an illegal memory address. The AVX2 instruction set extension also includes additional gather instructions that can be used with double-precision floating-point elements and/or quadword indices. These are listed in the summary table at the end of this chapter.

Table 15-3 shows some benchmark timing measurements for source code example Ch15_05. Note that the benchmark measurements for the assembly language function ConvertU8ToF32_Aavx2() are about the same as the C++ function ConvertU8ToF32_Iavx2() from source code example Ch04_07 (see Table 4-3).

***Table 15-3.*** *Pixel Conversion Algorithm Execution Times (Microseconds), 10,000,000 Pixels*

| CPU | ConvertU8ToF32_Cpp() | ConvertU8ToF32_Aavx2() | ConvertU8ToF32_Iavx2() |
|---|---|---|---|
| Intel Core i7-8700K | 3302 | 2820 | 2893 |
| Intel Core i5-11600K | 2741 | 2374 | 2456 |

# Summary

Table 15-4 summarizes the x86 assembly language instructions introduced in this chapter. This table also includes closely related instructions. Before proceeding to the next chapter, make sure you understand the calculation or operation that is performed by each instruction shown in Table 15-4.

***Table 15-4.*** *X86 Assembly Language Instruction Summary for Chapter 15*

| Instruction Mnemonic | Description |
|---|---|
| popcnt | Count number of bits set to 1 |
| vcvtdq2p[d\|s] | Convert packed doubleword integers to packed floating point |
| vcvtp[d\|s]2dq | Convert packed floating point to packed doubleword integers |
| vextracti128 | Extract packed integer values |
| vgatherdp[d\|s] | Gather packed floating-point values using doubleword indices |
| vgatherqp[d\|s] | Gather packed floating-point values using quadword indices |
| vpackss[wb\|dw\| | Packed signed integers using signed saturation |
| vpackus[wb\|dw\| | Packed unsigned integers using unsigned saturation |
| vpbroadcast[b\|w\|d\|q] | Broadcast integer value to all elements |
| vpmovmskb | Build mask using the most significant bit of each byte element |
| vpmovsx[bw\|bd\|bq] | Packed byte move with sign extension |
| vpmovsx[wd\|wq] | Packed word move with sign extension |
| vpmovsxdq | Packed doubleword move with sign extension |
| vpmovzx[bw\|bd\|bq] | Packed byte move with zero extension |
| vpmovzx[wd\|wq] | Packed word move with zero extension |
| vpmovzxdq | Packed doubleword move with zero extension |

# CHAPTER 16

■ ■ ■

# AVX2 Assembly Language Programming: Part 2

In Chapters 5 and 6, you learned how to code a variety of numerically oriented functions that performed calculations using floating-point arrays and matrices. In this chapter, you will learn how to code similar functions using assembly language and AVX2 instructions. You will also learn how to use several FMA instructions. The first source code example presents a least-squares calculation using double-precision floating-point arrays. The next three source code examples cover matrix-matrix and matrix-vector multiplication. The final source code example of this chapter illustrates a 1D discrete convolution. Besides these topics, the source code examples in this chapter also demonstrate the use of additional MASM operators and directives.

## Floating-Point Arrays

Listing 16-1 shows the assembly language source code for example Ch16_01. This example illustrates how to perform a least-squares calculation using double-precision floating-point arrays, AVX2 instructions, and FMA arithmetic. Before examining the source code, you may want to review the least-squares equations that were defined in Chapter 5 for source code example Ch05_01 since the same equations are used in this example.

*Listing 16-1.* Example Ch16_01

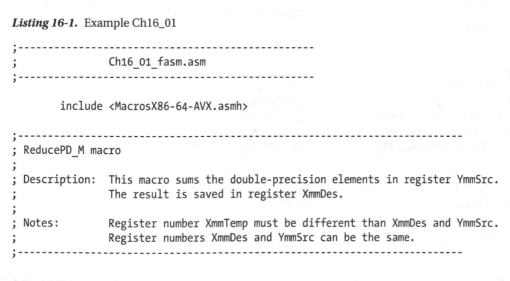

```
;------------------------------------------------
;                Ch16_01_fasm.asm
;------------------------------------------------

        include <MacrosX86-64-AVX.asmh>

;----------------------------------------------------------------------
; ReducePD_M macro
;
; Description:  This macro sums the double-precision elements in register YmmSrc.
;               The result is saved in register XmmDes.
;
; Notes:        Register number XmmTemp must be different than XmmDes and YmmSrc.
;               Register numbers XmmDes and YmmSrc can be the same.
;----------------------------------------------------------------------
```

© Daniel Kusswurm 2022

D. Kusswurm, *Modern Parallel Programming with C++ and Assembly Language*,
https://doi.org/10.1007/978-1-4842-7918-2_16

```
ReducePD_M macro XmmDes,YmmSrc,XmmTemp
        TempSS SUBSTR <YmmSrc>,2          ;<TempSS> = <YmmSrc> sans leading char
        XmmSrc CATSTR <x>,TempSS          ;<XmmSrc> = "x" + <TempSS>

        vextractf128 XmmTemp,YmmSrc,1    ;extract two high-order F64 values
        vaddpd XmmDes,XmmTemp,XmmSrc     ;reduce to two F64 values
        vhaddpd XmmDes,XmmDes,XmmDes     ;reduce to one F64 value
        endm


;-------------------------------------------------------------------------
; extern "C" void CalcLeastSquares_Aavx2(double* m, double* b, const double* x,
;   const double* y, size_t n);
;-------------------------------------------------------------------------


NSE     equ 4                                    ;num_simd_elements
        extern g_LsEpsilon:real8


        .code
CalcLeastSquares_Aavx2 proc frame
        CreateFrame_M LS_,0,64
        SaveXmmRegs_M xmm12,xmm13,xmm14,xmm15
        EndProlog_M

; Set m and b to zero (error values)
        xor eax,eax
        mov qword ptr [rcx],rax          ;m = 0
        mov qword ptr [rdx],rax          ;b = 0

; Validate arguments
        mov r10,qword ptr [rbp+LS_OffsetStackArgs]  ;r10 = n
        cmp r10,2
        jl Done                          ;jump if n < 2

        test r8,1fh
        jnz Done                         ;jump if x not 32b aligned
        test r9,1fh
        jnz Done                         ;jump if y not 32b aligned

; Initialize
        mov rax,-NSE                     ;rax = i
        vxorpd ymm12,ymm12,ymm12         ;packed sum_x = 0
        vxorpd ymm13,ymm13,ymm13         ;packed sum_y = 0
        vxorpd ymm14,ymm14,ymm14         ;packed sum_xx = 0
        vxorpd ymm15,ymm15,ymm15         ;packed sum_xy = 0

; Main processing loop
Loop1:  add rax,NSE                      ;i += NSE
        mov r11,r10                      ;r11 = n
        sub r11,rax                      ;r11 = n - i
        cmp r11,NSE
        jb @F                            ;jump if n - i < NSE
```

```
        vmovapd ymm0,ymmword ptr [r8+rax*8]     ;load x[i:i+3]
        vmovapd ymm1,ymmword ptr [r9+rax*8]     ;load y[i:i+3]

        vaddpd ymm12,ymm12,ymm0                  ;update packed sum_x
        vaddpd ymm13,ymm13,ymm1                  ;update packed sum_y
        vfmadd231pd ymm14,ymm0,ymm0             ;update packed sum_xx
        vfmadd231pd ymm15,ymm0,ymm1             ;update packed_sum_xy
        jmp Loop1

; Reduce packed sums to scalars
@@:     ReducePD_M xmm12,ymm12,xmm0              ;xmm12 = sum_x
        ReducePD_M xmm13,ymm13,xmm0              ;xmm13 = sum_y
        ReducePD_M xmm14,ymm14,xmm0              ;xmm14 = sum_xx
        ReducePD_M xmm15,ymm15,xmm0              ;xmm15 = sum_xy

; Process any residual elements
Loop2:  cmp rax,r10
        jae CalcLS                               ;jump if i >= n

        vmovsd xmm0,real8 ptr [r8+rax*8]        ;load x[i]
        vmovsd xmm1,real8 ptr [r9+rax*8]        ;load y[i]

        vaddsd xmm12,xmm12,xmm0                  ;update sum_x
        vaddsd xmm13,xmm13,xmm1                  ;update sum_y
        vfmadd231sd xmm14,xmm0,xmm0             ;update sum_xx
        vfmadd231sd xmm15,xmm0,xmm1             ;update sum_xy

        inc rax                                  ;i += 1
        jmp Loop2

CalcLS: vcvtsi2sd xmm5,xmm5,r10                  ;xmm5 = n
        vmulsd xmm0,xmm5,xmm14                   ;xmm0 = n * sum_xx
        vmulsd xmm1,xmm12,xmm12                  ;xmm1 = sum_x * sum_x
        vsubsd xmm0,xmm0,xmm1                    ;xmm0 = denom

        mov rax,7fffffffffffffffh               ;abs mask
        vmovq xmm1,rax
        vandpd xmm4,xmm0,xmm1                    ;xmm4 = fabs(denom)
        vcomisd xmm4,[g_LsEpsilon]
        jb Done                                  ;jump if denom < fabs(g_LsEpsilon)

; Compute and save slope
        vmulsd xmm0,xmm5,xmm15                   ;n * sum_xy
        vmulsd xmm1,xmm12,xmm13                  ;sum_x * sum_y
        vsubsd xmm2,xmm0,xmm1                    ;n * sum_xy - sum_x * sum_y
        vdivsd xmm3,xmm2,xmm4                    ;xmm3 = slope
        vmovsd real8 ptr [rcx],xmm3             ;save slope

; Compute and save intercept
        vmulsd xmm0,xmm14,xmm13                  ;sum_xx * sum_y
        vmulsd xmm1,xmm12,xmm15                  ;sum_x * sum_xy
```

```
        vsubsd  xmm2,xmm0,xmm1              ;sum_xx * sum_y - sum_x _ sum_xy
        vdivsd  xmm3,xmm2,xmm4              ;xmm3 = intercept
        vmovsd  real8 ptr [rdx],xmm3        ;save intercept

Done:   vzeroupper
        RestoreXmmRegs_M xmm12,xmm13,xmm14,xmm15
        DeleteFrame_M
        ret
CalcLeastSquares_Aavx2 endp
        end
```

Listing 16-1 opens with the definition of a macro named ReducePD_M. This macro emits code that sums the four double-precision floating-point elements of argument YmmSrc. This sum is then saved in the XMM register specified by macro argument XmmDes. Macro argument XmmTemp is an XMM register that holds an intermediate result.

Macro ReducePD_M begins with the statement TempSS SUBSTR <YmmSrc>,2. This statement employs the MASM operator SUBSTR to construct a macro text string whose value equals argument YmmSrc sans its leading character. For example, if YmmSrc equals *YMM12*, then TempSS equals *MM12*. The constant 2 instructs the SUBSTR operator to extract a substring from YmmSrc starting at character position number 2 (the first character in a macro text string is character number 1). Note that the angled brackets surrounding YmmSrc are required since they instruct MASM to treat YmmSrc as a string literal instead of performing a normal macro text substitution. The ensuing XmmSrc CATSTR <x>,TempSS statement builds a new macro text string named XmmSrc whose value is the concatenation of the letter *x* and the text value of TempSS. Thus, using macro ReducePD_M with YmmSrc equal to *YMM12* generates a new macro text string named XmmSrc whose value is *XMM12*. It is important to keep in mind that neither SUBSTR nor CATSTR is an executable x86-64 instruction; they are MASM operators that manipulate macro text strings.

The first executable instruction of macro ReducePD_M, vextractf128 XmmTemp,YmmSrc,1, copies the two high-order double-precision floating-point elements of register YmmSrc to register XmmTemp. The next instruction, vaddpd XmmDes,XmmTemp,XmmSrc, sums the double-precision floating-point elements in registers XmmTemp and XmmSrc. This is followed by a vhaddpd XmmDes,XmmDes,XmmDes instruction that yields the final sum in the low-order element of XmmDes.

Following its prologue, function CalcLeastSquares_Aavx2() sets the slope m (RCX) and intercept b (RDX) to 0.0. Setting these values to 0.0 allows the caller to determine if an error occurred during execution of CalcLeastSquares_Aavx2() (or if all values in array y are the same). The next block of code validates argument value n for size and array pointers x and y for proper alignment. This is followed by a code block that initializes packed sum variables sum_x (YMM12), sum_y (YMM13), sum_xx (YMM14), and sum_xy (YMM15) to all zeros.

The first code block in Loop1 verifies that there are at least four (NSE) elements remaining to be processed. Following this check, CalcLeastSquares_Aavx2() uses the instruction pair vmovapd ymm0,ymmword ptr [r8+rax*8] and vmovapd ymm1,ymmword ptr [r9+rax*8] to load x[i:i+3] and y[i:i+3] into registers YMM0 and YMM1, respectively. The next two instructions, vaddpd ymm12,ymm12,ymm0 and vaddpd ymm13,ymm13,ymm1, update sum_x and sum_y. This is followed by a vfmadd231pd ymm14,ymm0,ymm0 (Fused Multiply-Add of DPFP Values) instruction that updates sum_xx. More specifically, this instruction multiplies the double-precision floating-point elements in the second operand (YMM0) by the third operand (YMM0); it then adds these products to the elements in the first operand (YMM14) and saves the result in the destination operand (YMM14). The ensuing vfmadd231pd ymm15,ymm0,ymm1 instruction updates sum_xy.

Before continuing with the source code in Listing 16-1, a few words regarding x86 FMA instruction mnemonics are warranted. Each standard x86 FMA instruction[1] mnemonic employs a three-digit operand ordering scheme that specifies which operands to use for multiplication and addition (or subtraction). The first digit specifies the operand to use as the multiplicand; the second digit specifies the operand to use as the multiplier; and the third digit specifies the operand that the product is added to (or subtracted from). Like other x86 assembly language instructions, the execution result of an FMA instruction is always saved in the left-most (or destination) operand. Consider, for example, the instruction vfmadd132sd xmm10,xmm11,xmm12 (Fused Multiply-Add of Scalar DPFP Values). In this example, operand 1 is XMM10, operand 2 is XMM11, and operand 3 is XMM12. During execution of this instruction, the processor calculates xmm10[63:0] * xmm12[63:0] + xmm11[63:0]; it then saves this result in xmm10[63:0]. All FMA instructions support multiple operand orderings. For example, a function can also use vfmadd213sd and vfmadd231sd to perform scalar FMA arithmetic using double-precision floating-point values. For some algorithms, having multiple instruction mnemonics for the same FMA operation is advantageous since it reduces the number of register-to-register transfers. Appendix B contains a list of reference manuals published by AMD and Intel that you can consult for more information regarding other x86 FMA instructions.

Back to the code in Listing 16-1. Following execution of Loop1, CalcLeastSquares_Aavx2() uses macro ReducePD_M to reduce sum_x, sum_y, sum_xx, and sum_xy to scalar values. For-loop Loop2 handles any residual elements using scalar versions of the same instructions that Loop1 used. The first code block that follows label CalcLS calculates the common denominator for the least-squares slope and intercept. The ensuing code block contains assembly language instructions that verify the value of the denominator (denom). This block begins with a mov rax,7fffffffffffffffh instruction that loads register RAX with the mask value needed to compute a double-precision floating-point absolute value. It should be noted that the mov instruction is the only x86-64 assembly language instruction that can be used with a 64-bit wide immediate operand. All other instructions only support 8-, 16-, or 32-bit wide immediate operands, and these values are zero- or sign-extended if necessary. The next two instructions, vmovq xmm1,rax and vandpd xmm4,xmm0,xmm1, calculate fabs(denom). The ensuing instruction pair, vcomisd xmm4,[g_LsEpsilon] and jb Done, skips over the remaining least-squares calculating code if denom < fabs(g_LsEpsilon) is true.

The remaining code in CalcLeastSquares_Aavx2() is straightforward scalar double-precision floating-point arithmetic that calculates the final least-squares slope and intercept point. These values are then saved to the buffers pointed to by RCX and RDX. Here are the results for source code example Ch16_01:

```
Results from AvxCalcLeastSquares_Cpp
   slope:      -1.00874909
   intercept:  196.22610714

Results from AvxCalcLeastSquares_Aavx2
   slope:      -1.00874909
   intercept:  196.22610714
```

---

[1] Some AMD processors include FMA instructions that require four operands. These instructions are not discussed in this book.

# Floating-Point Matrices

In Chapter 5, you learned how to implement several common matrix calculating functions using C++ SIMD intrinsic functions. In this section, you will learn how to code some of these operations using x86-64 assembly language and AVX2 instructions. The first source code example covers matrix multiplication, while the second example highlights matrix multiplication using 4 × 4 matrices. The final example of this section demonstrates matrix-vector multiplication.

## Matrix Multiplication

The next source code example, named Ch16_02, illustrates how to perform single-precision floating-point matrix multiplication using AVX2 instructions. Listing 16-2 shows the assembly language source code for example Ch16_02, which is a redo of example Ch05_02. Before reviewing the source code in Listing 16-2, you may want to quickly revisit the matrix multiplication equations and diagrams (Figures 5-1, 5-2, and 5-3) presented in Chapter 5 for source code example Ch05_02.

***Listing 16-2.*** Example Ch16_02

```
;---------------------------------------------------
;                   Ch16_02_fasm.asm
;---------------------------------------------------

; Data for vmaskmovps masks
            .const
mask0       dword 8 dup(0)
mask1       dword 1 dup(80000000h), 7 dup(0)
mask2       dword 2 dup(80000000h), 6 dup(0)
mask3       dword 3 dup(80000000h), 5 dup(0)
mask4       dword 4 dup(80000000h), 4 dup(0)
mask5       dword 5 dup(80000000h), 3 dup(0)
mask6       dword 6 dup(80000000h), 2 dup(0)
mask7       dword 7 dup(80000000h), 1 dup(0)


;-------------------------------------------------------------------------
; extern "C" void MatrixMulF32_Aavx2(float* c, const float* a, const float* b,
;    const size_t* sizes);
;-------------------------------------------------------------------------

NSE     equ 8                               ;num_simd_elements
NSE_MOD equ 07h                             ;mask to calculate num_residual_cols

        .code
MatrixMulF32_Aavx2 proc frame
        push rbx
        .pushreg rbx
        push rsi
        .pushreg rsi
        push rdi
        .pushreg rdi
        push r12
```

```
        .pushreg r12
        push r13
        .pushreg r13
        push r14
        .pushreg r14
        push r15
        .pushreg r15
        .endprolog

; Load matrix sizes
        mov r13,qword ptr [r9]               ;r13 = c_nrows
        mov r14,qword ptr [r9+8]             ;r14 = c_ncols (also b_ncols)
        mov r15,qword ptr [r9+16]            ;r15 = a_ncols

; Load mask for vmaskmovps instruction
        mov r12,r14                          ;r12 = c_ncols
        and r12,NSE_MOD                      ;num_residual_cols = c_ncols % NSE

        mov rax,r12                          ;rax = num_residual_cols
        shl rax,5                            ;rax = num_residual_cols * 32
        mov r11,offset mask0                 ;r11 = address of mask0
        add rax,r11                          ;rax = address of maskX
        vmovdqu ymm5,ymmword ptr [rax]       ;ymm5 = maskX for vmaskmovps

        mov rax,-1                           ;rax = i

; General-purpose registers used in code below
;   rax     i                                   r9      j
;   rbx     matrix a element pointer (p_aa)     r10     k
;   rcx     matrix c                            r11     scratch
;   rdx     matrix a                            r12     num_residual_cols
;   rsi     matrix b element pointer (p_bb)     r13     c_nrows
;   rdi     &a[i][0]                            r15     a_ncols
;   r8      matrix b

; Repeat for each row in c
        align 16
Loop1:  inc rax                              ;i += 1
        cmp rax,r13
        jae Done                             ;jump if i >= c_nrows

        mov rdi,rdx                          ;rdi = &a[i][0]
        lea rdx,[rdx+r15*4]                  ;rdx = &a[i+1][0]
        xor r9,r9                            ;r9 = j

; Repeat while there are at least NSE columns in current row of c
        align 16
Loop2:  lea r11,[r9+NSE]                     ;r11 = j + NSE
        cmp r11,r14
        ja ChkRes                            ;jump if j + NSE > c_ncols
```

```
        mov rbx,rdi                               ;rbx = &a[i][0]
        lea rsi,[r8+r9*4]                         ;rsi = &b[0][j]
        vxorps ymm2,ymm2,ymm2                     ;initialize packed c_vals
        mov r10,r15                               ;r10 = a_ncols

; Calculate c[i][j:j+7]
        align 16
Loop3a: vbroadcastss ymm0,real4 ptr [rbx]        ;broadcast a[i][k]
        vfmadd231ps ymm2,ymm0,ymmword ptr [rsi]   ;ymm2 += a[i][k] * b[k][j:j+7]

        add rbx,4                                 ;rbx = &a[i][k+1]
        lea rsi,[rsi+r14*4]                       ;rsi = &b[k+1][j]
        dec r10                                   ;k -= 1
        jnz Loop3a                                ;repeat until done

; Save c[i][j:j+7]
        vmovups ymmword ptr[rcx],ymm2             ;save c[i][j:j+7]

        add r9,NSE                                ;j += num_simd_elements
        add rcx,NSE*4                             ;rcx = &c[i][j+8] (next SIMD group)
        jmp Loop2

ChkRes: test r12,r12                              ;num_residual_cols == 0?
        jz Loop1                                  ;jump if yes

        mov rbx,rdi                               ;rbx = &a[i][0]
        lea rsi,[r8+r9*4]                         ;rsi = &b[0][j]
        vxorps ymm2,ymm2,ymm2                     ;initialize packed c_vals
        mov r10,r15                               ;r10 = a_ncols

; Calculate c[i][j:j+NRC] (NRC is num_residual_cols)
        align 16
Loop3b: vbroadcastss ymm0,real4 ptr [rbx]        ;broadcast a[i][k]
        vmaskmovps ymm1,ymm5,ymmword ptr [rsi]    ;load b[k][j:j+NRC]
        vfmadd231ps ymm2,ymm1,ymm0                ;update product sums

        add rbx,4                                 ;rbx = &a[i][k+1]
        lea rsi,[rsi+r14*4]                       ;rsi = &b[k+1][j]
        dec r10                                   ;k -= 1
        jnz Loop3b                                ;repeat until done

; Save c[i][j:j+NRC]
        vmaskmovps ymmword ptr[rcx],ymm5,ymm2     ;save c[i][j:j+NRC]
        lea rcx,[rcx+r12*4]                       ;rcx = &c[i+1][0] (next SIMD group)
        jmp Loop1

Done:   vzeroupper
        pop r15
        pop r14
        pop r13
        pop r12
```

```
        pop rdi
        pop rsi
        pop rbx
        ret
MatrixMulF32_Aavx2 endp
        end
```

Recall from earlier source code examples that the address of an element in a C++ matrix can be calculated using integer multiplication and addition. For example, to calculate the address of matrix element a[i][j], one can use the expression &a[i * a_ncols + k]. In source code example Ch05_02, the for-loops in the C++ SIMD function MatrixMulF32_Iavx2() employed this technique since it is simple to code and easy to understand. Another alternative is to use pointers and pointer arithmetic in the for-loops for matrix element addresses. The advantage of this approach is that one can exploit the fact that constant offsets exist between matrix elements in different rows but in the same column (constant offsets also exist between consecutive elements in the same row). For example, the address of matrix element a[i+1][j] is &a[(i +1) * a_ncols + k], and the index offset difference between this element and element a[i][k] is a_ncols. When emitting code for a for-loop that references matrix elements using indices, a C++ compiler will often utilize pointer addition instead of integer multiplications and additions since eliminating the multiplications yields faster code. The assembly language source code in Listing 16-2 employs this same technique as you will soon see.

The assembly language source code in Listing 16-2 begins with a .const section that contains mask values for the vmaskmovps (Conditional SIMD Packed Loads and Stores) instruction. The operation performed by this instruction is explained later in this section. Each maskX definition in the .const section contains eight doubleword values. The text dup is a MASM operator that performs both storage allocation and data initialization. For example, the statement mask0 dword 8 dup(0) defines a storage location named mask0 and allocates space for eight doubleword values; it also initializes each doubleword value to 0x00000000. Then the next statement, mask1 dword 1 dup(80000000h), 7 dup(0), allocates storage space for one doubleword and initializes it to 0x80000000; this statement also allocates storage space for seven doubleword values and initializes these values to 0x00000000.

Function MatrixMulF32_Aavx2() begins its execution with a series of push instructions that save all used nonvolatile registers on the stack. Function MatrixMulF32_Aavx2() uses explicit push instructions and assembler directives instead of the macros CreateFrame_M, SaveXmmRegs_M, etc., since it does not use any nonvolatile SIMD registers or require any local stack space. Following its prologue, the matrix size values c_nrows, c_ncols (also b_ncols), and a_ncols are loaded into registers R13, R14, and R15 using a series of mov instructions. The next code block begins with the instruction pair mov r12,r14 and and r12,NSE_MOD, which calculates num_residual_cols = c_ncols % NSE. The next code block contains a series of instructions that load the mask for vmaskmovps into register YMM5. Note that this is the same operation that function MatrixMulF32_Iavx2() employed as part of its initialization code in source code example Ch05_02.

Immediately before the label Loop1 is the statement align 16. This assembler directive positions the ensuing inc rax instruction on a 16-byte boundary. The reason for doing this is that execution of a for-loop is often faster when the target of a jump instruction is aligned on a 16-byte boundary. The drawback of using the align directive in this manner is a slight increase in code size since the assembler must insert one or more "no operation" instructions to perform the alignment. Immediately following the inc rax instruction is the instruction pair cmp rax,r13 and jae Done, which terminates Loop1 when i >= c_nrows is true. The subsequent code block begins with a mov rdi,rdx instruction that loads &a[i][0] into register RDI. This is followed by a lea rdx,[rdx+r15*4] instruction that loads &a[i+1][0] into register RDX for the next iteration of Loop1. Note that R15 contains a_ncols; multiplying this value by 4 and adding it to RDX yields the address of &a[i+1][0]. Following the lea instruction is an xor r9,r9 instruction that initializes Loop2 index variable j to zero.

For-loop Loop2 begins each iteration with a `lea r11,[r9+NSE]` instruction that loads `j + NSE` into register R11. On x86 processors, the `lea` instruction is often used to perform add operations like this since it is usually faster than using two distinct instructions (e.g., `mov r11,r9` and `add r11,NSE`). If `j + NSE > c_ncols` is false, the ensuing code block performs several requisite initializations for Loop3a. Note that registers RBX and RSI are initialized with the addresses of matrix elements `a[i][0]` and `b[0][j]`, respectively. For-loop Loop3a, which repeats c_ncols times, calculates products for matrix elements `c[i][j:j+7]`. This for-loop begins each iteration with a `vbroadcastss ymm0,real4 ptr [rbx]` instruction that broadcasts `a[i][k]` to each element position in YMM0. The next instruction, `vfmadd231ps ymm2,ymm0,ymmword ptr [rsi]`, calculates `c[i][j:j+7] += a[i][k] * b[k][j:j+7]`. Following the FMA operation, the add `rbx,4` instruction updates RBX so that it points to element `&a[i][k+1]`. Execution of the ensuing `lea rsi,[rsi+r14*4]` instruction sets RSI to `&b[k+1][j]`. The `vmovups ymmword ptr[rcx],ymm2` instruction that follows Loop3a saves elements `c[i][j:j+7]`.

Following completion of Loop2, `MatrixMulF32_Aavx2()` uses the instruction pair `test r12,r12` and `jz Loop1` to skip Loop3b if `num_residual_cols == 0` is true. For-loop Loop3b computes products for matrix elements `c[i][j:j+NRC]` (NRC is num_residual_columns) using the same basic technique as Loop3a. Note that this for-loop uses a `vmaskmovps ymm1,ymm5,ymmword ptr [rsi]` instruction to load matrix elements `b[k][j:j+NRC]`. This vmaskmovps instruction only loads an element into register YMM1 if the most significant bit of the corresponding element in YMM5 is set to 1; otherwise, zero is loaded. For-loop Loop3a also uses a `vmaskmovps ymmword ptr[rcx],ymm5,ymm2` instruction to save matrix elements `c[i][j:j+NRC]`. Note that when using vmaskmovps to perform a store, element positions in the destination memory buffer are not altered if the corresponding element mask bit is set to zero. Here are the results for source code example Ch16_02:

```
Results for MatrixMulF32
Matrix compare passed
Results saved to file Ch16_02_MatrixMulF32_OXYGEN4.txt

Running benchmark function MatrixMulF32_bm - please wait
Benchmark times save to file Ch16_02_MatrixMulF32_bm_OXYGEN4.csv
```

Table 16-1 shows some benchmark timing measurements for source code example Ch16_02. These measurements were made using 250 × 250 matrices. The right-most column in this table shows the measurements for function `MatrixMulF32_Iavx2()` from Table 5-1. For matrix-matrix multiplication algorithm, the timing measurements for functions `MatrixMulF32_Aavx2()` and `MatrixMulF32_Iavx2()` are essentially the same.

*Table 16-1.* *Matrix Multiplication (Single-Precision) Execution Times (Microseconds)*

| CPU | MatrixMulF32_Cpp() | MatrixMulF32_Aavx2() | MatrixMulF32_Iavx2() |
|---|---|---|---|
| Intel Core i7-8700K | 12346 | 1596 | 1606 |
| Intel Core i5-11600K | 10379 | 1376 | 1380 |

# Matrix (4 × 4) Multiplication

The next source code example, named Ch16_03, illustrates how to perform 4 × 4 matrix multiplication using assembly language. It also demonstrates some of the performance advantages of using FMA arithmetic. Listing 16-3 shows the source code for example Ch16_03. The assembly language source code in this listing calculates the same equations that were defined in Figure 5-4. You may want to review these equations before examining the source code in Listing 16-3.

***Listing 16-3.*** Example Ch16_03

```
;--------------------------------------------------
;                 Ch16_03_fasm.asm
;--------------------------------------------------


;---------------------------------------------------------------------------
; Mat4x4MulCalcRowF32a_M macro
;
; Description:   This macro is used to compute one row of a 4x4 matrix
;                multiply using FMA instructions.
;
; Registers:     xmm0 = row b[0][]
;                xmm1 = row b[1][]
;                xmm2 = row b[2][]
;                xmm3 = row b[3][]
;                rcx = matrix c pointer
;                rdx = matrix a pointer
;                xmm4, xmm5 = scratch registers
;---------------------------------------------------------------------------

Mat4x4MulCalcRowF32a_M macro disp
        vbroadcastss xmm5,real4 ptr [rdx+disp]          ;broadcast a[i][0]
        vmulps xmm4,xmm5,xmm0                            ;xmm4  = a[i][0] * b[0][]

        vbroadcastss xmm5,real4 ptr [rdx+disp+4]         ;broadcast a[i][1]
        vfmadd231ps xmm4,xmm5,xmm1                       ;xmm4 += a[i][1] * b[1][]

        vbroadcastss xmm5,real4 ptr [rdx+disp+8]         ;broadcast a[i][2]
        vfmadd231ps xmm4,xmm5,xmm2                       ;xmm4 += a[i][2] * b[2][]

        vbroadcastss xmm5,real4 ptr [rdx+disp+12]        ;broadcast a[i][3]
        vfmadd231ps xmm4,xmm5,xmm3                       ;xmm4 += a[i][3] * b[3][]

        vmovaps xmmword ptr [rcx+disp],xmm4              ;save row c[i]
        endm

;---------------------------------------------------------------------------
; Mat4x4MulCalcRowF32b_M macro
;
; Description:   This macro is used to compute one row of a 4x4 matrix
;                multiply sans FMA instructions.
;
; Registers:     xmm0 = row b[0][]
;                xmm1 = row b[1][]
;                xmm2 = row b[2][]
;                xmm3 = row b[3][]
;                rcx = matrix c pointer
;                rdx = matrix a pointer
;                xmm4, xmm5 = scratch registers
;---------------------------------------------------------------------------
```

```
Mat4x4MulCalcRowF32b_M macro disp
        vbroadcastss xmm5,real4 ptr [rdx+disp]        ;broadcast a[i][0]
        vmulps xmm4,xmm5,xmm0                         ;xmm5  = a[i][0] * b[0][]

        vbroadcastss xmm5,real4 ptr [rdx+disp+4]      ;broadcast a[i][1]
        vmulps  xmm5,xmm5,xmm1                        ;xmm5  = a[i][1] * b[1][]
        vaddps xmm4,xmm5,xmm4                         ;xmm4 += a[i][1] * b[1][]

        vbroadcastss xmm5,real4 ptr [rdx+disp+8]      ;broadcast a[i][2]
        vmulps xmm5,xmm5,xmm2                         ;xmm5  = a[i][2] * b[2][]
        vaddps xmm4,xmm5,xmm4                         ;xmm4 += a[i][2] * b[2][]

        vbroadcastss xmm5,real4 ptr [rdx+disp+12]     ;broadcast a[i][3]
        vmulps  xmm5,xmm5,xmm3                        ;xmm5  = a[i][3] * b[3][]
        vaddps xmm4,xmm5,xmm4                         ;xmm4 += a[i][3] * b[3][]

        vmovaps xmmword ptr [rcx+disp],xmm4           ;save row c[i]
        endm

;---------------------------------------------------------------------------
; extern "C" void MatrixMul4x4F32a_Aavx2(float* c, const float* a, const float* b);
;---------------------------------------------------------------------------

        .code
MatrixMul4x4F32a_Aavx2 proc

; Load matrix b into xmm0 - xmm3
        vmovaps ymm0,ymmword ptr [r8]      ;xmm0 = row b[0][]
        vextractf128 xmm1,ymm0,1           ;xmm1 = row b[1][]
        vmovaps ymm2,ymmword ptr [r8+32]   ;xmm2 = row b[2][]
        vextractf128 xmm3,ymm2,1           ;xmm3 = row b[3][]

; Calculate matrix product c = a * b
        Mat4x4MulCalcRowF32a_M 0           ;calculate row c[0][]
        Mat4x4MulCalcRowF32a_M 16          ;calculate row c[1][]
        Mat4x4MulCalcRowF32a_M 32          ;calculate row c[2][]
        Mat4x4MulCalcRowF32a_M 48          ;calculate row c[3][]

        vzeroupper
        ret
MatrixMul4x4F32a_Aavx2 endp

;---------------------------------------------------------------------------
; extern "C" void MatrixMul4x4F32b_Aavx2(float* c, const float* a, const float* b);
;---------------------------------------------------------------------------

MatrixMul4x4F32b_Aavx2 proc
; Load matrix b into xmm0 - xmm3
        vmovaps ymm0,ymmword ptr [r8]      ;xmm0 = row b[0][]
        vextractf128 xmm1,ymm0,1           ;xmm1 = row b[1][]
```

```
        vmovaps ymm2,ymmword ptr [r8+32]      ;xmm2 = row b[2][]
        vextractf128 xmm3,ymm2,1              ;xmm3 = row b[3][]

; Calculate matrix product c = a * b
        Mat4x4MulCalcRowF32b_M 0              ;calculate row c[0][]
        Mat4x4MulCalcRowF32b_M 16             ;calculate row c[1][]
        Mat4x4MulCalcRowF32b_M 32             ;calculate row c[2][]
        Mat4x4MulCalcRowF32b_M 48             ;calculate row c[3][]

        vzeroupper
        ret
MatrixMul4x4F32b_Aavx2 endp
        end
```

Listing 16-3 opens with the definition of a macro named Mat4x4MulCalcRowF32a_M. This macro calculates one row of a 4 × 4 matrix multiplication using FMA instructions. Note that macro Mat4x4MulCalcRowF32a_M requires a single argument named disp. This argument corresponds to the displacement for row i of matrix a. The code emitted by macro Mat4x4MulCalcRowF32a_M employs a series of vbroadcastss and vfmadd231ps instructions to calculate matrix elements c[i][j:j+3]. Note that a vmovaps xmmword ptr [rcx+disp],xmm4 is used to save each row in matrix c. Unlike the matrix multiplication function in source code example Ch16_02, each row of a 4 × 4 matrix in this example is properly aligned on a double quadword boundary.

Following the definition of macro Mat4x4MulCalcRowF32a_M is another macro definition named Mat4x4MulCalcRowF32b_M. The code emitted by this macro differs from Mat4x4MulCalcRowF32a_M in that it uses distinct vmulps and vaddps instructions instead of a single vfmadd231ps instruction. The purpose of this macro is to carry out a simple performance experiment as you will soon see.

Following the macro definitions in Listing 16-3 is the assembly language code for function MatrixMul4x4F32a_Aavx2(), which calculates the product of two 4 × 4 matrices. This function begins with a vmovaps ymm0,ymmword ptr [r8] instruction that loads rows 0 and 1 of matrix b into register YMM0. The ensuing vextractf128 xmm1,ymm0,1 instruction copies the four high-order single-precision elements in YMM0 (matrix b row 1) to register XMM1. Execution of this instruction does not alter the four low-order single-precision elements of YMM0 (i.e., register XMM0), which holds matrix b row 0. Rows 2 and 3 of matrix b are then loaded into registers XMM2 and XMM3 using a similar sequence of instructions. Following the loading of matrix b, function MatrixMul4x4F32a_Aavx2() utilizes macro Mat4x4MulCalcRowF32a_M four times to calculate the matrix product c = a * b. Note that each use of macro Mat4x4MulCalcRowF32a_M uses a different displacement value, which corresponds to the row offset of matrix a.

The final function is Listing 16-3 is named MatrixMul4x4F32b_Aavx2(). This function is almost identical to the previous function but uses macro Mat4x4MulCalcRowF32b_M to perform the 4 × 4 matrix multiplication. Here are the results for source code example Ch16_03:

```
Results for MatrixMul4x4F32
Matrix a
        10.0           11.0           12.0           13.0
        20.0           21.0           22.0           23.0
        30.0           31.0           32.0           33.0
        40.0           41.0           42.0           43.0

Matrix b
        100.0          101.0          102.0          103.0
        200.0          201.0          202.0          203.0
        300.0          301.0          302.0          303.0
        400.0          401.0          402.0          403.0
```

```
Matrix c1
      12000.0         12046.0         12092.0         12138.0
      22000.0         22086.0         22172.0         22258.0
      32000.0         32126.0         32252.0         32378.0
      42000.0         42166.0         42332.0         42498.0

Matrix c2
      12000.0         12046.0         12092.0         12138.0
      22000.0         22086.0         22172.0         22258.0
      32000.0         32126.0         32252.0         32378.0
      42000.0         42166.0         42332.0         42498.0

Matrix c3
      12000.0         12046.0         12092.0         12138.0
      22000.0         22086.0         22172.0         22258.0
      32000.0         32126.0         32252.0         32378.0
      42000.0         42166.0         42332.0         42498.0

Matrix compare passed

Running benchmark function MatrixMul4x4F32_bm - please wait
.....................................................
Benchmark times save to file Ch16_03_MatrixMul4x4F32_bm_OXYGEN4.csv
```

Table 16-2 shows the benchmark timing measurements for source code example Ch16_03. The arrangement of this table differs from previous benchmark measurement tables since there are four function measurements for each processor. In Table 16-2, the measurements for function MatrixMulF32_Iavx2() were copied from Table 5-2. Note that there are meaningful performance gains between functions MatrixMul4x4F32a_Aavx2() (which used FMA instructions) and MatrixMul4x4F32b_Aavx2() (which used distinct multiply and add instructions).

***Table 16-2.*** *Matrix Multiplication (4 × 4, Single-Precision) Execution Times (Microseconds), 1,000,000 Multiplications*

| Function Name | Intel Core i7-8700K | Intel Core i5-11600K |
|---|---|---|
| MatrixMul4x4F32_Cpp() | 15344 | 14256 |
| MatrixMul4x4F32a_Aavx2() (FMA) | 3080 | 2468 |
| MatrixMul4x4F32b_Aavx2() (no FMA) | 3468 | 2878 |
| MatrixMul4x4F32_Iavx2() | 3227 | 2734 |

# Matrix (4 × 4) Vector Multiplication

Source code example Ch05_06 explained how to perform matrix-vector multiplication using a 4 × 4 matrix and array of 4 × 1 vectors. Listing 16-4 shows the assembly language source code for example Ch16_04, which performs the same matrix-vector multiplications. Before examining the source code in Listing 16-4, you may want to take another look at the equations shown in Figure 5-5 and the definition of structure Vec4x1_F32 in Listing 5-6 since both are used again in this example.

**Listing 16-4.** Example Ch16_04

```
;---------------------------------------------------
;                   Ch16_04_fasm.asm
;---------------------------------------------------


;------------------------------------------------------------------------
; Mat4x4TransposeF32_M macro
;
; Description:   This macro transposes a 4x4 matrix of single-precision
;                floating-point values.
;
;   Input Matrix                        Output Matrix
;   ------------------------------------------------------
;   xmm0    a3 a2 a1 a0                 xmm0    d0 c0 b0 a0
;   xmm1    b3 b2 b1 b0                 xmm1    d1 c1 b1 a1
;   xmm2    c3 c2 c1 c0                 xmm2    d2 c2 b2 a2
;   xmm3    d3 d2 d1 d0                 xmm3    d3 c3 b3 a3
;
; Scratch registers: xmm4, xmm5
;------------------------------------------------------------------------

Mat4x4TransposeF32_M macro
        vunpcklps xmm4,xmm0,xmm1             ;xmm4 = b1 a1 b0 a0
        vunpckhps xmm0,xmm0,xmm1             ;xmm0 = b3 a3 b2 a2
        vunpcklps xmm5,xmm2,xmm3             ;xmm5 = d1 c1 d0 c0
        vunpckhps xmm1,xmm2,xmm3             ;xmm1 = d3 c3 d2 c2

        vmovlhps xmm2,xmm0,xmm1              ;xmm2 = d2 c2 b2 a2
        vmovhlps xmm3,xmm1,xmm0              ;xmm3 = d3 c3 b3 a3
        vmovlhps xmm0,xmm4,xmm5              ;xmm0 = d0 c0 b0 a0
        vmovhlps xmm1,xmm5,xmm4              ;xmm1 = d1 c1 b1 a1
        endm

;------------------------------------------------------------------------
; extern "C" void MatVecMulF32_Aavx2(Vec4x1_F32* vec_b, const float* m,
;   const Vec4x1_F32* vec_a, size_t num_vec);
;------------------------------------------------------------------------

        .code
MatVecMulF32_Aavx2 proc

; Validate arguments
        test r9,r9
        jz Done                         ;jump if num_vec == 0
        test rcx,1fh
        jnz Done                        ;jump if vec_b not 32b aligned
        test rdx,1fh
        jnz Done                        ;jump if m not 32b aligned
        test r8,1fh
        jnz Done                        ;jump if vec_a 32b aligned
```

```
; Initialize
        mov rax,-16                             ;array offset
        vmovaps ymm0,ymmword ptr [rdx]          ;xmm0 = m row 0
        vextractf128 xmm1,ymm0,1                ;xmm1 = m ro1 1
        vmovaps ymm2,ymmword ptr [rdx+32]       ;xmm2 = m row 2
        vextractf128 xmm3,ymm2,1                ;xmm3 = m row 3

; Transpose m
        Mat4x4TransposeF32_M

; Calculate matrix-vector products
        align 16
Loop1:  add rax,16

        vbroadcastss xmm5,real4 ptr [r8+rax]    ;xmm5 = vec_a[i].W
        vmulps xmm4,xmm0,xmm5                    ;xmm4  = m_T row 0 * W vals

        vbroadcastss xmm5,real4 ptr [r8+rax+4]  ;xmm5 = vec_a[i].X
        vfmadd231ps xmm4,xmm1,xmm5               ;xmm4 += m_T row 1 * X vals

        vbroadcastss xmm5,real4 ptr [r8+rax+8]  ;xmm5 = vec_a[i].Y
        vfmadd231ps xmm4,xmm2,xmm5               ;xmm4 += m_T row 2 * Y vals

        vbroadcastss xmm5,real4 ptr [r8+rax+12] ;xmm5 = vec_a[i].Z
        vfmadd231ps xmm4,xmm3,xmm5               ;xmm4 += m_T row 3 * Z vals

        vmovaps xmmword ptr [rcx+rax],xmm4       ;save vec_b[i]

        dec r9                                   ;num_vec -= 1
        jnz Loop1                                ;repeat until done

Done:   vzeroupper
        ret
MatVecMulF32_Aavx2 endp
        end
```

Listing 16-4 commences with the definition of a macro named Mat4x4TransposeF32_M. This macro emits code that calculates the transpose of a 4 × 4 matrix. Macro Mat4x4TransposeF32_M requires rows 0–3 of the original matrix to be loaded into registers XMM0–XMM3, respectively, prior to its use. Following the transpose operation, registers XMM0–XMM3 contain the transposed matrix. Note that macro Mat4x4TransposeF32_M includes instructions that use registers XMM4 and XMM5 to hold intermediate results.

Figure 16-1 illustrates the sequence of instructions used to calculate the matrix transpose. The technique used here matches the one used in example Ch05_06. The first instruction, vunpcklps xmm4,xmm0,xmm1 (Unpack and Interleave Low Packed SPFP Values), interleaves the low-order single-precision floating-point elements of source operands XMM0 and XMM1 and saves the result in register XMM4. Then the next instruction, vunpckhps xmm0,xmm0,xmm1 (Unpack and Interleave High Packed SPFP Values), interleaves the high-order elements of registers XMM0 and XMM1. The ensuing instruction pair, vunpcklps xmm5,xmm2,xmm3 and vunpckhps xmm1,xmm2,xmm3, performs the same interleave operation using the elements for rows 2 and 3.

$$\mathbf{A} = \begin{bmatrix} 2 & 7 & 8 & 3 \\ 11 & 14 & 16 & 10 \\ 24 & 21 & 27 & 29 \\ 31 & 34 & 38 & 33 \end{bmatrix} \qquad \mathbf{A}^T = \begin{bmatrix} 2 & 11 & 24 & 31 \\ 7 & 14 & 21 & 34 \\ 8 & 16 & 27 & 38 \\ 3 & 10 & 29 & 33 \end{bmatrix}$$

Initial values

| 3.0 | 8.0 | 7.0 | 2.0 | XMM0 (row 0 of A) |
|---|---|---|---|---|

| 10.0 | 16.0 | 14.0 | 11.0 | XMM1 (row 1 of A) |
|---|---|---|---|---|

| 29.0 | 27.0 | 21.0 | 24.0 | XMM2 (row 2 of A) |
|---|---|---|---|---|

| 33.0 | 38.0 | 34.0 | 31.0 | XMM3 (row 3 of A) |
|---|---|---|---|---|

vunpcklps xmm4,xmm0,xmm1

| 14.0 | 7.0 | 11.0 | 2.0 | XMM4 |
|---|---|---|---|---|

vunpckhps xmm0,xmm0,xmm1

| 10.0 | 3.0 | 16.0 | 8.0 | XMM0 |
|---|---|---|---|---|

vunpcklps xmm5,xmm2,xmm3

| 34.0 | 21.0 | 31.0 | 24.0 | XMM5 |
|---|---|---|---|---|

vunpckhps xmm1,xmm2,xmm3

| 33.0 | 29.0 | 38.0 | 27.0 | XMM1 |
|---|---|---|---|---|

vmovlhps xmm2,xmm0,xmm1

| 38.0 | 27.0 | 16.0 | 8.0 | XMM2 (row 2 of A^T) |
|---|---|---|---|---|

vmovhlps xmm3,xmm1,xmm0

| 33.0 | 29.0 | 10.0 | 3.0 | XMM3 (row 3 of A^T) |
|---|---|---|---|---|

vmovlhps xmm0,xmm4,xmm5

| 31.0 | 24.0 | 11.0 | 2.0 | XMM0 (row 0 of A^T) |
|---|---|---|---|---|

vmovhlps xmm1,xmm5,xmm4

| 34.0 | 21.0 | 14.0 | 7.0 | XMM1 (row 1 of A^T) |
|---|---|---|---|---|

***Figure 16-1.*** *Transposition of a 4 × 4 matrix (single-precision floating-point) using* vunpcklps, vunpckhps, *vmovlhps, and* vmovhlps *vmovhlps*

Following the interleave instructions are a series of vmovlhps (Move Packed SPFP Values Low to High) and vmovhlps (Move Packed SPFP Values High to Low) instructions. Execution of the vmovlhps xmm2,xmm0,xmm1 instruction copies the two low-order single-precision floating-point elements of XMM0 (bits 63:0) to the same element positions of register XMM2 (bits 63:0) as shown in Figure 16-1. This instruction also copies the two low-order elements of XMM1 (bits 63:0) to the two high-order element positions of XMM2 (bits 127:64). Following execution of the vmovlhps xmm2,xmm0,xmm1 instruction, register XMM2 contains row 2 of the transposed matrix.

The next instruction, vmovhlps xmm3,xmm1,xmm0, copies the two high-order elements of XMM0 (bits 127:64) to the two low-order element positions of register XMM3 (bits 63:0). Execution of this instruction also copies the two high-order elements of register XMM1 (bits 127:64) to the two high-order element positions of register XMM3 (bits 127:64), which yields row 3 of the transposed matrix. The ensuing instruction pair, vmovlhps xmm0,xmm4,xmm5 and vmovhlps xmm1,xmm5,xmm4, computes rows 0 and 1 of the transposed matrix.

Function MatVecMulF32_Aavx2() begins with a series of instructions that validate num_vec for size and the various argument pointers for proper alignment. Following argument validation, the rows of matrix m are loaded into registers XMM0–XMM3 using the instructions vmovaps and vextractf128. The transpose of matrix m is then calculated using the previously defined macro Mat4x4TransposeF32_M.

Each iteration of Loop1 begins with an add rax,16 instruction that updates register RAX, which contains the displacement for vector arrays vec_a and vec_b. The next instruction, vbroadcastss xmm5,real4 ptr [r8+rax], broadcasts vector component vec_a[i].W to each element position of register XMM5. This is followed by a vmulps xmm4,xmm0,xmm5 instruction that multiplies row 0 of the transposed matrix (or column 0 of the original matrix) by vec_a[i].W as shown in Figure 16-2.

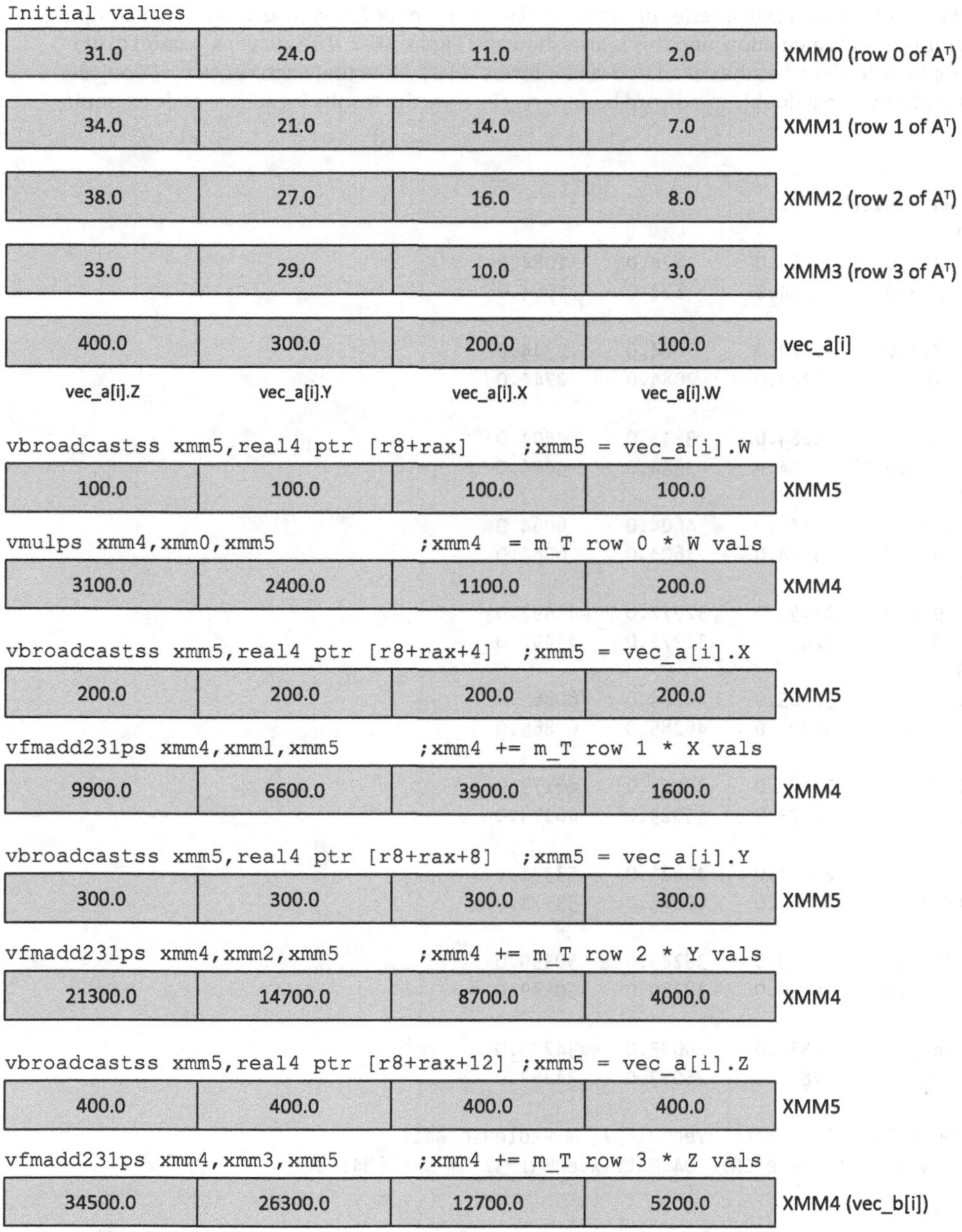

Initial values

| 31.0 | 24.0 | 11.0 | 2.0 | XMM0 (row 0 of A$^T$) |
|---|---|---|---|---|

| 34.0 | 21.0 | 14.0 | 7.0 | XMM1 (row 1 of A$^T$) |
|---|---|---|---|---|

| 38.0 | 27.0 | 16.0 | 8.0 | XMM2 (row 2 of A$^T$) |
|---|---|---|---|---|

| 33.0 | 29.0 | 10.0 | 3.0 | XMM3 (row 3 of A$^T$) |
|---|---|---|---|---|

| 400.0 | 300.0 | 200.0 | 100.0 | vec_a[i] |
|---|---|---|---|---|
| vec_a[i].Z | vec_a[i].Y | vec_a[i].X | vec_a[i].W | |

```
vbroadcastss xmm5,real4 ptr [r8+rax]      ;xmm5 = vec_a[i].W
```

| 100.0 | 100.0 | 100.0 | 100.0 | XMM5 |
|---|---|---|---|---|

```
vmulps xmm4,xmm0,xmm5              ;xmm4  = m_T row 0 * W vals
```

| 3100.0 | 2400.0 | 1100.0 | 200.0 | XMM4 |
|---|---|---|---|---|

```
vbroadcastss xmm5,real4 ptr [r8+rax+4]    ;xmm5 = vec_a[i].X
```

| 200.0 | 200.0 | 200.0 | 200.0 | XMM5 |
|---|---|---|---|---|

```
vfmadd231ps xmm4,xmm1,xmm5        ;xmm4 += m_T row 1 * X vals
```

| 9900.0 | 6600.0 | 3900.0 | 1600.0 | XMM4 |
|---|---|---|---|---|

```
vbroadcastss xmm5,real4 ptr [r8+rax+8]    ;xmm5 = vec_a[i].Y
```

| 300.0 | 300.0 | 300.0 | 300.0 | XMM5 |
|---|---|---|---|---|

```
vfmadd231ps xmm4,xmm2,xmm5        ;xmm4 += m_T row 2 * Y vals
```

| 21300.0 | 14700.0 | 8700.0 | 4000.0 | XMM4 |
|---|---|---|---|---|

```
vbroadcastss xmm5,real4 ptr [r8+rax+12]   ;xmm5 = vec_a[i].Z
```

| 400.0 | 400.0 | 400.0 | 400.0 | XMM5 |
|---|---|---|---|---|

```
vfmadd231ps xmm4,xmm3,xmm5        ;xmm4 += m_T row 3 * Z vals
```

| 34500.0 | 26300.0 | 12700.0 | 5200.0 | XMM4 (vec_b[i]) |
|---|---|---|---|---|

*Figure 16-2.* *Calculation of matrix (4 × 4) and vector (4 × 1) product using vbroadcastss, vmulps, and vfmadd231ps*

For-loop Loop1 concludes with a series of vbroadcastss and vfmadd231ps instructions that complete the matrix-vector product calculation, and this is also shown in Figure 16-2. The vmovaps xmmword ptr [rcx+rax],xmm4 instruction saves the calculated vector to vec_b[i]. Note that each Vec4x1_f32 object in array vec_b is aligned on a double quadword boundary. Here are the results for source code example Ch16_04:

```
Results for MatrixVecMulF32
Test case #0
vec_b1:      304.0        564.0        824.0       1084.0
vec_b2:      304.0        564.0        824.0       1084.0
Test case #1
vec_b1:      764.0       1424.0       2084.0       2744.0
vec_b2:      764.0       1424.0       2084.0       2744.0
Test case #2
vec_b1:     1224.0       2284.0       3344.0       4404.0
vec_b2:     1224.0       2284.0       3344.0       4404.0
Test case #3
vec_b1:     1684.0       3144.0       4604.0       6064.0
vec_b2:     1684.0       3144.0       4604.0       6064.0
Test case #4
vec_b1:    11932.0      22452.0      32972.0      43492.0
vec_b2:    11932.0      22452.0      32972.0      43492.0
Test case #5
vec_b1:    17125.0      31705.0      46285.0      60865.0
vec_b2:    17125.0      31705.0      46285.0      60865.0
Test case #6
vec_b1:    12723.0      23873.0      35023.0      46173.0
vec_b2:    12723.0      23873.0      35023.0      46173.0
Test case #7
vec_b1:    15121.0      27871.0      40621.0      53371.0
vec_b2:    15121.0      27871.0      40621.0      53371.0
Test case #8
vec_b1:    13789.0      26039.0      38289.0      50539.0
vec_b2:    13789.0      26039.0      38289.0      50539.0
Test case #9
vec_b1:     9663.0      17873.0      26083.0      34293.0
vec_b2:     9663.0      17873.0      26083.0      34293.0

Running benchmark function MatrixVecMulF32_bm - please wait
Benchmark times save to file Ch16_04_MatrixVecMulF32_bm_OXYGEN4.csv
```

Table 16-3 shows some benchmark timing measurements for source code example Ch16_04. The measurement numbers for function MatVecMulF32_Iavx2() in the right-most column of this table were obtained from Table 5-3. This is another example where the performance of the assembly language and C++ SIMD implementations of the same algorithm are about the same.

*Table 16-3.* *Matrix-Vector (4 × 4, 4 × 1) Multiplication Execution Times (Microseconds), 1,000,000 Vectors*

| CPU | MatVecMulF32_Cpp() | MatVecMulF32_Aavx2() | MatVecMulF32_Iavx2() |
|---|---|---|---|
| Intel Core i7-8700K | 5343 | 1555 | 1588 |
| Intel Core i5-11600K | 5084 | 1154 | 1155 |

# Signal Processing

The final source code example of this chapter, named Ch16_05, illustrates how to implement a 1D discrete convolution function using assembly language. Listing 16-5 shows the assembly language source code for example Ch16_05. Before examining the source code, you might want to review the sections in Chapter 6 that explained the mathematics of 1D discrete convolutions and the C++ SIMD source code in Listing 6-1. When reviewing these explanations, keep in mind that 1D discrete convolutions are often employed to carry out discrete convolutions in higher dimensions.

*Listing 16-5.* Example Ch16_05

```
;----------------------------------------------------
;               Ch16_05_fasm.asm
;----------------------------------------------------

            include <MacrosX86-64-AVX.asmh>

;--------------------------------------------------------------------
; extern "C" void Convolve1D_F32_Aavx2(float* y, const float* x, const float* kernel,
;    size_t num_pts, size_t kernel_size);
;--------------------------------------------------------------------

NSE     equ     8                           ;num_simd_elements
NSE2    equ     4                           ;num_simd_elements2

        .code
Convolve1D_F32_Aavx2 proc frame
        CreateFrame_M CV_,0,0,rbx,rsi,r12,r13,r14
        EndProlog_M

; Validate arguments
        mov r10,qword ptr [rbp+CV_OffsetStackArgs]   ;r10 = kernel_size (ks)
        test r10,1
        jz Done                             ;jump if ks is even
        cmp r10,3
        jb Done                             ;jump if ks < 3
        cmp r9,r10
        jb Done                             ;jump if num_pts < ks

; Initialize
        mov r11,r10                         ;r11 = ks
        shr r11,1                           ;r11 = ks2
        mov rsi,r9                          ;rsi = num_pts
        sub rsi,r11                         ;rsi = num_pts - ks2
```

```
        mov r14,r11
        neg r14                                         ;r14 = -ks2
        mov rax,r11                                     ;i = ks2

; General-purpose registers used in code below
;   rax       i                 r9      num_pts
;   rbx       k                 r10     kernel_size
;   rcx       y array           r11     ks2
;   rdx       x array           r12     scratch
;   rsi       num_pts - ks2     r13     scratch
;   r8        kernel            r14     -ks2

; Loop1 is outer-most for-loop
        align 16
Loop1:  cmp rax,rsi
        jge Done                                        ;jump if i >= num_pts - ks2

        lea r12,[rax+NSE]                               ;r12 = i + NSE
        cmp r12,rsi
        jg @F                                           ;jump if i + NSE > num_pts - ks2

        vxorps ymm0,ymm0,ymm0                           ;y[i:i+7] = 0
        mov rbx,r14                                     ;k = -ks2

; Calculate y[i:i+7]
        align 16
Loop2a: mov r12,rax                                     ;r12 = i
        sub r12,rbx                                     ;r12 = i - k
        lea r13,[rbx+r11]                               ;r13 = k + ks2

        vbroadcastss ymm2,real4 ptr [r8+r13*4]          ;ymm2 = kernel[k+ks2]
        vfmadd231ps ymm0,ymm2,ymmword ptr [rdx+r12*4]   ;update y[i:i+7]

        inc rbx                                         ;k += 1
        cmp rbx,r11
        jle Loop2a                                      ;jump if k <= ks2

        vmovups ymmword ptr [rcx+rax*4],ymm0            ;save y[i:i+7]
        add rax,NSE                                     ;i += NSE
        jmp Loop1

@@:     lea r12,[rax+NSE2]                              ;r12 = i + NSE2
        cmp r12,rsi
        jg @F                                           ;jump if i + NSE2 > num_pts - ks2

        vxorps xmm0,xmm0,xmm0                           ;y[i:i+3] = 0
        mov rbx,r14                                     ;k = -ks2

; Calculate y[i:i+3]
        align 16
Loop2b: mov r12,rax                                     ;r12 = i
```

```
        sub r12,rbx                              ;r12 = i - k
        lea r13,[rbx+r11]                        ;r13 = k + ks2

        vbroadcastss xmm2,real4 ptr [r8+r13*4]          ;xmm2 = kernel[k+ks2]
        vfmadd231ps xmm0,xmm2,xmmword ptr [rdx+r12*4]   ;update y[i:i+3]

        inc rbx                                  ;k += 1
        cmp rbx,r11
        jle Loop2b                               ;jump if k <= ks2

        vmovups xmmword ptr [rcx+rax*4],xmm0     ;save y[i:i+3]
        add rax,NSE2                             ;i += NSE2
        jmp Loop1

@@:     vxorps xmm0,xmm0,xmm0                     ;y[i] = 0
        mov rbx,r14                              ;k = -ks2

; Calculate y[i]
        align 16
Loop2c: mov r12,rax                              ;r12 = i
        sub r12,rbx                              ;r12 = i - k
        lea r13,[rbx+r11]                        ;r13 = k + ks2

        vmovss xmm2,real4 ptr [r8+r13*4]              ;xmm2 = kernel[k+ks2]
        vfmadd231ss xmm0,xmm2,real4 ptr [rdx+r12*4] ;update y[i]

        inc rbx                                  ;k += 1
        cmp rbx,r11
        jle Loop2c                               ;jump if k <= ks2

        vmovss real4 ptr [rcx+rax*4],xmm0        ;save y[i]
        inc rax                                  ;i += 1
        jmp Loop1

Done:   vzeroupper
        DeleteFrame_M rbx,rsi,r12,r13,r14
        ret
Convolve1D_F32_Aavx2 endp

;-------------------------------------------------------------------------
; extern "C" void Convolve1DKs5_F32_Aavx2(float* y, const float* x,
;   const float* kernel, size_t num_pts);
;-------------------------------------------------------------------------

KS      equ     5                                ;kernel_size
KS2     equ     2                                ;floor(kernel_size / 2)

Convolve1DKs5_F32_Aavx2 proc frame
        CreateFrame_M CV5_,0,16,r12
        SaveXmmRegs_M xmm6
        EndProlog_M
```

```
; Validate arguments
        cmp r9,KS
        jb Done                                 ;jump if num_pts < KS

; Initialize
        mov rax,KS2                             ;i = ks2
        mov r10,r9                              ;r10 = num_pts
        sub r10,KS2                             ;r10 = num_pts - KS2

        vbroadcastss ymm0,real4 ptr [r8]        ;ymm0 = packed kernel[0]
        vbroadcastss ymm1,real4 ptr [r8+4]      ;ymm1 = packed kernel[1]
        vbroadcastss ymm2,real4 ptr [r8+8]      ;ymm2 = packed kernel[2]
        vbroadcastss ymm3,real4 ptr [r8+12]     ;ymm3 = packed kernel[3]
        vbroadcastss ymm4,real4 ptr [r8+16]     ;ymm4 = packed kernel[4]

; General-purpose registers used in code below
;   rax     i                   r9      num_pts
;   rcx     y array             r10     num_pts -= ks2
;   rdx     x array             r11     j
;   r8      kernel              r12     scratch


        align 16
Loop1:  cmp rax,r10
        jge Done                                ;jump if i >= num_pts - ks2

        lea r11,[rax+KS2]                        ;j = i + KS2
        lea r12,[rax+NSE]                        ;r12 = i + NSE
        cmp r12,r10
        jg @F                                    ;jump if i + NSE > num_pts - ks2

; Calculate y[i:i+7]
        vmulps ymm6,ymm0,ymmword ptr [rdx+r11*4]          ;kernel[0] * x[j]
        vfmadd231ps ymm6,ymm1,ymmword ptr [rdx+r11*4-4]   ;kernel[1] * x[j-1]
        vfmadd231ps ymm6,ymm2,ymmword ptr [rdx+r11*4-8]   ;kernel[2] * x[j-2]
        vfmadd231ps ymm6,ymm3,ymmword ptr [rdx+r11*4-12]  ;kernel[3] * x[j-3]
        vfmadd231ps ymm6,ymm4,ymmword ptr [rdx+r11*4-16]  ;kernel[4] * x[j-4]

        vmovups ymmword ptr [rcx+rax*4],ymm6              ;save y[i:i+7]
        add rax,NSE                                       ;i += NSE
        jmp Loop1

; Calculate y[i:i+3]
@@:     lea r12,[rax+NSE2]                       ;r12 = i + NSE2
        cmp r12,r10
        jg @F                                    ;jump if i + NSE2 > num_pts - ks2

        vmulps xmm6,xmm0,xmmword ptr [rdx+r11*4]          ;kernel[0] * x[j]
        vfmadd231ps xmm6,xmm1,xmmword ptr [rdx+r11*4-4]   ;kernel[1] * x[j-1]
        vfmadd231ps xmm6,xmm2,xmmword ptr [rdx+r11*4-8]   ;kernel[2] * x[j-2]
        vfmadd231ps xmm6,xmm3,xmmword ptr [rdx+r11*4-12]  ;kernel[3] * x[j-3]
        vfmadd231ps xmm6,xmm4,xmmword ptr [rdx+r11*4-16]  ;kernel[4] * x[j-4]
```

```
          vmovups xmmword ptr [rcx+rax*4],xmm6              ;save y[i:i+3]
          add rax,NSE2                                      ;i += NSE2
          jmp Loop1

; Calculate y[i]
@@:       vmulss xmm6,xmm0,real4 ptr [rdx+r11*4]            ;kernel[0] * x[j]
          vfmadd231ss xmm6,xmm1,real4 ptr [rdx+r11*4-4]     ;kernel[1] * x[j-1]
          vfmadd231ss xmm6,xmm2,real4 ptr [rdx+r11*4-8]     ;kernel[2] * x[j-2]
          vfmadd231ss xmm6,xmm3,real4 ptr [rdx+r11*4-12]    ;kernel[3] * x[j-3]
          vfmadd231ss xmm6,xmm4,real4 ptr [rdx+r11*4-16]    ;kernel[4] * x[j-4]

          vmovss real4 ptr [rcx+rax*4],xmm6                 ;save y[i]
          inc rax                                           ;i += 1
          jmp Loop1

Done:     vzeroupper
          RestoreXmmRegs_M xmm6
          DeleteFrame_M r12
          ret
Convolve1DKs5_F32_Aavx2 endp
          end
```

Like source code example Ch06_01, the code in Listing 16-5 includes two 1D discrete convolution functions. The first function, Convolve1D_F32_Aavx2(), implements a 1D discrete convolution for a kernel whose size is an odd integer greater than or equal to three. The second function, Convolve1DKs5_F32_Aavx2, also implements a 1D discrete convolution but is optimized for a kernel size of five elements. As mentioned in Chapter 6, real-word signal processing algorithms frequently exploit convolution functions that are optimized for specific kernel sizes since these are often faster than their variable-size counterparts. In applications that make repeated use of fixed kernel 1D discrete convolutions, the performance gains will rapidly accumulate.

Following its prologue, function Convolve1D_F32_Aavx2() validates argument value kernel_size to ensure it is an odd integer greater than or equal to three. The next code block includes function initialization instructions that load ks2 (kernel_size / 2) into R11, num_pts – ks2 into RSI, and -ks2 into R14. Register RAX is also loaded with ks2 and will be used as loop index variable i in for-loop Loop1.

For-loop Loop1 begins each iteration with a code block that terminates the for-loop if i >= num_pts – ks2 is true. Then the next code block verifies that at least eight (NSE) elements are available. Following this check, Convolve1D_F32_Aavx2() uses a vxorps ymm0,ymm0,ymm0 to initialize y_vals[i:i+7] to zero. The ensuing mov rbx,r14 instruction loads -ks2 into RBX, which is used as index variable k in for-loop Loop2a.

For-loop Loop2a calculates output signal elements y[i:i+7]. During each iteration, the vbroadcastss ymm2,real4 ptr [r8+r13*4] instruction loads kernel[k+ks2] into each single-precision floating-point element of YMM2. The ensuing vfmadd231ps ymm0,ymm2,ymmword ptr [rdx+r12*4] instruction calculates y_vals[i:i+7] += x[i-k:i-k+7] * kernel[k+ks2]. This is the same calculation that was used in source code example Ch06_01 (see Figure 6-6). Following calculation of y[i:i+7], the vmovups ymmword ptr [rcx+rax*4],ymm0 instruction saves the result. The vmovaps instruction cannot be used here since output signal elements y[i:i+7] may not be aligned on a 32-byte boundary.

For-loop Loop2a continues to execute until fewer than NSE elements remain to be processed. For-loop Loop2b computes output signal elements y[i:i+3]. Note that the code in this for-loop is almost identical to the code in Loop2a with the main difference being the use of an XMM register (which holds NSE2 or four elements) instead of a YMM register for the FMA arithmetic. The final calculating for-loop, Loop2c, processes any residual elements using scalar FMA arithmetic. This loop will only execute if (num_pts – (ks2 * 2)) % NSE2 is not equal to zero.

The second assembly language function in Listing 16-5 is named Convolve1DKs5_F32_Aavx2(). This function implements a 1D discrete convolution for a five-element kernel. Following the prologue and argument validation code blocks, Convolve1DKs5_F32_Aavx2() uses five vbroadcastss instructions to load packed versions of kernel[0]-kernel[4] into registers YMM0-YMM4, respectively. The calculations carried out in for-loop Loop1 are the same as the previous function. However, it is important to note that there are no inner for-loops. Function Convolve1DKs5_F32_Aavx2() can use explicit sequences of vmulps and vfmadd231ps instructions since the size of the convolution kernel is fixed at five. Here are the results for source code example Ch16_05:

---

```
Executing Convolve1D_F32()
Results saved to file Ch16_05_Convolve1D_F32_Results_OXYGEN4.csv

Running benchmark function Convolve1D_F32_bm - please wait
Benchmark times saved to file Ch16_05_Convolve1D_F32_bm_OXYGEN4.csv
```

---

Table 16-4 shows the benchmark timing measurements for source code example Ch16_05. These measurements were made using a 1,000,000-element input signal and a five-element convolution kernel. Table 16-5 also shows the benchmark timing measurements for functions Convolve1D_F32_Iavx2() and Convolve1DKs5_F32_Iavx2() from source code example Ch06_01 (see Table 6-1) for comparison purposes. Note that on both processors, the assembly language implementation of the five-element kernel 1D discrete convolution function Convolve1DKs5_F32_Aavx2() is moderately faster that its C++ SIMD counterpart function Convolve1DKs5_F32_Iavx2().

*Table 16-4.* *1D Discrete Convolution (Single-Precision) Execution Times (Microseconds)*

| Function Name | Intel Core i7-8700K | Intel Core i5-11600K |
|---|---|---|
| Convolve1D_F32_Cpp() | 3262 | 2259 |
| Convolve1D_F32_Aavx2() | 398 | 342 |
| Convolve1D_F32_Iavx2() | 411 | 325 |
| Convolve1DKs5_F32_Aavx2() | 229 | 199 |
| Convolve1DKs5_F32_Iavx2() | 278 | 221 |

# Summary

Table 16-5 summarizes the x86 assembly language instructions introduced in this chapter. This table also includes several closely related instructions. Before proceeding to the next chapter, make sure you understand the calculation or operation that is performed by each instruction shown in Table 16-5.

***Table 16-5.*** *X86 Assembly Language Instruction Summary for Chapter 16*

| Instruction Mnemonic | Description |
|---|---|
| vfmadd132p[d\|s]vfmadd213p[d\|s]vfmadd231p[d\|s] | Packed floating-point fused-multiply-add |
| vfmadd132s[d\|s]vfmadd213s[d\|s]vfmadd231s[d\|s] | Scalar floating-point fused-multiply-add |
| vfmsub132p[d\|s]vfmsub213p[d\|s]vfmsub231p[d\|s] | Packed floating-point fused-multiply-subtract |
| vfmsub132s[d\|s]vfmsub213s[d\|s]vfmasub231s[d\|s] | Scalar floating-point fused-multiply-subtract |
| vmaskmovp[d\|s] | Conditional packed floating-point load/store |
| vmovhlps | Move packed single-precision floating-point values (high to low) |
| vmovlhps | Move packed single-precision floating-point values (low to high) |
| vunpckhp[d\|s] | Unpack and interleave packed floating-point values (high-order elements) |
| vunpcklp[d\|s] | Unpack and interleave packed floating-point values (low-order elements) |

# CHAPTER 17

■ ■ ■

# AVX-512 Assembly Language Programming: Part 1

In Chapters 7 and 8, you learned how to exploit the computational resources of AVX-512 using C++ SIMD intrinsic functions. The next two chapters explain how to use AVX-512 assembly language instructions to perform similar operations. The focus of this chapter is AVX-512 SIMD calculations and operations using 512-bit wide packed integer operands. AVX-512 SIMD calculations and operations using packed floating-point operands are covered in the next chapter.

As discussed in Chapter 7, AVX-512 is somewhat different than its predecessor AVX/AVX2 instruction set extensions. From a programming perspective, many AVX-512 instructions can be used just like their AVX or AVX2 counterparts. However, to fully maximize the computing potential of AVX-512, a function must explicitly exploit its novel capabilities as you will soon see. It is also important to keep in mind that AVX-512 is a collection of interrelated but distinct instruction set extensions. The discussions and source code examples in this and the next chapter assume that the host processor supports the following AVX-512 instruction set extensions: AVX512F, AVX512BW, AVX512DQ, and AVX512VL. The host operating system must also support AVX-512. For information regarding AVX-512 instruction set extensions that are not discussed in this book, you can consult the programming reference manuals listed in Appendix B.

## Integer Arithmetic

In this section, you will learn how to use AVX-512 instructions to perform basic integer arithmetic operations using 512-bit wide SIMD operands. The first source code example covers simple integer arithmetic. The second source code example illustrates simple integer arithmetic using zero masking and merge masking. This example also demonstrates how to use the AVX-512 opmask registers.

### Basic Operations

Listing 17-1 shows the assembly language source code for example Ch17_01. This example, which is a modified version of example Ch15_01, explains how to perform basic packed integer arithmetic using AVX-512 instructions and 512-bit wide operands. Source code example Ch17_01 also spotlights some of the minor assembly language programming differences that exist between AVX/AVX2 and AVX-512.

© Daniel Kusswurm 2022
D. Kusswurm, *Modern Parallel Programming with C++ and Assembly Language*,
https://doi.org/10.1007/978-1-4842-7918-2_17

***Listing 17-1.*** Example Ch17_01

```
;---------------------------------------------------
;               Ch17_01_fasm.asm
;---------------------------------------------------


;-----------------------------------------------------------------------
; extern void MathI16_Aavx512(ZmmVal c[6], const ZmmVal* a, const ZmmVal* b);
;-----------------------------------------------------------------------

        .code
MathI16_Aavx512 proc
        vmovdqa64 zmm0,zmmword ptr [rdx]          ;load a values
        vmovdqa64 zmm1,zmmword ptr [r8]           ;load b values

        vpaddw zmm2,zmm0,zmm1                     ;packed addition - wraparound
        vmovdqa64 zmmword ptr [rcx],zmm2          ;save result

        vpaddsw zmm2,zmm0,zmm1                    ;packed addition - saturated
        vmovdqa64 zmmword ptr [rcx+64],zmm2       ;save result

        vpsubw zmm2,zmm0,zmm1                     ;packed subtraction - wraparound
        vmovdqa64 zmmword ptr [rcx+128],zmm2      ;save result

        vpsubsw zmm2,zmm0,zmm1                    ;packed subtraction - saturated
        vmovdqa64 zmmword ptr [rcx++192],zmm2     ;save result

        vpminsw zmm2,zmm0,zmm1                    ;packed min values
        vmovdqa64 zmmword ptr [rcx+256],zmm2      ;save result

        vpmaxsw zmm2,zmm0,zmm1                    ;packed max values
        vmovdqa64 zmmword ptr [rcx+320],zmm2      ;save result

        vzeroupper                               ;clear upper YMM/ZMM bits
        ret
MathI16_Aavx512 endp

;-----------------------------------------------------------------------
; extern void MathI64_Aavx512(ZmmVal c[6], const ZmmVal* a, const ZmmVal* b);
;-----------------------------------------------------------------------


MathI64_Aavx512 proc
        vmovdqa64 zmm16,zmmword ptr [rdx]         ;load a values
        vmovdqa64 zmm17,zmmword ptr [r8]          ;load b values

        vpaddq zmm18,zmm16,zmm17                  ;packed qword addition
        vmovdqa64 zmmword ptr [rcx],zmm18         ;save result

        vpsubq zmm18,zmm16,zmm17                  ;packed qword subtraction
        vmovdqa64 zmmword ptr [rcx+64],zmm18      ;save result
```

```
        vpmullq  zmm18,zmm16,zmm17           ;packed qword multiplication
        vmovdqa64 zmmword ptr [rcx+128],zmm18 ;save products (low 64-bits)

        vpsllvq  zmm18,zmm16,zmm17           ;packed qword shift left
        vmovdqa64 zmmword ptr [rcx+192],zmm18 ;save result

        vpsravq  zmm18,zmm16,zmm17           ;packed qword shift right
        vmovdqa64 zmmword ptr [rcx+256],zmm18 ;save result

        vpabsq   zmm18,zmm16                 ;packed qword abs (a values)
        vmovdqa64 zmmword ptr [rcx+320],zmm18 ;save result

        ret                                  ;vzeroupper not needed
MathI64_Aavx512 endp
        end
```

Listing 17-1 begins with the definition of a function named MathI16_Aavx512(). This function illustrates the use of several AVX-512 packed integer instructions using 512-bit wide operands and 16-bit wide elements. Note that function MathI16_Aavx512() requires three arguments of type ZmmVal. This is the same C++ structure that was introduced in Chapter 7 (see Listing 7-1). Recall that the declaration of structure ZmmVal uses the C++ alignas(64) specifier, which means that each ZmmVal instance is properly aligned on a 64-byte boundary.

The first instruction of function MathI16_Aavx512(), vmovdqa64 zmm0,zmmword ptr [rdx], loads 512 bits (64 bytes) of packed integer data from the memory location pointed to by register RDX (argument value a) into register ZMM0. Unlike the AVX/AVX2 packed integer move instructions vmovdqa and vmovdqu, the AVX-512 packed integer move instructions vmovdqa[32|64] (Move Aligned Packed Integer Values) and vmovdqu[8|16|32|64] (Move Unaligned Packed Integer Values) employ a size suffix. This suffix is necessary to support zero masking and merge masking. You will learn more about masking operations later in this chapter. When zero masking and merge masking are not utilized, as in this example, a function can use a vmovdqa[32|64] or vmovdqu[8|16|32|64] instruction to perform packed integer loads or stores of 512-bit wide operands. These instructions also can be used to perform packed integer loads or stores using 128- or 256-bit wide SIMD operands.

The next instruction in Listing 17-1, vmovdqa64 zmm1,zmmword ptr [r8], loads argument value b into register ZMM1. This is followed by a vpaddw zmm2,zmm0,zmm1 instruction that performs packed integer addition using 16-bit wide integer elements. The ensuing vmovdqa64 zmmword ptr [rcx],zmm2 instruction saves the calculated sums to c[0]. The next instruction, vpaddsw zmm2,zmm0,zmm1, performs packed integer addition using 16-bit wide elements and saturated arithmetic. The subsequent vmovdqa64 zmmword ptr [rcx+64],zmm2 instruction saves this result to c[1]. Note that except for the ZMM register operands, MathI16_Aavx512() uses the instructions vpaddw and vpaddsw just like they were used in the AVX2 source example Ch15_01.

The ensuing code blocks in MathI16_Aavx512() illustrate the use of the vpsubw, vpsubsw, vpminsw, and vpmaxsw instructions using 512-bit wide operands and 16-bit wide integer elements. Note that the displacements on the vmovdqa64 save instructions are integral multiples of 64 since each ZMM register (and ZmmVal instance) is 64 bytes wide. The penultimate instruction of MathI16_Aavx512() is vzeroupper. Proper use of this instruction in functions that modify ZMM registers will be explained shortly.

The next function in Listing 17-1, MathI64_Aavx512(), demonstrates the use of AVX-512 instructions that perform SIMD arithmetic operations using packed quadword elements. Note that in this example, registers ZMM16, ZMM17, and ZMM18 are used to carry out the calculations. According to the Visual C++ calling convention, registers ZMM16–ZMM31 (and their corresponding XMM and YMM registers) are volatile, which means that they do not need to be preserved by a called function. The extra 16 SIMD registers provided by AVX-512 enable many functions to implement SIMD calculations without preserving any of the nonvolatile SIMD registers XMM6–XMM15, which results in faster execution times.

Function MathI64_Aavx512() begins its execution with the instruction pair vmovdqa64 zmm16,zmmword ptr [rdx] and vmovdqa64 zmm17,zmmword ptr [r8] that loads registers ZMM16 and ZMM17 with argument values a and b, respectively. The ensuing vpaddq zmm18,zmm16,zmm17 performs packed integer addition using quadword elements. The next instruction, vmovdqa64 zmmword ptr [rcx],zmm18, saves the calculated quadword sums to c[0]. The remaining instructions in MathI64_Aavx512() perform other packed integer operations using quadword elements including subtraction (vpsubq), multiplication (vpmullq), shift left logical (vpsllvq), shift right arithmetic (vpsravq), and absolute value (vpabsq).

You may have noticed that function MathI64_Aavx512() does not utilize a vzeroupper instruction prior to its ret instruction. Recall from the discussions in Chapter 14 that execution of a vzeroupper (or vzeroall) instruction prevents potential performance delays from occurring whenever the processor transitions from executing x86-AVX instructions to executing x86-SSE instructions. A vzeroupper instruction should always be used prior to returning from any function that modifies the upper 128 bits of registers YMM0–YMM15. This rule also applies if a function calls another function that might use x86-SSE instructions such as a C++ math library function. On processors that support AVX-512, the vzeroupper usage rule is extended to include the upper 384 bits of registers ZMM0–ZMM15. It is not necessary for a function to use vzeroupper if it only modifies registers YMM16–YMM31 or ZMM16–ZMM31. Here are the results for source code example Ch17_01:

Results for MathI16

| i | a | b | add | adds | sub | subs | min | max |
|---|---|---|-----|------|-----|------|-----|-----|
| 0 | 10 | 100 | 110 | 110 | -90 | -90 | 10 | 100 |
| 1 | 20 | 200 | 220 | 220 | -180 | -180 | 20 | 200 |
| 2 | 30 | 300 | 330 | 330 | -270 | -270 | 30 | 300 |
| 3 | 40 | 400 | 440 | 440 | -360 | -360 | 40 | 400 |
| 4 | 50 | 500 | 550 | 550 | -450 | -450 | 50 | 500 |
| 5 | 60 | 600 | 660 | 660 | -540 | -540 | 60 | 600 |
| 6 | 70 | 700 | 770 | 770 | -630 | -630 | 70 | 700 |
| 7 | 80 | 800 | 880 | 880 | -720 | -720 | 80 | 800 |
| 8 | 1000 | -100 | 900 | 900 | 1100 | 1100 | -100 | 1000 |
| 9 | 2000 | 200 | 2200 | 2200 | 1800 | 1800 | 200 | 2000 |
| 10 | 3000 | -300 | 2700 | 2700 | 3300 | 3300 | -300 | 3000 |
| 11 | 4000 | 400 | 4400 | 4400 | 3600 | 3600 | 400 | 4000 |
| 12 | 5000 | -500 | 4500 | 4500 | 5500 | 5500 | -500 | 5000 |
| 13 | 6000 | 600 | 6600 | 6600 | 5400 | 5400 | 600 | 6000 |
| 14 | 7000 | -700 | 6300 | 6300 | 7700 | 7700 | -700 | 7000 |
| 15 | 8000 | 800 | 8800 | 8800 | 7200 | 7200 | 800 | 8000 |
| 16 | -1000 | 100 | -900 | -900 | -1100 | -1100 | -1000 | 100 |
| 17 | -2000 | -200 | -2200 | -2200 | -1800 | -1800 | -2000 | -200 |
| 18 | 3000 | 303 | 3303 | 3303 | 2697 | 2697 | 303 | 3000 |
| 19 | 4000 | -400 | 3600 | 3600 | 4400 | 4400 | -400 | 4000 |
| 20 | -5000 | 500 | -4500 | -4500 | -5500 | -5500 | -5000 | 500 |
| 21 | -6000 | -600 | -6600 | -6600 | -5400 | -5400 | -6000 | -600 |
| 22 | -7000 | 700 | -6300 | -6300 | -7700 | -7700 | -7000 | 700 |
| 23 | -8000 | 800 | -7200 | -7200 | -8800 | -8800 | -8000 | 800 |
| 24 | 30000 | 3000 | -32536 | 32767 | 27000 | 27000 | 3000 | 30000 |
| 25 | 6000 | 32000 | -27536 | 32767 | -26000 | -26000 | 6000 | 32000 |
| 26 | -25000 | -27000 | 13536 | -32768 | 2000 | 2000 | -27000 | -25000 |
| 27 | 8000 | 28700 | -28836 | 32767 | -20700 | -20700 | 8000 | 28700 |
| 28 | 2000 | -31000 | -29000 | -29000 | -32536 | 32767 | -31000 | 2000 |

| 29 | 4000 | -30000 | -26000 | -26000 | -31536 | 32767 | -30000 | 4000 |
| 30 | -3000 | 32000 | 29000 | 29000 | 30536 | -32768 | -3000 | 32000 |
| 31 | -15000 | 24000 | 9000 | 9000 | 26536 | -32768 | -15000 | 24000 |

Results for MathI64

| i | a | b | add | sub | mul | sll | sra | abs |
|---|---|---|-----|-----|-----|-----|-----|-----|
| 0 | 64 | 4 | 68 | 60 | 256 | 1024 | 4 | 64 |
| 1 | 1024 | 5 | 1029 | 1019 | 5120 | 32768 | 32 | 1024 |
| 2 | -2048 | 2 | -2046 | -2050 | -4096 | -8192 | -512 | 2048 |
| 3 | 8192 | 5 | 8197 | 8187 | 40960 | 262144 | 256 | 8192 |
| 4 | -256 | 8 | -248 | -264 | -2048 | -65536 | -1 | 256 |
| 5 | 4096 | 7 | 4103 | 4089 | 28672 | 524288 | 32 | 4096 |
| 6 | 16 | 3 | 19 | 13 | 48 | 128 | 2 | 16 |
| 7 | 512 | 6 | 518 | 506 | 3072 | 32768 | 8 | 512 |

## Masked Operations

The next source code example, named Ch17_02, explains how to perform zero masking and merge masking using an AVX-512 opmask register. It also illustrates how to implement a SIMD ternary operation using packed quadword integers and 512-bit wide operands. Listing 17-2 shows the assembly language source code for example Ch17_02.

**Listing 17-2.** Example Ch17_02

```
;--------------------------------------------------
;               Ch17_02_fasm.asm
;--------------------------------------------------

        include <cmpequ.asmh>

;------------------------------------------------------------------------
; void MaskOpI64a_Aavx512(ZmmVal c[5], uint8_t mask, const ZmmVal* a,
;    const ZmmVal* b);
;------------------------------------------------------------------------

        .code
MaskOpI64a_Aavx512 proc
        vmovdqa64 zmm0,zmmword ptr [r8]         ;load a values
        vmovdqa64 zmm1,zmmword ptr [r9]         ;load b values

        kmovb k1,edx                            ;k1 = opmask

        vpaddq zmm2{k1}{z},zmm0,zmm1            ;masked qword addition
        vmovdqa64 zmmword ptr [rcx],zmm2        ;save result

        vpsubq zmm2{k1}{z},zmm0,zmm1            ;masked qword subtraction
        vmovdqa64 zmmword ptr [rcx+64],zmm2     ;save result
```

```
        vpmullq zmm2{k1}{z},zmm0,zmm1           ;masked qword multiplication
        vmovdqa64 zmmword ptr [rcx+128],zmm2    ;save products (low 64-bits)

        vpsllvq zmm2{k1}{z},zmm0,zmm1           ;masked qword shift left
        vmovdqa64 zmmword ptr [rcx+192],zmm2    ;save result

        vpsravq zmm2{k1}{z},zmm0,zmm1           ;masked qword shift right
        vmovdqa64 zmmword ptr [rcx+256],zmm2    ;save result

        vzeroupper
        ret
MaskOpI64a_Aavx512 endp

;-----------------------------------------------------------------------
; void MaskOpI64b_Aavx512(ZmmVal c[5], uint8_t mask, const ZmmVal* a,
;   const ZmmVal* b1, const ZmmVal* b2);
;-----------------------------------------------------------------------

MaskOpI64b_Aavx512 proc
        vmovdqa64 zmm0,zmmword ptr [r8]         ;load a values
        vmovdqa64 zmm1,zmmword ptr [r9]         ;load b1 values
        mov rax,[rsp+40]                        ;rax = b2
        vmovdqa64 zmm2,zmmword ptr [rax]        ;load b2 values

        kmovb k1,edx                            ;k1 = opmask

        vpaddq zmm0{k1},zmm1,zmm2               ;masked qword addition
        vmovdqa64 zmmword ptr [rcx],zmm0        ;save result

        vpsubq zmm0{k1},zmm1,zmm2               ;masked qword subtraction
        vmovdqa64 zmmword ptr [rcx+64],zmm0     ;save result

        vpmullq zmm0{k1},zmm1,zmm2              ;masked qword multiplication
        vmovdqa64 zmmword ptr [rcx+128],zmm0    ;save products (low 64-bits)

        vpsllvq zmm0{k1},zmm1,zmm2              ;masked qword shift left
        vmovdqa64 zmmword ptr [rcx+192],zmm0    ;save result

        vpsravq zmm0{k1},zmm1,zmm2              ;masked qword shift right
        vmovdqa64 zmmword ptr [rcx+256],zmm0    ;save result

        vzeroupper
        ret
MaskOpI64b_Aavx512 endp

;-----------------------------------------------------------------------
; void MaskOpI64c_Aavx512(ZmmVal* c, const ZmmVal* a, int64_t x1, int64_t x2);
;-----------------------------------------------------------------------
```

```
MaskOpI64c_Aavx512 proc
            vmovdqa64 zmm0,zmmword ptr [rdx]          ;load a values
            vpbroadcastq zmm1,r8                       ;broadcast x1 to zmm1
            vpbroadcastq zmm2,r9                       ;broadcast x2 to zmm2

; c[i] = (a[i] >= x1) ? a[i] + x2 : a[i]
            vpcmpq k1,zmm0,zmm1,CMP_GE                 ;k1 = a >= b mask
            vpaddq zmm0{k1},zmm0,zmm2                  ;masked qword addition
            vmovdqa64 zmmword ptr [rcx],zmm0           ;save result

            vzeroupper
            ret
MaskOpI64c_Aavx512 endp
            end
```

The first function in Listing 17-2, MaskOpI64a_Aavx512(), begins its execution with two vmovdqa64 instructions that load ZmmVal arguments a and b into registers ZMM0 and ZMM1, respectively. The next instruction, kmovb k1,edx (Move From and To Mask Register), copies the low-order eight bits of register EDX (argument value mask) to the low-order eight bits of opmask register K1; the high-order bits of register K1 are set to zero. Recall from the discussions in Chapter 10 that AVX-512 includes eight opmask registers named K0–K7 (see Figure 10-2). Most AVX-512 instructions can be used with an opmask register to perform either zero masking or merge masking. Besides the kmovb instruction, AVX-512 includes additional instructions that a function can use to perform opmask register addition, bitwise logical operations, and shifts. These instructions are listed in the end-of-chapter instruction summary table (Table 17-2).

Before continuing with the code of example Ch17_02, a few more words regarding opmask registers and their instruction mnemonics are warranted. The width of an AVX-512 opmask register is 64 bits; however, an AVX-512 instruction will only use or modify the exact number of low-order bits needed to carry out an operation. The high-order bits are either zeroed or ignored. The last letter of most opmask register instruction mnemonics signifies the size of the mask value (b = byte, w = word, d = doubleword, q = quadword). In the current example, function MaskOpI64a_Aavx512() uses the kmovb instruction since subsequent instructions manipulate quadword elements and each ZMM register can hold eight quadword values, which means only eight opmask register bits are needed. AVX-512 instructions can use registers K1–K7 to perform zero masking or merge masking. Opmask register K0 cannot be specified for these operations since AVX-512 instruction encodings use the encoding pattern for register K0 to implement unconditional processing. (One time-saving use of K0 is to load all ones into an opmask register. The instruction kxnorw k1,k0,k0 is often faster than kxnorw k1,k1,k1, especially when K1 is used in a subsequent gather or scatter instruction.) Returning to the code in Listing 17-2, the first instruction that follows the kmovb k1,edx instruction is vpaddq zmm2{k1}{z},zmm0,zmm1. This instruction performs conditional adds of the quadword elements in registers ZMM0 and ZMM1. The elements in these source operand registers are summed only if the corresponding bit position in opmask register K1 is set to 1. If the corresponding bit position in K1 is set to 0, the element in destination register ZMM2 is set to 0 as illustrated in Figure 17-1. Note that opmask register K1 in the vpaddq instruction is surrounded by curly braces; these are required. The {z} operand enables zero masking. Using an AVX-512 instruction with an opmask register sans the {z} operand selects merge masking as you will soon see. Most AVX-512 instructions support both zero masking and merge masking.

Initial values

| 512 | 16 | 4096 | -256 | 8192 | -2048 | 1024 | 64 | ZMM0 |
|-----|-----|------|------|------|-------|------|-----|------|

| 6 | 3 | 7 | 8 | 5 | 2 | 5 | 4 | ZMM1 |
|---|---|---|---|---|---|---|---|------|

| 0 | 1 | 1 | 1 | 1 | 0 | 1 | 1 | K1 (bits 0:7) |
|---|---|---|---|---|---|---|---|---------------|

vpaddq zmm2{k1}{z},zmm0,zmm1

| 0 | 19 | 4103 | -248 | 8197 | 0 | 1029 | 68 | ZMM2 |
|---|-----|------|------|------|---|------|-----|------|

**Figure 17-1.** *Execution of instruction vpaddq zmm2{k1}{z},zmm0,zmm1 (zero masking)*

Following the vpaddq instruction is a vmovdqa64 zmmword ptr [rcx],zmm0 instruction that saves the 512-bit wide result to c[0]. It should be noted that AVX-512 load/store instructions like vmovdqa64 also support zero masking and merge masking. The remaining code in function MaskOpI64a_Aavx512() illustrates the use of additional AVX-512 instructions using packed quadword elements and zero masking.

The next function in Listing 17-2, MaskOpI64b_Aavx512(), demonstrates how to perform merge masking. The first code block in this function contains a series of vmovdqa64 instructions that load argument values a, b1, and b2 into registers ZMM0, ZMM1, and ZMM2, respectively. This is followed by a kmovb k1,edx instruction that loads argument value mask into opmask register K1. The next instruction, vpaddq zmm0{k1},zmm1,zmm2, performs conditional adds of the quadword elements in registers ZMM1 and ZMM2. The quadword elements of ZMM1 and ZMM2 are summed only if the corresponding bit position in opmask register K1 is set to 1. If this bit is set to 0, the quadword element in destination operand ZMM0 remains unaltered as shown in Figure 17-2. Like the previous function, the subsequent code in MaskOpI64b_Aavx512() highlights the use of additional AVX-512 instructions using packed quadword elements and merge masking.

Initial values

| 888888 | 777777 | 666666 | 555555 | 444444 | 333333 | 222222 | 111111 | ZMM0 |
|--------|--------|--------|--------|--------|--------|--------|--------|------|

| 512 | 16 | 4096 | -256 | 8192 | -2048 | 1024 | 64 | ZMM1 |
|-----|-----|------|------|------|-------|------|-----|------|

| 6 | 3 | 7 | 8 | 5 | 2 | 5 | 4 | ZMM2 |
|---|---|---|---|---|---|---|---|------|

| 1 | 0 | 1 | 1 | 0 | 1 | 1 | 0 | K1 (bits 0:7) |
|---|---|---|---|---|---|---|---|---------------|

vpaddq zmm0{k1},zmm1,zmm2

| 518 | 777777 | 4103 | -248 | 444444 | -2046 | 1029 | 111111 | ZMM0 |
|-----|--------|------|------|--------|-------|------|--------|------|

**Figure 17-2.** *Execution of instruction vpaddq zmm0{k1},zmm1,zmm2 (merge masking)*

The final function in Listing 17-2 is named MaskOpI64c_Aavx512(). This function illustrates how to implement a SIMD ternary operator using an opmask register. The first instruction of this function, vmovdqa64 zmm0,zmmword ptr [rdx], loads argument value a into register ZMM0. This is followed by a vpbroadcastq zmm1,r8 instruction that broadcasts the quadword value in register R8 (argument value x1) to each quadword element position in ZMM1. Unlike AVX2, the AVX-512 vpbroadcast[b|w|d|q] instruction can use a general-purpose register as a source operand. The ensuing vpbroadcastq zmm2,r9 sets each quadword element in ZMM2 to the value in register R9 (argument value x2).

The next code block contains instructions that implement the SIMD ternary expression c[i] = (a[i] >= x1) ? a[i] + x2 : a[i]. Note that in this expression, the indices within the brackets signify SIMD quadword element positions. The first instruction of this code block, vpcmpq k1,zmm0,zmm1,CMP_GE (Compare Packed Integer Values into Mask), compares each quadword element in register ZMM0 to its counterpart element in register ZMM1. If the specified compare predicate CMP_GE is true, the corresponding bit position in opmask register K1 is set to 1; otherwise, it is set to 0. The next instruction, vpaddq zmm0{k1},zmm0,zmm2, sums counterpart quadword elements in ZMM0 and ZMM2 whose corresponding bit in opmask register K1 is set to 1. This quadword element sum is then saved in ZMM0 as illustrated in Figure 17-3. If the corresponding bit in opmask register K1 is set to 0, the quadword element in ZMM0 is not changed.

```
Initial values
```

| -800 | 700 | 600 | -500 | -400 | 300 | 200 | -100 | ZMM0 |
|------|-----|-----|------|------|-----|-----|------|------|

| 0 | 0 | 0 | 0 | 0 | 0 | 0 | 0 | ZMM1 |
|---|---|---|---|---|---|---|---|------|

| 42 | 42 | 42 | 42 | 42 | 42 | 42 | 42 | ZMM2 |
|----|----|----|----|----|----|----|----|------|

```
vpcmpq k1,zmm0,zmm1,CMP_GE
```

| 0 | 1 | 1 | 0 | 0 | 1 | 1 | 0 | K1 (bits 0:7) |
|---|---|---|---|---|---|---|---|---------------|

```
vpaddq zmm0{k1},zmm0,zmm2
```

| -800 | 742 | 642 | -500 | -400 | 342 | 242 | -100 | ZMM0 |
|------|-----|-----|------|------|-----|-----|------|------|

***Figure 17-3.*** *Execution of SIMD ternary operation using merge masking*

Compared to AVX and AVX2, AVX-512's incorporation of distinct opmask registers and its support for zero masking and merge masking provides software developers a significant amount of algorithmic flexibility. You will see additional examples of AVX-512 masking later in this chapter and in Chapter 18. Here are the results for source code example Ch17_02:

```
Results for MaskOpI64a (mask = 0x7b)

i      a     b     add      sub      mul      sll      sra
---------------------------------------------------------------
0     64     4     68        60       256     1024        4
1   1024     5   1029      1019      5120    32768       32
2  -2048     2      0         0         0        0        0
3   8192     5   8197      8187     40960   262144      256
4   -256     8   -248      -264     -2048   -65536       -1
5   4096     7   4103      4089     28672   524288       32
6     16     3     19        13        48      128        2
7    512     6      0         0         0        0        0
```

Results for MaskOpI64b (mask = 0xb6)

| i | a | b1 | b2 | add | sub | mul | sll | sra |
|---|---|----|----|-----|-----|-----|-----|-----|
| 0 | 111111 | 64 | 4 | 111111 | 111111 | 111111 | 111111 | 111111 |
| 1 | 222222 | 1024 | 5 | 1029 | 1019 | 5120 | 32768 | 32 |
| 2 | 333333 | -2048 | 2 | -2046 | -2050 | -4096 | -8192 | -512 |
| 3 | 444444 | 8192 | 5 | 444444 | 444444 | 444444 | 444444 | 444444 |
| 4 | 555555 | -256 | 8 | -248 | -264 | -2048 | -65536 | -1 |
| 5 | 666666 | 4096 | 7 | 4103 | 4089 | 28672 | 524288 | 32 |
| 6 | 777777 | 16 | 3 | 777777 | 777777 | 777777 | 777777 | 777777 |
| 7 | 888888 | 512 | 6 | 518 | 506 | 3072 | 32768 | 8 |

Results for MaskOpI64c (x1 = 0, x2 = 42)

| i | a | c |
|---|---|---|
| 0 | -100 | -100 |
| 1 | 200 | 242 |
| 2 | 300 | 342 |
| 3 | -400 | -400 |
| 4 | -500 | -500 |
| 5 | 600 | 642 |
| 6 | 700 | 742 |
| 7 | -800 | -800 |

# Image Processing

In Chapter 7, you learned how to implement a few common image processing techniques using AVX2 and C++ SIMD intrinsic functions. In this section, you will learn how to code some of these same algorithms using AVX-512 assembly language instructions. The first source code example spotlights a general-purpose image thresholding function, while the second source code example explains how to calculate basic statistics for a grayscale image.

## Image Thresholding

Recall from the discussions in Chapters 4 that image thresholding is an image processing technique that creates a mask image from a grayscale image. The mask image signifies which pixels in the original image are greater than a predetermined or algorithmically derived intensity threshold value. Other relational operators such as less than, equal, and not equal can also be used to create a mask image. Listing 17-3 shows the assembly language source code for example Ch17_03. This example, which is the assembly language counterpart of source code example Ch07_04, uses AVX-512 packed integer instructions to implement a general-purpose image thresholding function.

*Listing 17-3.* Example Ch17_03

```
;--------------------------------------------------
;                Ch17_03_fasm.asm
;--------------------------------------------------

            include <cmpequ.asmh>

NSE     equ     64                              ;num_simd_elements

;--------------------------------------------------------------------
; Macro PixelCmp_M
;--------------------------------------------------------------------

PixelCmp_M macro CmpOp
        align 16
@@:     add rax,NSE                             ;i += NSE
        vmovdqa64 zmm2,zmmword ptr [rdx+rax]    ;load src[i:i+63]
        vpcmpub k1,zmm2,zmm1,CmpOp              ;packed compare using CmpOp
        vmovdqu8 zmm3{k1}{z},zmm0               ;create pixel mask
        vmovdqa64 zmmword ptr [rcx+rax],zmm3    ;save des[i:i+63]
        sub r8,NSE                              ;r8 -= NSE
        jnz @B                                  ;repeat until done
        jmp Done
        endm

;--------------------------------------------------------------------
; extern void ComparePixels_Aavx512(uint8_t* des, const uint8_t* src, size_t num_pixels,
;   CmpOp cmp_op, uint8_t cmp_val);
;--------------------------------------------------------------------

        .code
ComparePixels_Aavx512 proc
; Validate arguments
        mov eax,1                      ;load error return code
        test r8,r8
        jz Done                        ;jump if num_pixels == 0
        test r8,3fh
        jnz Done                       ;jump if num_pixels % 64 != 0

        test rcx,3fh
        jnz Done                       ;jump if des not 64b aligned
        test rdx,3fh
        jnz Done                       ;jump if src not 64b aligned

        cmp r9,CmpOpTableCount
        jae Done                       ;jump if cmp_op is invalid

; Initialize
        mov eax,0ffh
        vpbroadcastb zmm0,eax          ;zmm0 = packed 0xff
        vpbroadcastb zmm1,byte ptr [rsp+40] ;zmm1 = packed cmp_val
        mov rax,-NSE                   ;i = -NSE
```

```
; Jump to target compare code
        jmp [CmpOpTable+r9*8]                    ;jump to specified compare code block

; Compare code blocks using macro PixelCmp_M
CmpEQ:  PixelCmp_M CMP_EQ
CmpNE:  PixelCmp_M CMP_NEQ
CmpLT:  PixelCmp_M CMP_LT
CmpLE:  PixelCmp_M CMP_LE
CmpGT:  PixelCmp_M CMP_GT
CmpGE:  PixelCmp_M CMP_GE

Done:   vzeroupper
        ret

; The order of values in following table must match enum CmpOp
; that's defined in Ch17_03.h.

        align 8
CmpOpTable equ $
        qword CmpEQ
        qword CmpNE
        qword CmpLT
        qword CmpLE
        qword CmpGT
        qword CmpGE
CmpOpTableCount equ ($ - CmpOpTable) / size qword

ComparePixels_Aavx512 endp
        end
```

Near the top of Listing 17-3 is the definition of a macro named PixelCmp_M. This macro emits instructions that implement a thresholding for-loop for the compare predicate specified by the macro parameter CmpOp. Supported compare predicates, which are defined in the assembly language header file cmpequ.asmh, include CMP_EQ, CMP_NEQ, CMP_LT, CMP_LE, CMP_GT, and CMP_GE. The first instruction of macro PixelCmp_M, add rax,NSE, updates for-loop index variable i so that it indexes the next block of 64 pixels in both the source and mask (destination) images. In this example, all source and mask image pixel values are 8-bit unsigned integers. The next instruction, vmovdqa64 zmm2,zmmword ptr [rdx+rax], loads pixel values src[i:i+63] into register ZMM2. Note that the use of the vmovdqa64 instruction means that each pixel block in source image src must be properly aligned on a 64-byte boundary. It should also be noted that it is acceptable to use the instruction vmovdqa64 to load 8-bit wide elements since neither zero masking nor merge masking is used here (AVX-512 does not include a vmovdqa8 instruction). There is no negative effect on performance since vmovdqa64 is simply performing an unconditional 512-bit wide copy.

Following the vmovdqa64 instruction is the AVX-512 instruction vpcmpub k1,zmm2,zmm1,CmpOp (Compare Packed Byte Values into Mask). This instruction compares each unsigned byte element in ZMM2 to its corresponding element position in ZMM1 using the compare predicate CmpOp. Prior to using macro PixelCmp_M, a function must broadcast the desired compare value to each byte element in register ZMM1 as you will soon see. Execution of vpcmpub sets each bit in opmask register K1 to 1 (compare predicate true) or 0 (compare predicate false). The next instruction, vmovdqu8 zmm3{k1}{z},zmm0, employs zero masking to create the required pixel mask as shown in Figure 17-4. Note that this figure uses the compare predicate CMP_GE for macro argument CmpOp. The ensuing vmovdqa64 zmmword ptr [rcx+rax],zmm3 instruction saves the calculated pixel mask to des[i:i+63]. The remaining instructions in macro PixelCmp_M are required to complete the for-loop.

Initial values

| OxFF | OxFF | OxFF | OxFF | OxFF | OxFF | OxFF | ... | OxFF | OxFF | OxFF | OxFF | OxFF | OxFF | OxFF | ZMM0 |
|------|------|------|------|------|------|------|-----|------|------|------|------|------|------|------|------|

| 100 | 100 | 100 | 100 | 100 | 100 | 100 | ... | 100 | 100 | 100 | 100 | 100 | 100 | 100 | ZMM1 (cmp_val) |
|-----|-----|-----|-----|-----|-----|-----|-----|-----|-----|-----|-----|-----|-----|-----|----------------|

| 229 | 232 | 36 | 127 | 144 | 12 | 45 | ... | 235 | 72 | 77 | 240 | 68 | 21 | 100 | ZMM2 (src[i:i+63]) |
|-----|-----|----|-----|-----|----|----|-----|-----|----|----|-----|----|----|-----|---------------------|

vpcmpub k1,zmm2,zmm1,CMP_GE

| 1 | 1 | 0 | 1 | 1 | 0 | 0 | ... | 1 | 0 | 0 | 1 | 0 | 0 | 1 | K1 |
|---|---|---|---|---|---|---|-----|---|---|---|---|---|---|---|----|

vmovdqu8 zmm3{k1}{z},zmm0

| OxFF | OxFF | 0x00 | OxFF | OxFF | 0x00 | 0x00 | ... | OxFF | 0x00 | 0x00 | OxFF | 0x00 | 0x00 | OxFF | ZMM3 |
|------|------|------|------|------|------|------|-----|------|------|------|------|------|------|------|------|

**Figure 17-4.** *Generation of pixel mask using AVX-512 instructions vpcmpub and vmovdqu8*

The next code item in Listing 17-3 is the assembly language function ComparePixels_Aavx512(). This function uses macro PixelCmp_M and an assembly language jump table to implement a general-purpose image thresholding function. Function ComparePixels_Aavx512() begins its execution with a code block that validates num_pixels for size. Note that in this example, num_pixels must be an integral multiple of 64. The next code block includes instructions that verify pixel buffers src and des for proper alignment on a 64-byte boundary. The final argument check validates cmp_op. This check is important since ComparePixels_Aavx512() uses cmp_op as an index into a jump table. Using an invalid value for cmp_op could cause the program to crash. Following argument validation, ComparePixels_Aavx512() employs the instruction pair mov eax,0ffh and vpbroadcastb zmm0,eax to set each byte element in register ZMM0 to OxFF. The next instruction, vpbroadcastb zmm1,byte ptr [rsp+40], loads cmp_val into each byte element of ZMM1.

Following initialization, ComparePixels_Aavx512() utilizes the instruction jmp [CmpOpTable+r9*8]. Execution of this instruction transfers program control to code block specified by the value in R9 (cmp_op). Toward the end of listing 17-3 is an assembly language jump table named CmpOpTable. This table contains labels of statements in ComparePixels_Aavx512() that use the macro PixelCmp_M to implement the for-loop for a specific compare predicate. It is important to note that the order of the quadword values in CmpOpTable matches the enumerated type CmpOp that is defined in the C++ header file Ch17_03.h. Here are the results for source code example Ch17_03:

```
Results for ComparePixels

Test #1
  num_pixels: 4194304
  cmp_op:     EQ
  cmp_val:    197
  Pixel masks are identical
  Number of non-zero mask pixels = 16424

Test #2
  num_pixels: 4194304
  cmp_op:     NE
  cmp_val:    222
  Pixel masks are identical
  Number of non-zero mask pixels = 4177927
```

```
Test #3
  num_pixels: 4194304
  cmp_op:     LT
  cmp_val:    43
  Pixel masks are identical
  Number of non-zero mask pixels = 703652

Test #4
  num_pixels: 4194304
  cmp_op:     LE
  cmp_val:    43
  Pixel masks are identical
  Number of non-zero mask pixels = 719787

Test #5
  num_pixels: 4194304
  cmp_op:     GT
  cmp_val:    129
  Pixel masks are identical
  Number of non-zero mask pixels = 2065724

Test #6
  num_pixels: 4194304
  cmp_op:     GE
  cmp_val:    222
  Pixel masks are identical
  Number of non-zero mask pixels = 556908
```

## Image Statistics

Listing 17-4 shows the assembly language source code for example Ch17_04. This example, which is the assembly language counterpart of example Ch07_05, illustrates how to calculate the mean and standard deviation of the pixels in a grayscale image. To make this example a bit more interesting, the statistical calculating functions only use pixel values that reside between two threshold limits. Before examining the source code in Listing 17-4, you may want to review the mean and standard deviation equations defined in Chapter 7 for source code example Ch07_05 since the same equations are used in this example.

***Listing 17-4.*** Example Ch17_04

```
;------------------------------------------------
;                 Ch17_04_fasm.asm
;------------------------------------------------

            include <cmpequ.asmh>
            include <MacrosX86-64-AVX.asmh>

; Image statistics structure. This must match the structure that's
; defined in Ch17_04.h
IS                      struct
PixelBuffer             qword ?
PixelMinVal             dword ?
```

```
PixelMaxVal            dword ?
NumPixels              qword ?
NumPixelsInRange       qword ?
PixelSum               qword ?
PixelSumSquares        qword ?
PixelMean              real8 ?
PixelStDev             real8 ?
IS                     ends


NSE      equ     64                            ;num_simd_elements

;-------------------------------------------------------------------------
; UpdateSumVars_M - update pixel_sums (zmm16) and pixel_sum_sqs (zmm17)
;
; Notes:    Register zmm5 contains pixel values pb[i:i+63].
;           Register zmm18 is used as a scratch register.
;-------------------------------------------------------------------------

UpdateSumVars_M macro EI
        vextracti64x2 xmm18,zmm5,EI         ;extract pixels pb[i+EI*16:i+EI*16+15]
        vpmovzxbd zmm18,xmm18               ;promote to dwords
        vpaddd zmm16,zmm16,zmm18            ;update loop pixel_sums
        vpmulld zmm18,zmm18,zmm18
        vpaddd zmm17,zmm17,zmm18            ;update loop pixel_sum_sqs
        endm

;-------------------------------------------------------------------------
; UpdateQwords_M - add dword elements in ZmmSrc to qword elements in ZmmDes
;-------------------------------------------------------------------------

UpdateQwords_M macro ZmmDes,ZmmSrc,ZmmTmp
        YmmSrcSuffix SUBSTR <ZmmSrc>,2
        YmmSrc CATSTR <y>,YmmSrcSuffix
        YmmTmpSuffix SUBSTR <ZmmTmp>,2
        YmmTmp CATSTR <y>,YmmTmpSuffix

        vextracti32x8 YmmTmp,ZmmSrc,1       ;extract ZmmSrc dwords 8:15
        vpaddd YmmTmp,YmmTmp,YmmSrc         ;add ZmmSrc dwords 8:15 and 0:7
        vpmovzxdq ZmmTmp,YmmTmp             ;promote to qwords
        vpaddq ZmmDes,ZmmDes,ZmmTmp         ;update ZmmDes qwords 0:7
        endm

;-------------------------------------------------------------------------
; SumQwords_M  - sum qword elements in ZmmSrc
;
; Note: Macro code below uses ymm29 and xmm30 as scratch registers.
;-------------------------------------------------------------------------

SumQwords_M macro GprDes,GprTmp,ZmmSrc
        YmmSrcSuffix SUBSTR <ZmmSrc>,2
        YmmSrc CATSTR <Y>,YmmSrcSuffix
```

```
        vextracti64x4 ymm29,ZmmSrc,1          ;ymm29 = ZmmSrc qword elements 4:7
        vpaddq ymm29,ymm29,YmmSrc             ;sum ZmmSrc qwords 4:7 and 0:3
        vextracti64x2 xmm30,ymm29,1           ;xmm30 = ymm29 qwords 2:3
        vpaddq xmm30,xmm30,xmm29              ;sum ymm29 qwords 2:3 and 0:1

        vpextrq GprTmp,xmm30,0                ;extract xmm30 qword 0
        vpextrq GprDes,xmm30,1                ;extract xmm30 qword 1
        add GprDes,GprTmp                     ;GprDes = scalar qword sum
        endm

;-------------------------------------------------------------------------
; extern "C" void CalcImageStats_Aavx512(ImageStats& im_stats);
;-------------------------------------------------------------------------

        extern CheckArgs:proc
        .code
CalcImageStats_Aavx512 proc frame
        CreateFrame_M CIS_,0,0
        EndProlog_M

; Validate values in im_stats
        mov qword ptr [rbp+CIS_OffsetHomeRCX],rcx    ;save im_stats ptr

        sub rsp,32                           ;allocate home area for CheckArgs
        call CheckArgs                       ;validate values im_stats
        or eax,eax
        jz Done                              ;jump if CheckArgs failed

        mov rcx,qword ptr [rbp+CIS_OffsetHomeRCX]    ;rcx = im_stats

; Initialize
        mov rdx,qword ptr [rcx+IS.PixelBuffer]  ;rdx = pb
        mov r8,qword ptr [rcx+IS.NumPixels]     ;r8 = num_pixels

        vpbroadcastb zmm0,byte ptr [rcx+IS.PixelMinVal]   ;pixel_min_vals
        vpbroadcastb zmm1,byte ptr [rcx+IS.PixelMaxVal]   ;pixel_max_vals

        vpxorq zmm2,zmm2,zmm2                 ;zmm2 = pixel_sums (8 qwords)
        vpxorq zmm3,zmm3,zmm3                 ;zmm3 = pixel_sum_sqs (8 qwords)

        xor r9,r9                            ;r9 = num_pixels_in_range
        mov rax,rdx                          ;rax = pixel_buffer
        add rax,r8                           ;rax = pixel_buffer + num_pixels

; Registers used in code below
;    rax     pixel_buffer+num_pixels      zmm0    pixel_min_vals
;    rcx     im_stats                     zmm1    pixel_max_vals
;    rdx     pixel_buffer                 zmm2    pixel_sums (8 qwords)
;    r8      num_pixels                   zmm3    pixel_sum_sqs (8 qwords)
;    r9      num_pixels_in_range          zmm4    pixel values
;    r10     scratch register             zmm5    pixel values in range (or zero)
;    r11     scratch register             zmm16 - zmm18 scratch registers
```

```
; Load next block of 64 pixels, calc in-range pixels
        align 16
Loop1:  vmovdqa64 zmm4,zmmword ptr [rdx]    ;load pb[i:i+63]
        vpcmpub k1,zmm4,zmm0,CMP_GE         ;k1 = mask of pixels GE PixelMinVal
        vpcmpub k2,zmm4,zmm1,CMP_LE         ;k2 = mask of pixels LE PixelMaxVal
        kandq k3,k1,k2                      ;k3 = mask of in-range pixels
        vmovdqu8 zmm5{k3}{z},zmm4           ;zmm5 = pixels in range (or zero)

        kmovq r10,k3                        ;r10 = in-range mask
        popcnt r10,r10                      ;r10 = number of in-range pixels
        add r9,r10                          ;update num_pixels_in_range

; Update pixel_sums and pixel_sums_sqs
        vpxord zmm16,zmm16,zmm16            ;loop pixel_sums (16 dwords)
        vpxord zmm17,zmm17,zmm17            ;loop pixel_sum_sqs (16 dwords)

        UpdateSumVars_M 0                   ;process pb[i:i+15]
        UpdateSumVars_M 1                   ;process pb[i+16:i+31]
        UpdateSumVars_M 2                   ;process pb[i+32:i+47]
        UpdateSumVars_M 3                   ;process pb[i+48:i+63]

        UpdateQwords_M zmm2,zmm16,zmm30     ;update pixel_sums
        UpdateQwords_M zmm3,zmm17,zmm31     ;update pixel_sum_sqs

        add rdx,NSE                         ;pb += NSE
        cmp rdx,rax                         ;more pixels?
        jb Loop1                            ;jump if yes

; Calculate final image statistics
        SumQwords_M r10,rax,zmm2            ;r10 = pixel_sum
        SumQwords_M r11,rax,zmm3            ;r11 = pixel_sum_sqs

        mov qword ptr [rcx+IS.NumPixelsInRange],r9  ;save num_pixels_in_range
        mov qword ptr [rcx+IS.PixelSum],r10         ;save pixel_sum
        mov qword ptr [rcx+IS.PixelSumSquares],r11  ;save pixel_sum_sqs

        vcvtusi2sd xmm16,xmm16,r9           ;num_pixels_in_range as F64
        dec r9                              ;r9 = num_pixels_in_range - 1
        vcvtusi2sd xmm17,xmm16,r9           ;num_pixels_in_range - 1 as F64
        vcvtusi2sd xmm18,xmm18,r10          ;pixel_sum as F64
        vcvtusi2sd xmm19,xmm19,r11          ;pixel_sum_sqs as F64

        vmulsd xmm0,xmm16,xmm19             ;num_pixels_in_range * pixel_sum_sqs
        vmulsd xmm1,xmm18,xmm18             ;pixel_sum * pixel_sum
        vsubsd xmm2,xmm0,xmm1               ;variance numerator
        vmulsd xmm3,xmm16,xmm17             ;variance denominator
        vdivsd xmm4,xmm2,xmm3               ;variance

        vdivsd xmm0,xmm18,xmm16             ;calc mean
        vmovsd real8 ptr [rcx+IS.PixelMean],xmm0  ;save mean
```

```
        vsqrtsd xmm1,xmm1,xmm4                  ;calc st_dev
        vmovsd real8 ptr [rcx+IS.PixelStDev],xmm1    ;save st_dev

Done:   vzeroupper
        DeleteFrame_M
        ret
CalcImageStats_Aavx512 endp
        end
```

Listing 17-4 opens with the definition of an assembly language structure named IS. This structure incorporates the data that is exchanged between the assembly language function CalcImageStats_Aavx512() and its caller.

Following the declaration of structure IS are three macro definitions. The first macro, UpdateSumVars_M, emits code that updates pixel_sums and pixel_sum_sqs during execution of Loop1 in CalcImageStats_Aavx512(). Note that macro UpdateSumVars_M requires an argument named EI. This argument specifies the block of 16 pixels that UpdateSumVars_M should process. The first instruction of UpdateSumVars_M, vextracti64x2 xmm18,zmm5,EI (Extract Packed Integer Values), copies 128 bits of integer data from ZMM5 to register XMM18. More specifically, this execution of this instruction extracts pixel values pb[i+EI*16:i+EI*16+15] from register ZMM5 and saves them in XMM18. The next instruction, vpmovzxbd zmm18,xmm18, size-extends the pixel values from bytes to doublewords, which facilitates doubleword arithmetic when updating pixel_sums and pixel_sum_sqs. The ensuing instruction triplet, vpaddd zmm16,zmm16,zmm18, vpmulld zmm18,zmm18,zmm18, and vpaddd zmm17,zmm17,zmm18, updates pixel_sums (ZMM16) and pixel_sum_sqs (ZMM17).

The next macro, UpdateQwords_M, adds the doubleword values in ZmmSrc to the quadword values in ZmmDes. This macro begins with a vextracti32x8 YmmTmp,ZmmSrc,1 instruction that extracts the eight high-order doublewords from ZmmSrc and saves them in register YmmTmp. The next macro instruction, vpaddd YmmTmp,YmmTmp,YmmSrc, sums the doubleword elements of YmmTmp (ZmmSrc doublewords 8:15) and YmmSrc (ZmmSrc doublewords 0:7). The ensuing instruction pair, vpmovzxdq ZmmTmp,YmmTmp and vpaddq ZmmDes,ZmmDes,ZmmTmp, size-promotes the doubleword elements of YmmTmp to quadwords and then adds these values to the quadword elements of ZmmDes.

The final macro in Listing 17-4, SumQwords_M, reduces the quadword elements of argument ZmmSrc to a scalar value and saves this result in general-purpose register Gpr. This macro begins with a vextracti64x4 ymm29,ZmmSrc,1 instruction that extracts the four high-order quadwords from ZmmSrc and saves these values in YMM29 (macro SumQwords_M uses YMM29 as a scratch register). The next instruction, vpaddq ymm29,ymm29,YmmSrc, sums the just extracted quadword elements with the four quadwords in YmmSrc (i.e., the four low-order quadwords of ZmmSrc). The ensuing instruction pair, vextracti64x2 xmm30,ymm29,1 and vpaddq xmm30,xmm30,xmm29, reduces the number of quadwords to two. The final three instructions of SumQwords_M, vpextrq GprTmp,xmm30,0, vpextrq GprDes,xmm30,1, and add GprDes,GprTmp, calculate the final scalar quadword sum.

Function CalcImageStats_Aavx512() begins its execution with a code block that validates the values in im_stats. In this function, argument validation is performed using the C++ function CheckArgs() primarily for demonstration purposes. Using a C++ function to perform runtime argument validation is often convenient in programs that include both a C++ and x86-AVX assembly language implementation of the same calculating function. Note that prior to calling CheckArgs(), CalcImageStats_Aavx512() saves register RCX (im_stats) in its home area on the stack. The reason for this register save is that RCX is a volatile register that CheckArgs() might modify. The mov rcx,qword ptr [rbp+CIS_OffsetHomeRCX] instruction that occurs after the call to CheckArgs() reloads RCX with argument value im_stats.

Following argument validation is a code block that performs the required initializations for Loop1. Note that the byte element registers ZMM0 and ZMM1 are loaded with IS.PixelMinVal and IS.PixelMaxVal, respectively. The vpxorq zmm2,zmm2,zmm2 instruction that follows initializes each quadword elements of ZMM2 (pixel_sums) to zero. Unlike AVX and AVX2, AVX-512 bitwise logical instructions incorporate a size suffix letter as part of the mnemonic. The ensuing vpxorq zmm3,zmm3,zmm3 instruction initializes each quadword element in pixel_sum_sqs to zero.

Each iteration of Loop1 commences with a vmovdqa64 zmm4,zmmword ptr [rdx] that loads pixel values pb[i:i+63] into register ZMM4. The next instruction, vpcmpub k1,zmm4,zmm0,CMP_GE, loads opmask register with a mask of all pixels in ZMM4 whose value is greater than or equal to PixelMinVal. This is followed by a vpcmpub k2,zmm4,zmm1,CMP_LE that loads K2 with a mask of all pixels in ZMM4 whose value is less than or equal to PixelMaxVal. The next instruction, kandq k3,k1,k2 (Bitwise Logical AND Masks), performs a bitwise logical AND of opmask registers K1 and K2. The result of this operation is a quadword mask of all pixels whose values reside between PixelMinVal and PixelMaxVal. The vmovdqu8 zmm5{k3}{z},zmm4 instruction that follows loads each byte element of ZMM5 with either an original pixel value (pixel is in range) or zero (pixel is out of range). After the vmovdqu8 instruction is the instruction triplet kmovq r10,k3, popcnt r10,r10, add r9,r10, which updates num_pixels_in_range (R9).

Following determination of in-range pixels, CalcImageStats_Aavx512() updates pixel_sums and pixel_sum_sqs. The code block that performs this action begins with the instruction pair vpxord zmm16,zmm16,zmm16 and vpxord zmm17,zmm17,zmm17. These instructions initialize registers ZMM16 and ZMM17 to hold intermediate doubleword results. Next is a series of UpdateSumVars_M usages that update ZMM16 (pixel_sums) and ZMM17 (pixel_sum_sqs) using the in-range pixel values of the current Loop1 iteration. Then the next action, UpdateQwords_M zmm2,zmm16,zmm30 and UpdateQwords_M zmm3,zmm17,zmm31, uses the just calculated intermediate results to update the quadword values in ZMM2 (pixel_sums) and ZMM3 (pixel_sum_sqs).

Upon completion of for-loop Loop1, CalcImageStats_Aavx512() uses the macro SumQwords_M twice to reduce packed quadword variables pixel_sum and pixel_sum_sqs to scalar values. Following this reduction, scalar double-precision floating-point arithmetic is used to calculate the final pixel mean and standard deviation. Note that the scalar code employs the AVX-512 instruction vcvtusi2sd (Convert Unsigned Integer to Scalar DPFP Value). Here are the results for source code example Ch17_04:

```
Results for CalcImageStats
image_fn:            ../../Data/ImageB.png
num_pixels:          2457600
c_PixelMinVal:       40
c_PixelMaxVal:       230

m_NumPixelsInRange:  2039471      | 2039471
m_PixelSum:          252932299    | 252932299
m_PixelSumSquares:   37534652095  | 37534652095
m_PixelMean:         124.018581   | 124.018581
m_PixelStDev:        54.986406    | 54.986406

Running benchmark function CalcImageStats_bm - please wait
Benchmark times save to file Ch17_04_CalcImageStats_bm_LITHIUM.csv
```

Table 17-1 shows some benchmark timing measurements for source code example Ch17_04. The rightmost column in this table shows the measurements for function CalcImageStats_Iavx512() from Table 7-3. Note that the assembly language function CalcImageStats_Aavx512() is a tad bit faster than its C++ SIMD counterpart function CalcImageStats_Iavx512().

*Table 17-1. Image Statistics Execution Times (Microseconds) Using ImageB.png*

| CPU | CalcImageStats_Cpp() | CalcImageStats_Aavx512() | CalcImageStats_Iavx512() |
|---|---|---|---|
| Intel Core i5-11600K | 3188 | 187 | 201 |

# Summary

Table 17-2 summarizes the x86 assembly language instructions introduced in this chapter. This table also includes closely related instructions. Before proceeding to the next chapter, make sure you understand the calculation or operation that is performed by each instruction shown in Table 17-2.

***Table 17-2.*** *X86 Assembly Language Instruction Summary for Chapter 17*

| Instruction Mnemonic | Description |
| --- | --- |
| kadd[b\|w\|d\|q] | Opmask register add |
| kand[b\|w\|d\|q] | Opmask register bitwise logical AND |
| kandn[b\|w\|d\|q] | Opmask register bitwise logical AND NOT |
| kmov[b\|w\|d\|q] | Opmask register move |
| knot[b\|w\|d\|q] | Opmask register bitwise logical NOT |
| kor[b\|w\|d\|q] | Opmask register bitwise logical OR |
| kortest[b\|w\|d\|q] | Opmask register bitwise logical OR test (sets RFLAGS.ZF and RFLAGS.CF) |
| kshiftl[b\|w\|d\|q] | Opmask register left shift logical |
| kshiftr[b\|w\|d\|q] | Opmask register right shift logical |
| ktest[b\|w\|d\|q] | Opmask register bitwise logical AND/ANDN test (sets RFLAGS.ZF and RFLAGS.CF) |
| kunpck[bw\|wd\|dq] | Opmask register unpack |
| kxnor[b\|w\|d\|q] | Opmask register bitwise logical exclusive NOR |
| kxor[b\|w\|d\|q] | Opmask register bitwise logical exclusive OR |
| vcvtusi2s[d\|s] | Convert unsigned integer to floating point |
| vextracti[32x4\|32x8] | Extract packed doubleword elements |
| vextracti[64x2\|64x4] | Extract packed quadword elements |
| vmovdqa[32\|64] | Move packed integer data (aligned) |
| vmovdqu[8\|16\|32\|64] | Move packed integer data (unaligned) |
| vpand[d\|q] | Packed integer bitwise logical AND |
| vpandn[d\|q] | Packed integer bitwise logical AND NOT |
| vpcmp[b\|w\|d\|q] | Packed signed integer compare |
| vpcmpu[b\|w\|d\|q] | Packed unsigned integer compare |
| vpor[d\|q] | Packed integer bitwise logical OR |
| vpxor[d\|q] | Packed integer bitwise logical exclusive OR |

# CHAPTER 18

■ ■ ■

# AVX-512 Assembly Language Programming: Part 2

In Chapters 5, 6, and 8, you learned how to code a variety of floating-point array and matrix calculating functions using C++ SIMD intrinsic functions. In this chapter, you will learn how to code similar functions using x86 assembly language and AVX-512 instructions. The first section includes source code examples that illustrate packed floating-point arithmetic using 512-bit wide operands. The second section focuses on using AVX-512 instructions to code functions that perform calculations using floating-point matrices. The chapter concludes with source code example that spotlights AVX-512 instructions in 1D discrete convolution functions.

## Floating-Point Arithmetic

In this section, you will learn how to perform elementary packed floating-point operations using AVX-512 instructions and 512-bit wide SIMD operands. The first source code example covers basic single-precision and double-precision floating-point arithmetic. The second source code example illustrates how to carry out packed floating-point compare operations.

### Basic Arithmetic

The first source code example of this chapter, named Ch18_01, demonstrates packed floating-point arithmetic using AVX-512. It also explains other features unique to AVX-512 including instruction-level rounding control and broadcast operations. Listing 18-1 shows the source code for example Ch18_01.

*Listing 18-1.* Example Ch18_01

```
;--------------------------------------------------
;                 Ch18_01_fasm.asm
;--------------------------------------------------

            .const
r8_AbsMask  qword 07fffffffffffffffh
r4_AbsMask  dword 07fffffffh
```

D. Kusswurm, *Modern Parallel Programming with C++ and Assembly Language*, https://doi.org/10.1007/978-1-4842-7918-2_18

```
;-------------------------------------------------------------------------
; extern "C" void PackedMathF32_Aavx512(ZmmVal c[9], const ZmmVal* a,
;    const ZmmVal* b);
;-------------------------------------------------------------------------

        .code
PackedMathF32_Aavx512 proc
        vmovaps zmm0,zmmword ptr [rdx]          ;zmm0 = a
        vmovaps zmm1,zmmword ptr [r8]           ;zmm1 = b

        vaddps zmm2,zmm0,zmm1                    ;SPFP addition
        vmovaps zmmword ptr[rcx],zmm2

        vaddps zmm2,zmm0,zmm1{rd-sae}            ;SPFP addition (round down toward -inf)
        vmovaps zmmword ptr[rcx+64],zmm2

        vsubps zmm2,zmm0,zmm1                    ;SPFP subtraction
        vmovaps zmmword ptr[rcx+128],zmm2

        vmulps zmm2,zmm0,zmm1                    ;SPFP multiplication
        vmovaps zmmword ptr[rcx+192],zmm2

        vdivps zmm2,zmm0,zmm1                    ;SPFP division
        vmovaps zmmword ptr[rcx+256],zmm2

        vminps zmm2,zmm0,zmm1                    ;SPFP min
        vmovaps zmmword ptr[rcx+320],zmm2

        vmaxps zmm2,zmm0,zmm1                    ;SPFP max
        vmovaps zmmword ptr[rcx+384],zmm2

        vsqrtps zmm2,zmm0                        ;SPFP sqrt(a)
        vmovaps zmmword ptr[rcx+448],zmm2

        vandps zmm2,zmm1,real4 bcst [r4_AbsMask]    ;SPFP abs(b)
        vmovaps zmmword ptr[rcx+512],zmm2

        vzeroupper
        ret
PackedMathF32_Aavx512 endp

;-------------------------------------------------------------------------
; extern "C" void PackedMathF64_Aavx512(ZmmVal c[9], const ZmmVal* a,
;    const ZmmVal* b);
;-------------------------------------------------------------------------

PackedMathF64_Aavx512 proc
        vmovapd zmm0,zmmword ptr [rdx]          ;zmm0 = a
        vmovapd zmm1,zmmword ptr [r8]           ;zmm1 = b

        vaddpd zmm2,zmm0,zmm1                    ;DPFP addition
        vmovapd zmmword ptr[rcx],zmm2
```

```
        vsubpd  zmm2,zmm0,zmm1              ;DPFP subtraction
        vmovapd zmmword ptr[rcx+64],zmm2

        vmulpd  zmm2,zmm0,zmm1              ;DPFP multiplication
        vmovapd zmmword ptr[rcx+128],zmm2

        vdivpd  zmm2,zmm0,zmm1              ;DPFP division
        vmovapd zmmword ptr[rcx+192],zmm2

        vdivpd  zmm2,zmm0,zmm1{ru-sae}      ;DPFP division (round up toward +inf)
        vmovapd zmmword ptr[rcx+256],zmm2

        vminpd  zmm2,zmm0,zmm1              ;DPFP min
        vmovapd zmmword ptr[rcx+320],zmm2

        vmaxpd  zmm2,zmm0,zmm1              ;DPFP max
        vmovapd zmmword ptr[rcx+384],zmm2

        vsqrtpd zmm2,zmm0                   ;DPFP sqrt(a)
        vmovapd zmmword ptr[rcx+448],zmm2

        vandpd  zmm2,zmm1,real8 bcst [r8_AbsMask]    ;DPFP abs(b)
        vmovapd zmmword ptr[rcx+512],zmm2

        vzeroupper
        ret
PackedMathF64_Aavx512 endp
        end
```

Listing 18-1 begins with a .const section that defines masks for single-precision and double-precision absolute values. Recall that the absolute value of a floating-point number can be calculated by setting its sign bit to zero. Following the .const section is the definition of function PackedMathF32_Aavx512(). This function illustrates the use of ordinary AVX-512 floating-point arithmetic instructions using packed single-precision operands. The first instruction of this function, vmovaps zmm0,zmmword ptr [rdx], loads ZmmVal argument value a into register ZMM0. This is followed by a vmovaps zmm1,zmmword ptr [r8] instruction that loads argument value b into register ZMM1. Following the vmovaps instructions is a vaddps zmm2,zmm0,zmm1 instruction that performs packed single-precision floating-point arithmetic. The next instruction, vmovaps zmmword ptr[rcx],zmm2, saves the resultant sums to c[0].

The subsequent vaddps zmm2,zmm0,zmm1{rd-sae} instruction also performs packed single-precision floating-point addition. The {rd-sae} operand included in this instruction specifies the rounding method that the processor should use during execution of vaddps. Recall from the discussions in Chapter 10 that control bits MXCSR.RC specify the rounding mode for most x86-AVX floating-point arithmetic instructions (a few x86-AVX instructions can specify an immediate rounding mode). On processors that support AVX-512, additional floating-point arithmetic and conversion instructions can specify a static (or per instruction) rounding mode that overrides the current rounding mode in MXCSR.RC.

In the current example, rd-sae instructs the processor to use round down toward -∞. Other static rounding mode options include round up toward +∞ (ru-sae), round to nearest (rn-sae), and round toward zero (rz-sae). The text sae signifies "suppress all exceptions" and is required when using a static rounding mode. This means the processor will not generate any floating-point exceptions or set any status flags in MXCSR during execution of an AVX-512 instruction that specifies a static rounding mode. It is important to note that static rounding modes are restricted to AVX-512 instruction forms that use only 512-bit wide register operands (e.g., vaddps zmm2,zmm0,zmmword ptr [rax]{rd-sae} is invalid); scalar floating-point arithmetic instructions that use only register operands can also specify a static rounding mode.

The remaining code in PackedMathF32_Aavx512() illustrates the use of additional AVX-512 packed single-precision floating-point instructions including vsubps, vmulps, vdivps, vminps, vmaxps, and vsqrtps. Note that except for the 512-bit wide operands, the use of these instructions is basically the same as it was for AVX.

Toward the end of function PackedMathF32_Aavx512() is the AVX-512 instruction vandps zmm2,zmm1,real4 bcst [r4_AbsMask]. This is an example of an instruction that exploits AVX-512's embedded broadcast capabilities. During execution of the vandps zmm2,zmm1,real4 bcst [r4_AbsMask] instruction, the processor performs a bitwise logical AND using each single-precision floating-point element in register ZMM1 and memory operand r4_AbsMask (0x7FFFFFFF). Using an embedded broadcast simplifies the coding of SIMD operations that require a constant value since it eliminates the need for an explicit broadcast instruction; it also preserves SIMD registers for other uses. Embedded broadcasts can be used with some (but not all) AVX-512 instructions that support memory operands. The element size of an embedded broadcast value must be 32 or 64 bits; 8- and 16-bit wide elements are not supported.

The next function in Listing 18-1 is PackedMathF64_Aavx512(), which is the double-precision counterpart of PackedMathF32_Aavx512(). Note that PackedMathF64_Aavx512() uses vaddpd, vsubpd, vmulpd, etc., to perform packed double-precision floating-point arithmetic using 512-bit wide operands. Also note that in this function, the second vdivpd instruction specifies a static rounding mode of ru-sae. The results for source code example Ch18_01 follow this paragraph. Value differences obtained when using a static rounding mode are shown in bold (the default rounding mode for Visual C++ programs is round to nearest).

```
Results for PackedMathF32
Group #0
  a:                36.333332      0.031250   |      2.000000     42.000000
  b:                -0.111111     64.000000   |     -0.062500      8.666667
  addps:            36.222221     64.031250   |      1.937500     50.666668
  addps {rd-sae}:   36.222218     64.031250   |      1.937500     50.666664
  subps:            36.444443    -63.968750   |      2.062500     33.333332
  mulps:            -4.037036      2.000000   |     -0.125000    364.000000
  divps:          -327.000031      0.000488   |    -32.000000      4.846154
  minps:            -0.111111      0.031250   |     -0.062500      8.666667
  maxps:            36.333332     64.000000   |      2.000000     42.000000
  sqrtps:            6.027714      0.176777   |      1.414214      6.480741
  absps:             0.111111     64.000000   |      0.062500      8.666667

Group #1
  a:                 7.000000     20.500000   |     36.125000      0.500000
  b:               -18.125000     56.000000   |     24.000000   -158.444443
  addps:           -11.125000     76.500000   |     60.125000   -157.944443
  addps {rd-sae}:  -11.125000     76.500000   |     60.125000   -157.944443
  subps:            25.125000    -35.500000   |     12.125000    158.944443
  mulps:          -126.875000   1148.000000   |    867.000000    -79.222221
  divps:            -0.386207      0.366071   |      1.505208     -0.003156
  minps:           -18.125000     20.500000   |     24.000000   -158.444443
  maxps:             7.000000     56.000000   |     36.125000      0.500000
  sqrtps:            2.645751      4.527693   |      6.010407      0.707107
  absps:            18.125000     56.000000   |     24.000000    158.444443
```

Group #2

| | | | | |
|---|---|---|---|---|
| a: | 136.777771 | 2.031250 | 32.000000 | 442.000000 |
| b: | -9.111111 | 864.000000 | -70.062500 | 98.666664 |
| addps: | 127.666656 | 866.031250 | -38.062500 | **540.666687** |
| addps {rd-sae}: | 127.666656 | 866.031250 | -38.062500 | **540.666626** |
| subps: | 145.888885 | -861.968750 | 102.062500 | 343.333344 |
| mulps: | -1246.197388 | 1755.000000 | -2242.000000 | 43610.664062 |
| divps: | -15.012195 | 0.002351 | -0.456735 | 4.479730 |
| minps: | -9.111111 | 2.031250 | -70.062500 | 98.666664 |
| maxps: | 136.777771 | 864.000000 | 32.000000 | 442.000000 |
| sqrtps: | 11.695203 | 1.425219 | 5.656854 | 21.023796 |
| absps: | 9.111111 | 864.000000 | 70.062500 | 98.666664 |

Group #3

| | | | | |
|---|---|---|---|---|
| a: | 57.000000 | 620.500000 | 736.125000 | 2.718282 |
| b: | -518.125000 | 456.000000 | 3.141593 | -298.600006 |
| addps: | -461.125000 | 1076.500000 | **739.266602** | **-295.881714** |
| addps {rd-sae}: | -461.125000 | 1076.500000 | **739.266541** | **-295.881744** |
| subps: | 575.125000 | 164.500000 | 732.983398 | 301.318298 |
| mulps: | -29533.125000 | 282948.000000 | 2312.604980 | -811.678955 |
| divps: | -0.110012 | 1.360746 | 234.315857 | -0.009103 |
| minps: | -518.125000 | 456.000000 | 3.141593 | -298.600006 |
| maxps: | 57.000000 | 620.500000 | 736.125000 | 2.718282 |
| sqrtps: | 7.549834 | 24.909838 | 27.131624 | 1.648721 |
| absps: | 518.125000 | 456.000000 | 3.141593 | 298.600006 |

Results for PackedMathF64
Group #0

| | | |
|---|---|---|
| a: | 2.7182818284590451 | 0.4342944819032518 |
| b: | 3.1415926535897931 | 2.7182818284590451 |
| addpd: | 5.8598744820488378 | 3.1525763103622970 |
| subpd: | -0.4233108251307480 | -2.2839873465557932 |
| mulpd: | 8.5397342226735660 | 1.1805347983576451 |
| divpd: | **0.8652559794322651** | 0.1597680113064094 |
| divpd {ru-sae}: | **0.8652559794322652** | 0.1597680113064094 |
| minpd: | 2.7182818284590451 | 0.4342944819032518 |
| maxpd: | 3.1415926535897931 | 2.7182818284590451 |
| sqrtpd: | 1.6487212707001282 | 0.6590102289822608 |
| abspd: | 3.1415926535897931 | 2.7182818284590451 |

Group #1

| | | |
|---|---|---|
| a: | 0.2828427124746190 | 7.0000000000000000 |
| b: | 0.6931471805599453 | -3.1415926535897931 |
| addpd: | 0.9759898930345643 | 3.8584073464102069 |
| subpd: | -0.4103044680853263 | 10.1415926535897931 |
| mulpd: | 0.1960516286937094 | -21.9911485751285518 |
| divpd: | 0.4080557786387158 | **-2.2281692032865350** |
| divpd {ru-sae}: | 0.4080557786387158 | **-2.2281692032865346** |
| minpd: | 0.2828427124746190 | -3.1415926535897931 |
| maxpd: | 0.6931471805599453 | 7.0000000000000000 |
| sqrtpd: | 0.5318295896944989 | 2.6457513110645907 |
| abspd: | 0.6931471805599453 | 3.1415926535897931 |

```
Group #2
  a:                    2.3025850929940459  |     0.3183098861837907
  b:                    1.0471975511965976  |     2.7182818284590451
  addpd:                3.3497826441906433  |     3.0365917146428356
  subpd:                1.2553875417974483  |    -2.3999719422752546
  mulpd:                2.4112614708051550  |     0.8652559794322651
  divpd:                2.1988067966382836  |     0.1170996630486383
  divpd {ru-sae}:       2.1988067966382840  |     0.1170996630486383
  minpd:                1.0471975511965976  |     0.3183098861837907
  maxpd:                2.3025850929940459  |     2.7182818284590451
  sqrtpd:               1.5174271293851465  |     0.5641895835477563
  abspd:                1.0471975511965976  |     2.7182818284590451

Group #3
  a:                    1.1283791670955126  |     1.4142135623730951
  b:                    3.1415926535897931  |    -1.5707963267948966
  addpd:                4.2699718206853055  |    -0.1565827644218014
  subpd:               -2.0132134864942808  |     2.9850098891679915
  mulpd:                3.5449077018110318  |    -2.2214414690791831
  divpd:                0.3591742442503331  |    -0.9003163161571062
  divpd {ru-sae}:       0.3591742442503332  |    -0.9003163161571061
  minpd:                1.1283791670955126  |    -1.5707963267948966
  maxpd:                3.1415926535897931  |     1.4142135623730951
  sqrtpd:               1.0622519320271968  |     1.1892071150027210
  abspd:                3.1415926535897931  |     1.5707963267948966
```

## Compare Operations

Listing 18-2 shows the assembly language source code for example Ch18_02. This example illustrates how to perform packed floating-point compare operations using AVX-512 instructions and 512-bit wide operands.

*Listing 18-2.* Example Ch18_02

```
;-------------------------------------------------
;               Ch18_02_fasm.asm
;-------------------------------------------------

        include <cmpequ.asmh>

;-----------------------------------------------------------------------
; extern "C" void PackedCompareF32_Aavx512(uint16_t c[8], const ZmmVal* a,
;   const ZmmVal* b);
;-----------------------------------------------------------------------

        .code
PackedCompareF32_Aavx512 proc
        vmovaps zmm0,zmmword ptr [rdx]      ;zmm0 = a
        vmovaps zmm1,zmmword ptr [r8]       ;zmm1 = b
```

```
        vcmpps k1,zmm0,zmm1,CMP_EQ_OQ          ;packed compare for EQ
        kmovw word ptr[rcx],k1                 ;save mask

        vcmpps k1,zmm0,zmm1,CMP_NEQ_OQ         ;packed compare for NEQ
        kmovw word ptr[rcx+2],k1               ;save mask

        vcmpps k1,zmm0,zmm1,CMP_LT_OQ          ;packed compare for LT
        kmovw word ptr[rcx+4],k1               ;save mask

        vcmpps k1,zmm0,zmm1,CMP_LE_OQ          ;packed compare for LE
        kmovw word ptr[rcx+6],k1               ;save mask

        vcmpps k1,zmm0,zmm1,CMP_GT_OQ          ;packed compare for GT
        kmovw word ptr[rcx+8],k1               ;save mask

        vcmpps k1,zmm0,zmm1,CMP_GE_OQ          ;packed compare for GE
        kmovw word ptr[rcx+10],k1              ;save mask

        vcmpps k1,zmm0,zmm1,CMP_ORD_Q          ;packed compare for ORD
        kmovw word ptr[rcx+12],k1              ;save mask

        vcmpps k1,zmm0,zmm1,CMP_UNORD_Q        ;packed compare for UNORD
        kmovw word ptr[rcx+14],k1              ;save mask

        vzeroupper
        ret
PackedCompareF32_Aavx512 endp

;-------------------------------------------------------------------------
; extern "C" void PackedCompareF64_Aavx512(uint8_t c[8], const ZmmVal* a,
;   const ZmmVal* b);
;-------------------------------------------------------------------------

PackedCompareF64_Aavx512 proc
        vmovapd zmm0,zmmword ptr [rdx]         ;zmm0 = a
        vmovapd zmm1,zmmword ptr [r8]          ;zmm1 = b

        vcmppd k1,zmm0,zmm1,CMP_EQ_OQ          ;packed compare for EQ
        kmovb byte ptr[rcx],k1                 ;save mask

        vcmppd k1,zmm0,zmm1,CMP_NEQ_OQ         ;packed compare for NEQ
        kmovb byte ptr[rcx+1],k1               ;save mask

        vcmppd k1,zmm0,zmm1,CMP_LT_OQ          ;packed compare for LT
        kmovb byte ptr[rcx+2],k1               ;save mask

        vcmppd k1,zmm0,zmm1,CMP_LE_OQ          ;packed compare for LE
        kmovb byte ptr[rcx+3],k1               ;save mask

        vcmppd k1,zmm0,zmm1,CMP_GT_OQ          ;packed compare for GT
        kmovb byte ptr[rcx+4],k1               ;save mask
```

```
        vcmppd k1,zmm0,zmm1,CMP_GE_OQ           ;packed compare for GE
        kmovb byte ptr[rcx+5],k1                ;save mask

        vcmppd k1,zmm0,zmm1,CMP_ORD_Q           ;packed compare for ORD
        kmovb byte ptr[rcx+6],k1                ;save mask

        vcmppd k1,zmm0,zmm1,CMP_UNORD_Q         ;packed compare for UNORD
        kmovb byte ptr[rcx+7],k1                ;save mask

        vzeroupper
        ret
PackedCompareF64_Aavx512 endp
        end
```

In Chapter 17, you learned how to perform AVX-512 compare operations using packed integer operands (see examples Ch17_02–Ch17_04). Recall that in these examples, the AVX-512 instructions vpcmp[b|w|d|q] and vpcmpu[b|w|d|q] saved their results in an opmask register. The AVX-512 floating-point counterpart compare instructions vcmpp[d|s] (Compare Packed DPFP | SPFP Values) also save their results in an opmask register as you will soon see.

Listing 18-2 opens with the definition of a function named PackedCompareF32_Aavx512(), which demonstrates how to perform packed floating-point compare operations using single-precision elements. The first two instructions of this function, vmovaps zmm0,zmmword ptr [rdx] and vmovaps zmm1,zmmword ptr [r8], load ZmmVal arguments a and b into registers ZMM0 and ZMM1, respectively. The next instruction, vcmpps k1,zmm0,zmm1,CMP_EQ_OQ, compares corresponding single-precision floating-point elements in ZMM0 and ZMM1 for equality. If the elements are equal, the corresponding bit position in opmask register K1 is set to 1; otherwise, it is set to 0. The compare predicate CMP_EQ_OQ used in the vcmpps instruction is defined in the assembly language header file include cmpequ.asmh (see Listing 14-2). Following the vcmpps instruction is a kmovw word ptr[rcx],k1 instruction that saves the resultant compare mask to c[0]. The word variant of instruction kmov[b|w|d|q] is used here since each ZMM register operand holds 16 single-precision floating-point elements. The remaining instructions in PackedCompareF32_Aavx512() demonstrate the use of other common floating-point compare predicates.

The next function in Listing 18-2 is named PackedCompareF64_Aavx512(). This function is the double-precision complement of PackedCompareF32_Aavx512(). Note that PackedCompareF64_Aavx512() employs the instructions vmovapd and vcmppd to perform packed double-precision floating-point loads and compares. Also note that PackedCompareF64_Aavx512() uses the kmovb instruction to save each compare result since each ZMM register contains eight double-precision floating-point values. Here are the results for source code example Ch18_02:

```
Results for PackedCompareF32
        a          b          EQ    NE    LT    LE    GT    GE    OD    UO
-----------------------------------------------------------------------
     2.0000     1.0000       0     1     0     0     1     1     1     0
     7.0000    12.0000       0     1     1     1     0     0     1     0
    -6.0000    -6.0000       1     0     0     1     0     1     1     0
     3.0000     8.0000       0     1     1     1     0     0     1     0
   -16.0000   -36.0000       0     1     0     0     1     1     1     0
     3.5000     3.5000       1     0     0     1     0     1     1     0
     3.1416    -6.0000       0     1     0     0     1     1     1     0
     1.4142        nan       0     0     0     0     0     0     0     1
   102.0000     0.7071       0     1     0     0     1     1     1     0
    77.0000    77.0000       1     0     0     1     0     1     1     0
```

| 187.0000 | 33.0000 | 0 | 1 | 0 | 0 | 1 | 1 | 1 | 0 |
| -5.1000 | -87.0000 | 0 | 1 | 0 | 0 | 1 | 1 | 1 | 0 |
| 16.0000 | 936.0000 | 0 | 1 | 1 | 1 | 0 | 0 | 1 | 0 |
| 0.5000 | 0.5000 | 1 | 0 | 0 | 1 | 0 | 1 | 1 | 0 |
| 6.2832 | 66.6667 | 0 | 1 | 1 | 1 | 0 | 0 | 1 | 0 |
| 0.7071 | 100.7000 | 0 | 1 | 1 | 1 | 0 | 0 | 1 | 0 |

```
Results for PackedCompareF64
         a          b      EQ   NE   LT   LE   GT   GE   OD   UO
-----------------------------------------------------------------
    2.0000     2.7183       0    1    1    1    0    0    1    0
    1.5708    -0.3183       0    1    0    0    1    1    1    0
   12.0000    42.0000       0    1    1    1    0    0    1    0
   33.3333     1.4142       0    1    0    0    1    1    1    0
    0.5000     5.4366       0    1    1    1    0    0    1    0
   -3.1416    -6.2832       0    1    0    0    1    1    1    0
  -24.0000   -24.0000       1    0    0    1    0    1    1    0
       nan   100.0000       0    0    0    0    0    0    0    1
```

# Floating-Point Matrices

In Chapter 8, you learned how to use AVX-512 C++ SIMD intrinsic functions to implement a variety of functions that utilized floating-point matrices. In this section, you will learn how to code some of these same functions using AVX-512 assembly language instructions. The first source example demonstrates calculation of a covariance matrix. This is followed by a source code example that implements matrix multiplication. The final source code example of this section spotlights matrix-vector multiplication.

## Covariance Matrix

Source code example Ch08_04 explained how to calculate a covariance matrix using AVX-512 C++ SIMD intrinsic functions. The next example of this chapter, named Ch18_03, illustrates how to calculate a covariance matrix using assembly language and AVX-512 instructions. Listing 18-3 shows the assembly language source code for example Ch18_03. Before examining this source code, you may want to review the covariance matrix equations defined in Chapter 8 since the same equations are used in example Ch18_03.

***Listing 18-3.*** Example Ch18_03

```
;--------------------------------------------------
;                 Ch18_03_fasm.asm
;--------------------------------------------------

        include <MacrosX86-64-AVX.asmh>

;-----------------------------------------------------------------------
; extern "C" void CalcCovMatF64_Aavx512(double* cov_mat, double* var_means,
;    const double* x, size_t n_vars, size_t n_obvs);
;-----------------------------------------------------------------------
```

```
NSE       equ     8                            ;num_simd_elements


          .code
CalcCovMatF64_Aavx512 proc frame
          CreateFrame_M COV_,0,0,rbx,r12,r13,r14,r15
          EndProlog_M

; Initialize
          mov r10,qword ptr [rbp+COV_OffsetStackArgs] ;r10 = n_obvs
          vcvtusi2sd xmm16,xmm16,r10                  ;convert n_obvs to F64
          mov rax,r10
          dec rax                               ;rax = n_obvs - 1
          vcvtusi2sd xmm17,xmm17,rax            ;convert n_obvs - 1 to F64
          mov rax,-1                            ;rax = i

;-----------------------------------------------------------------------
; Calculate var_means[i] (mean of row i in matrix x)
;
; General-purpose register use in code that calculates var_means[i]
;
;   rax      i                    r10     n_obvs
;   rbx      j                    r11     scratch register
;   rcx      cov_mat              r12     -----
;   rdx      var_means            r13     -----
;   r8       x                    r14     i * n_obvs
;   r9       n_vars               r15     -----
;-----------------------------------------------------------------------


          align 16
Loop1:    inc rax                              ;i += 1
          cmp rax,r9
          jae CalcCV                           ;jump if i >= n_vars

          mov r14,rax                          ;r14 = i
          imul r14,r10                         ;r14 = i * n_obvs
          mov rbx,-NSE                         ;rbx = j
          vxorpd zmm0,zmm0,zmm0                 ;sums[0:7] = 0

; Sum elements in row x[i]
          align 16
Loop2:    add rbx,NSE                          ;j += NSE
          mov r11,r10                          ;r11 = n_obvs
          sub r11,rbx                          ;r11 = n_obvs - j
          cmp r11,NSE
          jb @F                                ;jump if n_objs - j < NSE

          lea r11,[r14+rbx]                        ;r11 = i * n_obvs + j
          vaddpd zmm0,zmm0,zmmword ptr [r8+r11*8] ;sums[0:7] += x[i][j:j+NSE-1]
          jmp Loop2
```

```
; Update sums for row x[i] if 4 or more elements remain
@@:     vextractf64x4 ymm1,zmm0,1              ;reduce sums (4 elements)
        vaddpd ymm0,ymm0,ymm1
        mov r11,r10                            ;r11 = n_obvs
        sub r11,rbx                            ;r11 = n_obvs - j
        cmp r11,NSE/2
        jb @F                                  ;jump if n_objs - j < NSE / 2

        lea r11,[r14+rbx]                      ;r11 = i * n_obvs + j
        vaddpd ymm0,ymm0,ymmword ptr [r8+r11*8] ;sums[0:3] += x[i][j:j+NSE/2-1]
        add rbx,NSE/2                          ;j += NSE / 2

; Update sums for row x[i] if 2 or more elements remain
@@:     vextractf64x2 xmm1,ymm0,1              ;reduce sums (2 elements)
        vaddpd xmm0,xmm0,xmm1
        mov r11,r10                            ;r11 = n_obvs
        sub r11,rbx                            ;r11 = n_obvs - j
        cmp r11,NSE/4
        jb @F                                  ;jump if n_objs - j < NSE / 4

        lea r11,[r14+rbx]                      ;r11 = i * n_obvs + j
        vaddpd xmm0,xmm0,xmmword ptr [r8+r11*8] ;sums[0:1] += x[i][j:j+NSE/4-1]
        add rbx,NSE/4                          ;j += NSE / 4

; Update sums for row x[i] if 1 element remains
@@:     vhaddpd xmm0,xmm0,xmm0                 ;reduce sums (scalar element)
        cmp rbx,r10
        jae CalcM                             ;jump if j >= n_obvs

        lea r11,[r14+rbx]                      ;r11 = i * n_obvs + j
        vaddsd xmm0,xmm0,real8 ptr [r8+r11*8]  ;sum += x[i][j]

; Calculate var_means[i]
CalcM:  vdivsd xmm1,xmm0,xmm16                 ;var_means[i] = sum / n_obvs
        vmovsd real8 ptr [rdx+rax*8],xmm1      ;save var_means[i]
        jmp Loop1


;---------------------------------------------------------------------
; Calculate covariance matrix
;
; General-purpose register use in code that calculates cov_mat[i][j]
;
;   rax     i                    r10     n_obvs
;   rbx     j                    r11     scratch register
;   rcx     cov_mat              r12     i * n_vars
;   rdx     var_means            r13     k
;   r8      x                    r14     i * n_obvs
;   r9      n_vars               r15     j * n_obvs
;---------------------------------------------------------------------
```

```
CalcCV: mov rax,-1                              ;rax = i

        align 16
Loop3:  inc rax                                 ;i += 1
        cmp rax,r9
        jae Done                                ;jump if i >= n_vars

        vbroadcastsd zmm18,real8 ptr [rdx+rax*8]    ;zmm18 = var_means[i]

        mov r12,rax                             ;r12 = i
        imul r12,r9                             ;r12 = i * n_vars
        mov r14,rax                             ;r14 = i
        imul r14,r10                            ;r14 = i * n_obvs
        mov rbx,-1                              ;rbx = j

        align 16
Loop4:  inc rbx                                 ;j += 1
        cmp rbx,r9
        jae Loop3                               ;jump if j >= n_vars

        cmp rax,rbx                             ;is i > j?
        ja NoCalc                               ;jump if i > j (no calculation required)

        vxorpd zmm0,zmm0,zmm0                    ;sums = 0;
        vbroadcastsd zmm19,real8 ptr [rdx+rbx*8]    ;zmm19 = var_means[j]
        mov r15,rbx                             ;r15 = j
        imul r15,r10                            ;r15 = j * n_obvs
        mov r13,-NSE                            ;r13 = k

; Calculate cov_mat[i][j] product sums
        align 16
Loop5:  add r13,NSE                             ;k += NSE
        mov r11,r10                             ;r11 = n_obvs
        sub r11,r13                             ;r11 = n_obvs - k
        cmp r11,NSE
        jb @F                                   ;jump if n_objs - k < NSE

        lea r11,[r14+r13]                       ;r11 = i * n_obvs + k
        vmovupd zmm1,zmmword ptr [r8+r11*8]     ;load x[i][k:k+NSE-1]
        lea r11,[r15+r13]                       ;r11 = j * n_obvs + k
        vmovupd zmm2,zmmword ptr [r8+r11*8]     ;load x[j][k:k+NSE-1]
        vsubpd zmm3,zmm1,zmm18                  ;x[i][k:k+NSE-1] - var_means[i]
        vsubpd zmm4,zmm2,zmm19                  ;x[j][k:k+NSE-1] - var_means[j]
        vfmadd231pd zmm0,zmm3,zmm4              ;update cov_mat[i][j] product sums
        jmp Loop5

; Update cov_mat[i][j] product sums if 4 or more elements remain
@@:     vextractf64x4 ymm1,zmm0,1               ;reduce product sums (4 elements)
        vaddpd ymm0,ymm0,ymm1
        mov r11,r10                             ;r11 = n_obvs
        sub r11,r13                             ;r11 = n_obvs - k
```

```
        cmp r11,NSE/2
        jb @F                                  ;jump if n_objs - k < NSE / 2

        lea r11,[r14+r13]                      ;r11 = i * n_obvs + k
        vmovupd ymm1,ymmword ptr [r8+r11*8]    ;load x[i][k:k+NSE/2-1]
        lea r11,[r15+r13]                      ;r11 = j * n_obvs + k
        vmovupd ymm2,ymmword ptr [r8+r11*8]    ;load x[j][k:k+NSE/2-1]
        vsubpd ymm3,ymm1,ymm18                 ;x[i][k:k+NSE/2-1] - var_means[i]
        vsubpd ymm4,ymm2,ymm19                 ;x[j][k:k+NSE/2-1] - var_means[j]
        vfmadd231pd ymm0,ymm3,ymm4             ;update cov_mat[i][j] product sums
        add r13,NSE/2                          ;k += NSE / 2

; Update cov_mat[i][j] product sums if 2 or more elements remain
@@:     vextractf64x2 xmm1,ymm0,1              ;reduce product sums (2 elements)
        vaddpd xmm0,xmm0,xmm1
        mov r11,r10                            ;r11 = n_obvs
        sub r11,r13                            ;r11 = n_obvs - k
        cmp r11,NSE/4
        jb @F                                  ;jump if n_objs - k < NSE / 4

        lea r11,[r14+r13]                      ;r11 = i * n_obvs + k
        vmovupd xmm1,xmmword ptr [r8+r11*8]    ;load x[i][k:k+NSE/4-1]
        lea r11,[r15+r13]                      ;r11 = j * n_obvs + k
        vmovupd xmm2,xmmword ptr [r8+r11*8]    ;load x[j][k:k+NSE/4-1]
        vsubpd xmm3,xmm1,xmm18                 ;x[i][k:k+NSE/4-1] - var_means[i]
        vsubpd xmm4,xmm2,xmm19                 ;x[j][k:k+NSE/4-1] - var_means[j]
        vfmadd231pd xmm0,xmm3,xmm4             ;update cov_mat[i][j] product sums
        add r13,NSE/4                          ;k += NSE / 4

; Update cov_mat[i][j] product sums if 1 element remains
@@:     vhaddpd xmm0,xmm0,xmm0                 ;reduce product sums (scalar element)
        cmp r13,r10
        jae @F                                 ;jump if k >= n_obvs

        lea r11,[r14+r13]                      ;r11 = i * n_obvs + k
        vmovsd xmm1,real8 ptr [r8+r11*8]       ;load x[i][k]
        lea r11,[r15+r13]                      ;r11 = j * n_obvs + k
        vmovsd xmm2,real8 ptr [r8+r11*8]       ;load x[j][k]
        vsubsd xmm3,xmm1,xmm18                 ;x[i][j] - var_means[i]
        vsubsd xmm4,xmm2,xmm19                 ;x[j][i] - var_means[j]
        vfmadd231sd xmm0,xmm3,xmm4             ;update cov_mat[i][j] product sums

; Finish calculation of cov_mat[i][j]
@@:     vdivsd xmm1,xmm0,xmm17                 ;calc cov_mat[i][j]
        lea r11,[r12+rbx]                      ;r11 = i * n_vars + j
        vmovsd real8 ptr [rcx+r11*8],xmm1      ;save cov_mat[i][j]
        jmp Loop4

; No calculation needed - set cov_mat[i][j] = cov_mat[j][i]
NoCalc: mov r11,rbx                            ;r11 = j
        imul r11,r9                            ;r11 = j * n_vars
```

```
        add r11,rax                       ;r11 = j * n_vars + i
        vmovsd xmm0,real8 ptr [rcx+r11*8] ;load cov_mat[j][i]
        lea r11,[r12+rbx]                 ;r11 = i * n_vars + j
        vmovsd real8 ptr [rcx+r11*8],xmm0 ;save cov_mat[i][j]
        jmp Loop4


Done:   vzeroupper
        DeleteFrame_M rbx,r12,r13,r14,r15
        ret
CalcCovMatF64_Aavx512 endp
        end
```

The sole function in Listing 18-3 is named CalcCovMatF64_Aavx512(). Following its prologue is a code block that performs the requisite initializations for the covariance matrix calculating code. Note that argument n_obvs is passed to CalcCovMatF64_Aavx512() via the stack (recall that only the first four integer-type arguments are passed via registers). Like the C++ code in example Ch08_04, the assembly language code in Listing 18-3 consists of two major sections. The first section calculates the mean values (var_means) for each variable (or row) in data matrix x. The second section computes covariance matrix cov_mat. Recall from the discussions in Chapter 8 that a covariance matrix is always symmetrical. The calculating code in CalcCovMatF64_Aavx512() exploits this fact to reduce the number of calculations it must perform as you will soon see.

Each row of data matrix x (R8) contains the values (or observations) for a single variable (see Figure 8-1). Function CalcCovMatF64_Aavx512() employs two nested for-loops to calculate the mean of each row in matrix x. For-loop Loop1 is the outer-most for-loop. During each iteration, the top-most code block in Loop1 terminates the for-loop if i >= n_vars is true. If i >= n_vars is false, CalcCovMatF64_Aavx512() calculates and sets R14 equal to i * n_obvs, which represents the index of matrix element x[i][0]. It also uses a vxorpd zmm0,zmm0,zmm0 instruction to initialize sums[0:7] to zero.

The element summing code for row x[i] is split into four code blocks. The first summing code block, which starts at label Loop2, calculates sums[0:7] += x[i][j:j+7] using SIMD arithmetic. This block repeats until there are fewer than eight (NSE) elements remaining. Note that following execution of Loop2, the number of remaining elements in row x[i] is n_obvs % 8. The second summing code block for row x[i] opens with the instruction pair vextractf64x4 ymm1,zmm0,1 (Extract Floating-Point Values) and vaddpd ymm0,ymm0,ymm1. This reduces the number of intermediate sum values from eight to four. If four (NSE / 2) or more elements remain in row x[i], CalcCovMatF64_Aavx512() calculates sums[0:3] += x[i][j:j+3] using the instruction vaddpd ymm0,ymm0,ymmword ptr [r8+r11*8].

The third summing code block for row x[i] starts with the instruction pair vextractf64x2 xmm1,ymm0,1 and vaddpd xmm0,xmm0,xmm1 that reduces the number of intermediate sums from four to two. If two or more elements remain in the current row, function CalcCovMatF64_Aavx512() calculates sums[0:1] += x[i][j:j+1]. The final summing code block for row x[i] starts with the instruction vhaddpd xmm0,xmm0,xmm0 that reduces the number of intermediate sums in XMM0 from two to one. If one element remains in row x[i], the instruction vaddsd xmm0,xmm0,real8 ptr [r8+r11*8] adds this value to the sum in XMM0. Scalar double-precision arithmetic is then employed to calculate var_means[i].

The covariance calculating code in CalcCovMatF64_Aavx512() uses three nested for-loops to calculate each cov_mat[i][j] value. The outer two for-loops, Loop3 and Loop4, include instructions that update and maintain for-loop index variables i and j. The instruction vbroadcastsd zmm18,real8 ptr [rdx+rax*8] that appears near the top of Loop3 broadcasts var_means[i] to each element in ZMM18. In the code block that follows, integer multiplication is used to calculate i * n_vars and i * n_obvs. These values are used in later code blocks to load elements from matrices x and cov_mat. The reason for performing these calculations here is that they only need to be calculated each time index variable i is incremented, which occurs in the code block next to label Loop3.

For-loop Loop4 begins with a code block that calculates j += 1. This code block also includes instructions that terminate Loop4 if j >= n_vars is true. Following the updating of j, CalcCovMatF64_Aavx512() uses the instruction pair cmp rax,rbx and ja NoCalc to skip over the calculating code for cov_mat[i][j] if i > j is true. When i > j is true, CalcCovMatF64_Aavx512() can perform a matrix element copy since cov_mat is a symmetric matrix. More on this later. The next code block performs initializations necessary to calculate cov_mat[i][j]. Note that register ZMM19 is loaded with var_means[j] using the instruction vbroadcastsd zmm19,real8 ptr [rdx+rbx*8]. Also note the use of the instruction pair mov r15,rbx and imul r15,r10 to calculate j * n_obvs.

Like the mean calculating code, the assembly language code that calculates the requisite covariance matrix product sums is also split into four code blocks. The first code block, located at label Loop5, computes covariance matrix product sums using eight (NSE) elements. In the first product sums calculating code block, CalcCovMatF64_Aavx512() uses the instruction pair lea r11,[r14+r13] and vmovupd zmm1,zmmword ptr [r8+r11*8] to load elements x[i][k:k+NSE-1] into register ZMM1. Note that the lea instruction, which calculates i * n_obvs + k, can be used here since i * n_obvs was calculated prior to the start of Loop5. The next instruction pair, lea r11,[r15+r13] and vmovupd zmm2,zmmword ptr [r8+r11*8], loads elements x[j][k:k+NSE-1] into register ZMM2. This is followed by the instruction triplet vsubpd zmm3,zmm1,zmm18, vsubpd zmm4,zmm2,zmm19, and vfmadd231pd zmm0,zmm3,zmm4, which updates the product sums needed to calculate cov_mat[i][j]. Note that for-loop Loop5 repeats until fewer than eight elements remain.

The second product sums calculating code block begins with the instruction pair vextractf64x4 ymm1,zmm0,1 and vaddpd ymm0,ymm0,ymm1 that reduces the number of product sums from eight to four. If four or more elements are available, CalcCovMatF64_Aavx512() updates the product sums using matrix elements x[i][k:k+NSE/2-1] and x[j][k:k+NSE/2-1]. Note that the vsubpd and vfmadd231pd instructions in this code block use YMM instead of ZMM register operands.

Execution of the third product sums calculating code block starts with the instruction pair vextractf64x2 xmm1,ymm0,1 and vaddpd xmm0,xmm0,xmm1 that reduces the product sums from four to two. This block updates the product sums using matrix elements x[i][k:k+NSE/4-1] and x[j][k:k+NSE/4-1]. The final product sums calculating code block commences with a vhaddpd xmm0,xmm0,xmm0 that reduces the product sums to a scalar value. Scalar arithmetic is then employed to update the product sum with the last element if necessary. Following calculation of the product sums for cov_mat[i][j], CalcCovMatF64_Aavx512() uses scalar arithmetic to calculate the final covariance. Note that in the instruction vdivsd xmm1,xmm0,xmm17, register XMM17 contains n_obvs - 1, which was calculated in the initialization code block of CalcCovMatF64_Aavx512().

The code block that follows label NoCalc contains instructions that set cov_mat[i][j] = cov_mat[j][i] when a complete covariance matrix element calculation is not required. Here are the results for source code example Ch18_03:

```
Results for CalcCovMatF64
n_vars = 12, n_obvs = 103
Variable means
    0:      13.29       13.29
    1:      12.19       12.19
    2:      13.23       13.23
    3:      12.81       12.81
    4:      12.21       12.21
    5:      11.94       11.94
    6:      11.61       11.61
    7:      12.14       12.14
    8:      12.17       12.17
    9:      12.75       12.75
   10:      11.57       11.57
   11:      13.48       13.48
```

```
cmd1.m_CovMat
 51.47   -5.44    -4.02   -7.40    9.38    9.54    3.78   -4.88   -0.13   -5.57   -3.05 -0.13
 -5.44   46.43     0.65    3.14    6.77    5.55    7.53  -10.10    3.28   -9.78    2.20 -2.67
 -4.02    0.65    47.41   -3.05    8.95    0.26   -3.35    1.96    7.56    1.05    5.73 14.40
 -7.40    3.14    -3.05   49.82   -1.64    4.03   -0.29    6.52   -3.84   -0.89   -0.43  0.61
  9.38    6.77     8.95   -1.64   58.12    4.29    5.73  -15.49  -10.73    0.43   -1.55  3.88
  9.54    5.55     0.26    4.03    4.29   54.11    4.26   -2.84   -5.88   -1.29   -2.37 -4.08
  3.78    7.53    -3.35   -0.29    5.73    4.26   57.93   -2.79   -4.37    8.29   -0.89  0.75
 -4.88  -10.10     1.96    6.52  -15.49   -2.84   -2.79   52.06    4.30   -3.24   -0.22 -0.53
 -0.13    3.28     7.56   -3.84  -10.73   -5.88   -4.37    4.30   54.63   -7.42   -0.98  2.74
 -5.57   -9.78     1.05   -0.89    0.43   -1.29    8.29   -3.24   -7.42   50.77   -9.46  0.80
 -3.05    2.20     5.73   -0.43   -1.55   -2.37   -0.89   -0.22   -0.98   -9.46   44.26  1.52
 -0.13   -2.67    14.40    0.61    3.88   -4.08    0.75   -0.53    2.74    0.80    1.52 55.52

cmd2.m_CovMat
 51.47   -5.44    -4.02   -7.40    9.38    9.54    3.78   -4.88   -0.13   -5.57   -3.05 -0.13
 -5.44   46.43     0.65    3.14    6.77    5.55    7.53  -10.10    3.28   -9.78    2.20 -2.67
 -4.02    0.65    47.41   -3.05    8.95    0.26   -3.35    1.96    7.56    1.05    5.73 14.40
 -7.40    3.14    -3.05   49.82   -1.64    4.03   -0.29    6.52   -3.84   -0.89   -0.43  0.61
  9.38    6.77     8.95   -1.64   58.12    4.29    5.73  -15.49  -10.73    0.43   -1.55  3.88
  9.54    5.55     0.26    4.03    4.29   54.11    4.26   -2.84   -5.88   -1.29   -2.37 -4.08
  3.78    7.53    -3.35   -0.29    5.73    4.26   57.93   -2.79   -4.37    8.29   -0.89  0.75
 -4.88  -10.10     1.96    6.52  -15.49   -2.84   -2.79   52.06    4.30   -3.24   -0.22 -0.53
 -0.13    3.28     7.56   -3.84  -10.73   -5.88   -4.37    4.30   54.63   -7.42   -0.98  2.74
 -5.57   -9.78     1.05   -0.89    0.43   -1.29    8.29   -3.24   -7.42   50.77   -9.46  0.80
 -3.05    2.20     5.73   -0.43   -1.55   -2.37   -0.89   -0.22   -0.98   -9.46   44.26  1.52
 -0.13   -2.67    14.40    0.61    3.88   -4.08    0.75   -0.53    2.74    0.80    1.52 55.52

CompareResults - passed
```

## Matrix Multiplication

Listing 18-4 shows the assembly language source code for example Ch18_04. This example demonstrates matrix multiplication using AVX-512 instructions. Before reviewing the source code in Listing 18-4, you may want to review the matrix multiplication equations and diagrams (Figures 5-1, 5-2, and 5-3) presented in Chapter 5 for source code example Ch05_02. You may also want to review the source code for example Ch08_05, which implemented matrix multiplication using AVX-512 C++ SIMD intrinsic functions.

*Listing 18-4.* Example Ch18_04

```
;--------------------------------------------------
;               Ch18_04_fasm.asm
;--------------------------------------------------

        include <MacrosX86-64-AVX.asmh>

;----------------------------------------------------------------------------
; extern "C" void MatrixMulF32_Aavx512_TEST(float* c, const float* a, const float* b,
;    const size_t* sizes);
;----------------------------------------------------------------------------
```

```
NSE      equ 16                                ;num_simd_elements
NSE_MOD equ 0fh                                ;mask to calculate num_residual_cols


        .code
MatrixMulF32_Aavx512 proc frame
        CreateFrame_M MM_,0,0,rbx,rsi,rdi,r12,r13,r14,r15
        EndProlog_M

; Load matrix sizes
        mov r13,qword ptr [r9]                 ;r13 = c_nrows
        mov r14,qword ptr [r9+8]                ;r14 = c_ncols (also b_ncols)
        mov r15,qword ptr [r9+16]              ;r15 = a_ncols

; Calculate mask for resdiual column load and store
        mov r12,r14                            ;r12 = c_ncols
        and r12,NSE_MOD                        ;num_residual_cols = c_ncols % NSE

        mov r9,rcx                             ;save rcx
        mov rcx,r12                            ;rcx = num_residual_cols
        mov eax,1
        shl eax,cl                             ;eax = 2 ** num_residual_cols
        dec eax                                ;eax = 2 ** num_residual_cols - 1
        kmovw k1,eax                           ;k1 = mask for residual col load/store
        mov rcx,r9                             ;restore rcx

        mov rax,-1                             ;rax = i

;-----------------------------------------------------------------------------
; General-purpose registers used in code below
;    rax      i                              r9     j
;    rbx      matrix a element pointer (p_aa)   r10    k
;    rcx      matrix c                       r11    scratch
;    rdx      matrix a                       r12    num_residual_cols
;    rsi      matrix b element pointer (p_bb)   r13    c_nrows
;    rdi      &a[i][0]                       r14    c_ncols (b_ncols)
;    r8       matrix b                       r15    a_ncols
;-----------------------------------------------------------------------------

; Repeat for each row in c
        align 16
Loop1:  inc rax                                ;i += 1
        cmp rax,r13
        jae Done                               ;jump if i >= c_nrows

        mov rdi,rdx                            ;rdi = &a[i][0]
        lea rdx,[rdx+r15*4]                    ;rdx = &a[i+1][0]
        xor r9,r9                              ;j = 0

; Calculate c[i][j:j+NSE*2-1]
        align 16
Loop2:  lea r11,[r9+NSE*2]                     ;r11 = j + NSE*2
```

```
        cmp  r11,r14
        ja   @F                                  ;jump if j + NSE*2 > c_ncols

        mov  rbx,rdi                             ;rbx = &a[i][0]
        lea  rsi,[r8+r9*4]                       ;rsi = &b[0][j]
        vxorps zmm2,zmm2,zmm2                     ;c_vals[i][j:j+NSE-1] = 0
        vxorps zmm3,zmm3,zmm3                     ;c_vals[i][j+NSE:j+NSE*2-1] = 0
        mov  r10,r15                             ;k = a_ncols

        align 16
Loop3:  vbroadcastss zmm0,real4 ptr [rbx]        ;broadcast a[i][k]
        vfmadd231ps zmm2,zmm0,zmmword ptr [rsi]     ;zmm2 += a[i][k] * b[k][j:j+NSE-1]
        vfmadd231ps zmm3,zmm0,zmmword ptr [rsi+64] ;zmm3 += a[i][k] * b[k][j+NSE:j+NSE*2-1]

        add  rbx,4                               ;rbx = &a[i][k+1]
        lea  rsi,[rsi+r14*4]                     ;rsi = &b[k+1][j]
        dec  r10                                 ;k -= 1
        jnz  Loop3                               ;repeat until done

        vmovups zmmword ptr[rcx],zmm2            ;save c[i][j:j+NSE-1]
        vmovups zmmword ptr[rcx+64],zmm3         ;save c[i][j+NSE:j+NSE*2-1]

        add  r9,NSE*2                            ;j += NSE * 2
        add  rcx,NSE*2*4                         ;rcx = &c[i][j+NSE*2]
        jmp  Loop2

; Calculate c[i][j:j+NSE-1]
@@:     lea  r11,[r9+NSE]                        ;r11 = j + NSE
        cmp  r11,r14
        ja   @F                                  ;jump if j + NSE > c_ncols

        mov  rbx,rdi                             ;rbx = &a[i][0]
        lea  rsi,[r8+r9*4]                       ;rsi = &b[0][j]
        vxorps zmm2,zmm2,zmm2                     ;c_vals[i][j:j+NSE-1] = 0
        mov  r10,r15                             ;k = a_ncols

        align 16
Loop4:  vbroadcastss zmm0,real4 ptr [rbx]        ;broadcast a[i][k]
        vfmadd231ps zmm2,zmm0,zmmword ptr [rsi] ;zmm2 += a[i][k] * b[k][j:j+NSE-1]

        add  rbx,4                               ;rbx = &a[i][k+1]
        lea  rsi,[rsi+r14*4]                     ;rsi = &b[k+1][j]
        dec  r10                                 ;k -= 1
        jnz  Loop4                               ;repeat until done

        vmovups zmmword ptr[rcx],zmm2            ;save c[i][j:j+NSE-1]

        add  r9,NSE                              ;j += NSE
        add  rcx,NSE*4                           ;rcx = &c[i][j+NSE]
        jmp  Loop2
```

```
; Calculate c[i][j:j+NRC] (NRC is num_residual_cols)
@@:     test r12,r12                              ;num_residual_cols == 0?
        jz Loop1                                  ;jump if yes

        mov rbx,rdi                               ;rbx = &a[i][0]
        lea rsi,[r8+r9*4]                         ;rsi = &b[0][j]
        vxorps zmm2,zmm2,zmm2                      ;c_vals[i][j:j+NRC] = 0
        mov r10,r15                               ;k = a_ncols

        align 16
Loop5:  vbroadcastss zmm0,real4 ptr [rbx]         ;broadcast a[i][k]
        vmovups zmm1{k1},zmmword ptr [rsi]        ;load b[k][j:j+NRC]
        vfmadd231ps zmm2,zmm0,zmm1                ;zmm2 += a[i][k] * b[k][j:j+NRC]

        add rbx,4                                 ;rbx = &a[i][k+1]
        lea rsi,[rsi+r14*4]                       ;rsi = &b[k+1][j]
        dec r10                                   ;k -= 1
        jnz Loop5                                 ;repeat until done

        vmovups zmmword ptr [rcx]{k1},zmm2        ;save c[i][j:j+NRC]

        lea rcx,[rcx+r12*4]                       ;rcx = &c[i+1][0]
        jmp Loop1

Done:   vzeroupper
        DeleteFrame_M rbx,rsi,rdi,r12,r13,r14,r15
        ret
MatrixMulF32_Aavx512 endp
        end
```

The source code shown in Listing 18-4 is a modified version of the AVX2 matrix multiplication source code that you saw in example Ch16_02. Following its prologue, function MatrixMulF32_Aavx512() uses three mov instructions to load c_nrows, c_ncols (b_ncols), and a_ncols into registers R13, R14, and R15, respectively. The next code block includes instructions that calculate the mask needed to perform matrix element loads and stores for residual columns. This block begins with the instruction pair mov r12,r14 and and r12,NSE_MOD that calculates num_residual_cols. The ensuing mov r9,rcx instruction preserves register RCX (argument value c) in R9 for later use. The next four instructions calculate 2 ** num_residual_cols - 1. This value corresponds to the mask needed for residual column loads and stores. Note that the variable left shift instruction shl eax,cl requires the bit count to be loaded in register CL. This is the reason for the earlier preservation of register RCX. Following calculation of 2 ** num_residual_cols - 1, MatrixMulF32_Aavx512() uses a kmovw k1,eax to save the mask in opmask register K1. The ensuing mov rcx,r9 instruction restores register RCX to its original value. RAX is then initialized as index variable i.

The matrix multiplication calculating code in MatrixMulF32_Aavx512() employs multiple for-loops. The outer-most for-loop, Loop1, indexes each row in matrix c. Execution of this for-loop begins with a code block that tests i >= c_nrows. If this expression is true, the matrix multiplication is complete. The ensuing instruction pair, mov rdi,rdx and lea rdx,[rdx+r15*4], loads RDI with &a[i][0] and RDX with &a[i+1][0]. Registers RDI and RDX contain the address of rows in matrix a needed for the current and next iteration of Loop1 (register RDX could have been updated later but is done here for proximity to the mov rdi,rdx instruction since these instructions are related). The xor r9,r9 instruction initializes R9 to zero and is used as index variable j.

The next-level for-loop, Loop2, cycles through the columns of the current row in matrix c. Each iteration of Loop2 begins with an instruction sequence that checks if j + NSE * 2 > c_ncols is true. The reason for using NSE * 2 instead of NSE (16) is that the first calculating for-loop (Loop3) in MatrixMulF32_Aavx512() computes row-column inner products using NSE * 2 elements. More on this shortly. If j + NSE * 2 > c_ncols is false, the ensuing code block loads &a[i][0] into RBX and &b[0][j] into RSI. The next two instructions, vxorps zmm2,zmm2,zmm2 and vxorps zmm3,zmm3,zmm3, initialize elements c_vals[i][j:j+NSE-1] and c_vals[i][j+NSE:j+NSE*2-1] to zero.

Each iteration of Loop3 begins with a vbroadcastss zmm0,real4 ptr [rbx] instruction that broadcasts a[i][k] to each element in register ZMM0. The ensuing instruction pair, vfmadd231ps zmm2,zmm0,zmmword ptr [rsi] and vfmadd231ps zmm3,zmm0,zmmword ptr [rsi+64], calculates c_vals[i][j:j+NSE-1] += a[i][k] * b[k][j:j+NSE-1] and c_vals[i][j+NSE:j+NSE*2-1] += a[i][k] * b[k][j:j+NSE*2-1], respectively. Note that together, these two vfmadd231ps instructions calculate 32 row-column inner product sums whereas a single vfmadd231ps instruction would calculate only 16 row-column product sums. Doing this reduces the number of times Loop3 executes from a_ncols to a_ncols / 2, which improves performance since fewer for-loop jumps are performed. It also facilitates parallel execution of the vfmadd231ps instructions on processors that contain two AVX-512 FMA execution units. Increasing the number of calculations performed during each iteration of a for-loop as demonstrated in Loop3 is an optimization technique known as partial loop unrolling.

For-loop Loop3 repeatedly executes until fewer than 32 columns remain in row i of matrix c. The code block that follows Loop3 tests j + NSE > c_ncols. If true, at least 16 columns remain in row i. The code in for-loop Loop4 then calculates c[i][j:j+NSE-1] using a single vfmadd231ps instruction. Following execution of Loop4, MatrixMulF32_Aavx512() uses a test r12,r12 instruction to test num_residual_cols == 0. If false, Loop5 calculates row-column product sums for matrix elements c[i][j:j+NRC] (NRC = num_residual_cols). Note that the vmovups instructions in Loop5 use the previously calculated mask in opmkask register K1 to selectively load elements b[k][j:j+NRC] and save elements c[i][j:j+NRC]. Here are the results for source code example Ch18_04:

```
Results for MatrixMulF32
Matrix compare passed
Results saved to file Ch18_04_MatrixMulF32_LITHIUM.txt

Running benchmark function MatrixMulF32_bm - please wait
Benchmark times save to file Ch18_04_MatrixMulF32_bm_LITHIUM.csv
```

Table 18-1 shows the benchmark timing measurements for example Ch18_04. This table also includes the benchmark timing measurements for functions MatrixMulF32_Iavx2(), MatrixMulF32_Aavx2(), and MatrixMulF32_Iavx512() for comparison purposes. All measurements were made using 250 × 250 matrices. As you can see from the numbers in Table 18-1, the AVX-512 implementations of the matrix multiplication algorithm are noticeably faster that their AVX2 counterparts. It should be noted that the source code in function MatrixMulF32_Aavx512() delivers better performance when the destination matrix contains a minimum of 32 columns. It can, of course, be used to calculate products of smaller matrices.

*Table 18-1.* *Matrix Multiplication (Single-Precision) Execution Times (Microseconds)*

| Source Code Example | Function Name | Intel i5-11600K |
|---|---|---|
| Ch05_02 | MatrixMulF32_Iavx2() | 1380 |
| Ch16_02 | MatrixMulF32_Aavx2() | 1376 |
| Ch08_05 | MatrixMulF32_Iavx512() | 713 |
| Ch18_04 | MatrixMulF32_Aavx512() | 653 |

# Matrix (4 x 4) Vector Multiplication

In Chapter 8, you learned how to perform matrix-vector multiplications using a 4 × 4 matrix, an array of 4 × 1 vectors, and AVX-512 SIMD C++ intrinsic functions (see example Ch08_07). The next source code example of this chapter, named Ch18_05, demonstrates how to use AVX-512 assembly language instructions to perform the same calculations. Listing 18-5 shows the assembly language source code for example Ch18_05. Before examining this code, you may want to review the equations shown in Figure 5-5 and the definition of structure Vec4x1_F32 in Listing 5-6 since both are used again in this example.

***Listing 18-5.*** Example Ch18_05

```
;---------------------------------------------
;                 Ch18_05_fasm.asm
;---------------------------------------------

ConstVals    segment readonly align(64) 'const'

; Indices for matrix permutations
MatIndCol0   dword 0, 4, 8, 12, 0, 4, 8, 12, 0, 4, 8, 12, 0, 4, 8, 12
MatIndCol1   dword 1, 5, 9, 13, 1, 5, 9, 13, 1, 5, 9, 13, 1, 5, 9, 13
MatIndCol2   dword 2, 6, 10, 14, 2, 6, 10, 14, 2, 6, 10, 14, 2, 6, 10, 14
MatIndCol3   dword 3, 7, 11, 15, 3, 7, 11, 15, 3, 7, 11, 15, 3, 7, 11, 15

; Indices for vector permutations
VecIndW      dword 0, 0, 0, 0, 4, 4, 4, 4, 8, 8, 8, 8, 12, 12, 12, 12
VecIndX      dword 1, 1, 1, 1, 5, 5, 5, 5, 9, 9, 9, 9, 13, 13, 13, 13
VecIndY      dword 2, 2, 2, 2, 6, 6, 6, 6, 10, 10, 10, 10, 14, 14, 14, 14
VecIndZ      dword 3, 3, 3, 3, 7, 7, 7, 7, 11, 11, 11, 11, 15, 15, 15, 15
ConstVals    ends


;-----------------------------------------------------------------------
; extern "C" void MatVecMulF32a_Aavx512(Vec4x1_F32* vec_b, const float* m,
;    const Vec4x1_F32* vec_a, size_t num_vec);
;-----------------------------------------------------------------------

NVPI    equ    4                        ;num_vec_per_iteration

        .code
MatVecMulF32a_Aavx512 proc
        test r9,r9
        jz Done                         ;jump if num_vec is zero
        test rcx,3fh
        jnz Done                        ;jump if vec_b not 64b aligned
        test rdx,3fh
        jnz Done                        ;jump if m not 64b aligned
        test r8,3fh
        jnz Done                        ;jump if vec_a not 64b aligned

; Load indices for matrix and vector permutations
        vmovdqa32 zmm16,zmmword ptr [MatIndCol0]    ;m col 0 indices
        vmovdqa32 zmm17,zmmword ptr [MatIndCol1]    ;m col 1 indices
        vmovdqa32 zmm18,zmmword ptr [MatIndCol2]    ;m col 2 indices
```

```
        vmovdqa32 zmm19,zmmword ptr [MatIndCol3]    ;m col 3 indices

        vmovdqa32 zmm24,zmmword ptr [VecIndW]       ;W component indices
        vmovdqa32 zmm25,zmmword ptr [VecIndX]       ;X component indices
        vmovdqa32 zmm26,zmmword ptr [VecIndY]       ;Y component indices
        vmovdqa32 zmm27,zmmword ptr [VecIndZ]       ;Z component indices

; Load source matrix m and permute 4 copies of each column
        vmovaps zmm0,zmmword ptr [rdx]          ;zmm0  = matrix m
        vpermps zmm20,zmm16,zmm0                ;zmm20 = m col 0 (4x)
        vpermps zmm21,zmm17,zmm0                ;zmm21 = m col 1 (4x)
        vpermps zmm22,zmm18,zmm0                ;zmm22 = m col 2 (4x)
        vpermps zmm23,zmm19,zmm0                ;zmm23 = m col 3 (4x)

        mov rax,-NVPI                          ;rax = i
        mov r10,-64                            ;r10 = offset for vec_a & vec_b

        align 16
Loop1:  add rax,NVPI                           ;i += NVPI
        add r10,64                             ;update offset for vec arrays

        mov r11,r9                             ;r11 = num_vec
        sub r11,rax                            ;r11 = num_vec - i
        cmp r11,NVPI
        jb @F                                  ;jump if num_vec - i < NVPI

; Load next 4 source vectors and permute the components
        vmovaps zmm4,zmmword ptr [r8+r10]      ;zmm4 = vec_a[i:i+3]

        vpermps zmm0,zmm24,zmm4                ;zmm0 = vec_a W components
        vpermps zmm1,zmm25,zmm4                ;zmm1 = vec_a X components
        vpermps zmm2,zmm26,zmm4                ;zmm2 = vec_a Y components
        vpermps zmm3,zmm27,zmm4                ;zmm3 = vec_a Z components

; Perform matrix-vector multiplications (4 vectors)
        vmulps zmm4,zmm20,zmm0                 ;zmm4  = m col 0 * W
        vfmadd231ps zmm4,zmm21,zmm1            ;zmm4 += m col 1 * X
        vfmadd231ps zmm4,zmm22,zmm2            ;zmm4 += m col 2 * Y
        vfmadd231ps zmm4,zmm23,zmm3            ;zmm4 += m col 3 * Z

; Save matrix-vector products (4 vectors)
        vmovaps zmmword ptr [rcx+r10],zmm4     ;save vec_b[i:i+3]
        jmp Loop1

; Process residual vectors (if any)
@@:     cmp rax,r9
        jae Done                               ;jump if i >= num_vec

        align 16
Loop2:  vbroadcastss xmm0,real4 ptr [r8+r10]       ;xmm0 = vec_a[i] W components
        vbroadcastss xmm1,real4 ptr [r8+r10+4]     ;xmm1 = vec_a[i] X components
```

```
        vbroadcastss xmm2,real4 ptr [r8+r10+8]       ;xmm2 = vec_a[i] Y components
        vbroadcastss xmm3,real4 ptr [r8+r10+12]      ;xmm3 = vec_a[i] Z components

        vmulps xmm4,xmm20,xmm0                        ;xmm4  = m col 0 * W
        vfmadd231ps xmm4,xmm21,xmm1                   ;xmm4 += m col 1 * X
        vfmadd231ps xmm4,xmm22,xmm2                   ;xmm4 += m col 2 * Y
        vfmadd231ps xmm4,xmm23,xmm3                   ;xmm4 += m col 3 * Z

        vmovaps xmmword ptr [rcx+r10],xmm4            ;save vec_b[i]
        add r10,16                                   ;offset += 16
        inc rax                                      ;i += 1
        cmp rax,r9
        jb Loop2                                     ;jump if i < num_vec

Done:   vzeroupper
        ret
MatVecMulF32a_Aavx512 endp
        end
```

Listing 18-5 opens with the definition of a custom memory section (or segment) that contains constant values. The reason for creating a custom segment is that a normal MASM .const segment is aligned on a 16-byte boundary and the code in this example employs vmovdqa32 instructions to load 512-bit wide SIMD constants. The statement ConstVals segment readonly align(64) 'const' defines a memory segment named ConstVals that contains read-only data. The align(64) parameter instructs MASM to align this memory segment on a 64-byte boundary. The 'const' parameter specifies that MASM should combine the data defined in ConstVals with other 'const' segments (in this example, any name could be used here but 'const' is MASM's default). Memory segment ConstVals contains a series of 512-bit wide values that contain doubleword permutation indices. The first group of values, MatIndCol0 through MatIndCol3, contains the indices necessary to transpose a 4 × 4 matrix of single-precision floating-point values. The second group, VecIndW through VecIndZ, includes indices that rearrange the components of four 4 × 1 vectors. Following the vector permutation indices is the statement ConstVals ends, which signifies the end of segment ConstVals.

Function MatVecMulF32a_Aavx512() begins its execution with a series of checks that verify num_vec for size and 64-byte alignment of arguments vec_a, vec_b, and m. The next code block uses four vmovdqa32 instructions to load MatIndCol0 through MatIndCol3 into registers ZMM16–ZMM19, respectively. This is followed by a code block that also employs four vmovdqa32 instructions to load VecIndW through VecIndZ into registers ZMM24–ZMM27. Following the permutation index loads, MatVecMulF32a_Aavx512() uses vmovaps zmm0,zmmword ptr [rdx] to load matrix m into register ZMM0. The ensuing vpermps zmm20,zmm16,zmm0 instruction loads register ZMM20 with four copies of matrix m column 0. This is followed by a vpermps instruction triplet that loads registers ZMM21, ZMM22, and ZMM23 with four copies of columns 1, 2, and 3, respectively, as shown in Figure 18-1.

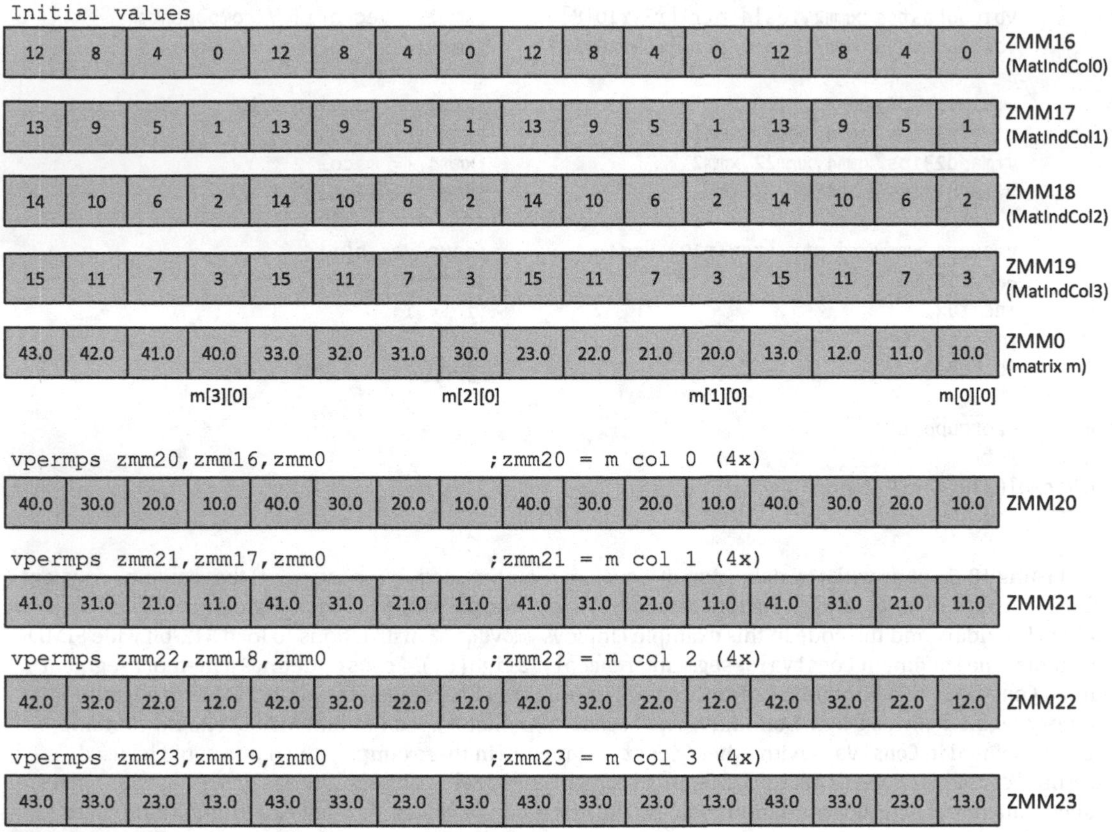

Initial values

| 12 | 8 | 4 | 0 | 12 | 8 | 4 | 0 | 12 | 8 | 4 | 0 | 12 | 8 | 4 | 0 | ZMM16 (MatIndCol0) |

| 13 | 9 | 5 | 1 | 13 | 9 | 5 | 1 | 13 | 9 | 5 | 1 | 13 | 9 | 5 | 1 | ZMM17 (MatIndCol1) |

| 14 | 10 | 6 | 2 | 14 | 10 | 6 | 2 | 14 | 10 | 6 | 2 | 14 | 10 | 6 | 2 | ZMM18 (MatIndCol2) |

| 15 | 11 | 7 | 3 | 15 | 11 | 7 | 3 | 15 | 11 | 7 | 3 | 15 | 11 | 7 | 3 | ZMM19 (MatIndCol3) |

| 43.0 | 42.0 | 41.0 | 40.0 | 33.0 | 32.0 | 31.0 | 30.0 | 23.0 | 22.0 | 21.0 | 20.0 | 13.0 | 12.0 | 11.0 | 10.0 | ZMM0 (matrix m) |

m[3][0]           m[2][0]           m[1][0]           m[0][0]

```
vpermps zmm20,zmm16,zmm0            ;zmm20 = m col 0 (4x)
```

| 40.0 | 30.0 | 20.0 | 10.0 | 40.0 | 30.0 | 20.0 | 10.0 | 40.0 | 30.0 | 20.0 | 10.0 | 40.0 | 30.0 | 20.0 | 10.0 | ZMM20 |

```
vpermps zmm21,zmm17,zmm0            ;zmm21 = m col 1 (4x)
```

| 41.0 | 31.0 | 21.0 | 11.0 | 41.0 | 31.0 | 21.0 | 11.0 | 41.0 | 31.0 | 21.0 | 11.0 | 41.0 | 31.0 | 21.0 | 11.0 | ZMM21 |

```
vpermps zmm22,zmm18,zmm0            ;zmm22 = m col 2 (4x)
```

| 42.0 | 32.0 | 22.0 | 12.0 | 42.0 | 32.0 | 22.0 | 12.0 | 42.0 | 32.0 | 22.0 | 12.0 | 42.0 | 32.0 | 22.0 | 12.0 | ZMM22 |

```
vpermps zmm23,zmm19,zmm0            ;zmm23 = m col 3 (4x)
```

| 43.0 | 33.0 | 23.0 | 13.0 | 43.0 | 33.0 | 23.0 | 13.0 | 43.0 | 33.0 | 23.0 | 13.0 | 43.0 | 33.0 | 23.0 | 13.0 | ZMM23 |

*Figure 18-1. Permutation of matrix columns using vpermps*

Each iteration of Loop1 begins with an add rax,NVPI instruction that calculates i += NVPI (NVPI = number of vectors per iteration). The next instruction, add r10,64, updates R10 so that it contains the correct offset for the next four vectors in arrays vec_a and vec_b. This is followed by a code block that terminates Loop1 if num_vec - i < NVPI is true (i.e., fewer than NVPI vectors remain). The ensuing vmovaps zmm4,zmmword ptr [r8+r10] instruction loads vectors vec_a[i:i+3] into register ZMM4. The X, Y, W, and Z components of these vectors are then reordered using a series of vpermps instructions. Figure 18-2 illustrates this operation in greater detail.

Initial values

| 12 | 12 | 12 | 12 | 8 | 8 | 8 | 8 | 4 | 4 | 4 | 4 | 0 | 0 | 0 | 0 | ZMM24 (VecIndW) |
|---|---|---|---|---|---|---|---|---|---|---|---|---|---|---|---|---|

| 13 | 13 | 13 | 13 | 9 | 9 | 9 | 9 | 5 | 5 | 5 | 5 | 1 | 1 | 1 | 1 | ZMM25 (VecIndX) |
|---|---|---|---|---|---|---|---|---|---|---|---|---|---|---|---|---|

| 14 | 14 | 14 | 14 | 10 | 10 | 10 | 10 | 6 | 6 | 6 | 6 | 2 | 2 | 2 | 2 | ZMM26 (VecIndY) |
|---|---|---|---|---|---|---|---|---|---|---|---|---|---|---|---|---|

| 15 | 15 | 15 | 15 | 11 | 11 | 11 | 11 | 7 | 7 | 7 | 7 | 3 | 3 | 3 | 3 | ZMM27 (VecIndZ) |
|---|---|---|---|---|---|---|---|---|---|---|---|---|---|---|---|---|

| 38.0 | 37.0 | 36.0 | 35.0 | 28.0 | 27.0 | 26.0 | 25.0 | 18.0 | 17.0 | 16.0 | 15.0 | 8.0 | 7.0 | 6.0 | 5.0 | ZMM4 (vec_a[i:i+3]) |
|---|---|---|---|---|---|---|---|---|---|---|---|---|---|---|---|---|
| a[3].Z | a[3].Y | a[3].X | a[3].W | a[2].Z | a[2].Y | a[2].X | a[2].W | a[1].Z | a[1].Y | a[1].X | a[1].W | a[0].Z | a[0].Y | a[0].X | a[0].W | |

vpermps zmm0,zmm24,zmm4          ;zmm0 = vec_a W components

| 35.0 | 35.0 | 35.0 | 35.0 | 25.0 | 25.0 | 25.0 | 25.0 | 15.0 | 15.0 | 15.0 | 15.0 | 5.0 | 5.0 | 5.0 | 5.0 | ZMM0 |
|---|---|---|---|---|---|---|---|---|---|---|---|---|---|---|---|---|

vpermps zmm1,zmm25,zmm4          ;zmm1 = vec_a X components

| 36.0 | 36.0 | 36.0 | 36.0 | 26.0 | 26.0 | 26.0 | 26.0 | 16.0 | 16.0 | 16.0 | 16.0 | 6.0 | 6.0 | 6.0 | 6.0 | ZMM1 |
|---|---|---|---|---|---|---|---|---|---|---|---|---|---|---|---|---|

vpermps zmm2,zmm26,zmm4          ;zmm2 = vec_a Y components

| 37.0 | 37.0 | 37.0 | 37.0 | 27.0 | 27.0 | 27.0 | 27.0 | 17.0 | 17.0 | 17.0 | 17.0 | 7.0 | 7.0 | 7.0 | 7.0 | ZMM2 |
|---|---|---|---|---|---|---|---|---|---|---|---|---|---|---|---|---|

vpermps zmm3,zmm27,zmm4          ;zmm3 = vec_a Z components

| 38.0 | 38.0 | 38.0 | 38.0 | 28.0 | 28.0 | 28.0 | 28.0 | 18.0 | 18.0 | 18.0 | 18.0 | 8.0 | 8.0 | 8.0 | 8.0 | ZMM3 |
|---|---|---|---|---|---|---|---|---|---|---|---|---|---|---|---|---|

**Figure 18-2.** *Permutation of vector components using vpermps*

Following the vector component permutations, MatVecMulF32a_Aavx512() uses a vmulps and three vfmadd231ps instructions to calculate four matrix-vector products (i.e., m * vec_a[i:i+3]). The vmovaps zmmword ptr [rcx+r10],zmm4 that follows saves the calculated matrix-vector products to vec_b[i:i+3]. Following execution of for-loop Loop1 is another for-loop named Loop2. This for-loop processes any residual vectors using FMA arithmetic. Note that for-loop Loop2 uses a series of vbroadcastss instructions to create packed versions of vec_a[i].W, vec_a[i].X, vec_a[i].Y, and vec_a[i].Z. This loop also employs vmulps and vfmadd231ps to calculate m * vec_a[i]. Here are the results for source code example Ch18_05:

```
Results for MatrixVecMulF32
Test case #0
vec_b1:      304.0      564.0      824.0     1084.0
vec_b2:      304.0      564.0      824.0     1084.0
Test case #1
vec_b1:      764.0     1424.0     2084.0     2744.0
vec_b2:      764.0     1424.0     2084.0     2744.0
Test case #2
vec_b1:     1224.0     2284.0     3344.0     4404.0
vec_b2:     1224.0     2284.0     3344.0     4404.0
Test case #3
vec_b1:     1684.0     3144.0     4604.0     6064.0
vec_b2:     1684.0     3144.0     4604.0     6064.0
```

```
Test case #4
vec_b1:    11932.0    22452.0    32972.0    43492.0
vec_b2:    11932.0    22452.0    32972.0    43492.0
Test case #5
vec_b1:    17125.0    31705.0    46285.0    60865.0
vec_b2:    17125.0    31705.0    46285.0    60865.0
Test case #6
vec_b1:    12723.0    23873.0    35023.0    46173.0
vec_b2:    12723.0    23873.0    35023.0    46173.0
Test case #7
vec_b1:    15121.0    27871.0    40621.0    53371.0
vec_b2:    15121.0    27871.0    40621.0    53371.0
Test case #8
vec_b1:    13789.0    26039.0    38289.0    50539.0
vec_b2:    13789.0    26039.0    38289.0    50539.0
Test case #9
vec_b1:     9663.0    17873.0    26083.0    34293.0
vec_b2:     9663.0    17873.0    26083.0    34293.0


Running benchmark function MatrixVecMulF32_bm - please wait
Benchmark times save to file Ch18_05_MatrixVecMulF32_bm_LITHIUM.csv
```

Not shown in Listing 18-5 is the function MatVecMulF32b_Aavx512(). The only difference between functions MatVecMulF32a_Aavx512() and MatVecMulF32b_Aavx512() is that the latter uses the instruction vmovntps (Store Packed SPFP Values Using Non-Temporal Hint) instead of vmovaps to save the calculated matrix-vector products. Recall from the discussions in Chapter 8 that a nontemporal memory hint notifies the processor that the data being saved will not be immediately referenced again. This allows the processor to (optionally) bypass its normal memory cache hierarchy, which minimizes cache pollution.

Table 18-2 shows the benchmark timing measurements for source example Ch18_05. This table also shows the benchmark timing measurements from source code example Ch08_07 for comparison purposes. Note that in both examples Ch08_07 and Ch18_05, the use of a nontemporal C++ SIMD intrinsic function or assembly language store instruction yielded a noteworthy improvement in performance due to minimization of cache pollution (in the current example, the processor does not update its cache hierarchy with the calculated vectors since it has been notified that the data will not be immediately referenced again).

*Table 18-2.* *Matrix-Vector (4 × 4, 4 × 1) Multiplication Execution Times (Microseconds), 1,000,000 Vectors*

| Source Code Example | Function Name | Store Intrinsic/Instruction | Intel i5-11600K |
|---|---|---|---|
| Ch08_07 | MatVecMulF32a_Iavx512() | _mm512_store_ps() | 1111 |
| Ch08_07 | MatVecMulF32b_Iavx512() | _mm512_stream_ps() | 708 |
| Ch18_05 | MatVecMulF32a_Aavx512() | vmovaps | 1093 |
| Ch18_05 | MatVecMulF32b_Aavx512() | vmovntps | 694 |

# Signal Processing

The final source code example of this chapter, Ch18_06, demonstrates 1D discrete convolutions using AVX-512 instructions. This example, shown in Listing 18-6, is the assembly language counterpart of source code example Ch08_08. Before examining the source code in Listing 18-6, you may want to review the source code for example Ch08_08 and the relevant sections in Chapter 6 that explained the mathematics of 1D discrete convolutions. Like the previous discrete convolution source code examples, the code and calculations presented in example Ch18_06 are somewhat specialized. If your programming interests reside elsewhere, you can either skim this section or skip ahead to the next one.

*Listing 18-6.* Example Ch18_06

```
;-------------------------------------------------
;                   Ch18_06_fasm.asm
;-------------------------------------------------

            include <MacrosX86-64-AVX.asmh>

;------------------------------------------------------------------------
; extern "C" void Convolve1D_F32_Aavx512(float* y, const float* x,
;   const float* kernel, size_t num_pts, size_t kernel_size);
;------------------------------------------------------------------------

NSE      equ      16                           ;num F32 elements in ZMM register

        .code
Convolve1D_F32_Aavx512 proc frame
        CreateFrame_M CV_,0,0,rbx,rsi,r12,r13,r14
        EndProlog_M

; Validate arguments
        mov r10,qword ptr [rbp+CV_OffsetStackArgs]   ;r10 = kernel_size (ks)
        test r10,1
        jz Done                               ;jump if ks is even
        cmp r10,3
        jb Done                               ;jump if ks < 3
        cmp r9,r10
        jb Done                               ;jump if num_pts < ks

; Initialize
        mov r11,r10                           ;r11 = ks
        shr r11,1                             ;r11 = ks2
        mov rsi,r9                            ;rsi = num_pts
        sub rsi,r11                           ;rsi = num_pts - ks2
        mov r14,r11
        neg r14                               ;r14 = -ks2
        mov rax,r11                           ;i = ks2


;------------------------------------------------------------------------
; General-purpose registers used in code below
;   rax      i                    r9       num_pts
;   rbx      k                    r10      kernel_size
;   rcx      y array              r11      ks2
;   rdx      x array              r12      scratch
;   rsi      num_pts - ks2        r13      scratch
;   r8       kernel               r14      -ks2
;------------------------------------------------------------------------
```

```
; Loop1 is outer-most for-loop
        align 16
Loop1:  cmp rax,rsi
        jge Done                                    ;jump if i >= num_pts - ks2

; Calculate y[i:i+NSE*2-1]
        lea r12,[rax+NSE*2]                          ;r12 = i + NSE * 2
        cmp r12,rsi
        jg @F                                        ;jump if i + NSE * 2 > num_pts - ks2

        vxorps zmm0,zmm0,zmm0                        ;y[i:i+NSE-1] = 0
        vxorps zmm1,zmm1,zmm1                        ;y[i+NSE:i+NSE*2-1] = 0
        mov rbx,r14                                  ;k = -ks2

        align 16
Loop2a: mov r12,rax                                  ;r12 = i
        sub r12,rbx                                  ;r12 = i - k
        lea r13,[rbx+r11]                            ;r13 = k + ks2

        vbroadcastss zmm5,real4 ptr [r8+r13*4]           ;zmm2 = kernel[k+ks2]
        vfmadd231ps zmm0,zmm5,zmmword ptr [rdx+r12*4]    ;update y[i:i+NSE-1]
        vfmadd231ps zmm1,zmm5,zmmword ptr [rdx+r12*4+64] ;update y[i+NSE:i+NSE*2-1]

        inc rbx                                      ;k += 1
        cmp rbx,r11
        jle Loop2a                                   ;jump if k <= ks2

        vmovups zmmword ptr [rcx+rax*4],zmm0         ;save y[i:i+NSE-1]
        vmovups zmmword ptr [rcx+rax*4+64],zmm1      ;save y[i+NSE:i+NSE*2-1]
        add rax,NSE*2                                ;i += NSE * 2
        jmp Loop1

; Calculate y[i:i+NSE-1]
@@:     lea r12,[rax+NSE]                            ;r12 = i + NSE
        cmp r12,rsi
        jg @F                                        ;jump if i + NSE > num_pts - ks2

        vxorps zmm0,zmm0,zmm0                        ;y[i:i+NSE-1] = 0
        mov rbx,r14                                  ;k = -ks2

        align 16
Loop2b: mov r12,rax                                  ;r12 = i
        sub r12,rbx                                  ;r12 = i - k
        lea r13,[rbx+r11]                            ;r13 = k + ks2

        vbroadcastss zmm5,real4 ptr [r8+r13*4]           ;zmm2 = kernel[k+ks2]
        vfmadd231ps zmm0,zmm5,zmmword ptr [rdx+r12*4]    ;update y[i:i+NSE-1]

        inc rbx                                      ;k += 1
        cmp rbx,r11
        jle Loop2b                                   ;jump if k <= ks2
```

```
        vmovups zmmword ptr [rcx+rax*4],zmm0    ;save y[i:i+NSE-1]
        add rax,NSE                             ;i += NSE
        jmp Loop1

; Calculate y[i:i+NSE/2-1]
@@:     lea r12,[rax+NSE/2]                      ;r12 = i + NSE / 2
        cmp r12,rsi
        jg @F                                    ;jump if i + NSE / 2 > num_pts - ks2

        vxorps ymm0,ymm0,ymm0                    ;y[i:i+NSE/2-1] = 0
        mov rbx,r14                              ;k = -ks2

        align 16
Loop2c: mov r12,rax                              ;r12 = i
        sub r12,rbx                              ;r12 = i - k
        lea r13,[rbx+r11]                        ;r13 = k + ks2

        vbroadcastss ymm5,real4 ptr [r8+r13*4]          ;ymm2 = kernel[k+ks2]
        vfmadd231ps ymm0,ymm5,ymmword ptr [rdx+r12*4]   ;update y[i:i+NSE/2-1]

        inc rbx                                  ;k += 1
        cmp rbx,r11
        jle Loop2c                               ;jump if k <= ks2

        vmovups ymmword ptr [rcx+rax*4],ymm0     ;save y[i:i+NSE/2-1]
        add rax,NSE/2                            ;i += NSE/2
        jmp Loop1

; Calculate y[i:i+NSE/4-1]
@@:     lea r12,[rax+NSE/4]                      ;r12 = i + NSE / 4
        cmp r12,rsi
        jg @F                                    ;jump if i + NSE / 4 > num_pts - ks2

        vxorps xmm0,xmm0,xmm0                    ;y[i:i+NSE/4-1] = 0
        mov rbx,r14                              ;k = -ks2

        align 16
Loop2d: mov r12,rax                              ;r12 = i
        sub r12,rbx                              ;r12 = i - k
        lea r13,[rbx+r11]                        ;r13 = k + ks2

        vbroadcastss xmm5,real4 ptr [r8+r13*4]          ;xmm2 = kernel[k+ks2]
        vfmadd231ps xmm0,xmm5,xmmword ptr [rdx+r12*4]   ;update y[i:i+NSE/4-1]

        inc rbx                                  ;k += 1
        cmp rbx,r11
        jle Loop2d                               ;jump if k <= ks2

        vmovups xmmword ptr [rcx+rax*4],xmm0     ;save y[i:i+NSE/4-1]
        add rax,NSE/4                            ;i += NSE / 4
        jmp Loop1
```

```
; Calculate y[i]
@@:      vxorps xmm0,xmm0,xmm0                      ;y[i] = 0
         mov rbx,r14                                ;k = -ks2

         align 16
Loop2e:  mov r12,rax                                ;r12 = i
         sub r12,rbx                                ;r12 = i - k
         lea r13,[rbx+r11]                          ;r13 = k + ks2

         vmovss xmm5,real4 ptr [r8+r13*4]           ;xmm2 = kernel[k+ks2]
         vfmadd231ss xmm0,xmm5,real4 ptr [rdx+r12*4] ;update y[i]

         inc rbx                                    ;k += 1
         cmp rbx,r11
         jle Loop2e                                 ;jump if k <= ks2

         vmovss real4 ptr [rcx+rax*4],xmm0          ;save y[i]
         inc rax                                    ;i += 1
         jmp Loop1

Done:    vzeroupper
         DeleteFrame_M rbx,rsi,r12,r13,r14
         ret
Convolve1D_F32_Aavx512 endp

;------------------------------------------------------------------------
; extern "C" void Convolve1DKs5_F32_Aavx512(float* y, const float* x,
;   const float* kernel, size_t num_pts);
;------------------------------------------------------------------------

KS       equ     5                                  ;kernel_size
KS2      equ     2                                  ;floor(kernel_size / 2)

Convolve1DKs5_F32_Aavx512 proc frame
         CreateFrame_M CV5_,0,0,r12
         EndProlog_M

; Validate arguments
         cmp r9,KS
         jb Done                                    ;jump if num_pts < KS

; Initialize
         mov rax,KS2                                ;i = ks2
         mov r10,r9                                 ;r10 = num_pts
         sub r10,KS2                                ;r10 = num_pts - KS2

         vbroadcastss zmm0,real4 ptr [r8]           ;zmm0 = packed kernel[0]
         vbroadcastss zmm1,real4 ptr [r8+4]         ;zmm1 = packed kernel[1]
         vbroadcastss zmm2,real4 ptr [r8+8]         ;zmm2 = packed kernel[2]
         vbroadcastss zmm3,real4 ptr [r8+12]        ;zmm3 = packed kernel[3]
         vbroadcastss zmm4,real4 ptr [r8+16]        ;zmm4 = packed kernel[4]
```

```
;-------------------------------------------------------------------------
; General-purpose registers used in code below
;   rax     i                   r9      num_pts
;   rcx     y array             r10     num_pts - ks2
;   rdx     x array             r11     j
;   r8      kernel              r12     scratch
;-------------------------------------------------------------------------

            align 16
Loop1:      cmp rax,r10
            jge Done                                ;jump if i >= num_pts - ks2

; Calculate y[i:i+NSE*2-1]
            lea r11,[rax+KS2]                       ;j = i + KS2
            lea r12,[rax+NSE*2]                     ;r12 = i + NSE * 2
            cmp r12,r10
            jg @F                                   ;jump if i + NSE * 2 > num_pts - ks2

            vmulps zmm5,zmm0,zmmword ptr [rdx+r11*4]            ;kernel[0] * x[j]
            vfmadd231ps zmm5,zmm1,zmmword ptr [rdx+r11*4-4]         ;kernel[1] * x[j-1]
            vfmadd231ps zmm5,zmm2,zmmword ptr [rdx+r11*4-8]         ;kernel[2] * x[j-2]
            vfmadd231ps zmm5,zmm3,zmmword ptr [rdx+r11*4-12]        ;kernel[3] * x[j-3]
            vfmadd231ps zmm5,zmm4,zmmword ptr [rdx+r11*4-16]        ;kernel[4] * x[j-4]

            vmulps zmm16,zmm0,zmmword ptr [rdx+r11*4+64]        ;kernel[0] * x[j]
            vfmadd231ps zmm16,zmm1,zmmword ptr [rdx+r11*4-4+64]     ;kernel[1] * x[j-1]
            vfmadd231ps zmm16,zmm2,zmmword ptr [rdx+r11*4-8+64]     ;kernel[2] * x[j-2]
            vfmadd231ps zmm16,zmm3,zmmword ptr [rdx+r11*4-12+64]    ;kernel[3] * x[j-3]
            vfmadd231ps zmm16,zmm4,zmmword ptr [rdx+r11*4-16+64]    ;kernel[4] * x[j-4]

            vmovups zmmword ptr [rcx+rax*4],zmm5               ;save y[i:i+NSE-1]
            vmovups zmmword ptr [rcx+rax*4+64],zmm16           ;save y[i+NSE:i+NSE*2-1]
            add rax,NSE*2                                      ;i += NSE * 2
            jmp Loop1

; Calculate y[i:i+NSE-1]
            lea r11,[rax+KS2]                       ;j = i + KS2
            lea r12,[rax+NSE]                       ;r12 = i + NSE
            cmp r12,r10
            jg @F                                   ;jump if i + NSE > num_pts - ks2

            vmulps zmm5,zmm0,zmmword ptr [rdx+r11*4]            ;kernel[0] * x[j]
            vfmadd231ps zmm5,zmm1,zmmword ptr [rdx+r11*4-4]         ;kernel[1] * x[j-1]
            vfmadd231ps zmm5,zmm2,zmmword ptr [rdx+r11*4-8]         ;kernel[2] * x[j-2]
            vfmadd231ps zmm5,zmm3,zmmword ptr [rdx+r11*4-12]        ;kernel[3] * x[j-3]
            vfmadd231ps zmm5,zmm4,zmmword ptr [rdx+r11*4-16]        ;kernel[4] * x[j-4]

            vmovups zmmword ptr [rcx+rax*4],zmm5               ;save y[i:i+NSE-1]
            add rax,NSE                                        ;i += NSE
            jmp Loop1
```

```
; Calculate y[i:i+NSE/2-1]
@@:     lea r12,[rax+NSE/2]                              ;r12 = i + NSE / 2
        cmp r12,r10
        jg @F                                           ;jump if i + NSE / 2 > num_pts - ks2

        vmulps ymm5,ymm0,ymmword ptr [rdx+r11*4]        ;kernel[0] * x[j]
        vfmadd231ps ymm5,ymm1,ymmword ptr [rdx+r11*4-4]   ;kernel[1] * x[j-1]
        vfmadd231ps ymm5,ymm2,ymmword ptr [rdx+r11*4-8]   ;kernel[2] * x[j-2]
        vfmadd231ps ymm5,ymm3,ymmword ptr [rdx+r11*4-12]  ;kernel[3] * x[j-3]
        vfmadd231ps ymm5,ymm4,ymmword ptr [rdx+r11*4-16]  ;kernel[4] * x[j-4]

        vmovups ymmword ptr [rcx+rax*4],ymm5            ;save y[i:i+NSE/2-1]
        add rax,NSE/2                                   ;i += NSE/2
        jmp Loop1

; Calculate y[i:i+NSE/4-1]
@@:     lea r12,[rax+NSE/4]                              ;r12 = i + NSE / 4
        cmp r12,r10
        jg @F                                           ;jump if i + NSE / 4 > num_pts - ks2

        vmulps xmm5,xmm0,xmmword ptr [rdx+r11*4]        ;kernel[0] * x[j]
        vfmadd231ps xmm5,xmm1,xmmword ptr [rdx+r11*4-4]   ;kernel[1] * x[j-1]
        vfmadd231ps xmm5,xmm2,xmmword ptr [rdx+r11*4-8]   ;kernel[2] * x[j-2]
        vfmadd231ps xmm5,xmm3,xmmword ptr [rdx+r11*4-12]  ;kernel[3] * x[j-3]
        vfmadd231ps xmm5,xmm4,xmmword ptr [rdx+r11*4-16]  ;kernel[4] * x[j-4]

        vmovups xmmword ptr [rcx+rax*4],xmm5            ;save y[i:i+NSE/4-1]
        add rax,NSE/4                                   ;i += NSE / 4
        jmp Loop1

; Calculate y[i]
@@:     vmulss xmm5,xmm0,real4 ptr [rdx+r11*4]          ;kernel[0] * x[j]
        vfmadd231ss xmm5,xmm1,real4 ptr [rdx+r11*4-4]    ;kernel[1] * x[j-1]
        vfmadd231ss xmm5,xmm2,real4 ptr [rdx+r11*4-8]    ;kernel[2] * x[j-2]
        vfmadd231ss xmm5,xmm3,real4 ptr [rdx+r11*4-12]   ;kernel[3] * x[j-3]
        vfmadd231ss xmm5,xmm4,real4 ptr [rdx+r11*4-16]   ;kernel[4] * x[j-4]

        vmovss real4 ptr [rcx+rax*4],xmm5              ;save y[i]
        inc rax                                         ;i += 1
        jmp Loop1

Done:   vzeroupper
        DeleteFrame_M r12
        ret
Convolve1DKs5_F32_Aavx512 endp
        end
```

Listing 18-6 contains two function definitions. The first function, Convolve1D_F32_Aavx512(), implements a 1D discrete convolution using a variable-width kernel. The second function, Convolve1DKs5_F32_Aavx512(), also implements a 1D discrete convolution but is optimized for a five-element kernel. Following its prologue, function Convolve1D_F32_Aavx512() validates arguments num_pts and kernel_size.

The code block that follows argument validation includes instructions that initialize R11 to ks2 = kernel_size / 2, RSI to num_pts - ks2, R14 to -ks2, and RAX (index variable i) to ks2. The outer-most for-loop of Convolve1D_F32_Aavx512(), named Loop1, repeatedly executes until all data points in the input signal array x have been processed.

In function Convolve1D_F32_Aavx512(), the 1D discrete convolution calculating code sections is partitioned into five sections. The code section that gets executed during an iteration of Loop1 depends on the number of remaining input signal points. If 32 or more input signal points remain (i.e., i + NSE * 2 > num_pts - ks2 is false), the first code section Loop2a calculates y[i:i+NSE*2-1] (NSE = 16). Similar to the matrix multiplication example that you saw earlier in this chapter, for-loop Loop2a employs 512-bit wide operands and dual vfmadd231ps instructions to carry out the requisite FMA calculations. Following completion of Loop2a, function Convolve1D_F32_Aavx512() uses two vmovups instructions to save y[i:i+NSE*2-1]. The add rax,NSE*2 instruction calculates i += NSE * 2 for the next iteration of Loop1.

The next code section, Loop2b, also exploits 512-bit wide SIMD operands but utilizes a single vfmadd231ps instruction to calculate y[i:i+NSE-1]. This code section executes only when the number of remaining signal points is between 16 and 31. Following execution of Loop2b, Convolve1D_F32_Aavx512() uses a single vmovups instruction to save y[i:i+NSE-1]. The ensuing add rax,NSE instruction calculates i += NSE for the next iteration of Loop1. The logic and structure of the remaining three code sections, Loop2c, Loop2d, and Loop2e, mimic Loop2a and Loop2b. These code sections calculate signal points y[i:i+NSE/2-1], y[i:i+NSE/4-1], and y[i] using 256-bit wide, 128-bit wide, and scalar operands, respectively.

Function Convolve1DKs5_F32_Aavx512() also calculates a 1D discrete convolution and is optimized for a five-element convolution kernel. The main difference between function Convolve1DKs5_F32_Aavx512() and function Convolve1D_F32_Aavx512() is that the former employs sequences of vmulps and vfmadd231ps instructions instead of for-loops to carry out the required calculations. Function Convolve1DKs5_F32_Aavx512() can use instruction sequences instead of for-loops since the size of the convolution kernel is always five elements. Note that function Convolve1DKs5_F32_Aavx512() will calculate an invalid output signal if it is called using a convolution kernel containing other than five elements. Here are the results for source code example Ch18_06:

```
Executing Convolve1D_F32()
Results saved to file Ch18_06_Convolve1D_F32_Results_LITHIUM.csv

Running benchmark function Convolve1D_F32_bm - please wait
Benchmark times saved to file Ch18_06_Convolve1D_F32_bm_LITHIUM.csv
```

Table 18-3 shows the benchmark timing measurements for source example Ch18_06. This table also shows the benchmark timing measurements from source code example Ch08_08 for comparison purposes. These measurements were made using a 1,000,000-element input signal array and a five-element convolution kernel. Like the matrix multiplication example that you saw earlier in this chapter, functions Convolve1D_F32_Aavx512() and Convolve1DKs5_F32_Aavx512() achieve better performance when the signal arrays contain a minimum of 32 usable elements since AVX-512 instructions can be exploited.

*Table 18-3. 1D Discrete Convolution (Single-Precision) Execution Times (Microseconds)*

| Source Code Example | Function Name | Intel i5-11600K |
| --- | --- | --- |
| Ch08_08 | Convolve1D_F32_Iavx512() | 242 |
| Ch08_08 | Convolve1DKs5_F32_Iavx512() | 200 |
| Ch18_06 | Convolve1D_F32_Aavx512() | 213 |
| Ch18_06 | Convolve1DKs5_F32_Aavx512() | 177 |

# Summary

Table 18-4 summarizes the x86 assembly language instructions introduced in this chapter. This table also includes closely related instructions. Before proceeding to the next chapter, make sure you understand the calculation or operation that is performed by each instruction shown in Table 18-4.

***Table 18-4.*** *X86 Assembly Language Instruction Summary for Chapter 18*

| Instruction Mnemonic | Description |
| --- | --- |
| vextractf[32x4\|32x8] | Extract packed single-precision floating-point elements |
| vextractf[64x2\|64x4] | Extract packed double-precision floating-point elements |
| vmovntp[d\|s] | Store packed floating-point values using nontemporal hint |
| vpermp[d\|s] | Permute packed floating-point elements |
| vpermilp[d\|s] | Permute in-lane packed floating-point elements |

# CHAPTER 19

∎∎∎

# SIMD Usage and Optimization Guidelines

Congratulations if you have made it this far. I hope that your x86-AVX SIMD journey has been informative and worthwhile. I would like to conclude this book with a chapter that briefly discusses some guidelines and techniques for x86-AVX SIMD usage and code optimization. The first section presents a few guidelines for x86-AVX SIMD software development. This section also outlines a few factors that you should consider regarding the use of C++ SIMD intrinsic functions vs. assembly language. The second section of this chapter elucidates some general guidelines for SIMD code development and workflow. The final section lists several techniques for x86-AVX SIMD code optimization.

In this chapter, I will use the term explicit SIMD to signify a function or algorithm that directly employs C++ SIMD intrinsic functions to carry out its calculations. This term also covers developer-coded x86-64 assembly language functions that use x86-AVX instructions. A non-explicit SIMD function is one that is coded sans any C++ SIMD intrinsic functions. Note that functions in this latter group might contain x86-AVX (or x86-SSE) SIMD instructions automatically generated by the C++ compiler.

## SIMD Usage Guidelines

The discussions and source code examples imparted in this book were designed to help you understand SIMD techniques and the computational capabilities of x86-AVX. At this juncture, you may be asking yourself if you should always use explicit SIMD code when developing a new algorithm that utilizes arrays or matrices. Or you may be wondering if you should refactor an existing code base so that it fully exploits explicit SIMD code. The answer to both questions is a resounding no.

As mentioned in the Introduction, software development using explicit SIMD code to accelerate the performance of computationally intense algorithms or functions should be regarded as a specialized programming tool that must be judiciously applied. The development of explicit SIMD code typically requires extra effort, even for software developers who are well versed in SIMD techniques and x86-AVX. SIMD code may also be harder to debug and maintain. The use of explicit SIMD code is often a trade-off between development effort, maintainability, and performance gains.

On many projects, it makes sense to utilize explicit SIMD code only in performance critical functions where the end user directly benefits from the performance gains of explicit SIMD code compared to C++ compiler generated code. For example, the performance gains of an explicitly coded SIMD function might not be noticed by the end user if the application saves the results on a file or database server. On the other hand, an application that incorporates an explicitly coded SIMD function to significantly reduce the time required to provide a critical result or enhance real-time responsiveness is an example where the extra effort of SIMD development can provide tangible benefits to the end user.

© Daniel Kusswurm 2022
D. Kusswurm, *Modern Parallel Programming with C++ and Assembly Language*,
https://doi.org/10.1007/978-1-4842-7918-2_19

The source code examples published in this book highlighted well-known algorithms in statistics, matrix operations, image processing, and signal processing. Specific functions were selected to illustrate a variety of SIMD instructions and coding techniques. Despite their diverse application domains, the SIMD calculating functions published in this book share one common attribute: they all carried out their calculations using arrays or matrices of integer or floating-point elements. Functions that perform computations using these types of data structures and types are often suitable for SIMD processing techniques.

# C++ SIMD Intrinsic Functions or x86 Assembly Language

While reading the preceding chapters, you may have asked yourself whether it is better to code explicit SIMD algorithms using C++ SIMD intrinsic functions or x86 assembly language. I think either option is acceptable. Both languages provide the means necessary to accelerate the performance of an algorithm. Moreover, similar SIMD coding patterns are frequently employed regardless of the language. As mentioned earlier in this book, most x86-AVX C++ SIMD intrinsic functions are simple wrappers for an underlying x86-AVX assembly language instruction. In those cases where this is not true, the C++ SIMD intrinsic function usually translates to a simple sequence of x86-AVX instructions.

Most software developers consider assembly language programming to be an arduous undertaking. However, and I am not the first person to articulate this, difficultly is different than unfamiliarity. Like any programming language, assembly language coding becomes easier as one gains more experience. Assembly language also provides additional opportunities to improve performance, which may be necessary to solve certain SIMD programming problems. For non-SIMD functions, assembly language coding is rarely advantageous. However, having the ability to read and comprehend x86-64 assembly language code is a valuable and often necessary skill for x86 SIMD developers, especially when referencing the documentation that describes the operation of each C++ SIMD intrinsic function. This skill is also a must if you want to examine and learn from the assembly language code emitted by a C++ compiler.

Many of the benchmark timing measurements published in this book showed similar results for the same algorithm coded using C++ SIMD intrinsic functions and x86-64 assembly language. The primary reason for the similar performance was that in most cases, the same coding arrangement was employed to underscore the programming similarities between C++ SIMD intrinsic function use and x86-64 assembly language. In a few source code examples, modest performance gains were achieved when a given function was coded using x86-64 assembly language. It has been my experience that for many (but certainly not all) SIMD functions, the use of assembly language can result in improved performance. However, the drawback of trying to squeeze out every nanosecond of performance is that this usually requires extra development effort. The amount of effort that you expend to achieve a specific level of performance should be tied to a specific benchmark timing measurement objective as discussed in the next section.

The one development scenario where I would discourage the use of explicit SIMD assembly language code on a project is when the same code needs to work on multiple platforms such as both Windows and Linux. The reason for this is that developing assembly language code that runs on both Windows and Linux can be a challenge given the disparate development tools and runtime calling conventions. It is sometimes a challenge just to get ISO-compliant C++ code to work on both platforms. If cross platform assembly language development is warranted on a project, carefully choose your development tools to minimize coding effort and future maintenance.

Regardless of which language you decide to use, you should always strive to keep any explicitly coded SIMD functions localized to minimize future maintenance. For an explicitly coded SIMD calculating function, either public class member or nonclass global, use standard data types (e.g., `int`, `int32_t`, `int64_t`, `float`, `double`, etc.) or pointers to simple structures for argument and return values. Avoid the use of C++ SIMD intrinsic data types such as `__m128`, `__m256`, and `__m512` for argument and return values. As mentioned earlier in this book, the C++ SIMD intrinsic functions and their associated data types are not defined in any ISO C++11 or later standard (platform-independent SIMD data types may be included in a future ISO C++XX standard). Localizing explicit SIMD functions will also simplify the process of porting your code to a non-x86 platform should you want to do this sometime in the future.

# SIMD Software Development Guidelines

For the most part, the development of explicit SIMD code is no different than non-SIMD code. When developing a SIMD algorithm, you still need to perform normal software design, coding, and test activities. However, SIMD development often requires additional testing and benchmarking to substantiate any anticipated performance gains.

The focus of this section is a simple workflow for SIMD software development. The workflow includes steps that are sometimes not carried out when performing non-SIMD software development. I make no claim that the described workflow is the only way to perform SIMD software development. Rather, I suggest that you peruse the workflow with the expectation that you will adapt it for a specific project or development environment. Here are the workflow steps:

- Identify Functions for SIMD Techniques

- Select Default and Explicit SIMD Instruction Sets

- Establish Benchmark Timing Objectives

- Code Explicit SIMD Functions

- Benchmark Code to Measure Performance

- Optimize Explicit SIMD Code

- Repeat Benchmarking and Optimization Steps

The remainder of this section discusses these workflow steps in greater detail.

## Identify Functions for SIMD Techniques

The first step of SIMD software development is to identify existing algorithms or functions that may benefit from a SIMD implementation. As mentioned earlier, functions most likely to benefit from SIMD techniques are those that carry out calculations using arrays or matrices. Functions that are I/O bound (e.g., delays caused by reading or writing to a file server, database server, etc.) are unlikely to see any performance gains. When evaluating code for possible SIMD implementation, focus on algorithms or functions where a SIMD implementation is expected to provide a tangible benefit to the end user (or overall application performance). For example, implementing an explicit SIMD image processing technique that enables the end user to see the resultant image appreciably sooner is something worth considering. A profiling tool, either IDE integrated or external, may be helpful in evaluating functions for possible SIMD conversion.

If you are developing a new algorithm or function, start with the creation of non-explicit SIMD code. There are two reasons for this. First, debugging a non-explicit SIMD function is often easier than debugging an explicit SIMD function. Second, once the non-explicit function is working, it can be used as a baseline for result correctness and benchmarking purposes. This function can also serve as the default function when a particular x86-AVX instruction set extension is not supported. More on this later.

## Select Default and Explicit SIMD Instruction Sets

The next step is to determine the default and SIMD instruction set extensions that your code will use. The default instruction set extension is simply the x86 instruction set that the C++ compiler uses for code generation. What to select here depends mostly on your target users. If you are developing a mainstream application for Windows or Linux, you may want or need to select a non-x86-AVX instruction set extension for the C++ compiler. One compelling reason for this approach is that the installed base of PCs still includes many devices with processors that don't support AVX, AVX2, or AVX-512. If you are developing a specialized application that targets recently marketed workstations or servers, you could select AVX or AVX2 as the default SIMD instruction set extension. The compiler switches needed to select a specific instruction set extension for Visual C++ and GNU C++ are reviewed in Appendix A.

Once you have selected the default SIMD instruction set extension, you need to decide which SIMD instruction set extension(s) to use in your own code. For a mainstream Windows or Linux application, it would not be unreasonable to specify SSE2 as the default SIMD instruction set extension and use AVX2 C++ SIMD intrinsic functions or AVX2 assembly language instructions in your own explicit SIMD code. For a specialized workstation or server application, you could select AVX2 for the compiler default instruction set and explicitly code AVX-512 functions.

It has been mentioned several times in this book, but it bears repeating one more time: your application must verify that the host processor supports any required x86 instruction set extensions. For example, if you have configured the C++ compiler to use AVX2 instructions, you should test for the presence of this instruction set extension during application startup, possibly inside function main(). It might also be a good idea to include a test for AVX2 or any other required x86 instruction set extensions during program installation. Doing this allows the install program to display a user-friendly error message if the program is installed on a computer with an incompatible processor.

Your application should also perform runtime checks to ensure that it executes appropriate functions depending on the capabilities of the host processor. Suppose, for example, you are developing an application performing an image processing operation. You have decided to configure the C++ compiler to emit SSE2 instructions but would like the end user to benefit from improved performance on a computer with a processor that supports AVX2. In this scenario, your application should contain two functions that perform the same image processing operation. The first (or baseline) function should be coded using standard C++ statements (i.e., non-explicit SIMD code). The second function can contain explicit SIMD code, either AVX2 C++ SIMD intrinsic functions or AVX2 assembly language instructions. When it comes time to carry out the image processing operation, your program can test a simple Boolean flag, which can be initialized during application startup. Your application would then call either the baseline function or the explicitly coded AVX2 function depending on the state of this flag.

## Establish Benchmark Timing Objectives

Following selection of the default and explicit SIMD instruction sets, establish some benchmarking timing objectives for your explicit SIMD functions. Try to use unambiguous and quantifiable objectives. For example, function Foo_Iavx2() must complete its calculations within $x$ milliseconds or be $x$ percent faster than baseline function Foo_Cpp().

## Code Explicit SIMD Functions

Once you have established your benchmarking timing objectives, you can code your explicit SIMD functions. As mentioned earlier in this section, it is usually a good programming practice to keep your explicit SIMD code localized to preclude future maintenance challenges.

## Benchmark Code to Measure Performance

The next workflow step is to perform benchmarking timing measurements of your explicit SIMD functions and the counterpart baseline function. There are several ways of doing this. One method is to employ a simple software stopwatch like the BmThreadTimer class used in many of this book's source code examples. The advantage of this approach is that it does not require any special drivers, compiler settings, or third-party tools to carry out the requisite timing measurements. For more precise timing measurements and/or insights into potential SIMD software bottlenecks, one of the profiler tools listed in Appendix B may be helpful.

## Optimize Explicit SIMD Code

During this workflow phase, experiment with different C++ SIMD intrinsic functions or x86-AVX assembly language instructions and different sequences. The reason for this is that different x86-AVX instructions or sequences of x86-AVX instructions sometimes yield different performance results. You should also try the optimization techniques discussed later in this chapter. When performing explicit SIMD function optimization, focus on the code blocks inside performance critical for-loops. Optimizing a code block that performs a one-time data initialization or transformation operation is unlikely to result in a significant increase in performance.

## Repeat Benchmarking and Optimization Steps

The last phase of the workflow is to repeat the benchmarking and optimization steps until you have achieved your benchmark timing objective or continued optimization attempts fail to yield any meaningful performance gains. If an explicitly coded SIMD function fails to yield adequate performance gains, consider not using it to avoid future maintenance tasks.

# Optimization Guidelines and Techniques

This section presents some optimization guidelines and techniques that you can use to improve the performance of your explicit SIMD code. The guidelines and techniques can also be employed during the initial coding of an explicit SIMD function.

Before looking at the guidelines and techniques, a few comments are warranted. First, the guidelines and techniques discussed in this section are suitable for use with SIMD code that will execute on x86 processors that support x86-AVX. However, different x86 microarchitectures sometimes exhibit different x86-AVX performance characteristics. This means that it is possible for a recommended optimization technique to improve performance on a specific processor microarchitecture but not yield any performance gains (or even degrade performance) on another. Always perform benchmarking timing measurements to confirm any performance gains. If you have the resources, try performing your benchmark timing measurements using a variety of processors from both AMD and Intel.

Second, none of the recommendations discussed in this section will ameliorate the performance of an inappropriate or poorly designed SIMD algorithm. The design of an algorithm is often the most critical component of its ultimate performance. Finally, I have limited the content of this section to basic optimization guidelines and techniques. It is not intended to be a comprehensive examination of x86-AVX SIMD optimization. Such an undertaking would minimally require several lengthy chapters or conceivably an entire book. Depending on your specific goals, you may want to consult the AMD and Intel optimization reference manuals listed in Appendix B for more information about x86-AVX SIMD code optimization.

## General Techniques

The following general techniques can be applied to improve the performance of x86 SIMD code:

- Use the C++ `alignas(n)` specifier to ensure that SIMD constants, small arrays, simple structures, etc., are aligned to their natural boundaries.

- Use `_aligned_malloc()` and `_aligned_free()` (Windows) or `aligned_alloc()` and `free()` (Linux) to dynamically allocate and release storage for properly aligned arrays and matrices (see source code files `OS.h` and `AlignedMem.h`).

- Use aligned loads and stores when SIMD data is known to be properly aligned.

- Favor the use of single-precision instead of double-precision floating-point values. An algorithm that uses double-precision floating-point values consumes more cache space and memory bandwidth compared to one that employs single-precision floating-point values.

- Use nontemporal stores (e.g., `_mm256_stream_ps()` or `vmovntps`) to minimize cache pollution (see examples Ch08_07 and Ch18_05). Recall that a nontemporal store provides a hint to the processor that the saved data will not be immediately accessed again, which helps minimize cache pollution. Always benchmark and verify the performance gains of any nontemporal store usage since an incorrectly used nontemporal store can decrease performance.

- Perform loop unrolling as follows:

  - Consider partially unrolling a for-loop by increasing the number of SIMD operations performed during each iteration (see example Ch18_04). For example, use two instances of `vfmadd231ps` (or two calls to `_mm256_fmadd_ps()`) to process 16 single-precision elements per iteration instead of a single call to `_mm256_fmadd_ps()` that processes eight elements per iteration. Doing this allows the code to better exploit the multiple SIMD execution units available on most modern x86 processors.

  - Consider fully unrolling small for-loops where the iteration count is known at compile time (see examples Ch05_04 and Ch16_03). Doing this eliminates for-loop control instructions and facilitates direct coding of constants, which often yields additional performance gains.

It is important to note that when using C++, the compiler may partially or fully unroll a for-loop automatically. Before manually unrolling any for-loops in your C++ SIMD code, you may want to check the assembly language code generated by the compiler. It is also important to keep in mind that loop unrolling increases code size and excessive unrolling may adversely affect performance. Always measure your manually unrolled for-loops to confirm any performance gains.

## Assembly Language Optimization Techniques

The following section includes techniques that can be utilized to improve the performance of x86 assembly language functions that use x86-AVX instructions. Additional information regarding these techniques can be found in the AMD and Intel reference manuals listed in Appendix B.

- Align multibyte data values, both scalar and SIMD, on their natural boundaries.

- Maintain frequently used data values and constants, both scalar and SIMD, in a register.

- Use volatile registers first; then use nonvolatile registers. This applies to both general-purpose and x86-AVX registers. Eliminating nonvolatile register saves and restores improves performance.

- Use the two or three operand forms of the `imul` instruction to multiply two signed integers when the full-width product is not needed. For example, use `imul rax,rcx` when a 64-bit truncated product is sufficient instead of `imul rcx`, which returns a 128-bit product in RDX:RAX. This guideline also applies to 32-bit signed integer multiplication (i.e., use `imul eax,ecx` instead of `imul ecx`).

- In performance-critical for-loops, avoid using the lea instruction with three effective address components (i.e., base register, index register, and displacement). On some processor x86 microarchitectures, the three-component form of the lea instruction is slower since it can only be dispatched to a single execution port; the two-component form can be dispatched to multiple execution ports.

- Arrange x86-AVX instructions to minimize or eliminate data dependencies. Instructions can also be staggered to hide any data dependencies (although doing this makes the code harder to read and maintain).

- On systems that support AVX-512, exploit the extra SIMD registers to avoid register spills. A register spill occurs when a function must temporarily save the contents of a register in memory to free the register for other calculations.

- Use the appropriate move instructions for SIMD loads and stores. For example, use vmovdq[a|u] for packed integers and vmovap[d|s] or vmovup[d|s] for packed floating-point values.

- Use the register-memory form of an x86-AVX instruction (e.g., vaddps ymm0,ymm1,ymmword ptr [rax]) to carry out a calculation with a single-use data value in memory. If the data value is needed for multiple calculations, load this value into a register.

- Do not use legacy x87-FPU floating-point instructions.

- Do not code functions that intermix x86-AVX and x86-SSE instructions. Doing this may cause performance degradation. It is also easier to perform maintenance on functions that do not intermix x86-AVX and x86-SSE instructions.

- Use the vzeroupper instruction as required to avoid x86-AVX to x86-SSE state transition penalties.

- Arrange performance critical code inside a for-loop to minimize loop-carried data dependencies.

- In performance critical for-loops, align conditional jump instruction (e.g., jz, jnz, jb, jbe, etc.) targets on a 16-byte boundary. To prevent large increases in code size, restrict the use of this technique to conditional jump instructions that regulate the number of times a for-loop executes.

Modern x86 processors employ both static and dynamic techniques to predict the target of a jump instruction. Incorrect branch predictions, which sometimes adversely affect performance, can be minimized if code blocks containing conditional jump instructions are arranged as follows:

- Use forward conditional jump instructions when the fall-through code is more likely to execute.

- Use backward conditional jump instructions when the fall-through code is less likely to execute.

The forward conditional jump approach is frequently used in code blocks at the beginning of a function to perform argument validation. This approach is also suitable in code blocks that carry out a terminating check at the top of a for-loop. Backward conditional jumps are typically employed in code blocks that perform a terminating check at the bottom a for-loop. Proper use of conditional jump instructions is important. You may want to consult one of the AMD or Intel optimization guides listed in Appendix B for more information about these optimization techniques.

# SIMD Code Complexity vs. Performance

In this section, two source code examples are presented that exemplify some of the trade-offs between SIMD code complexity and performance. Listing 19-1 shows the C++ SIMD source code for the first example named Ch19_01. This example includes two functions that calculate the mean and standard deviation of each row in a matrix.

*Listing 19-1.* Example Ch19_01

```cpp
//-------------------------------------------------
//                  Ch19_01_fcpp.cpp
//-------------------------------------------------

#include <immintrin.h>
#include <stdexcept>
#include "Ch19_01.h"
#include "MatrixF32.h"

void CalcRowStatsF32a_Iavx512(MatrixF32& x, std::vector<float>& row_means,
    std::vector<float>& row_sds)
{
    if (!CheckArgs(x, row_means, row_sds))
        throw std::runtime_error("CalcRowStatsF32a_Iavx512() - CheckArgs failed");

    size_t nrows = x.GetNumRows();
    size_t ncols = x.GetNumCols();
    const float* xx = x.Data();
    const size_t num_simd_elements = 16;

    for (size_t i = 0; i < nrows; i++)
    {
        // Calculate mean of row i in matrix x

        size_t j = 0;
        __m512 sums_f32x16 = _mm512_setzero_ps();

        // Repeat until fewer than 16 elements remain
        while (ncols - j >= num_simd_elements)
        {
            __m512 x_f32x16 = _mm512_loadu_ps(&xx[i * ncols + j]);

            sums_f32x16 = _mm512_add_ps(x_f32x16, sums_f32x16);
            j += num_simd_elements;
        }

        // 8 or more elements?
        if (ncols - j >= num_simd_elements / 2)
        {
            __m256 x_f32x8 = _mm256_loadu_ps(&xx[i * ncols + j]);
            __m512 x_f32x16 = _mm512_insertf32x8(_mm512_setzero_ps(), x_f32x8, 0);
```

```
        sums_f32x16 = _mm512_add_ps(x_f32x16, sums_f32x16);
        j += num_simd_elements / 2;
}


// 4 or more elements?
if (ncols - j >= num_simd_elements / 4)
{
    __m128 x_f32x4 = _mm_loadu_ps(&xx[i * ncols + j]);
    __m512 x_f32x16 = _mm512_insertf32x4(_mm512_setzero_ps(), x_f32x4, 0);

    sums_f32x16 = _mm512_add_ps(x_f32x16, sums_f32x16);
    j += num_simd_elements / 4;
}


// Reduce packed sums to scalar, then add any residual elements
float sum = _mm512_reduce_add_ps(sums_f32x16);

while (j < ncols)
{
    sum += xx[i * ncols + j];
    j += 1;
}


row_means[i] = sum / ncols;


// Calculate standard deviation of row i in matrix x

j = 0;
__m512 sum_sqs_f32x16 = _mm512_setzero_ps();
__m512 row_means_f32x16 = _mm512_set1_ps(row_means[i]);


// Repeat until fewer than 16 elements remain
while (ncols - j >= num_simd_elements)
{
    __m512 x_f32x16 = _mm512_loadu_ps(&xx[i * ncols + j]);
    __m512 t1_f32x16 = _mm512_sub_ps(x_f32x16, row_means_f32x16);
    __m512 t2_f32x16 = _mm512_mul_ps(t1_f32x16, t1_f32x16);

    sum_sqs_f32x16 = _mm512_add_ps(t2_f32x16, sum_sqs_f32x16);
    j += num_simd_elements;
}


// 8 or more elements?
if (ncols - j >= num_simd_elements / 2)
{
    __m256 x_f32x8 = _mm256_loadu_ps(&xx[i * ncols + j]);
    __m256 row_means_f32x8 = _mm256_set1_ps(row_means[i]);
    __m256 t1_f32x8 = _mm256_sub_ps(x_f32x8, row_means_f32x8);
    __m256 t2_f32x8 = _mm256_mul_ps(t1_f32x8, t1_f32x8);
    __m512 x_f32x16 = _mm512_insertf32x8(_mm512_setzero_ps(), t2_f32x8, 0);
```

```
            sum_sqs_f32x16 = _mm512_add_ps(x_f32x16, sum_sqs_f32x16);
            j += num_simd_elements / 2;
        }

        // 4 or more elements?
        if (ncols - j >= num_simd_elements / 4)
        {
            __m128 x_f32x4 = _mm_loadu_ps(&xx[i * ncols + j]);
            __m128 row_means_f32x4 = _mm_set1_ps(row_means[i]);
            __m128 t1_f32x4 = _mm_sub_ps(x_f32x4, row_means_f32x4);
            __m128 t2_f32x4 = _mm_mul_ps(t1_f32x4, t1_f32x4);
            __m512 x_f32x16 = _mm512_insertf32x4(_mm512_setzero_ps(), t2_f32x4, 0);

            sum_sqs_f32x16 = _mm512_add_ps(x_f32x16, sum_sqs_f32x16);
            j += num_simd_elements / 4;
        }

        // Reduce packed sum-of-squares to scalar, then add any residual elements
        float sum_sqs = _mm512_reduce_add_ps(sum_sqs_f32x16);

        while (j < ncols)
        {
            float temp1 = xx[i * ncols + j] - row_means[i];
            sum_sqs += temp1 * temp1;
            j += 1;
        }

        row_sds[i] = sqrt(sum_sqs / (ncols - 1));
    }
}

void CalcRowStatsF32b_Iavx512(MatrixF32& x, std::vector<float>& row_means,
    std::vector<float>& row_sds)
{
    if (!CheckArgs(x, row_means, row_sds))
        throw std::runtime_error("CalcRowStatsF32b_Iavx512() - CheckArgs failed");

    size_t nrows = x.GetNumRows();
    size_t ncols = x.GetNumCols();
    const float* xx = x.Data();
    const size_t num_simd_elements = 16;

    for (size_t i = 0; i < nrows; i++)
    {
        // Calculate mean of row i in matrix x

        size_t j = 0;
        __m512 sums_f32x16 = _mm512_setzero_ps();

        // Repeat until fewer than 16 elements remain
        while (ncols - j >= num_simd_elements)
```

```
    {
        __m512 x_f32x16 = _mm512_loadu_ps(&xx[i * ncols + j]);

        sums_f32x16 = _mm512_add_ps(x_f32x16, sums_f32x16);
        j += num_simd_elements;
    }

    // Reduce packed sums to scalar, then add any residual elements
    float sum = _mm512_reduce_add_ps(sums_f32x16);

    while (j < ncols)
    {
        sum += xx[i * ncols + j];
        j += 1;
    }

    row_means[i] = sum / ncols;

    // Calculate standard deviation of row i in matrix x

    j = 0;
    __m512 sum_sqs_f32x16 = _mm512_setzero_ps();
    __m512 row_means_f32x16 = _mm512_set1_ps(row_means[i]);

    // Repeat until fewer than 16 elements remain
    while (ncols - j >= num_simd_elements)
    {
        __m512 x_f32x16 = _mm512_loadu_ps(&xx[i * ncols + j]);
        __m512 t1_f32x16 = _mm512_sub_ps(x_f32x16, row_means_f32x16);
        __m512 t2_f32x16 = _mm512_mul_ps(t1_f32x16, t1_f32x16);

        sum_sqs_f32x16 = _mm512_add_ps(t2_f32x16, sum_sqs_f32x16);
        j += num_simd_elements;
    }

    // Reduce packed sum-of-squares to scalar, then process residual elements
    float sum_sqs = _mm512_reduce_add_ps(sum_sqs_f32x16);

    while (j < ncols)
    {
        float temp1 = xx[i * ncols + j] - row_means[i];
        sum_sqs += temp1 * temp1;
        j += 1;
    }

    row_sds[i] = sqrt(sum_sqs / (ncols - 1));
    }
}
```

Listing 19-1 opens with the definition of a function named CalcRowStatsF32a_Iavx512(). This function calculates row means and standard deviations using AVX-512 C++ SIMD intrinsic functions. Each iteration of the outer-most for-loop in CalcRowStatsF32a_Iavx512() begins with a call to _mm512_setzero_ps() that sets each single-precision floating-point element of sums_f32x16 to zero. The next code block contains a simple while loop that sums the elements of matrix x row i using 512-bit wide SIMD operands. Note that this while loop executes only if 16 or more elements are available in row i.

Following execution of the while loop, the number of elements that remain in row i can vary between 0 and 15. The next code block updates sums_f32x16 if eight or more elements remain in the current row. Note that this code block uses _mm256_loadu_ps() to load eight elements. This is followed by a call to _mm512_insertf32x8() that creates a 512-bit wide SIMD operand whose eight least significant single-precision floating-point elements contain the elements loaded by _mm256_loadu_ps(); the eight most significant elements are set to zero by the call to _mm512_setzero_ps(). Doing this facilitates the use of _mm512_add_ps() to update sums_f32x16.

The ensuing code block uses the same basic technique but only executes if four or more elements remain in the current row. The final section of the mean calculating code in CalcRowStatsF32a_Iavx512() begins with a call to _mm512_reduce_add_ps() that sums the single-precision floating-point elements of sums_f32x16. This is followed by a simple while loop that adds any residual elements to sum. Calculation of the mean for row i follows. The layout of the code that calculates row standard deviations mimics the mean calculating code. Note that these code blocks calculate sums of squares instead of plain sums.

The next function in Listing 19-1, CalcRowStatsF32b_Iavx512(), also calculates row means and standard deviations. This function also starts with a while loop that uses 512-bit wide SIMD operands to calculate the required intermediate sums for the row i mean. Unlike function CalcRowStatsF32a_Iavx512(), function CalcRowStatsF32b_Iavx512() omits the code blocks that utilized eight- and four-element SIMD arithmetic to update sums_f32x16. Note that following the reduction operation, the residual-element while loop will process 1-15 elements instead of 1–3 elements. Function CalcRowStatsF32b_Iavx512() also omits the eight- and four-element SIMD arithmetic code blocks from standard deviation calculating code.

Table 19-1 shows the benchmark timing measurements for source code example Ch19_01. Note that for each test case, matrix x contains 15 more columns than rows. This ensures that all code paths in function CalcRowStatsF32a_Iavx512() get executed. The right-most column of this table signifies the percent performance gain of function CalcRowStatsF32a_Iavx512() compared to function CalcRowStatsF32b_Iavx512().

**Table 19-1.** *Benchmark Timing Measurements for Source Code Example Ch19_01 (Microseconds)*

| Matrix Size | CalcRowStatsF32a_Iavx512() | CalcRowStatsF32b_Iavx512() | % Gain |
|---|---|---|---|
| 1024 × 1039 | 117 | 131 | 10.7 |
| 1536 × 1551 | 286 | 309 | 7.4 |
| 2048 × 2063 | 628 | 652 | 3.7 |
| 2560 × 2575 | 1084 | 1117 | 3.0 |
| 3072 × 3087 | 1616 | 1651 | 2.1 |
| 3584 × 3599 | 2225 | 2268 | 1.9 |
| 4096 × 4111 | 2928 | 2974 | 1.5 |

As you can see from the measurements in Table 19-1, the SIMD code in function CalcRowStatsF32a_Iavx512() yielded meaningful gains in performance compared to function CalcRowStatsF32b_Iavx512(). Note that the percentage gain drops as the size of the matrix increases. This trend is not surprising given that the number of residual columns is fixed at 15 while the total number of columns increases.

Before drawing any conclusions regarding SIMD algorithm complexity vs. performance, let's look at one other example. Source code example Ch19_02 contains two functions named Convolve1Dx2_F32a_ Iavx512() and Convolve1Dx2_F32b_Iavx512() that implement 2D discrete convolutions. Listing 19-2 shows the source code for function Convolve1Dx2_F32b_Iavx512(). The code for function Convolve1Dx2_F32a_ Iavx512() is the same code that you saw in source code example Ch08_09 (see function Convolve1Dx2_F32_ Iavx512() in Listing 8-9).

*Listing 19-2.* Example Ch19_02

```
//--------------------------------------------------
//                  Ch19_02_fcpp2.cpp
//--------------------------------------------------

#include <stdexcept>
#include <immintrin.h>
#include "Ch19_02.h"
#include "MiscTypes.h"

void Convolve1Dx2_F32b_Iavx512(CD_1Dx2& cd)
{
    if (!CheckArgs1Dx2(cd))
        throw std::runtime_error("Convolve1Dx2_F32b_Iavx512() - CheckArgs failed");

    indx_t ks = (indx_t)cd.m_KernelSize;
    indx_t ks2 = ks / 2;
    indx_t im_h = cd.m_ImH;
    indx_t im_w = cd.m_ImW;

    const std::vector<float>& im_src = cd.m_ImSrc;
    std::vector<float>& im_des = cd.m_ImDes;
    std::vector<float>& im_tmp = cd.m_ImTmp;
    const std::vector<float>& im_ker_x = cd.m_Kernel1Dx;
    const std::vector<float>& im_ker_y = cd.m_Kernel1Dy;

    const indx_t num_simd_elements = 16;
    const indx_t num_simd_elements2 = 8;
    const indx_t num_simd_elements3 = 4;

    // Perform 1D convolution (X)
    for (indx_t i = ks2; i < im_h - ks2; i++)
    {
        indx_t j = ks2;

        while (j < im_w - ks2)
        {
            if (j + num_simd_elements <= im_w - ks2)
            {
                // Use 512-bit SIMD arithmetic
                __m512 im_tmp_vals = _mm512_setzero_ps();
```

```
                    for (indx_t k = -ks2; k <= ks2; k++)
                    {
                        __m512 im_src_vals = _mm512_loadu_ps(&im_src[i * im_w + j - k]);
                        __m512 im_ker_vals = _mm512_set1_ps(im_ker_x[k + ks2]);

                        im_tmp_vals = _mm512_fmadd_ps(im_src_vals, im_ker_vals,
                                        im_tmp_vals);
                    }

                    _mm512_storeu_ps(&im_tmp[i * im_w + j], im_tmp_vals);
                    j += num_simd_elements;
                }
                else
                {
                    // Use scalar arithmetic
                    __m128 im_tmp_vals = _mm_setzero_ps();

                    for (indx_t k = -ks2; k <= ks2; k++)
                    {
                        __m128 im_src_vals = _mm_load_ss(&im_src[i * im_w + j - k]);
                        __m128 im_ker_vals = _mm_load_ss(&im_ker_x[k + ks2]);

                        im_tmp_vals = _mm_fmadd_ss(im_src_vals, im_ker_vals,
                                        im_tmp_vals);
                    }

                    _mm_store_ss(&im_tmp[i * im_w + j], im_tmp_vals);
                    j += 1;
                }
            }
        }

        // Perform 1D convolution (Y)
        indx_t j = ks2;

        while (j < im_w - ks2)
        {
            if (j + num_simd_elements <= im_w - ks2)
            {
                // Use 512-bit SIMD arithmetic
                for (indx_t i = ks2; i < im_h - ks2; i++)
                {
                    __m512 im_des_vals = _mm512_setzero_ps();

                    for (indx_t k = -ks2; k <= ks2; k++)
                    {
                        __m512 im_tmp_vals = _mm512_loadu_ps(&im_tmp[(i - k) * im_w + j]);
                        __m512 im_ker_vals = _mm512_set1_ps(im_ker_y[k + ks2]);

                        im_des_vals = _mm512_fmadd_ps(im_tmp_vals, im_ker_vals,
                                        im_des_vals);
                    }
```

```
            _mm512_storeu_ps(&im_des[i * im_w + j], im_des_vals);
        }

        j += num_simd_elements;
    }
    else
    {
        // Use scalar arithmetic
        for (indx_t i = ks2; i < im_h - ks2; i++)
        {
            __m128 im_des_vals = _mm_setzero_ps();

            for (indx_t k = -ks2; k <= ks2; k++)
            {
                __m128 im_tmp_vals = _mm_load_ss(&im_tmp[(i - k) * im_w + j]);
                __m128 im_ker_vals = _mm_load_ss(&im_ker_y[k + ks2]);

                im_des_vals = _mm_fmadd_ss(im_tmp_vals, im_ker_vals,
                                im_des_vals);
            }

            _mm_store_ss(&im_des[i * im_w + j], im_des_vals);
        }

        j += 1;
    }
  }
}
```

Like the previous example, the two discrete convolution calculating functions in this example differ in terms of SIMD complexity. Function Convolve1Dx2_F32a_Iavx512() uses 512-, 256-, and 128-bit wide SIMD operands to carry out FMA calculations using 16, 8, and 4 pixels, respectively. In Listing 19-2, the convolution code for function Convolve1Dx2_F32b_Iavx512() is simpler in that it only employs 512-bit wide SIMD operands. Both 2D discrete convolution functions exercise scalar FMA arithmetic to handle any residual row or column pixels.

Table 19-2 shows the benchmark timing measurements for example Ch19_02. These measurements were made using a 9 × 9 convolution kernel and test images containing random pixel values. The size of each test image was tweaked to include 15 extra pixels in each row and column. This ensures execution of all code paths in the convolution functions. As you can see from the measurements in Table 19-2, the performance of function Convolve1Dx2_F32a_Iavx512() is demonstrably faster than Convolve1Dx2_F32b_Iavx512(). Like the previous example, the percent gain drops as image size increases since the number of residual pixels is constant.

**Table 19-2.** *Benchmark Timing Measurements for Source Code Example Ch19_02 (Microseconds)*

| Nominal Image Size | Convolve1Dx2_F32a_Iavx512() | Convolve1Dx2_F32b_Iavx512() | % Gain |
|---|---|---|---|
| 1024 × 1024 | 1256 | 1444 | 13.0 |
| 2048 × 2048 | 5266 | 5514 | 4.5 |
| 3072 × 3072 | 12288 | 12729 | 3.5 |
| 4096 × 4096 | 22643 | 23203 | 2.4 |

If you scrutinize the SIMD code in functions `CalcRowStatsF32a_Iavx512()` (Ch19_01) and `Convolve1Dx2_F32a_Iavx512()` (Ch19_02), you will notice that the 256- and 128-bit SIMD code blocks exercise different size variants of the same C++ SIMD intrinsic functions used in the 512-bit SIMD code blocks. These functions also include some extra control logic to ensure correct execution of the 256- and 128-bit SIMD code blocks.

The source code examples in this section exemplify that for many (but certainly not all) SIMD algorithms, it often makes sense to develop code that fully exploits the SIMD resources of the host processor. However, coding streamlined SIMD functions like `CalcRowStatsF32b_Iavx512()` (Ch19_01) and `Convolve1Dx2_F32b_Iavx512()` (Ch19_02) might be appealing if you favor algorithmic simplicity in exchange for slightly slower performance. This approach might also make sense if you are developing SIMD code for an algorithm where the processing of residual elements is either inconsequential or irrelevant.

# Summary

Here are the key learning points for Chapter 19:

- Explicit SIMD code development is a specialized programming tool that should be thoughtfully utilized.

- Explicit SIMD techniques are suitable for functions that perform calculations using arrays or matrices.

- An explicitly coded SIMD function should provide tangible benefits to the end user.

- Always measure explicitly coded SIMD functions to confirm any anticipated performance gains.

- The coding and optimization of an explicit SIMD function is often a trade-off between development effort, performance gains, and future maintenance activities.

# APPENDIX A

■ ■ ■

# Source Code and Development Tools

Appendix A explains how to download and set up the source code. It also explains how to build and execute the source code examples using Visual Studio (Windows) or the GNU toolchain (Linux).

## Source Code Download and Setup

Use the following steps to download and set up the source code:

1. Create a source code master folder. Use `C:\Users\<UserName>\Documents\ModParProgCppAsm` (Windows) or `~/Documents/ModParProgCppAsm` (Linux). If you prefer, you can create the master folder at a different location. Note that if you do this, you will also need to adapt some subsequent instructions accordingly.

2. Using your favorite browser, navigate to the following GitHub website: `https://github.com/Apress/modern-parallel-programming-cpp-assembly`.

3. Click on the **Code** button and select **Download ZIP**.

4. Save the ZIP file in the master folder that you created in Step 1.

5. Open a File Manager window and navigate to the master folder.

6. Right-click on the downloaded ZIP file and select **Extract All...** (Windows) or **Extract Here** (Linux).

7. Windows Only: In the dialog box that appears, edit the folder name so that it matches the folder name created in Step 1. Click **Extract**.

8. Rename the subfolder `modern-parallel-programming-cpp-assembly-master` to Code.

9. Verify that the folder tree under Code matches the folder tree shown in Figure A-1.

© Daniel Kusswurm 2022
D. Kusswurm, *Modern Parallel Programming with C++ and Assembly Language*,
https://doi.org/10.1007/978-1-4842-7918-2

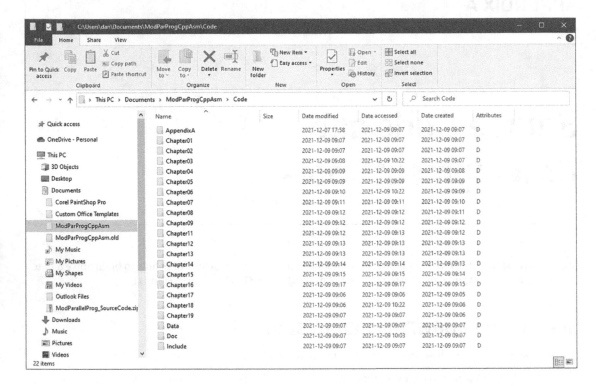

**Figure A-1.** *Source code folder tree*

In some source code examples, relative pathnames (e.g., `../../Data/ImageA.png`) are used to specify an image file. You may need to change these pathname strings if you use a folder structure that differs from the default one created in this section.

# Development Tools

The following section discusses the development tools that were used to create the source code examples. The content is partitioned into two subsections. The first subsection covers Visual Studio and Windows. The second subsection covers the GNU toolchain and Linux. You can read one or both subsections depending on your interests.

## Visual Studio and Windows

In this section, you will learn how to use Microsoft's Visual Studio development IDE to run the source code examples. You will also learn how to create a simple Visual Studio C++ project. The source code examples in this book were created using Visual Studio Professional 2019, but you can use any 2019 edition including the free Community edition. If any updates are required for Visual Studio 2022, they will be available on GitHub.

Visual Studio uses logical entities called solutions and projects to help simplify application development. A solution is a collection of one or more projects that are used to build an application. A project is a container object that organizes an application's files. A Visual Studio project is usually created for each buildable component of an application (e.g., executable file, dynamic-linked library, static library, etc.).

A standard Visual Studio C++ project includes two solution configurations named Debug and Release. As implied by their names, these configurations support separate executable builds for initial development and final release. A standard Visual Studio C++ project also incorporates two solution platforms. The default solution platforms are named Win32 and x64. These solution platforms contain the necessary settings to build 32-bit and 64-bit executables, respectively. The Visual Studio solution and project files for this book's source code examples include only the x64 platform.

## Running a Source Code Example

Use the following steps to execute any of the book's source code examples:

1.  Using File Explorer, double-click on the chapter's Visual Studio solution (.sln) file. The .sln file for each chapter is located in the chapter subfolder (e.g., C:\ Users\<UserName>\Documents\ModParProgCppAsm\Code\Chapter02).

2.  Select menu item Build | Configuration Manager. In the Configuration Manager dialog box, set Active Solution Configuration to **Release**. Then set Active Solution Platform to **x64**. Note that these options may already be selected.

3.  If necessary, select menu item View | Solution Explorer to open the Solution Explorer window.

4.  In the Solution Explorer window, right-click on a project to run (e.g., Ch02_01) and choose **Set as Startup Project**.

5.  Select menu item Debug | Start Without Debugging to run the program.

## Creating a Visual Studio C++ Project

In this section, you will learn how to create a simple Visual Studio project that includes both C++ and assembly language source code files. The ensuing paragraphs describe the same basic procedure that was used to create this book's source code examples and includes the following stages:

- Create a C++ project
- Enable MASM support
- Add an assembly language file
- Set project properties
- Edit the source code
- Build and run the project

You may need to adapt some of the instructions that follow depending on the configuration of Visual Studio.

### Create a C++ Project

Use the following steps to create a Visual Studio C++ solution and project:

1.  Start Visual Studio.

2.  Select File | New | Project.

3.  In the Create a new project dialog box, adjust the three drop-down box selections (located just below the Search for templates text box) to match those in Figure A-2. Then select **Console App** as shown in Figure A-2. Click **Next**.

4.  In the Configure your new project dialog box, enter Example1 in the Project name text box.

5.  Enter a location for the project in the Location text box or leave it unchanged to use the default location.

6.  In the Solution name text box, enter TestSolution.

7.  Verify that your Configure your new project dialog box matches Figure A-3 (the Location text can be different). Click **Create**.

8.  Select Build | Configuration Manager. In the Configuration Manager dialog box, choose **<Edit...>** under Active Solution Platforms (Figure A-4).

9.  In the Edit Solution Platforms dialog box, select **x86** (Figure A-5). Click **Remove**.

10. Click **Close** to close the Edit Solution Platforms dialog box. Click **Close** to close the Configuration Manager dialog box.

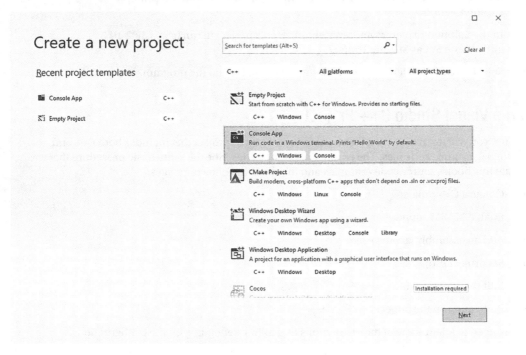

***Figure A-2.*** *Create a new project dialog box*

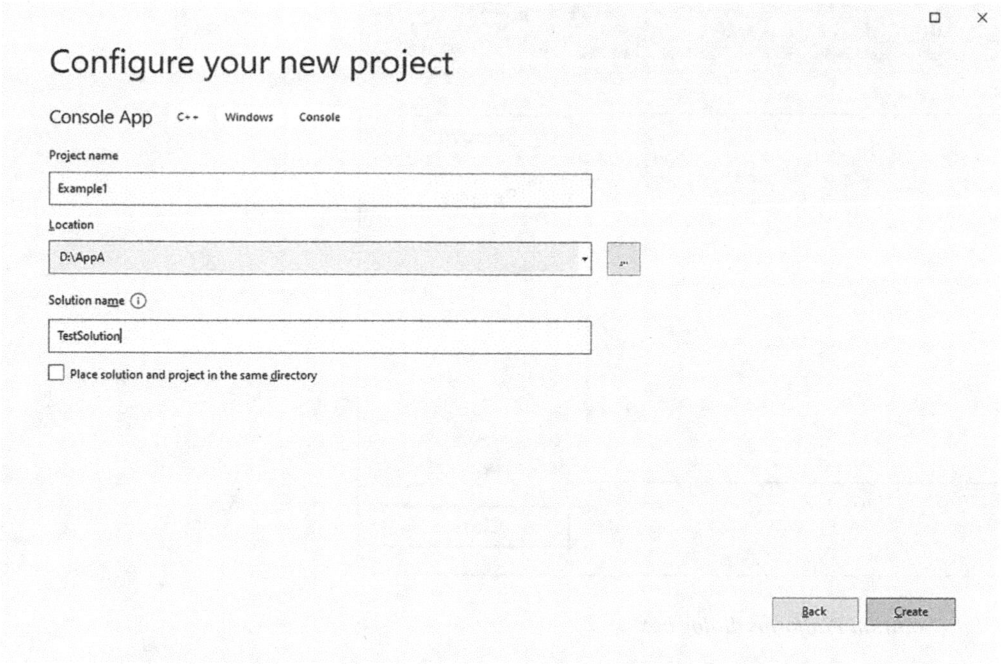

## Configure your new project

Console App    C++    Windows    Console

Project name

Example1

Location

D:\AppA

Solution name (i)

TestSolution

☐ Place solution and project in the same directory

Back    Create

**Figure A-3.** *Configure your new project dialog box*

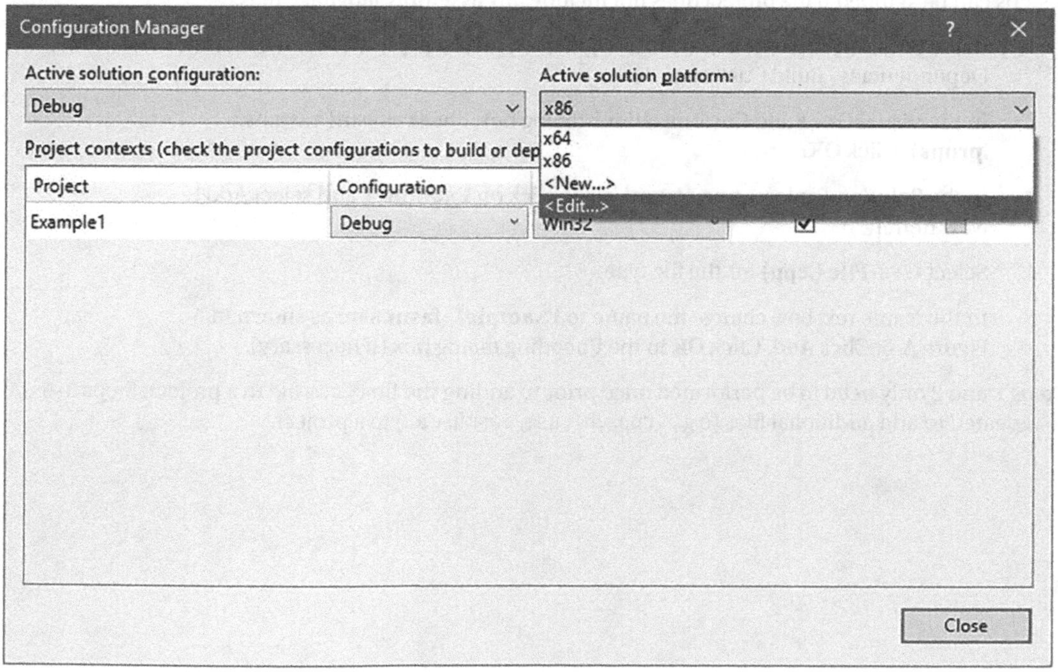

## Configuration Manager

Active solution configuration:          Active solution platform:

Debug                            x86

Project contexts (check the project configurations to build or dep

| Project | Configuration | | | |
|---------|---------------|--|--|--|
| Example1 | Debug | Win32 | ☑ | ☐ |

x64
x86
<New...>
<Edit...>

Close

**Figure A-4.** *Configuration Manager dialog box*

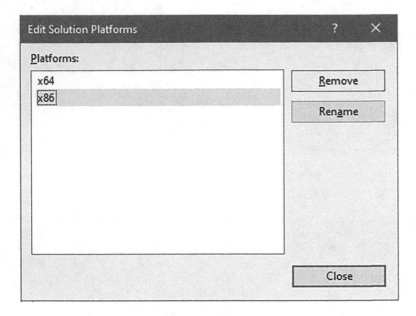

**Figure A-5.** *Edit Solution Platforms dialog box*

## Add an Assembly Language File

Perform the steps in this section to add an x86 assembly language file (.asm) to a Visual Studio C++ project. These steps can be skipped if the project does not include any assembly language files.

1. In the Solution Explorer tree control, right-click on **Example1** and select Build Dependencies | Build Customizations.

2. In the Visual C++ Build Customizations dialog box, check **masm(.targets, .props)**. Click **OK**.

3. In the Solution Explorer tree control, right-click on **Example1** and select Add | New Item.

4. Select **C++ File (.cpp)** for the file type.

5. In the Name text box, change the name to **Example1_fasm.asm** as shown in Figure A-6. Click **Add**. Click **OK** in the Encoding dialog box (if necessary).

Steps 1 and 2 only need to be performed once prior to adding the first .asm file to a project. Steps 3–5 can be repeated to add additional files (e.g., .cpp, .h, .asm, .asmh, etc.) to a project.

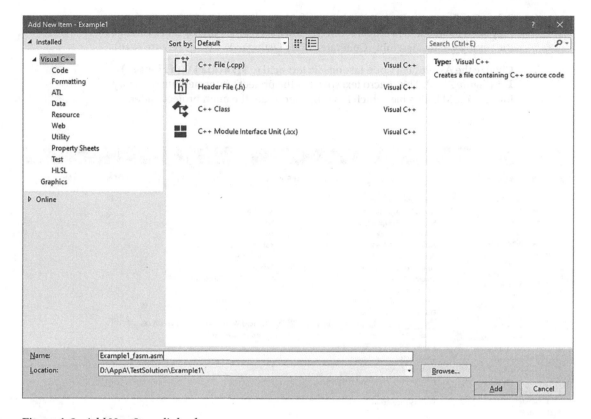

*Figure A-6.* *Add New Item dialog box*

## Set Project Properties

Perform the steps in this section to set the project's properties. The steps that enable listing files (steps 5–7) are optional.

1. In the Solution Explorer tree control, right-click on **Example1** and select **Properties**.

2. In the Property Pages dialog box, change the Configuration setting to **All Configurations** and the Platform setting to **All Platforms**. Note that one or both options may already be set.

3. Select Configuration Properties | C/C++ | Code Generation. Change the setting Enable Enhanced Instruction Set to **Advanced Vector Extensions (/arch:AVX)** (Figure A-7). You can also select /arch:AVX2 or /arch:AVX512.

4. Select Configuration Properties | C/C++ | Optimization. If necessary, change the setting Whole Program Optimization to **No** (Figure A-8) for reasons described later in this section.

5. Select Configuration Properties | C/C++ | Output Files. Change the setting Assembler Output to **Assembly Machine and Source Code (/FAcs)** (Figure A-9).

6. Select Configuration Properties | Microsoft Macro Assembler | Listing File (you may need to adjust the vertical scroll bar downward to see this option). Change the setting Enable Assembly Generated Code Listing to **Yes (/Sg)** (Figure A-10).

7. Change the Assembled Code Listing File text field to **$(IntDir)\%(filename). lst** (Figure A-10). This macro text specifies the project's intermediate directory for the MASM listing file, which is a subfolder under the main project folder.

8. Click **OK**.

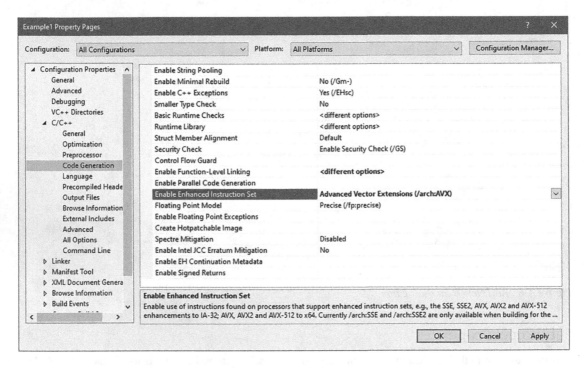

*Figure A-7. Property Pages dialog box – Enable Enhanced Instruction Set*

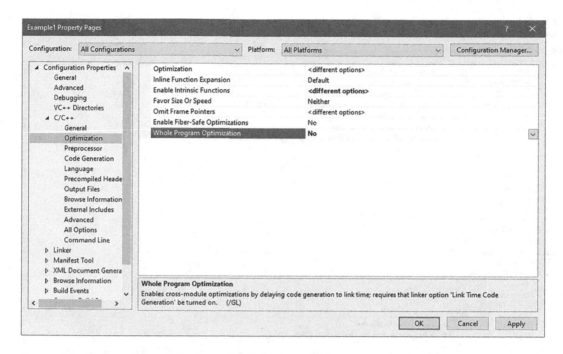

**Figure A-8.** *Property Pages dialog box – Whole Program Optimization*

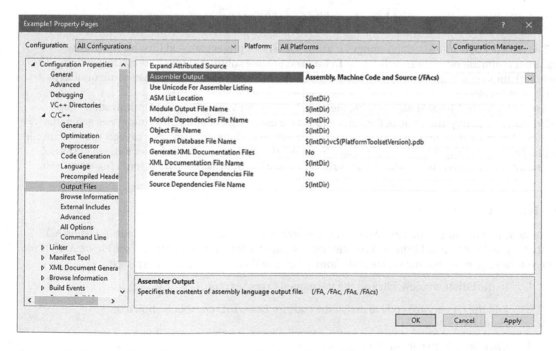

**Figure A-9.** *Property Pages dialog box – Assembler Output*

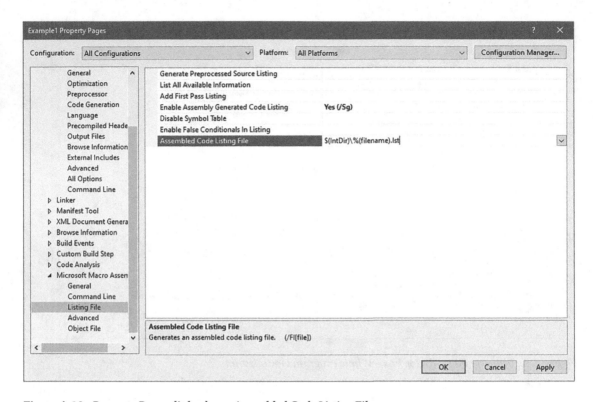

**Figure A-10.** *Property Pages dialog box – Assembled Code Listing File*

The default code optimization settings for a new Visual C++ project are /Od (disable) and /O2 (maximum optimization favor speed) for the Debug and Release solution configurations, respectively. The benchmark timing measurements published in this book were made using the Release configuration as described in Chapter 2.

According to the Visual Studio website, the default setting for Whole Program Optimization (step 4) is No. You can change the value of this setting to Yes (or use /GL), but doing this sometimes generates inaccurate benchmark timing measurements for C++ functions. There are also a few caveats that you should consider before enabling this option, especially in production code. For more information, see https://docs.microsoft.com/en-us/cpp/build/reference/gl-whole-program-optimization?view=msvc-160.

## Edit the Source Code

Use the steps that follow this paragraph to edit the source code so that it matches the code in Listing A-1. Note that the code shown in Listing A-1 is included in subfolder AppendixA\Example1 (see Figure A-1). If you prefer, you can cut and paste the source code from the files in this folder instead of typing it.

1. In the Editor window, click on the tab named Example1.cpp.

2. Edit the C++ source code to match the code for Example1.cpp that is shown in Listing A-1.

3. Click on the tab named Example1_fasm.asm.

4.   Edit the assembly language source code to match the code for Example1_fasm.
     asm that is shown in Listing A-1.

5.   Select File | Save All.

*Listing A-1.* Source Code for Example1

```cpp
//-------------------------------------------------
//                 Example1.cpp
//-------------------------------------------------

#include <iostream>
#include <iomanip>
#include <string>
#include <immintrin.h>

static void CalcZ_Iavx(float* z, const float* x, const float* y, size_t n);
extern "C" void CalcZ_Aavx(float* z, const float* x, const float* y, size_t n);

int main()
{
    const size_t n = 19;
    float x[n], y[n], z1[n], z2[n];

    // Initialize the data arrays
    for (size_t i = 0; i < n; i++)
    {
        x[i] = i * 10.0f + 10.0f;
        y[i] = i * 1000.0f + 1000.0f;
        z1[i] = z2[i] = 0.0f;
    }

    // Exercise the SIMD calculating functions
    CalcZ_Iavx(z1, x, y, n);
    CalcZ_Aavx(z2, x, y, n);

    // Display the results
    const char nl = '\n';
    const size_t w = 10;
    std::cout << std::fixed << std::setprecision(1);

    std::cout << std::setw(w) << "i";
    std::cout << std::setw(w) << "x";
    std::cout << std::setw(w) << "y";
    std::cout << std::setw(w) << "z1";
    std::cout << std::setw(w) << "z2" << nl;
    std::cout << std::string(60, '-') << nl;

    for (size_t i = 0; i < n; i++)
    {
        std::cout << std::setw(w) << i;
        std::cout << std::setw(w) << x[i];
```

```cpp
            std::cout << std::setw(w) << y[i];
            std::cout << std::setw(w) << z1[i];
            std::cout << std::setw(w) << z2[i] << nl;
    }
}

void CalcZ_Iavx(float* z, const float* x, const float* y, size_t n)
{
    size_t i = 0;
    const size_t num_simd_elements = 8;

    for (; n - i >= num_simd_elements; i += num_simd_elements)
    {
        // Calculate z[i:i+7] = x[i:i+7] + y[i:i+7]
        __m256 x_vals = _mm256_loadu_ps(&x[i]);
        __m256 y_vals = _mm256_loadu_ps(&y[i]);
        __m256 z_vals = _mm256_add_ps(x_vals, y_vals);

        _mm256_storeu_ps(&z[i], z_vals);
    }

    // Calculate z[i] = x[i] + y[i] for any remaining elements
    for (; i < n; i += 1)
        z[i] = x[i] + y[i];
}
```

```asm
;----------------------------------------------------
;                 Example1_fasm.asm
;----------------------------------------------------


;-----------------------------------------------------------------------------
; extern "C" void CalcZ_Aavx(float* z, const float* x, const float* x, size_t n);
;-----------------------------------------------------------------------------

NSE     equ 8                                   ;num_simd_elements

        .code
CalcZ_Aavx proc
        xor rax,rax                             ;i = 0;

Loop1:  mov r10,r9                              ;r10 = n
        sub r10,rax                             ;r10 = n - i
        cmp r10,NSE                             ;is n - i < NSE?
        jb Loop2                                ;jump if yes
```

```
; Calculate z[i:i+7] = x[i:i+7] + y[i:i+7]
        vmovups ymm0,ymmword ptr [rdx+rax*4]    ;ymm0 = x[i:i+7]
        vmovups ymm1,ymmword ptr [r8+rax*4]     ;ymm1 = y[i:i+7]
        vaddps ymm2,ymm0,ymm1                    ;z[i:i+7] = x[i:i+7] + y[i:i+7]
        vmovups ymmword ptr [rcx+rax*4],ymm2     ;save z[i:i+7]

        add rax,NSE                              ;i += NSE
        jmp Loop1                                ;repeat Loop1 until done

Loop2:  cmp rax,r9                               ;is i >= n?
        jae Done                                 ;jump if yes

; Calculate z[i] = x[i] + y[i] for remaining elements
        vmovss xmm0,real4 ptr [rdx+rax*4]        ;xmm0 = x[i]
        vmovss xmm1,real4 ptr [r8+rax*4]         ;xmm1 = y[i]
        vaddss xmm2,xmm0,xmm1                     ;z[i] = x[i] + y[i]
        vmovss real4 ptr [rcx+rax*4],xmm2        ;save z[i]

        inc rax                                  ;i += 1
        jmp Loop2                                ;repeat Loop2 until done

Done:   vzeroupper                               ;clear upper bits of ymm regs
        ret                                      ;return to caller
CalcZ_Aavx endp
        end
```

## Build and Run the Project

Use the following steps to build and run the project:

1.  Select Build | Build Solution.

2.  If necessary, fix any reported C++ compiler or MASM errors and repeat Step 1.

3.  Select Debug | Start Without Debugging.

4.  Verify that the output matches the console window shown in Figure A-11.

5.  Press any key to close the console window.

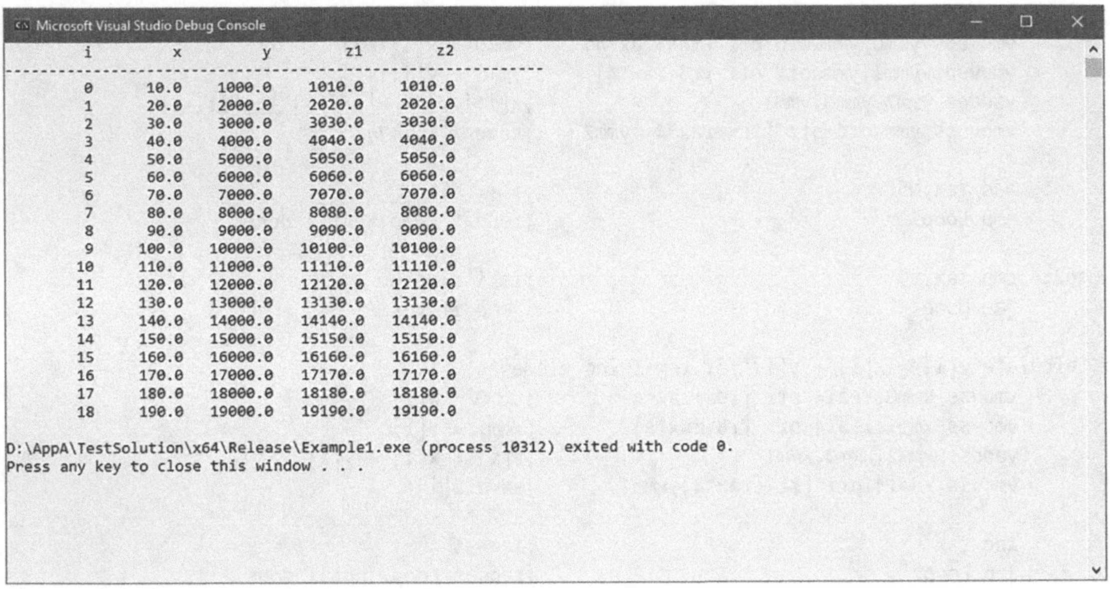

```
Microsoft Visual Studio Debug Console                                    —    □    ×
      i        x        y        z1        z2
-------------------------------------------------------
      0     10.0     1000.0    1010.0    1010.0
      1     20.0     2000.0    2020.0    2020.0
      2     30.0     3000.0    3030.0    3030.0
      3     40.0     4000.0    4040.0    4040.0
      4     50.0     5000.0    5050.0    5050.0
      5     60.0     6000.0    6060.0    6060.0
      6     70.0     7000.0    7070.0    7070.0
      7     80.0     8000.0    8080.0    8080.0
      8     90.0     9000.0    9090.0    9090.0
      9    100.0    10000.0   10100.0   10100.0
     10    110.0    11000.0   11110.0   11110.0
     11    120.0    12000.0   12120.0   12120.0
     12    130.0    13000.0   13130.0   13130.0
     13    140.0    14000.0   14140.0   14140.0
     14    150.0    15000.0   15150.0   15150.0
     15    160.0    16000.0   16160.0   16160.0
     16    170.0    17000.0   17170.0   17170.0
     17    180.0    18000.0   18180.0   18180.0
     18    190.0    19000.0   19190.0   19190.0

D:\AppA\TestSolution\x64\Release\Example1.exe (process 10312) exited with code 0.
Press any key to close this window . . .
```

*Figure A-11.* *Console window output for Example1*

# GCC and Linux

As mentioned in the Introduction, you can also build and execute the C++ SIMD source code examples (Chapters 2–9) using a Debian or Ubuntu distribution of Linux. This section explains how to do this.

## Additional Configuration

A few source code examples require libpng, which is a freely available library for processing PNG image files (www.libpng.org/pub/png). Perform the following steps to install this library on your computer:

1. Open a terminal window.

2. Type sudo apt install libpng-dev and press **Enter**.

3. Select **Yes** to install libpng if it is not already installed.

## Build and Run

Perform the following steps to build and run a source code example on Linux:

1. Open a terminal window in your home folder.

2. Using the cd command, change the current working directory to a source code example directory. For example, to build and execute source code example Ch02_01, type the following: cd Documents/ModParProgCppAsm/Code/Chapter02/Ch02_01. Press **Enter**.

3. Type make and press **Enter** to build source code example Ch02_01.

4. Type ./Ch02_01 and press **Enter** to run source code example Ch02_01.

# Make Utility

GNU Make ("Make") is a software development utility that facilitates automated program builds. It is typically installed on computers that run Linux. Make uses dependency rules to specify the source code (e.g., .cpp and .h) and intermediate (e.g., .o) files needed to build a target. A target can be any type of file but is often an executable file. Dependency rules are defined in a special file called a makefile. Each dependency rule includes one or more shell commands that instruct Make how to build a target or intermediate file.

The primary advantage of using Make is its ability to selectively execute commands based on changes that occur to a target's dependencies. For example, Make will recompile only the source code files that have changed since it was last run. It uses the last modified datetime stamp of each dependent file to accomplish this.

The remainder of this section briefly discusses the makefiles that were created for this book's source code examples. It is important to note that the subsequent paragraphs are not intended to be a tutorial on Make or how to create makefiles. Comprehensive usage information for Make and makefile dependency rule creation is available online at www.gnu.org/software/make/manual/.

Listing A-2 shows the makefile for source code example Ch02_01. Other source code examples use a makefile that is almost identical to the one discussed in this section except for the target name and the C++ compiler switches.

***Listing A-2.*** Makefile for Source Code Example Ch02_01

```
# Target, include, and object directories
TARGET = Ch02_01
INCDIR1 = .
INCDIR2 = ../../Include
OBJDIR = linobj
MTARG = -m64 -mavx

# include files
CPPINCFILES1 = $(wildcard $(INCDIR1)/*.h)
CPPINCFILES2 = $(wildcard $(INCDIR2)/*.h)
ASMINCFILES1 = $(wildcard $(INCDIR1)/*.inc)
ASMINCFILES2 = $(wildcard $(INCDIR2)/*.inc)

# .cpp files in current directory
CPPFILES = $(wildcard *.cpp)
CPPOBJFILES_ = $(CPPFILES:.cpp=.o)
CPPOBJFILES = $(patsubst %, $(OBJDIR)/%, $(CPPOBJFILES_))

# .s files in current directory
ASMFILES = $(wildcard *.s)
ASMOBJFILES_ = $(ASMFILES:.s=.o)
ASMOBJFILES = $(patsubst %, $(OBJDIR)/%, $(ASMOBJFILES_))

# Target object files
OBJFILES = $(CPPOBJFILES) $(ASMOBJFILES)
```

```
# g++ and assembler options - required
GPPOPT = $(MTARG) -O3 -std=c++14 -Wall -Wextra
ASMOPT = $(MTARG)

# g++ and assembler options - optional (uncomment to enable)
DEBUG = -g
LISTFILE_CPP = -Wa,-aghl=$(OBJDIR)/$(basename $<).lst -save-temps=obj
LISTFILE_ASM = -aghlms=$(OBJDIR)/$(basename $<).lst

# Create directory for object and temp files
MKOBJDIR := $(shell mkdir -p $(OBJDIR))

# Build rules
$(TARGET): $(OBJFILES)
	g++ $(MTARG) $(OBJFILES) -o $(TARGET)

# Note: full recompiles/assembles on any include file changes
$(OBJDIR)/%.o: %.cpp $(CPPINCFILES1) $(CPPINCFILES2)
	g++ $(DEBUG) $(LISTFILE_CPP) $(GPPOPT) -I$(INCDIR1) -I$(INCDIR2) -c $< -o $@

$(OBJDIR)/%.o: %.s $(ASMINCFILES1) $(ASMINCFILES2)
	as  $(DEBUG) $(LISTFILE_ASM) $(ASMOPT) -I$(INCDIR1) -I$(INCDIR2) $< -o $@

.PHONY:    clean

clean:
	rm -f $(TARGET)
	rm -rf $(OBJDIR)
```

The first line in Listing A-2, TARGET = Ch02_01, sets the makefile variable TARGET equal to the text string Ch02_01. Like most programming languages, a makefile can use variables (which are sometimes called macros) to streamline rule creation and eliminate duplication. The next three statements assign text strings to makefile variables INCDIR1, INCDIR2, and OBJDIR. The variables INCDIR1 and INCDIR2 define the directories that contain include files, while OBJDIR defines the directory that stores object modules and other temporary files.

The MTARG variable contains GNU C++ compiler code generation switches. The switch -m64 instructs the C++ compiler to generate x86-64 code. Then next switch, -mavx, directs the C++ compiler to emit AVX instructions. Other source examples employ different C++ compiler code generation switches. The -mavx2 switch enables AVX2 code generation. The AVX-512 source code examples use the following compiler switches: -mavx512f, -mavx512vl, -mavx512bw, and -mavx512dq. The -mfma switch instructs the C++ compiler to emit FMA instructions. The GCC C++ compiler also supports additional x86 code generation switches. For more information regarding these switches, see https://gcc.gnu.org/onlinedocs/gcc-10.3.0/gcc/x86-Options.html#x86-Options.

The remaining lines in Listing A-2 are the same for all source code example makefiles. The first few sections instruct Make to build lists of file names with extensions .h and .cpp. These sections also build lists of assembly language source code files with extensions .s and .inc (none of the Linux source code examples contain .s or .inc files but this capability is included for future use). Having Make build lists of file names eliminates the need to manually create file dependency lists that would be different for each source code example.

Let's take a closer look at the makefile statements that build the file lists. The statement CPPINCFILES1 = $(wildcard $(INCDIR1)/*.h) builds a list of all .h files located in the directory INCDIR1 and assigns this list to variable CPPINCFILES1. This statement uses the variable INCDIR1 that was defined in the previous group of statements. Note that the variable name INCDIR1 is surrounded by parenthesis and includes a leading $ symbol. This syntax is required when using a previously defined variable. The text wildcard is a Make function that performs file searches using a search pattern. In the current statement, wildcard searches INCDIR1 for all *.h files. The remaining statements in this block initialize variables CPPINCFILES2, ASMINCFILES1, and ASMINCFILES2 using the same wildcard technique.

The first statement of the next group, CPPFILES = $(wildcard *.cpp), builds a list of all .cpp files in the current directory and assigns this list to variable CPPFILES. Then the next two statements build a list of .o (object module) files that correspond to the .cpp files in the current directory and assign this list to CPPOBJFILES. The ensuing statement group uses the same technique to build a list of object modules that correspond to the .s (assembly language) files in the current directory and assigns this list to ASMOBJFILES. This is followed by the statement OBJFILES = $(CPPOBJFILES) $(ASMOBJFILES), which sets OBJFILES equal to a list of all object module files that are needed to build the executable file TARGET.

The next two makefile variables, GPPOPT and ASMOPT, contain option switches for the GNU C++ compiler and GNU assembler. These switches are required and should not be changed. The $(MTARG) option adds the C++ compiler switches defined earlier in the makefile. The -O3 option instructs the C++ compiler to generate the fastest possible code. The drawback of using this option is somewhat slower compile times. The -std=c++14 switch enables compilation of the C++ source code using ISO C++ 2014 features. The -Wall option enables nearly all GNU C++ compiler warning messages.

The next variable group controls optional features. The DEBUG variable instructs the GNU C++ compiler and assembler to generate debugging information for use with the GNU debugger (gdb). The variables LISTFILE_CPP and LISTFILE_ASM include switches that enable the generation of listing files. Note that the compiler and assembler listing files are saved in the OBJDIR directory.

Following the definition of LISTFILE_ASM is the statement MKOBJDIR := $(shell mkdir -p $(OBJDIR)). This statement instructs Make to create the subdirectory OBJDIR. Recall that this directory contains the target's object module files, temporary files, and listing files.

The build statement group begins with a $(TARGET): $(OBJFILES) dependency rule. This rule informs Make that TARGET depends on the object module files defined by the variable OBJFILES. The ensuing statement, g++ $(OBJFILES) -o $(TARGET), is the shell command that Make runs to build the executable file TARGET. More specifically, this command links the object modules defined by OBJFILES into a single executable file. Note that this makefile statement is indented with a tab character, which is required.

The next dependency rule, $(OBJDIR)/%.o: %.cpp $(CPPINCFILES1) $(CPPINCFILES2), notifies Make that each .o file in OBJDIR depends on a corresponding .cpp file in the current directory. Each .o file also depends on the include files defined by the variables CPPINCFILES1 and CPPINCFILES2. Make uses the ensuing shell command g++ $(DEBUG) $(LISTFILE_CPP) $(GPPOPT) -I$(INCDIR1) -I$(INCDIR2) -c $< -o $@ to compile a C++ source code file. In this statement, Make replaces the automatic variable $< with the name of the C++ file. It also replaces the automatic variable $@ with the name of the object module file. The -c switch instructs the g++ to skip the link step, while the -o switch directs g++ to save the output object module to file $@. A similar dependency rule and shell command pair are also used for any assembly language files.

The statement .PHONY: clean defines a fake (or nonfile) target named clean. Typing make clean in a terminal window instructs Make to execute shell commands rm -f $(TARGET) and rm -rf $(OBJDIR). These commands delete the file TARGET and remove the subdirectory OBJDIR. The make clean command is often used to force a complete rebuild of a target executable the next time Make is used.

■ ■ ■

# References and Resources

Appendix B lists the references that were consulted during the writing of this book. It also includes additional resources that you might find useful or interesting.

## C++ SIMD Intrinsic Function Documentation

Comprehensive C++ SIMD intrinsic function documentation is available at the following Intel website: www.intel.com/content/www/us/en/docs/intrinsics-guide/index.html. You can also download a copy of this documentation for offline use using the Download link located below the Categories list.

## X86 Programming References

The following section lists the principal x86 programming reference manuals published by AMD and Intel. These manuals cover both SIMD and non-SIMD programming topics.

*AMD64 Architecture Programmer's Manual: Volumes 1–5,* Publication Number 40332, www.amd.com/system/files/TechDocs/40332.pdf

*Software Optimization Guide for AMD Family 17h Processors,* Publication Number 55723, https://developer.amd.com/resources/developer-guides-manuals

*Software Optimization Guide for AMD Family 17h Processors 30h and Greater Processors,* Publication Number 56305, https://developer.amd.com/resources/developer-guides-manuals

*Software Optimization Guide for AMD EPYC 7003 Processors,* Publication Number 56665, https://developer.amd.com/resources/developer-guides-manuals

*Intel 64 and IA-32 Architectures Software Developer's Manual, Combined Volumes: 1, 2A, 2B, 2C, 2D, 3A, 3B, 3C, 3D, and 4,* www.intel.com/content/www/us/en/processors/architectures-software-developer-manuals.html

*Intel 64 and IA-32 Architectures Optimization Reference Manual,* www.intel.com/content/www/us/en/processors/architectures-software-developer-manuals.html

© Daniel Kusswurm 2022
D. Kusswurm, *Modern Parallel Programming with C++ and Assembly Language,*
https://doi.org/10.1007/978-1-4842-7918-2

# X86 Processor Information

The following sites contain useful information regarding x86 processors:

*AMD Processors*, `www.amd.com/en/processors`

*Intel Product Specifications*, `https://ark.intel.com/content/www/us/en/ark.html`

Wikipedia, *Advanced Vector Extensions*, `https://en.wikipedia.org/wiki/Advanced_Vector_Extensions`

Wikipedia, *List of AMD CPU Microarchitectures*, `https://en.wikipedia.org/wiki/List_of_AMD_CPU_microarchitectures`

Wikipedia, *List of Intel CPU Microarchitectures*, `https://en.wikipedia.org/wiki/List_of_Intel_CPU_microarchitectures`

# Software Development Tools

The following software development tools were used to develop the source code examples in this book:

GNU Compiler Collection, `www.gnu.org/software/gcc/`

GNU Make, `www.gnu.org/software/make`

Portable Network Graphics, `www.libpng.org/pub/png/libpng.html`

Visual Studio, `https://visualstudio.microsoft.com/`

# Algorithm References

The following resources were consulted to develop the algorithms used in the source code examples:

Forman S. Acton, *REAL Computing Made REAL – Preventing Errors in Scientific and Engineering Calculations*, ISBN 978-0486442211, Dover Publications, 2005

Tony Chan, Gene Golub, Randall LeVeque, *Algorithms for Computing the Sample Variance: Analysis and Recommendations*, The American Statistician, Volume 37 Number 3 (1983), p. 242–247

James F. Epperson, *An Introduction to Numerical Methods and Analysis, Second Edition*, ISBN 978-1-118-36759-9, Wiley, 2013

David Goldberg, *What Every Computer Scientist Should Know About Floating-Point Arithmetic*, ACM Computing Surveys, Volume 23 Issue 1 (March 1991), p. 5–48

Rafael C. Gonzalez and Richard E. Woods, *Digital Image Processing*, Fourth Edition, ISBN 978-0-133-35672-4, Pearson, 2018

Daniel Kusswurm, *Modern X86 Assembly Language Programming, Second Edition*, ISBN 978-1-4842-4062-5, Apress, 2018

Bryan Manly, *Multivariate Statistical Methods, A Primer, Second Edition*, ISBN 0-412-60300-4, Chapman and Hall, 1994

James E. Miller, David G. Moursund, Charles S. Duris, *Elementary Theory & Application of Numerical Analysis, Revised Edition*, ISBN 978-0486479064, Dover Publications, 2011

Anthony Pettofrezzo, *Matrices and Transformations*, ISBN 0-486-63634-8, Dover Publications, 1978

Hans Schneider and George Barker, *Matrices and Linear Algebra*, ISBN 0-486-66014-1, Dover Publications, 1989

Eric W. Weisstein, *Convolution*, Mathworld, http://mathworld.wolfram.com/Convolution.html

Eric W. Weisstein, *Correlation Coefficient*, Mathworld, http://mathworld.wolfram.com/CorrelationCoefficient.html

Eric W. Weisstein, *Covariance Matrix*, Mathworld, https://mathworld.wolfram.com/CovarianceMatrix.html

Eric W. Weisstein, *Least Squares Fitting*, Mathworld, http://mathworld.wolfram.com/LeastSquaresFitting.html

Eric W. Weisstein, *Matrix Multiplication*, Mathworld, http://mathworld.wolfram.com/MatrixMultiplication.html

David M. Young and Robert Todd Gregory, *A Survey of Numerical Mathematics, Volume 1*, ISBN 0-486-65691-8, Dover Publications, 1988

Wikipedia, *Algorithms for Calculating Variance*, https://en.wikipedia.org/wiki/Algorithms_for_calculating_variance

Wikipedia, *Grayscale*, https://en.wikipedia.org/wiki/Grayscale

*Body Surface Area Calculator*, www.globalrph.com/bsa2.htm

# C++ References

The following resources contain valuable information about C++ programming and the C++ Standard Template Libraries:

Nicolai M. Josuttis, *The C++ Standard Library – A Tutorial and Reference, Second Edition*, Addison Wesley, ISBN 978-0-321-62321-8, 2012

Bjarne Stroustrup, *The C++ Programming Language, Fourth Edition*, Addison Wesley, ISBN 978-0-321-56384-2, 2013

cplusplus.com, www.cplusplus.com

## Utilities, Tools, and Libraries

The following utilities, tools, and libraries may be of interest to readers of this book:

AMD μProf, https://developer.amd.com/amd-uprof/

cpuid, www.cpuid.com/

gprof, https://sourceware.org/binutils/docs/gprof/

Intel VTune Profiler, www.intel.com/content/www/us/en/develop/documentation/get-started-with-vtune/top.html

libcpuid, https://github.com/anrieff/libcpuid

# Index

© Daniel Kusswurm 2022
D. Kusswurm, *Modern Parallel Programming with C++ and Assembly Language*,
https://doi.org/10.1007/978-1-4842-7918-2

## ■ T, U

## ■ V, W

## ■ X, Y

## ■ Z

Printed in the United States
by Baker & Taylor Publisher Services